Closing the Justice Gap for Adult and Child Sexual Assault

Anne Cossins

Closing the Justice Gap for Adult and Child Sexual Assault

Rethinking the Adversarial Trial

palgrave
macmillan

Anne Cossins
Honorary Professor and former Professor of Law and Criminology
Faculty of Law
University of New South Wales
Sydney, Australia

ISBN 978-1-137-32050-6 ISBN 978-1-137-32051-3 (eBook)
https://doi.org/10.1057/978-1-137-32051-3

Cover illustration: r.classen/Shutterstock

This Palgrave Macmillan imprint is published by the registered company Springer Nature Limited
The registered company address is: The Campus, 4 Crinan Street, London, N1 9XW, United Kingdom

Contents

List of Figures

Chapter 1

List of Tables

Chapter 1

Chapter 4

Chapter 5

Chapter 7

Chapter 8

Chapter 11

Chapter 12

1
Introduction

1 Introduction

Rape and sexual assault are unique crimes because they are mostly perpetrated against female children, female adolescents and women.[1] In addition, both male and female victims are most likely to be abused by men or male adolescents with whom they are acquainted or related and most often in relationships of intimacy, trust and/or authority (Australian Bureau of Statistics [ABS], 2018; Held & McLaughlin, 2013; Office for National Statistics [ONS], 2018).

These relationships mean that perpetrators not only have relatively easy access to groom their victims but also are able to commit their crimes in circumstances of privacy and secrecy with few, if any, eyewitnesses or earwitnesses. Even the presence of forensic evidence is unusual due to the relatively fast degradation of bodily fluids (Cossins, Jayakody, Norrie, & Parkinson, 2016) and the common tendency for victims to

[1]The male pronoun is used for defendants and the female pronoun is used for complainants which reflects the empirical data that the majority of sex offenders are male and the majority of sexual assault complainants are female (Australian Bureau of Statistics, 2019a), although it is recognised that men, male adolescents and boys can also be victims of sexual assault.

A. Cossins, *Closing the Justice Gap for Adult and Child Sexual Assault*,
https://doi.org/10.1057/978-1-137-32051-3_1

delay their complaints to authorities. For adult sexual assault, in a word-against-word case, the issue of lack of consent can be impossible to prove beyond reasonable doubt, as several recent high-profile cases have shown.[2]

For these and other reasons, sexual assault against both adults and children have been the focus of numerous inquiries, independent reviews, Royal Commissions, media inquiries and feminist campaigns (see, for example, Angiolini, 2015; Australian Law Reform Commission, 2010a, 2010b; Cossins, 2010; Home Office, 2010; Jay, 2014; Royal Commission into Institutional Responses to Child Sexual Abuse, 2017a; Topping & Barr, 2018). As the data in this chapter shows, sexual assault requires considerable resources to investigate and prosecute (Angiolini, 2015). For example, sexual assault is the most common crime prosecuted in the higher courts of Australia's largest jurisdiction (New South Wales (NSW) (Cossins & Goodman-Delahunty, 2013), yet is characterised by high attrition rates and relatively low conviction rates at trial (ABS, 2019b; Fitzgerald, 2006; Royal Commission, 2017).

In this book, the term, 'sexual assault', is used to describe the range of sex offences that are committed against both adults and children since the term covers both penetrative and non-penetrative offences (such as non-consensual sexual touching), as well as sex offences committed with and without the use of force or threat of force. Sexual assault is not confined to penile penetration and may involve penetration by any other part of the body as well as by objects. Rape, on the other hand, usually refers to vaginal, anal or oral sexual penetration depending on the jurisdiction. Sometimes rape is restrictively defined as penile penetration only (see further Chapter 2).

One of the difficulties with prosecuting sexual assault against adults is the fact that the alleged sexual behaviours can involve sexual conduct that one day is legal, the next criminal, because unlike other criminal

---

[2]See, for example, https://www.news.com.au/national/nsw-act/courts-law/john-jarratt-found-not-guilty-of-sydney-rape/news-story/e3e5557b101c8bb2ec111d8f2d7f70b7; accessed 10 July, 2019; https://www.abc.net.au/news/2018-05-07/kings-cross-rape-case-that-put-consent-on-trial/9695858; accessed 10 July, 2019; https://www.theguardian.com/commentisfree/2018/mar/21/rape-complainant-loss-privacy-intrusive-investigations; accessed 10 July, 2019; https://www.smh.com.au/world/europe/jury-discharged-in-uk-rape-case-of-australian-cricketer-alex-hepburn-20190112-p50qyq.html; accessed 10 July, 2019.

offences, the crime includes activities that most adults engage in for much of their adult lives. Historically, the line between consent and non-consent has always been influenced by stereotypical expectations of how women and men 'naturally' behave so that rape is an offence that has pitted 'malicious' women and girls against men obeying their 'natural' urges. A considerable amount of research has shown that the investigation and prosecution of rape and sexual assault is plagued by rape myths that have been shown to influence the perceptions and decisions of police officers, prosecutors, lawyers, judges and jurors (Hohl & Stanko, 2015; Temkin & Krahé, 2008; see further Chapter 2).

The prevalence of rape and sexual assault and the historical lack of criminal justice sanctions for offenders has led to countless reforms in all adversarial jurisdictions since at least the 1970s. Many of these reforms are considered to be 'feminist-inspired, with the aim of redressing the criminal justice system's traditional gender bias in relation to rape' (Larcombe, 2011: 27). It could be a 'feminist success story' (Larcombe, 2011: 27) that so much reform has occurred after sexual assault law reform became part of the legislative agenda. However, more than a decade ago, Kelly, Lovett and Regan (2005: 30) reported that conviction rates had fallen even after significant law reform measures in England and Wales (E&W):

> despite widespread reform of statute law and, in many jurisdictions, procedural rules, the 1990s witnessed declining or static conviction rates. … Remarkably little research or legal commentary has, as yet, attempted to explain these common—and unexpected—international similarities.

They concluded that 'the two patterns in reported rape cases … over the past two decades … [are] a continuing and unbroken increase in reporting; and a relatively static number of convictions' (Kelly et al., 2005: 25). This chapter will investigate whether this is still the case.

Over the years many options and suggestions have been made regarding improvements to the way sexual assault is investigated and prosecuted. Larcombe (2011: 32) notes that the most sound reason, empirically, for low conviction rates is relatively low guilty plea rates which result in relatively high acquittal rates. Thus, it is necessary to focus on fact-finders and why they are prone to acquit rather than convict in both adult and child sexual assault trials, the subject of lengthy discussion in Chapter 2 in a review of the literature on jury decision-making in sexual assault trials.

Pether (2009: 240) has also observed that 'the contemporary data establish that statutory rape law reform, whether substantive … or procedural … including reform of police practices and judicial education, has had no effect on improving the rates of the prosecution of and conviction for rape'. Similar statements were made by the NSW Criminal Justice and Sexual Offences Taskforce (2005) about the situation in Australia's largest jurisdiction, New South Wales (NSW).

The question is, is this still the case in 2019? Even if conviction rates have continued to be low for child and adult sexual assault,

> for what purposes would … an increase [in conviction rates] be sought? And is the sole measure of future reforms to be their impact on conviction rates? (Larcombe, 2011: 29)

In other words, conviction rates are only one measure of the effectiveness of reforms that are focused on the investigation and prosecution of sexual assault. Other measures for assessing success include:

- Rates of reporting to police;
- Police investigations and police practices;
- Prosecution rates;
- Attrition rates;
- Guilty plea rates;
- Conviction rates at trial;
- Overall conviction rates (guilty pleas plus convictions at trial);
- Sentencing; and
- Victims' and complainants' satisfaction levels with the criminal justice process.

For example, Larcombe (2011: 29) argues that:

> while the current legal impunity for rape cannot be condoned, increasing conviction rates is not itself a valid objective of reform. … [S]trategies designed solely to increase rape conviction rates are more likely to work against, rather than in support of, feminist aims.

Overall, the successes of feminist-inspired law reform in the sexual assault arena are considered to represent a bleak picture. For example, Larcombe (2011) considers that 'the "gains" of post-1970s rape law reform are doubtful' since there is no evidence that law reform has decreased the prevalence of sexual assault, increased reporting rates or increased the chances of a conviction. While few discuss the possibility that low conviction rates could represent wrongful acquittals, Larcombe (2011: 30) notes that:

> The particular issue confronting policy-makers, feminists, criminologists and others, however, is to explain the trend in conviction rates postreform whereby the 'gap' between reporting and conviction rates for sexual offences has also widened. Indeed, leading UK researchers in this field have suggested that the 'justice gap' for sexual assault victim/survivors is now better described as a 'chasm'.

More recently, in its investigation of the criminal justice response to rape by *The Guardian* newspaper, Topping and Barr (2018, n.p.) observed:

> [a] few months ago … a long-time associate who campaigns against violence against women and girls … said [that] rape complainants were finding it increasingly difficult to get charges brought by the Crown Prosecution Service … [and] talked about a crisis in the criminal justice system's treatment of rape, which had been made worse this year by the so-called 'disclosure crisis' [of complainants' digital material] in rape trials. …[T]here had been a lot of … high profile rape trials, mainly involving young men, collapsing after digital material which compromised the prosecution's case was disclosed at the last minute. The overwhelming narrative was that women were making up rape allegations against innocent men, she said, when in fact there was a yawning gap in rape victims' access to justice.

The data in this chapter indicate that this 'yawning gap' is not just anecdotal but is an empirical fact, as discussed below. Not only is it necessary to explain relatively high attrition rates and relatively low conviction rates (at trial), it is also necessary to explain what can be done to deal with a situation where the focus of a sexual assault trial is still on the complainant's behaviour, as it has been historically, rather than the defendant's. While 'low prosecution rates are, in part, a result of the low chances of conviction' (Larcombe, 2011: 28), what is the cause of the low chances of conviction?

Understanding the reasons why victims of sexual assault fail to report or delay their reports for long periods of time, why cases fall out of the system at the investigative and prosecutorial stages and why cases do not result in a conviction 'is vital to improving the legal and criminal justice response' (Grubb & Turner, 2012: 444), as well as vital to the public's trust in that system. This book argues that it is the way that sexual assault trials are conducted that gives rise to the seemingly intractable problems of high attrition rates, low conviction and the re-traumatisation of complainants.

The remainder of this chapter examines the available data on the prevalence and reporting of adult and child sexual assault (CSA) in Australia and E&W, followed by the available data on prosecutorial and conviction rates in NSW and E&W, in order to provide background information for the chapters that follow.

I have chosen to compare E&W and NSW to illustrate how two jurisdictions on opposite sides of the world not only share many similarities but have responded in a variety of different ways to the same problems associated with the investigation and prosecution of rape and sexual assault. Each jurisdiction has much to offer and much to learn from the other. While this comparative analysis could have included another jurisdiction, such as Scotland or Canada, the amount of material became unwieldy such that it was necessary for the sake of clarity and the word limit to confine this book to just two.

2 What Do We Know About the Prevalence of Sexual Assault?

It is necessary to know how widespread the problem of sexual assault is in order to consider the appropriateness of criminal justice responses. While sexual violence is experienced by men, women and children, women and children bear the burden of sexual abuse worldwide (World Health Organization, 2014), including the burden of psychological trauma that is caused by sexual assault with all its attendant social and economic consequences.

2.1 Australia

In Australia, the latest Australian Bureau of Statistics (ABS) report on crime victimisation (ABS, 2018) reveals prevalence rates for sexual assault over a 12-month period: '[i]n the twelve months prior to interview, of the 18.0 million persons aged 18 years and over, 0.4% (77,400) [had] experienced at least one sexual assault'.[3] These findings were similar to those from the 2014–2015 survey with no significant change in sexual victimisation. In fact, since 2008–2009, there has been no change in rates of sexual victimisation of those over the age of 18 years.

Only 30% of these sexual assault victims 'had their most recent incident reported to police' which was the lowest rate of reporting compared to other personal crimes (physical assault, threatened assault and robbery) (ABS, 2018, Table 1). By comparison, Cox (2016: 42) found that just under one in five women reported their most recent sexual assault by a male to the police (162,800, 19.1%) in an analysis of the data from the 2012 Personal Safety Survey. However, very few incidents were prosecuted since 'just over one in 20 women indicated that the perpetrator had ended up in court. Although women were more likely to perceive an assault by a stranger as a crime, this did not result in

---

[3]The ABS survey collected data, via personal telephone interview, about people's experiences of crime victimisation for a range of selected personal and household crimes.

Table 1 Australia: victimisation rates for sexual assault for different age groups, per 100,000 (2017)

All ages (years)	0–9	10–14	15–19	20–24	25–34	35–44	45–54	55–64	65 & over
101.5	82.4	325.7	416.3	155.6	94.9	70.2	52.4	27.4	9.5

Source ABS (2018); http://www.abs.gov.au/AUSSTATS/abs@.nsf/DetailsPage/4510.02017?OpenDocument (Table 2)

a marked increase in prosecution for this perpetrator type' (Cox, 2016: 64).

Overall, Table 1 shows that victimisation rates are very much age-related since they peak in the 15–19-year age group, with these young people being the group that is most vulnerable to sexual assault followed by those aged 10–14 years. Although much of the debate and research often focuses on women's vulnerability to sexual assault, these statistics show that children are more likely to be sexually assaulted than adults.

In terms of gender, females (165.9 per 100,000) are 4.7 times more likely to be sexually assaulted than males (35.6 per 100,000). When victimisation rates for males and females are compared in the 10–14 and 15–19 age groups, the rate is even more stark for females: 548.6 per 100,000, and 763.1 per 100,000, respectively, compared to males in those two age groups: 114.9 per 100,000, and 85.0 per 100,000.

A recent Australian study of 7700 women aged 28–33 years found a prevalence rate for childhood experiences of sexual abuse of 14.5% (Coles, Lee, Taft, Mazza, & Loxton, 2015). This compares with the 2016 Personal Safety Survey (ABS 2017) which found that nearly one in ten Australians over the age of 18 years experienced sexual abuse *before* the age of 15 (7.7% or 1.4 million) (ABS, 2017). The majority of abusers were known to their victims (98% of male victims; 91% of female victims) although the most common perpetrator was known but non-familial. Males (65%) more likely to be abused by a non-familial person than females (47%).

In terms of adult sexual assault, the Personal Safety Survey conducted by the ABS (2017) from November 2016 to June 2017 also compiled data collected from Australian men and women aged 18 years and over about experiences of violence since the age of 15 years, including sexual violence. The Personal Safety Survey was previously conducted in 2012 and 2005.

A total of 1,585,100 Australian women had been sexually assaulted[4] since the age of 15. While the ABS (2017) did not calculate the prevalence of sexual assault, based on the estimated Australian population of 24,598,900 (ABS, 2017b) as at 30 June 2017, this total equates to an approximate prevalence of 6.4%. By contrast, a total of 384,800 Australian men had been sexually assaulted since the age of 15 years which equates to a prevalence rate of 1.6%.

Despite the popular belief in stranger rape, the majority of offenders were intimate partners/other relatives or people known to their victims, such as friends, housemates, acquaintances and neighbours. The vast majority of the Australian women who responded to the Personal Safety Survey (97.7%) had been sexually assaulted by a male perpetrator, while 87% had been sexually assaulted by a male known to them with the most common locations being the woman's home (40%) or the perpetrator's home (17%). Nearly 9 out of 10 women (87%) did not report the incident to the police.

For Australian men, 59.4% had been sexually assaulted by a female perpetrator while 70.3% had been sexually assaulted by a male or female known to them.

2.2 England and Wales

The Crime Survey for England and Wales (CSEW) (Office for National Statistics [ONS], 2018) estimated that 2.1% of the population or approximately 700,000 people aged 16–59 years were victims of sexual assault from 31 March 2016 to 31 March 2018. The definition of sexual assault used by the ONS (2018: 5) included: rape; attempted rape; assault by penetration attempted assault by penetration; causing sexual activity without consent; indecent exposure and unwanted sexual

---

[4]The ABS (2017) stated that the definitions for sexual assault that were used in the survey 'were based on actions which would be considered as offences under State and Territory criminal law'.

touching. Unwanted sexual touching was the most common sexual offence recorded for both male and female victims (ONS, 2018: 8).

Like Australia, the majority of cases do not enter the criminal justice system since less than one in five victims reported their experiences to the police. However, half of the recorded sexual offences (that is, those reported to police) did not proceed further because of evidentiary problems, 'reflect[ing] the challenges involved in investigating sexual offences, despite the majority of suspects being identified' (ONS, 2018: 2).

The majority of victims were female (approximately 560,000) compared to 140,000 male victims which means that '[w]omen were nearly four times as likely as men to have experienced sexual assault in the last year (3.4% compared with 0.9%)' (ONS, 2018: 8). Like Australia, the highest prevalence rates occurred in younger age groups: 16–19 years (female: 11.0%; male: 2.7%) and 20–24 years (female: 8.2%; male: 2.1%).

While the prevalence rate of sexual assault has fluctuated from year to year, the estimated prevalence rate for the year 31 March 2017–31 March 2018 is similar to the prevalence rate a decade ago (ONS, 2018: 9). Nonetheless, there was 'a significant increase' from 2.0% in the previous year to 2.7% in the year ending March 2018 as a result of:

- unwanted touching (increasing from 1.4 to 2.1%); and
- indecent exposure (increasing from 0.4 to 0.8%) (ONS, 2018: 9).

This relatively low prevalence rate compared to Australia is not directly comparable because of differences in definitions of sexual assault and the ages of those surveyed. But how does E&W compare with the rest of Europe? A review of the prevalence of sexual aggression[5] in 27 European Union countries (including Great Britain) found a wide variation in rates, both within and between countries, as a result of methodological differences in the 113 studies gathered (Krahé, Tomaszewska, Kuyper, & Vanwesenbeeck, 2014). The lifetime prevalence rates for females aged 12

[5]Defined as: 'behavior carried out with the intent or result of making another person engage in sexual activity or sexual communication despite his or her unwillingness to do so' (Krahé et al., 2014: 546).

to 25 years ranged from 9–83%, compared to 2–66% for males in the same age group.

The highest lifetime prevalence rates for females aged 12–25 years were found in the Netherlands (83.9%), Germany (63.5%), Sweden (60%) and Spain (50.1%), compared with Great Britain (17.8%) and Ireland (31.8%), the differences being attributed to wider definitions of sexual aggression, including non-physical conduct such as verbal sexual harassment. In addition, '[c]ulture-level variables, such as differences in sexual behavior patterns, gender roles, extent of sex education, and drinking culture, may be systematically related to variations in sexual aggression rates' (Krahé et al., 2014: 552–553).

While fewer studies documented the lifetime prevalence rates for males aged 12–25 years, the highest rates were reported in the Netherlands (66.3%), Spain (54.2%), Germany (45.0%) and Sweden (30.0%), compared with Great Britain (19.0%) and Ireland (8.1%).

3 The Importance of Prevalence Rates

Why should we care about the incidence and prevalence of adult and child sexual assault within a population? Despite the wide variation in rates between different jurisdictions, there are three important facts that can be discerned:

i. children and adolescents are more vulnerable to sexual assault than adults;
ii. the vast majority of sexual assault incidents are not reported to police; and
iii. females are more likely to be sexually assaulted than males.

It is only in recent decades that psychological studies have revealed just how mentally and physically damaging sexual assault can be, with victims reporting a wide range of problems from anxiety disorders, depression, eating disorders, symptoms of post-traumatic stress disorder (PTSD), sleeping disorders and suicidality (Chen et al., 2010; Coles et al., 2015;

Holmes & Sher, 2013; Jonas, Bebbington, McManus, & Meltzer, 2011; Walsh et al., 2012, 2014).

Since most sexual assaults and offenders are never dealt with by the criminal justice system, victims, their families and the community at large bear a significant social, health and economic burden because of the psychological impact of sexual assault. For children, CSA can lead to drug and/or alcohol abuse, suicide, suicide ideation, unemployment and mental health issues for life, as well as leaving them vulnerable to re-victimisation (see Chapter 2). The wasted potential of these young lives is a tragic loss to the individual victim and their families, as well as society more broadly. As the World Health Organization (WHO) (2014: viii) has observed:

> Such violence contributes to lifelong ill health—particularly for women and children—and early death. Many leading causes of death such as heart disease, stroke, cancer and HIV/AIDS are the result of victims of violence adopting behaviours such as smoking, alcohol and drug misuse, and unsafe sex in an effort to cope with the psychological impact of violence. Violence also places a heavy strain on health and criminal justice systems, social and welfare services and the economic fabric of communities.

Since the above prevalence rates reveal the relatively large numbers of victims of both adult and child sexual assault in Australia and E&W, can the criminal justice system ever deal with the extent of such a social problem? As a starting point, it is necessary to know how frequently sexual assault is being reported to police. Without such reports there is less likelihood of any reduction in the prevalence of sexual assault.

4 Recorded Rates of Sexual Assault by Police

As discussed above, the vast majority of adult and child victims of sexual assault do not report their experiences to the police. The complexity of the criminal justice process for victims if they report a sexual assault to the police is illustrated in Fig. 1, which also highlights the various drop-out points or points of attrition for sexual assault cases.

As Fig. 1 shows, a report must be made to the police for it to become official in the form of a recorded incident which may then lead to a preliminary investigation and charges if a suspect can be identified. This means that the police are the gatekeepers for the entry of all offences into the criminal justice system. While it is possible for no further action to be taken if the complainant does not wish to proceed with her/his complaint, the police may decide there is insufficient evidence to lay charges, a discretionary power that is influenced by, and influences, the types of cases that are successfully prosecuted. For the minority of sex offences that are reported to the police, attrition at various stages of the criminal justice system ensures that the vast majority of reports do not result in a prosecution or a conviction.

In a comparative analysis of studies in Australia, New Zealand, Canada and the UK, Daly and Bouhours (2010: 572) found that reporting rates varied from 6–20%, with rates of 14–18% in E&W and 12–20% in Australia. Overall, an average of 14% of sex offences were reported and, of these, Daly and Bouhours (2010) found that only 30% were prosecuted, 20% were adjudicated in court and 12.5% resulted in a conviction.

Research also shows that the typical features of stranger rape (such as the unpredictable location, injury, element of surprise and unknown assailant) have governed the response of police and prosecutors to non-stranger rapes and sexual assault (Daly & Bouhours, 2010; Grace, Lloyd, & Smith, 1992; Gregory & Lees, 1996; Harris & Grace, 1999; Temkin & Krahé, 2008), with higher attrition rates for cases involving a known assailant compared to those involving a stranger. For example, Daly and Bouhours (2010: 573–576) report:

> An important question for attrition research is whether the relative composition of aggravated and simple rapes, or of stranger rapes, reported to the police has changed over time. ... One explanation is that an increasing share of non-traditional rapes, which are more difficult to prove in court, are being reported to the police. ... [W]e identified a subsample of cases from our attrition sample that examined victim-offender relations

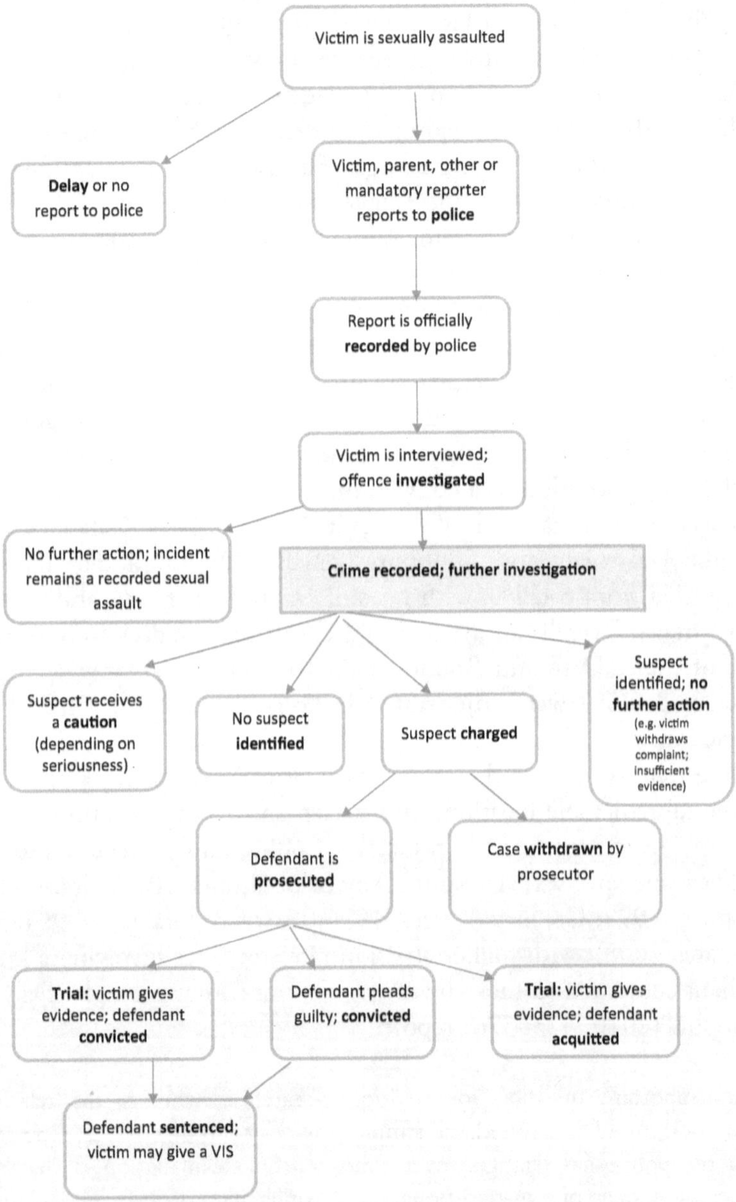

Fig. 1 Progress of a sexual offence through the criminal justice system

> as an attrition factor and then reread each to determine the stranger relationship share of offenses reported to the police. ... Our mini study found that stranger relations were a significantly higher share of cases reported to the police in the 1970s and 1980s (48 percent) than in the 1990s forward (26 percent). Although the sample size is small, the findings confirm that the stranger relations share of rapes reported to the police has decreased over time.

What do recent data tell us about rates of reporting to police?

4.1 Australia

Compared to crimes such as robbery, there was a sustained increase in the *recorded rates* of sexual assault during the 1990s which continued into the 2000s in Australia. A major contributor to this increase was a rise in the recorded rates of sexual assault involving young people. In fact, 'in the 10-year period between 1995 and 2005, the incidence of recorded sexual assault for children aged 0-14 years accounted for around 40 percent of all recorded sexual assaults' (Bricknell, 2008: 3).

From 2010–2017, the increase in recorded rates of all sexual assault in Australia continued from 18,862 to 24,957 in 2017, an increase that represented an eight-year high, a sixth annual increase in a row and an 8% increase on the previous year. Just over four-fifths of victims were female (82%) while the number of female victims increased by 9% compared with 2016, the largest annual increase since 2010 (ABS, 2018).

Compared to the previous decade, the incidence of recorded sexual assault for children aged 15–19 years was the highest out of all age groups for that period (ranging from 355.9 in 2010 to 416.3 in 2017) and accounting for 27.5% in 2010 and 24.8% in 2017 of all recorded sexual assaults. Even more worrying, the recorded rates for the combined age groups, 0–9, 10–14 and 15–19, accounted for the majority of all sexual assaults (63.6% in 2010; 54.4% in 2017) (ABS, 2018, Table 2).

By comparison, in 2018, the number of recorded victims of adult sexual assault increased for the seventh year in a row by 2% to 26,312, Australia-wide, compared with 24,957 in 2017 (ABS, 2018,

Table 1). Again, the majority of victims were female (84%) and just over half (55.7%) were aged between 10 and 19 years (ABS, 2018, Table 2). Overall, from 2010–2018, recorded victims of sexual assault increased by 40% 'which, after accounting for population growth, represents a 23% increase in the victimisation rate (from 86 victims to 105 victims per 100,000 persons)' (ABS, 2018, Table 1).

However, consistent with the prevalence data, girls and women are significantly more likely to be recorded victims of sexual assault than boys and men, compared to other crimes involving personal violence, in that the victimisation rate for females is more than five times that of males as set out in Table 2.

Despite the almost ten-year sustained increase in recorded rates of sexual assault in Australia there is limited information available about the reasons why most victims of sexual assault do not report to police.

For example, in 2015, the National Union of Students (NUS) conducted a survey of Australian female university students (N = 1366; 3.4% transsexual or intersex). The study reported that 72.8% of respondents had experienced sexual harassment or unwelcome sexual behaviour both on and off campus; 36.0% had experienced an unwanted sexual experience, including 17.8% who had experienced non-consensual penetration, or attempted penetration. Almost all female students (94.5%) who had experienced sexual assault, harassment or violence did not report the incident. Of those who did, 71.6% were dissatisfied with the outcome (NUS Women's Department, 2015).

Table 2 The victimisation rate, by sex of victim, for recorded victims of sexual offences compared to victims of select personal violence offences in Australia, 2018

	Homicide & related offences	Murder	Attempted murder	Manslaughter	Armed robbery	All sexual offences
Female	1.0	0.7	0.3	0.0	6.9	175.5
Male	2.0	1.1	0.7	0.2	25.6	33.1

Source ABS (2018, Table 2)

Table 3 Australian students' reasons for not reporting sexual assault to university

Reasons	Percentage
Not serious enough	40
Did not need help	40
Thought it would be too hard to prove	28
Did not know who to make the complaint to	25
Worried they wouldn't be believed	22
Did not know where to go/what to do to make the report	21
Felt embarrassed or ashamed	21
Did not want to hurt offender(s) or get them into trouble	17
Did not want anyone to know	16

Source Australian Human Rights Commission (2017: 129)

Although not representative of all sexual assault victims in Australia, a national survey of university students reported their reasons for not reporting to their university (Australian Human Rights Commission, 2017). The report found that 87% of Australian university students who experienced sexual assault did not make a formal report or complaint to anyone at their university in relation to the most recent incident. The most common reasons for not reporting were that students 'did not think it was serious enough or that they did not think they needed help' (Australian Human Rights Commission, 2017: 129) as set out in Table 3.

4.2 England and Wales

In 2015, the number of sex offences recorded by police in E&W was at its highest level since the introduction of the National Crime Recording Standard in 2002 which may reflect improvements in recording and/or the willingness of victims to report (Rook & Ward, 2016: 1–2). However, the Crime Survey for England and Wales (CSEW) conducted by the Office for National Statistics (ONS) (2018, Table 23) for all adults aged 16–59 years resident in households in England and Wales estimated that less than one in five (17%) victims reported their experience of non-consensual penetration to the police. While the survey did not 'provide information on whether other types of sexual offences were reported ..., reporting rates for these offences are likely to be lower than for rape and assault by penetration, given the nature of the offences' (ONS, 2018: 11).

As set out in Table 4, the three most common reasons for not reporting to the police were complainant embarrassment, a belief that the police could not help and a belief that reporting would be humiliating.

In 2011, the National Union of Students (2011) in the UK reported that of 2058 female students who participated in a survey, 14.3% had experienced a serious physical or sexual assault as a student; 68% had experienced either verbal or non-verbal harassment (such as sexual comments, flashing and groping); 12% reported stalking; more than 10% had been subject to serious physical violence; 16% per cent have experienced unwanted kissing, touching or molesting and 7% had been the victim of a serious sexual assault. Like the situation in Australia, reporting levels to the police were low for every type of assault as seen in the following categories (percentage who reported):

- stalking: 13%;
- serious sexual assault: 10%;
- less serious sexual assault: 2%;
- serious physical violence: 17%;
- less serious physical violence: 7%.

Table 4 Reasons for not reporting rape to police: CSEW (adults 16–59 years)

Reasons for not reporting	Percentage
Embarrassment	44
Didn't think they could help	33
Thought it would be humiliating	33
Didn't think they would believe me	25
Didn't want to go to court	21
Too trivial/not worth reporting	17
Didn't think they would do anything about it	17
Some other reasons	17
Feared more violence as a result of involving the police	16
Didn't think the police would be sympathetic	14
Private/family matter/not police business	10
Didn't want the person or people who did it to be punished	8
Dislike/fear of the police	2

Source ONS (2018: Table 23)

The latest figures reveal that, in E&W, '[t]he police recorded 150,847 sexual offences in the year ending March 2018' (ONS, 2018: 13), a figure that does not correspond with the data reported by the CSEW since 'police data cover a broader range of offences and includes offences against children and those living in institutions' (ONS, 2018: 13). Similar to the situation in Australia, both males and females 'aged 10 to 14, 15 to 19 and 20 to 24 years were disproportionately more likely to be victims of sexual offences recorded by the police than any other age group' (ONS, 2018: 13).

Like Australia, consistent with the prevalence data, girls and young women are significantly more likely to be victims than boys and young men compared to other crimes involving personal violence (see Table 5). Except for homicide, recorded incidents of offences involving non-sexual violence are relatively similar for males and females. However, for sexual offences, including rape, females report more than four times as many offences as males (84% vs 16% for sexual offences; 89% vs 11% for rape).

The ONS (2018: 15) reported that '[r]ape accounted for around one in three of police recorded sexual offences in the year ending March 2018 (36%)' compared to nearly one in seven victims of sexual assault who had reported rape in the CSEW survey, suggesting that 'victims are more likely to report rape … than other sexual offences'. Nonetheless, a

Table 5 The proportion of sexual offences, by sex of victim, for police-recorded crimes against the person in England and Wales, year ending March 2018[a]

	Violence against the person (%)	Homicide (%)	Violence with injury (%)	Violence without injury (%)	Sexual offences (%)	Rape (%)	Other sexual offences (%)
Female	53	26	45	52	84	89	81
Male	47	74	55	48	16	11	19

[a]Data taken from ONS (2018) Home Office Appendix Tables, Table 22 which states 'Police recorded crime data based on 37 forces that provided data via the Home Office Data Hub or in manual return. Data have not been reconciled with forces'. The data in Table 5 records offences rather than victims which means a victim may report more than one offence, making the number of offences higher than the number of victims who report

comparison of police-recorded data and data from the CSEW 'suggests that rapes within a relationship are less likely to be reported to the police than rapes committed by other perpetrators' (ONS, 2018:15).

While '[t]he number of police recorded sexual offences has almost tripled since the year ending March 2013', this is considered to be due to improvements in police recording methods and more victims coming forward, resulting in a 'sharp increase' for both rape and other sexual offences, with non-recent offences accounting for just over one quarter (26%) of all recorded sexual offences, a figure that has not changed in the last five years (ONS, 2018: 13; 14). Nonetheless:

> The increases don't reflect the level of victimisation having tripled. Although the CSEW has estimated an increase in prevalence over the same period, this increase is much smaller than seen in police recorded offences. (ONS, 2018: 14)

For recorded rates of CSA, the NSPCC (2018: 28–31) reported the statistics in Table 6 for England, Wales, Northern Ireland and Scotland for the period, 2016/2017.

In England, the rates of sexual offences per 10,000 children have doubled in the past four years probably because of the 'improved recording of sexual offences by the police and an increased willingness of victims to come foreword [sic] have contributed to this rise' (NSPCC, 2018: 28). The rate per 10,000 children in Wales was the highest in the UK while the rate in Northern Ireland was the lowest.

Table 6 Recorded sexual offences against children in the UK and Number of sexual offences per 10,000 Children (2016/2017)

Age of complainant	England	Wales	N. Ireland	Scotland
Under 16 years	43,522 (41.3)	2845 (51.1)	Not available	4097 (45.0)
Under 18 years	54,846 (46.5)	Not available	1875 (43.3)	Not available

Overall, it is not possible to compare the rates of recorded CSA between Australia and E&W. First, the rate for Australia is calculated by reference to the age of the victim at the time of report to police whereas the rates for E&W are calculated with reference to the age of the victim at the time of the offence. Thus, the rates for CSA that are reported by the ABS in Australia are an underestimation compared to E&W since they do not capture historical CSA incidents which are reported when the child becomes an adult. In addition, the data for Australia is for children aged 0–14 years at the time of reporting, compared to E&W (0–16 years at the time of the offence). See Table 7.

Table 7 Recorded sexual assault rates (per 100,000) for England, Wales and Australia

Jurisdiction	Child	All victims
Australia (2018)[a]	54.4 (0–9 years) 109.5 (10–14 years)[b]	105.3 (0–65 years & over)
NSW (2018)[c]	130.0 (0–9 years) 484.2 (0–14 years)	128.2
England and Wales (2018)[d]	Not available	98.1
England (2016–2017)[e]	413 (0–16 years)	Not available
Wales (2016/2017)[f]	511 (0–16 years)	Not available

[a]Australian Bureau of Statistics, *Recorded Crime—Victims, Australia, 2018*, Table 2; https://www.abs.gov.au/AUSSTATS/abs@.nsf/DetailsPage/4510.02018?OpenDocument
[b]This is the age at which the offence was reported to the police
[c]Australian Bureau of Statistics, *Recorded Crime—Victims, Australia, 2018*, Tables 6 and 7, https://www.abs.gov.au/AUSSTATS/abs@.nsf/DetailsPage/4510.02018?OpenDocument
[d]Office for National Statistics, *Crime in England & Wales, Year Ending December 2018—Appendix Tables*, Tables A7; https://www.ons.gov.uk/peoplepopulationandcommunity/crimeandjustice/datasets/crimeinenglandandwalesappendixtables
[e]National Society for the Prevention of Cruelty to Children, *How Safe Are Our Children?* (2018), 29 https://learning.nspcc.org.uk/media/1067/how-safe-are-our-children-2018.pdf. The recorded rate includes the following offences: rape of a child under 13 years, rape of a child under 16 years, sexual assault on a child under 1 year, sexual activity involving a child under 13 years, sexual activity involving a child under 16 years, sexual grooming, abuse of position of trust of a sexual nature (includes under 18s) and abuse of children through sexual exploitation (includes under 18s)
[f]Ibid.: 30. Includes same offences as above

5 Child Sexual Abuse: Delayed Reports to Police

Various factors affect the fact that delayed, rather than immediate disclosure is the key feature that characterises CSA (Cossins, 2010; Cashmore, Taylor, & Parkinson, 2017; Kelly & Karsna, 2017), leading to reports to police that involve allegations of sexual abuse that occurred months, years or even decades before.

For example, the Royal Commission into Institutional Responses to Child Sexual Abuse (2017a: 67) (the Royal Commission) in Australia reported that, of the 6875 survivors who gave evidence to the Commission in private sessions, 5518 victims provided disclosure information. Of those, four-fifths (80.8%) said they had not previously reported their abuse to the police. Similarly, the Children's Commissioner in England (2015: 7) estimated that only 1 in 8 victims of CSA (12.5%) come to the attention of the authorities.

The Royal Commission (2017a: 67) reported that:

> distrust of police and government can inhibit people from disclosing abuse. Some survivors chose not to disclose abuse because they thought they would not be believed. Others did disclose to police and were not believed. … Delayed reporting may be particularly common for [CSA] in institutional contexts where the perpetrator is in a position of trust or authority. An examination of [NSW] police data found the cases of [CSA] that had the greatest likelihood of delayed reporting involved alleged perpetrators who were in a position of authority in relation to the child. Cases that had the least delay in reporting were those where the person of interest was not known to the victim.

In 2010, I conducted a literature review of studies of disclosure patterns by children. These studies (updated and set out in Table 8) provide evidence of the key 'consistent patterns of children's reactions to sexual abuse' (that is, reported in at least two studies) (Cossins, 2010: 79). Overall, failure to disclose is influenced by the type of perpetrator, closeness of the relationship between offender and victim, the child's age at the onset of the abuse, repeated abuse and, possibly, threats and

Table 8 Patterns of disclosure of sexually abused children

Patterns	Study	Type of sample
1. A majority of children do not disclose immediately or within one month of the abuse	Baker and Duncan (1985)	Probability sample (UK)
	Finkelhor, Hotaling, Lewis, and Smith (1990)	Community sample (US)
	Anderson, Martin, Mullen, Romans, and Herbison (1993)	Community sample (NZ)
	Fleming (1997)	Community sample (Aust.)
	Smith et al. (2000)	National population sample (US)
	Kogan (2004)	National population sample (US)
	Alaggia (2004)	Mixed clinical/non-clinical (US)
	Ullman and Filipas (2005)	College students (US)
	London, Bruck, Ceci, and Shuman (2005)	Review of 11 retrospective studies
	Hebert, Tourigny, Cyr, McDuff, and Joly (2009)	Community sample (Canada)
	Connolly, Chong, Coburn, and Lutgens (2015)	Court judgments 1986–2012 (Canada)
2. A majority of children only disclose sexual abuse one or more years after it occurred, or not at all	Finkelhor et al. (1990)	
	Anderson et al. (1993)	
	Roesler and Wind (1994)	Clinical sample (US)
	Smith et al. (2000)	
	London et al. (2005)	
	Hebert et al. (2009)	
3. Children abused by strangers, or those abused by offenders outside their immediate family are more likely to disclose within one month	Arata (1998)	College students (US)
	Smith et al. (2000)	
	Kogan (2004)	
	Herbert et al. (2009)	
3a. Stranger abuse is a key predictor of rapid disclosure	Smith et al. (2000)	
	Priebe and Svedin (2008)	National Adolescent Sexuality Survey (Sweden)
	Connolly et al. (2015)	
4. Children abused by family members are more likely to delay disclosure longer than one month	Sauzier (1989)	Clinical sample (US)
	Anderson et al. (1993)	
	Arata (1998)	
	Smith et al. (2000)	
	Goodman-Brown et al. (2003)	Forensic sample (US)
	Kogan (2004)	
	Hershkowitz et al. (2005)	Forensic sample (Israel)
	Priebe and Svedin (2008)	
	Herbert et al. (2009)	
	Connolly et al. (2015)	
	Cashmore et al. (2017) (including trusted relationships)	Reports to police 1994–2014 (NSW & SA, Australia)

(continued)

Table 8 (continued)

Patterns	Study	Type of sample
5. Children who experience multiple abuse are less likely to disclose	Arata (1998) Smith et al. (2000) Kogan (2004)	
6. Less intrusive forms of abuse are more likely to be reported	Sauzier (1989) Arata (1998) Lev-Wiesel and First (2018) *cf* Smith et al. (2000)	Representative sample of school children (Israel)
7. The younger the child at the onset of abuse, the less likely she or he will disclose	Fleming (1997) (<12 yrs) Smith et al. (2000) Kogan (2004) (<7 yrs) Hershkowitz et al. (2005) Bunting (2014)	CSA reports to the police in Northern Ireland, 2008–2010
8. Threats and use of force may be associated with delay; data inconclusive	Smith et al. (2000) London et al. (2005)	
9. Authority figures (e.g. police) are the least common type of confidant	Russell (1983) Anderson et al (1993) Fleming (1997) Arata (1998) Smith et al. (2000) Kogan (2004) Priebe and Svedin (2008)	Community sample (US)
10. Friends are the most common type of confidant; disclosure to peers increases with age	Smith et al. (2000) Kogan (2004) London et al. (2005) Priebe and Svedin (2008) *cf* Fleming (1997) and Arata (1998) (mothers most common)	
11. Embarrassment, shame, being blamed or feeling responsible for the abuse are key factors that prevent children from reporting	Anderson et al. (1993) Roesler and Wind (1994) Fleming (1997) Goodman-Brown et al. (2003) Royal Commission into Institutional Responses to Child Sexual Abuse (2017a)	Reports to the Commission, 2013–2017
12. Males are less willing to disclose than females	Lev-Wiesel and First (2018) Royal Commission into Institutional Responses to Child Sexual Abuse (2017a)	

Source Updated from Cossins (2010)

use of force. Consistent with the data discussed in this chapter, the studies in Table 8 reveal that victims are least likely to disclose to the police compared to others, such as peers, and for reasons similar to adults—embarrassment and shame.

While sexual abuse within families is the type of abuse least likely to be disclosed, such delayed disclosure is compounded by the fact that repeated abuse is common in cases of intrafamilial sexual abuse (Fischer & McDonald, 1998; Goodman-Delahunty, 2014; Ventus, Antfolk, & Salo, 2017), a factor that is also implicated in delayed disclosure.

The delayed disclosure pattern of CSA victims means that reported offences will be skewed not only by extended delay, but also by the type of victim who is more likely to disclose, compared to other types of victims. As I observed in 2010 (Cossins, 2010: 82–83), the above studies show that:

> delay is a typical, rather than an aberrant, feature of child sexual abuse. This broad range of studies [in Table 8] ... shows that the patterns of disclosure are remarkably similar in relation to both general population samples (representative samples) and clinical/forensic samples (unrepresentative samples). The findings from these studies indicate that if a child does not report immediately or within one month it is likely that he or she will either not disclose for some years or not disclose at all.

5.1 The Consequences of Delayed Disclosure of CSA

Different studies have reported different associations between delayed reports and outcomes after report to the police. For example, in Northern Ireland, Bunting (2008) found that the shortest and longest delays were more likely to result in sanctions such as arrest, summons or formal caution, with the former coinciding with more immediate reporting and the latter coinciding with complaints made by adults. Similarly, Bunting (2014) found that more immediate reporting was associated with a greater likelihood of CSA cases being prosecuted for children aged 7–17 years (at the date of offence) (49%), compared with complaints reported a year or more later by the same age group (33%). However, these results were not replicated for historical complaints by female adults where there was a greater likelihood of a case proceeding if the complainant was less than 13 years at the time of offence (20% *cf* 4% if aged 13–17 years at offence).

In Australia, Cashmore et al. (2017: 52) investigated the association between delayed reporting and case outcomes, using CSA reports to the police from 1994–2014 in NSW and South Australia. In NSW, there was a total of 101,632 incidents during this period, with 80.5% being reported while the complainant was under 18 years of age. The majority involved female victims (80.4%). Delay was 'defined as the time between the incident and the reporting date and categorized as: same day, next day, 2 days–3 months, 3 months–1 year, 1–5 years, 5–10 years, 10–20 years, more than 20 years' (Cashmore et al., 2017: 52).

In NSW, the chances of a police report of CSA proceeding to prosecution was relatively low in the 2010s compared to the 1990s:

> In 1995, a suspect was identified in 94% of all child reports of sexual assault, and 'proceeded against', in 63% of these incidents. In 2014, a suspect was identified in only 55.4% of reported incidents, and proceeded against in only 33.5% of these incidents. Overall, legal proceedings were commenced in only 18.6% of the 2285 sexual assault incidents reported to police in 2014 compared with 59% in 1995. (Cashmore et al., 2017: 54)

When comparing offences reported in childhood versus adulthood, the authors noted the different outcomes:

> there was a marked decline in the proportion of cases proceeding to court between 1995 and 2014. This proportion was consistently highest for indecent assault offences reported in adulthood, peaking at 73% in 1995 and 79% in 2002 and dropping to 44% in 2014. There was a similar trend for sexual assault reported in both childhood and adulthood. Incidents of sexual assault and indecent assault reported during childhood, although more numerous, were less likely to proceed than those reported during adulthood, dropping to a low of 18% for sexual assault in 2010, followed by an increase to 32% in 2014. (Cashmore et al., 2017: 54)

Thus, reports of CSA were significantly more likely to proceed in the mid-1990s compared to the following decade with odds ratios of 3.04 for 1996 compared to 0.67 for 2014. Counter-intuitively, the likelihood of a case proceeding increased with longer delays up to 20 years whereas 'only

10% of sexual assault incidents reported on the same or the next day in 2014 proceeded' (Cashmore et al., 2017: 55), a finding that was independent of the age of the child at offence date. Nonetheless, cases involving a complainant who was aged 5 years or younger had the lowest probability of proceeding while legal action was more likely for male adolescents (41%) than female adolescents (33%) (Cashmore et al., 2017: 55–56), suggesting a bias against cases involving females.

The relationship between the suspect and the complainant also affected the likelihood of a reported incident of CSA proceeding to court, in that '[t]he most likely to proceed were child and adult reports of indecent assault involving suspects in positions of authority (49.5% for adult reports and 36.3% for child reports)' (Cashmore et al., 2017: 56). But the relationship was mediated by age at the time of report so that:

> [m]ore than double the proportion of incidents involving parents and guardians proceeded when the incident was reported in adulthood (44.7%) than in childhood (19.3%). This was also the case for adult reports of incidents involving other family members (45.9%) compared with child reports (20.8%). (Cashmore et al., 2017: 56)

While the likelihood of legal action proceeding 'increased with the age of the complainant at the time of the alleged offence', it also increased 'with the difference in age between the complainant' and the suspect, while '[t]he most likely to proceed were child and adult reports of indecent assault involving suspects in positions of authority' (Cashmore et al., 2017: 56).

A comparison of the two Australian jurisdictions, South Australia and NSW, found that, for 2012–2014, in NSW, 'legal action [only] commenced in 16.6% of child reports and 33.0% of adult reports of sexual assault' with similar figures for indecent assaults (19.3% of child reports and 35% of adult reports) (Cashmore et al., 2017: 59). By comparison:

> [t]he proportion of child reports that proceeded was two to three times higher in SA than in NSW, and higher (but not as markedly so) for adult reports. The reason for these differences is not clear, but may well reflect

> differences in policy and practice. There was some evidence that while in SA, cases were more likely to proceed to court, the prosecution was more likely to be dropped once at court. That is, the filters operated at different stages – in NSW in the decision whether to charge; in SA, in the decision whether to continue with the prosecution. (Cashmore et al., 2017: 59)

Overall, the following can be said about reported incidents of CSA in NSW:

- the odds of prosecution appear to be dependent on the jurisdiction;
- prosecution rates have dropped significantly since the 1990s compared to the mid-2010s;
- adult reports are more likely to proceed than reports made in childhood, even with long delays of up to 20 years;
- cases with a complainant aged 5 years or younger had the lowest probability of proceeding;
- legal action was more likely for male adolescents than female adolescents;
- the relationship between complainant and perpetrator affected prosecution rates, with cases involving those in positions of authority the most likely to proceed;
- complainant age mediated relationship in that if the incident was reported in adulthood, cases involving parents, guardians and other family members were more likely to proceed than if reported in childhood; and
- cases were more likely to proceed with increasing age of the complainant at the time of the incident and with increasing age difference between complainant and perpetrator.

6 Attrition Rates of Sexual Assault: The 'Justice Gap'

Sexual assault victims experience a 'justice gap' (Temkin & Krahé, 2008), with a significant difference between the number of reports to police and the number of cases that result in charges being laid and prosecuted, with attrition at each stage of the process from report through to trial, with lower conviction rates compared to other offence types.

Decades of research shows that the prosecution of adult and child sexual assault cases is characterised by:

i. relatively high attrition rates both after the first report to police and prior to trial;
ii. a relatively low guilty plea rate for those charged with a sex offence compared to other offences;
iii. a relatively low probability of conviction if a case goes to trial; and
iv. relatively high rates of success on appeal.

In a comparative analysis of adult rape cases in Australia, Canada and the UK, Daly and Bouhours (2010) found that only 14% of sex offences were reported, of which 30% were prosecuted, 20% were adjudicated in court, with 12.5% resulting in a conviction. In a study of the NSW criminal justice system, Fitzgerald (2006) reported that, in 2004, criminal charges were initiated for 19% of reported sexual offences against adults and 15% of reported sexual offences against children. In the higher courts, where most serious offences are prosecuted, defendants were less likely to plead guilty to charges of CSA (45%), or sexual offences against adults (23%) than defendants overall (70%). Conviction rates for at least one charge in the higher courts were also appreciably lower for CSA and adult sex offences (38% and 25%, respectively) than for all offence types (50%). Taylor (2007) also found that acquittal rates for adult sexual offences in Australian higher courts were notably higher (at around 60%) than for other serious crimes including homicide, assault and drug offences.

In 2007, Her Majesty's Crown Prosecution Service Inspectorate (HMCPSI) in the UK reported that police did not proceed with one-half to two-thirds of reports while of those that were sent to the Crown Prosecution Service (CPS), a third to one-half of cases were dropped. Of cases that went to trial, about half resulted in a guilty verdict, which represented about 6% of reports to police.

Have there been any improvements since the early 2000s? In 2018, data from the CPS showed that:

> three in five of rape-flagged prosecutions and four in five of prosecutions for other sexual offences resulted in a conviction. Of those that did not result in a conviction, over half were due to acquittals. A further 16% of rape-flagged cases and 13% of other sexual offences that did not result in a conviction were due to victim retraction, victim non-attendance or evidence of the victim not supporting the case. (ONS, 2018: 2)

However, these statistics do not give us the conviction rates as a result of guilty pleas versus convictions as a result of a trial verdict, or the percentage of cases that were not dropped or withdrawn, nor does this data reveal formal or informal 'plea bargaining' methods for obtaining guilty pleas.

Before discussing the attrition data in detail below, I want to consider the reasons why sexual offences, and rape in particular, are so difficult to prosecute, with less than 10% of reported cases resulting in a conviction such that 'one might argue that in England and Wales rape is effectively "decriminalized"' (Hohl & Stanko, 2015: 325). In fact, this book attempts to answer the question, 'What makes a rape complaint credible in the eyes of criminal justice agents, and what discredits a complainant?' (Hohl & Stanko, 2015: 325) in order to understand why few cases go to court and most drop out.

Law reformers like myself may have thought that reform to the substantive law governing sex offences, such as a clear definition of consent and the enactment of provisions covering the range of possible sexual assaults, would assist police and prosecutors in laying charges. Other reforms since the 1990s have focused on assisting victims at the time of their report to police and in giving evidence in court, including specialist police investigators in NSW and E&W, Sexual Assault Referral Centres which provide medical and psychological services to complainants in E&W, 'rape suites' in police stations in E&W, Joint Investigation Response Teams in NSW[6] and protections to enable

[6] See https://www.health.nsw.gov.au/parvan/jirt/Pages/default.aspx.

complainants to give evidence outside the courtroom such as closed-circuit television (CCTV) and pre-recording of evidence. Nonetheless, assistance to complainants does not appear to have affected either the attrition rate of sex offences nor increased conviction rates (see, for example, Hamlyn, Phelps, Turtle, & Sattar, 2004).

Below I examine the latest available data on the phenomenon of attrition in more detail.

6.1 England and Wales

While only a minority of sexual offences are reported to the police, recent data reveals that, of reported incidents, the vast majority either do not proceed beyond an initial police investigation, do not result in charges, or are not prosecuted. If cases go to trial, '[t]he UK has one of the lowest conviction rates for rape in Europe' (Hohl & Stanko, 2015: 324).

It is possible to identify attrition points at three key sites within the criminal justice system:

i. the police investigation stage where the case does not progress to charging a suspect due to:
   - complainant withdrawal;
   - police decision that no crime has occurred;
   - no suspect identified; or
   - insufficient evidence.
ii. the CPS decides not to prosecute because there is no realistic prospect of conviction which is affected by expectations about jury decision-making; and
iii. case withdrawn prior to trial.

The attrition rate is greatest at the police investigation stage, 'with victim withdrawal accounting for a large proportion of the attrition' (Hohl & Stanko, 2015: 326) as discussed below.

The latest data available from the ONS in E&W, published in 2018, reveals that attrition is the perennial problem associated with sexual offences and is a historic problem of at least the last two decades:

> [t]he proportion of complaints that result in … sanction detections, prosecutions and conviction – has declined noticeably. Whereas 24 percent of complaints resulted in a conviction in 1985, only 12 percent did so in 1995, and conviction rates have remained at around a low 7 percent since 2000 … [T]he series of legal changes, HMIC inspections, guideline revisions and government-commissioned reviews have not been accompanied by a reduction of the attrition problem. Attrition is still high, and getting worse, at every stage of the criminal justice process. (Hohl & Stanko, 2015: 326; references omitted)

Before discussing the ONS (2018) report on attrition rates, it is useful to discuss the study by Hohl and Stanko (2015) as a comparison. Hohl and Stanko (2015: 325) analysed 'a large, representative sample of rape complaints made to the UK's largest police force, the Metropolitan Police Service in London (MPS)' during April and May 2012 in order to determine the factors that affect attrition of rape complaints made by women.

From a sample of 587 cases, Hohl and Stanko (2015: 332–335) reported the following results. First, complainant withdrawal explained 48% of attrition of reported cases and was highest during the police investigation stage (67%) compared to pre-trial (12%). However, withdrawal was dependent on a victim's relationship with police in that 'the odds of victim withdrawal increase[d] by 308 percent if the victim ceased[d] cooperation with police'. Attendance at a Sexual Assault Referral Centre decreased the likelihood of withdrawal by 44% as did the police's ability to identify a suspect. Nonetheless, attendance at a Sexual Assault Referral Centre 'did not significantly reduce attrition through withdrawal for victims with mental health issues' (Hohl & Stanko, 2015: 337). As discussed in Chapter 4, the lack of trauma-informed care within the criminal justice system for complainants with mental health issues is a major barrier to successful prosecutions.

Complainant withdrawal was also influenced by the relationship with the suspect in that a 'current or previous intimate partnership … or previous consensual sex with the suspect (outside a relationship) nearly doubles the odds of withdrawal', although withdrawal was less likely when the suspect had a prior criminal record of any kind.

Of the remaining cases where the complainant wanted to continue:

- 19% were no-crimed by police (11% of case outcomes);
- 67% were designated no further action by police (39% of case outcomes);
- 14% were designated no further action by the CPS (8% of case outcomes);
- 22% involved ongoing police investigations;
- 6% were awaiting a CPS decision at the time of data collection; and
- only 9% of non-withdrawn cases were awaiting trial at the time of data collection (approximately six months after complaint to police).

The second attrition point found by the study was the decision by police to no-crime a rape incident, with this outcome accounting for:

- 19% of attrition in non-withdrawn cases; and
- 11% of all case outcomes.

For a comparison, in 2012/2013 the average no-criming rate for rape complaints in England and Wales was 12%, six times higher than for other victim-based crimes (2%; HMIC, 2014).

Hohl and Stanko (2015) reported that no-criming is influenced by various factors including:

- a previous false allegation by the complainant (increases the odds by 786%);
- evidence that contradicts the allegation (increases the odds by 585%);
- doubt about the truthfulness of the allegation (increases the odds by 240%);
- complainant inconsistencies (increase the odds by 443%);
- complainant's 'lack of understanding of consent' (increases the odds 540%);
- complainant mental health issues (increase the odds by 2.3 times); and
- complainants with learning difficulties (increase the odds by 4.4 times).

None of the allegations that were associated with a previous false allegation, complainant inconsistencies or police doubt were prosecuted (Hohl & Stanko, 2015: 325). By contrast, there was a 70% reduction in the odds of no-criming if a suspect had a prior criminal record.

Race and ethnicity also seem to be important variables since '[n]on-white suspects [had] 70 percent lower odds of no-criming, regardless [of] the ethnicity of the victim'. Complainant ethnicity also influenced the odds of no-criming since a case was two times more likely to be no-crimed if both the suspect and victim were white, and 11 times more likely if the victim was non-white, suggesting that 'white suspects are significantly … more likely to avoid further investigation than non-white suspects, in particular if their victim is non-white'.

The next point of attrition was a police investigation that resulted in no further action so that there was no referral to the CPS. This was the point at which the largest number of non-withdrawn cases suffered attrition (67%). The authors identified three factors that militated against attrition at this point, with the first being the most important:

- 'evidence and incident characteristics that lend the allegation credibility';
- a suspect who is a 'credible criminal'; and
- a complainant who is a 'credible victim'.

By contrast, if there was evidence that raised doubt about the complainant's account, there was a tenfold increase in the odds of no further action. While supporting evidence 'reduces the odds of attrition at this stage by 72 percent', a complainant's inconsistencies increased the odds of no further action by 295%.

Consistent with various rape myths discussed in Chapter 2, the 'odds of attrition … are halved if the victim physically resisted the assault, but increase by 470 percent if the victim delayed reporting' while the presence of victim injuries was a not statistically significant factor in attrition. Nonetheless, a suspect with a criminal record reduced the odds of attrition by 70%, irrespective of the type of offence.

Complainant behaviour also increased the likelihood of no further action including:

- a previous false allegation where that case had not been no-crimed (all cases);
- a history of consensual sex between the complainant and suspect (2.2 times);
- complainant mental health problems (1.5 times); and
- voluntary alcohol consumption prior to the assault (2.1 times).

Other factors *decreased* the likelihood of no further action by almost 60%, including:

- Victim support in the form of attendance at a Sexual Assault Referral Centre; and
- a video-recorded statement.

Interestingly, if a complainant was under the age of 13 years, these cases were 'nearly 4 times less likely to suffer attrition at this stage'.

Finally, the failure of the CPS to prosecute a case was the third point of attrition, accounting for 14% of non-withdrawn cases, and was based on factors that were very similar or the same as those that influenced police decisions:

- complainant inconsistencies (none of these cases were prosecuted);
- complainant mental health problems; and
- police doubts noted in the case file.

Race also played a part since a decision to lay charges by the CPS was 'significantly more likely if the victim and suspect were non-white … and if the suspect was a known sex offender'.

Overall, Hohl and Stanko (2015) found that 7% of cases were no-crimed, 40% resulted in no further action by police and 30% suffered attrition due to no further action by the CPS. Only 15% of non-withdrawn cases were awaiting trial at the time of data collection (Hohl

& Stanko, 2015: 335). While this study is a first in revealing the reasons behind police and prosecutorial decisions, complainants' reasons for withdrawing their complaints, their satisfaction with police responses, and their views about the validity of alleged false allegations, inconsistencies and police doubts would be required to complete the picture. As Hohl and Stanko (2015: 336) observe, the number of alleged false allegations in the sample (3.7%) is considerably higher than the prosecutions for making a false allegation of rape in 2011/2012 (0.2%).

However, complainants would probably be disturbed at the extent to which rape myths affected police decision-making since:

> voluntary alcohol consumption prior to the rape, a history of consensual sex with the perpetrator, mental health problems and learning difficulties, and a woman's 'misunderstanding' of the meaning of consent explain police decisions to discontinue a case. (Hohl & Stanko, 2015: 336)

Not surprisingly, given the history of how rape allegations have been dealt with in E&W over the centuries, it appears that:

> one of the most influential factors is the perceived credibility of the allegation … as seen through the eyes of the investigating police officer and prosecutor. Only 2 percent of complaints in which police officers noted doubt about the allegation resulted in a CPS charge. (Hohl & Stanko, 2015: 337)

Even independent evidence supporting a complaint of rape did not prevent attrition to a statistically significant extent, 'revealing a stark asymmetry between the non-significant impact of supporting evidence and the large, statistically significant effect of evidence that casts doubt on the allegation'.

As discussed in Chapter 4, a sexual assault complainant is more likely than not to be suffering from the symptoms of trauma, including PTSD, which means that the police, as a complainant's first contact with the criminal justice system, may unknowingly re-traumatise her through rude, ignorant or indifferent responses. We do not know how many cases drop out because a traumatised complainant cannot cope with an indifferent (or worse) police response. As discussed in Chapter 4, the creation of trust is a key element when dealing with trauma survivors. Training in the management of trauma victims would seem to be an essential part of police training in order to ensure that complainants participate in the criminal justice system rather than withdrawing. Yet reasons for not reporting or the withdrawal of a complaint include:

> a lack of trust in the police and criminal justice system, a fear of not being believed and taken seriously, and feeling 'raped all over again' by the way the police question both the victim and their account. The tentative trust required to report the rape is quickly lost when police officers communicate disbelief and disrespect or when the victim loses faith in the police to effectively investigate the case. (Hohl & Stanko, 2015: 327)

In light of Hohl and Stanko's (2015) study, which was limited to cases reported over a two-month period to one police service in 2012, let's look at attrition for a 3-year period as documented by the Ministry of Justice et al. (2013). Generally, the most serious sexual offences, including penetration and serious sexual assault, are reported which, in 2011/2012, accounted for 71% of all sex offences recorded by police (Ministry of Justice et al., 2013: 6).

Figures 2 and 3 display the typical inverted pyramid for the progression of sexual assault and rape offences through the criminal justice system, with convictions representing the pointy end of the pyramid. Because of the phenomenon of attrition, the number of cases decrease as they progress. In Fig. 2, sexual assault convictions represented between 1.1 to 1.3% of the estimated number of victims while rape convictions represented 1.1 to 1.8% of the estimated number of victims. In Fig. 3, sexual assault convictions represented 10.3% of recorded police incidents while rape convictions represented 6.8% of recorded police incidents. Thus, attrition in E&W was a significant problem nearly 10 years ago, with the vast majority of recorded rape and sexual assault incidents not proceeding to court.

Has the situation changed since 2012?

Between April 2017 and March 2018, the police recorded 150,847 sexual offences which is almost three times the number recorded since the year ending March 2012 as a result of improved police recording

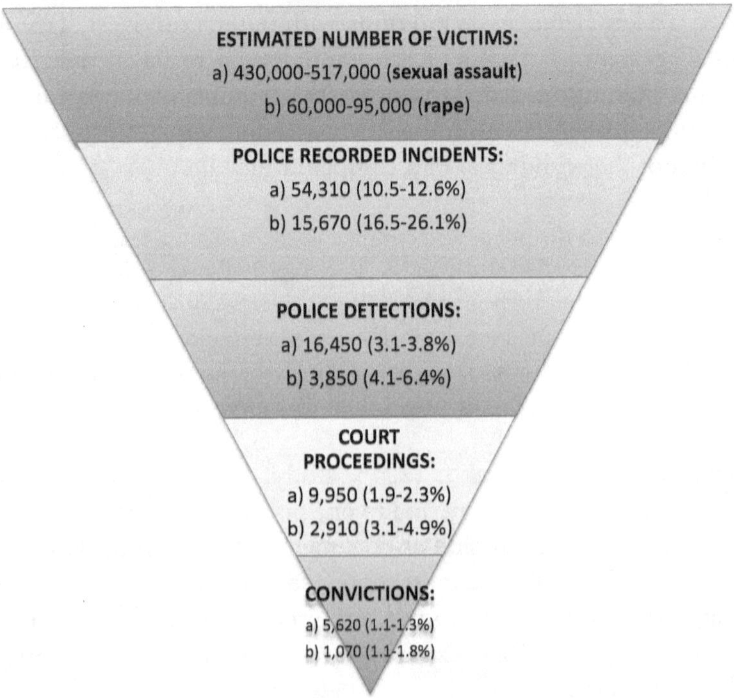

Fig. 2 Convictions for incidents of sexual assault & rape as a proportion of the estimated number of victims (3-year average E&W: 2009/2010, 2010/2011, 2011/2012)

practices (ONS, 2018: 13). Eighty-four per cent of victims were female while more than a third of recorded sexual offences were rape (36%). This figure compares with about one in seven people who said they were raped in the latest CSEW survey, suggesting that victims are more likely to report the most serious sexual offences to police. Nonetheless, 'rapes within a relationship [may be] less likely to be reported to the police than rapes committed by other perpetrators' (ONS, 2018: 15).

Police take longer with sexual offences to assign an outcome compared to other recorded crimes (ONS, 2018: 17) so that only 82% (123,440) were assigned an outcome for the year ending March 2018 with police taking an average of 73 days, compared to an average of 15 days for violence against the person and six days for all crimes. For rape offences,

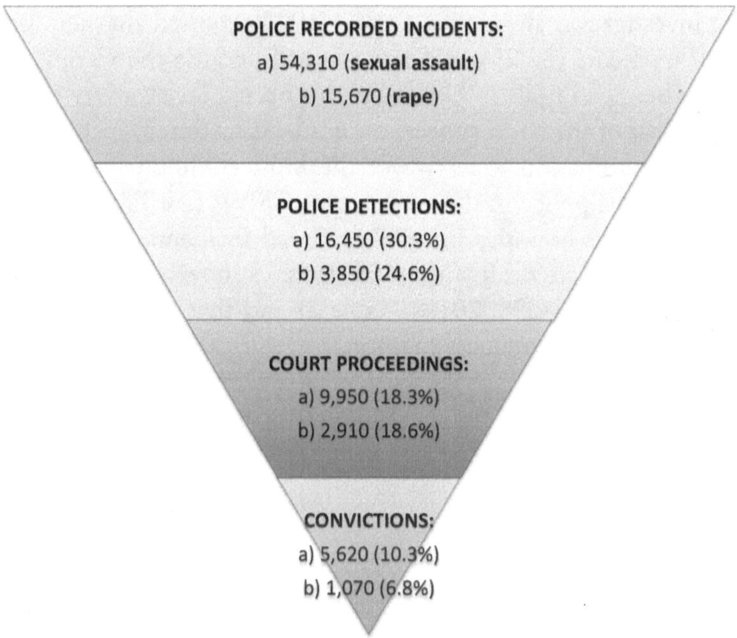

Fig. 3 Convictions for incidents of sexual assault & rape as a proportion of police-recorded incidents (3-year average E&W: 2009/2010, 2010/2011, 2011/2012)

the average number of days for the assignment of an outcome was 129 days (ONS, 2018: 17).

Overall, sexual offences 'are among those that take the longest amount of time to conclude' from offence to completion in court (ONS, 2018: 35). For 2017, the average completion time was more than a year (470 days) (ONS, 2018: 35), although the longest delay is 'between the date of the offence and the date the defendant was charged or summonsed' (ONS, 2018: 35) while these cases take longer to investigate. Compared to violence against the person offences, where the average time to complete was 204 days (median: 130), adult rape cases took an average of 1003 days (median: 524) while child rape cases took the longest to complete: an average of 4273 days (median: 2115 days).

Compared to the study by Hohl and Stanko (2015) where 48% of reported cases were attributed to complainant withdrawal (67% at the police investigation stage), the ONS (2018) reported that almost one-third of incidents (32.2%) did not proceed because the victim did not want further action taken. No doubt this occurs for a variety of reasons although fear of the court process cannot be discounted since embarrassment and humiliation were two of the most common reasons for not reporting to the police in the most recent CSEW (see Table 4).

Table 9 shows how the 150,847 recorded incidents of sexual assault for 2017–2018 were dealt with. CPS statistics show that the majority of victims are female (CPS, 2018a, Table 2) and that the vast majority of defendants in sexual offences cases are male (for the period April 2011–March 2018, an average of 98.5 defendants charged were male).

In particular, only 6% of the 150,847 recorded incidents resulted in a charge or summons with 51.3% being categorised as having evidential

Table 9 Police-recorded incidents of sexual offences, E&W, April 2017–March 2018

Outcome	Percentage (number)
Charged or summonsed	6.0 (9097)
Caution or warning	1.0 (1502)
Prosecution prevented/not in public interest	2.8 (4205)
Evidential difficulties/victim supported further action	19.1 (28,887)
Evidential difficulties/victim did not support further action	32.2 (48,586)
No suspect identified	15.5 (23,315)
Action undertaken by another body/agency	3.0 (4456)
Further investigation not in public interest	2.2 (3392)
No outcome assigned	18.2 (27,407)
Total	100% (150,847)

Source ONS (2018)

difficulties which meant that 'the police were unable to build a strong enough case' to prosecute, or the victim or offender could not be located (ONS, 2018: 18). Worryingly, the ONS (2018: 20) reported:

> a fall in the percentage of sexual offences that have been dealt with by charge or summons outcomes (from 13% in the year ending March 2016 to 6% in the year ending March 2018). This is partly because there are more cases yet to be assigned an outcome in the latest year. However, if those cases that are still under investigation are excluded, there is still a sharp fall in the charge or summons outcomes rate from 16% to 7% over the same time period.

Just as worrying is the fact that the absolute number of charges for sexual offences has also fallen 'from 17,571 in the year ending March 2016 to 14,071 in the year ending March 2018' (ONS 2018: 20) even though police-recorded sexual offences increased by 42% from 106,383 to 150,847. At the very least, one would expect about the same proportion of charges to be laid from one year to the next.

Perhaps not surprisingly, rape offences, which usually turn on the issue of consent, are less likely to result in a charge or summons compared to less serious sexual offences so that only 3% of the 53,970 recorded rape offences resulted in this outcome (ONS, 2018: 20).

Attrition happens not only at the investigation stage (with just over one-half of reported incidents not proceeding because of evidential difficulties, as stated above) but also at the CPS end. In relation to CPS charging decisions for the year ending March 2018, out of 6012 rape-flagged offences, just under half (47%) resulted in a decision to charge and progressed further. This meant that 2822 defendants were charged, which was a decrease of 23% from the previous year (ONS, 2018: 21).

When it comes to prosecutions, in 2017, there were 11,311 defendants proceeded against at magistrates' courts for all sexual offences, a 10% decrease from 2016. This reduction was 'similar to the reduction in the absolute number of police charges for sexual offences recorded in 2017 compared with the previous year'. Nonetheless, '[s]exual assault offences accounted for the highest proportion of defendants in 2017

(40%), followed by rape (28%)', proportions that have been stable for the preceding five years (ONS, 2018: 25).

A 7% decrease in convictions was also recorded for all courts E&W in 2017: 6960 offenders were found guilty of sexual offences, compared with 7511 in 2016 (ONS, 2018: 26). Nonetheless, between 2013 and 2016 there had been an increase in conviction rates while 'the number of offenders found guilty at all courts [in 2017] is 23% higher than in 2013'.

When conviction ratios are considered, that is, convictions as a proportion of the number of proceedings, it is possible to identify a third drop-off or attrition point in the criminal justice system. Between 2012 and 2013 there was a large decrease in the conviction ratio in E&W (61–52%). Since 2013, the conviction ratio for all sexual offences has been increasing annually so that it now exceeds the conviction ratio for 2012, that is, 61.4% in 2017 (ONS, 2018: 27), 63.7% in 2018 and 71.3% in 2019 (Ministry of Justice, 2019, Table 3.4).

However, these figures do not tell us the conviction rates *at trial*, nor do they discriminate between conviction rates at trial for different age groups of complainants or for female vs male complainants. This means we have no way of knowing if this increasing annual conviction rate is a result of higher guilty plea rates, fewer acquittals at trial or fewer marginal cases going to trial. For example, since 2017, the number of overall convictions for sexual offences decreased from 26,643 for the year ending March, 2017, to 23,248 for the year ending March, 2018 to 18,955 for the year ending March, 2019 (Ministry of Justice, 2019, Table 3.5), a decrease of 28.9% over that two-year period. This matches the decrease in the number of defendants found guilty in all courts of sexual offences for the years ending March, 2017 (7608), 2018 (6631) and 2019 (5284), a decrease of 30.5% (Ministry of Justice, 2019, Table 3.3).

The annual increase in conviction ratios since 2013 is not the case for rape offences since conviction ratios decreased from 41% in 2012 to 36% in 2017, although the variation in conviction ratios for different sex offences 'is driven by a number of factors, including the likelihood of a guilty plea for that offence, availability and accessibility of evidence, … sentence lengths, witness and victim support, [and] trial lengths' (ONS, 2018: 27). Unfortunately, the latest Ministry of Justice (2019) data does not provide separate conviction ratios for rape compared to other sexual offences.

While the CPS record a much larger number of convictions for rape than the Ministry of Justice (ONS, 2018: 29), the CPS recorded an 11% decrease in completed prosecutions for sexual offences, falling from 13,490 (year ending March 2017), to 12,005 (year ending March 2018) (ONS, 2018: 29; CPS, 2018a, Table 7). Similarly, completed rape-flagged prosecutions recorded a 13% decrease, from 5,190 (year ending March 2017) to 4517 (year ending March 2018), although this latter figure is 17% higher than the year ending March 2012 (ONS, 2018: 30).

However, a '[l]ower proportion of rape-flagged prosecutions resulted in convictions compared with other sexual offences for the year ending March 2018' (ONS, 2018: 30), with 58% resulting in a conviction (that is, 2635 prosecutions which amounts to a 62% decrease compared to the year ending March 2012). By comparison, 'four-fifths (80%) of prosecutions for other sexual offences resulted in a conviction (9,654 prosecutions)', the highest level since 2012 (ONS, 2018: 30). These rates include convictions as a result of guilty pleas and convictions at trial, although there was a lower guilty plea rate for rape-flagged offences than other sexual offences (34% vs 68%) for the year ending March 2018 (ONS, 2018: 31).

For the 42% of rape-flagged cases that did not result in a conviction, 59% resulted in an acquittal; 15% did not progress to trial due to a conflict of evidence, while 'victim retraction, victim non-attendance or evidence of the victim not supporting the case prevented 16% progressing further' (ONS, 2018: 30). Conflict in evidence has seen a 37% increase in cases not progressing since the year ending March 2012 (ONS, 2018: 30), an issue that no doubt influences perceptions of reasonable prospects of conviction based on satisfying the element of lack of consent.

For other sexual offences, there was a 10% decrease in convictions (9654, year ending March 2018) compared to the year ending 2017 (10,721) which matches a decrease in charges for the same period (ONS, 2018: 31).

6.2 Attrition of CSA Cases

Like adult sexual assault cases, attrition also characterises CSA incidents as they progress through the criminal justice system from the first report to police through to court proceedings. In E&W, Kelly and Karsna (2017: 29) reported that 53,811 CSA offences in E&W were recorded by the police in 2015/2016, although this figure includes 12,875 offences related to 'the publication/possession of obscene or protected sexual materials … which include crimes against adults as well as children' and abusing position of trust (which also includes offences against adults).

Figure 4 illustrates the 'considerable attrition as child sex offences proceed from the initial report to charge' (Kelly & Karsna, 2017: 33). Just under 'a quarter (24%) of recorded CSA offences resulted in a charge or summons', with evidential problems being 'the main barrier to a successful outcome'. Overall, 60% of cases were discontinued, including:

- 26% even where a suspect was identified because of insufficient evidence;
- 21% where the victim and/or parents did not support a prosecution; and
- 13% where no suspect was identified (Kelly & Karsna, 2017: 33).

6.3 Summary of Data in England and Wales

The following points can be made about the progress of sexual offences through the criminal justice system in E&W for the period 2017–2018:

- there has been a threefold increase in the number of recorded sexual offences since the year ending March 2012;
- 36% of recorded sexual offences were rape compared to the three-year period, 2009–2010 to 2011–2012 (22.4%);
- police take much longer to assign an outcome to sexual offences (average 73 days compared to 6 days for all crimes, a 12-fold difference);
- most sexual offences drop out at the police investigation stage;

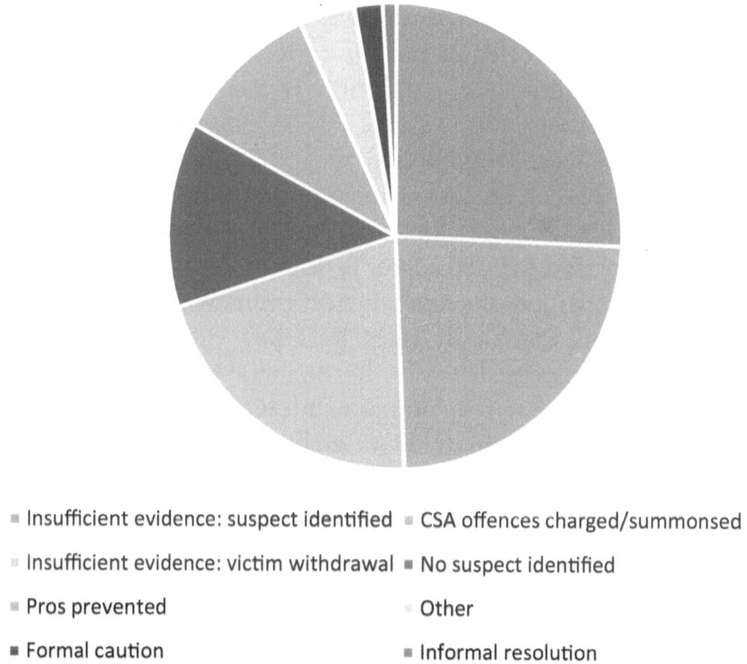

Fig. 4 Attrition of CSA offences prior to prosecution in E&W, year ending March 2016 (data taken from Kelly & Karsna, 2017)

- only 6% of sexual offences resulted in a charge or summons;
- 32.2% of cases did not proceed due to victim withdrawal;
- 51.3% of cases were categorised as having evidential difficulties;
- there was a 7% decrease in convictions in all courts in 2017 compared with 2016;
- from 2017–2019, the number of overall convictions (guilty pleas + verdicts) has decreased by 28.9%;
- the absolute number of charges also fell in 2017 compared to 2016 even though recorded sexual offences increased by 42% in that 12-month period, with a 10% decrease in the number of defendants prosecuted;

- the conviction ratio has increased over the last 3 years and was 71.3% in 2019 for sexual offences but there are no available details on the proportion of guilty pleas versus guilty verdicts.

While the CPS recently published the results of a review of sexual offences (CPS, 2018a), its narrow focus on failed instances of disclosure of evidence to the defence before trial, such as social media messages of the complainant and the defendant, is unlikely to offer solutions to the serious issue of attrition of sexual offences in E&W.

The above data graphically reveal just how difficult it is for these offences to be prosecuted, while the dramatic fall in the number of cases resulting in a charge or summons means that the criminal justice system in E&W is failing in its ability to deal with sexual offences. While there has been a dramatic increase in police-recorded sexual offences, as discussed above, the ONS (2018: 20) considers that the police are recording 'more sexual offences where it is difficult to achieve a charge or summons outcome', presumably due to evidential difficulties.

But what could these be, apart from the inability to locate a suspect or victim, or false complaints? While, historically, there is a strong cultural belief that rape complaints are often false, the incidence of sexual assault in the community compared with those that are reported suggests that false complaints are relatively low, as found in various studies (Kelly, 2010; Levitt & Crown Prosecution Service Equality and Diversity Unit, 2013; Saunders, 2012). Between 2–10% of reports are considered to be false or unfounded (Lisak, Gardinier, Nicksa, & Cote, 2010), although there are question marks over how police investigators define an unfounded or false allegation (Kelly, 2010). A review by the CPS (Levett & Crown Prosecution Service Equality and Diversity Unit, 2013: 3–4) found that out of 5651 prosecutions for rape in E&W between January 2011 and May 2012, there were only 35 prosecutions (0.6%) for making false allegations of rape and that 'a significant number of these cases involved young, often vulnerable people'.

More recently, Hohl and Conway (2017: 260) found that only 1.03% of 679 reports of sexual assault in a 2-month period to the MPS were retracted by complainants as false allegations. Nonetheless, McMillan

(2018: 9) found that 'police officers' estimate of false allegations varies widely from 5 to 90%' and that:

> gender stereotypes about women as deceitful, vengeful and ultimately regretful of sexual encounters, continue to pervade the thinking of some officers … [who] differentiate between 'types' of reports they consider to be false, and operate with a notional 'hierarchy' of presumed false allegations that ranges from vengeful/malicious to mistaken/confused, with a corresponding reducing level of culpability attributed to women for the supposedly false allegation.

Unlike other criminal trials, sexual assault trials are characterized by particular features, including the vulnerability of the prosecution's chief witness, lack of corroborating evidence (in the form of eyewitness testimony and forensic evidence), age-old myths and misconceptions about women and children who complain of sexual assault and the influence of sex offender registration schemes on court outcomes since such schemes do not encourage guilty pleas. This book will discuss these and other barriers to prosecuting sex offences at a time when sex offences are on the increase in terms of reports to police.

In the UK, for example, prosecutors can only prosecute a case if it meets the Full Code Test[7] which involves an evidential test and a public interest test. First, they 'must be satisfied that there is sufficient evidence to provide *a realistic prospect of conviction* against each suspect on each charge'. If so, prosecutors must then 'consider whether a prosecution is required in the public interest', a test that involves consideration of seven factors:

i. how serious the offence is;
ii. the level of culpability of the suspect;
iii. the circumstances of and the harm caused to the victim;
iv. the suspect's age and maturity at the time of the offence;
v. the impact on the community;
vi. whether or not prosecution a proportionate response; and

[7] See https://www.cps.gov.uk/publication/code-crown-prosecutors.

vii. whether there are sources of information requiring protection.[8]

Both tests are inherently subjective, particularly the assessment of whether or not witnesses are credible which is one of the criteria that informs the evidential test. This book will discuss how the trial process, which influences the types of cases that are investigated and prosecuted (Temkin & Krahé, 2008), is a hostile environment for complainants and the non-evidential reasons why so many cases are not prosecuted or result in acquittals.

However, a Home Office study by Thomas (2010: v) reported that '[c]ontrary to popular belief and previous government reports, juries actually convict more often than they acquit in rape cases (55% jury conviction rate)' and that other serious offences (such as attempted murder, manslaughter, and GBH) have lower conviction rates at trial than rape.

Thomas (2010) challenged a previous Home Office study by Kelly et al. (2005) which had concluded that rape convictions were less common than acquittals by juries, on the grounds that the study sample was small (181 verdicts) in a small number of courts. By contrast, Thomas's (2010) study included all verdicts in rape trials conducted before a jury in all courts in E&W between 2006–2008 ($N = 4310$). The study found that conviction rates at trial for rape varied according to the gender and age of the complainant, with high conviction rates for some female and male age groups (62%: females 13–15 years; 77%: males 16 + years; 75%: males < 13 years), and relatively lower conviction rates for males under the age of 16 years (51%) and female complainants over the age of 16 years (47%). Thus, Thomas (2010) concluded that there was no general jury bias against female complainants:

> an analysis of jury conviction rates in rape cases by both age and gender of the complainant … raises doubts about a general jury bias against female complainants. Jury conviction rates are not low for some female complainants and the lowest jury conviction rates in rape cases involve male complainants … as well as female complainants … . This suggests

[8]Ibid; accessed 8 October, 2019.

> that a jury's propensity to convict or acquit in rape cases is not necessarily due to juror attitudes to female complainants. There is no doubt the proportion of rape allegations reported to police that end in conviction is extremely low, but it is also clear that this not due to any widespread jury failure to convict in rape cases. (Thomas, 2010: 32)

However, what Thomas (2010) did not highlight was that the jury conviction rates for females over 16 years compared to males over 16 varied widely (47% vs. 77%) which is likely to be a significant difference and one that does, in fact, suggest that a jury's propensity to convict or acquit is due, in part, to jurors' attitudes towards female complainants.

Another age category in which the conviction rate involving female complainants was significantly lower than the conviction rate for male complainants was the under 13 years age group: 58% (females) compared to 75% (males). The only age category in which the jury conviction rate involving female complainants was higher than for males, was under 16 years of age: 62% versus 51%.

Nonetheless, Thomas (2010: 29) also found that the offence types with the lowest conviction rates were non-fatal offences against the person and sexual offences which 'appear to be ones where the jury has to choose between conflicting versions of events often in the absence of strong corroborating evidence'. As well, in 2007, conviction rates were lower for rape offences involving female complainants than for other violent offences, that is, 46% compared to manslaughter (83%), murder (79%) and robbery (77%) (Ministry of Justice, 2008). It has not been possible to update these figures since the Ministry of Justice (2019) data does not distinguish between male and female victims of these offences.

6.4 Australia: New South Wales

The most recent published data on the *progression* of sexual offences through the NSW criminal justice system is from 2014. Figure 5 shows the points of attrition for both child and adult sexual offences in NSW and the number and proportion of sexual offences at various stages of the criminal justice system. There are two main points of attrition:

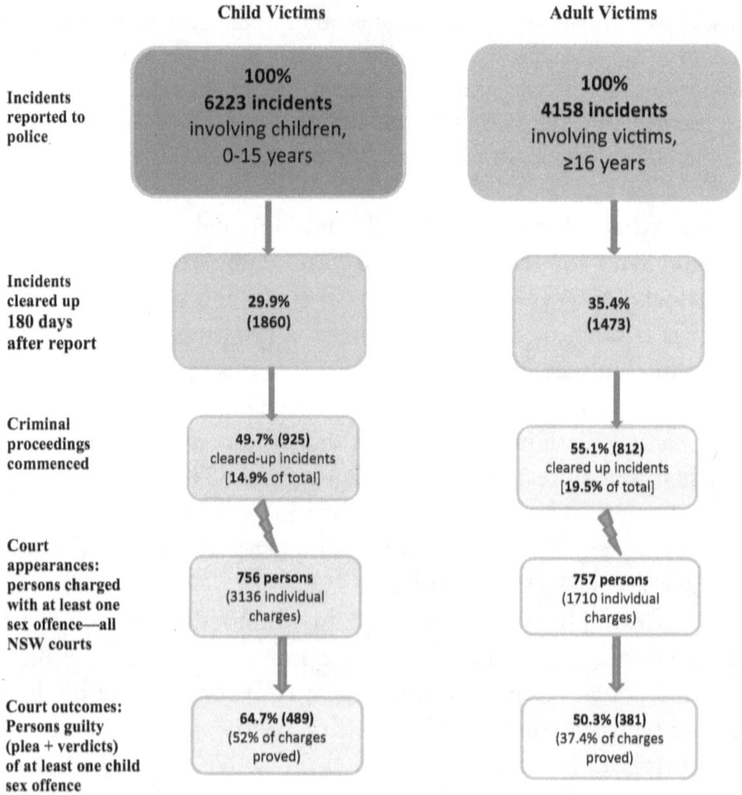

Fig. 5 The progress of sexual offences through NSW criminal justice system, 2014 (NSW Bureau of Crime Statistics and Research [NSWBOCSAR]) (https://www.scribd.com/document/273468462/Sexual-Attribution-Diagrams#). *Notes* (1) Incidents reported to police: includes recorded incidents of sexual assault, indecent assault, acts of indecency and other sexual offences. Incidents involving multiple victims are classified by the age of the youngest victim, (2) The number of court appearances (persons charged with at least one sexual offence) do not directly relate to the incidents recorded by police in 2014

i. police investigation: from the time of report to police to the commencement of proceedings; and
ii. prosecution: court appearances to finalisation of case (guilty/not guilty).

However, in Fig. 5 reported incidents 'are not linked to the court data' since police data records 'criminal incidents and the court data show finalised defendants and charges' (Fitzgerald, 2006: 2). As is typical with CSA, one defendant could have been involved with multiple incidents while a single incident could give rise to multiple charges. As well, annual court statistics 'do not necessarily arise from incidents recorded by police in the same year due to the time it takes to investigate an offence and for charges to be finalised in court' (Fitzgerald, 2006: 2).

In Fig. 5, there were a total of 10,381 sexual offence incidents for 2014, of which 60.0% involved a child. In 2004, only 48% of all sexual offence incidents involved a child (Fitzgerald, 2006).

Sexual offences first drop-out of the criminal justice system between report to police and clear-up. 180 days after report, a cleared criminal incident indicates that the police investigation is over, either because criminal proceedings have been commenced against a defendant or 'for another reason, such as withdrawal of the complaint' while '[i]ncidents that are not cleared are not likely to proceed any further' (Fitzgerald, 2006: 4). Clear-up rates can be affected by a number of factors, such as:

> (1) changes in the time taken by police to clear sexual assault incidents; (2) changes to the definition of what constitutes a 'cleared' sexual assault incident; and (3) changes in the number (and proportion) of cases where police are able to lay criminal charges. (O'Brien, Jones, & Korabelnikoff, 2008: 1)

For example, the third reason was found to be the most plausible by O'Brien et al. (2008) to explain the 63% fall in clearance of sexual assault incidents by the NSW police in 2006 on the grounds that there were:

> statistically significant decreases in the proportion of incidents involving physical injury, weapon use and co-occurring offences and a significant increase in the proportion of incidents where the victim and offender were known to one another.

In 2014, Fig. 5 shows that less than a third (29.9%) of child sex offence incidents and just over one-third of adult sex offence incidents (35.4%) were cleared up six months after report to police. Like the situation in E&W, the police investigation stage is the attrition point where the largest number of sexual offence incidents drop out of the criminal justice system (67.9% in 2014). This was also the case back in 2004 (Fitzgerald, 2006).

The second largest attrition point arises between clear-up and the commencement of criminal proceedings with nearly one-half of cleared child sex offences (49.7%) resulting in the commencement of proceedings, compared to 55.1% of incidents involving an adult victim. In 2004, these figures were 53% and 59%, respectively. In addition, Fig. 5 shows that in 2014, less than 20% of reported incidents involving a sex offence against a child or against an adult saw proceedings commenced (14.9%: child; 19.5%: adults), showing almost no change since 2004 (14.8%: child; 18.6%: adult) (Fitzgerald, 2006).

Court outcomes are measured by reference to the number of defendants who appeared in court, although defendants may have been charged with more than one offence as seen in Fig. 5 where the number of defendants and number of charges are listed. Figure 5 shows that 756 persons appeared in NSW courts in 2014 charged with at least one child sexual offence of whom 64.7% were found guilty either as a result of a guilty plea or guilty verdict. This compares with 547 persons in 2004 and a conviction rate of 44% (Fitzgerald, 2006). The 20% difference in conviction rate is likely due to an increase in the guilty plea rate.

While 757 persons appeared for at least one adult sexual offence in the NSW courts in 2014, only 50.3% were found guilty either as a result of a guilty plea or guilty verdict. This compares with 593 persons in 2004 and a conviction rate of 41.7% (Fitzgerald, 2006).

The higher conviction rate for child sex offences compared with adult sex offences is a phenomenon that has been relatively stable in NSW for the period 2006–2014 and is also seen in more recent data from the ABS, as discussed below. For the year 2004, Fitzgerald (2006: 7) explained that the higher conviction rate for sex offences against children was because these defendants:

> are much more likely to plead guilty (45%) than those appearing for sex offences against adults (23%) and much less likely to be acquitted of all charges after a trial.

Even though the data in Fig. 5 is now 6 years old, the NSW BOCSAR has documented the progression of adult and child sexual offences through the NSW criminal justice system since 2006 as set out in Table 10. This table shows that for the nine-year period, January 2006 to December 2014, the number of reported child sex offences in NSW increased by just over a third (35.8%) (4581 in 2006; 6223 in 2014) whereas the number of reported sex offences against an adult remained fairly constant.

For child sex offences, there was a steady increase in the proportion of reported cases that were cleared up by the police within 180 days from 2006 to 2010, after which, from 2011 to 2014, the clear-up rate began to fall (36.5% in 2010; 29.9% in 2014). For sex offences against adults, the clear-up rate rose from 30.7 to 37.2% in 2010, after which it dropped to 35.4% in 2014.

In relation to the proportion of cleared-up child sex offences cases in which proceedings were commenced, there was a steady decrease from 56.6% in 2006 to a low of 33.1% in 2010. By 2014, this figure had risen again to 49.7%. For the period, 2006–2014, less than 20% of reported incidents involving a sex offence against a child saw proceedings commenced, meaning that on a yearly basis, more than 80% of reported incidents were not prosecuted. In 2006 this figure was 14.5% which decreased to a low of 10.7% in 2012 with an increase to 14.9% by 2014.

For sex offences against adults, proceedings were commenced in 54.9% of cleared-up cases in 2006, a figure which also saw a decrease over time to 47.0% in 2011 with an increase to 55.1% in 2014. Similar to child sex offences, from 2006–2104, less than 20% of reported incidents involving a sex offence against an adult saw proceedings commenced. In 2006, this figure was 16.8% with an increase to 19.5% by 2014.

Thus, in NSW there appears to be a greater reluctance to commence proceedings when a case involves a child complainant, rather than an adult complainant of sexual assault.

On average, there were 638 persons who had court appearances for at least one child sex offence, although the conviction rate (guilty pleas and verdicts) increased from 58.0 in 2006 to 63.6% in 2014. Nonetheless,

Table 10 Sexual assault incidents reported to NSW police involving child and adult victims, 2006–2014 (NSWBOCSAR)[a]

Year	Incidents reported to police with child victim, 0–15 years	Incidents reported to police: Victim, aged ≥16 years
2006	Total: 4581 Cleared up: 25.6% Proceedings: 56.6% **14.5% of total** Court appearances: 591 Court outcomes: (guilty pleas + verdicts): **58.0%**	Total: 4037 Cleared up: 30.7% Proceedings: 54.9% **16.8% of total** Court appearances: 625 Court outcomes: (guilty pleas + verdicts): **50.6%**
2007	Total: 4488 Cleared up: 27.1% Proceedings: 61.2% **16.5% of total** Court appearances: 599 Court outcomes: (guilty pleas + verdicts): **56.8%**	Total: 4255 Cleared up: 29.5% Proceedings: 53.9% **15.9% of total** Court appearances: 634 Court outcomes: (guilty pleas + verdicts): **49.5%**
2008	Total: 4739 Cleared up: 28.0%% Proceedings: 57.8% **16.1% of total** Court appearances: 722 Court outcomes: (guilty pleas + verdicts): **58.4%**	Total: 4078 Cleared up: 32.0% Proceedings: 56.1% **17.9% of total** Court appearances: 637 Court outcomes: (guilty pleas + verdicts): **50.5%**
2009	Total: 5062 Cleared up: 29.0% Proceedings: 45.4% **13.2% of total** Court appearances: 627 Court outcomes: (guilty pleas + verdicts): **63.5%**	Total: 4011 Cleared up: 36.7% Proceedings: 49.4% **18.1% of total** Court appearances: 737 Court outcomes: (guilty pleas + verdicts): **54.4%**
2010	Total: 4886 Cleared up: 36.5% Proceedings: **33.1%** **12.1% of total** Court appearances: 603 Court outcomes: (guilty pleas + verdicts): **60.9%**	Total: 4119 Cleared up: 37.2% Proceedings: 49.3% **18.4% of total** Court appearances: 787 Court outcomes: (guilty pleas + verdicts): **50.2%**
2011	Total: 5636 Cleared up: 30.9% Proceedings: 37.2% **11.5% of total** Court appearances: 578 Court outcomes: (guilty pleas + verdicts): **62.8%**	Total: 4049 Cleared up: 36.0% Proceedings: 47.0% **16.9% of total** Court appearances: 739 Court outcomes: (guilty pleas + verdicts): **49.9%**

(continued)

Table 10 (continued)

Year	Incidents reported to police with child victim, 0–15 years	Incidents reported to police: Victim, aged ≥16 years
2012	Total: 5785 Cleared up: 29.3% Proceedings: 36.6% **10.7% of total** Court appearances: 620 Court outcomes: (guilty pleas + verdicts): **66.1%**	Total: 4059 Cleared up: 35.5% Proceedings: 50.3% **17.8% of total** Court appearances: 717 Court outcomes: (guilty pleas + verdicts): **46.6%**
2013	Total: 6260 Cleared up: 30.6% Proceedings: 47.5% **14.6% of total** Court appearances: 646 Court outcomes: (guilty pleas + verdicts): **59.0%**	Total: 3951 Cleared up: 34.0% Proceedings: 49.7% **16.9% of total** Court appearances: 715 Court outcomes: (guilty pleas + verdicts): **44.9%**
2014	Total: 6223 Cleared up: 29.9% Proceedings: 49.7% **14.9% of total** Court appearances: 756 Court outcomes: (guilty pleas + verdicts): **63.6%**	Total: 4158 Cleared up: 35.4% Proceedings: 55.1% **19.5% of total** Court appearances: 757 Court outcomes: (guilty pleas + verdicts): **42.0%**

[a]https://www.scribd.com/document/273468462/Sexual-Attribution-Diagrams#

Notes

1. Incidents reported to police: includes recorded incidents of sexual assault, indecent assault, acts of indecency and other sexual offences. Incidents involving multiple victims are classified by the age of the youngest victim
2. The number of persons charged with at least one sexual offence do not directly relate to the incidents recorded by police in the years 2006–2014
3. 'Cleared up' means incidents cleared up 180 days after report to police
4. 'Proceedings' means criminal proceedings commenced as a proportion of cleared-up incidents
5. 'Court appearances' means the number of persons who appeared in the NSW courts charged with at least one child sex offence or one sexual offence against an adult
6. 'Court outcomes' means found guilty of at least one child sex offence or one sex offence against an adult
7. Percentages calculated by author

there is no way of saying whether this increase was due to an increase in guilty pleas or an increase in guilty verdicts at trial (or both) since this data is not available. Although court appearances are not a subset of proceedings commenced, except for 2010 and 2012, in no other year did the number of persons with court appearances equal the number of proceedings commenced, suggesting another (smaller) attrition point.

By contrast, an average of 705 persons had court appearances per year for at least one sexual offence against an adult, although the conviction rate (guilty pleas and verdicts) *decreased* from 50.6 in 2006 to 42.0% in 2014. Again, there is no way of knowing whether this decrease was due to a decreasing guilty plea rate or decreasing guilty verdicts at trial, or both.

In 2004, Fitzgerald (2006: 4) concluded that for sexual offences reported to NSW police:

> criminal proceedings are initiated in only 15 percent of incidents involving a child victim and 19 percent of incidents involving adult victims. Of the charges that do reach court, slightly less than half result in a guilty finding. It follows that approximately eight percent of recorded incidents involving children and ten percent of recorded incidents involving adults result in a sexual offence being proven in court.

For sexual offences reported to NSW police in the period 2006–2014, there has been little improvement. On average, only 13.8% of incidents involving a child resulted in criminal proceedings, which is slightly lower than in 2004. Despite the increasing overall conviction rate in this period (an average of 61.0%), approximately 8% of recorded incidents involving children resulted in a guilty finding in court.

Similarly, on average, only 17.6% of sexual offence incidents against an adult resulted in criminal proceedings, which is slightly lower than in 2004. Because of the decreasing overall conviction rate in this period (on average, 48.7%), approximately 8% of recorded incidents involving adults resulted in a guilty finding in court.

Overall, the two main attrition points for sexual offences in NSW occur at the police investigation stage, that is, between reports to police and police clear-up (the largest attrition point) and, second, between clear-up and the decision to prosecute (the commencement of criminal proceedings). While there is a third attrition point at the prosecutorial stage, this constitutes the smallest attrition point because only a relatively small percentage of sexual offences reach this stage.

Decisions to prosecute are influenced by the difficulties in securing a conviction which means that prosecutors will only run those cases that have the highest chances of success according to the reasonable prospect of conviction test in NSW.[9]

Like E&W, prosecutions in NSW are guided by public interest considerations, with the general public interest being 'the paramount criterion' (NSW Office of Public Prosecutions, 2018, Guideline 4) as set out below:

> The question whether or not the public interest requires that a matter be prosecuted is resolved by determining:
>
> (1) whether or not the admissible evidence available is capable of establishing each element of the offence;
>
> (2) whether or not it can be said that there is no reasonable prospect of conviction by a reasonable jury (or other tribunal of fact) properly instructed as to the law; and if not
>
> (3) whether or not discretionary factors nevertheless dictate that the matter should not proceed in the public interest.

However, none of these matters are scientifically measurable or objective and require subjective evaluations based on experience, as recognised in Guideline 4 in relation to the reasonable prospect of conviction test which is:

> an exercise of judgment which will depend in part upon an evaluation of the weight of the available evidence and the persuasive strength of the prosecution case in light of the anticipated course of proceedings, including the circumstances in which they will take place. (NSW Office of Public Prosecutions, 2018)

Furthermore, the public interest in NSW will depend upon consideration of 23 factors, a list too long to set out here but including 'the youth, age, maturity, intelligence, physical health, mental health or special disability or infirmity of the alleged offender, a witness or a victim'. The subjective nature of all 23 factors means that the need for prosecution in the public interest is very much in the eye of the beholder,

[9]That is, 'can it be said that there is a reasonable prospect of conviction by a reasonable jury (or magistrate) properly instructed' (Crime and Misconduct Commission, Queensland, 2003: 52). This is the test in most Australian jurisdictions.

albeit one experienced in the criminal justice system, and one who is aware of the fact that 'the resources available for prosecuting are finite and should not be expended pursuing inappropriate cases'.

This, in turn, means that the highest chances of success will be in cases in which there is supporting evidence, although these are likely to represent a minority of sexual assault cases because of the common problem of delay in complaint, particularly CSA cases.

6.5 Comparison of Finalised Sexual Offences with Other Offences: What Happens at Trial?

The most up to date data available on *finalised* sexual offences in Australia comes from the ABS (2019b). Out of the total adjudicated (which does not include offences that are withdrawn or transferred), the overall conviction rate (guilty pleas and verdicts) for defendants charged with sexual offences (and related offences) in all Australian criminal courts for 2016–2017 and 2017–2018 was 82.8% in both years. This compares with overall conviction rates of 43.3 and 43.2%, respectively when calculated as a proportion of the total number of offences, as set out in Table 11.

Looking at the data for sexual assault (and related offences) in Table 11, the overall conviction rate (guilty pleas and verdicts) is slightly higher than homicide but significantly lower than acts intended to cause injury. As well, sexual assault and homicide are more likely to be transferred to lower courts (which suggests a plea deal involving a lesser offence) than acts intending to cause injury. Despite similarities between acquittal and conviction rates for homicide and sexual offences, the rate at which sexual assault cases are withdrawn by the prosecution is approximately double that for homicide which suggests a difference in case strengths between these two offences.

However, Table 12 gives us more detail about what happens in relation to a range of offences that go to trial and result in a guilty verdict by a fact-finder (judge or jury). Table 12, which focuses on data for NSW, reveals that many more sexual assault matters go to trial, rather than have guilty pleas, compared to all other offences in Table 12,

Table 11 Selected defendants finalised in all Australian criminal courts by principle offence, 2016–2017 to 2017–2018

Offence	Acquitted (%)[a]	Proven guilty (conviction rate[b]) (%)[a]	Total adjudicated (%)	Transferred (%)	Withdrawn by prosecution (%)	Total number
Homicide & related offences 2016–2017	7.6	41.8	49.5	39.4	9.1	967
2017–2018	8.8	39.8	48.2	40.1	8.4	993
Sexual assault & related offences 2016–2017	9.0	43.3	52.3	30.6	16.1	9437
2017–2018	8.9	43.2	52.1	31.5	15.3	9885
Robbery/extortion 2016–2017	2.3	50.8	53.2	34.0	12.7	4418
2017–2018	2.6	50.0	52.5	34.1	13.1	4993
Acts intended to cause injury 2016–2017	5.9	74.8	80.7	3.7	15.3	75,987
2017–2018	6.2	73.1	79.3	4.8	15.3	78,345

Source ABS (2019b, Table 4)
Notes
[a]Percentage of total number
[b]Guilty pleas + guilty verdicts
Percentages calculated by author using ABS (2019b data, Table 4)

except for homicide. This is because of the relatively lower guilty plea rate for sexual assault offences, which was 50.5% in 2016–2017, dropping to 44.0% in 2017–2018, compared to acts intended to cause injury, robbery/extortion, fraud, illicit drugs which have guilty plea rates between 70 and 90%.

Conviction rates as a proportion of total or adjudicated matters do not tell us about how different offences are assessed by fact-finders who must make decisions about the strength of the prosecution's case which includes assessments of witness credibility. As shown in Table 12, sexual assault had the lowest conviction rate *at trial* compared to the other offences listed, as represented by the percentage at 'c', that is, 49.8% in 2016–2017 and 46.9% in 2017–2018 which suggests that there is

Table 12 Selected defendants finalised by principle offence in NSW higher courts, 2016–2017 to 2017–2018

Offence	Acquitted	Guilty plea	Guilty verdict	Adjudicated outcomes	Trf'd	Withdrawn	Total
Homicide 2016–2017	21 (14.6%)	62 (43.1%)	48 a. 33.3% **b. 36.1%** ***c. 69.6%***	133 (92.4%)	0	5 (3.5%)	144
2017–2018	28 (19.0%)	64 (43.5%)	36 a. 24.5%: **b. 26.9%** ***c. 56.3%***	134 (91.2%)	0	5 (3.4%)	147
Sexual assault 2016–2017	148 (18.3%)	409 (50.5%)	147 a. 18.2% **b. 20.9%** ***c. 49.8%***	703 (86.8%)	0	74 (9.1%)	810
2017–2018	183 (23.3%)	345 (44.0%)	162 a. 20.7% **b. 23.4%** ***c. 46.9%***	693 (88.4%)	0	64 (8.2%)	784
Acts intended to cause injury 2016–2017	49 (7.4%)	491 (74.4%)	77 a. 11.7% **b. 12.2%** ***c. 61.1%***	629 (95.3%)	5 (0.76%)	17 (2.6%)	660
2017–2018	53 (8.0%)	502 (75.9%)	64 a. 9.7% **b. 10.4%** ***c. 54.7%***	618 (93.5%)	3 (0.45%)	28 (4.2%)	661
Robbery/ extortion 2016–2017	24 (%)	355 (83.1%)	31 a. 7.3% **b. 7.6%** ***c. 56.4%***	410 (96.0%)	0	9 (2.1%)	427
2017–2018	28 (6.3%)	356 (79.6%)	35 a. 7.8% **b. 7.4%** ***c. 55.6%***	420 (94.0%)	0	20 (4.5%)	447
Fraud 2016–2017	0	56 (84.8%)	6 a. 9.1% **b. 10.3%** ***c. 100%***	58 (87.9%)	0	7 (10.6%)	66
2017–2018	4 (4.0%)	72 (72.7%)	9 a. 9.1% **b. 10.5%** ***c. 69.2%***	86 (8.7%)	4 (4.0%)	9 (9.1%)	99
Illicit 2016–2017	27 (2.0%)	1236 (90.0%)	79 a. 5.8% **b. 5.9%** ***c. 74.5%***	1341 (97.6%)	10 (0.7%)	20 (1.5%)	1374

(continued)

Table 12 (continued)

Offence	Acquitted	Guilty plea	Guilty verdict	Adjudicated outcomes	Trf'd	Withdrawn	Total
2017–2018	24 (1.6%)	1356 (90.7%)	66 a. 4.4% **b. 4.5%** *c. 73.3%*	1458 (97.5%)	10 (0.7%)	22 (1.5%)	1495

Source ABS (2019b, Table 17)
Notes
a. Guilty as a proportion of total number of matters
b. Guilty as a proportion of adjudicated outcomes
c. Guilty verdict as a proportion of trials with jury/judge verdict
1. Percentages calculated using ABS (2019b data, Table 17)
2. Homicide includes 'and related offences'
3. Sexual assault includes 'and related offences'
4. 'Trf'd' means transferred to a lower court
5. 'Withdrawn' means case withdrawn by the prosecution
6. Percentages in brackets are a proportion of the total
7. The ABS does not report separate data for child and adult sexual offences

something different about how sexual assault matters are assessed by fact-finders compared to other offences.[10]

Out of all sexual assault matters where charges have been laid and the matter is set down for trial, Table 12 shows that only one-fifth will result in a conviction due to a combination of the relatively low conviction rate and the relatively high withdrawal rate of around 9% (only fraud offences had a similarly high withdrawal rate) compared to the other offences.

6.6 The Royal Commission into Institutional Responses to Child Sexual Abuse

The Royal Commission (2017b: 165) identified that, compared to many other crimes, CSA is characterised by:

- lower reporting rates: 'the Australian Bureau of Statistics Crime Victimisation Survey 2014–2015 reported that only 25 per cent of victims of sexual assault reported their most recent incident to police';

[10]Note that a direct comparison between the rates provided by the NSWBOCSAR and the ABS is not possible because of the different periods used by these two organisations, that is, January to December by the NSWBOCSAR and July to June by the ABS.

- higher attrition rates: 'police commenced proceedings in 28 per cent of child sexual abuse matters reported to police in the period 1 January 2010 to 31 December 2014' compared to 15% of reported matters in 2006;
- lower charging and prosecution rates: in a NSW study, legal proceedings were commenced in almost 17% of matters reported by children and 33% per cent of matters reported by adults (Cashmore et al., 2016);
- fewer guilty pleas: Table 11 shows that sexual assault offences and homicide had the lowest guilty plea rates, compared to a range of other offences;
- fewer convictions: Cashmore et al. (2016) reported that between 8 to 15% of all reported child sexual assault matters result in a conviction while NSW BOCSAR data allows an estimate of 8% of reported matters. As per Table 12, sexual assault matters had the lowest conviction rate at trial among other comparable offences, although the ABS does not provide separate data for child sexual assault matters.

When the Royal Commission (2017b) analysed all child sexual assault prosecutions that were finalised between July 2012 and June 2016, they found that 33% of defendants were convicted of all charges, 27% were convicted of at least one relevant charge and 40% were not convicted of any charge (Table 13). These matters involved convictions as a result of guilty pleas and verdicts at trial. No data was provided on the progression

Table 13 Outcomes of all child sexual assault matters in NSW courts, July 2012 to June 2016

Total matters	2604
***Convictions*:**	
All charges (%)	33
At least one relevant charge (%)	27
Trials as a proportion of total matters (%)	27.8
Convictions:	
All charges (%)	32
At least one relevant charge (%)	16
None (%)	52

Source Royal Commission into Institutional Responses to Child Sexual Abuse (2017b)

of child sexual assault matters after being reported to police. In terms of trial outcomes, Table 13 shows that 52% of matters resulted in a not guilty verdict, with a conviction rate at trial of 48%. Overall, between 2012–2013 and 2015–2016, the acquittal rate for CSA matters in NSW increased from 44 to 54% (Royal Commission, 2017b: 174).

Table 14 shows the number of CSA matters that are prosecuted in NSW courts, with the more serious offences being prosecuted in the higher courts (Supreme and District Courts). The conviction rate at trial was less than 50% in all NSW courts for the period, July 2012 to June 2016.

When CSA matters are compared to a range of other offences in Table 15, the overall conviction rate is lowest for adult sexual assault, followed by CSA, a finding that is consistent with the data reported in Table 12. This difference in the conviction rates at trial for child and adult sexual offences has been attributed to the fact that adult sexual assault matters commonly involve the issue of lack of consent which often involves word-against-word. The higher conviction rate for other

Table 14 All defendant appearances for all child sexual assault matters in NSW courts, July 2012–June 2016

NSW Courts	Convicted of at least one offence (guilty pleas + verdicts) (%)	Total matters	Convicted of at least one offence–guilty verdicts (%)	Total matters
Supreme Court	50	4	0	1
District Court	67	1215	49	408
Local Court	51	1015	47	264
Children's Court	62	370	47	52
Total	60	2604	48	725

Source Royal Commission into Institutional Responses to Child Sexual Abuse (2017b)

Note

1. 'The data relates to individual appearances in New South Wales courts, so, if an offender appeared more than once in relation to separate groups of charges, they would be counted more than once in the data' (Royal Commission, 2017b: 174; footnote 22)

Table 15 Comparison of conviction rates for child sexual assault matters with other offences in all NSW courts, July 2012–June 2016

Offence category	Overall conviction rate (%) (guilty pleas + guilty verdicts)
All offences	89
Adult sexual assault	50
Child sexual assault	60
Assault	70
Robbery	73
Illicit drugs	94

Source Royal Commission into Institutional Responses to Child Sexual Abuse (2017b)

offences listed in Table 15, such as assault and robbery, can be attributed to the higher guilty plea rates for these offences (see Table 12).

The Royal Commission (2017b: 169) cited various reasons why CSA cases are difficult to prosecute, many of which have been documented elsewhere:

- Word-against-word cases which typically have no eyewitnesses or medical or forensic evidence either due to delayed complaint and/or the fact that many child sex offences do not involve sexual acts that result in the exchange of bodily fluids (Cossins et al., 2016). In fact, jurors have trouble dealing with cases where there is no evidence to support a complainant's testimony (Goodman-Delahunty, Cossins, & Martschuk, 2016).
- Drop-out of cases due to complainant unwillingness.
- Delays of months, years or decades before a complainant's first report to police affect a complainant's memory, including about dates and details, thus affecting the police investigation including the ability to find supporting evidence. This chapter and previous studies confirm that the police investigation stage is where the largest number of CSA cases drop out of the criminal justice system (Fitzgerald, 2006; Wundersitz, 2003).
- Vulnerable witnesses: as discussed in Chapter 11, victims of CSA frequently suffer from a range of debilitating trauma symptoms which impact their memories and their ability to withstand the rigours of

the adversarial system. Child witnesses are particularly vulnerable to the cross-examination effect (see Chapter 8).

A recent study by Bailey, Powell, and Brubacher (2017) reveals the progression of CSA matters through the criminal justice system in two unnamed Australian jurisdictions (Jurisdictions A and B) which compared cases involving Indigenous and non-Indigenous complainants of CSA. The study not only reveals the main attrition points for CSA cases but it also reveals that the race of the complainant affects the attrition rate.

Although unnamed, the authors state that the Indigenous population of the two jurisdictions are '3% to 4% vs. 30%' (Bailey et al., 2017: 185). The only jurisdiction in Australia with an Indigenous population of 30% is the Northern Territory which would be Jurisdiction B while Jurisdiction A is likely to be Victoria, the authors' home state.

Jurisdiction A included 566 cases of child sexual abuse reports during 2011, of which 125 involved Indigenous complainants. The average age of all children at the time when the abuse was reported was 11.3 years. Jurisdiction B included 617 cases of child sexual abuse reports for mid-2009 to mid-2014, of which 364 cases involved Indigenous complainants with the mean age of all children at the time of their report being 12.2 years.

The progression of these cases through the criminal justice system is depicted in Figs. 6 (Jurisdiction A) and 7 (Jurisdiction B) (Bailey et al., 2017: 182), with percentages representing the proportion of active cases at each stage. Like adult sexual assault cases, both figures show a broad trend of significant case attrition at various points within the criminal justice system for CSA cases: at the police investigation stage, at the prosecution stage and at the trial stage, although for all types of cases, attrition at the police investigation stage (forensic disclosure) was greatest. In Jurisdiction B (Fig. 7), the conviction rate as a proportion of the total number of CSA cases was very similar, irrespective of the race of the complainant.

However, Fig. 6 reveals the differences in attrition rates between cases involving Indigenous versus non-Indigenous complainants in Jurisdiction A. The authors report that at each stage of the criminal justice

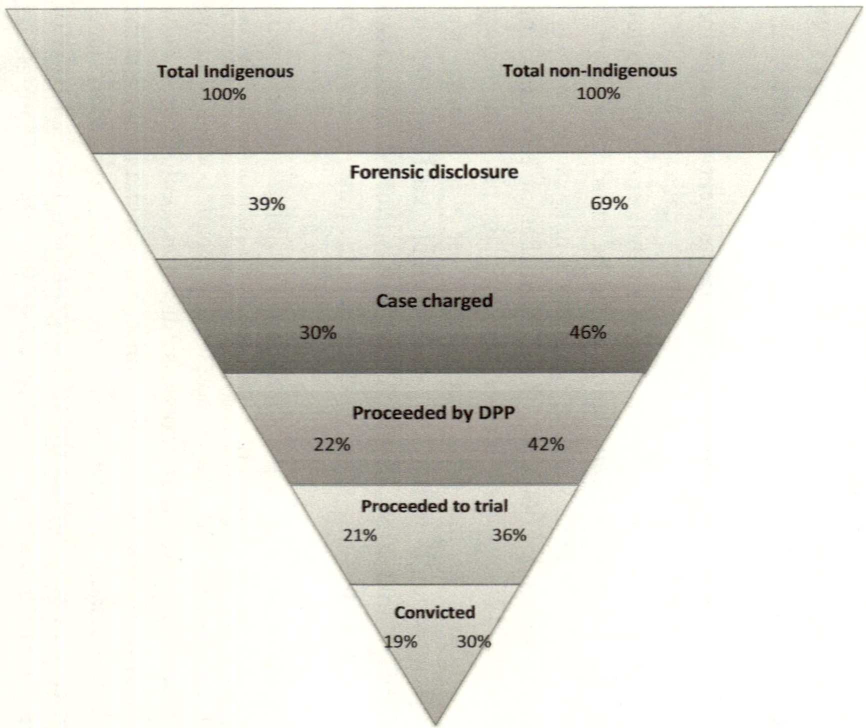

Fig. 6 Progression of reported CSA cases with respect to the complainant's Indigenous status: Jurisdiction A (Australia) (Bailey et al., 2017)

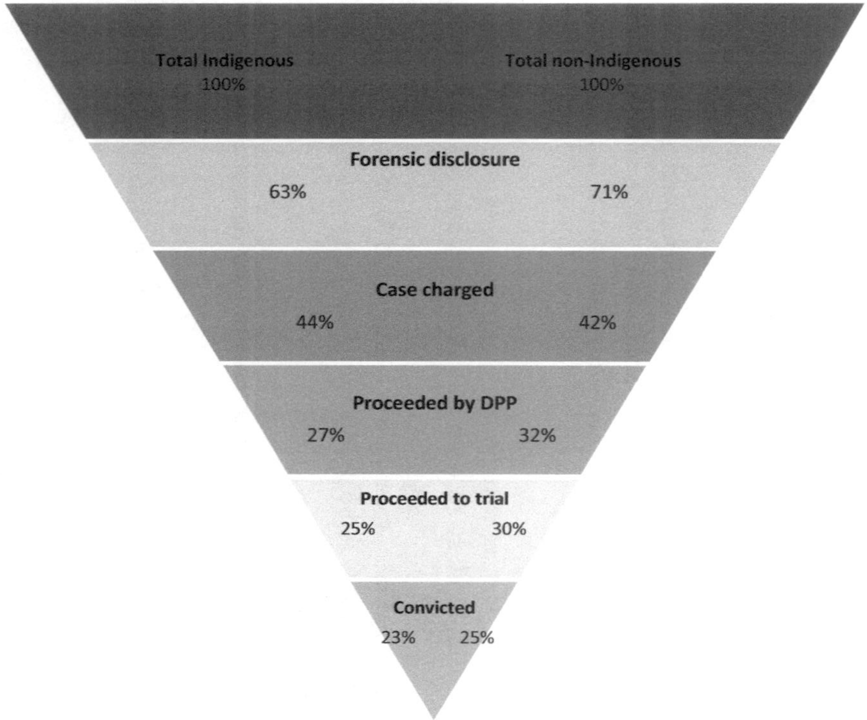

Fig. 7 Progression of reported CSA cases with respect to the complainant's Indigenous status: Jurisdiction B (Australia) (Bailey et al., 2017)

system, the differences in the proportion of Indigenous and non-Indigenous cases progressing were statistically significant (Bailey et al., 2017: 182), in that, cases were significantly more likely to drop out at each attrition point if the complainant was Indigenous. By contrast, in Jurisdiction B (Fig. 7), the only significant difference in attrition rates between Indigenous and non-Indigenous CSA cases was at the police investigation stage (forensic disclosure).

As well, this study reveals that, in both jurisdictions, Indigenous complainants were less likely to make a forensic disclosure of sexual abuse when they were interviewed by police, compared to non-Indigenous complainants. When the authors 'investigated how many cases progressed as a percentage of how many remained at each stage, rather than as a percentage of the whole', they found two significant attrition points for Indigenous CSA cases, compared to non-Indigenous cases:

1. Indigenous CSA cases were 30.0% (Jurisdiction A) and 7.9% (Jurisdiction B) more likely to drop out at the forensic disclosure stage; and
2. Indigenous CSA cases were 17.8% (Jurisdiction A) and 16.7% (Jurisdiction B) less likely to be proceeded by the prosecution (Bailey et al., 2017: 182–183).

The authors also reported several factors that may have affected the case attrition of Indigenous cases:

> In Jurisdiction A, Indigenous cases were 21% less likely to have a corroborating witness and 25% less likely to have physical evidence. In Jurisdiction B, Indigenous cases were 18% more likely to be severe and it was 18% less likely for the alleged offender to be a stranger in Indigenous cases than in non-Indigenous cases. (Bailey et al., 2017: 183)

When the authors analysed the factors that were associated with forensic disclosure—the lack of which was the main reason for case attrition at the police investigation stage—they found five variables that strongly predicted such disclosure in Jurisdiction A (Bailey et al., 2017: 184):

- *Race*: non-Indigenous complainants were almost three times more likely to make a forensic disclosure than Indigenous complainants (not found in Jurisdiction B);
- *Complainant Age*: 'cases of mid-aged children were 2.7 times more likely to contain a forensic disclosure than cases of younger children';
- *Prior allegation by complainant*: 'cases where the child had made a prior allegation were five times more likely to contain a forensic disclosure';
- *Delay*: cases with a delayed report of more than 12 months were almost twice as likely to contain a forensic disclosure (not found in Jurisdiction B);
- *Corroboration*: 'cases with at least one corroborating witness were 5.6 times more likely to contain a forensic disclosure than cases without'.

Thus, a prior allegation and a corroborating witness 'were significant predictors of forensic disclosure in both jurisdictions' (Bailey et al., 2017: 186). The fact that race was not a factor that affected forensic disclosure in Jurisdiction B, which had a significantly higher Indigenous population, suggests that there are different 'policing practices between the two jurisdictions' (Bailey et al., 2017: 186), such as more police experience in interviewing Indigenous complainants or more Indigenous police officers who conduct such interviews.

Overall, this study reveals the vulnerability of children who have been sexually abused in terms of their ability to disclose during a police interview, something that is probably unique to CSA complainants compared to adult complainants. The vulnerability of sexual assault victims is the key theme that flows through this book, a fact that adversarial criminal justice systems do not have the ability to address in adequate ways in order to address the attrition problem for both child and adult sexual assault cases.

6.7 Summary: The Similarities and Differences Between NSW and E&W

The following points can be made about the progress of sexual offences through the criminal justice system in NSW for the period 2006–2014:

- the number of reported child sex offences in NSW increased by just over a third (35.8%) from 2006 to 2014;
- the number of reported sex offences against an adult remained fairly constant;
- child sex offences constituted a much greater proportion of reported incidents in 2014 compared with 10 years previously;
- less than 20% of reported incidents involving a sex offence against a child or against an adult saw proceedings commenced;
- the conviction rate for child sex offences (guilty pleas and verdicts) increased from 58.0% in 2006 to 63.6% in 2014;
- by contrast, the conviction rate for adult sex offences (guilty pleas and verdicts) decreased from 50.6% in 2006 to 42.0% in 2014;
- the higher conviction rate for child sex offences compared with adult sex offences was relatively stable over this period;
- despite an increasing overall conviction rate in this period, approximately 8% of recorded incidents involving children resulted in a guilty finding in court;
- similarly, approximately 8% of recorded incidents involving adults resulted in a guilty finding in court;
- the two main attrition points for sexual offences in NSW occur at the police investigation stage, and between clear-up and the decision to prosecute (the commencement of criminal proceedings).

For the years 2016–2017 and 2017–2018 in NSW:

- many more sexual assault matters go to trial, rather than result in guilty pleas, compared to all other offences except homicide;
- sexual assault had the lowest conviction rate *at trial* compared to a number of other offences;
- out of all matters where charges were laid and the matter set down for trial, only one-fifth resulted in a conviction due to a combination of the relatively low conviction rate and the relatively high withdrawal rate.

In both NSW and E&W, the largest attrition point is the police investigation stage, followed by attrition at the prosecutorial stage, both before and after charges are laid. Australian studies show that police discriminate between cases based on the age, gender and race of the complainant, in that cases are *less* likely to proceed if a complainant is less than 5 years old; if the complainant is a child rather than an adult complainant of sexual abuse; if the complainant is Indigenous compared to non-Indigenous, and if the complainant is a male adolescent compared to female.

Overall, in NSW, less than 20% of reported incidents result in criminal proceedings, while in E&W, less than 10% result in charges or summons. Generally, sexual offences are characterised by low guilty plea rates. In relation to conviction rates, in E&W there has been a decreasing conviction rate for sexual offences in the last two years while, in NSW, there was a decrease in conviction rates for adult sexual offences between 2006 and 2014 but not for child sexual offences.

7 What to Do About the Attrition Problem?

The above data confirms previous research that shows that sexual offences are the, or one of the, hardest crimes to prosecute as a result of perennially low reporting rates, high attrition rates when reported, relatively low guilty plea rates, and relatively low conviction rates at trial (compared to other offences) at a time which has also seen criminal justice controls over sex offenders increasing (e.g. registration schemes and indefinite detention[11]) along with mandatory reporting of sex offences against children.

There is no other type of criminal offence which has the historical legacy and baggage of sexual assault (as discussed in Chapter 5) since it is a crime whose elements are defined with reference to the age of the victim (which has varied historically [Cossins, 2000]), and a notoriously difficult (and subjective) concept to pin down—consent. These elements make the evidentiary issues in relation to sexual assault one of the 'hardest crimes to prosecute'. It is taken for granted that those who are physically assaulted, robbed, defrauded of property or money or murdered do not consent to these criminal acts against them.

Not so the victim of a sexual assault since, historically, the mere presence of a woman or girl in public was sufficient justification for sexual touching by a male, although some women are still subject to this behaviour with little recourse. For example, a recent survey of Australian workers in the retail and fast food industries (Australian Human Rights Commission, 2019) found that female workers under the age of 30 years were more likely to be sexually harassed, including inappropriate touching, than in other industries.

In Australia, we have had a multitude of reports into the investigation and prosecution of sex offences (e.g. Australian Law Reform Commission, 2010a; Chapman, 2006; Law Reform Commission of Western Australia, 2008; Northern Territory Law Reform Commission, 1999; NSW Parliament, Legislative Council, Standing Committee on Law and

[11]A complicated framework now exists in many jurisdictions for the control and oversight of sex offenders. In Australia, for example, NSW was the first jurisdiction out of eight states and territories to introduce a sex offender register under the *Child Protection (Offenders Registration) Act 2000* (NSW). This was followed by the *Child Protection (Offenders Prohibition Orders) Act 2004* (NSW) which allows a local court under to grant a Child Protection Prohibition Order (CPPO) against an offender in order to prohibit particular conduct, such as restrictions on travel, or where and with whom they live if '(a) there is reasonable cause to believe, having regard to the nature and pattern of conduct of the person, that the person poses a risk to the lives or sexual safety of one or more children, or children generally, and (b) the making of the order will reduce that risk' (s 5(1)). Two years later, the *Crimes (Serious Sex Offenders) Act 2006* (NSW) introduced extended supervision orders so that the government could apply to the Supreme Court to supervise a serious sex offender, who posed a risk to the community, for up to five years. In 2013, this Act was renamed the *Crimes (High Risk Offenders) Act 2013* (NSW) and now provides for the continuing detention of high risk violent offenders including high risk sex offenders.

Justice, 2002; Parliament of Victoria, Crime Prevention Committee, 1995; Queensland Crime Commission and Queensland Police Service, 2000; Queensland Crime and Misconduct Commission, 2003; Royal Commission into Institutional Responses to Child Sexual Abuse, 2017; Royal Commission into the New South Wales Police Service, 1997; Victorian Law Reform Commission, 2004).

There have also been various studies in E&W into the 'attrition problem', including two early studies (Grace, Lloyd, & Smith, 1992; Harris & Grace, 1999) that were followed by a number of government-commissioned reports in the 2000s (HMIC & HMCPSJ, 2002, 2007; Home Office, 2000; Kelly, 2002; Kelly et al., 2005) followed by the Stern Report in 2010 (Stern, 2010), although this oft-cited report is only 'a review and does not contain fresh empirical evidence' (Hohl and Stanko (2015: 325).

While victim report studies, surveys and official reports tell us that the majority of perpetrators of sexual assault are known to their victims and that sexual assault is relatively prevalent, there is a cultural investment in media images of stranger attacks. In other words, only some rape cases capture public attention (DiBennardo, 2018), which leaves the public with the idea that rape is an exceptional, rather than a common everyday occurrence.

Official reports also reveal that the problems in relation to the investigation and prosecution of sex offences are very similar in both Australia and Britain. But despite various reports and inquiries, questions remain:

i. what other changes are needed to improve outcomes in sex offence cases which are prosecuted in the hostile environment of the adversarial system?
ii. Are these changes achieveable? Or have we reached the limits of change in the adversarial system?
iii. If so, what other alternatives can be envisaged?

Another question worth considering is that although there is some judicial recognition that the fair trial principle includes, in addition to the rights of the accused, the interests of sexual assault complainants and the community (Cossins, 2010), can that principle be re-invigorated to create a right to be treated in a way that no further psychological harm is done within the trial context?

As Sheehy (2012: 7) observes, 'the law in practice – as implemented by police, prosecutors, and defence counsel – has quite successfully resisted women's just demands for equal protection of the law'. However, how do we conceive of sexual assault complainants' 'rights' when criminal trials are underpinned by a defendant's right to a fair trial (which encompasses the right to silence, the prosecutorial burden of proof, the principle of innocent until proven guilty) and when rape myths are considered to be relevant to the issue of consent?

Answering these questions will involve some key challenges, such as:

- documenting, and critiquing the efficacy of the key sexual assault reform issues associated with the trial process in E&W and Australia, with a focus on Australia's largest jurisdiction by population, NSW, in relation to *both* adult and child sexual offences, given that younger age groups are more likely to be victims of sexual assault;
- analysis of the trial process itself rather than just focusing on the substantive law of rape and sexual assault, by considering both procedural (e.g. the cross-examination process) and evidence law impacts.
- historical analysis of the origins of adversarialism in order to identify the structures of power within the trial process and how they affect the prosecution's burden of proof, a burden that is elevated in sexual assault trials.
- jury and juror reasoning processes in sexual assault trials: review of key jury studies and a consideration of how adversarialism, itself, affects jury decision-making in sexual assault trials.
- alternatives to adversarialism such as specialist courts, restorative justice or trauma-informed systems.
- recognition that 'the most significant reforms needed are not so much legal reforms but reforms in the attitudes and perceptions' of society (Tolmie, 2012: 69), that is, laypeople who become jurors and legal professionals.

Possibly the biggest issue that prosecutors have to deal with is the cultural expectations associated with proving that a complainant's allegations of sexual touching/intercourse were non-consensual. In other words, the historical legacy of women's obligations to protect their sexual reputations permeates cultural expectations about women's social and sexual behaviour, as discussed in Chapter 2. Thus, the cultural environment of every sexual assault trial is likely to include some fact-finders who believe that the responsibility for 'managing predatory male sexuality' (Tolmie, 2012: 70) is on the female complainant, rather than the defendant, and that women and girls regularly lie about sexual assault.

This book will address these issues by considering the well-identified evidentiary problems in sexual assault cases, as well as possible reforms and alternatives to the adversarial system, some of which may not be achievable in current political climates. Nonetheless, the book is the first of its kind to consider these issues in relation to *both* adult and child sexual offences, and to develop a reform agenda based on the psychological impact of trauma. The lack of academic work on CSA is a major gap in the literature since, as discussed above, most reported sexual assault in Australia is committed against adolescents aged 15–19 years, followed by children aged 0–14 years compared to all other age groups. Similarly, in E&W, most reported sexual assault is committed against adolescents aged 16–19 years.

This book considers the attrition problem at a time when many reform options have already been introduced but satisfactory outcomes for victims are difficult to obtain. Because of the similarities between the criminal law and procedure of E&W and Australia, and the similarities in relation to low conviction and high attrition rates for sexual assault, these jurisdictions have much in common. Because of the different pace of reform and the different reform issues that have been tackled, each country has much to learn from the other.

This book is distinctive in its analysis of the trial process in addition to the substantive law of rape and sexual assault. Considerable progress in substantive law reforms have been made, such as abolition of the requirement for corroboration, rules restricting the admissibility of a complainant's counselling notes and her past sexual reputation and history (rape shield laws), and definitions of consent.

Despite significant reforms in NSW, in the 1980s, for example, conviction rates have declined since they were introduced, suggesting that it is the *trial process itself* that results in poor outcomes in sex offence cases, including wrongful acquittals and victim dissatisfaction. By engaging with the structures of power within the trial process, I consider how and at what points that process is weighted against complainants of sexual assault.

As discussed above, some feel a sense of failure in relation to sexual assault law reform with 'low rape conviction rates confirm[ing] the limitations of law for feminist anti-violence aims, making continued feminist engagement with rape law reform a project of questionable value' (Larcombe, 2011: 29). However, that sense of failure may be because researchers have been focusing on the wrong things. Every criminal trial has two narratives as exemplified in prosecutorial and defence opening and closing addresses. Feminists have not engaged sufficiently with these trial narratives, in particular, how the construction of the defence narrative, usually partially or wholly based on rape myths, influences trial outcomes and how such narratives could be prevented. As a former justice of the Canadian Supreme Court has observed:

> [s]peculative myths, stereotypes, and sexist assumptions about women who have been sexually assaulted have too often hindered the search for truth and imposed harsh and unnecessary burdens on complainants. … The most injurious myth is that women and children are not credible in this area of criminal law. (L'Heureux-Dubé, 2012: 3)

Low conviction rates produce a feedback effect which influences police investigations and prosecutors' assessments of the evidence, including the believability of the complainant. Thus, when police and prosecutors are assessing the reasonable prospects of conviction, they do so in light of a trial process that sends the message time and time again that any behaviour on the part of the complainant that could elicit victim-blame from the finder-of-fact will be detrimental to securing a conviction.

There is considerable research on the influence of both legal and extra-legal factors on the attrition of sexual assault cases, including prosecutors' charging decisions in sexual assault cases. While legal factors include the sufficiency and strength of the evidence, extra-legal factors tend to be associated with the characteristics of complainants, such as age (Harris & Grace, 1999), and mental health (Kelly et al., 2005; Hester, 2015), as well as complainant behaviour, such as the use of alcohol and/or drugs (Beichner & Spohn, 2005; Campbell, Wasco, Ahrens, Self, & Barnes, 2001; Spohn & Holleran, 2001), inconsistencies in evidence (Frohmann, 1991; Hester, 2015; Hohl & Stanko, 2015) and the type of relationship between victim and offender (Hester & Lilley, 2017; O'Neal, Tellis, & Spohn, 2015).

For example, O'Neal et al. (2015) examined the factors that influenced prosecutors' charging decisions in 47 intimate partner sexual assault cases in LA County, and reported that they consider both legal and extra-legal factors, including rape myths:

> Numerous themes emerged … that support the notion that attitudes toward IPSA [intimate partner sexual assault] influence prosecutors' initial decisions to prosecute. Whereas stranger rape is seen as a legitimate violent crime, IPSA is often seen as a trivial conflict between partners. For example, one prosecutor characterized a sexual assault as an incident involving miscommunication that could be remedied with marriage counselling. (O'Neill et al., 2015: 1249)

The extra-legal factors that influenced the filing of charges by prosecutors were associated with victim credibility and included a criminal record, affiliation with a gang, drinking at the time, being drunk, using illegal drugs, being unconscious, mental health issues, and inconsistent statements to police. In all cases involving one of the above factors, charges were not filed. In cases where there was no physical or verbal resistance, 28.6% of cases were filed compared to 64.3% of cases which involved physical and verbal resistance (O'Neill et al., 2015: 1248).

In case it be thought that the above study only pertains to US prosecutions, Hester and Lilley (2017) reported the results of a study involving 87 reported rape cases involving acquaintance (36.8%), domestic violence (31.0%), historical CSA (29.9%) or recent family (2.2%) from three police forces in England. Only 44 (50.6%) were deemed to be crimes which resulted in arrests, while just over half of those 'were referred to the CPS for charging decisions (23/87, 26%)' (Hester & Lilley, 2017: 181). Only 17 out of 23 resulted in charges being laid, which amounted to just under 'one in five (19%) for the whole sample' (ibid.).

Sixteen cases proceeded to trial after one victim dropped out while 10 out of 16 resulted in a conviction (62.5%) which represented 11.5% of the total reported sample (ibid.). Overall:

> Domestic violence and historical cases were more likely to be crimed than acquaintance rapes … Most arrests were in domestic violence cases … and [while] historical cases were significantly less likely to result in arrest … [t]he CPS were significantly more likely to lay charges in historical cases … and least likely to do so in acquaintance rapes … Historical cases were significantly more likely to result in conviction … With regard to vulnerability, victims/survivors of acquaintance rapes were significantly more likely to be recorded as drunk … Victims of historical child sexual abuse were significantly more likely to be recorded as having mental health problems. (ibid.: 181)

Interviews with police officers revealed that they viewed rape cases differently depending on the relationship between victim and offender, as well as victim age. Despite the fact that acquaintance cases were more recently reported, enabling the gathering of forensic material, these cases resulted in the smallest number of charges. Instead, nearly a third of complainants in these cases were 'referred by the police to counseling or mental health services' (ibid.: 182).

In terms of other extra-legal factors, complainants who had mental health problems 'tended not to have their cases progressed to charge' (ibid.: 185), something that happened most commonly with complainants of historical CSA cases. Thus, mental health issues and having a prior history of abuse increased attrition, as did police recording that the complainant was drunk. In fact, '[v]ictim/survivors with mental health issues or whom the police deemed drunk were least likely to have their cases proceed' (ibid.: 186). The authors also reported that 'resource constraints also appeared to affect the type and range of evidence collected in some instances with possible impacts on attrition' (ibid.: 186).

Overall, '[t]he relationship between the victim and suspect was a key feature in the pattern of attrition' and 'led to different attrition trajectories' (ibid.: 186), with acquaintance rapes more likely to be no-crimed and having 'the largest rate of attrition, with proportionately fewest arrests, charges, and few convictions, and included significantly more of the victims who had been drinking and were drunk' (ibid.). Intimate partner rapes were more likely to result in an arrest but these victims were more likely than others 'to withdraw due to fear and threats from the suspect' (ibid.). By contrast, cases involving adult complainants of historical CSA saw the highest rates of charge and conviction.

The authors concluded:

> If we are to … tackle attrition in rape cases … [and] the 'justice gap', it is important that we understand how these different types of cases progress … The legal and extra-legal factors that have been identified in the previous literature as increasing attrition, in particular relationship between victim and offender, vulnerability of victim, and evidential issues were all seen to play some part in the attrition and trajectories of the cases discussed here, but may be deemed to be relevant to different degrees depending on whether the cases involved acquaintance, intimate domestic violence, or historical child sexual abuse. (ibid.: 187)

For example, acquaintance rape cases were more recently reported but because of the prevalence of alcohol, 'the police were at times reluctant, or unable, to investigate fully the lack of consent by a very drunk victim' (ibid.: 187). By contrast, domestic violence rapes 'were often carried out in contexts of extreme threats and other violence', with complainants' being fearful of repercussions from the police and criminal justice involvement while historical CSA cases involved more mental health issues (ibid.). While the authors recognised that different complainants require different types of specialist support services in order to 'stick' with a case, absent complainant withdrawal, each type of case is still plagued by certain myths and prejudices regarding victim credibility.

8 The Contents of This Book

The comprehensive data reported in this chapter shows that there is a significant attrition problem of sexual offences in both E&W and Australia which has not improved within at least the last decade. Over the past 20 years, the pace of reform in Australia and E&W in relation to sexual assault trials has been relatively fast, at times controversial. But most reforms have focused on improvements to enable victims to give evidence in ways other than being present in the courtroom. No government has yet tackled the documented reasons for low conviction rates and high attrition rates. More needs to be done and I hope this book will push the reform agenda to another level.

The two studies on extra-legal factors discussed above reveal there is considerable cultural baggage associated with decision-making in these cases. Rather than examining the impact of police and prosecutorial decision-making as others have done (Alderden & Ullman, 2012; Beichner & Spohn, 2005; Bollingmo, Wessel, Eilertsen, & Magnussen, 2008; Cashmore, Taylor, & Parkinson, 2017; Kassin, Meissner, & Norwick, 2005; McMillan, 2018; Sleath & Bull, 2012; Temkin & Krahé, 2008), the focus on this book is on jury decision-making. However:

> [s]ome might argue that research on juror decision making should not necessarily be a high priority for future research because such a small percentage of sexual assault cases end up going to trial. (Lonsway & Archambault, 2012: 163)

While much has been written about the inadequacies of the traditional criminal justice system for dealing with sexual assault (see Chapter 5), few have addressed the victim-blaming processes inherent within the wider population that perpetuate and condone rape-supportive beliefs in the criminal justice system.

Like Lonsway and Archambault (2012), I believe that what happens at trial has a fundamental feedback effect on police and prosecutors' decision-making because their assessments of the strength of the evidence in any particular case, along with consideration of relevant public interest factors, is to determine whether or not a case has a reasonable prospect of conviction if sent to trial. Thus, police and prosecutors must try to 'second guess' what a fact-finder would decide in a sexual assault trial. In other words:

> If prosecutors do not believe they can persuade jurors to convict in a sexual assault case, they may charge and try fewer cases. Then as law enforcement investigators see that fewer cases are being charged and tried, they may forward fewer cases to the prosecutor's office. … Therefore, any change that is targeted at the final point in the attrition process has the potential to push for reforms all the way 'upstream'. (Lonsway & Archambault, 2012: 163)

Thus, reforms are needed to 'reformulate the perceived "convictability standard"' (Lonsway & Archambault, 2012: 163) in order to bridge the attrition gap from the time of the first report to police (the largest attrition point) to the point when decisions are made to file charges to the point where cases are sent to or withdrawn from trial. The cultural baggage that is brought into the courtroom when sexual offences are prosecuted—by defence counsel, prosecutors, judges and jurors—affects each of these attrition points.

In order to understand the outcomes in sexual assault trials, Chapters 1–4 discuss the nature and effects of adversarialism and jury decision-making in sexual assault trials by examining 40 years of jury studies on jury decision-making, including the factors that predict outcomes in sexual assault trials, such as the effect of alcohol consumption on perceptions of guilt.

Chapter 5, '*No Means Yes and Yes Means Anal*' summarises the results of studies on the prevalence of rape myth acceptance (RMA) in general populations, as well as mock jurors' beliefs about victims of CSA, followed by a discussion of the factors influencing victim blame and the independent effects of victim and participant characteristics on victim blaming. This is followed by a summary of the independent effects of victim stereotypicality and gender stereotypicality on jury decision-making, as well as the interactions between offence, victim and perpetrator stereotypicality. In light of all these studies, Chapter 5 concludes with a discussion of the heuristic-systematic processing model of juror decision-making and the implications for sexual assault trials.

Chapter 6, *The Nature and Effects of Adversarialism: Sites of Activation for Heuristic Reasoning Processes*, begins with a discussion of the role of evidence and procedural laws in sexual assault trials before focusing on activation statements in sexual assault trials, in the form of prosecution and defence opening addresses, and the points at which these activation statements and heuristics will have an impact on jury reasoning in adversarial trials. By analysing how jurors develop a narrative framework using the story model of jury decision-making, it is possible to identify how jurors develop a narrative based on heuristics and rape myths which is likely to be immune to judicial directions and jury deliberation.

Chapter 7, *Modernisation of the Substantive Law of Consent*, then discusses attempts at modernising the substantive law of consent in order to focus jurors' minds on a communicative model of consent and on whether a defendant's belief in consent was, objectively, reasonable. Two recent case studies reveal the limits of these law reform attempts with a final discussion about the need for more radical reforms in order to switch the focus of a sexual assault trial from the complainant's behaviours to the steps taken by the defendant to ascertain consent.

Chapter 8, *Cross-examination in sexual assault trials: Evidentiary safeguard or an opportunity to confuse?*, engages in an analysis of the culture of adversarialism within the criminal trial and the 'legitimated bullying' that is condoned within that culture through the cross-examination process, with a focus on the extent to which defence counsel cross-examination uses the factors associated with acquittals to manufacture inconsistencies in evidence. The chapter documents the many inquiries and studies into the impact of cross-examination on children's evidence, and the extensive research that shows that cross-examination is an unreliable method for testing the evidence of children, compared to the requirements of forensic interviewing. This discussion is then extended to the impact of cross-examination on the evidence of adult sexual assault complainants, including the impact of rape myths and stereotypes during cross-examination. The right to cross-examine as an absolute, unfettered right is questioned, with an analysis of the relevant case law in E&W and Australia.

Chapter 9 documents the various contemporary reforms to cross-examination, including: judicial control of improper questions and the intermediary scheme that operates in E&W compared to other countries including Australia. After considering evaluations of the role of intermediaries and research on their effectiveness, Chapter 9 concludes by considering whether or not the intermediary should adopt the role of specialist examiner in sexual assault trials.

Chapter 10 engages with the particular problems facing reformers of the sexual assault trial because of the extent to which fact-finders' verdicts and credibility assessments of complainants are influenced by a number of extra-legal factors, including rape myths and misconceptions about children. A discussion of special measures for the protection of vulnerable witnesses shows that these measures have not solved these problems, nor have the introduction of charters or codes of victims' rights which Chapter 10 reveals are not a panacea to the moralistic culture of the adversarial sexual assault trial.

Thus, the premise of Chapters 11 (*Achieving Best Evidence for Vulnerable Witnesses: The Use of Trauma-Informed Theory to Reform the Sexual Assault Trial*) and 12 (*Reform Measures: The Devil is in the Detail*) is the creation of a different model for achieving justice in sexual assault trials, one based on trauma-informed care. Using trauma-informed theory, principles and philosophy, Chapter 11 investigates the possibility of transforming the criminal justice process in sexual assault trials by importing a victim-focused model that addresses the needs of survivors/victims of sexual assault in order to do no further harm and to achieve best evidence. In doing so, Chapter 11 documents the triggers for re-traumatisation within the criminal trial, compares the processes of trauma-informed systems and considers the compatibility of trauma-informed care with the adversarial system. It concludes by discussing the requirements for creating a trauma-informed adversarial system.

In keeping with the above trauma-informed approach, Chapter 12 discusses the other reform measures that would be necessary to transform the sexual assault trial from one where the complainant's moral worthiness is 'on trial' to a fully functioning trauma-informed system. In doing so, it is necessary to reconceptualise the concept of fairness which in recent times has been recognised as including the rights, expectations and needs of complainants and the community generally.

These other reform measures include reforms to opening and closing addresses, mandatory training of all court personnel in trauma-informed principles, the creation of child- and complainant-friendly environments, the benefits of pre-recording of evidence, the introduction of time limited cross-examination and vetting of questions and changing the cross-examination process through the use of a professional examiner.

Finally, Chapter 12 discusses where restorative justice would fit into a new, trauma-informed model that has been devised for sexual assault trials by briefly reviewing the literature on restorative justice for sex offenders as a pre- or post-sentencing option and considering the compatibility of restorative justice theory and trauma-informed care.

References

Alaggia, R. (2004). Many ways of telling: Expanding conceptualizations of child sexual abuse disclosure. *Child Abuse & Neglect, 28,* 1213–1227.

Alderden, M. A., & Ullman, S. E. (2012). Creating a more complete and current picture examining police and prosecutor decision-making when processing sexual assault cases. *Violence Against Women, 18,* 525–551.

Anderson, J., Martin, J., Mullen, P., Romans, S., & Herbison, P. (1993). Prevalence of childhood sexual abuse experiences in a community sample of women. *Journal of American Academy of Child and Adolescent Psychiatry, 32,* 911–919.

Angiolini, E. (2015). *Report of the independent review into the investigation and prosecution of rape in London.* London: Crown Prosecution Service.

Arata, C. M. (1998). To tell or not to tell: Current functioning of child sexual abuse survivors who disclosed their victimization. *Child Maltreatment, 3,* 63–71.

Australian Bureau of Statistics (ABS). (2017). *4906.0—Personal safety, Australia, 2016.* https://www.abs.gov.au/ausstats/abs@.nsf/Lookup/by%20Subject/4906.0~2016~Main%20Features~Experience%20of%20Abuse%20before%20the%20age%20of%2015~27.

Australian Bureau of Statistics (ABS). (2018). *4510.0—Recorded crime—Victims, Australia, 2017*. http://www.abs.gov.au/ausstats/abs@.nsf/Lookup/by%20Subject/4510.0-2017-Media%20Release-Recording%20of%20sexual%20assaults%20reaches%20eight-year%20high%20(Media%20Release)-16.

Australian Bureau of Statistics (ABS). (2019a). *4510.0—Recorded crime—Victims, Australia, 2018*. https://www.abs.gov.au/AUSSTATS/abs@.nsf/Lookup/4510.0Main+Features12018?OpenDocument.

Australian Bureau of Statistics (ABS). (2019b). *4513.0—Criminal courts, Australia, 2017–18*. https://www.abs.gov.au/Ausstats/abs@.nsf/0/4BC54F34DFC618ACCA2573DA0016FB63?OpenDocument..

Australian Human Rights Commission. (2017). *Change the course: National report on sexual assault and sexual harassment at Australian Universities*. Sydney: AHRC. https://www.humanrights.gov.au/sites/default/files/document/publication/AHRC_2017_ChangeTheCourse_UniversityReport.pdf.

Australian Human Rights Commission. (2019). *Everyone's business: Survey on sexual harassment of members of the shop, distributive and allied employees' association*. Sydney: AHRC. https://humanrights.gov.au/sites/default/files/document/publication/ahrc_sda_survey_report_2019.pdf.

Australian Law Reform Commission. (2010a). *Family violence: A national legal response* (ALRC Report No. 114). Sydney: ALRC.

Australian Law Reform Commission. (2010b). *Family violence: Improving legal frameworks* (Consultation Paper). Sydney: ALRC.

Bailey, C., Powell, M., & Brubacher, S. P. (2017). The attrition of indigenous and non-indigenous child sexual abuse cases in two Australian jurisdictions. *Psychology, Public Policy, and Law, 23*, 178–190.

Baker, A., & Duncan, S. (1985). Child sexual abuse: A study of prevalence in Great Britain. *Child Abuse and Neglect, 9*, 457–467.

Beichner, D., & Spohn, C. (2005). Prosecutorial charging decisions in sexual assault cases: Examining the impact of a specialized prosecution unit. *Criminal Justice Police Review, 16*, 461–498.

Bollingmo, G. C., Wessel, E. M., Eilertsen, D. E., & Magnussen, S. (2008). Credibility of the emotional witness: A study of ratings by police investigators. *Psychology, Crime & Law, 14*, 29–40.

Bricknell, S. (2008). *Trends in violent crime* (Research Paper No. 359). Australian Institute of Criminology.

Bunting, L. (2008). Sexual offences against children: An exploration of attrition in the Northern Ireland criminal justice system. *Child Abuse & Neglect, 32,* 1109–1118.

Bunting, L. (2014). Exploring the influence of reporting delay on criminal justice outcomes: Comparing child and adult reporters of childhood sexual abuse. *Journal of Child Sexual Abuse, 23,* 577–594.

Campbell, R., Wasco, S. M., Ahrens, C. E., Self, T., & Barnes, H. E. (2001). Preventing the 'second rape': Rape survivors' experiences with community service provider. *Journal of Interpersonal Violence, 16,* 1239–1259.

Cashmore, J., Taylor, A., & Parkinson, P. (2017). The characteristics of reports to the police of child sexual abuse and the likelihood of cases proceeding to prosecution after delays in reporting. *Child Sexual Abuse & Neglect, 74,* 49–61.

Cashmore, J., Taylor, A., Shackel, R., & Parkinson, P. (2016). *The impact of delayed reporting on the prosecution and outcomes of child sexual abuse cases.* Sydney: Royal Commission into Institutional Responses to Child Sexual Abuse.

Chapman, L. (2006). *Review of South Australia rape and sexual assault law: Discussion paper.* Adelaide: Government of South Australia.

Chen, L. P., Murad, M. H., Paras, M. L., Colbenson, K. M., Sattler, A. L., Goranson, E. N., … Zirakzadeh, A. (2010). Sexual abuse and lifetime diagnosis of psychiatric disorders: Systematic review and meta-analysis. *Mayo Clinic Proceedings, 85,* 618–629.

Children's Commissioner. (2015). *Protecting children from harm: A critical assessment of child sexual abuse in the family network.* London: Children's Commissioner. https://www.childrenscommissioner.gov.uk/wp-content/uploads/2017/06/Protecting-children-from-harm-full-report.pdf.

Coles, J., Lee, A., Taft, A., Mazza, D., & Loxton, D. (2015). Childhood sexual abuse and its association with adult physical and mental health: Results from a national cohort of young Australian women. *Journal of Interpersonal Violence, 30,* 1929–1944.

Connolly, D. A., Chong, K., Coburn, P. I., & Lutgens, D. (2015). Factors associated with delays of days to decades to criminal prosecutions of child sexual abuse. *Behavioral Sciences & the Law, 33,* 546–560.

Cossins, A. (2000). *Masculinities, sexualities and child sexual abuse.* The Hague: Kluwer Law International.

Cossins, A. (2010). Time out for *Longman*: Myths, science and the common law. *Melbourne University Law Review, 34,* 69–105.

Cossins, A., & Goodman-Delahunty, J. (2013). Misconceptions or expert evidence in child sexual assault trials: Enhancing justice and jurors' 'common sense'. *Journal of Judicial Administration, 22*, 171–190.

Cossins, A., Jayakody, A., Norrie, C., & Parkinson, P. (2016). The Role of photographic and video documentation in the investigation and prosecution of child sexual assault. *Journal of Law and Medicine, 23*, 925–937.

Cox, P. (2016). *Violence against women: Additional analysis of the Australian Bureau Of Statistics' Personal Safety Survey, 2012: Key findings and future directions*. Sydney: Australian National Research Organisation for Women's Safety.

Crown Prosecution Service. (2018a). *Rape and serious sexual offence prosecutions: Assessment of disclosure of unused material ahead of trial*. https://www.cps.gov.uk/sites/default/files/documents/publications/RASSO-prosecutions-Assessment-disclosure-unused-material-ahead-trial_0.pdf. Accessed 2 October 2019.

Daly, K., & Bouhours, B. (2010). Rape and attrition in the legal process: A comparative analysis of five countries. In M. Tonry (Ed.), *Crime and justice: A review of research*. Chicago: University of Chicago Press.

DiBennardo, R. A. (2018). Ideal victims and monstrous offenders: How the news media represent sexual predators. *Socius: Sociological Research for a Dynamic World*. Open Epub. https://doi.org/10.1177/2378023118802512.

Finkelhor, D., Hotaling, G., Lewis, I. A., & Smith, C. (1990). Sexual abuse in a national survey of adult men and women: Prevalence, characteristics, and risk factors. *Child Abuse and Neglect, 14*, 19–28.

Fischer, D. G., & McDonald, W. L. (1998). Characteristics of intrafamilial and extrafamilial child sexual abuse. *Child Abuse & Neglect, 22*, 915–929.

Fitzgerald, J. (2006). *The attrition of sexual offences from the New South Wales criminal justice system* (Crime and Justice Bulletin, No. 92). Sydney: NSW Bureau of Crime Statistics and Research.

Fleming, J. M. (1997). Prevalence of childhood sexual abuse in a community sample of Australian women. *Medical Journal of Australia, 166*, 65–68.

Frohmann, L. (1991). Discrediting victims' allegations of sexual assault: prosecutorial accounts of case rejections. *Social Problems, 38*, 213–226.

Goodman-Delahunty, J. (2014). *Profiling parental child sex abuse* (Trends and Issues in Crime and Criminal Justice, No. 465, pp. 1–8). Canberra: Australian Institute of Criminology.

Goodman-Delahunty, J., Cossins, A., & Martschuk, N. (2016). *Jury reasoning in joint and separate trials of institutional child sexual abuse: An empirical study*. Sydney: Royal Commission into Institutional Responses to Child Sexual Abuse.

Goodman-Brown, T. B., Edelstein, R. S., Goodman, G. S., Jones, D. P. H., & Gordon, D. S. (2003). Why children tell: A model of children's disclosure of sexual abuse. *Child Abuse & Neglect, 27*, 525–540.

Grace, S., Lloyd, C., & Smith, L. (1992). *Rape: From recording to conviction.* London: Home Office Research Unit.

Gregory, S., & Lees, S. (1996). Attrition in rape and sexual assault cases. *British Journal of Criminology, 36,* 1–17.

Grubb, A., & Turner, E. (2012). Rape myth acceptance, gender role conformity and substance use on victim blaming. *Aggression and Violent Behavior, 17,* 443–452.

Hamlyn, B., Phelps, A., Turtle, J., & Sattar, G. (2004). *Are special measures working? Evidence from surveys of vulnerable and intimidated witnesses* (Home Office Research Study 283). London: Home Office.

Harris, J., & Grace, S. (1999). *A question of evidence? Investigating and prosecuting rape in the 1990s* (Home Office Research Study 196). London: Home Office.

Hebert, M., Tourigny, M., Cyr, M., McDuff, P., & Joly, J. (2009). Prevalence of childhood sexual abuse and timing of disclosure in a representative sample of adults from Quebec. *The Canadian Journal of Psychiatry, 54,* 631–636.

Held, M., & McLaughlin, J. (2013). Rape and sexual assault. *Georgetown Journal of Gender & Law, 15,* 155–194.

Hershkowitz, I., Horowitz, D., & Lamb, M. E. (2005). Trends in children's disclosure of abuse in Israel: A national study. *Child Abuse & Neglect, 29,* 1203–1214.

Hester, M. (2015). Reflections on criminal (in)justice in cases of rape. *Papers from the British Criminology Conference, 15,* 26–42.

Hester, M., & Lilley, S.-J. (2017). Rape investigation and attrition in acquaintance, domestic violence and historical rape cases. *Journal of Investigative Psychology and Offender Profiling, 14,* 175–188.

Hohl, K., & Conway, M. A. (2017). Memory as evidence: How normal features of victim memory lead to the attrition of rape complaints. *Criminology & Criminal Justice, 17,* 248–265.

Hohl, K., & Stanko, E. A. (2015). Complaints of rape and the criminal justice system: Fresh evidence on the attrition problem in England and Wales. *European Journal of Criminology, 12,* 324–341.

Holmes, K., & Sher, L. (2013). Dating violence and suicidal behavior in adolescents. *International Journal of Adolescent Medicine and Health, 25,* 257–261.

Home Office. (2000). *Setting the boundaries: Reforming the law on sexual offences*. London: Home Office.

Home Office. (2010). *The stern review: A report by Baroness Vivian Stern CBE of an independent review into how rape complaints are handled by public authorities in England and Wales*. London: Home Office.

HM Inspectorate for Constabulary & HM Crown Prosecution Service Inspectorate. (2002). *Report on the joint inspection into the investigation and prosecution of rape offences in England and Wales*. London: HMIC & HMCPSI.

HM Inspectorate for the Constabulary & HM Crown Prosecution Service Inspectorate. (2007). *Without consent: A report on the joint review of the investigation and prosecution of rape offences*. London: HMCPSI and HMIC.

Jay, A. (2014). *Independent inquiry into child sexual exploitation in Rotherham (1997–2013)*. https://www.rotherham.gov.uk/downloads/file/1407/independent_inquiry_cse_in_rotherham.

Jonas, S., Bebbington, P., McManus, S., & Meltzer, H. (2011). Sexual abuse and psychiatric disorder in England: Results from the 2007 Adult Psychiatric Morbidity Survey. *Psychological Medicine, 41,* 709–719.

Kassin, S. M., Meissner, C. A., & Norwick, R. J. (2005). 'I'd know a false confession if I saw one': A comparative study of college students and police investigators. *Law and Human Behavior, 29,* 211–227.

Kelly, L. (2002). *Routes to (in)justice: A research review on the reporting, investigation and prosecution of rape cases*. London: Her Majesty's Crown Prosecution Service Inspectorate.

Kelly, L. (2010). The (in)credible words of women: False allegations in European rape research. *Violence Against Women, 16,* 1345–1355.

Kelly, L., & Karsna, K. (2017). *Measuring the scale and changing nature of child sexual abuse and child sexual exploitation*. London: London Metropolitan University. https://cwasu.org/wp-content/uploads/2017/07/18871_CSA_Scoping_paper_web_FA.pdf.

Kelly, L., Lovett, J., & Regan, L. (2005). *A gap or a chasm? Attrition in reported rape cases* (Home Office Research Study No. 293). London: Home Office. https://webarchive.nationalarchives.gov.uk/20110218141141/http://rds.homeoffice.gov.uk/rds/pdfs05/hors293.pdf.

Kogan, S. M. (2004). Disclosing unwanted sexual experiences: Results from a national sample of adolescent women. *Child Abuse & Neglect, 28,* 147–165.

Krahé, B., Tomaszewska, P., Kuyper, L., & Vanwesenbeeck, I. (2014). Prevalence of sexual aggression among young people in Europe: A review of the evidence from 27 EU countries. *Aggression and Violent Behavior, 19,* 545–558.

Larcombe, W. (2011). Falling rape conviction rates: (Some) feminist aims and measures for rape law. *Feminist Legal Studies, 19,* 27–45.

Law Reform Commission of Western Australia. (2008). *Court intervention programs: Consultation* (Project No. 96). Perth: Law Reform Commission of Western Australia.

Levitt, A., & Crown Prosecution Service Equality and Diversity Unit. (2013). *Charging perverting the course of justice and wasting police time in cases involving allegedly false rape and domestic violence allegations: Joint report to the Director of Public Prosecutions.* London: CPS.

Lev-Wiesel, R., & First, M. (2018). Willingness to disclose child maltreatment: CSA vs other forms of child abuse in relation to gender. *Child Abuse & Neglect, 79,* 183–191.

L'Heureux-Dubé, C. (2012). Foreword: Still punished for being female. In E. A. Sheehy (Ed.), *Sexual assault in Canada: Law, legal practice and women's activism* (pp. 1–5). Ottawa: University of Ottawa Press.

Lisak, D., Gardinier, L., Nicksa, S. C., & Cote, A. M. (2010). False allegations of sexual assault: An analysis of ten years of reported cases. *Violence Against Women, 16,* 1318–1334.

London, K., Bruck, M., Ceci, S. J., & Shuman, D. W. (2005). Disclosure of child sexual abuse: What does the research tell us about the ways that children tell? *Psychology, Public Policy and Law, 11,* 194–226.

Lonsway, K. A., & Archambault, J. (2012). The 'justice gap' for sexual assault cases: Future directions for research and reform. *Violence Against Women, 18,* 145–168.

McMillan, L. (2018). Police officers' perceptions of false allegations of rape. *Journal of Gender Studies, 27,* 9–21.

Ministry of Justice. (2008). *Ministry of justice report: Judicial and court statistics 2007*. London: Ministry of Justice.

Ministry of Justice. (2019, March). *Criminal justice system statistics quarterly.* https://www.gov.uk/government/statistics/criminal-justice-system-statistics-quarterly-march-2019.

Ministry of Justice, Home Office & Office for National Statistics. (2013). *An overview of sexual offending in England and Wales. Statistical Bulletin.* London: Ministry of Justice, Home Office and Office for National Statistics.

National Union of Students. (2011). *Hidden marks: A study of women students' experiences of harassment, stalking, violence and sexual assault*. https://www.nus.org.uk/Global/NUS_hidden_marks_report_2nd_edition_web.pdf.

Northern Territory Law Reform Commission. (1999). *Final report on the laws relating to the investigation and prosecution of sexual assault in the North Territory*. Darwin: North Territory Law Reform Commission.

NSPCC. (2018). *How safe are our children? The most comprehensive overview of child protection in the UK*. NSPCC. https://learning.nspcc.org.uk/media/1067/how-safe-are-our-children-2018.pdf.

NSW Criminal Justice and Sexual Offences Taskforce. (2005). *Responding to sexual assault: The way forward*. Sydney: Attorney-General's Department of NSW.

NSW Office of the Director of Public Prosecutions. (2018). *ODPP Prosecution guidelines*. https://www.odpp.nsw.gov.au/prosecution-guidelines-0.

NSW Standing Committee on Law and Justice. (2002). *Report on child sexual assault prosecutions* (Parliamentary Paper No. 208; Report No. 22). Sydney: Parliament of NSW.

NUS Women's Department. (2015). *Talk about it: NUS women's department 2015 survey*. National Union of Students. https://d3n8a8pro7vhmx.cloudfront.net/nus/pages/144/attachments/original/1454369041/Talk_about_it_Survey_Report.pdf?1454369041.

O'Brien, K., Jones, C., & Korabelnikoff, V. (2008). *What caused the decrease in sexual assault clear-up rates?* (Crime and Justice Bulletin, No. 125). Sydney: NSW Bureau of Crime Statistics and Research.

Office for National Statistics. (2018). *Sexual offending: Victimisation and the path through the criminal justice system: An overview of sexual offending in England and Wales, using a range of national statistics and official statistics from across the crime and criminal justice system*. https://www.ons.gov.uk/peoplepopulationandcommunity/crimeandjustice/articles/sexualoffendingvictimisationandthepaththroughthecriminaljusticesystem/2018-12-13.

O'Neal, E. N., Tellis, K., & Spohn, C. (2015). Prosecuting intimate partner sexual assault: Legal and extra-legal factors that influence charging decisions. *Violence Against Women, 21*, 1237–1258.

Parliament of Victoria, Crime Prevention Committee. (1995). *Combating child sexual assault: An integrated model* (First Report Upon the Inquiry into Sexual Offences Against Children and Adults). Melbourne: Government Printer.

Pether, P. (2009). What is due to others: Speaking and signifying subject(s) of rape law. *Griffith Law Review, 18*, 237–258.

Priebe, G., & Svedin, C. G. (2008). Child sexual abuse is largely hidden from the adult society: An epidemiological study of adolescents' disclosures. *Child Abuse & Neglect, 32*, 1095–1108.

Queensland Crime and Misconduct Commission. (2003). *Seeking justice: An inquiry into the handling of sexual offences by the criminal justice system.* Brisbane: Crime and Misconduct Commission.

Queensland Crime Commission and Queensland Police Service. (2000). *Project axis-child sexual abuse in Queensland: Responses to the problem.* Brisbane: Queensland Crime Commission.

Roesler, T. A., & Wind, T. W. (1994). Telling the secret: Adult women describe their disclosures of incest. *Journal of Interpersonal Violence, 9*, 327–338.

Rook, P., & Ward, R. (2016). *Rook & Ward on sexual offences: Law & practice* (5th ed.). London: Sweet & Maxwell.

Royal Commission into Institutional Responses to Child Sexual Abuse. (2017a). *Final report: Nature and cause* (Vol. 2). Sydney: Royal Commission into Institutional Responses to Child Sexual Abuse.

Royal Commission into Institutional Responses to Child Sexual Abuse. (2017b). *Criminal justice report* (Executive Summary and Parts I–II). Sydney: Royal Commission into Institutional Responses to Child Sexual Abuse.

Royal Commission into Institutional Responses to Child Sexual Abuse. (2017c). *Criminal justice report* (Parts VII–X and Appendices). Sydney: Royal Commission into Institutional Responses to Child Sexual Abuse.

Royal Commission into the New South Wales Police Service. (1997). *The paedophile inquiry* (Vol. 5, Final Report). Sydney: The Government of the State of New South Wales.

Russell, D. E. (1983). The incidence and prevalence of intrafamilial and extrafamilial sexual abuse of female children. *Child Abuse & Neglect, 7*, 133–146.

Saunders, C. (2012). The trust, the half-truth, and nothing like the truth: Reconceptualising false allegations of rape. *British Journal of Criminology, 52*, 1152–1171.

Sauzier, M. (1989). Disclosure of child sexual abuse: For better or for worse. *Psychiatric Clinics of North America, 12*, 455–469.

Sheehy, E. A. (2012). *Introduction, sexual assault in Canada: Law, legal practice and women's activism* (pp. 7–21). Ottawa: University of Ottawa Press.

Sleath, E., & Bull, R. (2012). Comparing rape victim and perpetrator blaming in a police officer sample. *Criminal Justice and Behaviour, 39*, 646–665.

Smith, D., Letourneau, E. J., Saunders, B. E., Kilpatrick, D. G., Resnick, H. S., & Best, C. L. (2000). Delay in disclosure of childhood rape: Results from a national survey. *Child Abuse & Neglect, 24,* 273–287.

Taylor, N. (2007). *Juror attitudes and biases in sexual assault cases* (Trends and Issues in Crime and Criminal Justice, No. 344). Canberra: Australian Institute of Criminology.

Temkin, J., & Krahé, B. (2008). *Sexual assault and the justice gap: A question of attitude*. Oxford: Hart Publishing.

Thomas, C. (2010). *Are juries fair?* (Ministry of Justice Research Series No. 1/10). London: Ministry of Justice. www.justice.gov.uk/downloads/publications/research-and-analysis/moj-research/are-juries-fair-research.pdf.

Tolmie, J. (2012). New Zealand's Jane Doe. In E. A. Sheehy (Ed.), *Sexual assault in Canada: Law, legal practice and women's activism* (pp. 53–71). Ottawa: University of Ottawa Press.

Topping, A., & Barr, C. (2018, September 24). Revealed: Less than a third of young men prosecuted for rape are convicted. *The Guardian.* https://www.theguardian.com/society/2018/sep/23/revealed-less-than-a-third-of-young-men-prosecuted-for-are-convicted.

Ullman, S. E., & Filipas, H. H. (2005). Gender differences in social reactions to abuse disclosures, post-abuse coping, and ptsd of child sexual abuse survivors. *Child Abuse & Neglect, 29,* 767–782.

Victorian Law Reform Commission. (2004). *Sexual offences* (Final Report). Melbourne: Victorian Law Reform Commission.

Ventus, D., Antfolk, J., & Salo, B. (2017). The associations between abuse characteristics in child sexual abuse: A meta-analysis. *Journal Of Sexual Aggression, 23,* 167–180.

Walsh, K., Danielson, C. K., McCauley, J. L., Saunders, B. E., Kilpatrick, D. G., & Resnick, H. S. (2012). National prevalence of posttraumatic stress disorder among sexually revictimized adolescent, college, and adult household-residing women. *Archives of General Psychiatry, 69,* 935–942.

Walsh, K., Resnick, H. S., Danielson, C. K., McCauley, J. L., Saunders, B. E., & Kilpatrick, D. G. (2014). Patterns of drug and alcohol use associated with lifetime sexual revictimization and current posttraumatic stress disorder among three national samples of adolescent, college, and household-residing women. *Addictive Behaviors, 39,* 684–689.

World Health Organization. (2014). *Global status report on violence prevention 2014*. Luxemborg: WHO.

Wundersitz, J. (2003). *Child Sexual assault: Tracking from police incident report to finalisation in court*. Adelaide: Office of Crime Statistics and Research.

2

The Nature and Effects of Adversarialism: Jury Decision-Making in Sexual Assault Trials

1 Introduction

Sexual assault is a unique crime in that most victims are female and most offenders are male. The gendered nature of sexual assault explains why the crime is characterised by delayed complaints, no eyewitnesses and little or no forensic evidence because the essence of the crime is about power and control.

As discussed in Chapter 1, the crime is also characterised by low reporting rates, high attrition rates and, compared to other crimes, low guilty plea rates and relatively low conviction rates. Because of these low conviction rates, the focus of this and the next chapter is on jury decision-making in order to understand the decision-making processes of disparate groups of laypeople when faced with allegations of sexual assault by a child or adult complainant. In other words, police and prosecutorial decisions to drop a case or charge a suspect are made in the shadow of the adversarial trial where only about one-third to one-half of sexual assault trials will result in a guilty verdict.

Jury decision-making in criminal trials has been the focus of considerable academic interest over the years, largely because the criminal justice system invites laypeople to be the triers-of-fact within a complicated legal

A. Cossins, *Closing the Justice Gap for Adult and Child Sexual Assault*,
https://doi.org/10.1057/978-1-137-32051-3_2

process. Nonetheless, it is commonly believed that juries, as an integral part of the criminal justice system, get it 'right' most of the time (Bornstein & Greene, 2011) and that '"verdict, "correct result" and "justice" are co-terminous' (Hill & Winkler, 2000: 401).

In countries, such as the UK, the USA and Australia, there is a history of hundreds of years of jury decision-making without, until the mid-twentieth century, any measure of the extent to which jury decision-making constitutes the best way to decide guilt or innocence in a criminal trial. Although jury trials have diminished in importance in some jurisdictions, jury trials are still the most common form of adjudication in Australia for indictable offences, although judge-only trials are available in certain circumstances.[1]

In the UK, the most serious criminal offences are tried in Crown Court where a jury will be the trier of fact unless a judge-only trial is held[2] although the cases tried in the Crown Courts represent a minority of all criminal offences prosecuted. Nonetheless, jury trials are still relatively common in the prosecution of sex offences in the UK since Thomas (2010: 26–28) found that juries in England and Wales were more likely to return a verdict in relation to a sex offence than any other type of offence so that 'the single largest proportion of jury verdicts are for sexual offences (31%)', partly because defendants were more likely to plead not guilty to a sex offence compared to all other charges (except homicide and proceeds of criminal conduct).[3]

This chapter begins by considering the problems with jury decision-making in criminal trials, generally, and sexual assault trials, in particular. In Chapter 1, I discussed the under-reporting of sexual offences, the reasons why victims do not report and the attrition problem associated with those offences that are reported. This chapter, however, deals with the inherent shortcomings associated with using laypeople as the triers-of-fact in the type of trial where a complainant's testimony is likely to

---

[1]See, for example, *Criminal Procedure Act 1986* (NSW), s132A.

[2]Criminal Justice Act 2003 (UK), schedule 3.

[3]In a study of all charges (551,669) in the Crown Courts of England and Wales that resulted in outcomes between 1 October 2006 and 31 March 2008, Thomas (2010: iii) found that overall only 12% were decided by trial by jury. While most defendants (59%) pleaded guilty, only 36% of charges with a not guilty plea were heard in a jury trial.

be uncorroborated because of the very nature of how sexual assault is perpetrated. Typically, this means that in sexual assault trials there will be:

i. No ear- or eyewitnesses;
ii. A delayed complaint;
iii. No forensic evidence of the alleged sexual act, or the inability of forensic evidence to prove lack of consent;
iv. No confirmatory medical evidence of the sexual act;
v. The consumption of alcohol and/or drugs by the complainant and/or the defendant;
vi. Counter-intuitive responses by the victim during and after the sexual assault; and
vii. Word against word oral evidence.

As a result, the jury will be reliant on the inexact 'science' of credibility assessments (Clemens et al., 2010; Granhag & Strömwall, 2000; Granhag, Strömwall, & Hartwig, 2005) to determine guilt/innocence. Horvath and Brown (2010: 556) consider that:

> a psychological analysis of the criminal justice system is needed to understand its apparent resistance to decades of attempts at reforming rape law, and to develop procedures that are not inhibitory to people reporting offences or authorities' investigation and prosecution of them. In particular, an understanding of rape stereotypes and the attrition problem are needed if we are to restore faith in the criminal justice system.

To that end, this book canvases the impact of rape myths and misconceptions on jury decision-making, as well as providing a historical and theoretical analysis of the entrenched rape-supportive beliefs within the criminal justice system when it comes to the prosecution of sex offences. While jury decision-making is only one part of the problem associated with investigating and prosecuting sex offences, the question is whether the jury trial is the best mechanism for determining the guilt or innocence of defendants within the gendered structure of the criminal trial, particularly since juries are comprised of laypeople who bring a number of myths and misconceptions to the jury room about rape and the behaviour of sexual assault victims.

Juries are also unlikely to have 'worked with a group to reach a decision about a complex problem' (Gordon, 2015: 1) which involves high-stakes (freedom versus conviction and imprisonment). In other words, a jury trial requires the empanelment of twelve laypeople, most of whom are likely to lack:

> legal knowledge and training to hear evidence that has been carefully chosen … to make sense of sometimes conflicting facts, and to apply legal rules … in order to reach a verdict. (Blackwell & Seymour, 2014: 567)

This lack of juror expertise is particularly salient in light of research that suggests that juries exhibit a pro-acquittal bias or a leniency asymmetry effect as a result of deliberation and the 'liberation effect' (Kalven & Zeisel, 1966), as explained below.

In the next section, I provide an analysis of jury behaviour in order to provide the context for understanding the factors that predict verdicts in child and adult sexual assault trials. After reviewing the literature on those factors, this chapter will discuss:

i. jurors' perceptions of guilt based on 'commonsense' or 'life experience';
ii. the cultural climate in which sex offences are prosecuted; and
iii. a literature review of the extent to which laypeople adhere to misconceptions and myths about women, children and sexual assault and the influence of these myths/misconceptions on outcomes in sexual assault trials.

2 Jury Behaviour: Understanding Sexual Assault Trials

In order to understand the difficulties with prosecuting sexual assault trials, it is important to understand jury decision-making, in particular the two phenomena that have been reported in the literature: the majority effect and the leniency asymmetry effect, since both help explain the tendency towards acquittals in sexual assault trials.

To begin, I turn back to the mid-1950s when the first studies on jury behaviour were conducted and the Chicago Jury Project was launched. In documenting the results of this landmark study, Kalven and Zeisel (1966) found that while judges and jurors agreed on a verdict in 78% of cases, overall, jurors were more lenient than judges, acquitting twice as often compared to what judges would have decided. In explaining this degree of judge–jury disagreement, Kalven and Zeisel (1966: 495) hypothesised that, in trials with ambiguous evidence (the typical situation in a sexual assault trial), juries are 'liberated' from trial constraints and rely on their commonsense assumptions and beliefs to resolve doubts about the evidence.

This hypothesis, known as the 'liberation effect', implies that 'jury verdicts will be determined by the strength of the evidence ... but susceptible to non-evidentiary influences when the evidence is "close"' (Devine, Buddenbaum, Houp, Studebaker, & Stolle, 2009: 136). In a sexual assault trial, such extra-legal factors could include the race and ethnicity of the defendant and complainant, as well as rape myth acceptance (RMA) beliefs.

In a partial replication of Kalven and Zeisel's study, Eisenberg et al. (2005) also found a high rate of judge–jury agreement (75%) and a similar pattern of disagreement in that 'juries are much more likely to acquit when judges would convict than they are to convict when judges would acquit' (Eisenberg et al., 2005: 173). In other words, juries have a higher conviction threshold than judges, something that Kalven and Zeisel (1966: 189) believed was due to juries 'more stringent view of proof beyond a reasonable doubt'.

In their study involving the National Center for State Courts database where judges and juries classified the evidence in a case as medium or strong, Eisenberg et al's (2005) study confirmed this hypothesis. They found that judges were more likely to convict than juries across 19 different crimes in four different jurisdictions, although judges were less likely than juries to convict in cases of weak case strength. Overall, Eisenberg et al. (2005: 189) concluded that 'juries require stronger evidence to convict than judges':

> Judges' willingness to convict exceeds 50 percent of cases even when jurors regard the evidence as largely favourable to the defense—"3" on [a] 1–7 scale. As the evidence favouring the prosecution moves from "4" to "5", jurors willingness to convict soars to over 90 percent.

Eisenberg et al. (2005: 191) also found that 'judges' lower conviction threshold does not appear to be a function' of either case or legal complexity. Nor did they find any association between juror characteristics, case characteristics and locality. Overall, there was 'at least a 12 percent increase in probability of conviction' with a judge as adjudicator, although evidence strength dominates case outcomes in that 'stronger evidence of guilt is strongly associated with increased likelihood of conviction' (Eisenberg et al., 2005: 196, 198). Some juror characteristics, such as gender and educational levels, were associated with outcomes in some localities, in that male jurors were more likely to convict while increased educational levels corresponded with a likelihood of acquittal. In fact, Eisenberg et al. (2005: 201) suggested that 'education … also helps explain judge-jury disagreement'.

2.1 The Majority Effect

In addition to the higher conviction threshold of juries compared to judges, jury research has also revealed the existence of a 'majority effect' on jury decision-making. After conducting post-trial interviews, Kalven and Zeisel (1966) reported that the majority verdict of jurors prior to deliberation became the final verdict in 90% of 225 trials. This finding was supported by a later study which showed that the initial majority verdict of a jury 'approaches 100% when two-thirds or more of the jury favors [that] particular verdict' (Devine et al., 2004: 2070) for both actual jurors (Devine et al., 2004; Kalven & Zeisel, 1966; Sandys & Dillehay, 1995; Zeisel & Diamond, 1978) and mock jurors (Huang & Lin, 2014; MacCoun & Kerr, 1988).

This 'majority effect' has led to the view that deliberation has little impact on jury outcomes (Kalven & Zeisel, 1966; Devine, Buddenbaum, Houp, Stolle, & Studebaker, 2007; Salerno & Diamond, 2010) since it appears that the initial majority view (that is, the sum total of individual opinions) prevails throughout the deliberation process (Devine et al., 2004). In other words, it is believed that the real decision is made before deliberation begins (Kalven & Zeisel, 1966: 488) with some researchers 'using individual opinions ... as a surrogate for the group decisions of mock juries' (Sandys & Dillehay, 1995: 176). Indeed, reversed verdicts, where the final verdict differs to that of the majority at the beginning of deliberation, are relatively rare (Devine et al., 2004; Tanford & Penrod, 1986).

In sexual assault trials, for example, the ability of some jurors during deliberation to counteract the impact of issues such as gender and RMA on individual opinions may be limited if a majority favours an acquittal before deliberation takes place. This is particularly important when considering the leniency asymmetry effect.

2.2 The Leniency Asymmetry Effect

The robust finding that deliberating jurors (both actual and mock) are prone to a majority effect contrasts with a leniency or asymmetric effect which predicts that juror factions favouring acquittal are more likely to prevail than those favouring conviction. The existence of a 'leniency bias' emerged from research which showed that juries with *less than* a two-thirds majority at the beginning of deliberation tended to acquit or produce hung verdicts (MacCoun and Kerr, 1988; Tanford & Penrod, 1986). Tanford and Penrod (1986) found a strong leniency effect in simulated jury studies involving jurors drawn from a jury pool in Wisconsin. Their study found that not only did majorities tend to prevail (with only 14 out of 100 juries reversing the original majority), evenly split juries tended to acquit, suggesting 'a scheme in which majorities win, and evenly split juries tend towards acquittal' (Tanford & Penrod, 1986: 331).

Meta-analyses by MacCoun and Kerr (1988) and Devine et al. (2001) show that the likelihood of a majority prevailing depends on its size and the verdict it favours. A majority that favours acquittal is more likely to prevail than an equivalent majority that favours conviction, an issue for sexual assault trials because of the extent of RMA in the general community (discussed under Part 5, below). This tendency towards acquittal is now referred to as the 'leniency asymmetry effect' and has been attributed to the high threshold represented by the criminal standard of proof (Kerr & MacCoun, 2012) and the fact that the burden of proof is on the prosecution. Deliberation itself may also increase the influence of group norms such as a bias in favour of acquittals (Davis, 1980) or the influence of RMA within a jury.

The question for this chapter is whether or not the leniency asymmetry effect is greater in sexual assault trials compared with other criminal trials, and, if so, what reforms would be needed to minimise this effect. Because of the typical lack of corroborating evidence in a sexual assault trial, it is likely that jurors will fill in the gaps in evidence by relying on their biases and misconceptions in assessing the credibility of the complainant and defendant and in reaching a verdict. Before dealing with this question in more detail, we need to know more about the leniency asymmetry effect.

In a meta-analysis of 11 studies, MacCoun and Kerr (1988) found that pro-conviction majorities in simulated criminal jury trials prevailed only 67% of the time, compared to pro-acquittal majorities which prevailed 94% of the time. Juries that were evenly divided at the beginning ended up acquitting 81% of the time. These results suggest that juries will exhibit a leniency asymmetry when at least a two-thirds majority does not exist at the beginning of deliberation, resulting in a final verdict that favours the defendant (see also MacCoun, 1984; Tanford & Penrod, 1986).

The leniency asymmetry effect manifests in juries with evenly split, or weak majority pre-deliberation factions and has been reported in simulated jury studies (Huang & Lin, 2014; MacCoun & Kerr, 1988; Park, Kim, Lee, & Seo, 2005) but has not been reported in studies involving actual jurors (Devine et al., 2004; Hannaford-Agor, Hans, Mott, & Munsterman, 2002; Kalven & Zeisel, 1966; Sandys & Dillehay, 1995). However, it is necessary to determine if this apparent difference between real and mock jurors is real.

3 Leniency Asymmetry Effect: Is There a Difference Between Mock and Actual Jurors?

In a recent study involving 279 jury-eligible community members in Taiwan, Huang and Lin (2014: 370–371) reported that jurors' post-deliberation acquittal rate (71.7%) was significantly higher than the pre-deliberation acquittal rate (58.8%), suggesting a leniency effect as a result of deliberation. In fact, the acquittal rate was significantly higher in juries who were required to return a unanimous verdict, compared to those who were able to return a majority verdict. The prosecutor's case strength and the credibility of the defence case were the strongest predictors in both pre- and post-deliberation verdicts, with a positive correlation between jurors' aversion to wrongful conviction and their acquittal rate, post-deliberation (Huang & Lin, 2014: 371).

Huang and Lin (2014: 371) also found a strong majority effect in that the unanimous verdicts in 11 out of 14 juries reflected the initial majority position. As well, among the six hung juries, 'the majorities won more votes in two juries, with four juries maintaining the initial vote', while all the final majority verdicts reflected the initial position of the majorities. Huang and Lin (2014: 374, 375) concluded that deliberation 'not only has the effect of increasing jurors' aversion to wrongful conviction and their acquittal votes ... but also the effect of promoting the association between the two' and that 'deliberation led more jurors to be persuaded to switch from conviction to acquittal than vice versa'.

This is an issue that could be important for sexual assault trials since Huang and Lin (2014) proposed that the leniency asymmetry effect may be due to 'jurors' increased concern over wrongful conviction after deliberation' which is related to the high standard of proof in criminal trials

(Huang & Lin, 2014: 375). Because of this high standard of proof, it is thought that jurors perceive that guilt beyond reasonable doubt requires a high level of certainty (90–100%) before convicting (MacCoun & Kerr, 1988; Saks, 1997). Arguably, this standard:

> provides pro-acquittal jurors with a strategic advantage during debate in the jury room. Jurors favouring acquittal need only raise a single reasonable doubt in the minds of pro-conviction jurors, whereas jurors arguing for conviction must refute all reasonable doubts in the minds of pro-acquittal jurors. (MacCoun & Kerr, 1988: 26; citing Nemeth, 1977)

In sexual assault trials, for example, these 'reasonable' doubts often arise from the defence narrative which typically relies on widespread beliefs about appropriate and inappropriate victim behaviours, as discussed in Parts 4 and 5, below.

MacCoun and Kerr (1988) found that there was a leniency bias (that is, verdicts favouring acquittal) in juries that had deliberated under the reasonable doubt standard, compared to juries that had deliberated under the preponderance of the evidence standard used in civil trials. Their results suggested 'that deliberation tends to amplify the effects of these instructions' (MacCoun & Kerr, 1988: 30). They also found a leniency shift towards acquittal independent of the standard of proof manipulation, indicating that deliberation, of itself, produces a leniency bias but as a result of what aspects of deliberation they were not able to tell.

Ellison and Munro (2010: 83) reported the existence of a leniency bias when they found that 22 out of 26 mock juries (84.6%) in a simulated sexual assault trial shifted away from an initial guilty verdict to acquittal. In addition, they reported that 'jurors who were initially undecided … were significantly more likely to vote not guilty' (81% versus 19%). Of the 24 juries that initially contained undecided jurors ($n = 18$), all voted not guilty in the end. Ellison and Munro (2010: 83–84) found that guilt beyond reasonable doubt was:

> routinely relied upon by jurors who sought to convince peers against conviction and the inability to be sure of guilt on the basis of the evidence

> was by far the most common reason offered by those who shifted preference towards acquittal. ... [J]urors who campaigned for a not guilty verdict routinely asserted that conviction required 100% certainty. ... It is striking that only in a very small number of juries was this interpretation ever questioned.

By contrast, Sandys and Dillehay's (1995) study with actual jurors found that of the juries that were evenly divided at the beginning of deliberation, 71% ended up convicting, suggesting, instead, a severity effect. After interviews with 142 jurors who had served on felony trials, Sandys and Dillehay (1995) reported findings that were remarkably similar to those of Kalven and Zeisel (1966) in that there was 'a significant relationship between first-ballot votes and final verdicts', with the final verdict being consistent with the initial majority in 93% of trials (Sandys & Dillehay, 1995: 184). These results confirm that by the time the first vote is taken in a criminal trial, 'the jury has settled on a decision' and only rarely will it be altered by subsequent deliberations (Sandys & Dillehay, 1995: 188).

While Sandys and Dillehay (1995: 185) found that final verdicts were consistent with majority first-ballots in 75% of cases, evenly split juries produced guilty verdicts in 71% of cases, acquittals in 21% of cases and hung juries in 8%. These results do not support the leniency asymmetry effect found in simulated jury studies, nor do the results of Hannaford-Agor et al. (2002) who, in a study of 382 criminal trials, found that 23 out of 44 (52.3%) of evenly split juries produced guilty verdicts.

Given the differences between simulated jury studies and studies involving actual jurors, it is necessary to ask, do *actual* juries display a leniency effect? This question is particularly important for understanding outcomes in sexual assault cases. It was addressed by Devine et al. (2004) who examined the predictive validity of jurors' initial vote on final jury verdicts by studying 79 criminal juries to determine whether a leniency asymmetry effect exists. The authors predicted that juries with a two-thirds majority, pre-deliberation, would follow the majority view by the end of jury deliberation, while juries without a majority prior to deliberation would acquit in most cases.

Devine et al. (2004: 2080) found that the strength of both prosecution and defence evidence 'were strongly related to guilty verdicts', while evidence presentation quality and severity of the primary charge were 'positively associated with conviction', compared to defendant testimony which was 'negatively associated'. As had been predicted, 'the percentage of jurors favoring conviction on the first deliberation vote was very strongly related to final verdicts … as was the shift in the number of jurors favoring guilt between the first and second votes'.

As expected, 94% of juries acquitted when they exhibited a two-thirds pro-acquittal majority prior to deliberation, while 90% of juries with a two-thirds pro-conviction majority delivered a guilty verdict. On the other hand, the expectation that juries *without* a two-thirds majority would acquit was not reflected in their results. Instead of acquitting, 75% of these juries (that is, juries with 50, 58 or 42% of jurors favouring conviction) delivered guilty verdicts, irrespective of jury size (Devine et al., 2004: 2081).

As well, reversed verdicts were rare with only 5% of juries producing a final verdict opposite to that favoured by the majority at the outset of deliberation. As a result, Devine et al. (2004: 2089) suggested that 'the operative decision scheme in real juries might be characterized as "two-thirds majority, otherwise convict"' (compared to mock juries) which suggests that real jurors exhibit a severity bias.

Devine et al. (2004: 2092) concluded that three independent studies, including their own, found 'much less leniency bias in actual juries than would be expected from the substantial research involving mock juries'. In each of these three studies, close juries (those with, or close to, a 50/50 split) convicted 50–75% of the time. In a later study, in which jurors from 103 criminal trials were surveyed, Devine et al. (2007) reported that 56% of the juries in cases in which the first ballot vote was close convicted the defendant, concluding that this was further evidence *against* a leniency effect on the part of real juries, although only 16 juries met the criteria for a non-two-thirds majority in the study.

Nonetheless, these results raise the question as to why mock jurors would act differently to real jurors, since they are drawn from the same population of people eligible for jury duty. The results also 'evoke longstanding arguments about the alleged invalidity of the mock jury method' (Kerr & MacCoun, 2012: 597), with explanations for the difference focusing on the artificiality of simulated jury studies, the simplified materials used (such as written case summaries) and the non-court, laboratory setting, although the leniency effect has been seen in simulated jury studies that used short, written materials, as well as realistic videotaped trial simulations (MacCoun & Kerr, 1988). On the other hand, studies of real juries assume that jurors' post-trial accounts of their juries' initial votes and final verdicts are accurate.

3.1 Severity or Leniency Effect: How Do Real Juries Actually Behave?

In order to determine whether a leniency effect is an artefact of mock jury studies and whether actual juries exhibit a severity effect, Kerr and MacCoun (2012) re-analysed the data reported by Sandys and Dillehay (1995), Hannaford-Agor et al. (2002) and Devine et al. (2004).

By identifying the methodological errors in the above studies, Kerr and MacCoun (2012: 588–589) concluded there were 'potential biases' in the coding of the first ballot votes. In other words, the primary explanation for 'the apparent divergence of laboratory and field evidence on the leniency asymmetry' appears to be due to the assumption that the category of 'undecided/abstain' votes equated to 'not guilty' votes such that the two categories were collapsed into one.

Kerr and MacCoun (2012: 590) consider that there is no empirical or logical reason for this assumption so that when a first vote is taken, the undecideds/abstainers should either be excluded or should be equally distributed between guilty and not guilty votes in a study. The up-shot of the misclassification means that evenly split juries in a study would, with re-classification or by exclusion of the undecideds/abstainers, turn into pro-conviction juries, thus changing the results reported by the study. Since only evenly split juries are used as the parameter for assessing a leniency effect, a pro-conviction jury that is misclassified as an evenly split jury that ends up convicting represents a false measure of severity and the non-existence of a leniency effect.

By using different coding assumptions, Kerr and MacCoun (2012) conducted two re-analyses, the first of which split all undecideds and abstentions equally between the factions favouring guilty and not guilty, while the second excluded all juries with any undecided or abstaining jurors. Both of these are less biased methods for determining jurors' preferences. For both re-analyses, Kerr and MacCoun (2012) confirmed previous findings in the literature that:

i. initial majorities nearly always prevail (93.2 and 94%); and
ii. for the majorities that did not prevail, they were more likely to be pro-conviction majorities that ended up acquitting.

Overall, the severity effect evident in the studies of Devine et al. (2007), Sandys and Dillehay (1995) and Hannaford-Agor et al. (2002), as a result of the misclassification of undecideds/abstentions, was 'attenuated or eliminated' when re-coding methods were used (Kerr & MacCoun, 2012: 591). The asymmetry was reversed in relation to the data of Devine et al. (2004) and Sandys and Dillehay (1995) (although less dramatically in the latter), while a symmetric effect for split juries was found with the re-coding of the data of Hannaford-Agor et al. (2002). Thus, the so-called severity effect reported in these studies 'can plausibly be attributed, at least in part, to a biased coding assumption' (Kerr & MacCoun, 2012: 595).

The leniency effect in the above studies was not as large as that found in MacCoun and Kerr's (1988) study of mock jurors. Even so, there are good reasons to re-consider the status of mock jury research since such studies assemble large numbers of jurors who view the same trial compared to actual juries which represent 'one jury per case' (Kerr & MacCoun, 2012: 598). Thus, it is likely to be harder to test for a leniency effect in real juries. As well, mock jury studies typically create case scenarios where the evidence is equivocal or close in strength (as between prosecution and defence) in order to test for the effect of specific types of evidence or judicial instructions. And it is in close cases where a leniency effect is most likely to be detected (Kerr & MacCoun, 2012: 598), rather than being apparent in all cases. By comparison, actual jury trials are likely to involve cases with relatively strong evidence for the prosecution given the discretionary decision to prosecute and the resources involved (Kerr & MacCoun, 2012: 598) so that a comparison of mock jury trials and real trials must take into account that these trials are not comparable in terms of case strength.

In conclusion, this review of the literature on jury decision-making reveals that both mock juries and actual juries exhibit:

i. a higher conviction threshold compared to judges;
ii. a majority effect, with acquittals more likely to prevail than convictions; and
iii. a leniency asymmetric effect as a result of juries being prone to acquit, particularly when the prosecution and defence evidence is close in strength.

In other words, all three findings have major implications for sexual assault trials, particularly those relying mostly on the complainant's word against that of the defendant. It is possible that sexual assault trials with little or no supporting evidence are particularly prone to the leniency effect due to widespread rape-supportive beliefs within Western cultures and the influence of RMA on jury outcomes (see Parts 4 and 5, below).

3.2 Systematic Biases in Jury Decision-Making

One clear observation from jury research is that while jury decision-making is imperfect, it is not randomly so in that 'humans consistently exhibit systematic biases in their judgments' (Kerr, MacCoun, & Kramer, 1996: 687). In other words, jurors 'arrive at court fully loaded with prototypes … heuristics … and "commonsense notions" of justice and fairness' (Finkel, Burke, & Chavez, 2000: 1113).

Jurors' biases include imprecision in the assessment of evidence, 'sins' of commission whereby juries ignore a judicial warning which warns them not to reason in a particular way, and sins of omission (Kerr et al., 1996). These biases may be due to a number of factors such as the use of heuristic processing, as opposed to more effortful, systematic processing when assessing the evidence in a trial (Chaiken, 1980; Chaiken and Trope, 1999; Chen, Shechter and Chaiken, 1996; Eagly and Chaiken, 1993; Winter and Greene, 2007) and misunderstandings of judicial directions. The significance of heuristic versus systematic processing in jury trials is discussed in Chapter 3.

Because jurors find themselves in an out-of-the-ordinary, unstructured situation where they are under pressure to reach a unanimous decision with strangers, 'they tend to primarily consider the information that supports the group's existing preferences' (Gordon, 2015: 40; citing Straus, 2011) while 'groups seem to have difficulty accessing information that is not widely shared among members' (Kerr et al., 1996: 714).

This tendency to focus on evidence that supports the majority position is supported by the story model proposed by Hastie, Penrod, and Pennington (1983). Where a preference is favoured by a majority of jurors, the story model, discussed in detail in Chapter 3, would propose that the story constructed by jurors reflects the majority position which then impedes jurors from considering other evidence that supports an alternative story and verdict, thus reinforcing individual biases and perpetuating information bias (Gordon, 2015: 41). Indeed, enhanced bias or 'sins of commission by groups operating under majority-rule decision' are more likely in groups, such as juries, where the decision-making task has 'no clearly shared conceptual scheme for defining right or wrong answers' (Kerr et al., 1996: 714). One could then conclude that group decision-making 'is ill-advised' for the important job that juries undertake (Kerr et al., 1996: 714).

Kerr et al. (1996: 687) consider that there is no simple answer to the question whether individuals are more biased than groups, although it is hypothesised that groups are more susceptible to extra-legal information, such as racial or sexist biases, and other misconceptions because of the persuasive nature of jury deliberation (Davis, 1980; Kalven & Zeisel, 1966). In fact, Davis' (1980) social decision scheme (SDS) model proposes that members of a group make decisions through social decision schemes, such as a 'majority rules' decision scheme, which is consonant with the majority effect and the leniency asymmetry effect discussed above. Nonetheless, SDS theory is ultimately a mathematical model which seeks to predict group behaviour based on, first, where group members begin their deliberation and, second, the processes by which group members discuss their preferences to reach a group decision. It is, therefore, a theory that may not be able to account for the complexities of group dynamics.

Being a member of a group 'can ... have a profound impact on an individual's cognition and behavior' (Gordon, 2015: 13) in that 'every aspect of individual information processing may be altered' in a group (Kerr et al., 1996: 695), as illustrated in Fig. 1. When information is received by an individual, s/he engages in: attention, encoding, storage, retrieval, processing and response. For groups, the interpersonal nature of deliberation converts individual processing into: group attention, group encoding, group storage, group retrieval, group processing and group decision rule (Kerr et al., 1996).

As well, the tasks of the group expand dramatically with group decision-making, including maintenance of group harmony, relationships and attention, the consideration of multiple points of view and style of deliberation. Group discussion may enhance or hinder retrieval of

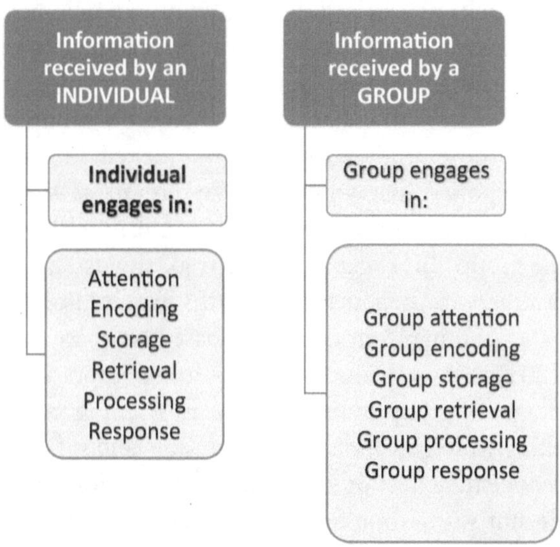

Fig. 1 From individual processing to group processing (based on Kerr et al., 1996)

information and enhance or correct individual biases, as well as having a corrective effect on individual misunderstandings of the facts and judicial instructions (Goodman-Delahunty, Cossins, & Martschuk, 2016).

It is possible that jury deliberations also reflect less responsibility by individuals as they begin to work as a group and play follow the leader, particularly as 'status hierarchies, group cohesion, group norms and group roles' emerge and develop (Gordon, 2015: 14). With high status individuals tending to lead group discussion, jurors 'participate in group discussion at markedly different rates', with higher status jurors being more influential in guiding the deliberation (Gordon, 2015: 15).

While juries are expected to represent community norms, a group of twelve people is unlikely to represent all possible sex, gender, racial, ethnic, cultural and religious norms in any given community. Even where diversity is present in a group, the phenomenon of group conformity means that group members may adopt others' incorrect decisions or interpretations, with human brains containing neurons for mimicking the actions of others (Gordon, 2015: 27–28). Thus, not every juror will necessarily engage in systematic, thoughtful, rational reasoning with some making quick, heuristic judgements, others not paying attention at all (referred to as 'social loafing': Simms & Nichols, 2014) and others going with the majority view.

Certainly, the effect of the majority choice on group behaviour, as documented in some studies (Clark, 2001; cited in Gordon, 2015), explains why majority first votes tend to prevail as the final verdict, suggesting that minority jurors eventually conform with the thinking of the dominant group. In a sexual assault trial, the extent to which individual jurors adhere to particular rape myths may lead to quick, heuristic judgements and dominant group norms based on these rape myths.

Gordon (2015: 35–37) argues that training jurors is the answer to the disadvantages of group dynamics, that is, training in 'effective group decision-making strategies and … collaboration' and information sharing in order to reduce the effect of status and social conformity and to ensure that jurors do not waste time figuring out how to work as a group, time better spent on analysing the evidence and applying the relevant judicial directions. Such training would require a large amount of resources, give the number of jurors who are called up for jury duty annually.

3.3 Is the Leniency Effect More Pronounced in Sexual Assault Cases Because of Jurors' Adherence to Rape Myths?

Compared to other criminal trials, sexual assault trials are more likely to be close cases because of a lack of the type of corroborating evidence that is typically admitted in other criminal trials, such as medical evidence of injuries, eyewitness evidence, DNA evidence, fingerprint or other forensic evidence. If the prosecution's chief witness is a child, his or her verbal and mental development can place them at a great disadvantage when giving evidence and being cross-examined (Cossins, 2009) which impacts on the quality of her/his evidence. In other words, sexual assault cases give rise to numerous doubts which are likely to be filtered through jurors' misconceptions about women, children and sexual assault.

Indeed, confirmation bias has been shown to influence people's assessment of the behaviour of others. Confirmation bias 'is the tendency to bolster a hypothesis by seeking consistent evidence while minimizing inconsistent evidence' (O'Brien, 2009) and has been confirmed in a number of experimental studies (Ask & Granhag, 2005; Hergovich, Schott, & Burger, 2010; Jonas, Schulz-Hardt, Frey, & Thelen, 2001; Jones & Sugden, 2001; Klayman, 1995; Kassin, Dror, & Kukucka, 2013).

For example, in an early study, Langer and Abelson (1974) recruited 40 clinical psychologists (from different theoretical backgrounds) who viewed a videotaped interview of a man with one of the authors. Half of the clinicians were told that the man was a job applicant while the other half were told that he was a patient. When the clinicians were asked to evaluate the man, the therapists with a traditional approach to therapy described the man as significantly more disturbed when they thought he was a patient compared to when they thought he was a job applicant.

If confirmation bias can occur with psychologists (Hergovich, Schott, & Burger, 2010; Langer & Abelson, 1974), police investigators (Ask & Granhag, 2005) and forensic scientists (Kassin et al., 2013), it is just as likely to occur in a jury when individual jurors believe in rape myths. A particular bias or heuristic cue—for example, that 'women who wear revealing clothing are asking for it'—may then be the filter or lens through which a complainant's evidence and credibility and other trial evidence is assessed in order to confirm the bias.

For example, Marks and Fraley (2006) investigated the extent to which people interpret information that confirms the sexual double standard in Western societies, which may be defined as positive cultural rewards for men who engage in sexual activity and negative cultural rewards for women who do the same. After 223 students read different vignettes which described 'a highly sexually active man or woman discussing his or her history of sexual activity' and the negative and positive comments they had received (Marks & Fraley, 2006: 21), participants were asked to recall the comments made. The authors found that participants 'tended to recall information that was consistent with a sexual double standard', which suggests that 'people are more likely to attend to evidence in which women are derogated as opposed to rewarded for sexual activity' (ibid.: 23). In other words:

> a cycle may occur such that people notice information that corroborates a double standard, which solidifies their belief in its existence, thereby making it all the more likely that they will continue to notice information that corroborates the double standard. (ibid.: 24)

As discussed in the next chapter, numerous studies reveal the extent to which laypeople endorse rape myth acceptance (RMA) and misconceptions about children and CSA, thus increasing the likelihood that in any one jury, a proportion of jurors will adhere to some of these myths and misconceptions. For example, the literature reveals that the higher an individual's level of RMA, the more likely s/he will blame the victim, and the less likely s/he will perceive the victim to be credible and the defendant to be culpable (Stewart & Jacquin, 2010). In fact, there is a positive correlation between relatively high levels of RMA and a tendency to acquit in sexual assault trials (Dinos, Burrowes, Hammond, & Cunliffe, 2015).

Although there is a leniency asymmetry effect in criminal trials, generally speaking, it may be too simplistic to conclude that a jury acts in exactly the same way as an individual when presented with a vignette about rape outside of a criminal justice setting. Jurors in a real trial engage in deliberation which may either modify or enhance the effect of any rape myths that exist within the jury room. Thus, it is necessary to understand the underlying psychological reasoning processes that might lead from RMA to an acquittal.

Is there a causal relationship between high levels of RMA and acquittals in sexual assault trials? Even asking the question presupposes that all sexual assault cases are identical in terms of evidence strength and complainant credibility and that RMA is the only factor that affects jury decision-making.

To answer this question, it is necessary to review the literature on the factors that affect jury verdicts in sexual assault trials. While there is a large literature on the relationship between the characteristics of jurors, victims and defendants, and criminal trial outcomes, the discussion in the next chapter focuses on sexual assault trials.

This discussion takes a closer look at the factors that have been shown to predict verdicts in sexual assault trials in order to explore whether the leniency effect could be more pronounced in those trials. It begins with studies that examine the legal factors that affect convictions in sexual assault cases, followed by a summary of the literature on jurors' and laypeople's perceptions of the behaviour of rape complainants and the literature on RMA in the general population.

References

Ask, K., & Granhag, P. A. (2005). Motivational sources of confirmation bias in criminal investigations: The need for cognitive closure. *Journal of Investigative Psychology and Offender Profiling, 2*, 43–63.

Blackwell, S., & Seymour, F. (2014). Prediction of jury verdicts in child sexual assault trials. *Psychiatry, Psychology & Law, 21*, 567–576.

Bornstein, B. H., & Greene, E. (2011). Jury decision making: Implications for and from psychology. *Current Directions in Psychological Science, 20*, 63–67.

Chaiken, S. (1980). Heuristic versus systematic information processing and the use of source versus message cues in persuasion. *Journal of Personality & Social Psychology, 39*, 752–766.

Chaiken, S. & Trope, Y. (Eds.). (1999). *Dual-process theories in social psychology*. New York: Guilford Press.

Chen, S., Shechter, D., & Chaiken, S. (1996). Getting at the truth or getting along: Accuracy versus impression-motivated heuristic and systematic processing. *Journal of Personality and Social Psychology, 71*, 262–275.

Clemens, F., Granhag, P. A., Strömwall, L. A., Vrij, A., Landström, S., ad Hjelmsäter, E. R., & Hartwig, M. (2010). Skulking around the dinosaur: Eliciting cues to children's deception via strategic disclosure of evidence. *Applied Cognitive Psychology, 24*, 925–940.

Cossins, A. (2009). Cross-examination in child sexual assault trials: Evidentiary safeguard or an opportunity to confuse? *Melbourne University Law Review, 33*, 68–104.

Davies, M. (1997). Taking the inside out: Sex and gender in the legal subject. In N. Naffine & R. J. Owens (Eds.), *Sexing the subject of law* (pp. 25–46). London: Sweet and Maxwell.

Davis, J. H. (1980). Group decision and procedural justice. In M. L. Fishbein (Ed.), *Progress in social psychology* (pp. 157–229). Hillsdale, NJ: Erlbaum.

Devine, D. J., Buddenbaum, J., Houp, S., Stolle, D. P., & Studebaker, N. (2007). Deliberation quality: A preliminary examination in criminal juries. *Journal of Empirical Legal Studies, 4*, 273–303.

Devine, D. J., Buddenbaum, J., Houp, S., Studebaker, N., & Stolle, D. P. (2009). Strength of evidence, extra evidentiary influence, and the liberation hypothesis: Data from the field. *Law and Human Behavior, 33*, 136–148.

Devine, D. J., Clayton, L. D., Dunford, B. D., Seying, R., & Pryce, J. (2001). Jury decision making: 45 years of empirical research on deliberating groups. *Psychology, Public Policy, and Law, 7*, 622–727.

Devine, D. J., Olafson, K. M., Jarvis, L. L., Bott, J. P., Clayton, L. D., & Wolfe, J. M. T. (2004). Explaining jury verdicts: Is leniency bias for real? *Journal of Applied Social Psychology, 34*, 2069–2098.

Dinos, S., Burrowes, N., Hammond, K., & Cunliffe, C. (2015). A systematic review of juries' assessment of rape victims: Do rape myths impact on juror decision-making? *International Journal of Law, Crime and Justice, 43*, 36–49.

Eagly, A. H., & Chaiken, S. (1993). Process theories of attitude formation and change: The elaboration likelihood and heuristic-systematic models. In A. H. Eagly & S. Chaiken (Eds.), *The psychology of attitudes* (pp. 303–350). Fort Worth, TX: Harcourt, Brace, & Janovich.

Eisenberg, T., Hannaford-Agor, P. L., Hans, V. P., Waters, N. L., Munsterman, G. T., Schwab, S. J., & Wells, M. T. (2005). Judge-jury agreement in criminal cases: A partial replication of Kalven and Zeisel's *The American Jury*. *Journal of Empirical Studies, 2,* 171–206.

Ellison, L., & Munro, V. E. (2010). Getting to (not) guilty: Examining jurors' deliberative processes in, and beyond, the context of a mock rape trial. *Social and Legal Studies, 30,* 74–97.

Finkel, N. J., Burke, J. E., & Chavez, L. J. (2000). Commonsense judgments of infanticide: Murder, manslaughter, madness, or miscellaneous? *Psychology, Public Policy, and Law, 6,* 1113–1137.

Goodman-Delahunty, J., Cossins, A., & Martschuk, N. (2016). *Jury reasoning in joint and separate trials of institutional child sexual abuse: An empirical study*. Sydney: Royal Commission into Institutional Responses to Child Sexual Abuse.

Gordon, S. G. (2015). *All together now: Using principles of group dynamics to train better jurors* (Scholarly Works, Paper 896, pp. 1–46). http://scholars.law.unlv.edu/facpub/896.

Granhag, P. A., & Strömwall, L. A. (2000). Effects of preconceptions on deception detection and new answers to why lie-catchers often fail. *Psychology, Crime, & Law, 6,* 197–218.

Granhag, P. A., Strömwall, L. A., & Hartwig, M. (2005). Eyewitness testimony: Tracing the beliefs of Swedish legal professionals. *Behavioral Sciences & the Law, 23,* 709–727.

Hannaford-Agor, P., Hans, V. P., Mott, N. L., & Munsterman, G. T. (2002). *Are hung juries a problem?* Williamsburg, VA: National Center for State Courts. http://www.ncsconline.org/WC/Publications/Res_Juries_HungJuriesProblemPub.pdf.

Hastie, R., Penrod, S., & Pennington, N. (1983). *Inside the jury*. Cambridge, MA: Harvard University Press.

Hergovich, A., Schott, R., & Burger, C. (2010). Biased evaluation of abstracts depending on topic and conclusion: Further evidence of a confirmation bias within scientific psychology. *Current Psychology, 29,* 188–209.

Hill, M., & Winkler, D. (2000). Juries: How do they work? Do we want them? *Criminal Law Forum, 11,* 397–443.

Horvath, M., & Brown, J. (2010). Between a rock and a hard place. *The Psychologist, 23,* 556–559.

Huang, K.-C., & Lin, C.-C. (2014). Mock jury trials in Taiwan: Paving the ground for introducing lay participation. *Law and Human Behavior, 38,* 367–377.

Jonas, E., Schulz-Hardt, S., Frey, D., & Thelen, N. (2001). Confirmation bias in sequential information search after preliminary decisions: An expansion of dissonance theoretical research on selective exposure to information. *Journal of Personality and Social Psychology, 80,* 557–571.

Jones, M., & Sugden, R. (2001). Positive confirmation bias in the acquisition of information. *Theory and Decision, 50,* 59–99.

Kalven, H., & Zeisel, H. (1966). *The American jury*. Chicago: University of Chicago Press.

Kassin, S. M., Dror, I. E., & Kukucka, J. (2013). The forensic confirmation bias: Problems, perspectives, and proposed solutions. *Journal of Applied Research in Memory and Cognition, 2,* 42–52.

Kerr, N. L., & MacCoun, R. J. (2012). Is the leniency asymmetry really dead? Misinterpreting asymmetry effects in criminal jury deliberation. *Group Processes and Intergroup Relations, 15,* 585–602.

Kerr, N. L., MacCoun, R. J., & Kramer, G. P. (1996). Bias in judgment: Comparing individuals and groups. *Psychological Review, 103,* 687–719.

Klayman, J. (1995). Varieties of confirmation bias. *Journal of Learning and Motivation, 32,* 385–418.

Langer, E., & Abelson, R. (1974). A patient by any other name: Clinician group difference in labelling bias. *Journal of Consulting and Clinical Psychology, 42,* 4–9.

MacCoun, R. J. (1984). Modeling the impact of extralegal bias and defined standards of proof on the decisions of mock jurors and juries. *Dissertation Abstracts International, 46,* 700B.

MacCoun, R. J., & Kerr, N. L. (1988). Asymmetric influence in mock jury deliberation: Jurors' bias for leniency. *Journal of Personality and Social Psychology, 54,* 21–33.

Marks, M. J., & Fraley, R. C. (2006). Confirmation bias and the sexual double standard. *Sex Roles, 54,* 19–26.

O'Brien, B. (2009). Prime suspect: An examination of factors that aggravate and counteract confirmation bias in criminal investigations. *Psychology, Public Policy, and Law, 15,* 315–334.

Park, K., Kim, S., Lee, E., & Seo, H. (2005). Social conformity and cognitive conversation during jury deliberation: A content analysis of deliberation arguments in the first officially simulated jury trial in Korea. *The Korean Journal of Social and Personality Psychology, 19,* 1–21.

Saks, M. J. (1997). What do jury experiments tell us about how juries (should) make decisions? *Southern California Interdisciplinary Law Journal, 6,* 1–53.

Salerno, J. M., & Diamond, S. S. (2010). The promise of a cognitive perspective on jury deliberation. *Psychonomic Bulletin & Review, 17,* 174–179.

Sandys, J., & Dillehay, R. C. (1995). First-ballot votes, predeliberation dispositions, and final verdicts in jury trials. *Law and Human Behavior, 19,* 175–195.

Simms, A., & Nichols, T. (2014). Social loafing: A review of the literature. *Journal of Management Policy and Practice, 15,* 58–67.

Stewart, D. N., & Jacquin, K. M. (2010). Juror perceptions in a rape trial: Examining the complainant's ingestion of chemical substances prior to sexual assault. *Journal of Aggression, Maltreatment & Trauma, 19,* 853–874.

Tanford, S., & Penrod, S. (1986). Jury deliberations: Discussion content and influence processes in jury decision making. *Journal of Applied Social Psychology, 16,* 322–347.

Thomas, C. (2010). *Are juries fair?* (Ministry of Justice Research Series No. 1/10). London: Ministry of Justice. www.justice.gov.uk/downloads/publications/research-and-analysis/moj-research/are-juries-fair-research.pdf.

Winter, R. J., & Greene, E. (2007). Juror decision-making. In F. Durso, R. S. Nickerson, S. T. Dumais, S. Lewandowsky, & T. J. Perfect (Eds.), *Handbook of applied cognition* (pp. 739–761). Chichester: Wiley.

Zeisel, H., & Diamond, S. S. (1978). The effect of peremptory challenges on jury and verdict: An experiment in a Federal District Court. *Stanford Law Review, 30,* 491–531.

3

Factors That Predict Outcomes in Sexual Assault Trials

1 Introduction

Jury research shows that verdicts in criminal trials vary according to the strength of the evidence presented by the prosecution and the defence (Devine, Clayton, Dunford, Seying, & Pryce, 2001). But because 'hard evidence' is usually lacking in sexual assault trials, it can be expected that jurors will rely on extra-legal factors (myths, biases and misconceptions) in deciding a case with ambiguous evidence such as a word-against-word case.

Studies of the legal and extra-legal variables that affect convictions in sexual assault cases go back to the 1960s and 1970s with findings that the degree of 'bad character' evidence about a complainant influences jurors' perceptions of her responsibility for the defendant's sexual conduct, which, in turn, may be associated with more lenient sentences for the defendant (Feldman-Summers & Lindner, 1976).

In their classic investigation of jury decision-making, Kalven and Zeisel (1966: 252–253) found that juries were four times more likely to convict in a sexual assault trial if the defendant was a stranger, if there was more than one assailant, or if the assault involved violence.

A. Cossins, *Closing the Justice Gap for Adult and Child Sexual Assault*,
https://doi.org/10.1057/978-1-137-32051-3_3

Although the authors did not specifically investigate the impact of variables associated with the complainant, they found that the degree of agreement between judges and juries in cases with one of the above three factors was 88%, compared to 40% in cases without one of these factors. Kalven and Zeisel (1966) hypothesised that the discrepancy between judge/jury agreement could be attributed to juries' focus on the behaviour of complainants, specifically the extent to which complainants were perceived to be responsible for their victimisation.

Nonetheless, sexual assault cases are not easy for judges to preside over. A study of a sample of US judges found that cases 'involving sexual offenses were rated by the judges as more difficult' compared to other criminal cases (Bumby & Maddox, 1999: 311). Specifically, 63.4% found sexual assault cases and 76.2% found CSA cases more or much more difficult from a legal/technical standpoint; 87.8% found sexual assault cases and 78.6% found CSA cases more or much more difficult from a personal/emotional standpoint, while 87.8% found both types of cases more or much difficult from a public scrutiny/pressure point of view.

Various reasons were given for these greater difficulties including, the 'rules of evidence make convictions more difficult and tend to promote hiding the truth'; 'ambiguity in evidence'; 'one-on-one crime'; 'lack of corroborating evidence/witness'; 'victim won't testify'; 'reluctance of juries to convict on testimony of only one witness'; 'assessing credibility of witness'; 'age of child witness'; and 'ease of defendant's injection of reasonable doubt into circumstances normally surrounding such a crime' (Bumby & Maddox, 1999: 312–313). As we will see below, these difficulties still characterise sexual assault trials two decades later.

2 Factors that Predict Outcomes in Sexual Assault Trials: Physical Evidence

Where the evidence is weak or ambiguous in a sexual assault trial, it can be expected that jurors will have expectations of corroborating evidence, such as medical and/or forensic evidence. For example, 57% of mock jurors agreed with the following statement, 'A physical examination by a doctor will almost always show whether a child has been sexually abused' in studies by Quas, Thompson, and Clarke-Stewart (2005) and Kovera and Borgida (1997).

Jurors' expectations of medical evidence have also been reported in simulated adult sexual assault cases. In a study of 233 jurors who participated in 27 simulated trials, Ellison and Munro (2009b: 376) found a 'widespread belief that genital trauma is an inevitable outcome of rape' contrary to a medical report in the trials which noted that the absence of genital injury 'was neither consistent nor inconsistent with rape' and instructions to jurors that 'the absence of physical injury did not rebut an allegation of rape'.

In a study involving 18 simulated sexual assault trials, Taylor and Joudo (2005) reported that, during deliberation, mock jurors attempted to 'fill in the gaps' in the evidence by speculating not only about the complainant's behaviour but also discussed the fact that there was no DNA evidence, and no medical evidence of injury (Taylor & Joudo, 2005: 61).

These studies raise the question, does the presence or absence of medical and/or forensic evidence affect outcomes in sexual assault cases? The literature that documents the impact of such evidence on the likelihood of prosecution and on outcomes in sexual assault trials reveals contradictory findings.

A few studies have found no association between medical evidence of sexual assault and the decision to prosecute or convict (Hagemann, Stene, Myhre, Ormstad, & Schei, 2011; Hansen, Mikkelsen, Sabroe, & Charles, 2010; Saint-Martin, Bouyssy, Jacquet, & O'Byrne, 2007), although 'differences in the legal systems in European countries [may] account for the lack of correlation between medical evidence and legal outcomes' (Cossins, Jayakody, Norris, & Parkinson, 2016: 931).

By comparison, the presence of positive medical evidence was the strongest predictor of conviction in actual CSA cases as reported by Bradshaw and Marks (1990). Similarly, Palusci, Cox, Cyrus, Heartwell, Vandervort, and Pott (1999) found that a positive medical finding was more likely to predict convictions in CSA cases compared to other factors such as behavioural symptoms displayed by the child complainant.

Out of a sample of 1547 cases of adult and child rape in South Africa, Jewkes, Christofides, Vetten, Jina, Sigsworth, and Lotts (2009) found that both non-genital and genital injuries were associated with the likelihood of CSA cases being prosecuted, compared to adult rape cases. In adult cases, a conviction was more likely if evidence of injury was presented by the prosecution, irrespective of the type of injury. Thus, convictions in the absence of injuries were found to be relatively low in South African courts, that is, 9% in adult sexual assault cases and 33% in CSA cases. By comparison, the presence of DNA evidence had no impact on outcomes in child or adult rape cases.

Similarly, McGregor, Du Mont, and Myhr (2002: 644) found that the extent of injuries documented by a medical examination (mild, moderate or severe) in 193 adult sexual assault cases had a significant positive association with the likelihood of charges being filed, while 'the only variable found to be associated with conviction was a clinical injury extent score of severe'.

When Du Mont and White (2007: 30–31) carried out a meta-analysis of studies that examined the impact of forensic and medical evidence on case outcomes, they reported that the '[c]ollection of biological/non-biological samples and the occurrence of ano-genital trauma were related to the legal resolution of cases in fewer than a third of pertinent studies'. In this study, a number of factors were associated with progression through the criminal justice system in sexual assault cases:

- 'documentation of injury was the strongest predictor of a positive legal outcome. In just under half (44%) of those studies that examined the presence of general physical injuries, a significant association was found'[1];
- the defendant's prior convictions and/or charges;
- multiple charges against the defendant;
- penetration;

[1]Quadara, Fileborn, and Parkinson (2013) note that the 'specificity of the legal context must be kept in mind in interpreting the implications' of evidence of the use of force for [non-American] jurisdictions since in many US states the use of force 'is an explicit component of the definition of rape and also shapes the notion of consent', compared to common law countries, such as Australia, and England and Wales.

- use of a weapon; and
- corroborating evidence from witnesses.

As well, progression through the criminal justice system was affected by perceptions of the complainant's character and behaviour, for example:

> whether her character or reputation were perceived as being negative … and her behaviours before (e.g., she engaged in "risk-taking" activities such as walking alone at night), during (e.g., she did not resist the assailant) and following an assault (e.g., she did not report the assault promptly to the police). (Du Mont & White, 2007: 49)

Other non-medical factors had a detrimental effect on case outcomes, leading to the conclusion that there is a correlation effect between socioeconomic status and character ('good' versus 'bad' victim):

> The composite profile of the victim least likely to see her assailant convicted is of an older, poorer woman, whose character or reputation is perceived negatively as she is deemed to have been sexually promiscuous, a sex worker, has a psychiatric history, drug abuse problem and/or a criminal record. (Du Mont & White, 2007: 30; references omitted)

In a review of the literature on the impact of forensic medical evidence in sexual assault prosecutions and outcomes, Quadara et al. (2013) reported that:

i. in half the studies reviewed, generally, 'forensic medical evidence was associated with positive a legal outcome', although 'a range of other evidentiary and credibility factors also have a role to play'.
ii. Evidence of severe or serious injury was 'most often associated with a positive legal outcome' although other 'biological evidence do[es] not appear to have any impact on legal outcomes'.
iii. No single factor was found to predict 'case progression or positive legal outcomes' because of 'complex interactions between numerous factors', including forensic evidence.

Overall, Quadara et al. (2013) concluded that:

> stereotypical beliefs around what constitutes 'real' rape ... and who is a 'deserving' victim ..., rather than the availability of forensic or medical evidence availability, continue to have a profound and significant [e]ffect on decision-making processes and case outcome for sexual offences.

The influence of 'hard evidence' is also reflected in decisions made by prosecutors to take cases to trial. An Australian study of the factors affecting the prosecution of 88 adult sexual assault cases found that there were statistically significant differences between cases that proceeded and cases that were withdrawn with seven, legally relevant variables predicting that a case would go to trial (Lievore, 2005: 5), including injury to the victim:

- the defendant was a stranger;
- the defendant was non-Caucasian;
- physical or verbal expression of non-consent by the victim;
- victim injury;
- use of force by the defendant;
- evidence of some threat, force, injury or weapon use;
- additional evidence linking the defendant to the offence.

While no single factor predicted prosecution, multivariate analyses found that 'cases were significantly more likely to proceed if the defendants used force and the victims actively expressed non-consent', both of which 'help to establish the mental element of the offence; that is, that the defendant knew the victim was not consenting, but intended to have sex regardless' (Lievore, 2005: 5).

In fact, prosecutorial discretion resulted in 38% of cases in the sample being withdrawn (Lievore, 2005). Of those that proceeded, 44% resulted in a conviction, although most were by way of a guilty plea. Thus, like police investigators, prosecutors represent guardians of 'the gateway to justice' (Spohn, Beichner, & Davis-Frenzel, 2002) since their discretion affects the type of cases that proceed to trial:

> prosecutors who pre-empt the views of the jury on the basis of various sociodemographic, personal or other extralegal variables may exclude

particular types of victims from justice. They may then fail to challenge and expand the bounds of convictability by dealing with actual juries to learn how to win believable but risky cases. (Lievore, 2005: 6)

While jurors might expect supporting medical or forensic evidence, it is uncommon for a sexual assault to result in demonstrable injury to the ano-genital area of adults and children (Cossins et al., 2016; Du Mont & White, 2007; Gray-Eurom, Seaberg, &Wears, 2002; Hansen et al., 2010; Heger, Ticson, Velasquez, & Bernier, 2002; Jina et al., 2015; Saint-Martin et al., 2007), or to result in the collection of forensic evidence.

The typicality of delayed complaint also prevents the collection of medical evidence while, in adult sexual assault cases, DNA evidence has no probative value in cases in which a defendant admits he had sex with the complainant but denies that it was non-consensual.

In a review of the literature on medical examinations involving suspected CSA, Cossins et al. (2016: 926) reported that 'there is a narrow window of time [around 72-96 hours] in which physical evidence may be recovered from the body of a pre-pubertal child', such as blood or semen, while injuries are generally absent due to the elasticity of the ano-genital tissues or because they are difficult to accurately detect (Cossins et al., 2016). As well, the 'competence among medical, law enforcement, forensic science, and legal professionals who deal with victims and their cases of sexual assault often negatively impact the integrity of medico-legal findings', as does active disbelief of a victim's allegations (Du Mont & White, 2013: 1231, 1232). Thus, both jurors' expectations of injury and prosecutors' filtering of cases based on lack of injury do not match the reality of most sexual assaults.

3 Factors that Predict Outcomes in Sexual Assault Trials: Other Corroborating Evidence

While the above studies were mostly limited to examining the impact of physical evidence on case outcomes in sexual assault trials, it is likely that a variety of legal factors are implicated in jury outcomes in these trials. In fact, mock jury studies predict that the overall strength of the prosecution's case is a significant factor in case outcomes (Bottoms et al., 2014). For example, in a large-scale, simulated jury study of CSA cases involving jury deliberation, when corroboration was provided by two other victims about being sexually abused by the same defendant, conviction rates increased significantly compared to a trial with no corroborating witnesses, irrespective of whether the corroborating evidence came from victim-witnesses, or victim-complainants in a joint trial (Goodman-Delahunty, Cossins, & Martschuk, 2016).

Studies show that evidence strength is also associated with convictions in actual sexual assault cases. When LaFree (1980) analysed 124 forcible rape cases from a large American city that were adjudicated between 1970 and 1975, he found that as 'the amount of prosecution evidence increased, the likelihood of guilty verdicts increased', with several factors having a greater impact on verdicts. The defendant's criminal record of sex offences, the seriousness of his prior sex offences, the number of offenders, and prompt report by the complainant all predicted guilty verdicts (LaFree, 1980: 843). In addition to the presence of bodily and/or genital trauma, Gray-Eurom, Seaberg and Wears' (2002) analysis of 801 sexual assault examinations over a 2-year period found that the victim's age (less than 18 years) and the use of a weapon by the assailant were also significantly associated with successful prosecutions.

A survey of Crown Prosecutors in New Zealand allowed Blackwell and Seymour (2014) to test the impact of nine independent variables in 137 completed CSA trials:

i. age of child at trial;
ii. presence of similar fact evidence[2];
iii. recent complaint evidence[3];
iv. presence of penile penetration;

[2]Similar fact evidence is also known as propensity, tendency or coincidence evidence and usually involves prior behaviours that are attributed to the defendant which are similar to the charges in the trial, such as prior charges/convictions, allegations from other witnesses about similar criminal conduct or other evidence of the defendant's association with similar events.

[3]Recent complaint evidence is usually given by a witness to whom the complainant first disclosed her allegation of sexual assault, such as a non-offending parent, counsellor, sibling, close friend, teacher or work colleague.

v. eyewitness evidence;
vi. two or more complainants in one trial;
vii. more than four charges;
viii. partial acknowledgement by the defendant;
ix. positive medical evidence;
x. presence of a venereal disease, or
xi. DNA evidence of the defendant in forensic samples.

The dependent variable was at least one guilty verdict for a sex offence.

The study found that the more evidential factors present in a CSA trial, the more likely it was for the jury to deliver a guilty verdict. Thus, 'the presence of any three or more of the nine evidential variables was significantly predictive of conviction' (Blackwell & Seymour, 2014: 573), and demonstrated the predictive value of overall evidence strength. Out of the above nine variables, the three that were most predictive of at least one guilty verdict were: the presence of similar fact evidence, eyewitness evidence and positive medical or DNA evidence.

This sample of cases also confirmed the fact that most CSA cases do not involve evidence to corroborate a complainant's allegations with only 10.9% of cases featuring similar fact evidence; 28.5% featuring medical evidence (although in two-thirds of those cases the medical evidence was equivocal); 10.2% featuring DNA evidence and 12.4% featuring eyewitness evidence (Blackwell & Seymour, 2014: 572; see also De Jong & Rose, 1991; Lewis, Klettke, & Day, 2014; Saint-Martin et al., 2007).

The paucity of corroborating evidence in a typical CSA trial means that in most cases, the credibility of the child complainant will be crucial to the jury verdict. Indeed, most charges in the 137-case sample resulted in acquittals (62.5%), confirming the relatively low conviction rate of sex offences seen in other studies (Daly & Bouhours, 2010; Fitzgerald, 2006; see review by Quadara, Fileborn, & Parkinson, 2013; see Chapter 1). This suggests that 'jurors require a high threshold of corroborative evidence to convict' (Blackwell & Seymour, 2014: 573),[4]

[4]This high threshold might be attributable to jurors' expectations of forensic evidence as a result of the so-called 'CSI-effect', although the existence of such an effect has been debated in the literature, with evidence for and against (Dioso-Villa, 2015; Holmgren & Fordham, 2011; Mancini, 2013; Schweitzer & Saks, 2007; Shelton, 2008).

a finding that supports the leniency effect observed in criminal trials, generally speaking.

Although Blackwell and Seymour (2014: 573) concluded that 'jurors' verdicts were dominated by evidential issues', they were unable to account for any variance in guilty verdicts that may have been attributed to extra-legal variables such as jurors' biases and misconceptions, nor the differential impact of legal and extra-legal factors in strong and weak cases. In other words, Blackwell and Seymour (2014) did not assess the extent to which the evidence in the 137 CSA trials was filtered through any CSA misconceptions held by jurors and jurors' expectations about how child complainants should behave. As a result, the omission of the effects of extra-legal factors may lead to inflated measures of the effects of legal, evidentiary variables.

By contrast, an analysis of 113 CSA trial transcripts in Victoria, Australia to determine how the presence of medical evidence impacts trial outcomes found that the most significant predictor of verdict was the behaviour of the child complainant:

> where the victims displayed some observable behavioral response to the alleged abuse, a guilty verdict was almost seven times more likely. (Lewis et al., 2014: 437)

These behaviours included: 'difficulty sleeping/nightmares, inappropriate displays of affection with parents, reluctance to undress, reluctance to bathe, displaying adult sexual behavior, withdrawing, problems at school, … promiscuity, depression, and suicidal ideation/attempts'. (Lewis et al., 2014: 435)

Counter-intuitively, the presence of medical evidence had no impact on guilty verdicts while the behaviour of 'acting out' was the only significant behavioural predictor of an acquittal, 'suggest[ing] that when child victims showed evidence of destructive behavior or contrary to what is expected …, a jury was more likely to discredit their account of the alleged abuse and therefore return a not guilty verdict' (Lewis et al., 2014: 438).

Nonetheless, small sample sizes for each factor in the study (medical evidence plus eleven different behavioural responses) suggest that further research is needed to confirm the findings of Lewis et al. (2014).

4 The Impact of Extra-Legal Factors on Outcomes in Sexual Assault Trials: Victim, Defendant and Juror Characteristics

In a large meta-analysis of jury studies to determine the impact of a range of juror, victim and defendant factors on outcomes in criminal trials, Devine and Caughlin (2014: 122) found that prior criminal record was one of two defendant characteristics that had a significant impact on guilty verdicts. However, 'the overall effect of defendant criminal record on guilty judgments … was only modest' and likely to depend on other variables such as the degree of similarity between the prior charges and the current charge.

By contrast, in a sexual assault trial, evidence of a defendant's prior criminal record is not likely to be a typical feature because of the extent to which sexual assault is an under-reported crime,[5] as discussed in Chapter 1. Because the focus of the typical adult sexual assault trial is whether or not the complainant consented, credibility assessments of the complainant mediate jurors' verdicts. In CSA cases, the fact that most children do not report the abuse to authorities for months or years means that the collection of medical evidence or inculpatory DNA evidence to prove the alleged sexual conduct is impossible. Even if there is prompt reporting or discovery of the abuse, medical examinations of children rarely show physical evidence of sexual abuse (Cossins et al., 2016; Johnson, 2004), while DNA evidence may not be available because of the type of sexual assault. Thus, the focus of the CSA trial is also on complainant credibility.

---

[5]In different jurisdictions, different rules of evidence govern the admissibility of evidence of a defendant's prior criminal conduct.

Because of the lack of so-called 'hard evidence' of a defendant's alleged sexual acts, 'jurors will turn to the only other information they have – their own expectations and beliefs' (Cossins, 2013: 95). This suggests that extra-legal variables, such as jurors' biases and misconceptions and/or defendant and complainant characteristics will have a significant impact on trial outcomes in sexual assault trials.

In an empirical study of jury decision-making in 18 simulated adult sexual assault trials,[6] Taylor and Joudo (2005) found a significant relationship between juror demographics, credibility and verdict, in that credibility ratings of the complainant were significantly associated with juror gender, socioeconomic status (SES) and jurors' political attitudes. In fact, jurors' pre-existing attitudes about sexual assault influenced their judgements about the credibility of the complainant and the guilt of the accused more than the facts of the case and the manner in which the evidence was given. Men 'tended to hold less favourable attitudes towards rape victims in general' and were significantly less likely to perceive the complainant as credible compared to women (Taylor & Joudo, 2005: 32).

Overall, the juror factors that were significantly associated with less favourable attitudes towards victims included being male, having a lower income and being politically conservative. In turn, these factors were linked to the belief that the defendant was not guilty. Those jurors who favoured a guilty verdict were significantly more likely to believe the defendant was guilty both before and after jury deliberation, to hold more positive attitudes towards victims, to believe the complainant to be highly credible, and to have low empathy for the defendant and higher empathy for the complainant (Taylor & Joudo, 2005: 56–57).

Although a majority of mock jurors (74%) favoured a not guilty verdict, half of this group believed the defendant was guilty, but did not believe the prosecution had proved their case beyond reasonable doubt (Taylor & Joudo, 2005: 48), a finding that is consistent with the

[6]This study involved a demographically diverse group of 210 mock jurors who were randomly assigned to 18 mock sexual assault trials, which used different modes of victim testimony (live evidence in court, evidence via CCTV or pre-recorded video) and simulated actual trial conditions. The jurors completed pre-deliberation and post-deliberation questionnaires (Taylor & Joudo, 2005: 22–25, 78–92).

high threshold that the standard of proof represents for laypeople and the leniency effect associated with jurors' verdicts.

The results of this study help explain the relatively low conviction rates in sexual assault trials in Australia and E&W, as discussed in Chapter 1. More mock jurors may have voted guilty and some of the hung juries may have become unanimous[7] if the jurors had been exposed to educational information. Such information may have challenged the type of myths and misconceptions that some mock jurors relied on when assessing the truth of the complainant's testimony since there was a 'high degree to which many jurors believed many of the myths which surround rape in general'. In particular, mock jurors had 'strong expectations about how a "real" victim would behave before, during and after an alleged sexual assault' which influenced their assessment of the complainant's credibility during deliberations (Taylor & Joudo, 2005: 59).

In fact, at least four decades of research shows that jurors' decisions in sexual assault trials are particularly influenced by extra-legal factors which may account for the relatively low conviction rates in such trials, compared to other offences, and may partly explain the leniency asymmetry effect in these trials. Historically,

> Distrust and contempt for the unchaste female accuser was formalised into a set of legal rules unique to rape cases. The most prominent rule allowed the use at trial of evidence of the complainant's unchaste conduct. These rules combined to shift the usual focus of a criminal trial from an inquiry into the conduct of the offender to that of the moral worth of the complainant.[8] (Galvin, 1986)

Although progressive judges have recognised that a complainant has 'her victimisation measured against the current rape mythologies',[9] unfortunately 'many judges show a conventional wisdom about human

---

[7]Of the 18 juries who deliberated, 16 could not reach a unanimous verdict within the time allowed while two returned unanimous not guilty verdicts (Taylor & Joudo, 2005: 46).

[8]Cited in *R v Seaboyer* (1991) 83 DLR (4th) 193, 218 (L'Heureux-Dube J).

[9]*R v Seaboyer* (1991) 83 DLR (4th) 193, 650 (L'Heureux-Dube J); see also Spigelman CJ in *JJB v R* (2006) 161 A Crim R 187.

behaviour which may represent the limitations of their background'.[10] Researchers have also recognised that the typical lack of eyewitness and forensic evidence in sexual assault trials means that a word-against-word trial is inherently 'unstable' (LaFree, 1980), thus inviting jurors to rely on other, external sources of information. This suggests that verdicts may depend less on the evidence and more on whether the complainant is considered to be worthy of the law's protection.

While there is no 'general propensity for female jurors to be harsher on criminal defendants than male jurors' (Devine & Caughlin, 2014: 122), Devine and Caughlin's (2014) recent meta-analysis of 11 focal characteristics of defendants and jurors found that juror gender has a significant impact on verdicts in both adult and child sexual assault trials. Female jurors are more likely to convict in those cases, particularly where the complainant is a child, compared to all other types of criminal trials (Devine & Caughlin, 2014: 122; see also Bottoms, Golding, Stevenson, Wiley, & Yozwiak, 2007).

Does this gender effect arise because men are more likely to adhere to rape myths and CSA misconceptions compared to women, or as a result of women's greater empathy for victims, or both? For example, studies with both student and community samples have found gender differences in empathy for victims, the believability of children as witnesses and attitudes towards CSA (Bottoms, 1993; Bottoms et al., 2014). Most recently, Bottoms et al. (2014: 789) found that 'women compared to men were more empathic toward child victims, more opposed to adult/child sex, more pro-women, … more inclined to believe children generally and … made more pro-victim judgments in hypothetical abuse cases'.

Victim age is also a key predictor of mock jurors' verdicts in CSA cases since age has been shown to affect 'perceptions of competence and trustworthiness' and hence credibility (Bottoms et al., 2007: 519; see also Bottoms et al., 2014). Generally, younger victims are perceived as more trustworthy compared to older children and teenagers, possibly because they are 'sexually naïve, lacking the knowledge and cognitive capacity to fabricate sexual encounters' (Bottoms et al., 2007: 519) and are unlikely

---

[10] *JJB v R* (2006) 161 A Crim R 187, [3] (Spigelman CJ).

to be the subject of allegations of drunkenness and sexual promiscuity during defence cross-examination. It is possible that age is a key factor in explaining the data in Chapter 1 that showed that the conviction rate for child sex offences compared to the conviction rate for adult sex offences was higher in NSW over an eight-year period.

For example, in a simulated jury study by Tabak and Klettke (2014), juries were significantly more likely to vote guilty when the complainant was aged 6 years compared to 11 or 15 years, although 'groups were less likely to reach a unanimous decision when the child was 11 years old' (Tabak & Klettke, 2014: 50). Age also affected credibility assessments of the complainant. A qualitative analysis of deliberation transcripts revealed that reasons for guilty verdicts when the complainant was 6-years-old included:

> 'the age of the child, the actions of the child after the fact, the language used in the child's statement', and 'he is totally guilty, as I don't believe a 6 year old would make it up and a 6 year old would not fantasise about those sorts of things'. Thus, mock jurors seemed to perceive a child of 6 years as less responsible and more vulnerable, trustworthy, and sexually naïve. (ibid.: 51)

In trials where the complainant was aged 11 years and prepubescent, jurors' comments suggested that:

> perceptions of competence and trustworthiness are not straightforward because this age group exhibits attributes of a child and emerging adult (i.e., sexual maturity). Thus, as the effect of age became more ambiguous, evidence and context of assault became more important. (ibid.: 51)

Thus, it appears that the mock jurors in this study linked age and sexual maturity with victim blaming and victim responsibility. While the 15-year-old complainant was perceived as 'more competent to recall the assault', she was also perceived 'as less trustworthy, less vulnerable, more responsible, and more likely to lie' (ibid.: 52), as well as having a greater ability to resist the abuse.

A meta-analysis by Whatley (1996) examined the degree of responsibility that observers impose on a female rape victim by investigating common variables associated with victim blame. The study found that the victim's clothing revealingness, and character significantly affected the likelihood that observers would blame a victim of sexual assault. As well, a victim with 'questionable' character is held to be more responsible than a more 'respectable' victim (Whatley, 1996: 90), as is the victim who is acquainted with the perpetrator (compared to a stranger).

In a meta-analysis of studies that examined the impact of victim behaviour and demeanour in CSA cases, Bottoms et al. (2007: 521) found that male mock jurors were more likely to attribute responsibility to victims who did not resist. This finding suggests that resistance is a gendered concept, with men judging females according to their expectations of how a victim ought to behave when faced with a threat. As well, actual jurors' verdicts were correlated with 'the child's facial expressions, gestures and movements, eye contact, nervousness, and manner of speaking'.

This suggests that jurors look for emotions that are expected of a sexual abuse victim, which are then used to make credibility assessments, as discussed in the next section.

5 The Impact of the Emotionality of the Victim/Complainant on Case Outcomes

When it comes to victim demeanour, various studies have shown that laypeople have particular expectations about emotional salience and CSA. Generally speaking, laypeople do not expect a neutral or non-emotional response from an abused child (Bederian-Gardner & Goldfarb, 2014; Wessel, Magnussen, & Melinder, 2013) and expect that children will commonly exhibit emotions such as fear and sadness (Bederian-Gardner & Goldfarb, 2014; Myers, Redlich, Goodman, Prizmich, & Imwinkelried, 1999; Regan & Baker, 1998), with emotional display being associated with increased guilty verdicts compared to calm emotional displays (Regan & Baker, 1998; see also Golding, Fryman, Marsil, & Yozwiak, 2003).

The same expectations appear to be true for adult complainants. For example, Ellison and Munro (2009a: 206–212) presented nine different video versions of a simulated sexual assault trial (in which the complainant's evidence was varied) to 233 mock jurors to investigate 'the influence upon juror deliberations of key behavioural cues involving lack of resistance, delayed reporting and calm complainant demeanour'. Because the evidence supporting the occurrence of the sexual assault was equivocal, jurors spent a large part of their deliberations discussing the complainant's emotional responses, as well as her '"appropriate" socio-sexual behaviour' before, during and after the alleged sexual assault to determine her veracity.

The factors that weighed in favour of a credible story were: the complainant's distress, her emotional state in court and her immediate complaint to the police. The factors that weighed against a credible story included the complainant's failure to resist or physically struggle, lack of significant injury, a three-day delay in complaint, and the complainant's calm, unemotional delivery of her evidence.

Ellison and Munro (2009a: 212, 214) concluded that 'mock jurors appeared to have little understanding of the psychological effects … that could influence a rape complainant's demeanour in court', while jurors' assumptions about 'the instinct to fight back, the compulsion to report immediately and the inability to control one's … emotions … clearly influenced' their deliberations and verdicts.

In a subsequent study, the authors examined whether or not expert testimony or an expansive judicial direction would address the popular misconceptions observed in mock jurors' deliberations. In simulated trials where the complainant displayed a calm, unemotional demeanour, delayed her complaint by three days or showed lack of resistance, jurors who received educational guidance 'were far more likely to offer thoughts on what could possibly account for the complainant's lack of emotionality' and were 'significantly more likely to state that they were untroubled' by the delayed complaint (Ellison & Munro, 2009b: 368, 370). However, no empirical analysis was carried out to determine the impact of the expert educational guidance on jury deliberations or case outcomes.

In a more recent study, when laypeople and professional child protection workers watched mock police interviews with child actors who disclosed physical abuse, Wessel et al. (2013) found that the emotions displayed by the children significantly affected the credibility ratings of the child and culpability ratings of the perpetrator given by both laypeople and professionals. The highest credibility ratings were for the sad, emotional expression 'followed by the neutral expression and a drop in perceived credibility when the witness displayed more positive emotional expression' (Wessel et al., 2013: 614).

In another study, the perceptions of college students and jurors about how emotional a sexually abused child was, 'were [also] highly predictive of their judgements', irrespective of the child's gender but not the child's age:

> Those who perceived the child to be more emotional were more likely to render guilty verdicts, view the child as credible, and view the defendant as less credible. Moreover, … these trends were especially robust when participants perceived the child who was shown as calm while testifying as being highly emotional. … Participants who perceived the child to be highly emotional were most likely to vote guilty. (Cooper, Quas, & Cleveland, 2014: 823)

By contrast, Bederian-Gardner and Goldfarb (2014: 840) found that both victim age and victim gender affected laypeople's expectations of the emotions of a sexually abused child. In particular, laypeople responded according to gender stereotypes in that they 'expected to see more sadness and fear from female than from male victims'. As well, the age of the child affected perceptions in that participants 'expected fear to be expressed more than sadness regardless of gender' for younger victims (aged 5 years) but expected anger to be the emotion displayed by the older, 13-year-old, male victim.

Other studies have also found that mock jurors, non-empanelled jurors called up for jury duty and actual jurors expect sexually abused children to display strong emotional reactions (Cossins, Goodman-Delahunty, & O'Brien, 2009; Goodman-Delahunty, Martschuk, & Cossins, 2017; McCauliff & Kovera, 2012). Indeed, the subjective nature of these expectations was recently demonstrated by Bederian-Gardner, Goldfarb and Goodman (2017) who found that the degree of empathy for participants predicted laypeople's assessments of a CSA victim's feelings, which, in turn, predicted ratings of perceived believability.

This means that there is a 'discrepancy between adults' expectations about child victims and how children actually behave when describing sexual abuse experiences' (Bederian-Gardner & Goldfarb, 2014: 841). Children do not necessarily display strong emotions when revealing their abuse experiences, 'often display[ing] relatively neutral emotion' (Bederian-Gardner & Goldfarb, 2014: 841; citing Sayfan, Mitchell, Goodman, Eisen, & Qin, 2008; Wood, Orsak, Murphy, & Cross, 1996). Importantly, Cooper et al. (2014: 825) observe that:

> Jurors' perceptions of emotion are important to consider in relation to some of the techniques commonly used to reduce a child's stress while testifying in open court, including screens, videotaped testimony, and closed circuit television .... These techniques, although often effective at reducing children's distress, may also lead to a child witness acting in a manner inconsistent with the expectations of jurors.

The authors suggest that education is needed to inform jurors about the 'variability in children's general emotional reactions' when giving evidence, and 'jurors' own potential biases about emotional displays in sexual abuse cases' (Cooper et al., 2014: 825) so that invalid considerations are not used to unfairly measure a child's credibility.

Mock jurors and observers also expect an adult complainant to be emotional when giving evidence (Taylor & Joudo, 2005). A number of studies show that an unemotional sexual assault victim is perceived as being significantly less credible compared to an emotional victim (Bollingmo, Wessel, Eilertsen, & Magnussen, 2008; Bollingmo, Wessel, Sandhold, Eilertsen, & Magnussen, 2009; Kaufman, Drevland, Wessel, Overskeid, & Magnussen, 2003; Klippenstine & Schuller, 2012; Lens, Doorn, Pemberton, & Bogaerts, 2014; Vrij & Fischer, 1997; Wessel, Drevland, Eilertsen, & Magnussen, 2006).

These effects have been found to be 'quite robust and turn up … across the complete age range of adults eligible for jury duty', as well as with experienced police investigators and judges (Bollingmo et al., 2009: 62). In addition, consistency in emotional response over time is important to people's perceptions of the believability of an allegation of sexual assault (Klippenstine & Schuller, 2012). It is also likely that these beliefs will influence jurors' perceptions of what is, and is not, a reasonable doubt even when they believe that the sexual assault occurred. In other words, '[t]he more ambiguous the available evidence, the greater the influence of general beliefs and sentiments' (Schuller et al., 2010: 760).

A related topic that has been investigated by Pickel and Gentry (2017) is the influence of observers' expectations of psychological harm on credibility assessments of rape complainants. Although it might be expected that evidence of high levels of psychological harm would result in more positive credibility assessments and guilty verdicts, research shows that this is too simple a conclusion. In the study by Pickel and Gentry (2017), undergraduate students were assigned to one of two simulated rape scenarios: a prototypical case in which the defendant was a stranger with the attack occurring late at night in a secluded area or a non-prototypical case in which the defendant was an acquaintance, with the attack occurring in the early evening in a private residence. The two scenarios were further manipulated by including either that the complainant was suffering from PTSD or from mild anxiety. Pickel and Gentry (2017) found that a diagnosis of PTSD was more congruent with jurors' expectations of harm in the prototypical scenario compared with the non-prototypical scenario. By contrast, in the non-prototypical case, jurors expected the complainant to be suffering from mild anxiety rather than PTSD.

As a result, Pickel and Gentry (2017: 265) found 'a significant interaction between prototypicality and harm level'. Participants in the prototypical condition rated the complainant as more credible when she was suffering from PTSD than mild anxiety, while those in the non-prototypical condition rated the complainant as more credible when she was suffering from mild anxiety than PTSD. Responsibility ratings of the complainant also reflected jurors' expectations in that they were lower:

i. in the prototypical condition than the non-prototypical condition;
ii. in the prototypical condition when the complainant was suffering PTSD compared to when she was suffering mild anxiety;
iii. in the non-prototypical condition when the complainant was suffering mild anxiety compared to when she was suffering PTSD.

Participants were more likely to vote guilty in the prototypical condition, although 'there was a greater proportion of guilty verdicts in the PTSD condition than the Mild Anxiety condition' (Pickel & Gentry, 2017: 267). The opposite was found in the non-prototypical condition. Interestingly:

> these differences were not related to the presence of a weapon, the victim's credibility, the severity of her physical injuries, her fear of being physically injured or killed, the extent to which she communicated that she did not want to have sexual intercourse, or the degree to which the perpetrator threatened to kill her. (Pickel & Gentry, 2017: 268)

Thus, 'the effect of harm on ratings of the victim's credibility is mediated by the extent to which the harm is in line with mock jurors' expectations' which were related to the prototypicality of the rape (Pickel & Gentry, 2017: 266). These findings suggest that credibility ratings and verdicts are not only assessed according to a complainant's behaviour before and during the sexual assault but also according to laypeople's expectations of post-rape trauma. However, these expectations do not necessarily reflect the findings from the literature on trauma, as discussed in Chapter 11.

6 The Influence of Victim Gender, Victim Race and Other Extra-Legal Factors on Case Outcomes

In a mock jury study involving 896 community volunteers aged 19 years or over, Feild (1979: 279) reported that verdicts were influenced by the race of the victim and the defendant, the physical attractiveness of the complainant, and the complainant's sexual history as well as her behaviour with the defendant prior to the alleged offence.

Although LaFree (1980) reported that as the strength of the prosecution's case increased, the likelihood of guilty verdicts also increased, he also found that as the time taken for the complainant to report increased, the chances of a guilty verdict decreased while the complainant's moral character and conduct (such as hitchhiking, at a bar by herself, out late at night) also predicted acquittals. Nonetheless, 'the single most important predictor [of a conviction] was the victim's race' in that men on trial for sexually assaulting black women were significantly less likely than other men of being convicted (LaFree, 1980: 846). This finding suggests that minority women are perceived to be less worthy of the law's protection.

Overall, men who sexually assaulted (i) black women, (ii) women who engaged in 'risky' behaviour, (iii) women outside their homes, (iv) women who delayed their complaint and (v) women who knew or were related to the defendant, were less likely to be convicted compared to other men. LaFree (1980: 848) concluded that these outcomes indicate that both authorities and fact-finders are influenced by their 'perceptions of the victim's behaviour and characteristics', as well as the characteristics of the defendant, all of which is mediated by cultural conceptions of rape.

LaFree, Reskin and Visher (1985) conducted post-trial interviews with 331 jurors in 38 forcible sexual assault trials between 1978 and 1980 where the complainant was at least 12 years old to examine the relationship between the following independent variables: (i) jurors' characteristics and attitudes; (ii) complainants' characteristics and behaviour; (iii) defendants' characteristics and behaviours; (iv) evidence and case characteristics. The dependent variable was jurors' pre-deliberation verdicts.

Neither the use of a weapon or victim injury significantly affected jurors' verdicts in cases where the defendant either denied the sexual act or said the sexual act was consensual. By contrast, jurors were influenced by the complainant's character and were 'less likely to believe in a defendant's guilt when the victim had reportedly engaged in sex outside marriage, drank or used drugs, or had been acquainted with the defendant'. In particular, jurors who had conservative sex-role attitudes were more likely to find the defendant innocent when the complainant used drugs or alcohol, compared to more liberal-minded jurors (LaFree et al., 1985: 397–399).

Jurors were also influenced by defendant characteristics in that they were more likely to vote guilty if he had few social ties, presented a negative courtroom appearance or had a previous criminal record.

Using the same dataset as LaFree et al. (1985), Reskin and Visher (1986) studied the impact of four types of corroborating evidence (a recovered weapon; victim injury, other physical evidence and eyewitness evidence) and extra-legal factors (defendant attractiveness; defendant's employment status; negative comments about the complainant's moral character; perceptions of victim carelessness) on jurors' pre-deliberation verdicts. All four types of corroborative evidence 'jointly explained almost one-fifth of the variation in jurors' judgments about the defendant's guilt', although a recovered weapon was the most influential (Reskin & Visher, 1986: 429).

While jurors did take account of evidence that corroborated the complainant's testimony, they '*selectively* interpreted' that evidence (Reskin & Visher, 1986: 436; emphasis added), giving more weight to evidence of force and seriousness of the sexual assault and less to eyewitness testimony.[11]

After controlling for the effects of corroborating evidence, attractive or employed defendants were less likely to be perceived as guilty, while jurors were more likely to believe in the defendant's innocence if the complainant had not, in their opinion, 'exercised sufficient caution or was of poor moral character'. In fact, these two variables about the complainant 'exerted the strongest independent effects on jurors' predeliberation verdicts' (Reskin & Visher, 1986: 431).

Overall, Reskin and Visher (1986: 434) found that their results supported Kalven and Zeisel's (1966) liberation hypothesis. As discussed in Chapter 2, the liberation effect is believed to arise in cases with ambiguous or weak evidence, such that juries' verdicts are more susceptible to the influence of extra-legal or non-evidentiary factors which, in turn, supports the existence of a leniency effect in sexual assault trials.

[11]Similarly, in another mock jury study, eyewitness testimony was found to increase credibility judgements of the child complainant but with no corresponding increase in guilty verdicts (Bottoms & Goodman, 1994).

In strong sexual assault cases (defined as having two or more types of corroborative evidence), jurors were more likely to believe in the defendant's guilt, compared to weak cases (those that had none or only one type of corroborating evidence). Out of the 38 sexual assault trials studied, '91 percent of the strong cases resulted in guilty verdicts in contrast to 53 percent of the weak cases' (Reskin & Visher, 1986: 434).

The strength of a sexual assault case also affected whether jurors considered extra-legal factors in coming to a decision. In cases where there were at least two types of corroborating evidence, jurors tended to ignore the complainant's and defendant's personal characteristics, although jurors' opinions about whether the complainant had failed to exercise sufficient caution still significantly affected assessments of the defendant's guilt in strong cases.

By contrast, in weak cases, jurors' verdicts were influenced by their own values, that is, their attitudes towards crime, as well as the characteristics of complainants and defendants. Defendants were more likely to be found innocent if the complainant had behaved carelessly or was judged to have been of low moral character. Thus, Reskin and Visher's (1986) study confirms the fact that the effects of evidence strength decrease when extra-legal factors are taken into account in statistical analyses, such that omitting the effects of these factors is likely to lead to inflated measures of the effects of legal factors on trial outcomes.

7 Summary

Generally speaking, verdicts in criminal trials, including sexual assault trials, vary according to the strength of the case evidence. While the above studies show that various legal factors predict verdicts in sexual assault trials (the defendant's prior criminal record, number of offenders, use of a weapon, medical evidence of victim injury, including ano-genital injury, other physical evidence, such as DNA, corroborating evidence from witnesses, prompt report to police and young age of complainant), they also tell us that jurors are influenced by various extra-legal factors that moderate the effects of legal factors. One of these is the relationship between victim and defendant so that jurors are more likely to convict when the parties are strangers to each other.

Studies on the influence of extra-legal factors have found that mock jury verdicts are influenced by juror demographics (gender and SES), as well as negative perceptions of the complainant's character or reputation (her sexual history, so-called 'risky' behaviours such as style of dress and her alcohol/drug use), the complainant's SES, her degree of resistance, and her emotional displays while giving evidence. Similarly, studies involving actual jurors have found that a complainant's negative moral character and 'risky' behaviour predicted acquittals, although a juror's gender and conservative or liberal value system influences their interpretation of a complainant's character. In addition, complainants' post-behavioural responses to sexual abuse influence verdicts in CSA trials.

Jurors have also been influenced by defendant characteristics, such as employment and SES, as well as the race and attractiveness of both the complainant and defendant and emotional displays by the complainant. It should be noted, however, that Devine and Caughlin (2014) concluded from their meta-analysis of juror and defendant characteristics and judgements of guilt that defendant race had limited impact in criminal trials, generally, while defendant attractiveness had no impact.

However, female jurors are 'notably more conviction prone' in sexual assault cases compared to other types of criminal cases, such that case type 'moderate[s] the relationship between juror gender and judgments of defendant culpability' (Devine & Caughlin, 2014: 118). Indeed, there is evidence to support Kalven and Zeisel's (1966) liberation hypothesis, discussed in Chapter 2, that juries' verdicts are more susceptible to the influence of extra-legal or non-evidentiary factors in cases with ambiguous or weak evidence, that is, with little or no corroborating evidence. It appears that the leniency effect observed in criminal trials will be exacerbated in sexual assault trials with ambiguous evidence and by the extent to which jurors rely, consciously or unconsciously, on one or more of the extra-legal factors discussed above which have been found to exert strong, independent effects on credibility ratings and verdict.

Key studies tell us that the match or mismatch between complainant and gender/victim stereotypes will influence jurors' credibility perceptions and verdicts. For most jurors in a sexual assault trial, it can be expected that 'many of their questions [will] remain … unanswered' and they will try 'to fill in the gaps … by drawing inferences about what may or may not have happened' (Taylor & Joudo, 2005: 61). Without corroborating evidence, it appears that jury deliberations create a vignette of consensual sex based on jurors' own assumptions and beliefs which then determines how they interpret the circumstances of the case at hand and the complainant's evidence (Taylor & Joudo, 2005).

These results suggest that reforms to the sexual assault trial need to focus on ways to counter the negative credibility perceptions of complainants which are based on both gender and victim stereotypes, since 'people may use their overall judgement of the gender stereotypicality of the complainant to anchor' other expectations about victim behaviour, such as emotionality (Schuller et al., 2010: 776). These issues are discussed in more detail in Chapter 5.

In the next chapter, I explore jurors' and laypeople's perceptions of guilt and responsibility in the context of drug and/or alcohol use by the complainant, given that a majority of adult sexual assaults involve consumption of these substances by either the complainant, the defendant or both.

References

Bederian-Gardner, D., & Goldfarb, D. (2014). Expectations of emotions during testimony: The role of communicator and perceiver characteristics. *Behavioral Sciences & the Law, 32*, 829–845.

Bederian-Gardner, D., Goldfarb, D., & Goodman, G. S. (2017). Empathy's relation to appraisal of the emotional child witness. *Applied Cognitive Psychology, 31*, 488–499.

Blackwell, S., & Seymour, F. (2014). Prediction of jury verdicts in child sexual assault trials. *Psychiatry, Psychology & Law, 21*, 567–576.

Bollingmo, G. C., Wessel, E. M., Eilertsen, D. E., & Magnussen, S. (2008). Credibility of the emotional witness: A study of ratings by police investigators. *Psychology, Crime & Law, 14*, 29–40.

Bollingmo, G. C., Wessel, E. M., Sandhold, Y., Eilertsen, D. E., & Magnussen, S. (2009). The effect of biased and non-biased information on judgments of witness credibility. *Psychology, Crime & Law, 15,* 61–71.

Bottoms, B. L. (1993). Individual differences in perceptions of child sexual assault victims. In G. S. Goodman & B. L. Bottoms (Eds.), *Child victims, child witnesses: Understanding and improving testimony* (pp. 229–261). New York: Guildford Press.

Bottoms, B. L., Golding, J., Stevenson, M., Wiley, T., & Yozwiak, J. (2007). Summary of factors affecting juror decisions in child sexual assault cases. In M. Toglia, J. Read, D. Ross, & R. Lindsay (Eds.), *Handbook of eyewitness psychology*. London: Lawrence Erlbaum Associates.

Bottoms, B. L., Peter-Hagene, L. C., Stevenson, M. C., Wiley, T. R. A., Schneider-Mitchell, T., & Goodman, G. S. (2014). Explaining gender differences in jurors' reactions to child sexual assault cases. *Behavioral Sciences & the Law, 32,* 789–812.

Bradshaw, T. L., & Marks, A. E. (1990). Beyond a reasonable doubt: Factors that influence the legal disposition of child sexual abuse cases. *Crime & Delinquency, 36,* 276–285.

Bumby, K. M., & Maddox, M. C. (1999). Judges' knowledge about sexual offenders, difficulties presiding over sexual offense cases, and opinions on sentencing, treatment, and legislation. *Sexual Abuse, 11,* 305–315.

Cooper, A., Quas, J. A., & Cleveland, K. C. (2014). The emotional child witness: Effects on juror decision-making. *Behavioral Science & the Law, 32,* 813–828.

Cossins, A. (2013). Expert witness evidence in sexual assault trials: Questions, answers and law reform in Australia and England. *International Journal of Evidence and Proof, 17,* 74–113.

Cossins, A., Goodman-Delahunty, J., & O'Brien, K. (2009). Uncertainty and misconceptions about child sexual abuse: Implications for the criminal justice system. *Psychiatry, Psychology & Law, 16,* 435–452.

Cossins, A., Jayakody, A., Norrie, C., & Parkinson, P. (2016). The Role of photographic and video documentation in the investigation and prosecution of child sexual assault. *Journal of Law and Medicine, 23,* 925–937.

Daly, K., & Bouhours, B. (2010). Rape and attrition in the legal process: A comparative analysis of five countries. In M. Tonry (Ed.), *Crime and justice: A review of research*. Chicago: University of Chicago Press.

De Jong, A. R., & Rose, M. (1991). Legal proof of child sexual abuse in the absence of physical evidence. *Pediatrics, 88,* 506–511.

Devine, D. J., & Caughlin, D. E. (2014). Do they matter? A meta-analytic investigation of individual characteristics and guilt judgments. *Psychology, Public Policy, and Law, 20,* 109–134.

Devine, D. J., Clayton, L. D., Dunford, B. D., Seying, R., & Pryce, J. (2001). Jury decision making: 45 years of empirical research on deliberating groups. *Psychology, Public Policy, and Law, 7,* 622–727.

Dioso-Villa, R. (2015). Is there evidence of a 'CSI-effect'? In K. J. Strom & M. J. Hickman (Eds.), *Forensic science and the administration of justice: Critical issues and directions.* Thousand Oaks, CA: Sage.

Du Mont, J., & White, D. (2007). *The uses and impacts of medico-legal evidence in sexual assault cases: A global review.* Geneva: World Health Organization. http://www.svri.org/sites/default/files/attachments/2016-01-19/medico.pdf.

Du Mont, J., & White, D. (2013). Barriers to the effective use of medico-legal findings in sexual assault cases worldwide. *Qualitative Health Research, 23,* 1228–1239.

Ellison, L., & Munro, V. E. (2009a). Of 'normal sex' and 'real rape': Exploring the use of socio-sexual scripts in (mock) jury deliberation. *Social and Legal Studies, 18,* 291–312.

Ellison, L., & Munro, V. E. (2009b). Reacting to rape: Exploring mock jurors' assessments of complainant credibility. *British Journal of Criminology, 49,* 202–219.

Feild, H. S. (1979). Rape trials and jurors' decisions: A psycholegal analysis of effects of victim, defendant, and case characteristics. *Law and Human Behavior, 3,* 261–284.

Feldman-Summers, S., & Lindner, K. (1976). Perceptions of victims and defendants in criminal assault cases. *Correctional Psychologist, 3,* 135–150.

Fitzgerald, J. (2006). *The attrition of sexual offences from the New South Wales criminal justice system* (Crime and Justice Bulletin, No. 92). Sydney: NSW Bureau of Crime Statistics and Research.

Galvin, H. (1986). Shielding rape victims in the state and federal courts: A proposal for the second decade. *Minnesota Law Review, 70,* 763–916.

Golding, J. M., Fryman, H. M., Marsil, D. F., & Yozwiak, J. A. (2003). Big girls don't cry: the effect of child witness demeanor on juror decisions in a child sexual abuse trial. *Child Abuse & Neglect, 27,* 1311–1321.

Goodman-Delahunty, J., Cossins, A., & Martschuk, N. (2016). *Jury reasoning in joint and separate trials of institutional child sexual abuse: An empirical study.* Sydney: Royal Commission into Institutional Responses to Child Sexual Abuse.

Goodman-Delahunty, J., Martschuk, N., & Cossins, A. (2017). What Australian jurors know and do not know about evidence of child sexual abuse. *Criminal Law Journal, 41,* 86–103.

Gray-Eurom, K., Seaberg, D. C., & Wears, R. L. (2002). The prosecution of sexual assault cases: Correlation with forensic evidence. *Annals of Emergency Medicine, 39,* 39–46.

Hagemann, C., Stene, L., Myhre, A., Ormstad, K., & Schei, B. (2011). Impact of medico-legal findings on charge filing in cases of rape in adult women. *Acta Obstetrics & Gynecology Scandanavia, 90,* 1218–1224.

Hansen, L., Mikkelsen, S., Sabroe, S., & Charles, A. (2010). Medical findings and legal outcomes in sexually abused children. *Journal of Forensic Sciences, 55,* 104–109.

Heger, A., Ticson, L., Velasquez, O., & Bernier, R. (2002). Children referred for possible sexual abuse: Medical findings in 2384 children. *Child Abuse and Neglect, 26,* 645–659.

Holmgren, J. A., & Fordham, J. (2011). The CSI effect and the Canadian and the Australian jury. *Journal of Forensic Sciences, 56*, S63–S71.

Jewkes, R., Christofides, N., Vetten, L., Jina, R., Sigsworth, R., & Lotts, L. (2009). Medico-legal findings, legal case progression, and outcomes in South African rape cases: Retrospective review. *PLoS Medicine, 6,* 1–9.

Jina, R., Jewkes, R., Vetten, L., Christofides, N., Sigsworth, R., & Loots, L. (2015). Genito-anal injury patterns and associated factors in rape survivors in an urban province of South Africa: A cross-sectional study. *BMC Women's Health, 15,* 1–14.

Johnson, C. F. (2004). Child sexual abuse. *The Lancet, 364,* 462–470.

Kalven, H., & Zeisel, H. (1966). *The American jury.* Chicago: University of Chicago Press.

Kaufman, G., Drevland, G. C. B., Wessel, E., Overskeidand, G., & Magnussen, S. (2003). The importance of being earnest: Displayed emotions and witness credibility. *Applied Cognitive Psychology, 17,* 21–34.

Klippenstine, M. A., & Schuller, R. A. (2012). Perceptions of sexual assault: Expectancies regarding the emotional response of a rape victim over time. *Psychology, Crime & Law, 18,* 79–94.

Kovera, M. B., & Borgida, E. (1997). Expert testimony in child sexual abuse trials: The admissibility of psychological science. *Applied Cognitive Psychology, 11,* 105–129.

LaFree, G. D. (1980). Variables affecting guilty pleas and convictions in rape cases: Toward a social theory of rape processing. *Social Forces, 58,* 833–850.

LaFree, G. D., Reskin, B. F., & Visher, C. A. (1985). Jurors' responses to victims' behaviour and legal issues in sexual assault trials. *Social Problems, 32,* 389–407.

Lens, K. M. E., Doorn, J., Pemberton, A., & Bogaerts, S. (2014). You shouldn't feel that way! Extending the emotional victim effect through the mediating role of expectancy violation. *Psychology, Crime, & Law, 20,* 326–338.

Lewis, T. T., Klettke, B., & Day, A. (2014). The influence of medical and behavioral evidence on conviction rates in cases of child sexual abuse. *Journal of Child Sexual Abuse, 23,* 431–441.

Lievore, D. (2005a). *Prosecutorial decisions in adult sexual assault cases* (Trends and Issues in Crime & Criminal Justice, No. 291, pp. 1–6).

Mancini, D. E. (2013). The 'CSI effect' in an actual juror sample: Why crime show genre may matter. *North American Journal of Psychology, 15,* 543–564.

McCauley, M. R., & Parker, J. F. (2001). When will a child be believed? The impact of the victim's age and juror's gender on children's credibility and verdict in a sexual-abuse case. *Child Abuse & Neglect, 25,* 523–539.

McGregor, M., Du Mont, J., & Myhr, T. (2002). Sexual assault forensic medical examination: Is evidence related to successful prosecution? *Annals in Emergency Medicine, 39,* 639–647.

Myers, J. E. B., Redlich, A. D., Goodman, G. S., Prizmich, L. P., & Imwinkelried, E. (1999). Jurors' perceptions of hearsay in child sexual abuse cases. *Psychology, Public Policy, and Law, 5,* 388–419.

Palusci, V., Cox, E., Cyrus, T., Heartwell, S., Vandervort, F., & Pott, E. (1999). Medical assessment and legal outcome in child sexual abuse. *Archives of Pediatric and Adolescent Medicine, 153,* 388–392.

Pickel, K. L., & Gentry, R. H. (2017). Mock jurors' expectations regarding the psychological harm experienced by rape victims as a function of rape prototypicality. *Psychology, Crime & Law, 23,* 254–273.

Quadara, A., Fileborn, B., & Parkinson, D. (2013). *The role of forensic medical evidence in the prosecution of adult sexual assault.* Canberra: Australian Institute of Family Studies.

Quas, J. A., Thompson, W. C., & Clarke-Stewart, K. A. (2005). Do jurors 'know' what isn't so about child witnesses? *Law and Human Behavior, 29,* 425–456.

Regan, P. C., & Baker, S. J. (1998). The impact of child witness demeanor on perceived credibility and trial outcome in sexual abuse cases. *Journal of Family Violence, 13,* 187–195.

Reskin, B. F., & Visher, C. A. (1986). The impacts of evidence and extralegal factors in jurors' decisions. *Law & Society Review, 20,* 423–438.

Saint-Martin, P., Bouyssy, M., & O'Byrne, P. (2007). Analysis of 756 cases of sexual assault in Tours (France): Medico-legal findings and judicial outcomes. *Medicine, Science and the Law, 47,* 315–324.

Sayfan, L., Mitchell, E. B., Goodman, G. S., Eisen, M. L., & Qin, J. (2008). Children's expressed emotions when disclosing maltreatment. *Child Abuse & Neglect, 32,* 1026–1036.

Schuller, R. A., McKimmie, B. M., Masser, B. M., & Klippenstine, M. A. (2010). Judgments of sexual assault: The impact of complainant emotional demeanor, gender and victim stereotypes. *New Criminal Law Review, 13,* 759–780.

Schweitzer, N. J., & Saks, M. J. (2007). The CSI effect: Popular fiction about forensic science affects the public's expectations about real forensic science. *Jurimetrics, 47,* 357–364.

Shelton, D. E. (2008). The 'CSI effect': Does it really exist? *National Institute of Justice Journal, 259,* 1–7.

Spohn, C., Beichner, D., & Davis-Frenzel, E. (2002). Prosecutorial justifications for sexual assault case rejection: Guarding the 'gateway to justice'. *Social Problems, 48,* 206–235.

Tabak, S. J., & Klettke, B. (2014). Mock jury attitudes towards credibility, age, and guilt in a fictional child sexual assault scenario. *Australian Journal of Psychology, 66,* 47–55.

Taylor, N., & Joudo, J. (2005) *The impact of pre-recorded video and closed circuit television testimony by adult sexual assault complainants on jury decision-making: An experimental study* (Research and Public Policy Series No. 68). Canberra: Australian Institute of Criminology.

Vrij, A., & Fischer, A. (1997). The role of displays of emotions and ethnicity in judgments of rape victims. *International Review of Victimology, 4,* 255–265.

Wessel, E. M., Drevland, G. C. B., Eilertsenand, D. E., & Magnussen, S. (2006). Credibility of the emotional witness: A study by court judges. *Law & Human Behavior, 30,* 221–230.

Wessel, E., Magnussen, S., & Melinder, A. M. D. (2013). Expressed emotions and perceived credibility of child mock victims disclosing physical abuse. *Applied Cognitive Psychology, 27,* 611–616.

Whatley, M. A. (1996). Victim characteristics influencing attributions of responsibility to rape victims: A meta-analysis. *Aggression and Violent Behavior, 1,* 81–95.

Wood, B., Orsak, C., Murphy, M., & Cross, H. J. (1996). Semistructured child sexual abuse interviews: Interview and child characteristics related to credibility of disclosure. *Child Abuse & Neglect, 20,* 81–92.

4

'Commonsense' or 'Life Experience': Jurors' Perceptions of Guilt

1 Introduction

Unlike other criminal offences, the main defences to a sexual assault charge include:

i. that no sexual act took place; or
ii. where lack of consent is an element of the offence, the defendant committed the sexual act but did so with the complainant's consent; or
iii. the defendant had a mistaken but honest belief in consent (see further Chapter 7).

While mistaken identification is sometimes an issue in both adult and child sexual assault trials, particularly in stranger-rape cases, more often than not the real issue is:

> the complainant's status as a victim. While jurors may question whether the complainant in any personal crime was actually victimized, only in sexual assault trials does this issue rise to the status of a major defense … either as challenge to the claim that the sex act occurred or the claim

A. Cossins, *Closing the Justice Gap for Adult and Child Sexual Assault*,
https://doi.org/10.1057/978-1-137-32051-3_4

> that the [complainant] did not consent. (LaFree, Reskin, & Visher, 1985: 392)

Because a legitimate defence to a charge of sexual assault is to argue the moral impropriety of the complainant by focusing on her 'risky' or sexualised behaviour, 'the rape victim becomes the defendant, that is, she is on trial to prove her innocence' (Field, 1979: 281). Not only must the prosecution prove the defendant's guilt beyond reasonable doubt but it must also prove the complainant's innocence, that is, her moral propriety, beyond reasonable doubt. While social attitudes in the period 2000–2020 are less conservative than previous decades (Bordini & Sperb, 2013; Klettke, Hallford, & Mellor, 2016), at least in relation to sex outside of marriage, other issues to do with a woman's sexuality are still based on the sexual double standard (Bordini & Sperb, 2013).

An excellent example of this double standard was evident in the 2014 documentary, *Slutphobia*,[1] which interviewed young men and women about their opinions of female promiscuity. Both men and women expressed a range of negative judgements about girls and women who have multiple sexual partners, compared to men who do the same.

As discussed later, a complainant's risky or immoral behaviour is taken to be evidence of implied consent in an adult sexual assault trial, or, if between the ages of 12–15 years, evidence that she is lying in a CSA trial. While the substantive law does not recognise a doctrine of implied consent in either Australia or E&W, such a concept arises as part of the defence narrative because evidence of 'risky' behaviour is deemed to be relevant to the issue of lack of consent on the part of fact-finders. In addition, historically, judges have implicitly condoned the existence of implied consent by reflecting social beliefs that rape can be categorised into 'real rape' where a woman or girl is attacked by a stranger but does not contribute to that attack, and less serious rape where the complainant's behaviours contributed to the defendant's sexual conduct.

In practice, any legal procedure or law of evidence that discriminates between different types of sexual assault cases based on complainant

---

[1] Directed by Sunny Bergman, produced by Valerie Shuit, screened on the SBS channel on free-to-air TV in Australia on 17 September 2017 (see http://www.sbs.com.au/news/video/340983363943/Slut-Phobia).

behaviour highlights the belief that the prosecution has to prove that the complainant did not impliedly consent to sex. There are many examples of culturally perceived implied consent 'based on a woman's conduct or lack of resistance', as if women are perceived to be '"walking around … in a state of constant consent to sexual activity"' (Benedet, 2014: 140; citing Fraser CJ in *Ewanchuk* (Alta CA), [1999] 1 SCR 330, [67]), particularly if they drink, take drugs, stay out late or wear certain styles of clothing.

Thus, there is a contradiction at the core of the sexual assault trial. Despite the fact that the broad definition of consent means free and voluntary agreement, and that a defendant has to have reasonably believed that the complainant was communicating her voluntary consent (see Chapter 7); and if there are no facts vitiating consent, such as unconsciousness, the defence can seek to disprove lack of consent by questioning the complainant about:

i. her sexual history (in certain circumstances, depending on the jurisdiction: see Chapter 7);
ii. her style of dress;
iii. her behaviour leading up to the alleged sexual assault (such as flirtation with the defendant or other men);
iv. her drug and alcohol consumption on the day/night in question;
v. her history of alcohol/drug consumption;
vi. her mental health history; and
vii. her delay in complaint.

All of these factors can be interpreted as amounting to implied consent by the jury. Historically and currently, these issues have been deemed to be relevant to the facts in issue and juries are, generally, not warned of the prejudicial reasoning involved in taking account of such factors.

Because the moral propriety of the complainant is allowed to be raised as an issue by the defence, jurors are invited to scrutinise the complainant's character and behaviours and permitted to consider a range of extra-legal factors in assessing her status and credibility as a victim. This then constitutes the *legal* basis for the use of extra-legal factors by jurors in sexual assault trials and is the heart of the problem with the conduct of sexual assault trials—the permissible resort to myths, bias and prejudice (masquerading as 'commonsense' or 'life experience') in order to determine the complainant's moral worth, and her degree of responsibility as a proxy for determining consent.

One issue that has been the subject of considerable research over several decades is the influence of a complainant's drug or alcohol consumption on jurors' and laypeople's perceptions of guilt and responsibility.

2 The Effect of Alcohol Consumption on Perceptions of Guilt

One of the most common features of a sexual assault case is alcohol, since approximately half to two-thirds of sexual assaults involve alcohol consumption by the victim and/or the offender (Abbey, Zawacki, Buck, Clinton, & McAuslan, 2004; Littleton, Grills-Taquechel, & Axsom, 2009; Scott-Ham & Burton, 2005). However, the extent to which perpetrators use alcohol and/or drugs (with or without the victim's knowledge) to facilitate sexual assault is not necessarily common knowledge, such that a victim's intoxication is open to misunderstandings by those within the criminal justice system, including jurors. Indeed, Kilpatrick, Resnick, Ruggiero, Conoscenti, and McCauley (2007: 58) reported that in the USA:

> the highest rape risk situation for both adult women and college women is not being rendered intoxicated and incapacitated by others; it is being taken advantage by a sexual predator after she has become intoxicated voluntarily.

Several studies have examined the impact of alcohol and/or drugs on laypeople's and jurors' perceptions of victim blame and defendant culpability (Abbey et al., 2004; Klippenstine, Schuller, & Wall, 2007; Lynch, Wasarhaley, Golding, & Simcic, 2013; Schuller & Wall, 1998; Simms, Noel, & Maisto, 2007; Stewart & Jacquin, 2010; Testa & Parks, 1996;

Ullman, Karabatsos, & Koss, 1999; Wall & Schuller, 2000; Wenger & Bornstein, 2006).

Overall, the results of these studies over a 20-year period have consistently found that jurors and laypeople perceive an intoxicated sexual assault complainant as less credible and more responsible than a non-intoxicated complainant. Such judgements are then likely to result in perceptions that the alleged sexual assault was consensual (Abbey, Ross, McDuffie, & McAuslan, 1996), particularly since research also shows that intoxicated offenders are perceived to be less responsible for their actions (Grubb & Turner, 2012).

Thus, the intoxicated victim is judged according to a 'double standard' which means that the combination of femaleness and alcohol consumption is perceived to be more morally reprehensible than maleness and alcohol consumption, perhaps because of the common cultural view that boys will be boys but girls must be 'good' (see Chapter 5, Table 1 for the degree of laypeople's agreement with rape myths about victim drunkenness). As Grubb and Turner (2012: 449) observe, this double standard is 'likely to impact upon decision making throughout the criminal justice process ... [and] to provide some explanation for the high attrition rate observed' in sexual assault cases.

For example, Schuller and Wall (1998) found that when mock jurors were presented with a complainant who had drunk alcohol, rather than a soft drink, they were less likely to view the complainant as credible and less likely to consider the defendant to be guilty.

In a study that investigated the effect of the voluntary and involuntary use of a drug (GHB)[2] or alcohol, Girard and Senn (2008) found that women's voluntary consumption of drugs prior to a sexual assault reduced perceived perpetrator responsibility and blame, and increased victim blame compared to other situations. However, when women were drugged (with drugs or alcohol) involuntarily, perpetrators were perceived to be more responsible than victims.

In the simulated trials conducted by Stewart and Jacquin (2010), mock jurors' decisions were influenced by the complainant's willingness to use a substance, as well as the type of substance (alcohol, GHB

---

[2]Gamma-hydroxybutyrate or GHB is an illegal intoxicant.

or marijuana). The complainant who willingly used a substance was viewed as less credible and more to blame for the sexual assault compared to a complainant who had unwillingly ingested a substance. Overall, however, ratings of guilt were unaffected by complainant willingness, with a large percentage of not guilty verdicts (69%), while almost two-thirds of jurors (64.8%) blamed the complainant for the defendant's conduct. Substance type accounted for much less variance in mock jurors' decisions, compared with complainant willingness. Counterintuitively, mock jurors 'assigned higher degrees of guilt to the defendant' when the complainant used alcohol compared to drugs, with 'jurors' perceptions of the complainant's credibility [being] highest when she unwillingly ingested GHB or marijuana' (Stewart & Jacquin, 2010: 869).

As expected, Steward and Jacquin (2010) found that jurors who scored high in RMA produced lower ratings of guilt compared to jurors with lower endorsement of rape myths. RMA also affected ratings of complainant and defendant credibility and blame. In line with other studies (see Table 1, Chapter 5), men and women differed significantly in their RMA scores with men, on average, being more likely to endorse rape myths than women.

When Lynch et al. (2013) investigated the effect of intoxication and who purchased the drinks on mock jurors' credibility ratings and verdicts, they also found that mock jurors were significantly less likely to render guilty verdicts and made lower credibility judgements of intoxicated complainants compared to non-intoxicated complainants. In fact, 'victim credibility was a significant mediator', with higher ratings of victim intoxication being associated with lower ratings of victim credibility 'which led to fewer verdicts' (Lynch et al., 2013: 3215). Consistent with research that has found that gender is one of the strongest predictors of verdicts in sexual assault trials (Devine & Caughlin, 2014; Klippenstine et al., 2007; Jimenez & Abreu, 2003; Schuller & Wall, 1998; Schutte & Hosch, 1997), male participants were significantly more likely to acquit the defendant and give lower credibility ratings of the complainant compared to female participants.

However, participants were nearly twice as likely to perceive the defendant as significantly less credible and to render guilty verdicts when he bought the drinks, compared to the situation when the complainant bought her own drinks. In fact, defendant credibility was a significant mediator which led to more guilty verdicts (Lynch et al., 2013: 3215). By contrast, participants rated the complainant as significantly less credible when she bought her own drinks, with credibility ratings of the complainant mediating the relationship between victim intoxication and verdict.

It seems remarkable that one simple change in the facts of a case could have such significant effects—that is:

> [w]hen the defendant bought the drinks, participants viewed the defense's case as significantly weaker than when the victim bought the drinks … and higher ratings of victim intoxication were associated with higher ratings of the defense's case strength. (Lynch et al., 2013: 3215)

When mock jurors were asked why they delivered a not guilty verdict in scenarios with an intoxicated victim, 44% questioned the complainant's credibility, such as her mental capacity, because of her intoxication (Lynch et al., 2013: 3216). The authors also suggest that stereotypes about female intoxication lead to the belief 'that women are more sexually responsive and responsible for their personal welfare when drinking alcohol' and are less likely to be perceived as victims because of their 'risky' or immoral behaviour (Lynch et al., 2013: 3217).

3 What Jurors Do not Know About the Vulnerability of Women and Children to Sexual Assault

Historically, women have been held responsible for their sexual behaviour so that female licentiousness versus moral propriety has influenced the development of the laws with respect to sexual assault. It is, thus, no surprise that 'women are blamed for alcohol-related rape because they are seen as having put themselves at risk' (Temkin & Krahé, 2008: 120). As discussed above, this level of blame demonstrates the double standards applied to men's and women's behaviours; that is, the cultural permission for men to act out their sexual urges without restrictions and the responsibility on women to protect their sexual and moral integrity (see Cossins, 2015 for a history of this double standard).

Defence questions about alcohol and drug consumption, style of dress, hitchhiking, staying out late at night, and frequenting bars alone, are all strategies for undermining a complainant's credibility in the eyes of jurors by invoking the concept of victim blame—that women and girls who behave in 'risky' ways invite sexual interest from men who cannot be blamed for accepting the invitation. This means that consent is viewed as something that can be communicated via a woman's behaviour rather than verbally so that there is a *presumption* of consent by women and girls who dress and behave in certain ways. Indeed, research on offenders' and others' attitudes about rape myths—that women enjoy forced sex, that women 'lead men on' or play 'hard to get' so that no means yes, and that drunk women are 'up for it' (see reviews in Abbey, 2011; Abbey et al., 2004; Table 1, Chapter 5)—reveal the prevalence of a presumption of consent, particularly in certain social settings such as bars and parties.

Because an intoxicated complainant is likely to invite probing questions from the defence about who bought the alcohol and about her moral culpability, prosecutors may decide not to proceed with cases that involve victim intoxication due to their perception that there is no reasonable prospect of conviction (Spohn & Holleran, 2001).

But let's think about the information the jury is *unlikely* to hear in a sexual assault trial. While the defence case will most likely focus on the complainant's so-called 'risky' behaviours, juries are unlikely to be told that '[t]he most consistent predictor of adolescent and adult sexual assault victimization is childhood sexual abuse' (Abbey et al., 2004: 284), thus remaining ignorant of the vulnerability of some women who are sexually assaulted as adults. Juries are also unlikely to hear about the fact that perpetrators of sexual violence commonly target women who are psychologically vulnerable (Testa, Van Zile-Tamsen, & Livingston, 2007). Between 50 and 60% of all sexually victimised women and girls are re-victimised in their lifetimes, and of those, between one-fifth to two-fifths will experience PTSD (Walsh et al., 2012).

Indeed, women's consumption of alcohol and drugs and their vulnerability to sexual assault are linked since '[r]ape victims report higher prevalence of public health problems including drug and alcohol use, abuse, and dependence compared to non-victims' (Walsh et al., 2014: 684). Such behaviours 'serve as a coping strategy for some women' which, in turn, increases their risk of repeat sexual victimisation (Abbey et al., 2004: 285; citing Kilpatrick, Acierno, Resnick, Saunders, & Best, 1997; see also Bryan et al., 2016; Collin-Vézina, Daigneault, & Hébert, 2013; Walsh et al., 2014).

This vulnerability, however, is ignored in sexual assault trials while classic, post-traumatic behaviour, such as drug and alcohol abuse, is transformed into the cultural narrative of a woman who is 'asking for it'. When Stanko and Williams (2009) analysed 677 rape complaints made to the Metropolitan Police Service in 2005, they found that 87% of complainants had at least one of four vulnerabilities; that is, they were under 18 years old, under the influence of drink or drugs at the time of the incident, recorded as having 'mental health issues' or were partners/former partners of the alleged assailant.

Another widespread belief is that a 'real' victim will physically resist the perpetrator and will have done nothing to encourage the assault. But the psychiatric and psychological literature reveals that some victims undergo a physiological process, known as the 'freeze response', which prevents physical resistance, while trauma symptoms contribute to delays in complaint and inconsistencies in evidence.

Arguably, the idea of physical resistance is a masculine view of how an attacker should be dealt with. But women and girls faced with the threat of sexual assault will respond in different ways because of their own experiences of, and cultural expectations to do with, resisting physical trauma. For example, the freeze response or tonic immobility is a typical response for those who have been previously sexually or physically victimised (Nurius, Norris, Macy, & Huang, 2004; Ogden & Minton, 2000; Siegmund, & Wotjak, 2007) and may result in the loss of any ability to move (Atara, 2015).

Tonic immobility is an involuntary, reflexive component of the fear response that is characterised by freezing or immobility in situations involving extreme fear and is considered to be an evolutionary response to perceived inescapable threats (Fusé, Forsyth, Marx, Gallup, & Weaver, 2007; Marx, Forsyth, Gallup, Fusé, & Lexington, 2008; Volchan et al.,

2011); that is, 'when the options of flight or fight are unavailable as a coping/defense mechanism' (Atara, 2015).

Galliano, Noble, Travis, and Puechl (1993) consider that tonic immobility helps explain the non-resistant response of many rape victims since they found that 37% of rape survivors in their study demonstrated immobility during their rape experiences. Similarly, Heidi, Marx, and Forsyth (2005) reported that over 52% of CSA survivors in their study had experienced tonic immobility. In fact, Bovin, Jager-Hyman, Gold, Marx, and Sloan (2008) found that tonic immobility during sexual assault was implicated in the severity of subsequent PTSD symptoms experienced by survivors while Heidi et al. (2005) also reported that those who reported tonic immobility during CSA had greater psychological impairment as adults.

It is useful to compare the symptoms of sexual victimisation with common rape myths held by laypeople. As seen in Table 1, any one of these symptoms can be readily translated into a cultural narrative that blames the complainant for the defendant's sexual conduct, or amounts to 'proof' that she is an unreliable witness.

While the use of alcohol and/or drugs is well-documented as a coping mechanism for those who have been sexually victimised, the vulnerability of sexual assault survivors to sexual re-victimisation is increased by alcohol and drug consumption since both produce cognitive deficits. This means that 'intoxication will make it difficult for [a woman] to recognize signs that suggest her companion has misunderstood' her lack of interest in having sex, and she may miss 'danger cues' that she would have noticed had she been sober (Abbey et al., 2004: 289; Davis, Stoner, Norris, George, & Masters, 2009). As well, '[a]lcohol impairs motor skills, thereby limiting a woman's ability to effectively resist sexual assault' (Abbey et al., 2004: 290; Davis, George, & Norris, 2004), while studies show that rapists purposely encourage their victims to drink in order to gain their sexual compliance (Abbey, 2011; Johnson, Wendel, & Hamilton, 1998; Kanin, 1985).

In summary, the information in Table 1 represents the information that every investigating police officer, prosecutor, judge and juror should know about. Yet there is a large gap between the reality of sexual assault and awareness of this reality by criminal justice system

Table 1 Comparison of symptoms of sexual victimisation with rape myths

Symptoms of sexual victimisation	Translation into rape myth[a]	Scientific explanation
• Use of alcohol, marijuana, other illicit drugs or non-medical prescription drugs[b]	• She invited the defendant's behaviour • 'She was asking for it' • 'It's her fault'	• PTSD & sexual re-victimisation consistently positively associated with all types of substance use by those reporting sexual assault and CSA
• Multiple psychiatric disorders: anxiety disorder, depression, eating disorders, PTSD, sleeping disorders and suicide attempts[c]	• Mentally unstable • 'She's lying or fantasising'	• Significant association between adult or child sexual assault and lifetime diagnosis of one or more psychiatric disorders, in particular PTSD
• Multiple and serial sexual partners[d] • Casual sex[e] • Teenage pregnancy[f] • Early onset of sexual activity[g] • Prostitution[h] • Sexual re-victimisation[i]	• Background of risky sexual behaviour • 'She was asking for it' • 'She got what she deserved'	• High-risk sexual behaviours 'serve to modulate emotional pain'[j] • Sexually risky behaviour by CSA survivors due to low self-worth, inability to 'prevent unwanted sexual advances', or 'needs for affection and acceptance'[k] • Reduced reality testing, awareness of danger and social supports • Social isolation • Drug or alcohol impairment • Learned powerlessness; tolerance of coercion, force, intimidation, pleading, and lack of affection in sexual relations[l]

(continued)

Table 1 (continued)

Symptoms of sexual victimisation	Translation into rape myth[a]	Scientific explanation
• Other high-risk behaviours: e.g. drinking to intoxication; suicide attempts, self-mutilation, running away, drug overdoses, unprotected sex[m] • Delinquent behaviour: e.g. physical assault; drug dealing; break, enter and steal, theft with force, use of weapons[n]	• Risky behaviour • 'She was asking for it' • 'She was out of control' • Unreliable witness	• Adolescents with lifetime PTSD at significantly greater risk of delinquent behaviour[o] • PTSD may lead to high-risk behaviours[p]: drinking to intoxication most frequent behaviour reported by sexually abused adolescents, followed by delinquent behaviour, major depressive episode and drug use[q]
• Failure to physically to resist the perpetrator	• A 'real' victim physically resists the perpetrator	• A significant minority or majority of victims will display tonic immobility (freeze response) during a sexual assault[r]

[a]See Table 1, Chapter 5 for a list of common rape myths
[b]Walsh et al. (2014: 687)
[c]Meta-analysis of 37 studies by Chen et al. (2010); Jonas, Bebbington, McManus, and Meltzer (2011); Danielson et al. (2010)
[d]Lalor and McElvaney (2010)
[e]Ibid.
[f]Ibid.
[g]Ibid.
[h]Ibid.
[i]Jonas et al. (2011); Trickett, Noll, and Putnam (2011); Walsh et al. (2014)
[j]Ibid.: 166; citing Polusny and Follette (1995)
[k]Steel and Herlitz (2005: 1150)
[l]Lalor and McElvaney (2010: 167)
[m]O'Hare, Shen, and Sherrer (2010); Danielson et al. (2010)
[n]Danielson et al. (2010)
[o]Ehring and Quack (2010)
[p]Van Dorn et al. (2005)
[q]Danielson et al. (2010)
[r]Heidi et al. (2005); Galliano et al. (1993)

personnel. Thus, sexual assault cases are investigated and prosecuted in a cultural climate of blame and judgement of the complainant's behaviours (Temkin & Krahé, 2008) which ultimately leads to an assessment of the complainant's moral worthiness for the law's protection. It appears that many within the criminal justice system consider that complainants who exhibit any of the symptoms of sexual victimisation in Table 1 are not worthy of that protection.

The next chapter discusses these issues in more detail, in particular the 'hostile' cultural climate in which sex offences are prosecuted.

References

Abbey, A. (2011). Alcohol's role in sexual violence perpetration: Theoretical explanations, existing evidence and future directions. *Drug and Alcohol Review, 30,* 481–489.

Abbey, A., Ross, L. T., McDuffie, D., & McAuslan, P. (1996). Alcohol and dating risk factors for sexual assault among college women. *Psychology of Women Quarterly, 20,* 147–169.

Abbey, A., Zawacki, T., Buck, P. O., Clinton, A. M., & McAuslan, P. (2004). Sexual assault and alcohol consumption: What do we know about their relationship and what types of research are still needed? *Aggression and Violent Behaviour, 9,* 271–303.

Atara, Y. (2015). Trauma from an enactive perspective: The collapse of the *knowing-how* structure. *Adaptive Behavior, 23,* 143–154.

Benedet, J. (2014). Sexual assault cases at the Alberta Court of Appeal: The roots of *Ewanchuk* and the unfinished revolution. *Alberta Law Review, 52,* 127–144.

Bordini, S., & Sperb, T. M. (2013). Sexual double standard: A review of the literature between 2001 and 2010. *Sexuality & Culture, 17,* 686–704.

Bovin, M. J., Jager-Hyman, S., Gold, S. D., Marx, B. P., & Sloan, D. M. (2008). Tonic immobility mediates the influence of peritraumatic fear and perceived inescapability on posttraumatic stress symptom severity among sexual assault survivors. *Journal of Traumatic Stress, 21,* 402–409.

Bryan, A. E. B., Norris, J., Abdallah, D. A., Stappenbeck, C. A., Morrison, D. M., Davis, K. C., … Zawacki, T. (2016). Longitudinal change in women's sexual victimization experiences as a function of alcohol consumption and sexual victimization history: A latent transition analysis. *Psychology of Violence, 6,* 271–279.

Chen, L. P., Murad, M. H., Paras, M. L., Colbenson, K. M., Sattler, A. L., Goranson, E. N., ... Zirakzadeh, A. (2010). Sexual abuse and lifetime diagnosis of psychiatric disorders: Systematic review and meta-analysis. *Mayo Clinic Proceedings, 85,* 618–629.

Collin-Vézina, D., Daigneault, I., & Hébert, M. (2013). Lessons learned from child sexual abuse research: Prevalence, outcomes, and preventive strategies. *Child and Adolescent Psychiatry and Mental Health, 7,* 1753–2000.

Cossins, A. (2015). *Female criminality: Infanticide, moral panics and the female body*. Basingstoke, UK: Palgrave Macmillan.

Danielson, C. K., Macdonald, A., Amstadter, A. B., Hanson, R., de Arellano, M. A., Saunders, B. E., & Kilpatrick, D. G. (2010). Risky behaviors and depression in conjunction with—or in the absence of—lifetime history of PTSD among sexually abused adolescents. *Child Maltreatment, 15*(1), 101–107.

Davis, K. C., Stoner, S. A., Norris, J., George, W. H., & Masters, N. T. (2009). Women's awareness of and discomfort with sexual assault cues: Effects of alcohol consumption and relationship type. *Violence Against Women, 15,* 1106–1125.

Davis, K. C., George, W. H., & Norris, J. (2004). Women's responses to unwanted sexual advances: The role of alcohol and inhibition. *Psychology of Women Quarterly, 28,* 333–343.

Devine, D. J., & Caughlin, D. E. (2014). Do they matter? A meta-analytic investigation of individual characteristics and guilt judgments. *Psychology, Public Policy, and Law, 20,* 109–134.

Ehring, T., & Quack, D. (2010). Emotion regulation difficulties in trauma survivors: The role of trauma type and PTSD symptom severity. *Behavior Therapy, 41,* 587–598.

Feild, H. S. (1979). Rape trials and jurors' decisions: A psycholegal analysis of effects of victim, defendant, and case characteristics. *Law and Human Behavior, 3,* 261–284.

Fusé, T., Forsyth, J. P., Marx, B., Gallup, G. G., & Weaver, S. (2007). Factor structure of the Tonic Immobility Scale in female sexual assault survivors: An exploratory and confirmatory factor analysis. *Journal of Anxiety Disorders, 21,* 265–283.

Galliano, G., Noble, L. M., Travis, L. A., & Puechl, C. (1993). Victim reactions during rape/sexual assault: A preliminary study of the immobility response and its correlates. *Journal of Interpersonal Violence, 8,* 109–114.

Girard, A. L., & Senn, C. Y. (2008). The role of the new 'date rape drugs' in attributions about date rape. *Journal of Interpersonal Violence, 23,* 3–20.

Grubb, A., & Turner, E. (2012). Rape myth acceptance, gender role conformity and substance use on victim blaming. *Aggression and Violent Behavior, 17,* 443–452.

Heidi, J. M., Marx, B. P., & Forsyth, J. P. (2005). Tonic immobility and childhood sexual abuse: A preliminary report evaluating the sequela of rape-induced paralysis. *Behavior Research and Therapy, 43,* 1157–1171.

Jimenez, J. A., & Abreu, J. M. (2003). Race and sex effects on attitudinal perceptions of acquaintance rape. *Journal of Counseling Psychology, 50,* 252–256.

Johnson, T. J., Wendel, J., & Hamilton, S. (1998). Social anxiety, alcohol expectancies and drinking-game participation. *Addictive Behaviors, 23,* 65–79.

Jonas, S., Bebbington, P., McManus, S., & Meltzer, H. (2011). Sexual abuse and psychiatric disorder in England: Results from the 2007 Adult Psychiatric Morbidity Survey. *Psychological Medicine, 41,* 709–719.

Kanin, E. J. (1985). Date rapists: Differential sexual socialization and relative deprivation. *Archives of Sexual Behavior, 14,* 219–231.

Kilpatrick, D. G., Acierno, R., Resnick, H. S., Saunders, B. E., & Best, C. L. (1997). A 2-year longitudinal analysis of the relationships between violent assault and substance use in women. *Journal of Consulting and Clinical Psychology, 65,* 834–847.

Kilpatrick, D. G., Resnick, H. S., Ruggiero, K. J., Conoscenti, L. M., & McCauley, J. (2007). *Drug-facilitated, incapacitated, and forcible rape: A national study.* Charleston, SC: National Crime Victims Research & Treatment Center.

Klettke, B., Hallford, D., & Mellor, D. (2016). Perceptions of credibility of sexual abuse victims across generations. *International Journal of Law and Psychiatry, 44,* 91–97.

Klippenstine, M. A., Schuller, R. A., & Wall, A.-M. (2007). Perceptions of sexual assault: The expression of gender differences and the impact of target alcohol consumption. *Journal of Applied Social Psychology, 37,* 2620–2641.

LaFree, G. D., Reskin, B. F., & Visher, C. A. (1985). Jurors' responses to victims' behaviour and legal issues in sexual assault trials. *Social Problems, 32,* 389–407.

Lalor, K., & McElvaney, R. (2010). Child sexual abuse, links to later sexual exploitation/high-risk sexual behavior, and prevention/treatment programs. *Trauma, Violence, & Abuse, 11,* 159–177.

Littleton, H., Grills-Taquechel, A., & Axsom, D. (2009). Impaired and incapacitated rape victims: Assault characteristics and post-assault experiences. *Violence and Victims, 24,* 439–457.

Lynch, K. R., Wasarhaley, N. E., Golding, J. M., & Simcic, T. (2013). Who bought the drinks? Juror perceptions of intoxication in a rape trial. *Journal of Interpersonal Violence, 28,* 3205–3222.

Marx, B. P., Forsyth, J. P., Gallup, G. G., Fusé, T., & Lexington, J. M. (2008). Tonic immobility as an evolved predator defense: Implications for sexual assault survivors. *Clinical Psychology Science and Practice, 15,* 74–90.

Nurius, P. S., Norris, J., Macy, R. J., & Huang, B. (2004). Women's situational coping with acquaintance sexual assault. *Violence Against Women, 10,* 450–478.

Ogden, P., & Minton, K. (2000). Sensorimotor psychotherapy: One method for processing traumatic memory. *Traumatology, 6,* 149–173.

O'Hare, T., Shen, C., & Sherrer, M. (2010). High-risk behaviors and drinking-to-cope as mediators of lifetime abuse and PTSD symptoms in clients with severe mental illness. *Journal of Traumatic Stress, 23,* 255–263.

Polusny, M., & Follette, V. (1995). Long-term correlates of child sexual abuse: Theory and review of the empirical literature. *Applied and Preventative Psychology, 4,* 143–166.

Schuller, R. A., & Wall, A.-M. (1998). The effects of defendant and complainant intoxication on mock jurors' judgments of sexual assault. *Pyschology of Women Quarterly, 22,* 555–573.

Schutte, J. W., & Hosch, H. M. (1997). Gender differences in sexual assault verdicts: A meta-analysis. *Journal of Social Behavior & Personality, 12,* 759–772.

Scott-Ham, M., & Burton, F. (2005). A study of blood and urine alcohol concentrations in cases of alleged drug-facilitated sexual assault in the UK over a 3-year period. *Journal of Clinical Forensic Medicine, 13,* 107–111.

Siegmund, A., & Wotjak, C. T. (2007). A mouse model of posttraumatic stress disorder that distinguishes between conditioned and sensitised fear. *Journal of Psychiatric Research, 41,* 848–860.

Simms, C. M., Noel, N. E., & Maisto, S. A. (2007). Rape blame as a function of alcohol presence and resistant type. *Addictive Behaviors, 32,* 2766–2776.

Spohn, C., & Holleran, D. (2001). Prosecuting sexual assault: A comparison of charging decisions in sexual assault cases involving strangers, acquaintances, and intimate partners. *Justice Quarterly, 18,* 651–688.

Stanko, E., & Williams, E. (2009). Reviewing rape and rape allegations in London: What are the vulnerabilities of the victims who report to the police?

In M. Horvath & J. Brown (Eds.), *Rape: Challenging contemporary thinking* (pp. 207–228). Collumpton, UK: Willan Publishing.

Steel, J., & Herlitz, C. (2005). The association between childhood and adolescent sexual abuse and proxies for sexual risk behavior: A random sample of the general population of Sweden. *Child Abuse & Neglect, 29,* 1141–1153.

Stewart, D. N., & Jacquin, K. M. (2010). Juror perceptions in a rape trial: Examining the complainant's ingestion of chemical substances prior to sexual assault. *Journal of Aggression, Maltreatment & Trauma, 19,* 853–874.

Temkin, J., & Krahé, B. (2008). *Sexual assault and the justice gap: A question of attitude.* Oxford: Hart Publishing.

Testa, M., & Parks, K. A. (1996). The role of women's alcohol consumption in sexual victimization. *Aggression and Violent Behavior, 1,* 217–234.

Testa, M., Van Zile-Tamsen, C., & Livingston, J. A. (2007). Prospective prediction of women's sexual victimization by intimate and nonintimate male perpetrators. *Journal of Consulting and Clinical Psychology, 75,* 52–60.

Trickett, P. K., Noll, J. G., & Putnam, F. W. (2011). The impact of sexual abuse on female development: Lessons from a multigenerational, longitudinal research study. *Development and Psychopathology, 23,* 453–476.

Ullman, S. E., Karabatsos, G., & Koss, M. P. (1999). Alcohol and sexual assault in a national sample of college women. *Journal of Interpersonal Violence, 14,* 603–625.

Van Dorn, R. A., Mustillo, S., Elbogen, E. B., Dorsey, S., Swanson, J. W., & Swartz, M. S. (2005). The effects of early sexual abuse on adult risky sexual behaviors among persons with severe mental illness. *Child Abuse and Neglect, 29,* 1265–1279.

Volchan, E., Souza, G. G., Franklin, C. M., Norte, C. E., Rocha-Rego, V., Oliveira, J. M., … Freire Coutinho, E. S. (2011). Is there tonic immobility in humans? Biological evidence from victims of traumatic stress. *Biological Psychology, 88,* 13–19.

Wall, A., & Schuller, R. (2000). Sexual assault and defendant/victim intoxication: Jurors' perceptions of guilt. *Journal of Applied Social Psychology, 30,* 253–274.

Walsh, K., Danielson, C. K., McCauley, J. L., Saunders, B. E., Kilpatrick, D. G., & Resnick, H. S. (2012). National prevalence of posttraumatic stress disorder among sexually revictimized adolescent, college, and adult household-residing women. *Archives of General Psychiatry, 69,* 935–942.

Walsh, K., Resnick, H. S., Danielson, C. K., McCauley, J. L., Saunders, B. E., & Kilpatrick, D. G. (2014). Patterns of drug and alcohol use associated with lifetime sexual revictimization and current posttraumatic stress disorder among three national samples of adolescent, college, and household-residing women. *Addictive Behaviors, 39*, 684–689.

Wenger, A. A., & Bornstein, B. H. (2006). The effects of victim's substance use and relationship closeness on mock jurors' judgments in an acquaintance rape case. *Sex Roles, 54*, 547–555.

5

'No Means Yes and Yes Means Anal': The Cultural Climate in Which Sex Offences Are Prosecuted

1 Introduction

Unlike other crimes against the person, such as a physical assault or robbery, sexual assault is an ambiguous category because it involves a socially normative activity, sex, in a cultural climate where movies, television, social media, advertisements, video games and pornography regularly depict consensual sexual encounters that involve coercion or force, often reinforcing male aggression and female passivity (Heyes, 2016; Oliver, 2016).

For example, when I searched for 'forced sex' on youtube.com in September 2017, I found over two million videos that matched my search, some more graphic than others. Another phenomenon of the internet culture is the emergence of creepshot websites[1] which are easily

Oliver (2005).

[1] http://jezebel.com/5921747/heres-a-new-totally-legal-reddit-hub-devoted-to-creep-shots; candidfashionpolice.com; creepshots.com.

A. Cossins, *Closing the Justice Gap for Adult and Child Sexual Assault*,
https://doi.org/10.1057/978-1-137-32051-3_5

accessible and contain thousands of photographs of women's body parts, unbeknownst to the women in the photos.[2]

In a cultural climate where forced or coerced sex is not always perceived as a criminal offence, messages via traditional and social media that sexually objectify women and girls and/or perpetuate rape myths are involved in maintaining rape-supportive beliefs (Ward, Merriwether, & Caruthers, 2006). Indeed, rape myths and sexual objectification are common in various media, gaming outlets, and advertisements (Driesmans, Vandenbosch, & Eggermont, 2015; Edwards, Turchik, Dardis, Reynolds, & Gidycz, 2011; Kahlor & Eastin, 2011; Stankiewicz & Rosselli, 2008) and have been shown to promote rape-supportive attitudes in newspaper readers (Franiuk, Seefelt, & Vandello, 2008), while Ferris, Smith, Greenberg, and Smith (2007: 500) reported that women are referred to as sexual objects almost six times per hour in reality dating shows. Overall, Oliver (2015: 9) considers that 'contemporary mainstream youth culture values lack of consent', with women conceived of as 'game' for hunting (Oliver, 2016), literally or figuratively. For many, sexual objectification is an everyday experience as Swim, Hyers, Cohen, and Ferguson (2001: 36) showed—diaries kept by 40 female college students for a fortnight revealed that 65% experienced at least one gender-based incident per week ('comments or behaviours that reflected … traditional gender role prejudice and stereotyping') while 23% experienced or witnessed sexual objectification.

But 'why is [our] culture obsessed with rape' (Williams, 2017, n.p.) and images of rape?

> There has never been any shortage of women getting raped in popular culture, but it seems to have reached a peak recently, from Broadchurch to Game of Thrones. … [T]he casual violence of rape in Game of Thrones becomes ever more ultra, and has such a playful quality that one almost forgets that there's anything to object to. … What is it doing to us as viewers[?] … [I]f rape on telly is culturally necessary, we need to ask why. (Williams, 2017, n.p.)

---

[2]Creepshots are photographs taken and distributed without the consent of the girl or woman who is depicted in them (Oliver, 2015).

Some have argued that the processes of sexual objectification of women and girls result in their dehumanisation (Vaes, Paladino, & Puvia, 2011) and depersonalisation, leading to the perception that they are less than human and have a lower moral status and inferior mental abilities (Loughnan et al., 2010). In other words, objectification theory proposes that:

> when [sexually] objectified, women are treated as bodies that exist for the use or consumption of others, stripped of their individuality and personality ... When this instrumental use of another person ... involves a denial of human characteristics, it becomes denigrating for the objectified. (Vaes et al., 2011: 774–775)

Vaes et al. (2011: 775) explained the phenomenon of dehumanization with respect to an individual's own 'in-group':

> people reserve full humanness to describe their own group, attributing a somewhat lesser humanity to the out-group ... . [T]he out-group is not necessarily completely deprived of humanness ...; it suffices that the other is attributed less human qualities relative to the in-group. (references omitted)

Referring to Haslam (2006), the authors go on to describe the distinction between different types of dehumanisation: '"*animalistic*" (i.e., the denial of uniquely human characteristics that distinguish us from animals such as civility and refinement) and "*mechanistic dehumanization*" (i.e., the denial of core human nature traits, such as emotionality, openness, and depth)' (Vaes et al., 2011: 775).

Vaes et al. (2011: 775; 778) were the first to carry out a series of studies to 'compare male *and* female objectified and non-objectified targets and directly measure the extent to which they elicit human versus animal associations'. When heterosexual male and female participants viewed a range of male and female advertising images, classified as either objectified women (sportive women, mother figures and career women), or objectified men (father figures, sportive men and career men), 'objectified women were the only targets that were less associated with human-related words'. Interestingly, 'both male and female participants dehumanized the objectified female targets to the same extent'.

In order to tease out the reasons for this latter finding, Vaes et al. (2011: 780–781) carried out a second study and found that female participants expressed affinity 'judgments of vulgarity and superficiality' in relation to images of objectified women compared to male participants who expressed affinity 'judgments of sexiness'. In fact, the index used to measure affinity 'moderated male and female participants' dehumanization of objectified and personalized women', revealing that the more female participants distanced themselves from sexualised images of women, and judged them to be vulgar and superficial, the more they tended to dehumanize them. By contrast, men's sexual attraction to objectified female images explained their subsequent dehumanization of them, although 'male participants who indicated feeling more distant from objectified female targets saw objectified and [non-objectified] women as equally (non) human'.

When male and female participants were primed with sex-related or neutral words before viewing non-objectified images of attractive and non-attractive women in a third study, the authors reported that 'good-looking female targets do not need to be presented in a sexually objectified fashion per se to be dehumanized by men. Instead, an active sex goal in men is a sufficient condition to both objectify and dehumanize good-looking female targets' (Vaes et al., 2011: 781).

In the context of sexual assault, it is likely that processes of naming and shaming (such as, 'slut', 'ho', 'whore', and 'prick-teaser') result in a woman's or girl's dehumanisation, her rights to bodily integrity and justify her violation, as the phenomenon of gang rape of unconscious young women so graphically demonstrates, as discussed below.

From a theoretical perspective, the hunting of women and girls for sexual conquest might be associated with war-prone societies. Because 'rape is endemic during war', Zurbriggen (2010: 538) argues that the needs of societies involved in war include a type of masculinity that produces effective soldiers: toughness, aggression, restricted emotional display and the ability to dehumanise the enemy. Such dehumanisation is widely perpetuated through pornography, the use of which has been shown to be positively correlated with RMA, sexually aggressive behaviours, less progressive gender role attitudes and less empathy for rape victims (Allen, Emmers, Gebhardt, & Giery, 1995; Linz, Donnerstein, & Penrod, 1988; Malamuth, Addison, & Koss, 2000; Milburn, Mather, & Conrad, 2000; Peter & Valkenburg, 2009; Wright, Tokunaga, & Kraus, 2015; Zillmann & Bryant, 1982).

Creepshot videos are a new method for dehumanising women which force victims of sexual assault 'to see their rape through the eyes of their rapists and the by-standers who saw it as a "Facebook" moment' where victims are described as 'living corpses' and 'dragged, dropped, violated, abused, and raped' (Oliver, 2015: 3). These videos extend the reach and power of rapists who treat the abuse as a 'spectator sport' which inevitably has a winner and a loser. The victim may be traumatised for an indefinite period since anyone on the internet can view a victim's violation:

> the valorization of non-consensual sex has reached the extreme where sex with unconscious girls ... has become a goal of some boys and men. ... In 2010 at Yale, fraternity brothers marched around the freshman dorms chanting, 'No means yes, yes means anal'. (Oliver, 2015: 4)

In fact, Oliver (2015: 1) documents too many anecdotes illustrating the mindset of male college students who view women as 'rapebait' and consider that consent is irrelevant to their entitlement to sex: '[w]hatever their desires, these college men are *saying* that they want non-consensual sex' (emphasis in original) which is usually obtained through 'the use of drugs and alcohol to incapacitate their prey':

> Young men's attitudes towards consent are formed by exposure to pornography ... in which rape victims are depicted as enjoying sexual assault. ... They have watched enough pornography to be convinced by the fantasy that whatever a woman says, and whether or not she is conscious, she enjoys it. For, within the pornutopia, the fantasy is that women enjoy violent sex, even abuse, conscious or not. (Oliver, 2015: 2; 3; see also Oliver, 2016)

For example, in the Vanderbilt rape case:

> Surveillance video showed Brandon Vandenburg helping to carry [his girlfriend] into his dorm room, where testimony showed he handed out condoms to three of his teammates and egged them on. The 23-year-old former player also took cellphone videos of the June 2013 dorm room rape and emailed them to friends in California while the crime was ongoing. (*New York Post*, 4 November 2016)[3]

Surveillance videos depicted the victim being dragged down a hallway, and dropped more than once while posted videos revealed that she was raped several times, including sodomy with a water bottle. None of the men who received Vandenburg's videos of the rape reported it to the police.

In November 2016, Harvard University suspended its men's soccer team from competing in the remainder of the soccer season after the discovery of a nine-page document which ranked the women soccer players according to their sex appeal, with vulgar comments being attached to their photos, including nicknames and sexual positions, such as 'missionary', 'Doggy style', 'The Triple Lindy' and 'cowgirl' (*New York Post*, 3 November 2016).[4]

In 2017, an unconscious 15-year-old schoolgirl was allegedly raped by a male student at an exclusive boys' school in Sydney, Australia. Another boy filmed the assault with the video being circulated between dozens of students in a private Facebook messenger group. The schoolgirl only found out about the sexual assault and the video after being informed by text message. The schoolgirl's principal wrote in a message to parents:

> We live in a privileged, advantaged society where women have access to education as a matter of right … . And yet girls and women are still subject to abuse or assault or violence of every kind. … Sexual assault is not a story of alcohol consumption or revealing fashions. Nor is it a story of bravado. It is a story of violence and crime and must be afforded its due gravity. (Allum, 2017)

---

[3]http://nypost.com/2016/11/04/vanderbilt-football-gang-rape-instigator-gets-17-years. Vandenburg was sentenced to 17 years, with no minimum sentence; accessed 6 April 2017.

[4]http://nypost.com/2016/11/03/harvard-cancels-mens-soccer-season-over-sex-scouting-report/; accessed 6 April 2017.

But what causes educated, young men to film rape or rank women according to their sex appeal, or to chant, '"My name is Jack, I'm a necrophiliac, I fuck dead girls"' or 'to incapacitate "hot" girls using punch spiked with the drug Rohypnol' (Oliver, 2015: 5)? Indeed, RMA is high among young groups of men who make up fraternity clubs and sporting groups (Bleecker & Murnen, 2005; Forbes, Adams-Curtis, Pakalka, & White, 2006; Foubert, Brosi, & Bannon, 2011; Hayes, Abbott, & Cook, 2016; Lutz-Zois, Moler, & Brown, 2015; Murnen & Kohlman, 2007).

Perhaps those fantasies are ultimately about accruing cultural power through the dehumanisation of women and girls. The extensive literature on the endorsement of men's rape-supportive beliefs and their interest in, or propensity for, committing sexual assault (Abbey & McAuslan, 2004; Edwards, Bradshaw, & Hinsz, 2014; Lisak & Miller, 2002; Lutz-Zois et al., 2015) suggests that men who rape see their victims as objects or property to be used not only for their sexual pleasure but also for the power gained through the processes of dehumanisation.

Oliver (2015: 6) argues that '[r]aping an unconscious woman is the ultimate power trip, proving absolute dominance over another human being' who has been utterly dehumanised during the process of rendering her unconscious and violating her. Nonetheless, that process of dehumanisation begins with a culture that tolerates, supports or condones rape-supportive beliefs and activities.

If '[p]ornography has penetrated mainstream culture ... [into] our everyday lives'; if creepshot photos of women's body parts and videos of gang rape are now circulated widely on social media so that 'rape has become a spectator sport' and 'a form of public entertainment' (Oliver, 2015: 5), *then the criminal justice system is prosecuting rape in a rape-supportive culture* with few procedures to guard against jurors' adherence to rape-supportive beliefs.

Do the dual processes of sexual objectification and dehumanisation take place within the sexual assault trial, when rape myths are used to characterise a complainant's behaviour before, during and after her alleged violation? Arguably, rape myths serve a particular function in a sexual assault trial—it is perhaps too simplistic to say that they distinguish 'real' rape from fabricated allegations, or distinguish stranger rape from acquaintance rape (McKimmie, Masser, & Bongiorno, 2014) since non-stranger rapes can and do result in convictions. Specifically, rape myths serve as a measure of the character or moral worth of the complainant at the same time as they constitute the means by which the female body is sexed according to the cultural values associated with femaleness (Cossins, 2015).

The processes of the criminal trial (opening addresses, oral evidence which is cross-examined, closing addresses, judicial summing-up) are opportunities for:

i. defence counsel and judges to objectify complainants so that they will be less likely to be associated with human-like qualities;
ii. female jurors to distance themselves from an objectified complainant (judging her to be vulgar and superficial); and
iii. male jurors to sexually objectify the complainant and judge her to be less than human.

Thus, rape myths within the sexual assault trial are the means by which complainants are dehumanised, thus confirming their low moral worthiness.

Rape law reformers have to deal with some serious questions, including why defence counsel are permitted to construct a narrative based on cultural fantasies about women and girls who dream of rough sex, or the beliefs that women and girls invite rape because of the clothing they wear or because they drink or take drugs or get into a man's car or flirt. The cultural message that is sent via these beliefs is that once a woman or girl ceases to police her own body and behaviours then it is culturally acceptable for her to be sexually assaulted.

In fact, the criminal justice system is an institutional site which has, historically, encouraged beliefs that protect men from punishment for sexual assault as a result of judicial warnings about the 'unreliable' evidence of women and children; the historical requirement for corroboration of the evidence of sexual assault complainants; the historical relevance of a woman or girl's sexual history/reputation to the issue of consent, and the largely uncontrolled cross-examination of complainants about their sexual histories, sexual behaviour, drug and alcohol consumption, delay in complaint, mental health history and so on. In other words, further evidence for the existence of a rape culture arises when the criminal justice system reinforces rape myths through its processes and procedures.

Since rape myths justify sexual assault, minimise its harms and assign responsibility for the sexual violation to the victim herself, the denial of the validity of a complainant's evidence in a sexual assault trial through the above methods reinforces any rape-supportive beliefs held by jurors which, in turn, has the potential to negatively impact their interpretation of the trial evidence, their assessments of complainant and defendant credibility, the assignment of blame and responsibility and ultimately their verdicts.

In summary, a rape culture exists where the sexual objectification of women and girls has become a widespread, endemic cultural phenomenon which leads to inaccurate beliefs about women's and girls' rights to bodily integrity and beliefs that permit male sexual access to their bodies irrespective of whether consent has been given. Together these beliefs are known as 'rape myths'.

2 Rape Myth Acceptance (RMA) Studies

Traditional gender role beliefs define how female bodies are expected to behave in that the 'degree to which an observer adheres to traditional gender role beliefs is ... a key factor when assigning levels of responsibility blame' to a victim in a rape scenario (Grubb & Turner, 2012: 447). It can also be expected that those with high levels of RMA will endorse the view that women who do not behave according to these gender role expectations invite male sexual aggression and are responsible for it.

In fact, RMA studies support but do not prove that English-speaking, Western countries are characterised by a 'rape culture' which has been defined as 'a complex of beliefs that encourages male sexual aggression and supports violence against women' (Buchwald, Fletcher, & Roth, 1993: vii). But questions remain: why is rape 'the logical and psychological extension of a dominant-submissive, competitive, sex role stereotyped culture' (Burt, 1980: 229)? Where does CSA fit into a rape culture? If some people consider that the use of drugs/alcohol or being sexually active is relevant to a complainant's credibility, the question is why?

A review of the psychological literature confirms that laypeople, jurors, law students and lawyers hold a range of myths and misconceptions about sexual assault, CSA and complainants (see Cossins, 2008; Cossins & Goodman-Delahunty, 2013; Goodman-Delahunty, Cossins, & O'Brien, 2010, 2011; Newcombe, van den Eynde, Hafner, & Jolly, 2008; Tabak & Klettke, 2014; Taylor, 2007; Temkin & Krahé, 2008). Essentially, the findings from these studies:

> suggest that information about the victim affects rape attributions in terms of a 'main effect', i.e. it shapes perceptions irrespective of other variables. Several studies, however, provide evidence of an 'interaction effect', indicating that information about the victim affects some perceivers more than others. (Temkin & Krahé, 2008: 46)

Some of these misconceptions amount to long-standing, historical myths about the propensity of 'immoral' or 'promiscuous' women and girls to lie about being sexually assaulted. The question is, what impact do these misconceptions and myths have on jury decision-making? Are jurors able to put aside these beliefs when carrying out the important task of delivering a verdict in a sexual assault trial?

The summary in Chapter 4 of the influence of alcohol and drug consumption on perceptions of victim and perpetrator blame raises the broader issue of RMA in the general population from which jurors are drawn.

2.1 Prevalence of Rape Myths: General Population Surveys

In 2013, the Department of Health in Victoria, Australia conducted a large, cross-sectional community survey of Australians aged 16 years and older which involved more than 17,500 telephone interviews on a range of topics relating to violence against women (VicHealth, 2014). The survey followed two previous ones that had been conducted in 1995 and 2009. For example, in response to the statement, 'Women are more likely to be raped by someone they know than a stranger', a majority of respondents agreed in all three surveys: 76% (1995); 70% (2009) and 64% (2013). However, since 1995, there has been a statistically significant decrease in agreement that women are less likely to be sexually assaulted by a stranger (VicHealth, 2014: 10–11). This contrasts with recorded crime statistics for NSW that show that sexual assault victims are 6.4 times more likely to be sexually assaulted by someone known to them than a stranger (ABS, 2019a, Table 11).

As well, there was a statistically significant increase in agreement that 'Rape results from men not able to control their need for sex' between 2009 (35%) and 2013 (43%), although very little agreement that 'A man is less responsible for rape if drunk/affected by drugs at the time' (8%, 2009; 9%, 2013) (VicHealth, 2014: 14).[5]

Although a majority of survey respondents agreed that 'Women rarely make false claims of rape', a significant minority disagreed with this statement, a finding that was constant from 1995 to 2013 (41%, 1995; 40%, 2009; 41%, 2013).[6] When the 2013 respondents were faced with the statement, 'A lot of times women who say they were raped led the man on and later had regrets', 38% agreed while only 10% agreed that 'If a woman doesn't physically resist— even if protesting verbally— then it isn't really rape'. As well, 12% agreed that 'If a woman goes to a room alone with a man at a party, it is her fault if she is raped'.[7] Almost one-fifth of respondents agreed that 'If a woman is raped while drunk/affected by drugs she is at least partly responsible' (18%, 2009; 19%, 2013), while slightly fewer proportions of respondents agreed that 'Women often say "no" when they mean "yes"' (18%, 1995; 14%, 2009; 16%, 2013).

Overall, the survey reported that while demographic factors had a 'modest influence on understanding and attitudes', age, gender and place of birth were the most influential factors. The groups that were found to have a lower understanding of violence against women and were less likely to reject violence-supportive attitudes were:

---

[5]There was no data supplied for 1995 regarding these questions.

[6]As discussed in Chapter 1, false allegations of rape are uncommon (Lisak, Gardiner, Nicksa, & Cote, 2010; Rumney, 2006).

[7]These latter two statements were not part of the 1995 and 2009 surveys.

i. men;
ii. those aged 16–24 years, particularly males;
iii. people born overseas in non-English speaking countries.

Indeed, those 'with a high level of support for gender equality have a higher level of understanding of violence against women and are less inclined to endorse violence-supportive attitudes', leading to the supposition that the influence of gender and age may be due to 'the rise of "raunch culture", a greater emphasis on individuals looking after themselves and a belief that gender equality has been achieved' (VicHealth, 2014: 20).

In 2018, a survey of 3922 adults conducted for the End Violence Against Women Coalition in Great Britain found 'a worrying confusion both about what rape is, and how much harm rape does' (End Violence Against Women Coalition, 2018: 2), issues that are likely to affect jurors' decision-making. The key findings were (ibid., 2–3):

- A third (33%) of respondents thought it is not 'usually rape if a woman is pressured into having sex but there is no physical violence';
- A third of men and 21% of women believed if a woman flirted on a date it generally would not be rape, even if she did not consent to sex;
- Almost a quarter (24%) did not believe that, in most cases, sex without consent in long-term relationships is rape;
- Respondents over 65 had the most troubling attitudes to rape, with a third not believing that non-consensual sex in marriage or a relationship was rape, compared with 16% of people aged 16–24;
- 11% of respondents believed that the more sexual partners a woman has, the less harm she will experience from rape;
- 40% thought it is never or usually not rape to remove a condom without a partner's consent;
- 11% were unsure or believed it is not usually not rape to have sex with a woman who is asleep or too drunk to consent.

2.2 Rape Myth Acceptance (RMA) Studies

In the first meta-analysis of the associations between RMA and demographic, attitudinal, and behavioural factors since the 1990s, Suarez and Gadalla (2010)[8] reported data from 37 studies involving 11,487 individuals, and found the following demographics factors, in descending order, were significantly associated with RMA:

i. *Gender*: men endorsed RMA at a higher rate than women;
ii. *Race/ethnicity*: Whites had lower RMA endorsement than those of other races/ethnicities;
iii. *Education*: those with higher education levels had lower levels of RMA endorsement (Suarez & Gadalla, 2010: 2019).

In terms of sociocultural attitudes, '[h]igher levels of RMA were strongly associated with higher levels of other oppressive beliefs', including ageism, classism, racism, homophobia and religious intolerance. As well, higher endorsement of RMA was significantly more likely in those with 'oppressive and adversarial attitudes against women', such as acceptance of interpersonal violence and acceptance of rape and victim-blaming attitudes (Suarez & Gadalla, 2010: 2020).

In terms of behavioural/situational factors, there was a significant relationship between sexual aggression and RMA, as there was with elite athlete status, being a playboy and using degrading images of women (Suarez & Gadalla, 2010: 2023–2024).

Overall, this meta-analysis confirms that RMA continues to be as prevalent, at least in North America, as it was in 1990s (see Lonsway & Fitzgerald, 1994). Given that the internet and social media sites are borderless and the extent to which North American culture permeates other English-speaking, Western countries, this meta-analysis also has implications for the criminal justice systems in Britain and Australia.

---

[8]Suarez and Gadalla (2010: 2027) caution that their meta-analysis has limitations because the 37 studies examined were not equivalent in terms of methodologies, and they used different RMA scales (e.g. RMAS or IRMAS) with an overrepresentation of student samples and White participants in North America.

Studies show that RMA is one of the most consistent predictors of victim blame in sexual assault scenarios (Grubb & Turner, 2012; Schuller & Wall, 1998; Suarez & Gadalla, 2010; Temkin & Krahé, 2008; Wenger & Bornstein, 2006). Mock jurors with high RMA scores are less likely to perceive the defendant to be guilty, compared to their low RMA-scoring counterparts (Stewart & Jacquin, 2010).

The attribution of blame to rape victims is considered to be influenced by an individual's particular cognitive and emotional biases which are based on 'widely shared, normative perceptions of role-conforming behaviour of men and women that restrict the range of what is considered rape and provide a basis for assigning responsibility to victims of rape' (Temkin & Krahé, 2008: 48).

These biases influence an individual's perception and interpretation of the context in which the alleged sexual assault occurred, as well as the victim's and defendant's credibility. Known as attribution theory (Weiner, 1980, 1985), this theory proposes that if individuals are able to attribute a victim's situation to a cause within the victim's control, this reduces sympathy for, and increases anger and blame towards, the victim. This means that 'sympathy and anger mediate the relationship between controllability and helping' (Sperry & Siegel, 2013: 17), although this process is influenced by an individual's perceived similarity to, or empathy with, the victim. For example, Sperry and Siegel (2013: 21) found that sympathy for a victim 'mediated the relationships between [victim] responsibility and helping, credibility, and to a lesser extent verdict'.

Indeed, victim sympathy may account for the documented differences between men and women in terms of levels of RMA.

But what are rape myths? Burt (1980: 217) was the first to define the concept of rape myths in the literature as 'prejudicial stereotyped, or false beliefs about rape, rape victims, and rapists'. More broadly, they can be defined as:

> commonly held beliefs about what a typical rape situation looks like which influence the decision-making process and guilty assessment of lay people as well as jurors. (van der Bruggen & Grubb, 2014: 524)

As 'oversimplified and rigid cognitive schemas ... [they] supply a structure around which information provided in a trial can be organized' (McKimmie et al., 2014: 2275; references omitted). They explain the degree of blame attributed to complainants compared to defendants in various studies that have investigated the effect of complainant characteristics and behaviours using hypothetical rape scenarios.

Research has consistently shown that mock jurors who display relatively higher levels of RMA are significantly more likely to blame rape victims and less likely to blame offenders compared to those who display relatively lower levels (Basow & Minieri, 2011; Cohn, Dupuis, & Brown, 2009; Hammond, Berry, & Rodriguez, 2011; Hockett, Saucier, Hoffman, & Craig, 2009; Temkin & Krahé, 2008). While rape myths may vary across time and place, 'they consistently follow a pattern whereby, they *blame the victim for their rape, express a disbelief in claims of rape, exonerate the perpetrator and allude that only certain types of women are raped*' (Grubb & Turner, 2012: 445; emphasis in original).

For example, Willmott, Boduszeka, Debowskac, and Woodfield (2018) conducted a mock jury study which found that 'complainant believability was significantly negatively associated with rape myth acceptance' and that 'defendant believability [was] significantly positively associated with [Acceptance of Modern Myths about Sexual Aggression] scores', both before and after jury deliberation and verdict. The authors concluded that:

> [s]uch relationships display the important role that pre-trial bias appears to have upon juror decision making, with rape attitudes shown to be directly associated with juror beliefs in a defendant's account of an alleged rape, though unsurprisingly, not with that of the complainant. Such findings directly support those reported in prior research in that, greater acceptance of sexually aggressive myths appears to reduce a juror's propensity to believe a rape complainant's testimony. (Willmott et al., 2018: ibid., 33)

Thus, complainant believability was significantly positively associated with guilty verdicts while defendant believability was significantly negatively associated with guilty verdict decisions (ibid.).

There are, however, inconsistencies in the definitions of rape myths and in the methodologies used to measure RMA in a certain cohort (Suarez & Gadalla, 2010: 2012), such as community members, university students and jurors. The Rape Myth Acceptance Scale (RMAS) developed by Burt (1980) has been used in several studies despite its documented limitations (Buhi, 2005; Lonsway & Fitzgerald, 1994, 1995) and is the most commonly used tool for measuring RMA (Suarez & Gadalla, 2010). In order to address the limitations of the RMAS, Payne et al. (1999) developed and validated the Illinois Rape Myth Acceptance Scale (IRMAS) as a standard measure of rape myth acceptance in a particular population, although other psychometric tools also exist for measuring rape myths (see Grubb & Turner, 2012 for a summary).

As set out in Table 1 below, the IRMAS (Payne et al., 1999) contains seven categories with a total of 45 items, of which 40 are rape myth statements.[9] Table 1 lists the seven main RMA categories and the degree of agreement with those myths from a variety of populations, including US college students, US military and naval academies, UK police officers and Norwegian community members from five recent studies which have used the IRMAS.

The wide range of sample types of the five studies listed in Table 1 illustrates that RMA varies within different population groups and also between men and women. Overall, one-fifth or more of participants in each study agreed with, 'If a woman is raped while she is drunk, she is at least somewhat responsible for letting things get out of control' and 'Rape accusations are often used as a way of getting back at men'.

British police officers displayed the *lowest* levels of RMA in relation to common rape myths such as:

i. 'If a woman is raped while she is drunk, she is at least somewhat responsible for letting things get out of control' (11.7% (M); 20.6% (F));

[9]The higher the score on the IRMAS, the greater the degree of RMA by an individual, with the highest possible score being 240 (in a range from 40–240).

Table 1 Recent rape myth studies categorised according to the seven IRMAS[a] categories

Categories of rape myths	Agreement* (%)	Studies and sample type
1. 'She asked for it' (e.g. drunk)		
If a woman is raped while she is drunk, she is at least somewhat responsible for letting things get out of control	41	Aronowitz, Lambert, and Davidoff (2012) *Sample*: 237 college students
	20	Vandiver and Dupalo (2012) *Sample*: 585 students, Texas State University
	36.0 (M) 32.3 (F)	Carroll, Rosenstein, Foubert, Clark, and Korenman (2016) *Sample*: students from the US Military Academy (1169); the US Naval Academy (1916) & a mid-western, public university (393)
	11.7 (M) 20.6 (F)	Sleath and Bull (2012)[#] *Sample*: 123 police officers from two UK Police Forces aged 27–54 years
A woman who "teases" men deserves anything that might happen	22.9 (M) 15.7 (F)	Bendixen, Hendriksen, and Nøstdahl (2014) *Random sample*: 475 Norwegians, aged 20–60 years
	3.0	Vandiver and Dupalo (2012)
When a woman allows petting to get to a certain point, she is implicitly agreeing to have sex	18.3 (M) 13.3 (F)	Bendixen et al. (2014)
If a woman makes out with a man, it is okay for him to push for sex	63.0	Aronowitz et al. (2012)

(continued)

Table 1 (continued)

Categories of rape myths	Agreement* (%)	Studies and sample type
When women are raped, it's often because the way they said "no" was ambiguous	6.7 (M) 3.1 (F)	Bendixen et al. (2014)
	14.2 (M) 8.6 (F)	Carroll et al. (2016)
	5.0 (M) 7.9 (F)	Sleath and Bull (2012)
	8.0	Vandiver and Dupalo (2012)
When a woman is raped, she usually did something careless to put herself in that situation	5.0 (M) 2.1 (F)	Bendixen et al. (2014)
A woman who dresses in skimpy clothes should not be surprised if a man tries to force her to have sex	22.2 (M) 17.8 (F)	Carroll et al. (2016)
	1.7 (M) 3.2 (F)	Sleath and Bull (2012)
	21	Vandiver and Dupalo (2012)[b]
When women go around wearing low-cut tops or short skirts, they're just asking for trouble	0.0 (M) 4.8 (F)	Sleath and Bull (2012)
A woman who "teases" men deserves anything that might happen	5.0 (M) 2.7 (F)	Carroll et al. (2016)
	1.7 (M) 1.6 (F)	Sleath and Bull (2012)
If a woman goes home with a man she doesn't know, it is her own fault if she is raped	0 (M) 7.9 (F)	Sleath and Bull (2012)
When a woman is a sexual tease, eventually she is going to get into trouble	18.3 (M) 20.6 (F)	Sleath and Bull (2012)
A woman who goes to the home or apartment of a man on the first date is implying that she wants to have sex	0.0 (M) 6.4 (F)	Sleath and Bull (2012)

(continued)

Table 1 (continued)

Categories of rape myths	Agreement* (%)	Studies and sample type
2. 'It wasn't really rape' (e.g. no physical evidence)		
If a woman does not physically fight back, you can't really say that it was rape	10.0 (M) 8.2 (F)	Bendixen et al. (2014)
	7.4 (M) 5.7 (F)	Carroll et al. (2016)
	0.0 (M) 1.6 (F)	Sleath and Bull (2012)
	7.0	Vandiver and Dupalo (2012)
A rape didn't happen if the women has no bruises or marks	5.0 (M) 3.4 (F)	Bendixen et al. (2014)
	0 (M) 1.6 (F)	Sleath and Bull (2012)
If the rapist doesn't have a weapon, you really can't call it rape	0.7 (M) 0.4 (F)	Carroll et al. (2016)
	0 (M) 1.6 (F)	Sleath and Bull (2012)
	1.0	Vandiver and Dupalo (2012)
If a woman doesn't physically resist sex—even when protesting verbally—it really can't be considered rape	3.3 (M) 1.6 (F)	Sleath and Bull (2012)
If a woman claims to have been raped but has no bruises or scrapes, she probably shouldn't be taken too seriously	0 (M) 3.2 (F)	Sleath and Bull (2012)
If someone came to me and claimed they were raped, my first reaction would be to not believe them	5.0	Vandiver and Dupalo (2012)

(continued)

Table 1 (continued)

Categories of rape myths	Agreement* (%)	Studies and sample type
3. 'He didn't mean to' (e.g. he was sexually aroused)		
Men do not usually intend to force sex on women, but sometimes they get too sexually carried away	13.3 (M) 13.8 (F)	Bendixen et al. (2014)
	31.8 (M) 18.6 (F)	Carroll et al. (2016)
	16.7 (M) 9.5 (F)	Sleath and Bull (2012)
	28.0	Vandiver and Dupalo (2012)
Rape happens when a man's sex drive gets out of control	33.1 (M) 23.2 (F)	Carroll et al. (2016)
	8.3 (M) 4.8 (F)	Sleath and Bull (2012)
	28.0	Vandiver and Dupalo (2012)
When men rape, it is because of their strong desire for sex	21.7 (M) 15.9 (F)	Sleath and Bull (2012)
Rapists are usually sexually frustrated individuals	11.7 (M) 12.7 (F)	Sleath and Bull (2012)
When a man is very sexually aroused, he may not even realize that the woman is resisting	5.0 (M) 14.3 (F)	Sleath and Bull (2012)
4. 'She wanted it' (e.g. secret desire to be raped)		
Forced sex is a turn on	23.0	Aronowitz et al. (2012)
Although most women wouldn't admit it, they generally find being physically forced into sex a real "turn on"	9.1 (M) 8.9 (F)	Carroll et al. (2016)
	0.0 (M) 3.2 (F)	Sleath and Bull (2012)
Although most women wouldn't admit it, they generally like being physically forced to have sex	8.0	Vandiver and Dupalo (2012)
Many women find being forced to have sex very arousing	1.7 (M) 1.6 (F)	Sleath and Bull (2012)

(continued)

Table 1 (continued)

Categories of rape myths	Agreement* (%)	Studies and sample type
Even though the woman may call it rape, she probably enjoyed it	8.3 (M) 5.2 (F)	Bendixen et al. (2014)
Many women secretly desire to be raped	2.0 (M) 2.6 (F)	Carroll et al. (2016)
	0 (M) 1.6 (F)	Sleath and Bull (2012)
	2.0	Vandiver and Dupalo (2012)
Some women prefer to have sex forced on them so they don't have to feel guilty about it	0.0 (M) 1.6 (F)	Sleath and Bull (2012)
Many women actually enjoy sex after the guy uses a little force	8.3 (M) 6.4 (F)	Sleath and Bull (2012)
5. 'She lied'		
Rape accusations are often used as a way of getting back at men	24.4 (M) 14.1 (F)	Carroll et al. (2016)
	31.7 (M) 28.6 (F)	Sleath and Bull (2012)
	24.0	Vandiver and Dupalo (2012)
A lot of women lead a man on and then they cry rape	17.9 (M) 12.7 (F)	Carroll et al. (2016)
	18.3 (M) 20.6 (F)	Sleath and Bull (2012)
	16.0	Vandiver and Dupalo (2012)
Women who are caught having an illicit affair sometimes claim that it was rape	60.0 (M) 65.1 (F)	Sleath and Bull (2012)
Many so-called rape victims are actually women who had sex and "changed their minds" afterwards	40.0 (M) 34.9 (F)	Sleath and Bull (2012)
A lot of times, women who claim they were raped just have emotional problems	6.7 (M) 19.1 (F)	Sleath and Bull (2012)

(continued)

Table 1 (continued)

Categories of rape myths	Agreement* (%)	Studies and sample type
6. 'Rape is a trivial event' (e.g. women tend to exaggerate)		
Women tend to exaggerate how much rape affects them	3.3 (M) 2.8 (F)	Bendixen et al. (2014)
	5.2 (M) 3.9 (F)	Carroll et al. (2016)
	0.0 (M) 3.2 (F)	Sleath and Bull (2012)
	4.0	Vandiver and Dupalo (2012)
If a woman is willing to "make out" with a guy, then it's no big deal if he goes a little further and has sex	3.4 (M) 2.2 (F)	Carroll et al. (2016)
	1.7 (M) 6.4 (F)	Sleath and Bull (2012)
	3.0	Vandiver and Dupalo (2012)
Rape isn't as big a problem as some feminists would like people to believe	1.7 (M) 4.8 (F)	Sleath and Bull (2012)
Being raped isn't as bad as being mugged and beaten	0.0 (M) 1.6 (F)	Sleath and Bull (2012)
If a woman isn't a virgin, then it shouldn't be a big deal if her date forces her to have sex	0.0 (M) 1.6 (F)	Sleath and Bull (2012)
7. 'Rape is a deviant event' (e.g. perpetrated by strangers)		
It is usually only women who dress suggestively that are raped	9.2 (M) 4.9 (F)	Carroll et al. (2016)
	1.7 (M) 3.2 (F)	Sleath and Bull (2012)
Men from nice middle-class homes almost never rape	4.3 (M) 2.7 (F)	Carroll et al. (2016)
	1.7 (M) 1.6 (F)	Sleath and Bull (2012)
	2.0	Vandiver and Dupalo (2012)

(continued)

Table 1 (continued)

Categories of rape myths	Agreement* (%)	Studies and sample type
Rape is unlikely to happen in the woman's own familiar neighbourhood	4.0 (M) 2.2 (F)	Carroll et al. (2016)
	0.0 (M) 1.6 (F)	Sleath and Bull (2012)
	1.0	Vandiver and Dupalo (2012)
Rape mainly occurs on the "bad" side of town	0.0 (M) 1.6 (F)	Sleath and Bull (2012)
Usually, it is only women who do things like hang out in bars and sleep around that are raped	1.7 (M) 4.8 (F)	Sleath and Bull (2012)
In reality, women are almost never raped by their boyfriends	3.3 (M) 1.6 (F)	Sleath and Bull (2012)
Rape almost never happens in the woman's own home	1.7 (M) 4.8 (F)	Sleath and Bull (2012)

[a]Payne, Lonsway, and Fitzgerald (1999)
[b]Note this study listed this rape myth under 'deviant event' however it is better categorised under "she asked for it" myth
*M = male; F = female
#Results rounded to one decimal place
Notes
1. In their studies, Aronowitz et al. (2012) and Carroll et al. (2016) used the IRMA Short Form
2. Bendixen et al. (2014) chose 11 items from the IRMAS, relating to five of the seven items: 'trivialisation of the crime, definition of rape, male intention, victim desire - enjoyment and victim precipitation'
3. Sleath and Bull (2012) used the 40 item IRMAS
4. Vandiver and Dupalo (2012) used the 19 item IRMAS

ii. 'A woman who dresses in skimpy clothes should not be surprised if a man tries to force to have sex with her' (1.7% (M); 3.2 (F));
iii. 'If a woman does not physically fight back, you can't really say that it was rape' (0.0% (M); 1.6% (F));
iv. 'Rape happens when a man's sex drive gets out of control' (8.3% (M); 4.8% (F)); and
v. 'Although most women wouldn't admit it, they generally find being physically forced into sex a real "turn on"' (0.0% (M); 3.2% (F)).

These low levels of RMA may have been partly due to the fact that almost one-third of the police officers (30.9%) had 'received specialist training to deal with rape victims' (Sleath & Bull, 2012: 650). However:

> no significant effect was found for specialist rape victim training regarding levels of victim blaming. ... This lack of effect is troubling, since it would be expected that specialist training to deal with sexual offenses would contain aspects that would address misperceptions about rape victims. (Sleath & Bull, 2012: 661)

Compared to other population groups listed in Table 1, British police officers exhibited the highest levels of RMA in relation to (vi) 'Rape accusations are often used as a way of getting back at men' (31.7% (M); 28.6% (F)), and (vii) 'A lot of women lead a man on and then they cry rape' (18.3% (M); 20.6% (F)). They also exhibited high levels of RMA in relation to (viii) 'Women who are caught having an illicit affair sometimes claim that it was rape' (60.0% (M); 65.1% (F)); and (ix) 'Many so-called rape victims are actually women who had sex and "changed their minds" afterwards' (40.0% (M); 34.9% (F)).

Sleath and Bull (2012: 659–660) reported that high levels of RMA among this group of police officers had a significant effect on the extent to which, individually, they blamed the victim, with both male and female offices displaying similar levels of victim blame. Specific types of rape myths were found to predict victim-blaming, that is, those that fell within the categories, 'She wanted it' and 'He didn't mean to'. Victim-blame was significantly higher when the perpetrator was an acquaintance compared to when he was a stranger.

By contrast, US students (a younger cohort) showed relatively higher levels of agreement with rape myths (i) to (v) and almost as high levels of agreement with myths (vi) and (vii). Generally, the community group of Norwegians displayed relatively low levels of agreement with all rape myths with their highest level of agreement being with 'A woman who "teases" men deserves anything that might happen' (5% (M); 2.7% (F)).

2.3 The Factors Influencing Victim Blame

One key question raised by the literature is what RMA scales are really measuring. Some consider RMA to be a measure of hostility towards women (Lonsway & Fitzgerald, 1994), or more broadly a measure of attitudes that deny the existence of rape and CSA (Forbes, Adam-Curtis, & White, 2004; Suarez & Gadalla, 2010; citing Cromer & Freyd, 2007). But what is the social purpose of rape myths about women and children? Before addressing this question, I discuss what is known about the factors influencing victim blame.

The literature reveals that '[t]here are a number of variables which have been found to influence the degree' of victim blame, 'including perceiver's beliefs, victim characteristics and situational aspects ... which are likely to influence every situation in a unique and unpredictable manner' (Grubb & Turner, 2012: 444). Because it is 'vital' to understand the different types of observer or mock juror characteristics, and the way in which they influence jury decision-making (Grubb & Turner, 2012), the following discussion summarises the latest meta-analyses of RMA studies, as well as the results of a study of a large representative sample of laypeople in the UK.

Temkin and Krahé (2008: 75) carried out a study with the general public 'to test the proposition that the justice gap is due ... to the influence of ... attitudes towards rape'. They used the Female Precipitation subscale of the Perceived Causes of Rape Scale (Cowan & Quinton, 1997) which included the following propositions that rape is caused by:

1. women who tease men;
2. women who allow men to intimately touch them;
3. women's use of drugs or alcohol;
4. women who dress sexy;
5. women allowing the situation to get out of control; and
6. women who do unsafe things (such as being out alone, hitch-hiking).

They also conducted an online survey of 2176 members of the UK general public (age range, 18–69 years[10]), using the 16-item Acceptance of Modern Myths about Sexual Aggression Scale (Gerger, Kley, Bohner, & Siebler, 2007), an instrument that is considered to measure subtler stereotypical beliefs about women and rape.

Rape scenarios were varied in terms of the use of force and complainant intoxication, as was the relationship between complainant and defendant (strangers, acquaintances with no prior sexual relationship, and ex-partners with a prior sexual relationship). All scenarios contained a verbal statement of non-consent by the complainant.

Participants' judgements about defendants and complainants 'were affected both by participants' acceptance of rape myths and by information activating stereotypes about rape' (Temkin & Krahé, 2008: 117). Ratings of defendant liability were directly influenced by the nature of the relationship in that the defendant was perceived as most liable when he was a stranger, compared to an acquaintance and ex-partner. Defendant liability was also greater when he used force than when he took advantage of the complainant's intoxication (Temkin & Krahé, 2008: 103). In the scenarios where the complainant was intoxicated, defendant liability ratings did not vary according to the type of relationship. However, the more that participants agreed with female precipitation myths and modern rape myths, the more leniency was displayed towards the defendant, generally, but especially when he was an ex-partner.

The complainant was blamed significantly less when the defendant was a stranger and she was also accorded less blame when subject to force than when she was intoxicated. Overall, complainant blame was correlated with rape-supportive attitudes in that the more participants endorsed rape myths, the more blame was attributed to the complainant.

Temkin and Krahé (2008: 107–108) concluded that 'differences in rape-supportive attitudes' affected participants' interpretations of rape scenarios. While, on average, men showed greater acceptance than women of female precipitation beliefs and modern myths about sexual

[10]This is the age range of those who can be selected for jury duty in England and Wales: Section 1, Juries Act 1974 (UK).

aggression, 'men and women did not differ substantially in their perceptions of defendant liability' or in relation to complainant blame. Despite a verbal statement of non-consent being included in the scenarios so that the key element of the crime of sexual intercourse without consent was satisfied, use of heuristics in the form of rape myths influenced participants' 'appraisal of the evidence to the disadvantage of the complainant' (Temkin & Krahé, 2008: 119). In other words, defendant liability and complainant blame were influenced by the relationship between the parties, the amount of force used by the defendant and the degree of intoxication of the complainant.

Temkin and Krahé (2008) concluded that schematic information processing[11] is responsible for the different assessments of liability and blame so that the more sexual assault cases deviate from the stranger-rape stereotype, the more likely the case facts will be judged according to pre-existing RMA.

Bieneck and Krahé (2011) carried out a series of mock jury experiments with a group of undergraduate students to determine whether there is a special leniency bias in sexual assault cases compared to robbery cases by measuring victim and perpetrator blame. They found that perpetrator blame was significantly higher in the robbery scenarios compared to the rape scenarios. As expected, more blame was attributed to the rape victim than the robbery victim (Bieneck & Krahé, 2011: 1790).

When the use of force and intoxication was varied, the victim was blamed more (and the perpetrator was blamed less) when she was intoxicated by alcohol than when force was used on her. When the perpetrator was a stranger, more blame was attributed to him than when he was an acquaintance or ex-partner while victim blame increased when he was

[11] Encoding of memories involves the formation of 'general or associative semantic representations (schemata) of new input based on prior experience. This schematic processing is based on abstracted mental representations that structure or organize some aspect of past experience, and schematic memory structures influence the processing of new information' (Agres & Wiggins, 2015: 152). This means that our pre-existing knowledge and beliefs influences how we perceive and interpret events and experiences. As Agres and Wiggins (2015: 152) explain: 'Piaget [et al., 1952], who considered schemata to be the building blocks of knowledge, discussed how new information is incorporated into existing schemata in the processes of assimilation … . When the new information is too dissimilar to be integrated, accommodation occurs, in which the schematic structure itself must change to accommodate the new information.'

an acquaintance or ex-partner. There was also a significant interaction between type of crime and coercive strategy:

> When the perpetrator exploited the fact the victim was drunk … perceived perpetrator blame decreased in the rape cases but not in the robbery cases. … Similarly, if the victim was too drunk to resist … she was blamed more in the rape cases but not in the robbery cases. (Bieneck & Krahé, 2011: 1791)

Even when force was used, perpetrator blame was higher in the robbery cases than in the rape cases. As well, perpetrator blame decreased when the perpetrator was an acquaintance or ex-partner in the rape cases but no corresponding decrease was seen in the robbery cases. Victim blame also 'increased in the rape cases the closer the relationship, but remained unaffected … in the robbery cases' (Bieneck & Krahé, 2011: 1793). The authors concluded:

> These patterns can be seen as a reflection of schematic information processing because neither victim intoxication nor victim-perpetrator relationship are critical features of the legal definition of rape. (Bieneck & Krahé, 2011: 1793)

Because victim-perpetrator relationship and victim intoxication trigger stereotypical thinking about the veracity of a rape allegation, the authors concluded that a 'special leniency bias' exists in rape cases since background information about the victim 'operated differently' for different crimes (Bieneck & Krahé, 2011: 1794). Perpetrator and victim blame was constant in the robbery cases irrespective of the type of background information whereas perpetrator and victim blame varied as a function of victim intoxication and victim–perpetrator relationship.

It is likely that the reason for this variation was due to the legal issue of lack of consent which is an element of the offence in adult sexual assault cases but not in robbery cases. Thus, it appears that background information, that is, victim behaviour and victim–perpetrator relationship, was used by mock jurors as proxy measures to decide whether lack of consent existed when no other information was available.

2.4 The Independent Effects of Victim and Participant Characteristics on Victim Blaming

Because of the difficulties with differentiating between the independent effects of victim characteristics versus participant characteristics, van der Bruggen and Grubb (2014) carried out a literature review in order to summarise what is known about their separate effects on victim blaming in rape scenarios. These characteristics included gender, sexuality, victim carelessness, degree of resistance and the victim/perpetrator relationship.

In relation to victim resistance, the results have been consistent over a twenty-year period: 'victims who do not resist tend to be blamed the most', although non-resistant male victims are blamed more than their female counterparts (van der Bruggen & Grubb, 2014: 526). A number of studies also show that victims are blamed more in date-, acquaintance- and marital-rape scenarios than stranger-rape scenarios (van der Bruggen & Grubb, 2014).

By comparison, the influence of *observer/participant* characteristics on victim blame is not well known, partly due to the difficulties in accessing representative cohorts of laypeople or jurors. What does emerge from the literature is that male, heterosexual participants are more likely to endorse rape myths *and* blame rape victims compared to female, heterosexual, and male, homosexual participants (van der Bruggen & Grubb, 2014).

Thus, participant gender is widely accepted as having a significant influence on perceptions of victim blame (see studies cited in van der Bruggen & Grubb, 2014: 527), with men more likely than women to blame rape victims for their victimisation, irrespective of the gender of the victim and the type of rape (stranger, date, acquaintance or marital). If, as it appears, men are more likely to identify and sympathise with the offender and are more likely to judge the victim's character, this has 'immense implications for the criminal justice system' (van der Bruggen & Grubb, 2014: 527) in terms of wrongful acquittals.

Indeed, RMA appears to act as a mediating variable between participant gender and victim blame, thus explaining men's higher propensity for blaming rape victims (Suarez & Gadalla, 2010) and voting guilty in sexual assault trials (Devine & Caughlin, 2014). The various stereotypes that make up RMA are believed to be used by mock jurors when assessing ambiguous evidence, blame and responsibility (McKimmie et al., 2014) since 'offense-related and victim-related schemas influence impressions about the blameworthiness of the defendant and complainant' (Stuart, McKimmie, & Masser, 2016: 2).

As well, participant gender role attitudes or levels of benevolent sexism have been shown to influence RMA, in that the higher the degree of benevolent sexism the more a rape victim is blamed (Grubb & Turner, 2012; van der Bruggen & Grubb, 2014), especially in date-rape scenarios compared to stranger-rape scenarios (Grubb & Turner, 2012). Other studies have found an indirect relationship between stereotypical gender role attitudes and victim blame, with such attitudes 'act[ing] as mediating variables between observer gender and degree of [victim] blame' (van der Bruggen & Grubb, 2014: 528).

2.5 Investigating the Independent Effects of Victim Stereotypicality and Gender Stereotypicality

While '[t]he exact relationship between gender role conformity, rape myth acceptance and victim blaming is unclear', Grubb and Turner (2012: 447) suggest that 'gender role conformity enhances RMA and ergo victim blaming by reinforcing cognitive schema that support the traditional stereotypical notion that rape victims are deserving of their misfortune'. The studies below provide some answers.

When Masser, Lee, and McKimmie (2010) investigated the independent effects of victim stereotypicality (verbalised non-consent, some physical resistance and assisting the police investigation) compared to gender stereotypicality ('bad' mother versus 'good' mother behaviour), they found that it was only when victims behaved in counter-stereotypical ways that the gender stereotypicality of the complainant affected mock jurors' perceptions of blame.

In a later study, McKimmie et al. (2014: 2278) investigated the impact of victim stereotypicality independently of gender stereotypicality 'in the context of stereotypical [stranger-rape] and counter-stereotypical [acquaintance-rape] offenses'. Victim stereotypicality amounted to the victim pushing the perpetrator away, trying to stop the removal of her clothes and cooperation with the police. Counter-stereotypicality involved no resistance and unwillingness to cooperate with police. Like other studies, RMA was a significant predictor of verdict by community participants, with higher endorsement of rape myths predicting acquittals and higher ratings of victim blame. The participants were also more likely to vote guilty and had more positive perceptions of the victim when the offence was stereotypical (stranger-rape) and when the victim was stereotypical (actively resisted).

While victim stereotypicality 'had no effect or a lesser effect on participants' perceptions in the stranger rape condition' (McKimmie et al., 2014: 2287), in the acquaintance-rape condition, a counter-stereotypical victim resulted in more victim blame, less defendant blame and fewer guilty verdicts. While most participants voted guilty in both conditions, not guilty verdicts were rarer in the stranger-rape condition compared to the acquaintance-rape condition. Reasons for guilty verdicts focused on the defendant's menacing behaviour in the stranger-rape scenario from which participants probably implied that the victim was not consenting, such that the victim's behaviour had less salience.

By contrast, in the acquaintance-rape scenario, reasons for both guilty and not guilty verdicts focused on the victim's behaviour (stereotypical or not) and, from that, whether she had consented. In both conditions, the most frequent reason for a not guilty verdict was that the victim's behaviour had 'put her at risk of rape' (McKimmie et al., 2014: 2293). Overall, the victim's behaviour in the acquaintance-rape condition was commented on three times more commonly when it was counter-stereotypical than when it was stereotypical, confirming the results of other studies that the issue of consent is dependent on the victim's behaviour in an acquaintance-rape situation. The authors concluded that their results:

> suggest that perceivers generally start with the 'real rape' crime prototype … in attempting to interpret what happened and how blame should be apportioned … . [T]his classification may motivate different questions to

> be asked of the evidence, leading to a 'step-down' through the hierarchy of schemas and, subsequently, the use of victim stereotypes to evaluate the complainant in counter-stereotypical cases. (McKimmie et al., 2014: 2294)

Ellison and Munro (2013) conducted a qualitative study with 160 jury-eligible mock jurors who were presented with four mini rape trials that included a number of elements common to acquaintance rape cases, and played in real time by professional actors and barristers. The ambiguous facts involved a complainant and defendant who had been in an eight-month relationship which had ended two months previously. During a meeting at the complainant's home, when they drank coffee, wine and talked, they kissed as the defendant was leaving. Although the defendant tried to initiate sexual intercourse, the complainant asked him to stop and pushed his hands away. The defendant admitted that sexual intercourse had taken place but maintained that it had been consensual. Evidence from a forensic specialist showed that the complainant had suffered bruises and scratches consistent with considerable force but had sustained no internal bruising. The mock jurors were told that this evidence neither confirmed nor contradicted the complainant's rape allegation.

Analysis of jury deliberations revealed jurors' reasons for believing or disbelieving the complainant's version of events. Jurors considered all keys elements of the facts by comparing them to those in a stranger rape scenario although they described the circumstances as 'more "delicate"', 'more of a "grey area"' and, therefore, found it more difficult to convict. While jurors used the stranger rape scenario as the 'standard' against which to judge the alleged sexual assault, they also held a set of expectations about the rules and 'conventions' of heterosexual relationships (Ellison & Munro, 2013: 310):

> [n]otwithstanding the fact that our jurors received an extended judicial direction which ... emphasised that rape by an acquaintance or intimate partner is no less serious than rape by a stranger, our findings suggest that jurors continued to struggle to convict because of engrained expectations regarding resistance and sexual miscommunication. (Ellison & Munro, 2013: 303)

As a result, they invoked a number of gendered 'scripts' which incorporated very traditional elements, including the belief that women had 'primary responsibility for acting as sexual gatekeepers' (Ellison & Munro, 2013: 310). Such understandings of heterosexual communications have the effect of transforming the trial into one that investigates the conduct of the complainant and positioning the defendant as the contradictory, passive, yet '"red-blooded"' man who is unable to control his urges and 'pushes his luck' according to what the woman does or says. Thus, the complainant was viewed as the active instigator of sexual relations, the one with total control. While jurors were aware of the 'communicative conventions' for sexual intimacy through various 'indirect verbal and non-verbal cues', these conventions turn out to be implicitly gendered:

> A number of jurors observed that the complainant had 'egged on' or encouraged the defendant by allowing him into her home, offering him a glass of wine, engaging him in friendly conversation over the course of a few hours, kissing him, and generally creating a comfortable ambience ... with jurors—male and female—frequently censuring the complainant for giving out 'mixed messages' ... or ... 'being a prick-tease'. (Ellison & Munro, 2013: 311)

This belief in the responsibility of women to control intimate encounters then allows jurors to determine the 'reasonableness' of a defendant's mistaken belief as to consent, or the reasonableness of the steps he took to make sure there was consent, depending on the jurisdiction (see further, Chapter 7).

As Ellison and Munro (2013: 311; 312) observe, their findings are consonant with other studies that have shown people's greater preoccupation with the complainant's conduct rather than the defendant's, as discussed above, thus 'testif[ying] to the strength and reach of these socio-sexual "scripts" ... [to] afford a more lenient treatment to defendants'. Jurors with these views thus excluded the possibility that a woman could have a social occasion with an ex-partner in the home they used to share, without sex being the inevitable outcome if the man so desired: 'jurors clearly relied upon a series of expectations regarding "appropriate" forms of behaviour towards ex-partners … [and] reflected on their own experiences with relationship breakdown to determine what (sexual) meaning might reasonably be imposed', such that the complainant was seen as being far too welcoming, 'needy, clingy or still in love with the defendant' while the defendant took the opportunity to '"try his luck"' (Ellison & Munro, 2013: 312–313), with the ability of the complainant to withdraw consent becoming an unreasonable possibility after a consensual kiss.

Narratives of revenge also featured in the deliberations. Despite no evidence, jurors decided that the defendant had '"moved on"', while the complainant had tried to rekindle the relationship and had made a false allegation when that failed. While some jurors challenged these views, no views were reported that suggested the defendant had gone to the complainant's home to rekindle the relationship and when that did not work, he raped her:

> the onus was typically placed upon the complainant to correct any potential misreading of her behaviour by communicating her lack of consent unequivocally … [T]his stretched to … a de facto requirement, that the complainant physically resist and/or use force where it was clear that her verbal protestations were not being taken on board by a defendant whom many perceived as having diminished deciphering skills *on account of his aroused condition.* (Ellison & Munro, 2013: 314; emphasis in original)

Jurors compared the complainant's lack of resistance with that of a woman confronted by a stranger, where the risk of serious violence would leave a woman '"petrified"', '"like jelly"', rather than the less traumatised complainant who, with no history of domestic violence, would be 'more inclined to "fight tooth and nail"' (Ellison & Munro, 2013: 314–315).

Although the jurors in this study were presented with evidence from a forensic medical examiner that it is common for rape victims to display no vaginal injury as a result of sexual assault, 'several jurors continued to voice the (unfounded) counterview that genuine resistance to an unwanted sexual attack would inevitably result in "some kind of tearing" or "inside trauma"' (Ellison & Munro, 2013: 317–318). Overwhelmingly, jurors believed that there would be evidence of internal damage and the lack of it equated with sexual arousal and, therefore, consent.

Even though the complainant sustained bruises to her chest, wrist and upper thigh, jurors advanced unsubstantiated explanations for her '"superficial-ish"' injuries, with the most common suggestions being that 'the complainant had self-inflicted the injuries to bolster the credibility of her false rape allegation, that she had sustained them accidentally in … a separate sexual or other physical activity, or that she was simply prone to bruising easily', that the parties had previously enjoyed '"rough"', '"raunchy"' or violent sex or that the encounter was a particularly passionate one as they '"reignit[ed] an old flame"'. The eccentricity of these views suggested they were drawn from '(media-informed) scripts about the intensity and urgency of heterosexual "reunion sex"'. A suggestion by some jurors that 'a woman could freeze during a sexual attack out of fear or shock' was rejected by others who considered such a response was only plausible in a stranger rape attack where there was a risk of additional violence (Ellison & Munro, 2013: 315).

As a result of their doubts, 80% of the 20 juries returned not guilty verdicts while 71% of jurors in post-deliberation questionnaires said that the previous relationship between the complainant and defendant was an important or a highly important factor in arriving at their verdicts (Ellison & Munro, 2013: 318–322).

However, in an ambiguous fact situation, jurors' own experiences or media-informed beliefs constitute a limited source of information for assessing the behaviour of two people whom they had never met and creating a narrative in which to understand an alleged sexual assault, such as the assertion that '"love makes people do crazy things"' (Ellison & Munro, 2013: 314). The authors concluded: 'on the whole, jurors displayed a striking willingness to construct a range of unsupported hypotheses regarding the parties' prior sexual relationship', even though no evidence of it had been raised in the simulated trial, although some assumed the defence had been prevented from doing so (Ellison & Munro, 2013: 319; 320).

In summary, these deliberations contain gendered assumptions about women's and men's behaviour (clingy, needy complainant, her need for revenge when rejected), media-driven views of heterosexual relations (to account for injuries) and the sympathy displayed to, and/or excuses made for, the defendant who may have merely misunderstood the complainant's behaviour, and, sexually aroused, could not control himself.

Whether jurors view the facts of an acquaintance rape case from the point of view of what they believe a stranger rape entails, or because jurors believe acquaintance rape cases are 'inherently "less clear-cut"' because the facts trigger 'expectations regarding "appropriate" forms of soci-sexual behaviour … and presumptions regarding the will and capacity of victims to resist' (Ellison & Munro, 2013: 302), the fact remains that these cases, which constitute the majority that are reported to police, are processed in a system that is not capable of recognising the distinguishing features of acquaintance rape and sexual assault so that most female victims 'are effectively barred from being acknowledged as victims of rape' (Ellison & Munro, 2013: 302; quoting Temkin & Krahé, 2008: 50). The authors recommend that while it is important to educate jurors about the realities of acquaintance versus stranger rapes, education

> alone will be insufficient to overcome some of the obstacles that render jurors reluctant to convict in such cases. Instead, a thorough interrogation of prevailing expectations regarding socio-(hetero)sexual behaviour and communication is required, alongside renewed efforts to disavow jurors of the assumption that a victim's 'normal' response to rape would be to fight back aggressively, receiving and causing injury (including internal injury) as a result. (Ellison & Munro, 2013: 321)

In Chapters 11 and 12, I discuss the reforms that would be necessary to overcome the obstacles to prosecuting (acquaintance) rape cases.

The key limitation of Ellison and Munro's study (2013) is that they did not undertake empirical analyses to examine the relationships between jurors' RMA, misconceptions, credibility determinations and verdicts, nor was any coding data for the deliberations reported. Nor did the authors determine the extent to which educational/judicial guidance changed mock jurors' misconceptions, or the relationship between mock jurors' exposure to educational/judicial guidance, their credibility perceptions and verdicts.

More recently, Smith and Skinner (2017) used court observations to explore the extent of rape myths in 28 sexual assault trials in E&W. They found that:

> rape myths were used extensively in every trial and were a routine way for the defence to undermine prosecution witnesses' credibility. ... Rape myths were used to portray victim/survivor behaviour as either normal or 'abnormal'. For example, juries were told to evaluate whether the demeanour of victim/survivors was 'consistent' with expectations; namely, that they were visibly distressed immediately after the offence, when initially reporting, and at trial. (Smith & Skinner, 2017: 449)

Other rape myths utilised by defence counsel included (Smith & Skinner, 2017: 449–452):

- the normality of physical resistance (e.g. 'Squirming is the word [Victim/Survivor] uses throughout. She doesn't do anything else ... What would you do?' (Smith & Skinner, 2017: 449));
- the abnormality of delayed complaints to police;
- revenge as a motive for complaint;
- the abnormality of maintaining contact with the accused; and
- inconsistencies by a complainant as evidence of dishonesty.

By focusing on 'normal' versus 'abnormal' behaviour, defence counsel created a dichotomy between so-called rational and irrational behaviour, thus calling into question the veracity of complainants. They also 'over-simplified' the context of sexual assault by controlling the complainant's answers by making statements with which she was required to either agree or disagree; for example, 'You had no reason to not tell the police'; 'The text messages show, don't they, an attempt to patch up a relationship' and 'He's quite a bit shorter than you, isn't he?'. On the positive side:

> comments made by prosecution barristers and judges aimed to challenge these [myths]. In fact, prosecution barristers resisted stereotypes at some

> point in every full trial, often by outlining the possible reasons for the victim/survivor's 'suspicious' behaviour. (Smith & Skinner, 2017: 453)

While myth-busting directions can be given by judges in sexual assault trial (Judicial Studies Board, 2010), 'judges did not give the full directions listed, but rather summarized their essence and ignored the concrete examples provided' (Smith & Skinner, 2017: 462). Although myth-busting comments were utilised by prosecutors during the trial, many prosecution comments:

> were not particularly complementary about victim/survivors. For example, the T1 prosecution barrister called the three victim/survivors 'stupid' and 'odd' instead of asserting that their actions are common after sexual victimisation. … [O]ne barrister, who was observed in both prosecution and defence roles, used myth-busters when prosecuting, yet invoked myths when defending. (Smith & Skinner, 2017: 453)

Indeed, myth-busting directions can also go the other way and be used to warn juries 'to be cautious about believing the victim/survivor because of their distress' (Smith & Skinner, 2017: 454). Overall, Smith and Skinner (2017: 454) did not find:

> any link between the use of myth-busters and conviction rates. This is not surprising since any challenge to the relevance of myths was strongly undermined by defence barristers and several factors meant they were kept relevant for juries.

But should myths, stereotypes and other inaccurate information about how a sexual assault complainant ought to behave be allowed in sexual assault trials at all? Myth-busting judicial directions implicitly recognise the unfairness of sexual assault trials because defence counsel are generally not constrained in relation to the myths and prejudices they may introduce during cross-examination of the complainant, as well as during their opening and closing addresses. Indeed, in the above study, defence barristers 'challenge[d] myth-buster directions in their closing speeches' by asserting that certain stereotypes might be relevant in the case at hand (Smith & Skinner, 2017: 454). For example:

> [Victim/Survivor] didn't bite, kick or scream ... You don't have to ... but it is good evidence in cases where that does happen and so you may think it's useful to know that she didn't bite, kick or scream. (Smith & Skinner, 2017: 455)

2.6 Summary

The above discussion reveals the existence of engrained, cultural stereotypes that influence people's perceptions of the responses of female sexual assault victims, including the cultural expectations that a truthful victim will act in particular ways and will not have 'encouraged' the defendant through her 'risky' behaviours. A complainant's behaviours are, therefore, used as a proxy for determining lack of consent, thus raising the question, what are the implications of victim behaviours that do not match expectations associated with the stranger-rape stereotype?

Rape myths are based on simplified, 'model' or 'ideal' (that is, gendered) behaviours for women, with victim and gender stereotypes 'serv[ing] to absolve the perpetrator' where there is a mismatch between a complainant's behaviour and the expected behaviours of the 'real' rape victim (Schuller, McKimmie, Masser, & Klippenstine, 2010). Many rape myths embody a belief that:

i. men have a need for, and a right to, have sex;
ii. it is the responsibility of women to control this need; and
iii. women encourage men's need for sex through their dress and flirtatious behaviours which constitutes implicit consent.

Because the 'consensual sexual script is generally agreed upon within cultures and across genders', it is common for defence counsel to adopt this script when challenging a complainant's account by pointing to stereotypical behaviours that 'characterize consensual sex' in order to undermine the complainant's credibility (McKimmie et al., 2014: 2296), with counter-intuitive behaviours well known to be the focus of defence counsel strategies in court (Cossins, 2009; Smith & Skinner, 2017; Zajac, Gross, & Hayne, 2003; Zajac & Hayne, 2003).

Suarez and Gadalla (2010: 2027) have argued that 'rape prevention programs must be broadened to incorporate strategies' that address the beliefs associated with RMA. But how are we to deal with RMA within sexual assault trials to address the use of rape myths, not only by jurors but also by judges and lawyers? How are we to eliminate the acceptance of styles of cross-examination which feed on rape myths and victim blame by turning everyday behaviours by both young men and women, such as dancing, drinking, flirting and staying out late at night, into a narrative that 'she was asking for it'? How are we to educate jurors about the fact that many of the symptoms of sexual victimisation, such as alcohol and drug use (see Table 1, Chapter 4), are misused by the defence to undermine a complainant's credibility?

Adherence to rape myths enables denial of the reality of sexual assault—that stranger-rape is comparatively rare, and that victims react in a variety of ways and do not always display expected physical or emotional reactions (Alderden & Ullman, 2012), such that counter-intuitive and 'risky' behaviours are misinterpreted by laypeople. Overall, RMA and the belief that women and girls commonly lie about sexually assault affects a number of 'real world issues' (Grubb & Turner, 2012: 445), such as:

i. that stranger-rape represents the model for judging the behaviours of victims who are sexually assaulted by relatives, partners, ex-partners, friends or acquaintances;
ii. 'inaccurate portrayal[s] and perception of the number of false rape allegations' (Grubb & Turner, 2012: 445), thus denying the true prevalence of sexual assault;
iii. victims' beliefs in their own victimisation, their ability to recognise what happened to them as sexual assault and, hence, reporting rates. For example, LeMaire, Oswald, and Russell (2016: 332) found that victims with higher RMA endorsement 'were less likely to label their past sexual assault experience as rape';
iv. police investigations and prosecutorial decisions (Frohmann, 1991; Spears & Spohn, 2006; Spohn & Holleran, 2001; Temkin & Krahe, 2008) since prosecutors filter out those cases 'unlikely to result in a

conviction because of questions about the victim's character, ... [and] behavior' (Spears & Spohn, 2006: 501); and

v. jury decision-making.

The fact that men are more likely to endorse RMA than women suggests that a jury dominated by men would be more likely to return a not guilty verdict in a sexual assault trial, particularly in cases where the evidence is ambiguous and/or the complainant's conduct before, during or after the assault is perceived as 'risky' or blame-worthy behaviour. Indeed the 'strong positive association between RMA and sexual aggression and other hostile attitudes' (Suarez & Gadalla, 2010: 2025) towards women suggests that a complainant's conduct and credibility will be central to a jury that is dominated by those with hostile attitudes towards women.

3 Interactions Between Offence, Victim and Perpetrator Stereotypicality

It goes without saying that the effect of extra-legal factors on jury decision-making in sexual assault trials is complex so that it is important to understand the relationship between the key aspects of a sexual assault trial: the type of offence (stranger vs acquaintance); the victim's characteristics and behaviours; and the perpetrator's characteristics and behaviours. A number of mock jury studies have been able to provide further insights into the interactive effects of various stereotypes on credibility assessments and verdicts.

Schuller et al. (2010) examined the difference between mock jurors' endorsement of gender stereotypes compared to victim stereotypes in determining the influence of myths and misconceptions on jurors' decision-making. Based on existing research that suggested that 'emotionality [of the complainant] is ... congruent with the feminine stereotype', Schuller et al. (2010: 768; 770) explored 'if, and how, perceptions of emotionality interact with victim and gender stereotypes to influence judgments of sexual assault victims'; that is, whether or not both '"good" women and "good" victims should be emotionally expressive'.

In their study, the calm and unemotional victim was perceived as being less representative of both women and rape victims in general, while the complainant who physically and verbally resisted the defendant was perceived to be more like a 'real' victim. Compared to the victim who only resisted verbally, the physically resistant complainant's claim of sexual assault was rated as more believable. Believability was also higher for the emotionally distressed complainant, compared to the calm/controlled victim. However, the influence of emotional distress was only found when the complainant was gender stereotypic, that is, when she was portrayed as a 'good' mother compared to the complainant who was portrayed as a 'bad' mother. Significantly more blame for the sexual assault was apportioned to the 'bad' mother (counter gender stereotypic behaviour) compared to the 'good' mother while the validity of the claims made by the 'bad' mother and the non-emotional, 'good' mother were both perceived to be low.

Schuller et al. (2010) concluded that the validity of a sexual assault claim is viewed through two stereotypical prisms, in that a complainant's allegation and credibility is measured according to the expectations associated with her gender and with a 'typical' victim; that is, a victim who conforms to gender expectations and acts like a 'typical' victim (high emotionality and physically resistant) will be viewed more positively. But this raises the question, isn't the concept of the typical victim, itself, a gendered concept? Has the literature ignored this relationship?

Masser et al. (2010) also manipulated gender and victim stereotypes in order to determine the independent effects of good/bad gender stereotypes versus real/not real victim stereotypes on mock juror attributions of blame in sexual assault scenarios. They found that gender stereotypicality (good mother versus bad mother behaviour) only influenced blame attributions when the complainant acted like a counter-stereotypical victim, that is, by not physically resisting the perpetrator, although it was not clear from their research why victim stereotypes were not considered to be based on gendered stereotypes.

In other words, the concept of a stereotypical victim is not gender neutral because of the cultural climate in which sex offences are prosecuted and the historical origins of victim stereotypes (as discussed above). Thus, blame attributions appear to depend on gendered expectations of female victim behaviour so that the good mother/bad mother stereotype reinforces the concept of stereotypical and counter-stereotypical victim behaviour in particular circumstances.

McKimmie et al. (2014) carried out a further study to examine the independent effects of offence prototypicality and victim stereotypicality on mock jurors' perceptions in simulated sexual assault scenarios which involved acquaintance and stranger rape scenarios. The study was based on the concept of cognitive schemas (stereotypes and crime prototypes) for interpreting case evidence and witness credibility.

Generally speaking, it appears that the less a complainant matches the qualities of a stereotypical rape victim, the more she will be blamed for the defendant's sexual behaviour (Masser et al., 2010; McKimmie et al., 2014) which supports the view that victim stereotypicality is a gendered concept. However, because there are several variables in each different sexual assault case, such as the type of relationship between complainant and defendant, degree of resistance, and the social context in which the sexual act occurred, understanding the precise schemas or stereotypes that operate, and the point at which they operate in a trial, is 'critically important ... in identifying how to understand and overcome their potentially negative influence' (McKimmie et al., 2014: 2277). It is also important to understand how offence prototypes interact with victim and gender stereotypes.

To this end, McKimmie et al. (2014) carried out a study with 420 community members who read rape scenarios which described either a stranger or an acquaintance rape incident. These two scenarios were manipulated for victim stereotypicality:

i. the complainant physically resisted the removal of her clothing and cooperated with police;
ii. the complainant did not physically resist (only asking the defendant to stop) and did not fully cooperate with police.

The authors found that RMA was a significant predictor on outcomes, 'with stronger endorsement of rape myths associated with a lower likelihood of a guilty verdict', as well as lower ratings of complainant credibility and defendant blame, and higher ratings of victim blame

(McKimmie et al., 2014: 2283; 2285). However, guilty verdicts were more likely 'when the offense was stereotypic [stranger rape] and also when the victim was stereotypic [physically resistant]'. In this context, '[p]articipants had more positive perceptions of the complainant and the prosecution case and less positive evaluations of the defendant and the defense case' (McKimmie et al., 2014: 2287).

It was only in the acquaintance rape scenario that victim stereotypicality influenced participants' views of the complainant which were more positive than when the victim's behaviour was counter-stereotypical. With the latter behaviour, participants were *less* likely to find the defendant guilty and the complainant was perceived as less credible and more to blame.

Comments provided by participants who read the acquaintance rape/counter-stereotypical scenario were even more illuminating, such as '"[c]omplainant's decisions or behaviour on the night put her at risk of rape"' which was the most frequent reason for a not guilty verdict (McKimmie et al., 2014: 2289; 2293), confirming the views expressed in other studies that women's behaviours incite rape. This study shows that mock jurors focused on the complainant's behaviour when the defendant was an acquaintance, but focused on the defendant's behaviour in the stranger rape situation, such that a woman's 'risky' behaviour is used to measure her degree of responsibility, indicating that jurors judge victim behaviour through the lens of gender expectations.

Thus, perceptions of sexual assault are gendered and contextual so that when the parties are known to each other, these perceptions appear to depend on the female complainant's behaviour which will be measured through the lens of stereotypical expectations about female victims' behaviours such as physical resistance, and not leading a man on. Thus, the main comments made by participants in the acquaintance rape scenario 'focused on establishing whether consent to the sexual act was given or implied' (McKimmie et al., 2014: 2294), results which assist in considering reform options for the vast majority of sexual assaults, that is, where the defendant is known to the complainant.

Interestingly, Süssenbach, Eyssel, Rees, and Bohner (2017) found that when participants in their mock jury study were given the opportunity to select more information about a complainant or a defendant in a rape trial scenario, those with higher RMA scores showed a preference for information about the complainant. These results supported their hypothesis that:

> RMA functions in terms of a cognitive schema that actively guides information search when individuals are confronted with a rape case, resulting in a focus away from the perpetrator and toward the victim, whose characteristics and behavior are at the heart of most rape myths. (ibid., 2332)

More recently, Bongiorno, McKimmie, and Masser (2016) found that when presented with counter-stereotypic victim behaviour, mock jurors who were culturally similar to perpetrators considered them to be less guilty and less deserving of punishment, compared to those who were culturally dissimilar. This increased leniency shown towards culturally similar perpetrators was explained by increases in victim blame and decreases in perpetrator blame.

However, it is not possible to determine whether laypeople 'start with the "real rape" crime prototype … in attempting to interpret what happened and how blame should be apportioned' (McKimmie et al., 2014: 2294), since it is also possible that laypeople begin with moral assumptions about women who complain of sexual assault and judge the complainant's behaviour accordingly. As McKimmie et al. (2014: 2294) recognised:

> the 'complainant's decisions or behaviour on the night put her at risk of rape' was the most frequently given reason for [a not guilty] verdict. This theme was most dominant in the acquaintance rape/counter-stereotypical victim condition.

This suggests that in acquaintance rape cases, jurors begin with an assessment of the female complainant's behaviour in order to determine whether her behaviour amounts to implied consent.

Finally, Stuart et al. (2016: 9) found that when they manipulated perpetrator and victim characteristics, 'typical rape victims' were seen by mock jurors as significantly more weak or vulnerable, frightened, helpless, scared, sad and depressed, ashamed and embarrassed and to have lower self-esteem than women in general. Typical rapists were perceived to be significantly more aggressive, angry towards women, insensitive, impulsive and significantly less socially skilled than men in general. When they examined the influence of offence, victim and perpetrator stereotypes on perceptions of victim and defendant behaviour, they found that mock jurors perceived the victim more positively and the perpetrator more negatively when both the offence and victim were described as stereotypical (stranger rape, aggressive force, victim who physically resisted).

However, perpetrator stereotypicality had no effect on perceptions of the victim's behaviour while the effect of victim stereotypicality did not differ as a function of offence stereotypicality. Instead, victim stereotypicality predicted how the perpetrator was perceived: the perpetrator was perceived as more stereotypical when the victim was stereotypical than when she was counter-stereotypical, thus confirming the finding from other studies that a female victim's behaviour influences perceptions of responsibility and that victim stereotypes are gendered concepts.

Because the authors also found that victim stereotypicality affected perceptions of offence stereotypicality, this suggests that gendered assumptions about women are the default stereotype that guides mock jurors' perceptions of blame, responsibility and consent, including perceptions of the defendant's behaviour. Since particular victim behaviours are not elements of a sexual assault offence, the complainant's behaviour should not logically affect perceptions of a perpetrator's conduct. Nonetheless, her behaviour appears to be the filter through which judgements about the alleged sexual conduct are made, suggesting that, for example, a resistant victim colours observers' perceptions of the defendant's conduct compared with a non-resistant victim.

The saliency of this approach by jurors makes sense when the cultural context in which these perceptions are made is taken into account—a context which is populated by images of sexually 'provocative' women and girls who enjoy forcible sex together with images of sexually entitled men, as discussed above. In other words, if predatory sexual relations are culturally normative, then a female victim's response may be the only measure for determining lack of consent.

In summary, the above studies show:

i. the less that a complainant matches the qualities of a stereotypical rape victim, the more she will be blamed for the defendant's sexual behaviour, suggesting that victim stereotypes are gendered concepts;
ii. gender stereotypicality only influences blame attributions when the complainant acts like a counter-stereotypical victim;
iii. mock jurors perceive a victim more positively and the perpetrator more negatively when both the offence and victim are described as stereotypical, (stranger rape, aggressive force, victim who physically resisted);
iv. guilty verdicts are more likely in stranger rape cases and also when the victim acts in stereotypic ways, such as being physically resistant;
v. when the victim's behaviour is counter-stereotypical, the defendant is less likely to be found guilty and the complainant is perceived as less credible and more to blame;
vi. perpetrator stereotypicality has no effect on perceptions of a victim's behaviour;
vii. victim stereotypicality predicts how the perpetrator is perceived—the perpetrator is perceived as more stereotypical when the victim is stereotypical than when she is counter-stereotypical;
viii. victim stereotypicality affects perceptions of offence stereotypicality;
ix. the effect of victim stereotypicality did not differ as a function of offence stereotypicality;
x. mock jurors focus on the complainant's behaviour when the defendant is an acquaintance, but focus on the defendant's behaviour in stranger rape scenarios;
xi. mock jurors who are culturally similar to perpetrators consider them to be less guilty and less deserving of punishment, as a result of increases in victim blame and decreases in perpetrator blame;
xii. overall, a female victim's behaviour influences perceptions of responsibility for both parties, leading to the conclusion that gendered perceptions of victim stereotypicality are the driving force behind credibility assessments and verdicts in sexual assault trials.

Is it possible to prevent jurors from relying on stereotypical, gendered perceptions of female complainants' behaviours? Arguably, the sexual assault trial is a gendered cultural space, with both male and female

Table 2 Cultural expectations of victims' responses to rape compared to documented responses of victims to trauma

Expected features of a rape scenario	Expected (masculine) responses to trauma/threats	Documented responses of victims to trauma/threats
Location: public space	Scream, shout to alert passers-by	Silence due to tonic immobility or freeze response
Resistance	Physical resistance, fight	Freeze response
Injury	Demonstrable injuries	Lack of resistance minimises injuries Medically unusual for genital injuries
Complaint	Immediate complaint	Delayed response due to shame, psychological trauma, self-blame

gender stereotypes influencing perceptions of complainants, and, in turn perceptions of defendants, as illustrated in Table 2.

As Table 2 demonstrates, there is a huge gap between 'commonsense' expectations about how sexual assault victims should respond and the reality of a sexual assault victim's psychological and physiological responses to trauma. How to bridge this gap will be discussed in Chapters 11 and 12.

4 Mock Jurors' Beliefs About Victims of Child Sexual Abuse

The type and extent of the misconceptions held by laypeople about children's reliability as witnesses and their responses to CSA have been established in a number of studies (Cossins, 2008; Cossins, Goodman-Delahunty, & O'Brien, 2009; Goodman-Delahunty, Martschuk, & Cossins, 2017a) so that the influence of jurors' pre-existing misconceptions on their perceptions of credibility and verdict cannot be discounted in filling in the gaps in evidence in CSA trials.

Like the studies involving adult sexual assault trials, these studies also demonstrate the centrality of a child's credibility to jurors' decision-making. As with adult complainants, the believability of a child's story and her/his credibility are predictors of defendant guilt, although laypeople's perceptions of credibility are mediated by their age, gender, education and misconceptions. Nonetheless, CSA trials feature an added complicating factor due to the range of misconceptions that laypeople hold about children's ability to give reliable evidence.

Juror gender exerts a significant main effect in that men are more sceptical than women about children's claims of sexual abuse and rate children as less believable, less credible and less competent and more culpable for the abuse than do women (Bottoms & Goodman, 1994; Clark & Nightingale, 1997; Crowley, O'Callaghan, & Ball, 1994; Devine & Caughlin, 2014; Gabora, Spanos, & Joab, 1993; Golding, Bradshaw, Dunlap, & Hodell, 2007; Goodman-Delahunty et al., 2010; McCauley & Parker, 2001; Orcutt, Goodman, Tobey, Batterman-Faunce, & Thomas, 2001; Quas, Bottoms, Haegerich, & Nysse-Carris, 2002).

Compared to women, men give higher estimates of false reports by children (Quas et al., 2002) while '[w]omen tend to be more positive about children's competence as witnesses, their ability to identify assailants, and their memory for trauma' (McCoy & Gray, 2007). As well, juror characteristics are related to the type of misconceptions jurors hold about CSA and children's reliability as witnesses in that men are significantly more likely to endorse misconceptions about CSA than women (Cossins, 2008; Goodman-Delahunty et al., 2010).

The more positive views held by women about children's claims of sexual abuse are evident in the results that have shown that female jurors and jury-eligible citizens are more likely to convict in a CSA trial, compared to their male counterparts (Devine & Caughlin, 2014).

An Australian study on the misconceptions held by a representative sample of jury-eligible citizens investigated their knowledge about children's memory, reliability, suggestibility and responses to sexual abuse (Cossins et al., 2009). The results showed that gender, age and educational attainment were associated with the degree of endorsement of CSA misconceptions. On average, participants correctly answered only 4% of the 20 items contained in a questionnaire created for the study although they 'held the most erroneous views about children's ability to provide reliable and truthful accounts of their experiences' (Cossins et al., 2009: 441).

A majority of participants were unsure about 35% of the questionnaire items and 'reported high rates of uncertainty … [about] a number of statements that might affect a juror's perception of a child's credibility'. These included uncertainty about: whether a child would avoid the abuser, that abused children show strong emotional reactions, that a physical examination rarely provides evidence of sexual abuse and that non-leading, open-ended questions are unlikely to lead children to make false claims of sexual abuse (Cossins et al., 2009: 440; 442).

This lack of understanding of children's reactions to sexual abuse and children's memory and reliability as witnesses influences mock jurors' credibility assessments and verdicts. For example, Gabora et al. (1993) found that jurors' endorsements of misconceptions were associated with low ratings of complainant credibility, fewer guilty verdicts and higher ratings of defendant credibility. Similar results were reported by Goodman-Delahunty et al. (2011) in that endorsement of CSA misconceptions by mock jurors negatively impacted their ratings of complainant credibility and their verdicts in simulated CSA trials, with the impact of jurors' misconceptions on verdict being mediated by the perceived credibility of the child complainant.

More recently, Goodman-Delahunty et al. (2017a) conducted a study with a large group of actual jurors ($n = 1931$) called for jury duty in order to assess their beliefs and attitudes about CSA, including their knowledge about children's memory, suggestibility and reactions to sexual abuse. The authors reported that, generally, although '[m]ore than two-thirds of jurors thought that children's memories were accurate, and that children could be trusted to provide reliable evidence', nearly two-thirds (62.4%) 'believed that children could … be persuaded by an adult to say something untruthful' (Goodman-Delahunty et al., 2017a: 93). As well, 'approximately one third of the jurors had some doubts or reservations about children's capacity as reliable witnesses and their suggestibility, and would be reluctant to convict a defendant on the basis of evidence given by a child' (ibid.). The misconceptions that attracted the greatest level of incorrect agreement and greatest levels of uncertainty were:

i. A medical examination almost always shows whether or not a child was sexually abused;
ii. Children are easily coached to make false claims of sexual abuse;
iii. Children aged 7–8 years are easily manipulated to give false reports of sexual abuse;
iv. Children sometimes make false claims of sexual abuse to get back at an adult;
v. A child victim of sexual abuse will avoid their abuser; and
vi. Children who are sexually abused display strong emotional reactions afterwards.

Generally, we know that jurors with greater knowledge and fewer misconceptions about CSA are more likely to believe a complainant and to convict, than jurors with less knowledge and more misconceptions about CSA; and that the perceived credibility of the child complainant mediates verdict (Goodman-Delahunty et al., 2011; Goodman-Delahunty, Cossins, & Martschuk, 2016).

Table 3 lists the types of misconceptions about children and CSA identified in various studies since 1992. It documents the extent to which jurors and/or laypeople agreed with these misconceptions. Misconceptions are listed in the table according to the extent to which participants *incorrectly* agreed with them, commencing with those that had the highest levels of incorrect agreement.

The top five misconceptions focus on the falsity of a child's allegation and the belief that a medical examination will show evidence of the abuse, with studies showing relatively high levels of agreement that children's abuse claims are often false and that children are easily manipulated into making false claims of abuse.

Even for misconceptions with relatively low levels of agreement, Cossins et al. (2009) and Goodman-Delahunty et al. (2017a) reported relatively high levels of uncertainty about: 'Children are sometimes led by an adult to report they have been abused when they have not'; 'Repeatedly asking children general, open-ended questions (e.g. what

Table 3 Laypeople's and jurors' misconceptions about children's responses to sexual abuse and suggestibility as witnesses[a]

Beliefs	Agreement(%)*	Study
1. Abuse claims made by 4- or 8-year- olds are false	77[b]	Quas et al. (2005)
1a. Abuse claims often prove to be false	>33	Morison and Greene (1992)
2. A psychologist can tell whether a child's description of an event has been influenced by another adult	68	Quas et al. (2005)
3. A physical examination by a doctor will almost always show whether a child has been sexually abused	57	Quas et al. (2005) Kovera and Borgida (1997)
	21.4 (46.7 uncertain)	Cossins et al. (2009)
	29.4 (25.3 uncertain)	Goodman-Delahunty et al. (2017a)
4. Children are easily manipulated into giving false reports of sexual abuse	53	Kovera and Borgida (1997)
	>50	Quas et al. (2005)
	>50	Morison and Greene (1992)
	8.8 (51.1 uncertain)	Cossins et al. (2009)
	23.6 (38.1 uncertain)	Goodman-Delahunty et al. (2017a)
4a. Children are sometimes led by an adult to report they have been abused when they have not	29.7 (61.2 uncertain)	Cossins et al. (2009)
4b. Children can be persuaded by an adult to say something untruthful	62.4 (31.5 uncertain)	Goodman-Delahunty et al. (2017a)
5. Child sexual abuse will result in physical damage and physical evidence	>50	Kovera and Borgida (1997)
	>50	Morison and Greene (1992)
6. Repeatedly asking children general, open-ended questions (e.g. what happened?) leads them to make false claims of sexual abuse	46	Quas et al. (2005)
	4.1 (49.8 uncertain)	Cossins et al. (2009)

(continued)

Table 3 (continued)

Beliefs	Agreement(%)*	Study
7. Most sexually abused children exhibit bizarre sexualised behaviour	41	Quas et al. (2005)
7a. Children who are abused display strong emotional reactions	26.6 (51.7 uncertain)	Cossins et al. (2009)
	47.8 (31.1 uncertain)	Goodman-Delahunty et al. (2017a)
8. A victim of sexual abuse will avoid the abuser	34.1 (42.3 uncertain)	Cossins et al. (2009)
	43.2 (29.6 uncertain)	Goodman-Delahunty et al. (2017a)
9. A typical victim would resist, cry out for help or escape the offender	>33	Morison and Greene (1992)
	20.8 (30.2 uncertain)	Cossins et al. (2009)
9a. A sexually abused child typically cries out for help and tries to escape	19.5 (26.1 uncertain)	Goodman-Delahunty et al. (2017a)
9b. Child victims of sexual abuse respond in a similar way to the abuse	16.8 (38.7 uncertain)	Goodman-Delahunty et al. (2017a)
10. Children sometimes make up false claims of sexual abuse for revenge	33	Quas et al. (2005)
	7.5 (60.5 uncertain)	Cossins et al. (2009)
10a. Children sometimes make up stories about being sexually abused when they actually have not	5.9 (63.1 uncertain)	Cossins et al. (2009)
10b. Children sometimes make false claims of sexual abuse to get back at an adult	25.7 (42.7 uncertain)	Goodman-Delahunty et al. (2017a)
11. Children cannot remember events well enough to be reliable witnesses	31	Quas et al. (2005)
11a. Children can be trusted to give reliable statements	66.5 (31.7 uncertain)	Goodman-Delahunty et al. (2017a)
11b. Children can accurately remember past events	68.9 (27.6 uncertain)	Goodman-Delahunty et al. (2017a)
11c. Memories of children aged 7–8 years about traumatic events are not as accurate as those of adults	13.4 (22.3 uncertain)	Goodman-Delahunty et al. (2017a)

(continued)

Table 3 (continued)

Beliefs	Agreement(%)*	Study
12. Inconsistencies in a child's report is evidence of lying	29 29 2.1 (35.5 uncertain) 8.1 (20.2 uncertain)	Quas et al. (2005) Morison and Greene (1992) Cossins et al. (2009) Goodman-Delahunty et al. (2017a)
13. When a child discloses more details over time, this indicates the report is false	25 6.9 (20.7 uncertain)	Quas et al. (2005) Goodman-Delahunty et al. (2017a)
14. Few child sex abuse cases are based on physical evidence	23.1 [64.6 uncertain]	Cossins et al. (2009)
15. Children who retract their reports have fabricated 15a. Children who change their reports of sexual abuse were probably lying in the first place	21 21 1.7 (24.7 uncertain) 9.7 (25.9 uncertain)	Quas et al. (2005) Morison and Greene (1992) Cossins et al. (2009) Goodman-Delahunty et al. (2017a)
16. Delay in complaint is evidence of lying	9 1.8 (13.8 uncertain)	Quas et al. (2005) Cossins et al. (2009)
17. Stepfathers are more likely to abuse children than natural fathers 17a. The perpetrator of CSA is normally a stranger to the child 17b. A friend or family member is less likely to sexually abuse a child than a stranger	16.5 (51.6 uncertain) 4.1 (19.7 uncertain) 15.8 (14.8 uncertain)	Cossins et al. (2009) Cossins et al. (2009) Goodman-Delahunty et al. (2017a)

(continued)

Table 3 (continued)

Beliefs	Agreement(%)*	Study
18. Repeatedly asking children specific questions (e.g. did he touch your private parts?) often leads them to make false claims of sexual abuse	58 17.3 (67.7 uncertain)	Quas et al. (2005) Cossins et al. (2009)
18a. Repeating questions such as 'What happened? What else happened?' leads children to make false abuse claims	16.8 (39.8 uncertain)	Goodman-Delahunty et al. (2017a)

[a]Table 3 is an updated version of Table 1 in Cossins (2008)

[b]Specifically, 49% of jurors/laypeople believed that 10–30% of sexual abuse claims were false and 28% of jurors and laypeople believed that 35->50% of claims were false (Quas et al., 2005)

*Percentages are quoted where they are provided by the study in question

happened?) leads them to make false claims of sexual abuse'; 'Children who are abused display strong emotional reactions' and 'A victim of abuse will avoid their abuser'. The extent to which jurors incorrectly agree with, or are uncertain about, particular misconceptions suggests that jurors may be vulnerable to defence counsel suggestions that reinforce these misconceptions, the most common being allegations of a false complaint.

5 The Heuristic-Systematic Processing Model of Juror Decision-Making

The above summary of the literature invites the difficult question as to whether the decision-making capacities of laypeople as jurors are inadequate for the complex tasks required of them in sexual assault trials, since almost every aspect of the realities of sexual assault are in conflict with 'commonsense' beliefs about victims and perpetrators.

In order to understand why the disputed evidence in a sexual assault trial invites the use of myths, prejudices and misconceptions, the theoretical framework proposed by Chaiken and colleagues which describes a dual-process model of jurors' decision-making—the heuristic-systematic processing model—is described below (Chaiken, 1980; Chaiken & Trope, 1990; Chen, Shechter, & Chaiken, 1996; Eagly & Chaiken, 1993; see also Gigerenzer, Todd, & the ABC Research Group, 1999).

What we know about jury decision-making, generally, is that:

i. 'jurors' decisions involve a complex and nuanced set of cognitive processes that transform difficult choices into easier ones by amplifying one alternative perspective on the evidence and deflating competing perspectives' (Winter & Greene, 2007: 741);
ii. individuals, generally, hold particular beliefs and attitudes that affect their reasoning processes and 'bias reasoning performance'; and
iii. when jurors are 'faced with complicated cognitive tasks' and lack the motivation or ability to understand and interpret the evidence, they will rely on heuristic cues to determine guilt (Chen & Chaiken, 1999; Winter & Greene, 2007).

Gigerenzer and Gaissmaier (2011: 454) define a heuristic as:

> a strategy that ignores part of the information, with the goal of making decisions more quickly, frugally, and/or accurately than more complex methods.

The heuristic-systematic processing model posits that two particular processes mediate individual decision-making. Heuristic processing, sometimes referred to as the conflict 'between the "head" and the "heart"' (Süssenbach, Albrecht, & Bohner, 2017: 292; citing Gawronski & Bodenhausen, 2014: 448), involves little or no scrutiny of evidence and low cognitive effort because the individual uses (persuasive) heuristic cues or generalisations about human behaviour, such as 'there's no smoke without fire' or 'children always lie', or other stereotypes to arrive at a decision. This is also known as implicit evaluation (as opposed to explicit evaluation: Süssenbach, Albrecht et al., 2017) and is an inherently unreliable method since heuristics are derived from individual beliefs and experience which may not accurately reflect the human behaviour that is the subject of a criminal trial.

Heuristic processing tends to be relied on when individuals are required to process ambiguous or incongruent evidence (which typically arises in a circumstantial evidence case, such as a sexual assault trial) but lack the ability or motivation to engage in systematic processing. This latter type of reasoning involves greater scrutiny of the evidence and higher cognitive effort, particularly as the complexity of the evidence increases. The higher a person's motivation and the less his or her emotional involvement in a case, the more likely he or she will engage in systematic processing (Maheswaran & Chaiken, 1991).

The use of heuristics will depend on the degree of emotional involvement of the fact-finder which is likely to be influenced by levels of RMA, identification with the complainant or the defendant and individual experiences of similar crimes, along with factors such as gender, age and education.

Studies show that individuals also use heuristics when under time pressures or when there is a large amount of information to process (Bröder, 2000; Newell, Weston, & Shanks, 2003; Rieskamp & Hoffrage, 2008; Rieskamp & Otto, 2006). For example, judges and magistrates rely on heuristics to determine bail and sentencing decisions when under time constraints as a result of heavy caseloads (Brehmer, 1994; Dhami & Ayton, 2001). Dhami and Ayton (2001: 160) found that a majority of the British magistrates in their study showed inconsistency in bail decisions even though all were 'highly confident' that they had made appropriate decisions. Their decisions were based on a 'fast and frugal model' that utilised heuristics:

> magistrates based their bail decisions on one cue [either defendant or crime-control related] and they differed as to the information they used. ... Finally, magistrates' explicit statements of cue use did not match that proposed by the models of their decision making policies. (ibid.)

In fact, Dhami (2003) found that 'the fast and frugal model' correctly predicted 92% and 85% of all magistrates' decisions in two London courts, respectively.

Because '[t]here is an inverse-U-shaped relation between level of accuracy and amount of information, computation, or time', sometimes heuristics can be useful, decision-making strategies (Gigerenzer & Gaissmaier, 2011: 454). However, caution is required in legal settings, since, as Bieneck and Krahé (2011: 1786–1787) observe, 'legal decision making is normatively required to be data [or evidence] driven'; that is, the verdict in a criminal case is supposed to be based on an interpretation and weighing of the admissible evidence. However:

> decisions made in the legal context are potentially susceptible to the same biases and limitations that characterise social information processing in general, such as the tendency to interpret information selectively by concentrating on what is consistent with the perceiver's pre-existing attitudes. (ibid.)

The stereotypes that make up various rape myths, for example, represent 'generalized knowledge structures' (Bieneck & Krahé, 2011: 1787) which are used to attribute blame and responsibility, assess witness credibility and arrive at a verdict. The use of such generalisations presents a major problem for the criminal justice system since 'legal definitions of sexual assault typically do not contain references to' factors, such as 'the type of victim-perpetrator relationship' or the victim's behaviour (ibid.).

Within a criminal justice setting, the use of heuristics is also problematic because this form of decision-making 'does not search through all available information, does not weigh information in an optimal way, does not integrate all relevant information and bases its decision on only one cue' (Dhami & Ayton, 2001: 161).

For example, a study of sentencing decisions by prosecutors found that they 'considered only a limited number of factors and neglected factors that are legally relevant and rated as highly important' as a result of relying on 'simple decision heuristics' (von Helversen & Rieskamp, 2009: 387; 388). While the use of heuristics depends on the legal task, some evidence shows that 'that the position of the decision-maker in the decision hierarchy has an important influence on the strategies' applied so that the inability to rely on another's decision might result in a decision-maker using compensatory measures such as heuristics (ibid., 389). The authors conclude that '[t]o change the decision process, it appears necessary to additionally formulate "procedural" rules (in addition to "factual" rules) that specify how factors should be used in arriving at a decision' (ibid.).

A number of factors may influence jurors' interpretations, motivations and emotional involvement in the evidence and facts of a case, such as pre-trial publicity (which may establish a pro-prosecution bias), activation statements by trial counsel and judges (discussed in Chapter 6), individuals' own experiences of similar crimes or events, as well as their own skills, competencies and individual differences such as gender, age and education (Devine & Caughlin, 2014) and their beliefs in the constancy of human behaviour.

Heuristic cues may arise from any one of these influences or other persuasive factors to do with the trial such as the impressive reputation of an expert witness, 'the heinous character of the crime [or] the horrific nature of certain evidence' (Winter & Greene, 2007: 746). An individual's processing style influences his/her understanding of evidence and, therefore, the quality of his/her reasoning. In a complex trial or one relying solely on circumstantial evidence, 'difficulties in comprehension may spark different processing strategies. For example, confusion may lead to a recourse to heuristics' (Honess & Charman, 2002: 73) and incomplete or inadequate interpretation of the evidence.

Charman, Honess, and Levi (2001) found that when jurors' comprehension difficulties triggered heuristic processing, this was associated with poorer evidence recall. This type of reasoning may also influence jurors to make up their minds early in the trial (also known as predecisional distortion: Carlson & Russo, 2001) and, once that occurs, 'they stop thinking about the evidence too hard' (Honess & Charman, 2002: 74). Both judges and jurors are susceptible to heuristic reasoning when gaps in the evidence give rise to confusion.

In order to determine whether or not jurors in a sexual assault trial use heuristic cues based on their degree of RMA, it is necessary to assess the extent to which they engage in systematic (or explicit) processing of the evidence compared with less effortful, heuristic (or implicit) reasoning.

To this end, Süssenbach, Albrecht et al. (2017) investigated implicit and explicit evaluations of two rape scenarios: the first represented the facts of a stranger-rape while the second, an acquaintance-rape scenario, deviated from the facts of the 'real' rape. By focusing on the processes that influence verdict and blame attributions, they found that:

> situational (i.e. specifics of the rape case) and personal factors (i.e. RMA) influence implicit judgments of a rape case (just as they influence explicit judgments). … [T]he results imply that people's gut responses to a case add to the explanation of their final explicit judgment – particularly for people with a low NFC [need for cognition], who do not like to engage in effortful processing, this effect was pronounced. (ibid., 299)[12]

Specifically, those with higher RMA levels, men, and those in the 'non-real-rape' case were more likely to be 'strongly pro-perpetrator and anti-victim'. As well, 'participants' implicit associations regarding the rape case predicted their explicit case judgments' (ibid., 299). Thus, implicit evaluations are influenced by situational and individual factors which, in turn, influence explicit judgements, such as verdict and blame. However, the authors noted that, '[a]lthough people with a low NFC showed a particularly pronounced relationship between implicit and explicit judgments', this effect was also evident in those with high NFC, although weaker. Thus, as suggested by the large literature on RMA, the participants in this study 'seem to have relied to varying degrees on their first gut response to the case. This gut response— just like the later explicit verdict— was already influenced by a situational variation, the manipulation of the rape case, and attitudinal differences' (ibid., 300).

In summary, this study shows, for the first time, clear evidence of the association between implicit evaluations and explicit judgements (verdict, blame). Even though 'a certain amount of influence of one's gut response on explicit case judgments is to be expected and acceptable', it is important to ask under which conditions the influence of implicit evaluations or heuristics (such as RMA) can be reduced in order to increase the likelihood of more effortful, systematic reasoning in sexual assault trials (ibid., 301).

Indeed, Eyssel and Bohner (2011) showed that when participants read a vignette of a rape case, those who had high RMA and received more

---

[12]Need for cognition (NFC) is 'a personality variable that reflects the extent to which individuals enjoy … engag[ing] in effortful cognitive activities' (Süssenbach, Albrecht et al., 2017: 294).

irrelevant evidence were less likely to blame the defendant, suggesting that the irrelevant information increased the impact of RMA, possibly through heuristic processing.

Süssenbach, Albrecht et al. (2017) suggest that 'more propositional processing should be encouraged specifically among' those with low NFC such as encouraging observers/jurors to look for information that contradicts their 'gut' reaction or initial judgement since:

> considering the opposite is assumed to be an effective corrective strategy, as it counters biases such as biased information search … . Future research should thus examine whether such an instruction reduces the impact of first implicit case evaluations on individuals' final verdict. (ibid., 301; references omitted)

6 Summary: Jury Decision-Making in Sexual Assault Trials

The jury is inevitably open to criticism when it comes to their role as fact-finders in criminal cases since they comprise a group of laypeople with little or no legal training. A number of studies have shown that juries are not impartial fact-finders since they are prone to taking into account extra-legal or legally irrelevant information in delivering a verdict. In sexual assault trials, this chapter has shown that jurors' decisions are influenced by both the strength of the evidence against the defendant *and* their biases and misconceptions about adult and child victims of sexual assault. In particular, both jurors and mock jurors have been shown to focus primarily on the complainant's behaviour in acquaintance rape scenarios, and primarily on the defendant's behaviour in stranger rape scenarios.

Overall, the summary of the literature in this chapter reveals that observers in simulated sexual assault trials make judgements in relation to blame, credibility and verdict based on the case facts (also known as situational factors), including not only the strength of the prosecution's evidence, but also based on variables that are unrelated to the elements of the offence. These include: the relationship between complainant and defendant, the complainant's behaviour prior to, during and after the offence (such as, consumption of drugs/alcohol, clothing revealingness, lack of physical resistance, delay in reporting), as well as observers' attitudes and adherence to rape myths and misconceptions about children and CSA, that is, factors personal to the decision-maker.

Generally speaking, the more a sexual assault case contains elements that accord with negative victim and gender stereotypes (or with stereotypes about lying children) and the more unlike the 'real rape' stereotype, the more likely it is that blame will be attributed to the complainant and observers will be more likely to find the defendant not guilty. Meta-analyses show that the higher an individual's level of RMA, the more likely it is that an individual will make negative judgements about the complainant and the prosecution's case and acquit the defendant. Similarly, jurors who are more likely to endorse misconceptions about children and CSA are less likely to believe the complainant and more likely to acquit.

Because decision-making is based on an interaction between case factors (legal and extra-legal) and an individual's personal beliefs, it would be inaccurate to conclude that only stranger or 'real' rape scenarios will result in convictions. For example, we know that women are more likely than men to vote guilty in both adult and child sexual assault cases. However, it can be expected that the more ambiguous the prosecution evidence, the more doubts will be created in observers' and jurors' minds and the more they will rely on extra-legal factors to deliver a verdict.

The effects of evidence strength decrease when extra-legal factors are taken into account in statistical analyses, such that omitting the effects of these factors leads to inflated measures of the effects of legally relevant evidence. However, it is worth asking, what do we expect jurors to do when a sexual assault case is word against word, there is little or no evidence to support the complainant's allegations and defence counsel are permitted to undermine the complainant's evidence by relying on myths, prejudice and stereotypes in opening and closing addresses, and when testing the complainant's evidence during cross-examination?

On the other hand, how logical is it for jurors to rely on stereotypes about human behaviour, guesswork and misconceptions to reach a verdict even in word against word cases? Overall, the research on jurors' decision-making reveals that:

i. when jurors are faced with complicated cognitive tasks, such as a case involving ambiguous evidence, and lack the motivation or ability to understand and interpret the evidence, they will rely on heuristic cues to determine guilt, rather than systematic, more effortful processing of the evidence;
ii. there is clear evidence of the association between implicit (heuristic) evaluations (that is, 'gut response') and explicit judgements (verdict, blame).

What can be done to reduce the influence of implicit evaluations or heuristics (such as RMA and misconceptions about CSA) in order to increase the likelihood of more effortful, systematic reasoning in sexual assault trials?

These issues are discussed in the following chapters.

References

Abbey, A., & McAuslan, P. (2004). A longitudinal examination of male college students' perpetration of sexual assault. *Journal of Consulting and Clinical Psychology, 72*, 747–756.

Agres, K., & Wiggins, G. A. (2015). Schematic processing as a framework for learning and creativity in CBR and CC. In *Proceedings of the ICCBR 2015 workshops*. Frankfurt, Germany. http://ceur-ws.org/Vol-1520/paper16.pdf.

Alderden, M. A., & Ullman, S. E. (2012). Creating a more complete and current picture examining police and prosecutor decision-making when processing sexual assault cases. *Violence Against Women, 18*, 525–551.

Allen, M., Emmers, T., Gebhardt, L., & Giery, M. A. (1995). Exposure to pornography and acceptance of rape myths. *Journal of Communication, 45*, 5–26.

Allum, J. (2017, April 7). SCEGGS principal speaks out over alleged rape of student and violence against women. *The Wentworth Courier*.

Aronowitz, T., Lambert, C. A., & Davidoff, S. (2012). The role of rape myth acceptance in the social norms regarding sexual behaviour among college students. *Journal of Community Health Nursing, 29,* 173–182.

Australian Bureau of Statistics (ABS). (2019a). *4510.0—Recorded crime—Victims, Australia, 2018.* https://www.abs.gov.au/AUSSTATS/abs@.nsf/Lookup/4510.0Main+Features12018?OpenDocument.

Basow, S. A., & Minieri, A. (2011). 'You owe me': Effects of date cost, who pays, participant gender, and rape myth beliefs on perceptions of rape. *Journal of Interpersonal Violence, 26,* 479–497.

Bendixen, M., Hendriksen, M., & Nøstdahl, R. K. A. (2014). Toward rape and attribution of responsibility to rape victims in a Norwegian community sample. *Nordic Psychology, 66,* 168–186.

Bieneck, S., & Krahé, B. (2011). Blaming the victim and exonerating the perpetrator in cases of rape and robbery: Is there a double standard? *Journal of Interpersonal Violence, 26,* 1785–1797.

Bleecker, E. T., & Murnen, S. K. (2005). Fraternity membership, the display of degrading sexual images of women, and rape myth acceptance. *Sex Roles, 53,* 487–493.

Bongiorno, R., McKimmie, B. M., & Masser, B. M. (2016). The selective use of rape-victim stereotypes to protect culturally similar perpetrators. *Psychology of Women Quarterly, 40,* 398–413.

Bottoms, B. L., & Goodman, G. S. (1994). Perceptions of children's credibility in sexual assault cases. *Journal of Applied Social Psychology, 24,* 702–732.

Brehmer, B. (1994). The psychology of linear judgment models. *Acta Psychologica, 87,* 137–154.

Bröder, A. (2000). Assessing the empirical validity of the 'take-the-best' heuristic as a model of human probabilistic inference. *Journal of Experimental Psychology: Learning, Memory, and Cognition, 26,* 1332–1346.

Buchwald, E., Fletcher, P., & Roth, M. (1993). Preamble. In E. Buchwald, P. Fletcher, & M. Roth (Eds.), *Transforming a rape culture* (p. vii). Minneapolis: Milkweed Editions.

Buhi, E. R. (2005). Reliability reporting practices in rape myth research. *Journal of School Health, 75,* 63–66.

Burt, M. R. (1980). Cultural myths and supports for rape. *Journal of Personality & Society, 38,* 217–230.

Carlson, K. A., & Russo, J. E. (2001). Biased interpretation of evidence by mock jurors. *Journal of Experimental Psychology: Applied, 7,* 91–103.

Carroll, M. H., Rosenstein, J. E., Foubert, J. D., Clark, M. D., & Korenman, L. M. (2016). Rape myth acceptance: A comparison of military service academy and civilian fraternity and sorority students. *Military Psychology, 28*, 306–317.

Chaiken, S. (1980). Heuristic versus systematic information processing and the use of source versus message cues in persuasion. *Journal of Personality & Social Psychology, 39*, 752–766.

Chaiken, S., & Trope, Y. (1990). *Dual-process theories in social psychology*. New York: Guilford Press.

Charman, E. A., Honess, T. M., & Levi, M. (2001). Juror competence and processing style in making sense of complex trial information. In R. Roesch, R. R. Corrado, & R. J. Dempster (Eds.), *Psychology in the courts: International advances in knowledge* (pp. 83–96). London: Routledge.

Chen, S., & Chaiken, S. (1999). The heuristic-systematic model in its broader context. In S. Chaiken & Y. Trope (Eds.), *Dual-process theories in social psychology* (pp. 73–96). New York: Guilford Press.

Chen, S., Shechter, D., & Chaiken, S. (1996). Getting at the truth or getting along: Accuracy versus impression-motivated heuristic and systematic processing. *Journal of Personality and Social Psychology, 71*, 262–275.

Clark, H. L., & Nightingale, N. N. (1997). When jurors consider recovered memory cases: Effects of victim and juror gender. *Journal of Offender Rehabilitation, 25*, 87–104.

Cohn, E. S., Dupuis, E. C., & Brown, T. M. (2009). In the eye of the beholder: Do behaviour and character affect victim and perpetrator responsibility for acquaintance rape? *Journal of Applied Social Psychology, 39*, 1513–1535.

Cossins, A. (2008). Children, sexual abuse and suggestibility: What laypeople think they know and what the literature tells us. *Psychiatry, Psychology and Law, 15*, 153–170.

Cossins, A. (2009). Cross-examination in child sexual assault trials: Evidentiary safeguard or an opportunity to confuse? *Melbourne University Law Review, 33*, 68–104.

Cossins, A. (2015). Female criminality: Infanticide, moral panics and the female body. Basingstoke, UK: Palgrave Macmillan.

Cossins, A., & Goodman-Delahunty, J. (2013). Misconceptions or expert evidence in child sexual assault trials: Enhancing justice and jurors' 'common sense'. *Journal of Judicial Administration, 22*, 171–190.

Cossins, A., Goodman-Delahunty, J., & O'Brien, K. (2009). Uncertainty and misconceptions about child sexual abuse: Implications for the criminal justice system. *Psychiatry, Psychology & Law, 16*, 435–452.

Cowan, G., & Quinton, W. (1997). Cognitive style and attitudinal correlates of the perceived causes of rape scale. *Pyschology of Women Quarterly, 21,* 227–245.

Cromer, L. D., & Freyd, J. J. (2007). What influences believing child abuse disclosures? The roles of depicted memory persistence, participant gender, trauma history and sexism. *Psychology of Women Quarterly, 2,* 227–245.

Crowley, M. J., O'Callaghan, M. G., & Ball, P. J. (1994). The juridical impact of psychological expert testimony in a simulated child sexual abuse trial. *Law and Human Behavior, 18,* 89–105.

Devine, D. J., & Caughlin, D. E. (2014). Do they matter? A meta-analytic investigation of individual characteristics and guilt judgments. *Psychology, Public Policy, and Law, 20,* 109–134.

Dhami, M. K. (2003). Psychological models of professional decision making. *Psychological Science, 14,* 175–180.

Dhami, M. K., & Ayton, P. (2001). Bailing and jailing the fast and frugal way. *Journal of Behavioral Decision Making, 14,* 141–168.

Driesmans, K., Vandenbosch, L., & Eggermont, S. (2015). Playing a videogame with a sexualized female character increases adolescents' rape myth acceptance and tolerance toward sexual harassment. *Games for Health Journal, 4,* 91–94.

Eagly, A. H., & Chaiken, S. (1993). Process theories of attitude formation and change: The elaboration likelihood and heuristic-systematic models. In A. H. Eagly & S. Chaiken (Eds.), *The psychology of attitudes* (pp. 303–350). Fort Worth, TX: Harcourt, Brace, & Janovich.

Edwards, K. M., Turchik, J. A., Dardis, C. M., Reynolds, N., & Gidycz, C. A. (2011). Rape myths: History, individual and institutional-level presence, and implications for change. *Sex Roles, 65,* 761–773.

Edwards, S. R., Bradshaw, K. A., & Hinsz, V. B. (2014). Denying rape but endorsing forceful intercourse: Exploring differences among responders. *Violence and Gender, 1,* 188–193.

Ellison, L., & Munro, V. E. (2013). Better the devil you know? 'Real Rape' stereotypes and the relevance of a previous relationship in (Mock) juror deliberations. *The International Journal of Evidence & Proof, 17,* 299–322.

End Violence Against Women Coalition. (2018). *Attitudes to sexual consent research.* https://www.endviolenceagainstwomen.org.uk/wp-content/uploads/1-Attitudes-to-sexual-consent-Research-findings-FINAL.pdf.

Eyssel, F., & Bohner, G. (2011). Schema effects of rape myth acceptance on judgments of guilt and blame in rape cases: The role of perceived entitlement to judge. *Journal of Interpersonal Violence, 26,* 1579–1605.

Ferris, A. L., Smith, S. W., Greenberg, B. S., & Smith, S. L. (2007). The content of reality dating shows and viewer perceptions of dating. *Journal of Communications, 57,* 490–510.

Forbes, G. B., Adams-Curtis, L. E., & White, K. B. (2004). First and second-generation of measures of sexism, rape myths and related beliefs, and hostility towards women: Their inter-relationships and association with college students' experiences with dating aggression and sexual coercion. *Violence Against Women, 10,* 236–261.

Forbes, G. B., Adams-Curtis, L. E., Pakalka, A. H., & White, K. B. (2006). Dating aggression, sexual coercion, and aggression-supporting attitudes among college men as a function of participation in aggressive high school sports. *Violence Against Women, 12,* 441–455.

Foubert, J. D., Brosi, M. W., & Bannon, R. S. (2011). Pornography viewing among fraternity men: Effects on bystander intervention, rape myth acceptance and behavioral intent to commit sexual assault. *Sexual Addiction and Compulsivity, 18,* 212–231.

Franuik, R., Seefelt, J. L., & Vandello, J. A. (2008). Prevalence of rape myths in headlines and their effects on attitudes towards rape. *Sex Roles, 58,* 790–801.

Frohmann, L. (1991). Discrediting victims' allegations of sexual assault: prosecutorial accounts of case rejections. *Social Problems, 38,* 213–226.

Gabora, N. J., Spanos, N. P., & Joab, A. (1993). The effects of complainant age and expert psychological testimony in a simulated child sexual abuse trial. *Law and Human Behavior, 17,* 103–119.

Gawronski, B., & Bodenhausen, G. V. (2014). Implicit and explicit evaluation: A brief review of the associative-propositional evaluation model. *Social and Personality Psychology Compass, 8,* 448–462.

Gerger, H., Kley, H., Bohner, G., & Siebler, F. (2007). The acceptance of modern myths about sexual aggression (AMMSA) scale: Development and validation in German and English. *Aggressive Behavior, 33,* 422–440.

Gigerenzer, G., & Gaissmaier, W. (2011). Heuristic decision making. *Annual Review of Psychology, 62,* 451–482.

Gigerenzer, G., Todd, P. M., & The ABC Research Group (Eds.). (1999). *Simple heuristics that make us smart.* New York: Oxford University Press.

Golding, J. M., Bradshaw, G. G., Dunlap, E. E., & Hodell, E. C. (2007). The impact of mock jury gender composition on deliberations and conviction rates in a child sexual assault trial. *Child Maltreatment, 12,* 182–190.

Goodman-Delahunty, J., Cossins, A., & Martschuk, N. (2016). *Jury reasoning in joint and separate trials of institutional child sexual abuse: An empirical study*. Sydney: Royal Commission into Institutional Responses to Child Sexual Abuse.

Goodman-Delahunty, J., Cossins, A., & O'Brien, K. (2010). Enhancing the credibility of complainants in child sexual assault trials: The effect of expert evidence and judicial directions. *Behavioral Sciences & the Law, 28*, 769–783.

Goodman-Delahunty, J., Cossins, A., & O'Brien, K. (2011). A comparison of expert evidence and judicial directions to counter misconceptions in child sexual abuse trials. *Australian and New Zealand Journal of Criminology, 44*, 196–217.

Goodman-Delahunty, J., Martschuk, N., & Cossins, A. (2017a). What Australian jurors know and do not know about evidence of child sexual abuse. *Criminal Law Journal, 41*, 86–103.

Grubb, A., & Turner, E. (2012). Rape myth acceptance, gender role conformity and substance use on victim blaming. *Aggression and Violent Behavior, 17*, 443–452.

Hammond, E. M., Berry, M. A., & Rodriguez, D. N. (2011). The influence of rape myth acceptance, sexual attitudes, and belief in a just world on attributions of responsibility in a date rape scenario. *Legal and Criminological Psychology, 16*, 242–252.

Haslam, N. (2006). Dehumanization: An integrative review. *Personality and Social Psychology Review, 10*, 252–264.

Hayes, R. M., Abbott, R. L., & Cook, S. (2016). It's her fault: Student acceptance of rape myths on two college campuses. *Violence Against Women, 22*, 1540–1555.

Heyes, C. J. (2016). Dead to the world: Rape, unconsciousness, and social media. *Signs: Journal of Women in Culture and Society, 41*(2), 361–383.

Hockett, J. M., Saucier, D. A., Hoffman, B. H., & Craig, A. W. (2009). Oppression through acceptance? Predicting rape myth acceptance and attitudes toward rape victims. *Violence Against Women, 15*, 877–897.

Honess, M., & Charman, E. A. (2002). Members of the jury—Guilty of incompetence? *The Psychologist, 15*, 72–75.

Judicial Studies Board. (2010). *Crown court bench book: Directing the jury*. https://issuu.com/forensicmed/docs/crown_court_benchbook_-_judicial_studies_board/276.

Kahlor, L., & Eastin, M. S. (2011). Television's role in the culture of violence toward women: A study of television viewing and the cultivation of rape myth acceptance in the United States. *Journal of Broadcasting & Electronic Media, 55*, 215–231.

Kovera, M. B., & Borgida, E. (1997). Expert testimony in child sexual abuse trials: The admissibility of psychological science. *Applied Cognitive Psychology, 11,* 105–129.

LeMaire, K. L., Oswald, D. L., & Russell, B. L. (2016). Labeling sexual victimization experiences: The role of sexism, rape myth acceptance, and tolerance for sexual harassment. *Violence and Victims, 31,* 332–346.

Linz, D. G., Donnerstein, E., & Penrod, S. (1988). Effects of long-term exposure to violent and sexually degrading depictions of women. *Journal of Personality and Social Psychology, 55*(5), 758–768.

Lisak, D., & Miller, P. M. (2002). Repeat rape and multiple offending among undetected rapists. *Violence and Victims, 17,* 73–84.

Lisak, D., Gardinier, L., Nicksa, S. C., & Cote, A. M. (2010). False allegations of sexual assault: An analysis of ten years of reported cases. *Violence Against Women, 16,* 1318–1334.

Lonsway, K. A., & Fitzgerald, L. F. (1994). Rape myths: In review. *Psychology of Women Quarterly, 68,* 133–164.

Lonsway, K. A., & Fitzgerald, L. F. (1995). Attitudinal antecedents of rape myth acceptance: A theoretical and empirical examination. *Journal of Personality and Social Psychology, 68,* 704–711.

Loughnan, S., Haslam, N., Murnane, T., Vaes, J., Reynolds, C., & Suitne, C. (2010). Objectification leads to depersonalization: The denial of mind and moral concern to objectified others. *European Journal of Social Pyschology, 40,* 709–717.

Lutz-Zois, C. J., Moler, K. A., & Brown, M. J. (2015). Mechanisms for the relationship between traditional masculine ideologies and rape myth acceptance among college men. *Journal of Aggression, Maltreatment and Trauma, 24,* 84–101.

Maheswaran, D., & Chaiken, S. (1991). Promoting systematic processing in low motivation settings: Effect of incongruent information on processing and judgment. *Journal of Personality and Social Psychology, 61,* 13–25.

Malamuth, N. M., Addison, T., & Koss, M. (2000). Pornography and sexual aggression: Are there reliable effects and can we understand them? *Annual Review of Sex Research, 11,* 26–91.

Masser, B. M., Lee, K., & McKimmie, B. M. (2010). Bad woman, bad victim? Disentangling the effects of victim stereotypicality, gender stereotypicality and benevolent sexism on acquaintance rape victim blame. *Sex Roles, 62,* 494–504.

McCauley, M. R., & Parker, J. F. (2001). When will a child be believed? The impact of the victim's age and juror's gender on children's credibility and verdict in a sexual-abuse case. *Child Abuse & Neglect, 25,* 523–539.

McCoy, M. L., & Gray, J. M. (2007). The impact of defendant gender and relationship to victim on juror decisions in a child sexual abuse case. *Journal of Applied Social Psychology, 37,* 1578–1593.

McKimmie, B. M., Masser, B. M., & Bongiorno, R. (2014). What counts as rape? The effect of offense prototypes, victim stereotypes, and participant gender on how the complainant and defendant are perceived. *Journal of Interpersonal Violence, 29,* 2273–2303.

Milburn, M. A., Mather, R., & Conrad, S. D. (2000). The effects of viewing r-rated movie scenes that objectify women on perceptions of date rape. *Sex Roles, 43,* 645–664.

Morison, S., & Greene, E. (1992). Juror and expert knowledge of child sexual abuse. *Child Abuse & Neglect, 16,* 595–613.

Murnen, S. K., & Kohlman, M. H. (2007). Athletic participation, fraternity membership, and sexual aggression among college men: A meta-analytic review. *Sex Roles, 57,* 145–157.

Newcombe, P. A., van den Eynde, J., Hafner, D., & Jolly, L. (2008). Attributions of responsibility for rape: Differences across familiarity of situation, gender, and acceptance of rape myths. *Journal of Applied Social Psychology, 38,* 1736–1754.

Newell, B. R., Weston, N. J., & Shanks, D. R. (2003). Empirical tests of a fast-and-frugal heuristic: Not everyone 'takes-the-best'. *Organizational Behavior & Human Decision Processes, 91,* 82–96.

Oliver, K. (2015). *Rape as spectator sport and* creepshot *entertainment: Social media and the valorization of lack of consent* (ASJ Occasional Papers, OP 10). http://op.asjournal.org/rape-as-spectator-sport-and-creepshot-entertainment/.

Oliver, K. (2016). *Hunting girls: Sexual violence from the hunger games to campus rape*. New York: Columbia University Press.

Orcutt, H. K., Goodman, G. S., Tobey, A. E., Batterman-Faunce, J. M., & Thomas, S. (2001). Detecting deception in children's testimony: Factfinders' abilities to reach the truth in open court and closed-circuit trials. *Law and Human Behavior, 25,* 339–372.

Payne, D. L., Lonsway, K. A., & Fitzgerald, L. F. (1999). Rape myth acceptance: Exploration of its structure and its measurement using the *Illinois Rape Myth Acceptance Scale*. *Journal of Research in Personality, 33,* 27–68.

Peter, J., & Valkenburg, P. M. (2009). Adolescents' exposure to sexually explicit internet material and notions of women as sex objects: Assessing causality and underlying processes. *Journal of Communication, 59,* 407–433.

Piaget, J., Cook, M., & Norton, W. (1952). *The origins of intelligence in children* (Vol. 8). New York: International Universities Press.

Quas, J. A., Bottoms, B. L., Haegerich, T. M., & Nysse-Carris, K. L. (2002). Effects of victim, defendant, and juror gender decisions in child sexual assault cases. *Journal of Applied Social Psychology, 32,* 1993–2021.

Quas, J. A., Thompson, W. C., & Clarke-Stewart, K. A. (2005). Do jurors 'know' what isn't so about child witnesses? *Law and Human Behavior, 29,* 425–456.

Rieskamp, J., & Hoffrage, U. (2008). Inferences under time pressure: How opportunity costs affect strategy selection. *Acta Psychologica, 127,* 258–276.

Rieskamp, J., & Otto, P. E. (2006). SSL: A theory of how people learn to select strategies. *Journal of Experimental Psychology: General, 135,* 207–236.

Rumney, P. N. (2006). False allegations of rape. *The Cambridge Law Journal, 65,* 128–158.

Schuller, R. A., McKimmie, B. M., Masser, B. M., & Klippenstine, M. A. (2010). Judgments of sexual assault: The impact of complainant emotional demeanor, gender and victim stereotypes. *New Criminal Law Review, 13,* 759–780.

Schuller, R. A., & Wall, A.-M. (1998). The effects of defendant and complainant intoxication on mock jurors' judgments of sexual assault. *Pyschology of Women Quarterly, 22,* 555–573.

Sleath, E., & Bull, R. (2012). Comparing rape victim and perpetrator blaming in a police officer sample. *Criminal Justice and Behaviour, 39,* 646–665.

Smith, O., & Skinner, T. (2017). How rape myths are used and challenged in rape and sexual assault trials. *Social & Legal Studies, 26,* 441–466.

Spears, J. W., & Spohn, C. C. (2006). The effect of evidence factors and victim characteristics on prosecutors' charging decisions in sexual assault cases. *Justice Quarterly, 14,* 501–524.

Sperry, K., & Siegel, J. T. (2013). Victim responsibility, credibility, and verdict in a simulated rape case: Application of Weiner's attribution model. *Legal and Criminological Psychology, 18,* 16–29.

Spohn, C., & Holleran, D. (2001). Prosecuting sexual assault: A comparison of charging decisions in sexual assault cases involving strangers, acquaintances, and intimate partners. *Justice Quarterly, 18,* 651–688.

Stankiewicz, J. M., & Rosselli, F. (2008). Women as sex objects and victims in print advertisements. *Sex Roles, 58,* 579–589.

Stewart, D. N., & Jacquin, K. M. (2010). Juror perceptions in a rape trial: Examining the complainant's ingestion of chemical substances prior to sexual assault. *Journal of Aggression, Maltreatment & Trauma, 19,* 853–874.

Stuart, S. M., McKimmie, B. M., & Masser, B. M. (2016). Rape perpetrators on trial: The effect of sexual assault–related schemas on attributions of blame. *Journal of Interpersonal Violence, 34,* 310–336.

Suarez, E., & Gadalla, T. M. (2010). Stop blaming the victim: A meta-analysis on rape myths. *Journal of Interpersonal Violence, 25,* 2010–2035.

Süssenbach, P., Albrecht, S., & Bohner, G. (2017). Implicit judgments of rape cases: An experiment on the determinants and consequences of implicit evaluations in a rape case. *Psychology Crime and Law, 23,* 291–304.

Süssenbach, P., Eyssel, F., Rees, J., & Bohner, G. (2017). Looking for blame: Rape myth acceptance and attention to victim and perpetrator. *Journal of Interpersonal Violence, 32,* 2323–2344.

Swim, J. K., Hyers, L. L., Cohen, L. L., & Ferguson, M. J. (2001). Everyday sexism: Evidence for its incidence, nature, and psychological impact from three daily diary studies. *Journal of Social Issues, 57,* 31–53.

Tabak, S. J., & Klettke, B. (2014). Mock jury attitudes towards credibility, age, and guilt in a fictional child sexual assault scenario. *Australian Journal of Psychology, 66,* 47–55.

Taylor, N. (2007). *Juror attitudes and biases in sexual assault cases* (Trends and Issues in Crime and Criminal Justice, No. 344). Canberra: Australian Institute of Criminology.

Temkin, J., & Krahé, B. (2008). *Sexual assault and the justice gap: A question of attitude.* Oxford: Hart Publishing.

Vaes, J., Paladino, P., & Puvia, E. (2011). Are sexualized women complete human beings? Why men and women dehumanize sexually objectified women. *European Journal of Social Psychology, 41,* 774–785.

van der Bruggen, M., & Grubb, A. (2014). A review of the literature relating to rape victim blaming: An analysis of the impact of observer and victim characteristics on attribution of blame in rape cases. *Aggression and Violent Behavior, 19,* 523–531.

Vandiver, D. M., & Dupalo, J. R. (2012). Factors that affect college students' perceptions of rape: What is the role of gender and other situational factors? *International Journal of Offender Therapy and Comparative Criminology, 57,* 592–612.

VicHealth. (2014). *Australians' attitudes to violence against women: Findings from the 2013 National Community Attitudes towards Violence Against*

Women Survey (NCAS). Melbourne: Australia Victorian Health Promotion Foundation.

von Helversen, B., & Rieskamp, J. (2009). Predicting sentencing for low level crimes: Comparing models of human judgment. *Journal of Experimental Psychology: Applied, 15,* 375–395.

Ward, L. M., Merriwether, A., & Caruthers, A. (2006). Breasts are for men: Media, masculinity ideologies, and men's beliefs about women's bodies. *Sex Roles, 55,* 703–714.

Weiner, B. (1980). A cognitive (attribution)-emotion-action model of motivated behavior: An analysis of judgments of help-giving. *Journal of Personality and Social Psychology, 39,* 186–200.

Weiner, B. (1985). An attributional theory of achievement motivation and emotion. *Psychological Review, 92,* 548–573.

Wenger, A. A., & Bornstein, B. H. (2006). The effects of victim's substance use and relationship closeness on mock jurors' judgments in an acquaintance rape case. *Sex Roles, 54,* 547–555.

Williams, Z. (2017, April 10). From Elle to Game of Thrones, why is culture obsessed with rape? *The Guardian*. theguardian.com/tv-and-radio/2017/apr/10/rape-culture-elle-game-thrones-zoe-williams.

Willmott, D., Boduszek, D., Debowska, A., & Woodfield, R. (2018). Introduction and validation of the juror decision scale (JDS): An empirical investigation of the story model. *Journal of Criminal Justice, 57,* 26–34.

Winter, R. J., & Greene, E. (2007). Juror decision-making. In F. Durso, R. S. Nickerson, S. T. Dumais, S. Lewandowsky, & T. J. Perfect (Eds.), *Handbook of applied cognition* (pp. 739–761). Chichester: Wiley.

Wright, P. J., Tokunaga, R. S., & Kraus, A. (2015). A meta-analysis of pornography consumption and actual acts of sexual aggression in general population studies. *Journal of Communication, 66,* 183–205.

Zajac, R., Gross, J., & Hayne, H. (2003). Asked and Answered: Questioning children in the courtroom. *Psychiatry, Psychology and Law, 10,* 199–209.

Zajac, R., & Hayne, H. (2003). I Don't Think That's What Really Happened: The effect of cross-examination on the accuracy of children's reports. *Journal of Experimental Psychology, 9,* 187–195.

Zillmann, D., & Bryant, J. (1982). Pornography, sexual callousness, and the trivialization of rape. *Journal of Communication, 32,* 10–21.

Zurbriggen, E. L. (2010). Rape, war, and the socialization of masculinity: Why our refusal to give up war ensures that rape cannot be eradicated. *Psychology of Women Quarterly, 34,* 538–549.

6

The Nature and Effects of Adversarialism: Sites of Activation for Heuristic Reasoning Processes

1 Background: The Role of Evidence and Procedural Laws in Sexual Assault Trials

Historically, the laws of evidence and procedure have used four methods to deal with unreliable or prejudicial evidence:

(i) exclusionary rules of evidence;
(ii) a requirement for corroboration in relation to the evidence of accomplices, sexual assault complainants and children;
(iii) cross-examination of witnesses; and
(iv) judicial warnings.

The accepted wisdom about the rules of evidence and procedure that apply in a criminal trial is that they impose a structure which ensures fairness for both the defence and the prosecution. However, historically, the prosecution was often prevented from fully explaining the context in which an alleged sexual assault occurred through legal restrictions preventing the admission of similar fact or propensity evidence

A. Cossins, *Closing the Justice Gap for Adult and Child Sexual Assault*,
https://doi.org/10.1057/978-1-137-32051-3_6

against the accused (Cossins, 2011a, 2013a) and the general, historical trend to hold separate rather than joint trials where more two or more complainants made allegations against the same defendant (Cossins, 2011b).

Instead, the criminal law developed various rules and procedures to highlight the assumed unreliability of the evidence of sexual assault complainants, rather than providing evidence about a defendant's propensities.

Historically, children's evidence faced stringent competency rules in some jurisdictions before reforms were introduced.[1] Still, today, trials may not proceed when the complainant has an intellectual disability,[2] even though intellectually disabled children are at greater risk of sexual abuse compared to all other groups (Hershkowitz, Lamb, & Horowitz, 2007; Jones et al., 2012; Wissink, van Vugt, Moonen, Stams, & Hendriks, 2015).

For more than a century, both women's and children's evidence was subject to judicial warnings about the quality of their evidence so that, for example, in Australia, a sexual assault trial may contain up to eleven warnings in addition to standard judicial directions about the burden of proof and the role of the jury.[3] This means that the criminal trial process in sexual assault cases has been peculiarly weighted against complainants whose evidence continues to be filtered through the lens of rape myths and misconceptions, as discussed in the previous chapters.

The sexual assault trial represents a gendered structure of power relations that emerged, historically, as a result of the belief that women's and girls' evidence about being sexually assaulted was unreliable unless corroborated (either by eyewitnesses, immediate complaint and/or physical evidence of injury). These beliefs were documented and repeated over

[1]See, for example, *Evidence Act 1995* (NSW), s 12; Youth Justice and Criminal Evidence Act 1999 (UK), s 53.

[2]In 2011, in South Australia, sexual assault charges against a bus driver were dropped by the prosecution because the intellectually disabled complainants were unable to give oral testimony in court without assistance. In 2015, the South Australian Parliament enacted legislation to enable such children to give evidence with the aid of an electronic device or a communication assistant: s 13A(2)(c)(ii), *Evidence Act 1929* (SA).

[3]The specific directions or warnings that a jury can receive in a sexual assault trial in Australia were summarised in *R v BWT* (2002) 54 NSWLR 241, 250–251 by Wood CJ at CL.

hundreds of years by legal commentators such as Bracton (1268/1968) and Blackstone (1765–1769).

For example, the jury warning regarding delay in complaint is derived from an ancient prescription that a woman's failure to immediately raise the 'hue and cry' after being raped was a defence to her allegation of rape (Bronitt, 1998). The history of the law of rape was, according to Blackstone (1765–1769), derived from Saxon law[4]:

> in order to prevent malicious accusations, … the woman should immediately after, 'dum recens fuerit maleficium' ['while the injury is recent'], go to the next town, and there make discovery to some credible persons of the injury she has suffered; and afterwards should acquaint the high constable of the hundred, the coroners, and the sheriff with the outrage. … At present there is no time of limitation fixed: … but the jury will rarely give credit to a stale complaint.

This 'hue and cry' requirement was unlikely to have been a practice that traumatised women and girls could readily engage in, particularly if it required revealing their loss of chastity.

Evidence about the veracity of a sexual assault complaint is not interpreted by lawyers or jurors objectively, but subjectively based on pre-existing cultural beliefs. Indeed, the specific substantive law and rules of evidence and procedure that apply in a sexual assault trial mirror cultural forms of the moral regulation of women and girls (Cossins, 2015), and encourage particular types of jury reasoning about women's and children's tendency to lie about being sexual assaulted, their promiscuity, and/or desires for revenge.

For many victims, the sexual assault trial is an ordeal, sometimes described as bad or worse than the original abuse (Cossins, 2019), a place where the complainant's behaviour is on trial. There are limited ways of preventing a sexual assault trial from turning into a character assassination of the complainant by defence counsel, while complainants, with no legal representation, have no control over the trial process. The authority of the state justifies a complainant's re-traumatisation with a variety of

[4]Probably first recorded by William Glanvil (1170) and Henry Bracton (1268).

defence allegations about her character and past still permitted, including drug and alcohol use, psychiatric history and past criminal offences.

Thus, there is a huge risk for complainants who choose to participate in a sexual assault trial—re-traumatisation is a documented phenomenon, as discussed in Chapter 11, and one reason that women and children do not proceed with their complaints.[5]

We also have no methods for vetting jurors to discover the rape myths (or heuristics) they adhere to while juries do not give reasons for their decisions in criminal trials. Thus, jurors are free to use heuristics to decide the key legal issues in an adult sexual assault trial: did she consent and what was his state of mind? Without eyewitnesses and other supporting evidence, the defendant's denial will generally be measured by reference to the complainant's behaviour.

As discussed in Chapter 5, numerous studies reveal the extent to which laypeople endorse the misconceptions associated with RMA and the fact that the higher an individual's level of RMA, the more likely s/he will blame the victim, and the less likely s/he will perceive the victim to be credible and the defendant to be culpable (Stewart & Jacquin, 2010). In fact, there is a positive correlation between relatively high levels of RMA and a tendency to acquit in sexual assault trials (Dinos, Burrowes, Hammond, & Cunliffe, 2015).

Therefore, jury decision-making in a sexual assault trial takes place within a context that is historically gendered despite the fact that the structure of the criminal trial reflects the principles that operate to ensure that the defendant receives a fair trial:

(i) burden of proof on the prosecution;
(ii) criminal standard of proof (beyond reasonable doubt) which is higher than the civil standard of proof (balance of probabilities);
(iii) defendant's right to remain silent; and
(iv) lack of a burden on the defendant to mount a case or prove his/her innocence.

[5]See, e.g. the story of 14-year-old Amy in 'Rape on Trial', *Insight*, SBS Television, 27 February 2018.

However, it is very the structure of the trial (together with the criminal standard of proof) that encourages the early questioning of the prosecution's case by the jury (see Hypothesis 1 in Fig. 1). By digging deeper, however, it is apparent that the emphasis on hypothesising (rather than investigation) as a way of determining guilt or innocence in a criminal trial has encouraged the development of a very particular requirement in sexual assault trials that is not apparent in other criminal trials; that is, proof of the moral worthiness of the adult or child complainant in order to prove her veracity as a witness and, in turn, the facts in issue:

(i) in a CSA trial, the commission of the alleged sexual conduct by the defendant;
(ii) in an adult sexual assault trial, typically lack of consent and knowledge of lack of consent on the part of the defendant.

Very early in a criminal trial, the jury is faced with competing hypotheses which encourages jurors to engage in a hypothesis-testing process (Carlson & Russo, 2001) whereby they determine the likelihood of the competing prosecution and defence hypotheses. Studies show that defence addresses to the jury can influence verdicts (Haegerich & Bottoms, 2000) by including empathy-inducing statements about the defendant such as asking the jury to put themselves in his or her shoes. When a fact-finder favours a particular outcome during the trial before delivering their final verdict, this early preference influences their interpretation of subsequent evidence. This process is known as pre-decisional distortion (Carlson & Russo, 2001; DeKay, 2015) and amounts to 'a form of self-fulfilling prophecy in which the decision-maker is especially likely to choose the initially preferred option' (DeKay, 2015: 405). Indeed, in Chapter 2, a review of the literature showed that juror verdicts before deliberation had a greater tendency to prevail after deliberation.

The effect of stereotypes in criminal trials has been examined by Haegerich, Salerno, and Bottoms (2013), specifically the effect of juvenile stereotypes on pre- and post-deliberation judgements in a mock trial in which the defendant was a juvenile offender. Jurors' adherence to two stereotypes ('Wayward Youth' and 'Super-predator') were measured and, in some mock trials, were encouraged by attorneys' arguments.

The authors found that that the more jurors adhered to the 'Super-predator' stereotype, the more likely they were to vote guilty, although the effects of jurors' pre-existing biases were somewhat minimised after jury deliberation.

Jurors' stereotypes were also 'activated' before and during the trial. The first type of activation involved a verbal statement introducing the study which also included statements about either 'Super-predators' or 'Wayward Youth' in the stereotype conditions, compared to the control. The second type of activation took place within the trial transcript, where participants in the Super-predator condition:

> were given the prosecuting attorney's opening statements and closing arguments with an added paragraph that emphasized the problem of 'Superpredators' who commit serious crimes, informing jurors that the defendant in this case is a perfect example of a 'Superpredator'. (Haegerich et al., 2013: 86)

A similar paragraph emphasised the problem of Wayward Youths in the second stereotype condition.

It was only in the 'Super-predator' condition that jurors were more likely to find the defendant guilty (100%) compared to jurors in the control and 'Wayward Youth' trials. Jurors' *activated* biases (compared to their pre-existing biases) were maximised after jury deliberation, especially in robbery cases. In addition, the effect of counsels' activating and biasing statements was 'significant regardless of jurors' own pre-existing beliefs about juvenile offenders' (Haegerich et al., 2013: 90).

The question then is, '[w]hy would preexisting stereotypes be minimized after deliberation, while activated stereotypes [were] maximized after deliberation?' (Haegerich et al., 2013: 91). The authors speculate that jurors controlled their pre-existing biases 'due to normative concerns about self-presenting as a biased person' or due to correction by other jurors, although 'if most jurors … share beliefs about a defendant before deliberation, then that jury will be more likely to render a verdict in line with those beliefs after deliberation' (Haegerich et al., 2013: 91).

By contrast, the expression of activated biases may be less likely to be controlled where those biases come from authoritative sources (such as trial counsel) and where they are shared by the group, something that would become apparent during deliberation. As well, since all jurors will have heard the activated biases during the trial, this 'might result in most members of the jury focusing on stereotype-consistent information' as relevant information during deliberation (Haegerich et al., 2013: 91). Thus, jury deliberation can both maximise or minimise biases.

Even though jurors in the study were told that defence and prosecution opening/closing addresses did not amount to evidence, the findings show that 'the manner in which case material is presented' in a trial can influence verdicts, 'putting the fairness of the legal system in jeopardy' (Haegerich et al., 2013: 89). Thus, controlling the content of counsels' 'biasing statements about the defendant during opening and closing arguments might be more important in decreasing juror bias' (Haegerich et al, 2013: 90) than other strategies.

The authors note that Haegerich and Bottoms (2000) showed how jurors in CSA trials tended to ignore judicial instructions to ignore counsels' opening/closing addresses or were unaware of the impact of such statements on their decision-making. Thus, Haegerich et al (2013: 90) recommend that judges could:

> inform jurors about the potential bias that attorneys' statements may have on their decision making, even without their awareness, and that they can attempt to resist such biases by being more cognitively aware, critically evaluating the evidence and the conclusions that the attorneys assert about what happened.

This research raises two key questions:

(i) What are the implications of the above research for the sexual assault trial?
(ii) Would judicial instructions solve the endemic problem of the effect of RMA and misconceptions on jury decision-making? (see Chapter 12).

2 Activation Statements in Sexual Assault Trials

In an adult sexual assault trial where consent is a fact in issue, the prosecution's hypothesis is that the defendant committed the alleged sexual conduct *without* the complainant's consent (Hypothesis 1 in Fig. 1).

In a CSA trial, where consent is usually not a fact in issue, the prosecution's hypothesis is that the defendant committed the alleged sexual conduct.

From the outset, however, Hypothesis 1 is under attack from the defence when the defence encourages any pre-existing juror biases and the use of heuristic reasoning by activating particular gender, victim and/or offence stereotypes (Hypothesis 2 in Fig. 1). By contrast, Hypothesis 2 remains untested unless the defence opens a case since the defendant is not required to mount a defence or give evidence. Thus, the defence does not have to provide any evidence to support Hypothesis 2 and, instead, relies on the general prevalence of RMA and misconceptions about children among laypeople called up for jury duty.

The acceptance of a defence hypothesis based on myths, prejudice and misconceptions constitutes the implicit acceptance by the criminal justice system of the *relevance* of such speculation in a sexual assault trial. Thus, the defence is not required to satisfy an evidential burden when relying on particular gender, victim and/or offence stereotypes in their cross-examination of the complainant which she must refute because of the burden on her to prove her lack of consent (or to prove that the sexual assault occurred), as the prosecution's chief witness.

Since the defence narrative in a sexual assault trial is driven by defence hypotheses that undermine a complainant's credibility and since the main vehicle for this narrative is cross-examination, there is little or no opportunity for the prosecution to attack the defence narrative. Even re-examination by a prosecutor is designed to restore a witness's credibility rather than disprove any defence narrative about the complainant's moral unworthiness.

If the defence narrative is bolstered by judicial comments and warnings about delayed complaint and lack of corroboration, which also

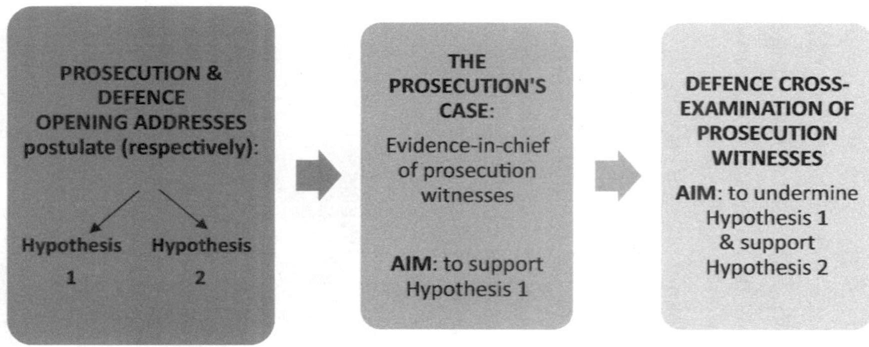

Fig. 1 The parts of a criminal trial that encourage hypothesis-testing by the jury

pertain to a complainant's credibility, this can potentially reinforce activated stereotypes and any doubts held by jurors about the defendant's guilt.

For example, in a study that tested the impact of pro- and anti-rape myth bias statements on the individual verdicts of 90 UK university students, participants who received pro-rape myth guidance 'were significantly more likely than those receiving anti-rape myth guidance to be confident that the defendant was innocent', regardless of mock jurors' levels of RMA (Gray, 2006: 78). These results suggest that even jurors with low levels of RMA can be influenced by pro-rape myth statements by court personnel, although rape myth supportive statements may be more influential on men than women (Gray, 2006).

How does the structure of the adversarial trial encourage defence hypothesis-testing reasoning (Clifford, 2003), given that a hypothesis is not merely a statement of the criminal charges but comprises a *story* including elements such as motive, opportunity, desire and relationship? As described in Fig. 2, a criminal trial has a number of sites or structural components which encourage hypothesis-testing.

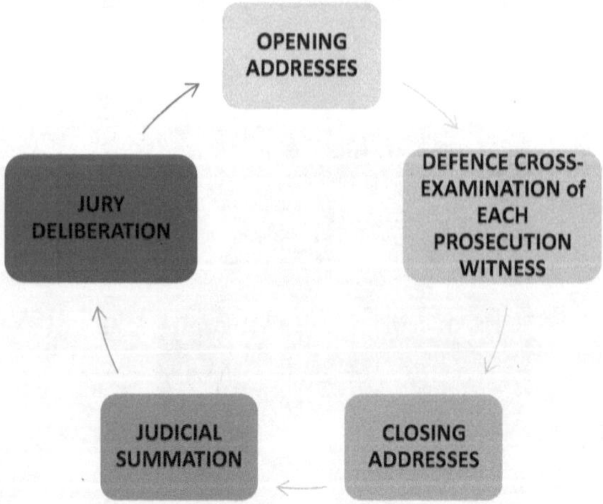

Fig. 2 Sites of activation: heuristics within a criminal trial

2.1 Prosecution and Defence Opening Addresses

Before any evidence is admitted, adversarial criminal trials permit counsel to address the jury. The purpose of the prosecution's opening address is to outline the case for the prosecution, that is, to provide a summary of the charges against the defendant, the evidence to be presented and witnesses to be called in order to support the prosecution's hypothesis—that the defendant is guilty of the charges in question.

The purpose of defence counsel's opening address is to undermine the prosecution's hypothesis by denying guilt and, in a sexual assault trial, proposing an alternative explanation for the events leading up to the charges, such as revenge by the complainant or a desire for victims' compensation. Thus, the defence opening address encourages jurors to engage in heuristic processing by using heuristic cues (or short cuts) to filter the evidence presented in the prosecution's case, in particular the complainant's testimony.

Because opening addresses do not amount to evidence, jurors are presented with opposing hypotheses before any actual evidence has been admitted. Thus, opening addresses may discourage jurors from interpreting the trial evidence in order to devise their own hypotheses since the interpretative process has been done for them. While jurors are not prevented from devising alternative hypotheses, to do so requires them to put the prosecution and defence hypotheses to one side and engage with the evidence in a deeper way, something that not all jurors will be capable of, as discussed in Chapter 5, in relation to the dual processing model of jury decision-making.

Because the burden of proving the charge(s) against the defendant lies with the prosecution, the prosecution's case follows the opening addresses. The prosecution opens its case by calling witnesses to give oral evidence, and/or by adducing other evidence (such as medical and forensic evidence, exhibits and/or CCTV footage) in order to prove that the defendant is guilty of the charge(s) beyond reasonable doubt. In other words, the aim of all the evidence adduced by the prosecution is to support Hypothesis 1 in Fig. 1.

During the prosecution case, the aim of defence cross-examination of prosecution witnesses is to undermine Hypothesis 1 by styles of questioning that create doubt about the credibility of prosecution witnesses, thereby supporting Hypothesis 2. As noted above, there is no balancing process which allows the prosecution to test Hypothesis 2 unless the defence opens a case and calls witnesses to give evidence. Thus, in a sexual assault trial, jurors are faced with determining the plausibility of the complainant's version of events compared with the defence's hypothesis which, by the end of the trial, may not have been tested. As well, we know that presentation order of evidence affects decision-making, that is, the most recent evidence or information can have the strongest impact (Dahl, Brimacombe, & Lindsay, 2009; Lagnado and Harvey, 2008), such as the defence closing address which closes the trial.

The way that criminal trials are conducted, with a step-by-step process of adducing each item of evidence and calling each witness, also encourages jurors to reach premature conclusions (Carlson & Russo, 2001: 91). Carlson and Russo (2001: 91) found that preventative instructions did not stop mock jurors and actual jurors from engaging in pre-decisional distortion, that is, 'jurors' biased interpretation of new evidence to support whichever verdict is tentatively favoured as a trial progresses'. Distortion of evidence can also occur as a result of jurors' prior beliefs or misconceptions about crime, victims and defendants. But even if jurors hold no prior beliefs or are able to put them aside, 'jurors naturally establish a tentative favourite side (or leading verdict) early in the trial and then evaluate new evidence as overly supportive of that currently leading verdict' (Carlson & Russo, 2001: 92).

Models of juror decision-making, such as the widely cited story model (Pennington & Hastie, 1986, 1992), predicts that jurors construct sometimes competing narratives of the events leading up to the charges in question from their interpretation of the evidence, their assessment of witness credibility, their own knowledge of the world and human behaviour. Eventually, according to Pennington and Hastie (1986), one story will emerge that makes the most sense based on coverage, coherence and uniqueness.

2.2 Jurors' Narrative Framework

Most criminal trials involve conflicting accounts of events as presented by the prosecution and the defence, with different witnesses and exhibits 'convey[ing] pieces of a historical puzzle in a jumbled temporal sequence' and inevitable gaps in the chronology of events (Pennington & Hastie, 1988: 521). Jurors reconcile these accounts and bridge the gaps by constructing a narrative framework that provides a commonsensical story of events and actions (Pennington & Hastie, 1992) which may contain imaginary elements based on jurors' life experiences and expectations (Ellison & Munro, 2009a, 2009b).

The descriptive, 'story model' of jury deliberation has been widely accepted in the literature as a way of explaining jury deliberation and the final verdicts (Blume, Johnson, & Paavola, 2007; Devine, 2012; Huntley & Costanzo, 2003). It has supplanted various mathematical models of jury decision-making due to the latter's assumptions about jurors weighing and adding all the evidence in a machine-like way, rather than the evolution of possible stories that fit with the evidence that has been accepted by jurors (Devine, 2012).

Willmott, Boduszeka, Debowskac, and Woodfield (2018: 31–32) observe that while 'widely regarded as the dominant explanation of juror-level decision making' there was no empirical testing of the factors underlying the story model. To that end, they developed the Juror Decision Scale in order to examine 'the Story Model's conceptualisation of individual juror decision formation (certainty principles) to be examined' (ibid., 32).[6] They found that their results:

[6]Willmott et al. (2018: 29) describe the Juror Decision Scale as 'a 16-item self-report measure designed to assess individual juror decision making ... The measure consists of three subscales; Complainant Believability (seven items), Defendant Believability (seven items), and Decision Confidence (two items), with all items scored on a 5-point Likert scale ... Higher scores on the Complainant Believability subscale indicates greater juror/respondent belief in the complainant's story, with lower scores indicating reduced belief in a complainant's account. Higher scores on the Defendant Believability sub-scale indicates greater juror/respondent belief in the defendant's story, with lower scores indicating a reduced belief. Higher scores on the Decision Confidence subscale indicates greater juror/respondent confidence in the accuracy of the verdict decision given'.

> support[ed] Pennington and Hastie's (1992) assertions that prior to selecting a verdict, jurors appear to assess competing witness accounts in terms of a subscribed set of certainty principles, in order to determine which story they deem most believable, before voting accordingly.

In fact, while the elements of the story model (coverage, coherence, completeness, plausibility and uniqueness, all of which are explained below) 'are clearly important determinants upon individual decision formation …, these assessments appear to be influenced in themselves by preconceived attitudes jurors hold' (ibid., 33).

Through the story model, jurors construct a causal explanation of events from evidence presented at trial and their own 'related world knowledge' (Pennington & Hastie, 1988: 522). Because the story model assumes that jurors actively process trial information, jurors are believed to sift through the evidence, 'focusing on some elements and discarding others' (Devine, 2012: 27) while simultaneously making inferences in order to create a chain of events or actions that are causally related to one another to create a plausible story (Pennington & Hastie, 1988: 522).

This storyline mirrors the model of classical storytelling that we see in books and films. Each story is comprised of 'interrelated *episodes*' and each episode contains an initiating event, goals, actions, consequences, and the psychological states of the protagonists (Pennington & Hastie, 1988: 522; emphasis in original). As the authors observe:

> [e]xpectations about the kinds of information necessary to make a story tell the juror when important pieces of the explanation structure are missing and when inferences must be made. (Pennington & Hastie, 1988: 522)

Thus, the process involves subjective assessments based on jurors' own beliefs, knowledge and life experiences, that is, 'existing cognitive structures such as *scripts* that involve common sequences of events and *stereotypes* that link categories of people or objects with typical attributes' (Devine, 2012: 27; emphasis in original). In other words, the story model proposes that jurors are not:

> undifferentiated automatons who make decisions based on a rational, standardized processing of the evidence. Instead, jurors' stories are viewed as heavily influenced by their life experiences and perceptions at trial. (Devine & Caughlin, 2014: 111)

Deliberating jurors may come up with multiple stories with a majority eventually accepting one story as more complete and coherent than others. The construction of alternative stories is considered to 'play an important role in evidence evaluation' and in determining jurors' confidence in their final decision (Pennington & Hastie, 1988: 530) while story variability 'corresponds to variability in decisions'. Jurors assess the competing prosecution and defence hypotheses according to 'certainty principles' (Pennington & Hastie, 1988, 1992). In order to obtain a unanimous decision, jurors have to assess each story for its *coverage*, that is, the extent to which each story explains and accounts for the different types of trial evidence; for *coherence*, that is, how internally consistent a story is; a story's *completeness*, that is, no elements of the story are missing; its *plausibility*, that is, the likelihood of it occurring and its *uniqueness*, that is, the confidence of jurors in any one particular story compared to other possible stories (Pennington & Hastie, 1988: 522). Only when all these certainty principles are present will a particular story be accepted by a juror. Verdicts will be based on the story that best satisfies these criteria:

> it is not just the coherence of one story that affects decisions ... but rather it is the strength of one story compared with the alternative that is important. (Pennington & Hastie, 1988: 530)

Nonetheless, the agreed story may include fictional elements because jurors' inferences to fill gaps in the evidence may not accord with the facts of the case but, instead, accord with their pre-existing cognitive schema concerning human behaviour. In a context of competing and conflicting accounts, subjectivity is an unavoidable part of jurors' explanation-driven interpretation of trial evidence. Although jurors hear and see the same evidence, their narratives differ based on their own subjective frameworks. In other words, they may focus on evidence that is consistent with their life experiences and ignore or reject evidence that is not (Carlson &

Russo, 2001). Thus, jurors do not merely interpret trial testimony and other evidence based on the directions given to them by the trial judge, they actively process that information to 'fit' with their own experiences of, and beliefs about, human behaviour. This will involve assessments of witness credibility (such as, 'she looked like she was lying', 'he looked like an honest man'), as well as characteristics of the defendant and complainant, such as their race and gender.

Devine (2012) observes that '[t]he ultimate test of a descriptive model is whether it reproduces (or explains) known outcomes' and notes that:

> all models of jury decision making incorporate the well-established strength-in-numbers effect associated with faction size …: initial majorities, especially strong ones, tend to prevail. (Devine, 2012: 21, 39)

Based on the empirical evidence (Pennington & Hastie, 1986, 1988, 1992; Devine, 2012: 29, 39) concludes that the story model 'has emerged as the leading model in the juror decision-making literature' since it 'provides a simple, powerful and compelling depiction of juror decision making'.

Devine (2012) recently extended the story model by formulating the 'director's cut' model which incorporates juror and defendant characteristics that may influence jurors' decision-making and verdicts:

(i) juror race, gender, socioeconomic status, trust in the legal system and need for cognition; and
(ii) defendant race, socioeconomic status, prior criminal record, physical attractiveness and courtroom demeanor.

Devine and Caughlin (2014: 111) explain that:

> the director's cut model says that jurors' initial mental representations of trial-related events are determined by juror and defendant characteristics along with any information acquired before the trial via the media, the nature of the charges, and the attorneys' opening statements.

Crucially, these initial mental representations or 'existing cognitive structures' constitute the filter or frame for jurors' subsequent interpretation of trial evidence and provide:

> the basis for formulating one or more stories, which are then translated into mental models for evaluation. How stories fare when tested via mental simulation then has direct implications for a juror's preferred verdict. (Devine & Caughlin, 2014: 111)

Figure 3 shows how the director's cut model links a number of juror and defendant characteristics 'to jurors' judgments about criminal guilt via criminal-related stereotypes and case-related scripts' (Devine & Caughlin, 2014: 112). First, the model is premised on interaction between jurors' 'existing cognitive structures' (that is, criminal stereotypes and scripts), the characteristics of the particular case, evidence presented and defendant characteristics (Devine & Caughlin, 2014: 111). I have added another box to the diagram, entitled 'trial influences' which, arguably, also influence jurors' script-driven inferences in addition to case characteristics, although these trial influences, such as judicial directions, must compete with several other influences. The justification for including trial influences is discussed later .

Out of this interaction, jurors construct an 'initial mental representation of the trial', although criminal stereotypes and scripts will vary depending on the criminal charge and victim characteristics. Stereotypes are defined as 'person-related categories consisting of a central label and associated behavioral attributes', while scripts are defined as 'sets of related events that are understood to occur in a causal sequence' (Devine & Caughlin, 2014: 111).

From the mental model of trial events emerges one or more stories. Arguably, a better description is the term, 'narrative', since the story model and director's cut models rely on a narration of events, which may or may not be accurate, based on 'inferences about what is true', and what is 'stored in memory and made accessible via the activation of jurors' stereotypes and scripts' (Devine & Caughlin, 2014: 111), that is, heuristic cues.

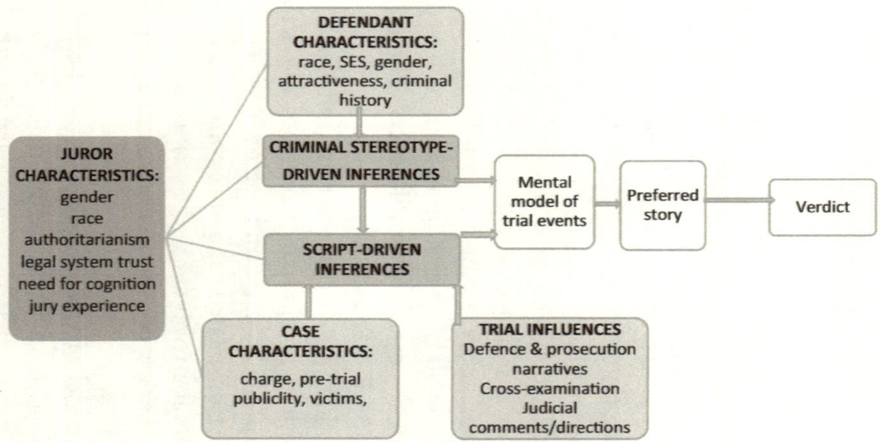

Fig. 3 'Director's cut' model linking juror and defendant characteristics to juror decisions (Adapted from Devine & Caughlin, 2014: 112; with additions by author)

Although Devine and Caughlin (2014) consider that 'jurors' stereotypes and scripts are a function of life experiences', stereotypes may be adhered to as a result of 'cultural knowledge', that is, ways of understanding certain people and situations based on media sources (such as TV crime shows) as well as gossip and rumour. Rape myths fall into this category. Jurors may have a number of beliefs about rape victims which amount to a stereotype even though jurors may have had no experience of, or contact with, a rape victim.

Under the director's cut model, rape myths would amount to a standard script involving adherence to a particular victim/gender stereotype (real victim vs unreal victim) as well as a particular criminal stereotype (such as stranger rape) which would lead jurors to process the trial evidence to form either a pro-conviction or pro-acquittal narrative depending on the extent to which the complainant and defendant matched the script and stereotypes.

In a rape trial, we know that men exhibit higher levels of RMA than women so that male jurors would be more likely to be 'attitudinally predisposed' (Devine & Caughlin, 2014: 111) to favour the narrative of events proposed by the defence while female jurors would be more likely to be 'attitudinally predisposed' to favour the narrative of events proposed by the prosecution. Similarly, adherence to a particular criminal stereotype (e.g. that rape is a violent crime) may predispose a juror to interpret the trial evidence as either fitting or not fitting that stereotype. As well, particular defendant characteristics may predispose a juror to view the defendant as a 'typical' criminal, thus triggering a particular criminal stereotype as portrayed in Fig. 3 above. For example, a high SES defendant on trial for sexual assault may be less likely to trigger a criminal stereotype but more likely to trigger a negative victim stereotype, thus leading jurors to construct a narrative in which the defendant has been wrongly accused.

The question is, does the research support the director's cut model proposed by Devine and Caughlin (2014)? After conducting a meta-analysis they concluded:

(i) 'the focal characteristics of defendants and jurors ... [set out in Fig. 3] have weak to modest overall relationships with juror predeliberation judgments of criminal culpability';
(ii) 'Most of these relationships are likely moderated by other variables and will accordingly vary across trial contexts';
(iii) 'The nature of the participants used in research does not appear to have a sizable or consistent effect on estimates of the relationship between participant characteristics and guilt judgments';
(iv) 'The relationship between two juror characteristics (authoritarianism and gender) and judgments of defendant culpability likely varies by case type'. (Devine & Caughlin, 2014: 119–120)

For example, juror education level, prior experience as a juror, defendant physical attractiveness, defendant gender and defendant race produced little or no effect on case outcomes, although there may be case types in which one or more of these characteristics does produce 'a stronger relationship with guilt judgments' (Devine & Caughlin, 2014: 120). However, the effect of juror gender is much more significant in sexual assault trials, particularly those involving children, compared to other criminal cases where female jurors are significantly more likely to convict than male jurors.

The authors found that several characteristics 'yielded effects on juror guilt judgments large enough to have some practical significance': defendant SES, defendant criminal record, juror authoritarianism and juror trust in the legal system (Devine & Caughlin, 2014: 122), so that low defendant SES, prior criminal record, high levels of juror authoritarianism and trust in the legal system were each associated to some extent with convictions. However, case type will mediate the effect of these characteristics:

> juror authoritarianism was a better predictor of guilt judgments for cases involving general homicide ... and the death penalty ... than adult sexual assault cases .... This may be because sexual crimes rarely involve third-party eyewitnesses and often present jurors with a difficult choice regarding the issue of consent. (Devine & Caughlin, 2014: 123)

Research on the influence of misconceptions and extra-legal biases in sexual assault trials confirms the existence of cognitive schemas that are used to categorise the expected behaviours of women and children before, during and after a sexual assault as discussed in Chapter 5. Based on the above findings regarding juror characteristics, as well as findings from RMA studies and other related studies summarised in Chapter 5, how might the conceptual model look for the sexual assault trial?

I have created Fig. 4 to incorporate the influence of victim characteristics on jury decision-making in terms of the inferences driven by jurors' adherence to victim stereotypes. Depending on the gender of the complainant, this stereotype can incorporate gender stereotypes. Thus, Fig. 4 summarises the possible characteristics that drive the creation of criminal stereotypes, victim stereotypes and script-driven inferences by jurors. Like Fig. 3, I have included trial influences to take account of the effect of prosecution, defence and judicial reliance on scripts or stereotypes in the information they present to a jury. The justification for including trial influences is set out below.

2.3 The Story Model and Pre-decisional Distortion

The story model takes no account of pre-decisional distortion and 'presume[s] jurors' unbiased interpretation' of new evidence. Thus, it does not account for the possibility that pre-decisional distortion can 'facilitate the emergence of one story over the others' (Carlson & Russo, 2001: 92). While Carlson and Russo (2001) suggest ways in which pre-decisional distortion could be incorporated into the story model of jury decision-making, arguably, it is the criminal trial process that encourages pre-decisional distortion. In their study, Carlson and Russo (2001: 96–99) found that:

(i) Mock jurors (university students) engaged in pre-decisional distortion when delivering individual verdicts in both civil and criminal simulated lawsuits, 'despite multiple instructions to suspend judgment until all the evidence had been presented';

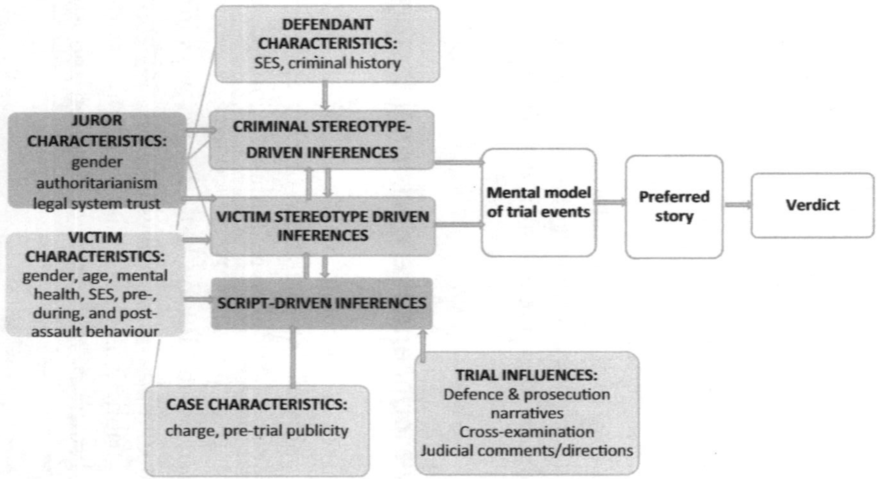

Fig. 4 Adaptation of the 'Director's cut' model linking juror, defendant and victim characteristics to juror decisions in sexual assault trials (Adapted from Devine & Caughlin, 2014: 112)

(ii) Jurors (average age: 40–45 years) who had completed jury orientation at a Wisconsin courthouse also engaged in pre-decisional distortion but were more biased than the younger mock students;
(iii) Actual jurors' judgements showed twice as much distortion, greater reliance on their prior beliefs and greater confidence in their favoured verdicts, compared to the mock jurors, with jurors' prior beliefs being a reliable predictor for their verdicts;
(iv) The higher confidence level of jurors was due, in part, to their tendency to use their prior beliefs early in the decision-making process whereas the younger mock jurors successfully followed instructions to ignore their prior beliefs.

Because Carlson and Russo (2001) used written affidavits rather than actual or videotaped testimony and excluded judicial directions and jury deliberation, it is possible that a real trial with complete testimony, cross-examination, judicial instructions and jury deliberation would amplify the effects of pre-decisional distortion because, as discussed above, trials are structured around competing narratives from the prosecution and the defence. In fact, trial processes *encourage* jurors to attach themselves to one side or the other through the processes of evidence-in-chief and adversarial cross-examination, competing experts, opening and closing addresses of counsel, and, sometimes, presentation of a defence case. As well, jurors' attachment to one hypothesis over another may also include variables such as defendant SES, the personal appeal of competing lawyers (Gunnell & Ceci, 2010) and/or the behaviour of the complainant in the witness box which are impossible to control for.

But why does pre-decisional distortion occur? Carlson and Russo (2001: 99) argue that it is driven by the need for coherence:

> Jurors seek to formulate a coherent account of the evidence presented, one that is coherent with their prior beliefs, counsels' opening arguments, the judge's instructions to the jury, and so on.

Although individual beliefs which favour one side over the other may be counteracted by the deliberation process, the liberation hypothesis, discussed in Chapter 2, asserts that where the prosecution evidence is weak or ambiguous, as in sexual assault cases, jurors are susceptible to non-evidentiary influences that is, extra-legal factors, such as race, ethnicity, gender and RMA beliefs.

Carlson and Russo (2001: 99) believe that the story model of jury decision-making could 'be extended to incorporate predecisional distortion' since '[d]riven by the goal of coherence, new evidence is distorted toward the currently leading [or favoured] verdict to make it more compatible with the currently dominant story'. However, the key finding by Carlson and Russo (2001) is the influence of prior beliefs on pre-decisional distortion, a finding that has been confirmed by the recent study of Willmott et al. (2018) (as discussed above). Thus, models of jury decision-making need to account for these beliefs as well as other research that has reported the relationship between rape myths/misconceptions and verdicts. In fact, Carlson and Russo (2001: 99) propose something simpler:

> Jurors need only harmonize new evidence with the currently leading verdict by distorting the evidence to conform to the emerging story that supports the leading story.

Depending on the leading verdict, that story is also likely to mirror the narrative proposed by either the prosecution or the defence. Thus, 'at any time during a trial, there is a dominant story, or rather a leading verdict and a corresponding story, that best accounts for the evidence' which is based on jurors' prior beliefs (or heuristics) in order to attain the 'goal of coherence' (Carlson & Russo, 2001: 100), with these beliefs driving the interpretation of each new item of evidence. In other words, pre-decisional distortion of the evidence is used by jurors to attain coherence with prior beliefs which explains the influence of rape myths and misconceptions on credibility assessments of complainants and verdicts in sexual assault trials.

However, few mechanisms within the criminal trial process are designed to discourage pre-decisional distortion other than judicial instructions. In NSW, for example, jurors are *encouraged* to use their subjective knowledge and experiences of 'human affairs':

> you represent a cross section of the community—a cross section of its wisdom and its sense of justice. You are expected to use your individual qualities of reasoning; your experience; and your understanding of people and human affairs. In particular, … you are expected to use your common sense and your ability to judge your fellow citizens, so that you bring to the jury room … your own experience of human affairs, which must necessarily be as varied as the twelve of you. (Judicial Commission, 2017: [7-020])

However, in E&W, in order to address the danger of jury assumptions based on jurors' life experiences, the *Crown Court Compendium* (Judicial College, 2018: 20–23) states that, '[d]epending on the evidence and arguments advanced in the case', judicial guidance to the jury may be necessary in relation to the complainant's evidence:

(1) Of untruthfulness:
   (a) Delay in making a complaint.
   (b) Complaint made for the first time when giving evidence.
   (c) Inconsistent accounts given by the complainant.
   (d) Lack of emotion/distress when giving evidence.

(2) Of truthfulness:
   (a) A consistent account given by the complainant.
   (b) Emotion/distress when giving evidence.

(3) Of consent and/or belief in consent:
   (a) Clothing worn by the complainant said to be revealing or provocative.
   (b) Intoxication (drink and/or drugs) on the part of the complainant while in the company of others.
   (c) Previous knowledge of, or friendship/sexual relationship between, the complainant and the defendant. In this regard it may be necessary to alert the jury to the distinction between submission and consent.
   (d) Some consensual sexual activity on the occasion of the alleged offence.

(e) Lack of any use or threat of force, physical struggle and/or signs of injury. Again it may be necessary to alert the jury to the distinction between submission and consent.

For example:

> It would be understandable if some of you came to this trial with assumptions about rape. You may have ideas about what kind of person is a victim of rape or what kind of person is a rapist. You may also have ideas about what a person will do or say when they are raped. But it is important that you dismiss these ideas when you decide this case. From experience we know that there is no typical rape, typical rapist or typical person that is raped. Rape can take place in almost any circumstance. It can happen between all different kinds of people. And people who are raped react in a variety of different ways. So you must put aside any assumptions you have about rape. All of you on this jury must make your judgement based only on the evidence you hear from the witnesses and the law as I explain that to you. (Judicial College, 2018: 20–24)

However, the phenomenon of pre-decisional distortion as illustrated in the 'Director's cut' model (Fig. 3) which links juror and defendant characteristics to juror decisions as well as my adaptation of the 'Director's cut' model (Fig. 4) which links juror, defendant and victim characteristics to juror decisions in sexual assault trials suggests that judicial instructions will have limited impact. In other words, judicial instructions must compete with juror characteristics that manifest as a pro-defence bias, as well as jurors' interpretations of the complainant and her background, the defendant's characteristics (e.g. low vs high SES, prior or no criminal history) and case characteristics (stranger rape vs acquaintance rape), including prosecution and defence narratives, all of which will be used to create a coherent narrative from jurors' points of view. Judicial instructions at the end of a trial about not making assumptions about rape victims will be too late since '[o]nce jurors have distorted the evidence, it may be impossible for them to reconstruct an unbiased version of that same evidence' (Carlson & Russo, 2001: 100).

In a sexual assault trial, an untested defence narrative will also reinforce pre-decisional distortion along with the case, victim and defendant characteristics that influence jurors to select the most coherent story. While the prosecution narrative, which is based on the evidence presented in the trial, is always tested by the defence, the defence narrative is often composed of myth and speculation. For example, a prosecution narrative such as 'the defendant took advantage of the complainant, plied her with alcohol and despite being told to leave her apartment, he climbed into her bed and had intercourse with her against her will', will be supported by the complainant's evidence and any other relevant evidence.

By contrast, the opposing defence narrative, such as 'the complainant invited the defendant back to her home where they drank a bottle of wine together and she invited him to stay the night' will remain untested unless the defence calls witnesses and other evidence to support the narrative. While jurors may be instructed that prosecution and defence opening/closing addresses do not amount to evidence, they provide the context or framework in which the trial evidence is interpreted and represent the starting point for any pre-decisional distortion.

Carlson and Russo's (2001: 98) study found that, compared to mock jurors, actual jurors' prior beliefs 'creat[ed] differential receptivity to the evidence'—those who favoured one side over the other interpreted each affidavit according to their favoured side while their favouritism was driven by their prior beliefs. Thus, if a juror uses experiential reasoning (Gunnell & Ceci, 2010) by relying on heuristics in his/her decision-making, such as, 'a woman who invites a man back to her home is asking for trouble', then the narrative that coheres with these heuristics is likely to dominate.

This raises the question: what is the impact of prior beliefs, including RMA, in creating pre-decisional distortion in a sexual assault trial? No study has examined this question, or whether or not jury deliberation rectifies or reinforces pre-decisional distortion in a sexual assault trial. Given the commonality of rape myths and misconceptions, if a majority of jurors adhere to them, deliberation is likely to have a reinforcing effect, while hung juries may represent the situation where groups of jurors adhere to opposing beliefs.

What determines jurors' early commitment to a particular verdict is likely to involve the type of reasoning described in the heuristic-systematic processing model in Chapter 5, which explains jurors' early commitment to one side or the other. This model also explains the role of rape myths in jury decision-making since heuristic processing:

> emphasizes 'vibes', emotions, and stereotypical thinking from past events … [and] is also associated with solving problems that rely on life lessons and experience that elude articulation and logical analysis … and is particularly prone to logical shortcuts or heuristics … . The rational [systematic processing model] …, on the other hand, is intentional and effortful. It is logic-driven; it is active, conscious, and requires justification via evidence … and it makes possible complex generalization, comprehension of cause and effect, and high levels of abstraction and complex reasoning. (Gunnell & Ceci, 2010: 853; references omitted)

The question, therefore, is whether or not law reform can counteract the impact of rape myths, heuristic processing and pre-decisional distortion. I will examine this question in the next chapter when documenting the history of the modernisation of the substantive law of consent in both E&W and NSW.

References

Blackstone, W. (1765–1769). *Commentaries on the laws of England* (Book 4, Chapter 15 of Offenses Against the Persons of Individuals). Oxford: The Clarendon Press.

Blume, J. H., Johnson, S. L., & Paavola, E. C. (2007). Every juror wants a story: Narrative relevance, third party guilt and the right to present a defense. *American Criminal Law Review, 44*, 1069–1113.

Bracton, H. (1268/1968). *Bracton on the laws and customs of England* (S. Thorne, Trans.). Cambridge, MA: Harvard University Press.

Bronitt, S. (1998). The rules of recent complaint: Rape myths and the legal construction of the 'reasonable' rape victim. In P. Easteal (ed), *Balancing The Scales, Rape Law Reform and Australian Culture* (pp. 41–59). Sydney: Federation Press.

Carlson, K. A., & Russo, J. E. (2001). Biased interpretation of evidence by mock jurors. *Journal of Experimental Psychology: Applied, 7*, 91–103.

Clifford, B. (2003). Methodology: Law's adopting and adapting to psychology's methods and findings. In D. Carson & R. Bull (Eds.), *Handbook of psychology in legal contexts* (pp. 605–624). Chichester: Wiley.

Cossins, A. (2011a). Similar facts and consent in sexual assault cases: Filling in the gap left by the high court in *Phillips*. *Monash University Law Review, 37*, 47–88.

Cossins, A. (2011b). The behaviour of persistent sex offenders: Implications for the prosecution of child sex offences in joint trials. *Melbourne University Law Review, 35*, 821–864.

Cossins, A. (2013a). The legacy of the *Makin* case 120 years on: Legal fictions, circular reasoning and some solutions. *Sydney Law Review, 35*, 731–759.

Cossins, A. (2015). *Female criminality: Infanticide, moral panics and the female body*. Basingstoke, UK: Palgrave Macmillan.

Cossins, A. (2019). Why her behaviour is still on trial: The absence of context in the modernisation of the substantive law on consent. *The University of New South Wales Law Journal, 42*, 462–499.

Dahl, L. C., Brimacombe, C. A. E., & Lindsay, D. S. (2009). Investigating investigators: How presentation order influences participant–investigators' interpretations of eyewitness identification and alibi evidence. *Law and Human Behavior, 33*, 368–380.

DeKay, M. L. (2015). Predecisional information distortion and the self-fulfilling prophecy of early preferences in choice. *Current Directions in Psychological Science, 24*, 405–411.

Devine, D. J. (2012). *Jury decision making: The state of the science*. New York: New York University Press.

Devine, D. J., & Caughlin, D. E. (2014). Do they matter? A meta-analytic investigation of individual characteristics and guilt judgments. *Psychology, Public Policy, and Law, 20*, 109–134.

Dinos, S., Burrowes, N., Hammond, K., & Cunliffe, C. (2015). A systematic review of juries' assessment of rape victims: Do rape myths impact on juror decision-making? *International Journal of Law, Crime and Justice, 43*, 36–49.

Ellison, L., & Munro, V. E. (2009a). Of 'normal sex' and 'real rape': Exploring the use of socio-sexual scripts in (mock) jury deliberation. *Social and Legal Studies, 18*, 291–312.

Ellison, L., & Munro, V. E. (2009b). Reacting to rape: Exploring mock jurors' assessments of complainant credibility. *British Journal of Criminology, 49*, 202–219.

Glanvil, W. (1170/1965). *The treatise on the laws and customs of the realm of England* (G. Hall & G. Derek, Eds.). London: Nelson.

Gray, J. M. (2006). Rape myth beliefs and prejudiced instructions: Effects on decisions of guilt in a case of date rape. *Legal and Criminological Psychology, 75,* 75–80.

Gunnell, J. J., & Ceci, S. J. (2010). When emotionality trumps reason: A study of individual processing style and juror bias. *Behavioral Sciences & the Law, 28,* 850–877.

Haegerich, T. M., & Bottoms, B. L. (2000). Empathy and jurors' decisions in trials involving child sexual assault allegations. *Law and Human Behavior, 24,* 421–448.

Haegerich, T. M., Salerno, J. M., & Bottoms, B. L. (2013). Are the effects of juvenile offender stereotypes maximized or minimized by jury deliberation? *Psychology, Public Policy & Law, 19,* 81–97.

Hershkowitz, I., Lamb, M. E., & Horowitz, D. (2007). Victimisation of children with disabilities. *American Journal of Orthopsychiatry, 77,* 629–635.

Huntley, J. E., & Costanzo, M. (2003). Sexual harassment stories: Testing a story-mediated model of juror decision-making in civil litigation. *Law and Human Behavior, 27,* 29–51.

Jones, L., Bellis, M. A., Wood, S., Hughes, K., McCoy, E., Eckley, L., … Officer, A. (2012). Prevalence and risk of violence against children with disabilities: A systematic review and meta-analysis of observational studies. *The Lancet, 380,* 899–907.

Judicial College. (2013–2019). *Equal treatment bench book.* https://www.judiciary.uk/wp-content/uploads/2018/02/equal-treatment-bench-book-february2018-v5-02mar18.pdf.

Judicial Commission of NSW. (2017, Update). *Criminal trial courts benchbook.* www.judcom.nsw.gov.au/publications/benchbks/criminal/index.html.

Lagnado, D. A., & Harvey, N. (2008). The impact of discredited evidence. *Psychonomic Bulletin and Review, 15,* 1166–1173.

Pennington, N., & Hastie, R. (1986). Evidence evaluation in complex decisions-making. *Journal of Personality and Social Psychology, 51,* 242–258.

Pennington, N., & Hastie, R. (1988). Explanation-based decision making: Effects of memory structure on judgment. *Journal of Experimental Psychology: Learning Memory and Cognition, 14,* 521–533.

Pennington, N., & Hastie, R. (1992). Explaining the evidence: Tests of the story model for juror decision making. *Journal of Personality and Social Psychology, 62,* 189–206.

Stewart, D. N., & Jacquin, K. M. (2010). Juror perceptions in a rape trial: Examining the complainant's ingestion of chemical substances prior to sexual assault. *Journal of Aggression, Maltreatment & Trauma, 19,* 853–874.

Willmott, D., Boduszek, D., Debowska, A., & Woodfield, R. (2018). Introduction and validation of the juror decision scale (JDS): An empirical investigation of the story model. *Journal of Criminal Justice, 57,* 26–34.

Wissink, I. B., van Vugt, E., Moonen, X., Stams, G.-J., & Hendriks, J. (2015). Sexual abuse involving children with an intellectual disability (ID): A narrative review. *Research in Developmental Disabilities, 36,* 20–35.

7

Modernisation of the Substantive Law of Consent

1 Introduction: Modernisation of the Substantive Law of Consent

Beginning in the 1970s in the USA (Klein, 2015), there have been a number of important reforms to the substantive laws governing sex offences in various countries around the world, including E&W, Scotland,[1] Canada,[2] New Zealand and all Australian states and territories (Australian Law Reform Commission (ALRC), 2010a: 1129–1176). The question is whether any of these reforms have been sufficient to counteract the rape myths that we know influence jurors' verdicts in sexual assault trials.

Generally speaking, the concept of consent has been central to law reform in these countries and has driven the development of rape law into the arena of sexual autonomy. Nonetheless, the legal concept of 'consent' '*presupposes what it undermines*, namely *women's full-blown sexual agency*' (du Toit, 2007: 59; emphases in original) as discussed in the case studies below.

[1] *Protection of Children and Prevention of Sexual Offences (Scotland) Act* 2005.

[2] Criminal Code (R.S.C., 1985, c. C-46) ss 273.1, 273.2, 274, 275, 276, 277, & 278.

A. Cossins, *Closing the Justice Gap for Adult and Child Sexual Assault*,
https://doi.org/10.1057/978-1-137-32051-3_7

In other words, RMA beliefs create the cultural conditions in which normative sexual relations can involve non-consensual sex with a woman by a man whose belief in consent is considered to be reasonable. The two case studies discussed in this chapter illustrate this proposition and the paradox at the heart of the substantive law of rape—that it is possible for:

i. a woman who does not communicate her consent to be deemed to consent; and
ii. a defendant to have a reasonable belief about a woman's consent even though it is accepted that she did not consent,

both of which undermine the concept of her sexual autonomy.

In light of the research on rape myths which shows that RMA is one of the most consistent predictors of victim blame in sexual assault scenarios, this chapter[3] discusses how sexual assault law reform, which has been based on a 'communicative' model of consent, has been subsequently undermined. Options for reform are discussed in light of the community standards expected under a 'communicative' model of consent.

In order to focus the discussion, the relevant law from NSW and E&W are used as examples while similar provisions in other jurisdictions are footnoted. NSW is used as the main example because that jurisdiction underwent the most recent changes to its sexual assault provisions in order to deal with, among other things, the difficulties with proving lack of consent (NSW Criminal Justice and Sexual Offences Taskforce, 2006) and the problems associated with the fault element, that is, the defendant's state of mind. It is also the jurisdiction that was used as a model by the Australian Law Reform Commission (ALRC) (2010a) in recommending amendments to the fault element in other Australian jurisdictions (ALRC, 2010a: 1165). In addition, in May 2018, the NSW Attorney-General asked the NSW Law Reform Commission (NSWLRC) to review sexual assault law in NSW after a rape

---

[3]Based on the article by Cossins (2019).

complainant in a controversial rape case told her story on national television.[4] This case will be discussed in the second case study. In October 2019, the NSWLRC released a set of draft proposals in relation to consent (NSWLRC, 2019), as discussed below.

The type of sexual conduct defined as rape has evolved from a requirement to prove the use of force or violence to mere proof of lack of consent even in circumstances with no overt threats, evidence of violence or physical resistance by the complainant (Forster, 2009; Quilter, 2015). Cowan (2007b: 94–95) discusses the evolution of the law of rape from an offence which was only enlivened if force had been used 'against the will' of the complainant to an offence which is enlivened if there has been a 'violation of [her] sexual autonomy'.

Many countries modernised their substantive laws on sex offences in light of empirical evidence about the low reporting rates of sexual assault, high attrition rates and low conviction rates (see, for example, Criminal Justice and Sexual Offences Taskforce, 2005; Home Office, 2000; HM Inspectorate of Constabulary & HM Crown Prosecution Service Inspectorate, 2002) or because the substantive law was out-dated, reflecting the knowledge and attitudes of former centuries where 'the laws were designed to protect [the] property interests' of men (Quilter, 2015: 101):

> the focus on (forced) penile-vaginal penetration … reflect[ed] a historic conceptualisation of rape as … [theft] whereby rape provisions were constructed and intended to protect a father from the loss of a virgin daughter's value as a transferable asset, or to protect a husband from his loss of exclusive conjugal rights, rather than to protect the physical and sexual integrity of the victim. (Forster, 2009: 836; footnotes omitted; see also Home Office, 2000, 2002; Law Commission, 2000; Scottish Law Commission, 2007)

Forster (2009: 837) summarises three significant 'waves of reform' of the substantive law on sexual assault which began in the 1970s in the USA, followed by reform in the 1980s in NSW, Canada and New Zealand and then in the 2000s in E&W, Scotland, South Africa and other Australian

[4] 'I am that girl', *4Corners*, ABC Television, 7 May 18; www.lawreform.justice.nsw.gov.au/Pages/lrc/lrc_current_projects/Consent/Consent.aspx; accessed 9 May 18.

states. In many jurisdictions, this modernisation has involved three key reforms (United Nations Department of Economic and Social Affairs Division for the Advancement of Women, 2010: 28):

i. a statutory definition of consent;
ii. an objective test for determining the defendant's state of mind or knowledge; and
iii. a list of evidential and conclusive presumptions about consent, or of circumstances vitiating consent.[5]

Modernisation has seen the concept of consent develop into a communicative model where the *capacity* to freely agree is the measure for assessing lack of consent. For example, in NSW in 2007, the then Attorney-General observed that:

> Modernisation of the law relating to consent, in particular, is aimed at bringing about both a cultural shift in the response to victims of sexual assault by the community and by key participants within the criminal justice system. (Hatzistergos, 2007: 3584)

Despite this modernisation, the fact remains that the prosecution must prove beyond reasonable doubt that a complainant did not consent and that the defendant had no knowledge, or, in some jurisdictions, was reckless about informing himself of her lack of consent. There is no legislative restriction that prevents victim-blaming attitudes from being taken into account by fact-finders.

[5]In E&W, a presumptions method is used, that is, an evidential presumption of non-consent is raised where certain circumstances exist (Sexual Offences Act 2003, ss 75 and 76) which may be rebutted by evidence to the contrary from the defendant compared to the approach in NSW, Scotland and Canada where a list of vitiating circumstances has been enacted which mean there is no consent in those circumstances (*Crimes Act 1900* (NSW), s 61HA(4) & (5); Canadian Criminal Code, s 273.1(2)); Sexual Offences (Scotland) Act 2009, ss 13–14). Rook and Ward (2016: 5) note that the evidential presumptions 'very rarely arise in practice'.

2 The Fact-Finder's Task in an Era of Modernisation

An example of how modernisation of the law operates can be seen in NSW where the common law term, 'rape', is no longer used in relation to sexual offences.[6] Instead, s 61I of the *Crimes Act* 1900 (NSW) criminalises sexual intercourse without consent:

> Any person who has sexual intercourse with another person without the consent of the other person and who knows that the other person does not consent to the sexual intercourse is liable to imprisonment for 14 years.

The fact-finder must be satisfied that the prosecution has proved the following three elements beyond reasonable doubt:

1. that the defendant had sexual intercourse with the complainant at the time and place alleged;
2. without the complainant's consent; and
3. the defendant did so knowing that the complainant did not consent.

Under s 61HA of the *Crimes Act*, sexual intercourse is defined more broadly and uses gender-neutral terms unlike E&W. It includes penetration of any part of the body by any object or any part of another person's body:

> 1. … 'sexual intercourse' means:
>
>   (a) sexual connection occasioned by the penetration to any extent of the genitalia (including a surgically constructed vagina) of a female person or the anus of any person by:

[6] *Crimes Act 1900* (NSW), s 63. Penetration is still described as rape in other Australian jurisdictions: Victoria (*Crimes Act 1958*, s 38); Queensland (*Criminal Code 1899*, s 349); South Australia (*Criminal Law Consolidation Act 1935*, s 48); Tasmania (*Criminal Code 1924*, s 185). It is described as 'sexual intercourse without consent' in Australia's two territories (the Australian Capital Territory (ACT) (*Crimes Act 1900*, s 54) and the Northern Territory (*Criminal Code*, s 192), while in Western Australia (WA) it is described as 'sexual penetration without consent' (*Criminal Code*, s 325).

(i) any part of the body of another person, or
(ii) any object manipulated by another person, except where the penetration is carried out for proper medical purposes, or

(b) sexual connection occasioned by the introduction of any part of the penis of a person into the mouth of another person, or
(c) cunnilingus, or
(d) the continuation of sexual intercourse as defined in paragraph (a), (b) or (c).

In NSW, a statutory definition of consent was enacted in 2007[7] as a result of a year-long review of the prosecution of sexual offences by the Criminal Justice and Sexual Offences Taskforce (2005) (the Taskforce).[8] In relation to adult sex offences, the Taskforce recommended a statutory definition of consent which was based on the definition under s 74 of the *Sexual Offences Act 2003* (UK)[9]:

> a person consents if he agrees by choice, and has the freedom and capacity to make that choice.

Although the definition in E&W 'is not a model of tight drafting' since 'the parameters of "freedom" are not clear' (Rook & Ward, 2016: 79), it was premised on the understanding that 'free agreement would assist in making it clear that absence of protest, resistance or injury does not necessarily mean the complainant consented' (Rook & Ward, 2016: 4).

The courts in E&W have given a 'wide interpretation to the definition of consent' under s 74 which has resulted in 'a focus on the autonomy of the complainant' (Rook & Ward, 2016: 4) and appears to cover the situation where a complainant freezes, 'utters no protest and offers no physical resistance' (Rook & Ward, 2016: 77). Overall, this definition

---

[7]Under the *Crimes Amendment (Consent—Sexual Offences) Act 2007* (NSW)).

[8]The author was involved in lobbying the then Attorney-General, Mr. Bob Debus, to set up this taskforce in December 2004. As a member of the taskforce and because I was subsequently involved in drafting the legislation which introduced a statutory definition of consent in NSW, the discussion in this chapter allows me to reflect on the impact of this particular definition and other reforms that resulted from the work of the Taskforce.

[9]For the background to the *Sexual Offences Act 2003*, see Rook and Ward (2016: 3–9).

recognises that '[o]ne does not consent to sex in general. One consents to this act of sex with this person at this time and in this place'.[10] Judges in E&W are required to instruct juries to counteract the influence of stereotypical assumptions about sexual behaviour and consent as set out in the *Crown Court Compendium* (Judicial College, 2019: 20–1).[11]

An issue that has arisen in E&W is whether or not compliance in the face of being groomed for sex amounts to consent under the UK definition. In *R v Ali (Yasir Ifran)*,[12] the complainant was groomed for sexual exploitation and complied with the defendant's demands for sex. The Court of Appeal stated that although:

> grooming does not necessarily vitiate consent, it starkly raises the possibility that a vulnerable or immature individual may have been placed in a position in which he or she is led merely to acquiesce rather than to give proper and real consent. One of the consequences of grooming is that it has a tendency to limit or subvert the alleged victim's capacity to make free decisions.[13]

Grooming also has the effect of creating an 'environment of dependency' whereby the complainant is confused or oblivious to their right to say no.[14] Overall, the E&W case law reveals a number of important principles so that there is no requirement for the prosecution to prove (i) verbal or physical behaviour (such as 'no' or active resistance) by the complainant to indicate lack of consent; or (ii) that 'absence of consent was communicated to the defendant'; or (iii) that the complainant 'was incapable of saying "no"' (Rook & Ward, 2016: 115).

Based on the statutory definition in E&W, s 61HE(2) of the *Crimes Act 1900* sets out the definition of consent in NSW:

---

[10] *R v Cooper* [2009] UKHL 42, [27] (Baroness Hale).

[11] See *Miller* [2010] EWCA Crim 1578.

[12] [2015] EWCA Crim 1279.

[13] Ibid., [58] (Fulford LJ).

[14] Ibid. See also *C v R* [2012] EWCA 2034 in which a step-daughter was groomed for sexual exploitation from the age of five to 25.

> A person 'consents' to sexual intercourse if the person freely and voluntarily agrees to the sexual intercourse.[15]

The NSWLRC (2019) recently recommended the enactment of a provision to clarify this definition by ensuring consent pertains to the particular time of the alleged sexual activity,[16] as well as a provision which clarifies that a person may withdraw their consent at any time.[17] These clarification provisions would be unnecessary but for the age-old assumption that a woman's consent to sex *at any time* has, in the past, been interpreted as consent to sex at a later time and consent to all types of sexual activities.

When the definition of consent in NSW was first enacted it was accompanied by an expanded list of circumstances in which consent is deemed to be vitiated or negated, although such circumstances presume consent unless the vitiating circumstance is proved beyond reasonable doubt.[18] Around Australia, all jurisdictions except the Australian Capital Territory (ACT) have enacted a statutory definition of consent using

---

[15]In NSW, those under the age of 16 years do not have the capacity to give consent, compared to the situation in England and Wales where, if a complainant is aged 13 years or over, the prosecution must prove lack of consent (see *Sexual Offences Act* 2003 (UK), s 5).

[16]Draft s 61HI(1): A person consents to a sexual activity if, at the time of the sexual activity, the person freely and voluntarily agrees to the sexual activity (NSWLRC, 2019: 9).

[17]Draft s 61HI(2): A person may, by words or conduct, withdraw consent to a sexual activity at any time before or during the sexual activity. Sexual activity that occurs after consent has been withdrawn occurs without consent (NSWLRC, 2019: 9).

[18]In NSW, consent is negated if any of the circumstances under s 61HE(5) and (6) of the *Crimes Act* are satisfied:

(5) A person does not consent to sexual intercourse: (a) if the person does not have the capacity to consent to the sexual intercourse, including because of age or cognitive incapacity, or (b) if the person does not have the opportunity to consent to the sexual intercourse because the person is unconscious or asleep, or (c) if the person consents to the sexual intercourse because of threats of force or terror (whether the threats are against, or the terror is instilled in, that person or any other person), or (d) if the person consents to the sexual intercourse because the person is unlawfully detained. Section 61HE(5) is only relevant where there is apparent consent to sexual intercourse but the consent is negatived because of lack of capacity to consent or because it was induced by force or terror (*R v XHR* [2012] NSWCCA 247 [69] (Beazley JA)). Section 61HE(6) states: A person who consents to sexual intercourse with another person: (a) under a mistaken belief as to the identity of the other person, or (b) under a mistaken belief that the other person is married to the person, or (c) under a mistaken belief that the sexual intercourse is for health or hygienic purposes (or under any other mistaken belief about the nature of the act induced by fraudulent means), does not consent to the sexual intercourse.

either 'free agreement',[19] 'free and voluntary agreement'[20] or 'consent freely and voluntarily given'[21] while Scotland and Canada use the words 'free agreement' and 'voluntary agreement', respectively.[22] These jurisdictions also recognise that certain circumstances, such as the use of force, intimidation or complainant incapacity, negate consent.[23]

After a NSW government review of the statutory definition of consent in 2013, it was concluded that since:

> over 2,500 people have been charged and appeared before the higher courts for sexual assault and aggravated sexual assault offences in the years 2008 to 2012, the limited number of appeals identified leads the Review to conclude that the statutory definition is understood and is working in NSW's courts. (NSW Department of Attorney-General & Justice, 2013: 18)

However, this review had no way of considering the impact of the definition of consent in cases of acquittals so that there is no way of knowing the extent to which subjective decision-making by fact-finders is involved in deciding whether the elements of the offence under s 61I of the *Crimes Act* have been satisfied.

In a word-against-word case, the research tells us the credibility of the complainant is crucial (see Chapters 5 and 6). But because detecting deception is a complex task which is complicated by limited time in which to make an assessment of a trial witness, observers typically 'rely on heuristics' (Vrij, Granhag, & Porter, 2010: 98), that is, mental shortcuts about human behaviour, as discussed in Chapter 6. Because both laypeople and legal professionals are no better at assessing whether someone is telling the truth than tossing a coin (Ekman, O'Sullivan,

---

19 *Crimes Act 1958* (Vic), s 36; *Criminal Code 1924* (Tas), s 2A(1).

20 *Criminal Law Consolidation Act 1935* (SA), s 46(2); *Criminal Code*, s 192(1).

21 *Criminal Code 1899* (Qld), s 348(1); *Criminal Code* (WA), s 319(2).

22 *Sexual Offences (Scotland) Act 2009*, s 12; *Criminal Code* (Can), s 273.1(1).

23 See: *Criminal Code 1899* (Qld), s 348(2); *Criminal Code 1924* (Tas), s 2A(2); *Criminal Code 1983* (NT), s 192(2); *Criminal Code Compilation Act 1913* (WA), s 319(2); *Crimes Act 1900* (ACT), s 67; *Crimes Act 1958* (Vic), s 36(2); *Criminal Code* (Can), s 273.1(2); *Sexual Offences (Scotland) Act 2009*, ss 13(2), 14(2). Under the *Sexual Offences Act 2003* (UK), ss 75(2), 76(2) provide for evidential and conclusive presumptions about consent, respectively.

& Frank, 1999; Kassin, Meissner, & Norwick, 2005; Porter, Woodworth, & Birt, 2000; Vrij et al., 2010) and use inaccurate demeanour cues to determine veracity (DePaulo et al., 2003; Mann, Vrij, & Bull, 2004; Strömwall & Granhag, 2003; Vrij et al., 2010), jurors' subjective assessments are likely to involve unconscious biases, such as rape myths.

As discussed in Chapter 5, heuristic processing, sometimes referred to as the conflict between the head and the heart (Gawronski & Bodenhausen, 2014), involves little or no scrutiny of the evidence and low cognitive effort because the individual uses (persuasive) heuristic cues or generalisations and stereotypes about human behaviour to arrive at a decision. This is an inherently unreliable method since heuristics are derived from individual beliefs and experience which may not accurately reflect the human behaviour that is the subject of a criminal trial.

For example, the 'anchoring heuristic' which involves 'strong but often inaccurate intuitive judgments of a [person's] general trustworthiness quickly upon seeing his or her face for the first time' means that jurors have a 'tendency to make insufficient adjustments from an initial value or assessment (the anchor) resulting in a final decision that is biased toward that anchor' (Vrij et al., 2010: 99). It is likely, for example, that jurors use the anchoring heuristic with a sexual assault complainant since she is the defendant's accuser. In a sexual assault trial, heuristics are magnified because of the cultural context in which sexual relations are judged (Bennett Capers, 2012–2013; Cossins, 2003; Randall, 2010).

3 The Problems with a Statutory Definition of Consent

A statutory definition has the effect, supposedly, of introducing a communicative model of consent which, as a minimum standard of sexual behaviour (Pineau, 1989), emphasises the 'sexual autonomy' of the parties in the absence of force or coercion (Rumney, 2001) rather than a model in which the complainant is 'a passive recipient [which] reinforc[es] stereotyped binaries such as active/passive and possessing/possessed' (Taskforce, 2006: 34; 33; see also ALRC, 2010a: 1169; Munro, 2008).

However, the sexual autonomy of women is a relational concept that has been historically dependent on women's economic and legal dependence on men and cultural expectations associated with regulating women's moral propriety. The sexual autonomy of men has a different historical meaning so that men's sexual autonomy and women's sexual autonomy cannot be equated:

> The meaningful consent assumed as possible by rape law is associated with the traditional liberal notions of free will, contractualism, free negotiation, formal equality, assertiveness, competitiveness, and so on. (du Toit, 2007: 58)

Thus, 'the dividing line between real consent and mere submission may be difficult to draw' (ALRC, 2010a: 1147) since the legislative definition of consent is broad enough to encompass states of mind from intense desire to 'reluctant acquiescence' (Rook & Ward, 2016: 74) in a context of unequal power relations. A definition of consent based on free agreement supposedly 'directs attention … to the context in which agreement to intercourse is given or refused' and, in theory, allows a fact-finder to consider 'the power dynamics and cultural pressures that operate to constrain a person's freedom and capacity to make sexual choices' (Munro, 2008: 944).

However, such a broad scope is a two-edged sword since '[t]erms such as freedom, choice and capacity can be interpreted in radically divergent and often minimalist ways' (Munro, 2008: 944; see also Munro, 2017), with little or no recognition of the economic, cultural or religious context in which a complainant's consent appeared to be given. As such, fact-finders are not required to make an assessment of the actual capacity of the complainant to make a free choice in the cultural context in which she finds herself, for example, as a partner subject to threats or violence, as an employee who cannot afford to lose her job or because of a large age difference between her and the defendant.

For an offence which involves the interpretation of sexual behaviour, there are many points where subjective and heuristic reasoning is possible, if not encouraged by the substantive law on sexual assault. In a culture where rape myths are promoted by pornographic depictions of 'consensual' sex (such as her provocative behaviour and submission to his natural, uncontrollable desires and coercive persuasions) and where pornography is viewed by millions, a communicative model of consent may seem rather passé to defendants and fact-finders, as illustrated in Case Study Two below.

In essence, the sexual assault trial does not operate in a cultural vacuum but in a context imbued with a 'profound suspicion of female sexuality' (Munro, 2008: 936) so that the consent threshold will be a floating standard, dependent on the facts of each particular case and the subjective interpretation of those facts by fact-finders (judge or jurors). The effect of a communicative model of consent is easily counteracted by beliefs that a complainant has behaved in culturally unacceptable ways.

The model presumes that men and women communicate about, and engage in, sexual behaviour from positions of social and economic equality when, in reality, many sexual interactions are characterised by inequality, control and/or exploitation (Cowan, 2007a; Munro, 2017), as discussed in Chapter 5. For example, those who have been sexually abused as children or raped as adults are more susceptible to repeated sexual victimisation (Stanko & Williams, 2009)[24] which gives pause to the communicative model of consent since many perpetrators target those vulnerable to re-victimisation. However, social messages and advertising campaigns position women's vulnerability to sexual assault as the problem (Munro, 2017) rather than men's predatory behaviour, suggesting that the communicative model of consent is premised on the legitimacy of men's predation and women's need to protect themselves.

Because the prosecution must prove beyond reasonable doubt that the complainant did not 'freely and voluntarily agree to the sexual intercourse' in NSW, the fact-finder must consider the behaviour and words of the complainant at the time of the sexual intercourse. A communicative model of consent may have no effect in changing the attitudes of fact-finders if normative judgements about women's passive sexuality and conformity to 'feminine' behaviour continue to influence credibility assessments and verdicts. In such a cultural context, the fact-finder is invited to subjectively assess whether a complainant's verbal and/or

[24]See Chapter 4, Table 1, Comparison of symptoms of sexual victimisation with rape myths.

physical lack of agreement was sufficient, since there is no formula for deciding how much verbal or physical behaviour amounts to a *lack* of free and voluntary consent.

For example, does submission in relation to a command from a defendant amount to free and voluntary agreement? Does acquiescence gained by any means short of actual violence amount to free and voluntary agreement? Does acquiescence to vaginal sexual intercourse mean consent to other forms of penetration? These questions highlight the fact that consent is an empty concept whose meaning arises from context and, crucially, from interpretation of that context. In every sexual assault trial, consent is a vessel that will be filled by the moral and cultural values of the fact-finder.

The NSWLRC (2019) has sought to address this issue by recommending provisions that would ensure that if there is an absence of communication by the complainant regarding consent that absence cannot be taken to be a (silent) acquiescence to consent.[25] Nonetheless, these recommended provisions would do nothing to address the situation where a complainant complies with a defendant's demands out of fear.

In NSW, juries will be told that 'a person who does not offer actual physical resistance to a sexual activity is not, by reason only of that fact, to be regarded as consenting to the sexual intercourse'.[26] But how will fact-finders deal with little or no physical resistance, particularly since some studies in Chapter 3 showed that laypeople expect some degree of physical resistance to be convinced that a complainant was not consenting?

In order to ameliorate some of the myths surrounding sexual assault, further assistance is provided to the fact-finder under s 61HE(8) of the NSW *Crimes Act* about the grounds 'on which it may be established that a person does not consent to a sexual activity'. However, these grounds, which include '*substantially* intoxicated by alcohol or

[25] Draft s 61HJ(1)(A): 'A person does not consent to a sexual activity if the person does not do or say anything to communicate consent' (NSWLRC, 2019: 13). Draft s 61HI(4): 'A person who consents to a particular sexual activity is not, by reason only of that fact, to be taken to consent to any other sexual activity' (NSWLRC, 2019: 10).

[26] *Crimes Act 1900* (NSW), s 61HE(9).

any drug' (emphasis added), 'intimidatory or coercive conduct, or other threat' and 'abuse of a position of authority or trust', do not automatically negate consent.[27]

Section 61HE(8) is only relevant where there is 'apparent consent ... but the consent is negatived' because one of the above grounds is made out.[28] In other words, the prosecution must still prove a lack of consent by the complainant.[29] In relation to intoxication, s 61HE(8)(a) contains no definition of 'substantially' and does not address the situation where a complainant is affected by alcohol and/or drugs but not substantially so, but is still vulnerable to predation. Furthermore, what does 'substantially' mean from a medical point of view in terms of degrees of impairment? Laypeople are not qualified to determine whether a complainant was substantially or not substantially intoxicated. The provision also takes no account of the fact that alcohol affects different people differently depending on factors such as gender, weight and age which are related to a person's ability to breakdown alcohol.[30]

For example, if there was no blood alcohol or drug testing or other medical assessment of the complainant's state at the time in question, a fact-finder's assessment of intoxication will be entirely subjective unless the complainant was unconsciousness. Arguably, it is insufficient to leave a complainant's level of intoxication (or being stupified, the term used in E&W) to guesswork by laypeople on a case by case basis. The problem with determining intoxication from a layperson's point of view is discussed in Case Study Two below.[31]

---

[27] Section 61HE(10) of the *Crimes Act 1900* (NSW) states that: 'this section does not limit the grounds on which it may be established that a person does not consent to sexual intercourse'.

[28] *R v XHR* [2012] NSWCCA 247, [69] (Beazley JA).

[29] The NSWLRC (2019: 13) proposes one simple list of circumstances which make it clear that consent does not exist in these circumstances.

[30] In England and Wales, intoxication is dealt with under s 75(2)(f), *Sexual Offences Act 2003* and has received much criticism since it 'applies mainly to the "drug rape" scenario' and implies a distinction between voluntary and involuntary intoxication (Leahy, 2014a: 257).

[31] Even if the NSWLRC's (2019: 14) recommendation that the wording be changed from 'substantially' to 'so affected by alcohol or another drug as to be incapable of consenting to the sexual activity', this still requires guesswork on the part of the fact-finder.

4 Proving the Mental Element of the Offence

The third element (or mental element) to be satisfied by the prosecution beyond reasonable doubt under s 61I of the *Crimes Act* in NSW is that the defendant had sexual intercourse *knowing* that the complainant did not consent. Prior to the 2007 amendments in NSW, the so-called *Morgan* defence[32] was available to a defendant which stated that a defendant's honest belief in consent encompassed an unreasonable belief in consent. In other words, an honest belief, even if based on unreasonable grounds, constituted a sufficient rebuttal to the prosecution's argument that the defendant knew the complainant was not consenting.

This honest belief is known as the subjective standard, a measure that did little to protect the vulnerability of women to sexual assault and preserved men's sexual access to women who did not consent in a context where women in the 1970s were still regarded as unreliable witnesses. In particular, 'the existence of the defence ... privileged particular ... social beliefs and sent out a message about the power relationships in society' (Banks, 2008: 235).

In NSW, the Taskforce (2005: 45) stated that reform was needed for several reasons:

i. an assertion of an honest belief is almost impossible to refute, 'regardless of how unreasonable the belief is';
ii. the validity of a defence based on unreasonable grounds reinforced the myth 'that women desire to be overpowered';
iii. inadequate protection 'of the autonomy of people to participate in sexual activity'; and
iv. to ensure 'that a reasonable standard of care is taken to ascertain whether a person is consenting'.

[32] *DPP v Morgan* [1976] AC 182.

The Taskforce (2005) recommended consideration of the Canadian reform[33] which abolishes belief in consent as a defence unless based on reasonable grounds, thus allowing for an objective assessment of the circumstances by the fact-finder. The subjective conception of belief in consent has since been legislatively amended in various jurisdictions to introduce an objective standard regarding consent (with a focus on the reasonableness of the defendant's belief) which has been adopted in E&W,[34] New Zealand[35] and Scotland[36] although the tests are not wholly objective.

For example, E&W did 'not adopt a test based on what a reasonable man would have believed'; rather the jury is able to take into account the defendant's 'personal characteristics' in considering the reasonableness of his belief because the legislation states that whether a belief is reasonable depends on 'all the circumstances' (Rook & Ward, 2016: 163–165). This is but a short step from *Morgan* since, as Rook and Ward (2016: 166) ask, '[w]hich characteristics are properly relevant to the defendant's ability to appreciate the risk that the complainant was not consenting?'

---

[33] *Criminal Code*, RSC 1985, c C-46, s 273.2 which states: 'It is not a defence to a charge under section 271, 272 or 273 that the accused believed that the complainant consented to the activity that forms the subject-matter of the charge, where (a) the accused's belief arose from the accused's (i) self-induced intoxication, or (ii) recklessness or wilful blindness; or (b) the accused did not take reasonable steps, in the circumstances known to the accused at the time, to ascertain that the complainant was consenting'.

[34] *Sexual Offences Act 2003*, s 1 which states: 'A person (A) commits an offence if—(a) he intentionally penetrates the vagina, anus or mouth of another person (B) with his penis, (b) B does not consent to the penetration, and (c) A does not reasonably believe that B consents. (2) Whether a belief is reasonable is to be determined having regard to all the circumstances, including any steps A has taken to ascertain whether B consents'.

[35] *Crimes Act 1961* (NZ), s 128(2) which states: '(2) Person A rapes person B if person A has sexual connection with person B, effected by the penetration of person B's genitalia by person A's penis, (a) without person B's consent to the connection; and (b) without believing on reasonable grounds that person B consents to the connection'. Section 128(3) is in like terms.

[36] *Sexual Offences (Scotland) Act 2009*, s 1 which states: 'If a person ("A"), with A's penis— (a) without another person ("B") consenting, and (b) without *any reasonable belief* that B consents, penetrates to any extent, either intending to do so or reckless as to whether there is penetration, the vagina, anus or mouth of B then A commits an offence, to be known as the offence of rape'. Section 2 is in like terms but refers to sexual assault by penetration with a part of the body.

Although self-induced intoxication is not a permissible factor in NSW,[37] and E&W (Rook & Ward, 2016: 173), what about a psychiatric condition[38] or autism? Or delusional and/or cultural beliefs about women's availability for sex? Or a sex addiction? In the absence of clear, legislative guidance, fact-finders are able to consider any characteristics they think are relevant. In the face of largely unaccountable jury decision-making, it is one thing for lawmakers to intentionally overturn a *Morgan*-type defence and another for fact-finders to understand and follow that intention, as illustrated in the two case studies below.

Unlike NSW, other jurisdictions have not 'included both recklessness and an objective test in the one provision' which defines sexual assault or rape (Dobinson & Townsley, 2008: 164), as set out in Table 1, which sets out the scope of the mental element for prosecuting sexual intercourse without consent in different jurisdictions. For example, in E&W, while intention to have intercourse must be proved by the prosecution beyond reasonable doubt, the law has been simplified by removing the concept of recklessness, with 'reasonable belief' in all the circumstances being the standard of care required. However, the introduction of an objective standard in E&W in 2003 'does not appear to have significantly impacted trial practices and outcomes' (Larcombe, Fileborn, Powell, Hanley, & Henry, 2016: 614), with no significant increase in conviction rates since its introduction in 2004.

When enacting reforms to overcome the *Morgan* defence, the NSW Government was not prepared to go as far as Canada by enacting a purely objective test.[39] Instead, it enacted s 61HA(3) of the *Crimes Act* (subsequently re-enacted as s 61HE(3)) which sets out the knowledge requirement to be proved by the prosecution and creates an additional fault element in addition to what already existed at common law.[40]

---

[37]See *Crimes Act 1900*, s 61HA(3)(e).

[38]See *R v MM* [2011] EWCA Crim 1291; *B v R* [2013] EWCA Crim 3.

[39]It is debatable whether there is much difference, in practice, between '(1) an honest belief held by a defendant which may have been reasonable in the circumstances and (2) a belief which a reasonable man, placed in the defendant's circumstances, may have held' (*R v MM* [2011] EWCA Crim 1291, [54] (Pitchford LJ).

[40]Section 61HE(3)(a) and (b) of the NSW *Crimes Act* represent a codification of the common law while 61HE(3)(c) eliminates a *Morgan*-type defence. Proof of the mental element (the defendant's 'guilty mind') differs around Australia. Three of the code states, Queensland, Tasmania

Table 1 Scope of the mental element for prosecuting sexual intercourse without consent in different jurisdictions

	NSW[a]	NSWLRC (2019) recommendations	E&W[b]	Scotland[c]	Canada[d]
Knowledge	Y	Y[e]	N	Y	N
Recklessness	Y	Y	N	Y	Y
Reasonable belief or belief on reasonable grounds	Y	Y[f]	Y	Y	Y
Requirement to take steps or reasonable steps	Y	Y[g]	Y	Y	Y
Intention	N	N	Y	Y	Y
Honest belief on unreasonable grounds	N	N	N	N	N

[a] *Crimes Act 1900*, s 61I
[b] Sexual Offences Act 2003, ss 1 and 2
[c] Sexual Offences (Scotland) Act 2009, ss 1–3, 16
[d] Canadian Criminal Code, s 265(1)
[e] Draft s 61HK(1): wording to be changed from 'if an accused knows' to an accused 'is taken to know' (NSWLRC, 2019: 20)
[f] Draft s 61HK(1)(c): 'any belief that the [accused] has, or may have, that the [complainant] consents to the sexual activity is not reasonable in the circumstances' (NSWLRC, 2019: 21)
[g] Draft s 61HK(2): trier of fact 'must have regard to all the circumstances of the case, including whether the accused person said or did anything to ascertain if the [complainant] consented to the sexual activity, and if so, what the [accused] said or did' (NSWLRC, 2019: 22)

Thus, the fact-finder must decide whether the prosecution has proved beyond reasonable doubt that the defendant actually knew the complainant did not consent, or was reckless as to whether she was

and WA make it an offence if a person intends to have sexual intercourse without consent: *Criminal Code 1899* (Qld), s 349; *Criminal Code Act 1924* (Tas), s 13; *Criminal Code Compilation Act 1913* (WA), s 325. In the ACT, the NT, South Australia and Victoria, the fault element for sexual intercourse without consent is intention and knowledge or intention and recklessness: *Crimes Act 1900* (ACT), s 92D; *Criminal Code* (NT), s 194(2); *Criminal Law Consolidation Act 1935* (SA), 48(1); *Crimes Act 1958* (Vic), s 38(2)(a).

not consenting,[41] or had no reasonable grounds for believing that the complainant was consenting. If the prosecution relies on proving lack of reasonable grounds, it must show that:

i. the defendant did not honestly believe that the complainant was consenting, or
ii. if he did have an honest belief in consent, that he had no reasonable grounds for that belief.[42]

Similar to the position in E&W, s 61HE(1)(c) requires the jury to determine whether the defendant's subjective belief was reasonable.

Nonetheless, there are several trigger points for the use of heuristics by a fact-finder under s 61HA(3) because '[s]ubjective fault elements, such as recklessness, knowledge and honest belief, emphasise the perspective of a particular defendant' (ALRC, 2010a: 1163).

While amounting to a reform measure, in that the requirement for the jury to consider 'all the circumstances', including any steps taken by the defendant, amounts to an endorsement of the communicative model of consent (NSW Department of Attorney-General & Justice, 2013: 22), the jury is actually being invited 'to scrutinize the complainant's behaviour' (Temkin & Ashworth, 2004: 342) because there is no legislative guidance about what would or would not amount to a belief based on reasonable grounds. In other words, '[t]he legal gaze … always returns

[41] If the prosecution cannot prove that the defendant knew the complainant was not consenting under s 61HE(3)(a) of the NSW *Crimes Act*, recklessness may be established either because the defendant: '(a) realised there was a possibility the complainant was not consenting to that particular act but went ahead and performed it anyway or; (b) did not even think about whether the complainant was consenting … in other words he did not care whether she was consenting' (*R v Lazarus*, District Court of NSW, 4 May 2017, 2013/00242040, unreported (Judge Tupman), p. 11). Thus, in NSW, both 'advertent and inadvertent recklessness remain part of the legal landscape' (Monaghan & Mason, 2016: 255; see also Dobinson & Townsley, 2008: 162). In reality, 'recklessness' embodies the notion of reasonableness in the circumstances so that if a defendant did not advert to the possibility that the complainant was consenting 'then it is illogical that [he] could have also taken reasonable steps to ascertain consent' (Dobinson & Townsley, 2008: 165). Nonetheless, s 61HA(3)(c) was not intended to change the law on recklessness and case law indicates that inadvertent recklessness is still part of the legal landscape in NSW (Monaghan & Mason, 2016: 255–256).

[42] *AM v R* [2011] NSWCCA 237, [22] (Harrison J); *O'Sullivan v R; Flanders v R; Tohu v R; NRH v R* [2012] NSWCCA 45, [114] (Davies and Garling JJ); *Lazarus* [2016] NSWCCA 52; *R v Lazarus* [2017] NSWCCA 279.

to the body of the woman' (Cowan, 2007b: 95). While the communicative model of consent seeks to rectify this, essentially the model is contractual so that it denies the conditions of inequality that define many sexual encounters. The idea of 'free choice' and the power to 'bargain' denies the existence of economic, social and religious contexts in which women and girls are groomed, coerced and/or subject to threats to submit, that is, entrapped by prevailing cultural norms.

Thus, a legal definition of consent that includes a defence for an accused who 'reasonably believed' or 'believed on reasonable grounds' in the complainant's consent requires the fact-finder to interpret consent by focusing on the complainant's words and actions, that is, the defendant's knowledge is assessed with reference to her behaviour and credibility which is an inherently subjective process. Indeed, the apparent objective standard under s 61HE(3)(c) fits like a perfect jigsaw piece into the traditional conduct of the sexual assault trial. This is because its structure has, historically, encouraged the jury to focus on the complainant's behaviour in order to determine what 'signals' she was sending to the defendant and invites the jury to blame the victim for the defendant's belief. Thus, the inquiry remains the same whether the standard is subjective (an honest belief) or objective (a reasonable belief).[43]

Although 'the law demands full-blown sexual agency in women' (du Toit, 2007: 62), through the interpretation of consent and reasonable belief, fact-finders have the power to erase 'women's sexual freedom', turning her into a passive subject, 'at the same time [as] demanding a very high level of sexual responsibility' (ibid.). It is also this paradox that defence counsel exploit during cross-examination since they can easily tap into entrenched social expectations about women's and rape victims' behaviours, thus providing jurors with 'reasonable' doubts.

Indeed, 'reasonableness' is a relative concept. Even if a reasonable belief standard can be justified on the grounds that there has to some

[43]The recommendation for reform by the NSWLRC (2019: 21) (see draft below) does nothing to change this focus since the change in wording was merely designed to 'encourage fact-finders to assess the reasonableness of a belief holistically, in light of all relevant circumstances'. Whatever way it is expressed, the concept of reasonableness requires the fact-finder to focus on the complainant's behaviour, rather than that of the defendant. Draft s 61HK(1)(c): 'any belief that the [accused] has, or may have, that the [complainant] consents to the sexual activity is not reasonable in the circumstances' (NSWLRC, 2019: 21).

measure for protecting bodily integrity and sexual autonomy, Munro (2008: 945) considers that 'it is less than clear that [reasonable belief] will operate in practice to hold defendants to a higher level of accountability'. A wide range of rape myths associated with female intoxication, sexually enticing behaviour and standards of morality, allow fact-finders to formulate their own criteria of reasonableness in all the circumstances since the literature shows that juries and laypeople interpret lack of resistance, lack of medical injuries, lack of force and complainant intoxication as indicative of consent (Du Mont & White, 2007). As discussed in the previous chapters, the progression of sexual assault cases through the criminal justice system is affected by perceptions of the complainant's character and behaviour (Du Mont & White, 2007; Quadara, Fileborn, & Parkinson, 2013).

Thus, heuristics can render an actual lack of consent by a complainant ineffective because of cultural beliefs about 'real rape'. Snap judgements based on heuristics may blind the fact-finder to the applicable law, as discussed in Case Studies One and Two below:

> [p]eople typically react to ethical dilemmas by first forming snap judgments and then rationalising or modifying [them] through further reflection. … These snap judgments are not arbitrary, but are generally based on rough rules of thumb or heuristics … . The *soundness of the judgments will then depend on the reliability of the heuristics involved*. (Crowe & Sveinsson, 2017: 149; emphasis added)

5 Looking at 'All the Circumstances'

In considering whether the defendant had an honest belief and whether there were reasonable grounds for that belief, the fact-finder must 'have regard to all the circumstances of the case':

a. including any steps taken by the person to ascertain whether the alleged victim consents to the sexual activity, but
b. not including any self-induced intoxication of the person (NSW *Crimes Act*, s 61HE(4)).

Thus, 'it is no longer acceptable for a person not to have turned their mind to the issue of consent' such that there must be evidence of the positive steps taken (NSW Department of Attorney-General & Justice, 2013: 22). In practice, this is not how the law has been interpreted in two key judge-only trials, as discussed in the case studies below.

A finding that no steps or inadequate steps were taken amounts to constructive knowledge of lack of consent (Monaghan & Mason, 2016: 249) although 'it is misleading to describe the test' in NSW (*Crimes Act*, s 61HE(3)(c)) (ibid., 259) as objective since it contains both subjective and objective elements. But because 'reasonable grounds' is not a mathematical formula and has no objective standard to refer to, the test relies entirely on how individual fact-finders interpret all the circumstances in a particular case which is subject to their own heuristics, misconceptions and beliefs about human sexual behaviour. Even less objective is the fact that every jury verdict is idiosyncratic since each jury of twelve people will most likely never again sit as a jury on a sexual assault case.

Before the enactment of the NSW reforms, the draft Bill[44] attempted to address rape myths by stating that 'all the circumstances of the case' did not include 'the personal opinions, values and general social and educational development' of the defendant, in order to remind the fact-finder that the defendant's belief had to be based on objectively reasonable grounds. That particular qualification was subsequently omitted from the amending legislation. Despite its attempt to challenge cultural stereotypes, the draft Bill did not address the source of rape myths, that is, the fact-finder. The most recent recommendations for reform by the NSWLRC (2019: 22) also do not address the source of rape myths, although it recommends that 'all the circumstances' include 'whether the accused person said or did anything to ascertain if the [complainant] consented to the sexual activity, and if so, what the [accused] said or did'.

Perhaps the biggest problem with s 61HE(3)(c) is that it *assumes* that the fact-finder will not make unreasonable inferences about the complainant's behaviour in deciding whether reasonable grounds existed

---

[44]Crimes Amendment (Consent-Sexual Assault Offences) Bill 2007 Consultation Draft, s 61R(3)b).

for the defendant's belief. From one fact-finder to the next, it is impossible to know what community standards each of them will consider to be reasonable. With no criteria specified in the NSW legislation as to what community standards are expected and those that are prohibited, it is an entirely subjective process.

By comparison, Victoria originally imposed an irrebuttable presumption under s 37(1)(a) of its *Crimes Act 1958*:

> The fact that a person did not say or do anything to indicate free agreement to a sexual act … is enough to show that the act took place without that person's free agreement.

As Banks (2008: 233) observes, the above provision 'neatly avoids the dilemma of having to decide whether a defendant had acted like a reasonable person and … what characteristics this reasonable person might be endowed with'.[45]

Despite the fact that the aim of the law on rape is to preserve 'human dignity',[46] the law still permits sexual intercourse with a non-consenting person, thus permitting the physical and mental traumatisation of a person who does not consent.

Two case studies illustrate the inadequacies of using a reasonableness standard for assessing the state of a defendant's knowledge about consent.

6 Case Study One: Sexual Assault in the Context of a Professional Relationship

When the NSW Court of Criminal Appeal (NSWCCA) in *R v XHR* [2012] NSWCCA 247 interpreted the knowledge requirement set out

---

[45]This provision has since been repealed and s 36(2)(l) of the *Crimes Act 1958* (Vic) enacted instead as a 'circumstance' that vitiates consent:

Circumstances in which a person does not consent to an act include, but are not limited to, the following …

(l) the person does not say or do anything to indicate consent to the act.

[46]*R v Kitchener* (1993) 29 NSWLR 696, 697 (Kirby P); emphasis added.

in s 61HE of the NSW *Crimes Act* (formerly, s 61HA), it revealed the faulty reasoning that fact-finders can fall into when dealing with the subjective notion of consent. The defendant was a massage therapist who digitally penetrated the complainant while he was massaging her on 28 April 2011. He was charged with committing sexual intercourse without consent (under *Crimes Act*, s 61I), although he denied the charge. He also stated in his police interview that a full body massage did not include a massage of the genital area.[47]

The complainant said that the defendant had removed her underwear and digitally penetrated her and that she had called out 'No' when she saw his head moving towards her groin. The prosecution argued that the defendant had not taken any steps to determine whether the complainant consented to digital penetration while being massaged.

At the conclusion of the Crown case, the defendant asked the trial judge to direct a verdict of acquittal because there was 'no case to answer'. The judge agreed on the grounds that the evidence was not capable of proving 'the requisite guilty knowledge on the part of the accused'.[48]

But how had the trial judge arrived at this decision?

On appeal, the prosecution argued that the judge, as fact-finder, had found that the prosecution had to prove that the complainant *communicated* her lack of consent to the defendant *prior* to the act of sexual intercourse in order to establish the mental element for the offence. In his reasons, the judge had said that:

> It is abundantly clear from the complainant's evidence that at no stage did she say or indicate ... in any way that she did not consent to the various things he did to her, and in particular the touching or massaging of her vagina and clitoris.[49]

In other words, the judge looked to the complainant's behaviour in order to determine if the defendant knew that she did not consent, rather than looking for any steps the defendant had taken to ascertain whether

[47] *R v XHR* [2012] NSWCCA 247, [97] (Beazley JA; Hall and Campbell JJ agreeing).

[48] Ibid., [10].

[49] Ibid., [32].

the complainant consented, as required under 61HE(4)(a) of the NSW *Crimes Act*.

The NSW Court of Criminal Appeal (NSWCCA) agreed with the prosecution's interpretation that the trial judge must have made his decision:

> on the basis that the Crown was required to establish communication of absence of consent prior to the acts of sexual intercourse occurring. Otherwise, his Honour's reference to there being no communication of absence of consent would have been entirely irrelevant.[50]

As a result of this decision, prosecutors do not have to prove that the complainant communicated her lack of consent *before* a sexual act in order to prove that the defendant knew she did not consent. Indeed, to expect a person who is the recipient of medical or alternative therapies to announce beforehand that they do not consent to sexual intercourse would be nonsensical.

In *XHR*, the trial judge did what fact-finders are encouraged to do as a result of the substantive law on consent—he focused on the complainant's behaviour rather than focusing on any steps taken by the defendant to determine if the complainant was consenting. The NSWCCA noted:

> His Honour may have considered that the stark difference between the complainant's evidence of the assault and the [defendant's] denial ... simply meant there was no issue that no steps were taken by the [defendant] to ascertain whether the complainant was consenting .... However, ... [s 61HE(4)(a)] does not involve a mechanical approach to its application. If the evidence discloses that the accused person took no steps to ascertain whether the person consented, any further consideration of that matter cannot merely be put to one side.[51]

If an experienced trial judge gets it wrong, can we be confident that juries get it right? Clearly, the requirement to have regard to any steps taken by

---

[50] Ibid., [47].

[51] Ibid., [61].

the defendant to ascertain consent (s 61HE(4)(a)) is not a failsafe provision, because, unlike trial judges, juries do not have to provide reasons for their decisions. Thus, juries would still able to reason, for example, that it was not necessary for a defendant to take any steps to ascertain that a complainant was consenting since her particular behaviour (flirting, drinking habits, etc.) was enough, on its own, to signal her consent.

RMA studies show that laypeople and jurors, using their 'ordinary human experience', consider that certain flirtatious and/or 'risky' behaviours are relevant because they 'rationally affect (directly or indirectly) the assessment of the probability' of whether the defendant knew that the complainant was or was not consenting.[52] For jurors who believe in rape myths, it would be possible to reason that a complainant was sending a message that she was open to sex which would be relevant to the defendant's state of mind as to consent, such that there were reasonable grounds for his belief as to consent.

In fact, the NSWCCA alluded to the possibility of a jury ignoring the requirement to consider any steps taken by the defendant when it recognised the 'ordinary human' interpretation of the situation when a complainant and defendant have been in a relationship:

> The relevance of whether an accused person took any steps to ascertain consent is inextricably bound up with all the other factors in the case. The words of the section expressly indicate this is so, but it must follow as a matter of ordinary human experience. Thus, if the accused and complainant are in an ongoing relationship, the failure to take steps to ascertain consent *may not be surprising* and so may *not be of any or much assistance* in the fact finding task.[53]

However, the facts in *XHR* were quite different since the defendant and complainant were 'in a relationship of service provider and client' for massage, not sex, so that 'the failure to take steps to ascertain consent … would likely be very relevant to' the defendant's knowledge of whether or not the complainant was consenting.[54] Thus, the fact-finder *was*

[52]This is the relevance test under s 55 of the *Evidence Act 1995* (NSW).
[53]*XHR* [2012] NSWCCA 247, [62] (Beazley JA); emphases added.
[54]Ibid.

required to consider the steps taken by the defendant before deciding if there was sufficient evidence to prove the defendant's knowledge beyond reasonable doubt.[55]

7 Case Study Two: Sexual Assault in the Context of a 'One Night Stand'—Proving the Impossible?

The controversial *Lazarus* case[56] is the most recent case in NSW to consider the problem of proving the defendant's knowledge about consent. The case attracted a huge amount of commentary from the traditional and social media both before and after Luke Lazarus was charged with sexual assault, possibly because he was from a wealthy family who was assumed to have taken advantage of a naïve 18-year-old virgin.[57] He underwent two trials, two appeals and was eventually acquitted. Even though, on appeal, the error made by the trial judge in his second trial may have led to his wrongful acquittal, the prosecution was not permitted to try him for a third time.

In 2013, Lazarus was charged under s 61I of the *Crimes Act 1900* (NSW) that in the early morning of 12 May 2013 he had sexual intercourse without consent with an 18-year-old woman in a laneway behind the Soho nightclub in Sydney's Kings Cross. At Lazarus's first trial, the prosecution had argued that Lazarus knew that the complainant was not consenting 'or was at least reckless as to whether or not she was consenting'.[58]

The jury found Lazarus guilty on 19 February 2015. He was sentenced to five years with a non-parole period of three years imprisonment but

[55] Ibid., [63].

[56] *Lazarus v R* [2016] NSWCCA 52; *R v Lazarus* [2017] NSWCCA 279; *R v Lazarus*, District Court of NSW, 4 May 2017, 2013/00242040, unreported (Judge Tupman).

[57] See most recently: 'I am that girl', *4Corners*, ABC TV, 7 May 2018.

[58] *Lazarus* [2016] NSWCCA 52, [25] (Fullerton J).

only served 11 months before his conviction was quashed on appeal by the NSWCCA[59] which also ordered a re-trial.

The re-trial on 3 April 2017 was a judge-alone trial in which Judge Tupman found Lazarus not guilty, a decision that attracted considerable controversy.[60] It is instructive to look at the facts of the case to understand why Lazarus was successful in his first appeal, and why, after a re-trial he was found not guilty, as well as why a second appeal overturned Judge Tupman's verdict, since the re-trial and appeals turned on the issue of proof of the defendant's knowledge of lack of consent.

On the night of 11 May and in the early hours of 12 May 2013, the complainant, Saxon Mullins,[61] had consumed between 10 and 13 standard drinks, including the consumption of most of a 600 ml Coke bottle half-filled with bourbon, before ending up in a laneway with Lazarus.[62] In the re-trial, Judge Tupman accepted that the Coke bottle contained 10 standard drinks of bourbon but that Saxon had consumed only seven standard drinks since she assumed that Saxon did not finish her bottle of bourbon and Coke.[63] The contrary assumption, based on the evidence that Saxon and her friends were trying to save money by mixing their own drinks, is that Saxon consumed the whole bottle which amounted to 10 standard drinks. After doing so, Saxon described herself as: 'quite tipsy. I was jelly I guess. Yes, pretty tipsy I would say'.[64]

---

[59] *Lazarus* [2016] NSWCCA 52.

[60] See, for example: http://www.abc.net.au/news/2017-05-06/luke-lazarus-case-should-make-us-reconsider-consent/8502144; www.smh.com.au/lifestyle/news-and-views/opinion/why-the-acquittal-of-luke-lazarus-goes-to-the-heart-of-rape-culture-in-australia-20170727-gxjvvp.html; www.theguardian.com/society/2017/jul/21/this-doesnt-get-to-be-over-for-me-the-case-that-put-consent-on-trial; www.dailytelegraph.com.au/news/nsw/luke-lazarus-case-womans-facebook-post-thanks-friends-for-support/news-story/efd325368f4ea5bd0766db5df659a93b; http://www.dailymail.co.uk/news/article-4475860/Luke-Lazarus-parties-Vaucluse-rape-charge-dropped.html; www.mamamia.com.au/woman-luke-lazarus-case/; see most recently 'I am that girl', *4Corners*, ABC TV, 7 May 2018; http://www.dailymail.co.uk/news/article-5701341/Saxon-Mullins-case-sparks-sexual-consent-laws-review-losing-virginity-outside-Kings-Cross-club.html.

[61] A non-publication order protected the identity of the complainant: *R v Lazarus*, District Court of NSW, 4 May 2017, 2013/00242040, unreported, (Judge Tupman) although this order was subsequently overturned which allowed Saxon Mullins to tell her story on national Australian television (see 'I am that girl', *4Corners*, ABC TV, 7 May 2018).

[62] *Lazarus* [2016] NSWCCA 52, [40] (Fullerton J).

[63] *Lazarus*, District Court of NSW, 4 May 2017, 2013/00242040, unreported, pp. 16–18.

[64] *Lazarus* [2017] NSWCCA 279, [13] (Bellew J).

Judge Tupman accepted that Saxon had consumed another three standard drinks during the rest of the night, taking judicial notice of the amount of alcohol in the types of drinks consumed.[65] Despite the NSW provision that states a person cannot be taken to have consented if they are substantially intoxicated by alcohol or drugs (NSW *Crimes Act*, s 61HA(6)(a)), Saxon was not considered to have been substantially affected by the drinks she had consumed.[66]

The lack of a context informed by alcohol intoxication meant that it was possible for the defence to attack Saxon's credibility by obtaining concessions from her about the amount of physical contact she had before the sexual intercourse and her lack of resistance. No counter evidence was offered by the prosecution to show that a person, whose mental and physical capacities are substantially impaired by alcohol, cannot be expected to offer resistance.

Unfortunately, Judge Tupman's decision about Saxon's alcohol consumption was hampered by a lack of expert evidence, as she recognised:

> There is no evidence of an expert nature ... about the levels of alcohol which might have been present in the complainant's blood and the likely impact it would have had on her levels of functioning, physical and cognitive. The Court is well aware that this sort of expert evidence is readily available and is called frequently in this Court. It was not called in this trial.[67]

The issue of complainant intoxication is controversial not least because there is a view that the negation of consent in circumstances of substantial intoxication extends 'the criminal law to catch people who might not otherwise be regarded as criminals' (Dobinson & Townsley, 2008: 161). Arguably, proof by the prosecution of the knowledge requirement beyond a reasonable doubt is sufficient protection. Possibly the bigger problem is that even with expert evidence about the effects of alcohol, inexpert laypeople are left to determine the physiological effects

[65] *Lazarus*, District Court of NSW, 4 May 2017, 2013/00242040, unreported, p. 18.
[66] Ibid., 52–53.
[67] Ibid., 52.

of alcohol on a complainant's capacity to consent. There is no way of knowing how many cases involving intoxicated complainants result in acquittals, rather than intoxication being taken into account as evidence of negation of consent. Similarly, there is no way of knowing whether adequate jury directions about the law on intoxication has an effect on negating rape myths about intoxicated complainants.

Without the benefit of expert evidence, Judge Tupman based her findings on the evidence of Saxon, her friends, her observations of the complainant's behaviour on CCTV footage and 'the application of common sense and [her] experience of the world', including as a trial judge of 21 years.[68] Using that experience, Judge Tupman was satisfied that Saxon was 'able to perform some physical and cognitive tasks, including walking from the World Bar to McDonalds to get some food, without any apparent difficulty' with no signs of stumbling or falling on the street or in the Soho nightclub,[69] concluding that '[t]his evidence does not support [Saxon's] own assessment of her level of intoxication'. Thus, Judge Tupman did not take into account Saxon's intoxication when deciding whether or not she had consented to anal intercourse or whether or not Lazarus had a belief in consent based on reasonable grounds.

However, the use of common sense and experience of the world is an unreliable method for determining the effect of alcohol on a particular individual, unless that experience of the world involves regular, reliable assessments of the behaviour of people affected by different levels of alcohol.

7.1 Alcohol Intoxication

According to the drinkwise website,[70] in Australia a standard drink contains 10 grams of alcohol which is, on average, how much the

---

[68] Ibid., 52.

[69] Ibid., 52–53.

[70] http://drinkwise.org.au/standard-drinks-calculator/#; accessed 30 November 2017; see also Andatech Resource Centre, How Many Standard Drinks to .05?; http://www.andatech.com.au/resource/how-many-standard-drinks-to-05/; accessed 1 December 2018.

human body can breakdown in one hour. However, a number of factors including age, gender and weight determine how quickly a person processes alcohol, with women's bodies less able to do so compared to men's because they are composed of more fat tissue and contain less water.[71] In the six hours during which she was drinking, Saxon consumed between 100 and 130 g of alcohol. If a body on average can only process 10 g per hour, at 4 am when she was allegedly raped by Lazarus, Saxon would still have had between 40 and 70 g of alcohol in her bloodstream.

Generally, two standard drinks per hour raise a person's blood-alcohol level (BAC) to 0.05%, the legal limit of blood alcohol for drivers in Australia. If a person continues to drink, one standard drink per hour thereafter will maintain their BAC at 0.05%. Since Saxon began her drinking by consuming around seven to 10 standard drinks within an hour, she would have been four to five times over the legal limit.

In a sexual assault trial where intoxication is an issue, fact-finders need to be aware of the stages of alcohol intoxication, as set out in Table 2. This table shows that as the concentration of alcohol in the blood increases, a person experiences decreased inhibitions and loss of judgement and control, their response to external stimuli decreases as does their ability to make quick decisions due to decreased reaction time, they become disoriented and mentally confused, their speech becomes slurred and their balance is impaired. Many of these symptoms were described by Saxon.

Rather than expert evidence about the effects of alcohol on Saxon's mental, emotional and physical state, both trials relied on Saxon's evidence and that of other prosecution witnesses about Saxon's degree of intoxication, as well as CCTV footage of Saxon and her friends on the street and in the Soho nightclub before she was led by Lazarus into a laneway.

After more drinks at the Soho nightclub, Saxon testified that she was 'slurring my words and I was kind of a bit uneasy on my feet I guess

[71] See http://www.andatech.com.au/resource/factors-affecting-blood-alcohol-level; accessed 1 December 2018.

Table 2 Dubowski's stages of acute alcohol intoxication[a]

Blood Alcohol Concentration (%W/V; mg/100 ml of blood)	Stage	Clinical signs/symptoms
0.01–0.05	Sobriety	Behaviour nearly normal by ordinary observation
0.03–0.12	Euphoria	• Mild euphoria, sociability, talkativeness; • Increased self-confidence; • Decreased inhibitions; diminution of attention, judgement and control; • Loss of efficiency in finer performance tests
0.09–0.25	Excitement	• Emotional instability, decreased inhibitions; • Loss of critical judgement; • Impairment of memory and comprehension; • Decreased sensitory response; increased reaction time; • Some muscular incoordination
0.18–0.30	Confusion	• Disorientation, mental confusion, dizziness; • Exaggerated emotional states (fear, anger, grief, etc.); • Disturbances of sensation and of perception of colour, form, motion and dimensions; • Decreased pain sense; • Impaired balance, muscular incoordination, staggering gait, slurred speech

(continued)

you would say',[72] suggesting that she was between the stages of 'excitement' and 'confusion' as set out in Table 2, with a possible blood alcohol content of approximately 0.20. After further drinks were consumed at the World Bar, Saxon testified that she was:

[72] *Lazarus v R* [2017] NSWCCA 279, [15] (Bellew J).

Table 2 (continued)

Blood Alcohol Concentration (%W/V; mg/100 ml of blood)	Stage	Clinical signs/symptoms
0.25–0.4	Stupor	• Apathy, general inertia, approaching paralysis; • Markedly decreased response to stimuli; • Marked muscular incoordination; inability to stand or walk; • Vomiting; incontinence of urine and faeces; • Impaired consciousness; sleep or stupor
0.35–0.5	Coma	• Complete unconsciousness; coma; anaesthesia; • Depressed or abolished reflexes; • Subnormal body temperature; • Incontinence of urine and faeces; • [Impairment] of circulation and respiration; • Possible death
0.45+	Death	• Death from respiratory arrest

[a]Table taken from Dubowski (1977: 94). This table is still in current use in the literature; see Connell (2015); McKee, Widder, Paton-Gay, Kirkpatrick, and Engels (2016)

> drunk yes and more I guess just amplified the affect (sic) that was already there. So just slurring words and dancing funny and that kind of thing.[73]

Saxon and her friends continued to go back and forth between the World Bar and the Soho nightclub so that around 3.30 am when she first met the defendant, she testified that:

> I was drunk yeah, and I was pretty out of it I guess and just very I don't know, drunk is the only way I can really think to describe it.[74]

[73]Ibid., [16].

[74]Ibid., [18].

Her descriptions of slurred words, 'dancing funny' and 'pretty out of it' also suggest that Saxon was in the stages of 'excitement' or 'confusion' which, as Table 2 shows, includes disorientation ('out of it'), disturbances of motion and impaired balance ('dancing funny') and slurred speech.

As a result of her BAC, Saxon may have also experienced a loss of critical judgement, impairment of comprehension and mental confusion, the more so in a dimly lit nightclub with which she was unfamiliar, making her vulnerable to sexual predation. With exaggerated emotional states (such as fear which she later described was the reason for obeying Lazarus's commands), Saxon's perceptions may have been disturbed, interfering with her ability to orient herself once she was in the laneway, while slowed reaction times and muscular incoordination may have impeded her ability to run or resist Lazarus's sexual overtures. If she experienced an exaggerated fear response, then her brain may have induced the freeze response as discussed below.

In two UK cases, *R v Bree*[75] and *R v Hysa,*[76] the Court of Appeal recognised that an intoxicated complainant may lack the capacity to freely consent even though she was not unconsciousness: 'as a matter of practical reality, capacity to consent may evaporate well before a complainant becomes unconscious'.[77] While NSW requires a complainant to be substantially intoxicated (a term that is undefined), in *Hysa* the Court of Appeal held that the prosecution is not required to prove that the complainant was so intoxicated that she was incapable of physical resistance or communication. Thus, a person who is walking and talking may still lack the capacity to consent. Case law in E&W is also clear that even though a complainant may have no memory of having said no, lack of memory cannot be used to conclude that sexual intercourse was consensual.[78]

Thus, it is possible that Saxon was substantially intoxicated by alcohol, one of the grounds upon which it may be established a person does not consent to sexual intercourse and for determining Lazarus's state of mind.

---

75 [2007] EWCA Crim 804.

76 [2007] EWCA Crim 2056.

77 *R v Bree* [2007] EWCA Crim 804, [34] (Sir Igor Judge P).

78 *Hysa* [2007] EWCA Crim 2056; *R v Tambedou* [2014] EWCA Crim 954.

Because Saxon's vulnerability is likely to have been noticeable to someone in Lazarus's position, can it be said that his honest belief as to consent was based on reasonable grounds?

7.2 Honest Belief and Reasonable Grounds

In light of the trial judge's decision to acquit Lazarus in his second trial, the following discussion considers the scope and meaning of s 61HE(3)(c) (NSW *Crimes Act*), that is, whether a defendant 'has no reasonable grounds for believing' that the complainant has consented.

While s 61HE(3)(c) 'does impose an objective test, in the sense that … the grounds which might lead to a belief of consent must be objectively reasonable',[79] this test may be confusing for a jury which cannot consider whether the defendant's belief was a reasonable belief in the sense of asking what a reasonable person might have believed about the complainant's consent. Instead, fact-finders must consider what the defendant, himself, actually believed in all the circumstances and decide whether the accused had reasonable grounds for his belief.[80] As stated previously, the test is partly subjective and partly objective because fact-finders must put themselves in the shoes of the defendant and decide whether the complainant's lack of consent would have been obvious to someone with the mental capacity of the defendant in those circumstances.[81]

These circumstances include: the complainant's and defendant's relationship; their actions and words, the nature of the sexual act and the 'condition' of the complainant at the time of the sexual act.[82]

Discovering the subjective belief of the defendant and testing it from an objective standpoint to determine its reasonableness is a difficult task without an actual admission by the defendant. However, fact-finders can

[79] *Lazarus* [2016] NSWCCA 52, [156] (Fullerton J).

[80] Ibid. It is clear from all the case law that 'it is the belief of the accused, and not that of the hypothetical reasonable person in the position of the accused, which has to be reasonable' (*Re Conlon* (1993) 69 A Crim R 92, 98 (Hunt CJ at CL)).

[81] *O'Sullivan v R; Flanders v R; Tohu v R & NRH v R* [2012] NSWCCA 45, [125] (Davies and Garling JJ).

[82] *Lazarus* [2016] NSWCCA 52, [144] (Fullerton J; quoting the trial judge).

infer from the evidence that the defendant must have known and that he did indeed know that the complainant was not consenting[83] which supposedly involves an objective standpoint, although in reality it is the subjective interpretation by the fact-finder.

A matter that received little coverage in Lazarus's second trial was the fact that Saxon was a virgin with little or no experience of sexual matters.[84] When Saxon met Lazarus,[85] he told her that he was a part-owner of the Soho nightclub and invited her to a VIP area of the club. Instead of a VIP area, Lazarus led her into a deserted laneway, thus deliberately misleading her about his intentions which were to take her to an isolated area for sex. In the 50-metre lane, Lazarus walked her to the end where they were out of sight of CCTV cameras in order to add her to his 'trophy list' of women as he stated in evidence. Here they kissed, although the complainant was unsure for how long, which would accord with her state of alcohol intoxication. She then decided she wanted to leave, telling Lazarus:

> I need to go back to my friend. I have to meet my friend.
> No, stay here with me.
> No, I really need to go.

At this stage, Lazarus's tone of voice was 'conversational' and despite kissing, Saxon communicated that she wanted to leave and did not want to have sex. When she turned away, Lazarus pulled her underwear down about three inches, a gesture that made his sexual intentions clear.[86] When Saxon pulled them up and told him that she had to leave, Lazarus ordered her to: 'Put your fucking hands on the wall'. Saxon's clear desire to leave, as well as Lazarus's aggressive tone of voice and swearing indicates that he was aware that Saxon was not consenting to his overture of pulling down her pants:

---

[83] Ibid.

[84] *Lazarus* [2017] NSWCCA 279, [26] (Bellew J).

[85] Facts taken from ibid., [19]–[31].

[86] *R v Lazarus*, District Court of NSW, 4 May 2017, 2013/00242040, unreported, p. 31 (Judge Tupman).

> The complainant described the respondent's tone of voice at that point as frustrated and impatient, and more aggressive than it had been during the previous conversation. She put her hands on a nearby wooden fence. She explained why she did so, saying:
>
> I was just scared I guess, I didn't know what to do so I just did what he said.[87]

With her relatively high BAC causing confusion and disorientation, it is possible that Saxon quite simply did not 'know what to do'. The physiological process, known as the 'freeze response' or tonic immobility, is an involuntary, reflexive component of the fear response that is characterised by freezing in situations involving extreme fear 'when the options of flight or fight are unavailable as a coping/defense mechanism' (Atara, 2015), as discussed in Chapter 2. A significant minority or majority of victims will display tonic immobility during a sexual assault (Galliano, Noble, Travis, & Puechl, 1993; Heidi, Marx, & Forsyth, 2005).

It is doubtful that Lazarus could have had an honest belief on reasonable grounds that Saxon was consenting when he unsuccessfully attempted sexual intercourse up against the fence. When Saxon complied with Lazarus's order to put her hands against a fence, this looks like an act of submission, rather than free and voluntary agreement. In any case, after her submission he took no steps to ascertain whether she was consenting. This raises a key question for both the concept of consent and knowledge by the defendant—what degree of coercion is 'incompatible with the freedom to exercise genuine sexual choice' (Leahy, 2014a: 246) and incompatible with reasonable grounds for the defendant's belief in consent?

After attempting vaginal intercourse unsuccessfully (which is when Saxon revealed that she was a virgin), Lazarus then pulled her stockings and underwear down to her ankles and ordered her to: 'Just get on your hands and knees and arch your back'. But with no experience in sexual matters, to what was Saxon consenting? And how would Lazarus be able to form a reasonable belief in Saxon's consent to *anal* intercourse without taking steps to ascertain whether she was consenting to vaginal

[87] *Lazarus* [2017] NSWCCA 279, [24] (Bellew J).

intercourse, or anal intercourse or merely doing what she was told? When Saxon obeyed, Lazarus penetrated her anus, which she found to be painful. Despite the fact that Saxon told him to stop and kept saying throughout the alleged assault that 'I have to go back to my friend', he continued.

Saxon's level of intoxication and the freeze response explains her obedience to Lazarus's commands, and her helplessness in the face of a sexual act she did not consent to. Her demeaning position, on the ground, on her hands and knees quite clearly demonstrates the power dynamic between them.

After she made her way to Kings Cross Railway station, Saxon called her friend, Brittany, who found her in a great deal of distress. She reported the incident to the police and later underwent a medical examination at a nearby hospital, the results of which were consistent with penile-anal intercourse having taken place.

During cross-examination, Saxon 'specifically denied the suggestion that she did not, at any stage, tell [Lazarus] to stop whilst penile-anal intercourse was occurring'.[88]

7.3 The First Appeal

After being convicted at his first trial, Lazarus successfully appealed on the grounds that the trial judge's directions were in error.[89] He argued that the following direction implied that the trial judge had directed the jury that the defendant had to prove the complainant was consenting:

> the accused's position is that the penile-anal intercourse he had with [the complainant] was consensual and that her consent was evidenced by her actions. If you consider that [the complainant's] actions *caused a belief in the mind of the accused* that she was consenting to penile-anal intercourse

[88] Ibid., [31].

[89] *Lazarus* [2016] NSWCCA 52, [21] (Fullerton J; with whom Hoeben CJ at CL and Adams J agreed).

> with him *and* you consider that such a belief was a reasonable one, then the third element would not have been proven.[90]

Fullerton J accepted that 'one way' of interpreting the words that the complainant's actions 'caused the appellant to have a belief that she was consenting' 'was to remind the jury that it was the appellant's case ... that he believed she was consenting, not that she was directing them that it was for the appellant to prove' the fact of lack of consent.[91] Although it is difficult to read the latter interpretation into the above directions, the NSWCCA concluded that the trial judge's directions about how the jury should 'approach their consideration of the appellant's state of mind' were in error.[92] Lazarus' conviction was quashed and a re-trial was ordered.

7.4 Was the Jury's Verdict Unreasonable?

Lazarus had also appealed on the grounds that the jury's verdict was unreasonable because there was insufficient evidence upon which the jury could have been satisfied beyond reasonable doubt that Lazarus knew the complainant was not consenting.[93]

The NSWCCA disagreed, deciding that the jury's verdict was reasonable because of the circumstances in which the sexual intercourse occurred:

> The explanation the complainant gave for participating in non-consensual anal intercourse ... was to the effect that although ... she willingly went into the laneway at his invitation (... in the expectation that she was being ushered to a VIP area) and willingly kissed the appellant ... she did not consent to anal intercourse (or sexual intercourse at all) but unwillingly submitted to it, and the pain that it entailed, out of fear.[94]

---

[90] Ibid., [145]; emphasis added.

[91] Ibid., [155].

[92] Ibid., [158].

[93] Ibid., [118].

[94] Ibid., [107].

The NSWCCA also considered that Saxon's intoxication was relevant to proving the defendant's knowledge of that fact, including whether the prosecution had established that Lazarus had no reasonable grounds for believing that Saxon was consenting.[95] Overall, the appeal question as to whether the evidence was sufficient to prove that Lazarus had, actual knowledge of lack of consent, or was reckless about consent or did not have a belief in consent:

> obliges this Court to consider all the circumstances bearing on that question including ... any steps taken by the appellant to ascertain whether the complainant was consenting.[96]

What the trial evidence did show is that Lazarus had:

> made no enquiry of the complainant before or during intercourse as to whether she was willing to have anal intercourse (or intercourse at all), or whether she was willing for him to proceed to try to achieve penetration when, even on his evidence, she expressed pain and declared that she was 'a virgin'.[97]

The NSWCCA concluded that it was 'not open ... for the appellant to invite this Court to find as a fact that it was conduct of the complainant preparatory to the anal intercourse that followed'.[98]

After undertaking a review of all the evidence, the NSWCCA was 'satisfied that the evidence allows for the jury to have concluded that the appellant was at least reckless as to whether the complainant was consenting to anal intercourse and to have concluded that was his state of mind when he had anal intercourse with her'.[99] As a result, it was open to the jury to find the defendant guilty. Thus, a jury and three judges of the NSWCCA considered that there was sufficient evidence to prove that Lazarus either knew that Saxon was not consenting to anal intercourse

---

[95] Ibid., [115].
[96] Ibid., [130].
[97] Ibid.
[98] Ibid., [135].
[99] Ibid., [136].

or was reckless as to consent or had no reasonable grounds for his belief as to consent.

7.5 The Re-Trial

After winning his appeal against conviction, Lazarus was retried in a judge-alone trial on 3 April 2017. Saxon's pre-recorded evidence from the first trial was used as her evidence-in-chief.[100] There were several types of evidence that the trial judge took into account in deciding whether or not Saxon has consented to anal intercourse. First, she took into account:

> The grounds on which it may be established that a person does not consent to sexual intercourse, includes if the person has sexual intercourse while substantially intoxicated by alcohol or any drug.[101]

As discussed above, Judge Tupman decided that Saxon was not substantially intoxicated by alcohol in deciding whether Saxon freely and voluntarily consented to sexual intercourse.[102] However, because of Saxon's immediate complaint to her friend, Brittany, and subsequent complaints to her sister and the police a few hours later, Judge Tupman found that 'the evidence does establish, beyond reasonable doubt that the complainant, in her own mind, did not consent to the anal sexual intercourse that occurred'.[103]

The key issue in the re-trial was Lazarus's knowledge about Saxon's lack of consent. Central to this issue was Saxon's lack of physical resistance from the time Lazarus ordered her to put her hands on the fence to the end of penile-anal intercourse. Even though the NSW *Crimes Act* states that 'a person who does not offer actual physical resistance to sexual intercourse is not, by reason only of that fact, to be regarded as consenting

---

[100] *Criminal Procedure Act 1986* (NSW), s 306B. Judge Tupman granted leave for further oral evidence-in-chief to be given by the complainant in order to clarify certain evidence.

[101] *Crimes Act 1900* (NSW), s 61HE(8)(a).

[102] *Lazarus*, District Court of NSW, 4 May 2017, 2013/00242040, unreported, p. 10 (Judge Tupman).

[103] Ibid., 70.

to the sexual intercourse' (s 61HE(9)), Saxon's lack of physical resistance was considered to have informed Lazarus's state of mind:

> the evidence of both the complainant and the accused is that whilst ever this anal penetration and anal intercourse was occurring, the complainant did nothing physical to prevent the sexual intercourse from continuing.[104]

However, it appears that Judge Tupman was unaware of the freeze response, its relative frequency among rape victims[105] and the fact that it can be mistaken for consent. Crucially, she preferred the evidence of Lazarus, rather than Saxon's, finding that Saxon's obedience to Lazarus's command to get on the ground had:

> a bearing on what his state of mind was about her consent … When … the complainant moved backwards when the accused was trying to penetrate her vagina and then as again I find moved backwards and forwards when he successfully then penetrated her anus, that too is relevant in assessing his state of mind about her consent to a continuation of … anal intercourse, even if … in her own mind, the complainant was not consenting to this.[106]

Thus, Judge Tupman looked to Saxon's behaviour in order to determine if the defendant knew that she did not consent, rather than looking for any steps taken by the defendant to ascertain whether Saxon had consented, as required under s 61HE(4)(a). This failure by the trial judge was a key issue in the second appeal.

Overall, Judge Tupman found that Lazarus was a witness of credibility and that Saxon's evidence was unreliable in many respects so that her Honour rejected Saxon's evidence that she had asked Lazarus to stop during the anal intercourse. In fact, Saxon's failure to say the word, 'stop',

---

[104] Ibid., 37.

[105] Heidi et al. (2005) reported that over 52% of CSA survivors in their study had experienced tonic immobility while Galliano et al. (1993) reported that 37% of rape survivors had experienced tonic immobility.

[106] *Lazarus*, District Court of NSW, 4 May 2017, 2013/00242040, unreported, p. 41 (Judge Tupman).

was central to Judge Tupman's conclusion that there was no evidence to support the proposition that Lazarus actually 'knew that the complainant was not consenting to the act of sexual intercourse'.[107]

Judge Tupman also found that there was no evidence to establish that Lazarus was reckless as to whether the complainant was consenting and finally concluded that 'the evidence establishes that the accused had a genuine and honest belief that the complainant was consenting'.[108] In addition, Judge Tupman was satisfied that the prosecution had not proved that Lazarus's belief was not based on reasonable grounds because of evidence from one female defence witness about 'contemporary morality':

> I do not accept … [the Crown's argument about the unlikelihood of a virgin consenting to anal intercourse as her first sexual experience] … particularly so when looking at the event together with the evidence of the young people who gave character evidence [for Lazarus] and especially the young woman to whose evidence I have just recently referred. Their evidence allowed some insight into the contemporary morality of that group of young people.[109]

This 'contemporary morality' included anecdotal evidence from one female friend of Lazarus's that anal intercourse during a one-night stand was not uncommon among her age group. As an easy short-cut or heuristic, 'contemporary morality' appears to have been used as a justification for Lazarus's behaviour despite the obvious questions that arise: how is one woman's experience representative of 18-year-old virgins? Was this young woman an expert in contemporary sexual morés? Had she carried out a survey of her age group? Are there no other 'contemporary moralities'?

The use of anecdotal evidence combined with an ill-defined term such as 'contemporary morality' appears to preclude the possibility that anal sex could be based on unreasonable grounds and, like many other heuristics, nullifies the important attempt at law reform under s 61HE(4)(a)

---

[107]Ibid., 71.
[108]Ibid.
[109]Ibid., 72.

of the NSW *Crimes Act* to focus on any steps taken by the defendant. Essentially, a resort to 'contemporary morality' amounts to a justification of a cultural practice in which sexual intercourse with a non-consenting woman (so that a man can expand his 'trophy list' of women) is not a criminal offence. In this way, 'contemporary morality' could be used to justify any sexual act in any circumstances, a step not that far from the *Morgan* defence.

The rationale for the finding that Saxon did not consent to sexual intercourse but that Lazarus had reasonable grounds for his belief that she was consenting makes no sense:

> when she was told to get down on the ground on all fours and arch her back, she did so as requested and *participated* in a further attempt to penetrate her vagina by moving back and forward as the accused attempted to do that. When that did not work and he started to insert his penis into her anus she pushed back towards him and then back and forwards as the anal intercourse took place.[110]

How is it possible to make a finding that a woman who is not consenting actively participated in sexual intercourse by facilitating it? Although physical resistance is not a requirement for establishing lack of consent, it appears that Saxon's lack of physical resistance was fatal to the prosecution's case:

> she did not say 'stop' or 'no'. She did not take any physical action to move away from the intercourse or attempted intercourse, either when they were standing up, or when she was down on the ground … I accept that this … amounts to reasonable grounds, in the circumstances for the accused to have formed the … genuine belief, that in fact the complainant was consenting to what was occurring even though it was quick, unromantic, … and … may not occurred if each had been sober.[111]

[110]Ibid., 73; emphasis added.

[111]Ibid., 73–74.

Judge Tupman did not turn her mind to the possibility that Saxon submitted to sex because of the implied threat in Lazarus's aggressive order and that 'her real intention [was] not to have sex but to avoid the harm threatened' (Cowan, 2007b: 98).

Thus, like the decision in *XHR* above, Judge Tupman decided that Saxon was required to communicate her lack of consent through physical resistance during an intimate encounter with a stranger. In essence, the use of the heuristic, 'contemporary morality', blinded Judge Tupman to the applicable law which in NSW had overturned the *Morgan* defence. Irrespective of contemporary morality and the lack of physical resistance, the fact-finder in *Lazarus* could not have been satisfied that the defendant had reasonable grounds for his belief as to consent unless she had investigated the steps taken by Lazarus to form his belief.

7.6 The Second Appeal

After Judge Tupman found Lazarus not guilty, the prosecution appealed[112] against that finding on two grounds, that is, whether Her Honour had:

i. erred in taking into account Lazarus's self-induced intoxication for the purpose of determining whether he had no reasonable grounds for believing that the complainant consented to the sexual intercourse; and
ii. erred in failing to take into account any steps taken by Lazarus to ascertain whether the complainant was consenting when making a finding about his knowledge of consent,[113] with the Crown arguing that … 'a "step" must be something more than just a state of mind'.[114]

The first ground was dismissed while the second ground was upheld. Despite the fact that Lazarus's acquittal was quashed, the NSWCCA refused to order a re-trial.

[112]Under the *Crimes (Appeal and Review) Act 2001* (NSW), s 107.
[113]*Lazarus* [2017] NSWCCA 279, [9] (Bellew J).
[114]Ibid., [137].

Like the trial judge in *XHR*, Judge Tupman had failed to properly apply the law regarding the defendant's state of mind even though the decision of the NSWCCA in *XHR* had been clear that:

i. a fact-finder must consider the reasonable steps taken by a defendant to ascertain whether the complainant was consenting; and
ii. in a judge-alone trial, the judge's reasons must 'demonstrate, either expressly or by implication, that such a principle has been applied'.[115]

Instead, the NSWCCA found that when Judge Tupman delivered her verdict, she had failed to consider the steps taken by Lazarus:

> nowhere in her Honour's reasons is there any reference, express or implied, to [s 61HE(4)(a)], and thus no express or implied statement of the relevant principle. Those factors alone support a conclusion that the principle was not applied, and that error is established.[116]

The NSWCCA said the word, 'step', should take 'its natural and ordinary meaning', that is, 'doing something positive' according to the dictionary meaning: 'to undertake measures to do something with a view to the attainment of some end'.[117] Thus:

> a 'step' … must involve the taking of some positive act. However, … a positive act does not necessarily have to be a physical one. A positive act … extends to include a person's consideration of, or reasoning in response to, things or events which he or she hears, observes or perceives.[118]

Even though the NSWCCA upheld the appeal on this ground, the Court refused to order a re-trial since it would be 'oppressive to put [Lazarus] to the expense and worry of a third trial'[119] so that such an order 'would … give rise to oppression and unfairness'.[120]

---

[115] *XHR* [2012] NSWCCA 247, [51] (Beazley JA).
[116] *Lazarus* [2017] NSWCCA 279, [144] (Bellew J).
[117] Ibid., [146].
[118] Ibid., [147].
[119] Ibid., [163].
[120] Ibid., [168].

While referring to the fact that it was not the fault of Lazarus that both judges in his two trials had made errors, it is notable that the NSWCCA did not weigh up the unfairness to Lazarus against the unfairness to Saxon and the community in general who also were not at fault for these judicial errors. If this case had been a high-profile terrorism or murder case, would the NSWCCA have also refused to order a re-trial?

8 Discussion and Conclusion

The above discussion shows that the historical shift to defining rape with reference to a lack of consent has been accompanied by inquiries into the defendant's perception of consent, that is, what he himself believed, a notion that has the power to undermine a complainant's experience. In order to prevent this, the defendant's subjective perception became subject to an objective test of reasonableness in order to prevent the *Morgan*-type situation where an unreasonable belief in consent could trump a complainant's lack of consent, as recognised in the amending legislation in NSW:

> The subjective [*Morgan*] test is outdated. It reflects archaic views about sexual activity. It fails to ensure a reasonable standard of care is taken to ascertain a person is consenting before embarking on potentially damaging behaviour. An objective test is required to ensure the jury applies its common sense regarding current community standards. (Hatzistergos, 2007)

In particular, the aim of recent reforms has been to refocus the trial on the defendant's actions by investigating the steps he took so that the fact-finder can determine the reasonableness of his belief in consent. While consent is, generally, inferred from a complainant's verbal and non-verbal behaviour, because of the unequal power relations in which sexual assault frequently occurs and the commonality of the freeze response, the notion of consent must be re-configured to take into account physiological as well as cultural responses to fear, intimidation and coercion.

Because it is not possible to analyse the reasons of actual juries, the reasons in two judge-alone trials reveal the ease with which the requirements for establishing the reasonableness of a defendant's belief about consent can be misunderstood or misapplied. As stated above, if experienced judges get it wrong, can we expect juries with no legal experience to apply the law correctly?

Both *Lazarus* and *XHR* reveal that the law reform enacted in NSW in 2007 in the form of:

i. a definition of consent ('free and voluntary agreement'); and
ii. a third option for satisfying the knowledge requirement, viz. the requirement that the defendant's belief about consent was based on reasonable grounds,

has not necessarily achieved its aims.

The errors made by the trial judges in *XHR* and *Lazarus* raise a number of questions:

i. How does the law capture non-verbal sexual negotiation?
ii. Is it possible for the law to deal with submission in the face of persuasion, coercion or fear?
iii. Should the definition of consent and reasonable grounds include a reference to body language (such as the freeze response)?
iv. Should there be a rebuttable presumption against consent if there is no verbal or physical communication of consent by the complainant, with an evidential onus on the defendant to rebut the presumption?

The legal definition of consent assumes that clear, verbal communication is the norm within a sexual context. The dilemma from a legal point of view is how to capture the reality of sexual negotiation which often occurs in the presence of alcohol, late at night and between young people for whom assertive legal language such as, 'do you freely and voluntarily agree to have sexual intercourse?' is antithetical to the vernacular of that age group.

While the provisions governing consent and reasonable belief attempt to provide guidance on the circumstances in which consent will negated, they provide little guidance for the grey area of human behaviour where forms of persuasion, coercion and/or abuse of power are commonly used to gain someone's consent, as the #MeToo phenomenon demonstrates (Cossins, 2020).

Although the 'introduction of an objective fault element discourages the assumption of consent, including in the context of a previous consensual relationship or family violence' (ALRC, 2010a: [25.165]), any standard of reasonableness is subject to current community standards or 'contemporary morality' about sexual behaviour which filters fact-finders' interpretations of the evidence. For example, an objective test has '"frequently resulted in the defence counsel drawing on information about the complainant's sexual history, or to appeal to rape myths in order to show that the defendant could have held that belief"' (ALRC, 2010a: 1166; reference omitted).

Thus, there are limits to the ability of law reform to bring about a desired cultural change in relation to community standards and how those standards are applied by fact-finders (ibid., 1125–1126) if standards of sexual behaviour remain nebulous and undefined. Without explicit legislative guidance, standards of consent and reasonableness will vary from fact-finder to fact-finder since the idea of free and voluntary agreement is entirely contextual. In fact, focus groups of sexual assault workers, legal professionals and community members have perceived the objective standard to be 'biased in favour of the defendant and created an onus on the victim to resist or protest'; to 'enable jury members to apply outdated assumptions about inferred or continuing consent', and 'to believe that consent was present when a former sexual partner does not protest or resist' (Larcombe et al., 2016: 617).

In 2007, the NSW government missed an important opportunity to convey a message about community standards and 'to impose affirmative duties that would have recognised true sexual autonomy' (Banks, 2008: 235) rather than the unsatisfactory situation in *Lazarus* where sexual intercourse with a non-consenting woman was found not to be a criminal offence (even if the verdict was overturned on appeal).

In fact, *XHR* and *Lazarus* illustrate Munro's (2008: 947) observation that modernising legislation contains:

> legal standards that at first sight appear to be exacting [but] will often fail to translate into demanding thresholds when removed from the lofty isolation of abstract theorizing and transposed into the messy realities of everyday socio-sexual life.

While the decisions in *XHR* and *Lazarus* were not ignorant of the applicable law, research on the use of heuristics to deal with complex fact situations allows us to understand the judicial errors made. The focus on a complainant's behaviour appears to be deeply rooted in both legal and social cultures. In *XHR*, the trial judge expected the complainant to have communicated her lack of consent to digital penetration while receiving a massage even though she had not sought sexual services from the defendant. The judge, thus, relied on the age-old notion that a complainant is responsible for protecting herself and doing something physical to stop a sexual assault, rather than the defendant having to take steps to obtain consent, as if women need to be perpetually prepared for men's sexual desires.

In *Lazarus*, the trial judge also focused on the complainant's behaviour, interpreting what she did not say, and what she did not do as signalling her consent to the defendant with reference to the heuristic, 'contemporary morality'. Thus, the trial judge decided that Saxon's lack of verbal and physical resistance formed the reasonable grounds for Luke Lazarus's belief in consent, thus ignoring the context in which Saxon's behaviour was governed by where Lazarus had taken her (a deserted laneway), what he had ordered her to do and her fear or freeze response. This produced the contradictory finding that the complainant had not consented to anal intercourse but that the defendant's belief in consent was based on reasonable grounds. In accepting Lazarus's evidence about his belief, Her Honour failed to examine the steps taken by the defendant to form his belief and concluded that he had no knowledge of Saxon's lack of consent, a position similar to the common law position under *Morgan*. Arguably, submission to a defendant's commands in a deserted laneway is not the behaviour envisaged by free and voluntary agreement and not the basis upon which any reasonable belief could be formed.

In neither appeal was there 'comprehensive judicial consideration of the level of coercion that is incompatible' (Leahy, 2014a: 246) with 'free and voluntary agreement' and with an honest belief based on reasonable grounds. In order to institute real change and provide consistency on 'what constitutes genuine sexual choice' (ibid., 247), it is necessary for legislation to not only provide the parameters around free and voluntary agreement beyond various vitiating factors but also guidance on what does and does not amount to reasonable grounds for a belief in consent.

If the law requires the defendant's subjective state of mind to be taken into account, it should also require defendants to take into account the complainant's subjective state of mind (rather than his assumptions about her state of mind) when the issues of consent and reasonable grounds for belief in consent are being decided. In other words:

> a right to consent is only meaningful if accompanied by a corresponding right to refuse, and this question of available options should be assessed from the individual's own point of view. (Cowart, 2004: 514; cited in Cowan, 2007b: 98)

This means that reasonable grounds for belief should be made with reference to the complainant's actual circumstances, such as age, inebriation, and access to help. For example, Saxon was an inexperienced, inebriated, 18-year-old virgin alone with Lazarus in a dark alleyway with no access to help and in a state of fear.

Because there are no objective criteria set out in the NSW legislation for determining what amounts to an honest belief on reasonable grounds, heuristics such as 'contemporary morality' fill the gap. I am reminded of MacKinnon's insight that 'rape law takes women's usual response to coercion—acquiescence, the despairing response to hopelessness to unequal odds—and calls that consent' (MacKinnon, 1989: 168). With the smokescreen of 'contemporary morality', rape becomes indistinguishable from normative sexual relations.

While consent is a vessel that will be filled by the moral values of the fact-finder, the solution:

> is not to abandon consent as the transformative channel between the permissible and the condemnable, but to reformulate it in a way that enables it to take greater account of the peculiarities of context, constraint, and construction. (Munro, 2008: 941)

The concept of free and voluntary agreement only gets us so far since it does not solve the fundamental problem of heuristic reasoning in sexual assault trials. Indeed, in any sexual assault trial, there will be a hierarchy of experiences which are in competition with each other. But whose experience of the world will triumph when there is nothing else to assist the fact-finder? In *Lazarus* there was the:

i. actual belief of Lazarus who had had numerous sexual experiences, and had intimate knowledge of the nightclub owned by his family where he appears to have sought out young women to create a 'trophy list';
ii. experiences of a middle-aged judge in a privileged position with 21 years as a judicial officer who relied on the heuristic of 'contemporary sexual morality' in 2017 (in other cases it will be the combined experiences of 12 laypeople from various backgrounds);
iii. actual belief of an 18-year-old complainant with no previous sexual experience who was arguably substantially affected by alcohol.

With such a hierarchy of experiences, both judges and jurors can only use their own subjective 'experience of the world' which is unlikely to include information about human physiology, such as the freeze response, and exaggerated emotional responses (such as fear) of those affected by alcohol.

It is an unsatisfactory state of affairs for a fact-finder's 'experiences of the world' to mean that a young, inexperienced woman's submission to an aggressive order in a deserted, dark laneway amounts to reasonable grounds for belief in consent. And for that fact-finder to fail to ask (i) why a sexually experienced defendant needed to aggressively order a young woman to do his bidding if he believed she was consenting; and (ii) why a defendant's desire for anal sex with a woman on all fours was not seen by the fact-finder as an act of power and subjugation to secure her compliance, rather than evidence of 'contemporary morality'.

Although reforms aimed at introducing a communicative model of consent may have won the battle in terms of a definition of consent that endorses autonomy, the war is lost by a model that permits 'contemporary morality' to justify the subjective state of mind of a defendant in relation to the offence of sexual intercourse without consent.

Solutions need to recognise that consent and reasonable belief are relational concepts, dependent on the parties' understandings but also influenced by the internalised cultural norms and beliefs of the fact-finder. How does one legislate in relation to such emotionally and psychologically complex issues? In particular, how does the law make the defendant's belief referable to the complainant's lack of consent, as illustrated in Fig. 1?

As discussed above, many jurisdictions have imposed a requirement on the defendant to take reasonable steps to ascertain consent. But the case studies in this chapter reveal that experienced fact-finders have failed to focus on the defendant's behaviour as required using a reasonableness standard. Further guidance is, therefore, necessary to inform fact-finders that consent and reasonableness are related concepts, such that the sole focus of the trial is not on the complainant's words and behaviours but encompasses the corresponding words and behaviours of the defendant who may actually have created the circumstances in which the sexual assault occurred.

The NSWLRC's (2019) response to this problem is the introduction of new jury directions to address the common misconceptions associated with sexual assault. These directions, discussed in Chapter 10, are unlikely to address the problem of requiring the fact-finder to apply the communicative model of consent by investigating the steps taken by the defendant to ascertain consent.

One way to ensure a broader focus on the defendant's behaviour is the following rebuttable presumption:

i. if a fact-finder decides beyond reasonable doubt that the complainant did not consent, the defendant is guilty of the offence of sexual intercourse without consent *unless* the fact-finder is satisfied that the

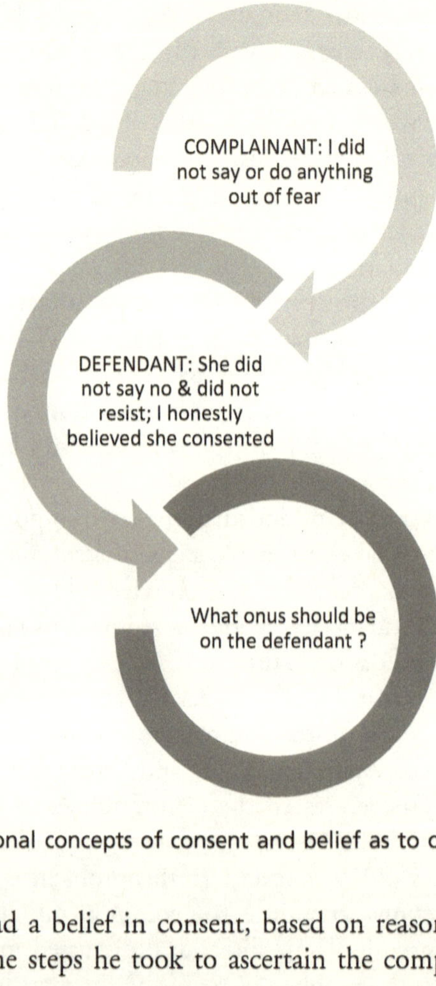

Fig. 1 The relational concepts of consent and belief as to consent

defendant had a belief in consent, based on reasonable grounds, as a result of the steps he took to ascertain the complainant's state of mind;

ii. the fact-finder must take into account what the defendant did, or did not do and what the defendant said, or did not say, in determining whether reasonable grounds existed.

This would impose an evidentiary threshold before a decision could be made that a defendant's belief was based on reasonable grounds which, in turn, may require the defendant to satisfy an evidential onus about the steps he took to ascertain consent.[121] This approach would hopefully ensure that a fact-finder could not ignore the requirements regarding the steps taken by the defendant, as happened in *Lazarus* and *XHR*, before delivering a verdict.

The law on consent should also prevent the use of particular heuristics about the sexual availability of women from the fact-finder's inquiry into reasonable grounds, in order to prevent fact-finders using heuristics to avoid considering steps taken by the defendant. Thus, further qualifications should be added to s 61HE(4)(a) of the NSW *Crimes Act*, as set out below:

The following matters are insufficient to amount to reasonable grounds for a defendant's belief in consent, either on their own or together:

i. the complainant's style of dress;
ii. the complainant's consumption of alcohol or drugs;
iii. the complainant's silence; and/or
iv. the complainant's lack of physical resistance.

Relevant judicial directions would need to be drafted to warn fact-finders about the physiological response known as the freeze response to explain that there may be good reasons why a complainant remained silent or offered no physical resistance. This might assist in preventing fact-finders from using silence/lack of resistance as reasonable grounds for a defendant's belief in consent, as happened in *Lazarus*.

The above reform takes into account Cowan's (2007b: 101; emphasis in original) view that the 'law should look to the substantive question of whether or not the acts were mutual … and how they were *negotiated*' rather than the binary of a passive victim saying yes or no to an active protagonist.

[121]This was a recommendation of the Victorian Law Reform Commission (2004: lxxii). Recommendation 174 stated: 'The accused must produce some evidence that he had an honest belief that the complainant consented before this matter can be left to the jury. The mere assertion by an accused that he believed the complainant was consenting shall not constitute sufficient evidence of an honest belief as to consent'. This was also a recommendation of the United Nations Department of Economic and Social Affairs (2010: 26).

In this way, a defendant's belief would become referable to the complainant's state of mind in order to prevent the situation where a fact-finder can decide that a defendant is not guilty of an offence for having sex with a non-consenting person. This approach may also prevent the use of heuristics like 'contemporary morality' to reason that because a complainant was silent or did not resist, the defendant's belief was reasonable in the circumstances.

Since fact-finders are not educated about the freeze response and the effect of inebriation on behaviour, guidance is also needed on what does not amount to free and voluntary consent. Thus, an extension of the matters that negate consent is warranted:

> The fact that a person froze, or was unable to respond to a sexual act, or did not say or do anything to indicate free agreement in response to a sexual act is enough to show that the act took place without that person's consent.

Amendments are also needed to take into account the fact that free and voluntary agreement is unlikely in circumstances of coercion even without physical violence. In NSW, for example, ss 61HE(8)(b) and (c) of the *Crimes Act* state that 'the grounds on which it may be established that a person does not consent to sexual intercourse' include 'intimidatory or coercive conduct, or other threat' and 'the abuse of a position of authority or trust', respectively. However, these subsections do not take into account the range of unequal relationships in which a person may submit to sexual intercourse rather than freely and voluntarily agreeing.

Thus, these grounds ought to be extended to include the situation where a complainant was in a position of inequality with respect to the defendant as a result of economic, social, cultural and/or religious reasons, or as a result of being groomed for sex.

In order to deal with the problem in *Lazarus*, where no expert evidence was adduced by the prosecution to assist the fact-finder in determining whether Saxon was substantially intoxicated, the word 'substantially' should be removed from the legislation in NSW since this word has no medical meaning. It should be replaced with medically accurate terminology which explains the relationship between specific blood-alcohol levels and particular behaviours (as set out in Table 2) in order to provide the fact-finder with accurate guidance about the relationship between different levels of alcohol consumption and the effect on critical judgement, emotional stability, comprehension and memory, muscular coordination and balance, visual perceptions and speech and degrees of consciousness.

References

Atara, Y. (2015). Trauma from an enactive perspective: The collapse of the *knowing-how* structure. *Adaptive Behavior, 23,* 143–154.

Australian Law Reform Commission. (2010a). *Family violence: A national legal response* (ALRC Report No. 114). Sydney: ALRC.

Banks, S. (2008). An honest but mistaken belief in London legislation: Consent, controversy and sexual offence reform in New South Wales. *The Law Teacher, 42,* 228–235.

Connell, M. (2015). Expert testimony in sexual assault cases: Alcohol intoxication and memory. *International Journal of Law and Psychiatry, 42–43,* 98–105.

Cossins, A. (2003). Saints, sluts and sexual assault: Rethinking the relationship between sex, race and gender. *Social and Legal Studies, 12,* 77–103.

Cossins, A. (2019). Why her behaviour is still on trial: The absence of context in the modernisation of the substantive law on consent. *The University of New South Wales Law Journal, 42,* 462–499.

Cossins, A. (2020). Feminist criminology in a time of 'digital feminism': Can the #MeToo Movement create fundamental cultural change? In S. Walklate, K. Fitz-gibbon, J. M. Maher & J. McCulloch (Eds.), *Emerald handbook in criminology, feminism and social change* (pp. 69–94). Bingley, UK: Emerald Publishing.

Cowan, S. (2007a). Freedom and capacity to make a choice: A feminist analysis of consent in the criminal law of rape. In V. Munro & C. Stychin (Eds.), *Sexuality and the law: Feminist engagements* (pp. 51–71). London: Routledge.

Cowan, S. (2007b). Choosing freely: Theoretically reframing the concept of consent. In R. Hunter & S. Cowan (Eds.), *Choice and consent: Feminist engagements with choice and subjectivity* (pp. 91–105). Abingdon: Routledge-Cavendish.

Cowart, M. (2004). Consent, speech act theory, and legal disputes. *Law and Philosophy, 23,* 495–525.

Criminal Justice and Sexual Offences Taskforce. (2006). *Responding to sexual assault: The way forward*. Sydney: Attorney-General's Department.

Crowe, J., & Sveinsson, L. (2017). Intimidation, consent and the role of holistic judgments in Australian rape law. *University of Western Australia Law Review, 42,* 136–154.

DePaulo, B. M., Lindsay, J. L., Malone, B. E., Muhlenbruck, L., Charlton, K., & Cooper, H. (2003). Cues to deception. *Psychological Bulletin, 129,* 74–118.

Dobinson, I., & Townsley, L. (2008). Sexual assault law reform in NSW: Issues of consent and objective fault. *Criminal Law Journal, 32,* 152–172.

Dubowski, K. M. (1977). *Manual for analysis of ethanol in biological liquids: Final report.* Washington, DC: Department of Transportation, National Highway Traffic Safety Administration.

Du Mont, J., & White, D. (2007). *The uses and impacts of medico-legal evidence in sexual assault cases: A global review*. Geneva: World Health Organization. http://www.svri.org/sites/default/files/attachments/2016-01-19/medico.pdf.

du Toit, L. (2007). The conditions of consent. In R. Hunter & S. Cowan (Eds.), *Choice and consent: Feminist engagements with choice and subjectivity* (pp. 58–73). Abingdon: Routledge-Cavendish.

Ekman, P., O'Sullivan, M., & Frank, M. G. (1999). A few can catch a liar. *Psychological Science, 10,* 263–266.

Forster, C. (2009). Sexual offences law reform in Pacific island countries: Replacing colonial norms with international good practices standards. *Melbourne University Law Review, 33,* 833–864.

Galliano, G., Noble, L. M., Travis, L. A., & Puechl, C. (1993). Victim reactions during rape/sexual assault: A preliminary study of the immobility response and its correlates. *Journal of Interpersonal Violence, 8,* 109–114.

Gawronski, B., & Bodenhausen, G. V. (2014). Implicit and explicit evaluation: A brief review of the associative-propositional evaluation model. *Social and Personality Psychology Compass, 8,* 448–462.

Hatzistergos, The Hon. John, Attorney-General, Second Reading Speech. (2007, November 7). *Crimes Amendment (Consent—Sexual Assault Offences) Bill 2007*, *Parliamentary Debates* (NSW Legislative Council, 3584).

Heidi, J. M., Marx, B. P., & Forsyth, J. P. (2005). Tonic immobility and childhood sexual abuse: A preliminary report evaluating the sequela of rape-induced paralysis. *Behavior Research and Therapy, 43,* 1157–1171.

HM Inspectorate for Constabulary & HM Crown Prosecution Service Inspectorate. (2002). *Report on the joint inspection into the investigation and prosecution of rape offences in England and Wales.* London: HMIC & HMCPSI.

Home Office. (2000). *Setting the boundaries: Reforming the law on sexual offences.* London: Home Office.

Home Office. (2002). *Protecting the public: strengthening protections against sex offenders and reforming the law on sexual offences.* London: Home Office.

Judicial College. (2017). *The Crown Court Compendium: Part 1: Jury and trial management and summing up.* www.judiciary.gov.uk/wp-content/uploads/2016/06/crown-court-compendium-pt1-jury-and-trial-management-and-summing-up-feb2017.pdf. Accessed 24 May 2017.

Judicial College. (2019). *The Crown Court Compendium: Part 1: Jury and trial management and summing up.* https://www.judiciary.uk/wp-content/uploads/2016/06/Crown-Court-Compendium-Part-I-December-2019-amended-19.02.20.pdf.

Kassin, S. M., Meissner, C. A., & Norwick, R. J. (2005). 'I'd know a false confession if I saw one': A comparative study of college students and police investigators. *Law and Human Behavior, 29,* 211–227.

Klein, R. (2015). An analysis of thirty-five years of rape reform: A frustrating search for fundamental fairness. *Akron Law Review, 41,* 981–1057.

Larcombe, W., Fileborn, B., Powell, A., Hanley, N., & Henry, N. (2016). 'I think it's rape and I think he would be found not guilty': Focus group perceptions of (un)reasonable belief in consent in rape law. *Social & Legal Studies, 25,* 611–629.

Law Commission. (2000). *Consent in sexual offences.* London: Law Commission.

Leahy, S. (2014a). Reform of Irish rape law: The need for a legislative definition of consent. *Common Law World Review, 43,* 231–263.

Mackinnon, C. (1989). *Toward a feminist theory of the state.* Harvard, MA: Harvard University Press.

Mann, S., Vrij, A., & Bull, R. (2004). Detecting true lies: Police officers' ability to detect suspects' lies. *Journal of Applied Psychology, 89,* 137–149.

McKee, J., Widder, S. L., Paton-Gay, J. D., Kirkpatrick, A. W., & Engels, P. (2016). Ten year review of alcohol use and major trauma in a Canadian province: Still a major problem. *Journal of Trauma Management & Outcomes, 10,* 1–9.

Monaghan, J., & Mason, G. (2016). Reasonable reform: Understanding the knowledge of consent provision in section 61HA(3)(c) of the Crimes Act 1900 (NSW). *Criminal Law Journal, 40,* 246–261.

Munro, V. E. (2008). Constructing consent: Legislating freedom and legitimating constraint in the expression of sexual autonomy. *Akron Law Review, 41,* 923–956.

Munro, V. E. (2017). Shifting sands? Consent, context and vulnerability in contemporary sexual offences policy in England and Wales. *Social & Legal Studies, 26,* 417–440.

NSW Criminal Justice and Sexual Offences Taskforce. (2005). *Responding to sexual assault: The way forward*. Sydney: Attorney-General's Department of NSW.

NSW Department of Attorney-General and Justice. (2013). *Review of the consent provision for sexual assault offences in the crimes act 1900*. Sydney: Department of Attorney-General and Justice.

NSW Law Reform Commission. (2019). *Consent in relation to sexual offences: Draft proposals*. Sydney: NSW Law Reform Commission.

Pineau, L. (1989). Date rape: A feminist analysis. *Law and Philosophy, 8,* 217–243.

Porter, S., Woodworth, M., & Birt, A. R. (2000). Truth, lies, and videotape: An investigation of the ability of federal parole officers to detect deception. *Law and Human Behavior, 24,* 643–658.

Quadara, A., Fileborn, B., & Parkinson, D. (2013). *The role of forensic medical evidence in the prosecution of adult sexual assault*. Canberra: Australian Institute of Family Studies.

Quilter, J. (2015). From raptus to rape: A history of the requirements of resistance and injury. *Law & History, 2,* 89–113.

Randall, M. (2010). Sexual assault law, credibility, and 'ideal victims': Consent, resistance, and victim blaming. *Canadian Journal of Women and the Law, 22,* 397–435.

Rook, P., & Ward, R. (2016). *Rook & Ward on sexual offences: Law & practice* (5th ed.). London: Sweet & Maxwell.

Rumney, P. N. (2001). The review of sexual offences and rape: Another false dawn. *Modern Law Review, 64,* 890–910.

Scottish Law Commission. (2007). *Report on rape and other sexual offences*. Edinburgh: Scottish Law Commission.

Stanko, E., & Williams, E. (2009). Reviewing rape and rape allegations in London: What are the vulnerabilities of the victims who report to the police? In M. Horvath & J. Brown (Eds.), *Rape: Challenging contemporary thinking* (pp. 207–228). Collumpton, UK: Willan Publishing.

Strömwall, L. A., & Granhag, P. A. (2003). How to detect deception? Arresting the beliefs of police officers, prosecutors and judges. *Psychology, Crime & Law, 9*, 19–36.

Temkin, J., & Ashworth, A. (2004). The Sexual Offences Act 2003: (1) Rape, sexual assaults and the problems of consent. *Criminal Law Review*, 328–346.

United Nations Department of Economic and Social Affairs, Division for the Advancement of Women. (2010). *Handbook for legislation on violence against women* (UN Doc ST/ESA/329).

Victorian Law Reform Commission. (2004). *Sexual offences* (Final Report). Melbourne: Victorian Law Reform Commission.

Vrij, A., Granhag, P., & Porter, S. (2010). Pitfalls and opportunities in nonverbal and verbal lie detection. *Psychological Science in the Public Interest, 11*, 89–121.

8

Cross-Examination in Sexual Assault Trials: Evidentiary Safeguard or an Opportunity to Confuse?

1 Introduction

One of the key features of the adversarial criminal trial is the giving of oral evidence by witnesses and the testing of that evidence through cross-examination, a process considered to be fundamental for ensuring that the defendant receives a fair trial (see, for example, Article 6 of the European Convention on Human Rights [ECHR]) because of its utility for testing a witness's veracity:

> inordinate faith is placed in the capacity of the skilful cross-examiner to expose the dishonest, mistaken or unreliable witness, and to uncover inconsistency and inaccuracy in oral testimony. Consequently, it is viewed as a fundamental right of the accused in a criminal trial to have the evidence of the prosecution witness tested by live cross-examination. (Ellison, 1999: 35)

This chapter is based on Cossins (2009). It has been updated and also considers the problems faced by adult complainants during cross-examination.

A. Cossins, *Closing the Justice Gap for Adult and Child Sexual Assault*,
https://doi.org/10.1057/978-1-137-32051-3_8

However, this oral tradition within a culture of adversarialism combines to produce entrenched patterns of manipulating a vulnerable witness's oral evidence through leading questions using complex vocabulary, sentence construction and syntax (Brennan, 1995; Hanna, Davies, Crothers, & Henderson, 2012; Davies, Henderson, & Hanna, 2010; Zajac, Gross, & Hayne, 2003), all of which has been described as 'legitimated bullying' (Henning, 2006: 136).

Apart from the requirement based on the old common law rule in *Browne v Dunn* (1893) 6 R 67 (HL) that a cross-examiner must actually put challenges to an opponent's witness to allow that witness, in fairness, to respond, the defence is entitled to raise reasonable doubts, with historically few legal limits on the methods for doing so and no limits on the use of stereotypes or rape myths. In Chapters 4 and 5, research studies revealed that the more that jurors endorse rape myths which are based on common stereotypes, the more likely they will blame the complainant, perceive the defendant as low in culpability and return not guilty verdicts.

It is a long-held objective of cross-examination to use witness questioning to communicate with the jury rather than the witness (Rook & Ward, 2016: 1555), thus resulting in zealous control of a witness's answers. This may be contrasted with the approach of forensic questioning which aims to obtain reliable evidence from a witness through open-ended, non-leading questions.

Because cross-examination is most likely to impact the quality of children's evidence, this chapter begins with an analysis of the problems facing child complainants within adversarial trials, followed by an analysis of the effect of cross-examination on adult witnesses.

2 A Culture of Adversarialism: 'Legitimated Bullying'?

Cross-examination of witnesses is based on the logically flawed assumption that cross-examination style questions will not affect the evidence of a witness who is telling the truth and that any change to a witness's examination-in-chief is a change towards the truth. However, for children, cross-examination is that part of court proceedings where their interests and rights 'are most likely to be ignored or sacrificed' (Brennan, 1995: 73). Because of this, the CSA trial has been described as 'a legally sanctioned' forum (Eastwood & Patton, 2002: 4) in which children can be emotionally traumatised by the unregulated behaviour of defence counsel and by questions children do not understand or cannot answer (Australian Law Reform Commission and Human Rights and Equal Opportunity Commission [ALRC & HREOC] 1997: 343; Davies et al., 2010).

More so than adults, children, as a group, are disadvantaged by a criminal justice process that is not underpinned by trauma-informed principles (as discussed in Chapter 11), and, therefore, 'does not allow their full and equal participation' (Scottish Executive Central Research Unit, 2002: i) even though their evidence will be central to the prosecution's case in a CSA trial.

Historical and recent analyses show that trials involving sex offences are governed by specific rules of evidence, warnings and methods of cross-examination that were originally based on cultural beliefs about women's and children's propensity for promiscuity and lying (Boniface, 1994; Cossins, 2000; NSW Department for Women, 1996; Smart, 1990). These beliefs are well entrenched not least because of the pronouncements by judges throughout the centuries[1] of Lord Hale's belief that rape is an accusation easy to make yet hard to prove (Hale, 1736/1971: 635). This view that has been used as the basis for justifying protections for the accused (Coyle, Field, Wilson, Cuthbert, & Miller, 2009; Criminal Justice and Sexual Offences Taskforce, 2006; Eastwood, Kift, & Grace, 2006) without concomitant consideration of the fair treatment of child witnesses.

---

[1]See, for example, *Kelleher v R* (1974) 131 CLR 534, 543 (Barwick CJ); *R v Rosemeyer* [1985] VR 945, 963 (Ormiston J); *Question of Law Reserved on Acquittal Pursuant to Section 351(1A) Criminal Law Consolidation Act (No 1 of 1993)* (1993) 59 SASR 214, 227 (Perry J); *Leoni v State*, 44 Ala 110, 113 (Peters J) (1870); see also at 114 (Peck CJ); *Bute v Illinois*, 333 US 640, 681 (Douglas J for Douglas, Murphy and Rutledge JJ) (1948); *Johnson v Alaska*, 501 P 2d 762, 766 (Boney CJ for Boney CJ, Rabinowitz, Connor and Erwin JJ) (Alaska, 1972); *United States v Wiley*, 492 F 2d 547, 554 (Bazelon CJ) (DC Cir, 1973); *R v Sherrin* [No 2] (1979) 21 SASR 250, 254 (King CJ); *R v Henry* (1968) 53 Cr App R 150, 153 (Salmon LJ).

Nonetheless, few reforms have recognised or addressed the inaccuracies produced during cross-examination, partly because of the way these prejudicial beliefs play out in the adversarial trial, particularly during cross-examination. While the last decade has seen major reforms in E&W and all Australian jurisdictions to address children's vulnerabilities through the use of CCTV, remote rooms and pre-recorded evidence (Cossins, 2010a; Davies et al., 2010; Spencer & Lamb, 2012), the history of sexual assault law reform shows that the process of cross-examination process remains the most unregulated part of the adversarial trial (Caruso, 2012; Cossins, 2010a).

The centrality of cross-examination to the adversarial trial demonstrates the oft-repeated belief that it is the most effective method for testing a witness's truthfulness and the accuracy of their testimony, though its actual effectiveness has been in dispute for many years (Davies et al., 2010). Yet the focus of the adversarial trial on two lawyers (prosecution and defence counsel) locked in verbal battle where one wins and the other loses is a verbal representation of a physical battle (Langbein, 2003) and is likely to have a considerable impact on the well-being of a child: 'the contest between a child … and a defence advocate [will be] far from equal' (Scottish Executive Central Research Unit, 2002: 16), with the child's vulnerability and the adversarial nature of cross-examination combining to produce a relationship of power easily exploited by defence counsel.

As discussed in Chapter 11, this power relationship will be heightened where the traumatic effects of cross-examination trigger the feelings of powerlessness experienced by a child as a result of the original sexual abuse (Dulcan & Wiener, 2006; Westcott & Page, 2002). Indeed, the adversarial trial has no mechanisms for recognising the prevalence of PTSD suffered by sexually abused children (and adults) and, therefore, no ability to apply trauma-informed care principles to the adversarial trial (see Chapter 11).

Many lawyers will argue that '[e]vidence which has not been subjected to the conventional safeguards of the adversarial trial process [should be] viewed with considerable suspicion' (Ellison, 1999: 35). However, the answers given by a child in response to cross-examination within the power relationship in an adversarial trial are highly suspect, not because of the qualities of the child but because of the risk that confusion, suggestion and/or a child's deference to an authority figure will produce inaccurate evidence, as *Ward v R* [2017] VSCA 37 demonstrates below. While a child's evidence during cross-examination may be the best evidence *for the defendant*, based on a review of relevant studies, the best evidence given by a child will be evidence that is *not* subject to standard cross-examination techniques.

Arguably, 'the extent to which truth is prejudiced by the use of these tactics' (Brennan, 1995: 73) is a question that must be addressed on the grounds that the fairness of a trial is to be measured by reference to not only the rights of the accused but also the rights of victims.

3 The Impact of Cross-Examination on Children's Evidence

Over the past decades, several inquiries and studies into the prosecution of child sex offences, and children as witnesses within the criminal justice system have found that:

- cross-examination is one of the worst parts of testifying for children since it is stressful and anxiety-inducing (Eastwood & Patton, 2002; Plotnikoff & Woolfson, 2009, 2012; Zajac, Jury, & O'Neill, 2009) and may re-trigger the original emotions associated with being abused in children suffering from post-traumatic stress disorder (PTSD) and other trauma symptoms[2];
- children are often subject to aggression, humiliation, harassment and accusations of lying from defence counsel (Cashmore & Trimboli, 2005; Eastwood & Patton, 2002; Plotnikoff & Woolfson, 2009, 2012; Powell, Westera, Goodman-Delahunty, & Pichler, 2016; Victorian Law Reform Commission [VLRC], 2004);
- the most damaging part of cross-examination for children is being accused of lying (Eastwood & Patton, 2002). In a 2002 report into the prosecution of CSA in NSW, the NSW Parliament's Standing

[2]These symptoms are documented in Chapter 11.

Committee on Law and Justice (NSWSCLJ) reported the views of many that the cross-examination of children was an abusive process, a fact also reported 15 years later by the Royal Commission into Institutional Responses to Child Sexual Abuse (2017b) in its *Criminal Justice Report*.

- children are subject to complex, developmentally inappropriate and repetitive questioning and questions that are deliberately designed to confuse and create inconsistencies (Cashmore & Trimboli, 2005; Davies et al., 2010; Eastwood & Patton, 2002; Hanna et al., 2012);
- the linguistic style of defence lawyers is *least* likely to match that of the child compared to other investigative professionals (Cashmore & Trimboli, 2005; Davies, Henderson, & Seymour, 1997; Davies et al., 2010; Plotnikoff & Woolfson, 2009; Zajac & Hayne, 2003; Zajac et al., 2003);
- when comparing the professional manner of lawyers and interviewers towards children, only defence lawyers were rated by researchers as being aggressive, sarcastic or accusatory towards a child (Cashmore & Trimboli, 2005);
- when comparing the fairness of all court participants towards them, defence lawyers were rated as the least fair by the 43 child complainants in Cashmore and Trimboli's study (2005); and
- compared to prosecutors, defence lawyers are more likely to use closed and leading questions resulting in the cross-examination effect, as discussed below, which has a dramatic impact on the accuracy of children's evidence, including changes in testimony away from the truth.

Most recently, the Royal Commission into Institutional Responses to Child Sexual Abuse (2017a: 75) reported that:

> [m]any survivors have told us how daunting they found the criminal justice system [and] … that they felt that they were the ones on trial. Some survivors told us that the cross-examination process was as bad as the child sexual abuse they suffered. Many survivors told us that they found the process re-traumatising and offensive.

The Royal Commission (2017a: 75) also noted that in their private sessions and public hearings, they had:

> heard from the families of young victims and victims with disability about the particular difficulties these victims face in giving evidence. Police and prosecutors have given us examples of complainants, especially children, breaking down during cross-examination, in some cases with the result that the prosecution has failed.

Overall, consultations and research by the Royal Commission (2017a: 75) concluded that, 'at least in some cases, the way in which complainants are questioned by police, prosecutors and defence counsel has itself compromised their evidence'.

A recent development in relation to children's evidence is that the inconsistencies produced during the cross-examination of children are being used by defendants to find appeals against convictions on the grounds that the 'inconsistencies so damaged [the complainant's] credibility and reliability that none of the convictions can stand' (*Ward* [2017] VSCA 37, [3], Maxwell P and Redlich JA; see also *R v W and M* [2011] EWCA Crim 1926).

In order to deal with such an appeal in *Ward*, the Victorian Court of Appeal (VSCA) was required to examine how defence counsel can discharge their obligations under the rule in *Browne v Dunn* (1897) 6 R 67 at the same time as 'achieving their forensic objective of seeking to undermine the credibility and reliability of a child witness' (*Ward* [2017] VSCA 37, [9]). The Court observed that:

> the cross-examination of a child complainant ... is a task of considerable complexity, requiring great care and sensitivity. ... The first challenge is to formulate questions which are age-appropriate ... as a matter of basic fairness to the child witness ... . Unless the questions are age-appropriate, answers which appear to create inconsistencies ... are unlikely to serve the desired purpose of creating a doubt in the minds of the jury or ... of persuading this Court that the jury 'must have a doubt' about the evidence. ... [T]he child witness must be given the opportunity to say whether something they have said, and which the accused disputes, is

> true. This is the obligation of fairness … [under] the rule in *Browne v Dunn*. (*Ward* [2017] VSCA 37, [10]–[12])

The problem that few jurisdictions have addressed in terms of reform is that challenging a child witness using typical suggestive statements (such as 'I put it to you that you XYZ did not happen' or 'I put it to you that your evidence is a pack of lies') is bound to create 'a significant risk' that the child will accept such suggestions without understanding their meaning or the implications of agreeing with the cross-examiner (*Ward* [2017] VSCA 37, [12]). Thus, the rule in *Browne v Dunn* (1897) 6 R 67 can create unfairness in relation to child witnesses as discussed further below.

In *W and M* [2011] EWCA Crim 1926, the defence had appealed on the grounds that the eight-year-old complainant had retracted her allegations under cross-examination when she answered 'No' to two tagged questions: 'S did not put his willy in your bum, did he?' and 'S did not put his willy in your minnie, did he?'[3] The EWCA identified the difficulties when a child's evidence is such that 'a jury could not safely convict' as a result of contradictions made under cross-examination.[4] Nonetheless, the EWCA rejected the appellants' arguments that the complainant's evidence should have been withdrawn from the jury and concluded that her retractions were unreliable because they were obtained by the use of highly suggestive questioning:

> Most of the questions which produced the answers which were chiefly relied upon … constituted the putting of direct suggestions with an indication of the answer: 'This happened, didn't it?' Or: 'This didn't happen, did it?' The consequence of that is … that it can be very difficult to tell whether the child is truly changing her account or simply taking the line of least resistance.[5]

In Australia, a country that still has not fully embraced the research that shows that cross-examination is an unreliable method for testing

---

[3]EWCA Crim 1926, [25].

[4]Ibid., [33].

[5]Ibid., [31].

the evidence of children, these grounds of appeal have sometimes been successful. For example, in *O'Reilly v R* [2015] VSCA 19, a case in which the complainant required an interpreter, the complainant gave very clear descriptions of multiple occasions of sexual abuse by the defendant. Despite this evidence and the misunderstandings caused by the interpreter's translation of complex cross-examination questions, the VSCA decided that the cross-examination was a reliable method for concluding that the complainant had actually recanted part of his police interview. The Crown had argued:

> simply because a child gives evidence about a particular sexual episode … and the child is unable to confirm that [evidence] … that fact alone can't result in the conviction being necessarily unsafe and unsatisfactory. One needs to look to the explanations. One needs look to the precision of the cross examination and whether or not it was recanted. If it was recanted, then clearly … the ground is made good. If it's short of recantation and it can be explained by memory lapse … and it was not a witness who was not telling the truth at any time, then the conviction isn't necessarily unsafe.[6]

Thus, the prosecution submitted that 'it was self-evident from the transcript that the complainant was operating under some confusion as to the import of the questions that were being put to him, and that those questions were themselves attenuated by a degree of ambiguity'.[7] At issue was the likely impact of stress on the complainant's recall as a result of the lengthy cross-examination (which took place over two days) and the effect of stress on memory recall. The prosecution noted that:

> [the complainant's] memory lapse was explicable by reference to the rigours of cross examination, which the complainant was self-evidently finding stressful, as well as the difficulties and confusion inherent in the interpretation process. … [I]t was scarcely surprising that the complainant might struggle to recall events that occurred so many years before, having

---

[6] *O'Reilly v R* [2015] VSCA 19, [49].

[7] Ibid., [51].

> given an account of those matters in 2007, in the [recorded police interview], when his memory would have been fresher than it was by the time of the special hearing.[8]

The VSCA held that the evidence given in support of three of the charges:

> was of such a questionable form as to leave us with a real doubt as to whether the appellant's guilt has been properly established in relation to those matters. Having considered the evidence as a whole, ... we are of the view that the verdicts ... are, relevantly, unsafe and unsatisfactory, and cannot be permitted to stand.[9]

This case highlights the problem that arises where a child merely agrees with defence counsel's suggestive, tagged statements. In other words, a child's agreement is more likely to be the result of this subtle form of coercion than a statement of the truth, as discussed below. As such, the criminal justice system may be perpetuating injustice in the name of fairness to the accused 'by taking unfair advantage of children's emotional and intellectual stage of development' (NSWSCLJ, 2002: 78). In fact, as the *Ward* case demonstrates below, because of age-inappropriate cross-examination, a child's evidence is easily distorted and her/his credibility easily undermined since we know that jurors' verdicts are influenced by the consistency of evidence and the credibility of the complainant (Cashmore & Trimboli, 2006).

Studies have found that jurors base their perceptions of a child's credibility and their decisions on the type of questions posed by attorneys. For example, Klemfuss, Quas, and Lyon (2014) found that the different types of questions asked by defence counsel and prosecutors of children were predictive of trial outcomes. After analysing 42 criminal court transcripts from CSA cases in Los Angeles County they found that although prosecutors asked more questions than defence attorneys, the latter asked significantly more suggestive questions:

[8] Ibid., [53]–[54].

[9] Ibid., [81]–[82].

> for both types of attorneys, ... the increased use of suggestive questions seemed to slightly increase the likelihood of [acquittals], particularly for defense attorneys. ... Cases that ended in acquittals were characterized by lower rates of option-posing questions and higher rates of suggestive questions by defense attorneys out of all the questions posed to the child. (Klemfuss et al., 2014: 783–784; 786)

Possibly, the most surprising finding was the fact that the content of questions matters more than a child's responses:

> While children's responses were neither directly nor indirectly related to case outcome, attorneys' questions were ... [which] suggest[s] that juries may be more sensitive to information provided by attorneys (both in statements and in questions to children) [than children's responses]. (ibid.: 785–786)

Such a finding confirms the views that the purpose of cross-examination is to use the witness to make a series of declarations and statements (Caruso, 2012; Henderson, 2014) which conveys the defence case to the jury but is untested by the prosecution. Indeed, such a 'finding is disturbing given that suggestive questions le[a]d to the most minimal responding and have been consistently shown to cause inaccurate responding, particularly in children' (Klemfuss et al., 2014: 786).

In a later study, Mugno, Klemfuss, and Lyon (2016: 191) found that mock jurors rated the child more favourably during direct examination than cross-examination, with the 'greater proportion of suggestive and leading questions' during cross-examination probably explaining less favourable views of the child. Indeed, 'the effect of questioning style is apparent even when responses from child witnesses are minimal' which is likely due to the content of those questions, with jurors then 'extrapolating this information to estimate the child's credibility' (ibid.: 193).

Some might consider these problems to be a feature of CSA trials before technological changes were made to the way children give evidence in court. Yet even with the advent of specially designed rooms from which evidence is given via CCTV, cross-examination is still the most traumatising aspect of giving evidence for children with the treatment of children by defence counsel and the styles and types of cross-examination questions remaining unchanged, at least in Australian jurisdictions (Cashmore & Trimboli, 2005, 2006; Eastwood & Patton, 2002; Royal Commission into Institutional Responses to Child Sexual Abuse, 2017a; *Ward* [2017] VSCA 37).

The damage that cross-examination can do to a child's testimony, as well as their mental health, lies in the fact that, after disclosure, children may be involved with a range of professionals, including police, doctors, counsellors and child welfare agencies, who 'convey … the message that they have done the right thing to tell someone, that they are not in trouble and that they are not responsible for the assault' (NSWSCLJ, 2002: 61). By contrast, cross-examination 'go[es] against everything else that a child has been told' because s/he may be accused of lying, making up stories, wanting to cause trouble for the defendant or being coached by their mother or other adults (ibid.).

While there is a common belief (discussed below) that greater regulation by judicial officers will solve the problems associated with the cross-examination of children, 'there is a wide variation as to what judges allow during cross-examination' (Eastwood & Patton, 2002: 125), since some do not recognise age-inappropriate questioning. It will also be much more difficult for a judge to know when to intervene in a line of questioning that is intended to confuse or create inconsistencies in the evidence, rather than one that is aggressive or intimidating (ibid.; see also Davies et al., 2010).

This variation is likely to be even greater now in NSW since, with the appointment of only two specially trained judges who sit on CSA cases (see, further, Chapter 9, other untrained judicial officers still preside over the bulk of CSA cases in NSW.

There is also a conflict for judges between their role in controlling cross-examination and their duty to protect the rights of the accused which may produce judicial resistance to intervening in cross-examination. In 2002, the NSWSCLJ considered that the answer lay in imposing a duty on trial judges to protect witnesses under the age of 18 years and recommended that s 41 of the NSW *Evidence Act 1995* be amended to impose a positive duty on judicial officers to intervene in relation to improper questions (for all witnesses). However, this reform has not had the desired effect. Anecdotal evidence (Cossins, 2009), as well as evidence from a study by Cashmore and Trimboli (2006) suggests that NSW judicial officers infrequently utilise s 41 to protect children from improper questions. As discussed later, Hopkins and Boyd (2010) made similar findings in interviews with practitioners.

While the Judicial Commission of NSW (2017 update) recommends that judges set ground rules for the developmentally appropriate cross-examination of child witnesses, there is no mandatory, legislative requirement to do so in NSW. By contrast, in E&W, ground rules hearings are now conducted in CSA cases where an intermediary has been appointed to advise the court on the communication abilities of the child complainant (see Chapter 9).

Indeed, the most common response about how children are treated by the criminal justice system has been to recommend the education of judges and lawyers about the dynamics of child abuse and child development (see Hopkins & Boyd, 2010; Caruso, 2012; Criminal Justice Sexual Offences Taskforce, 2006; Davies et al., 2010; NSWSCLJ, 2002). However, Cashmore and Trimboli (2006) found that educational packages for judges had no discernible effect on the cross-examination process in the CSA trials they evaluated. In fact, the study confirmed anecdotal evidence that judges are reluctant to intervene to protect a child witness from badgering during cross-examination.[10]

In the seventeen trials observed (from March to December 2004), judicial intervention was found to be least common 'to protect the child witness from badgering or oppressive questioning, [or] to support and encourage the child', with only 20.6% of judicial interventions being made to control cross-examination (Cashmore & Trimboli, 2005: 52; 54), compared to interventions for clarifying questions or answers.

Although judicial intervention varied considerably according to the trial judge, it did not vary according to the complainant's age or the style of questioning by the defence. In fact, those judges who had received

[10]The study evaluated a 'specialist jurisdiction' which was established in 2003 after recommendations made by the NSWSCLJ (2002) to address the obstacles associated with CSA prosecutions, although it did not amount to a specialist court. Eleven trials were heard in the 'specialist jurisdiction' and six were held in a comparison registry (Sydney).

education packages about inappropriate questioning of children intervened *less* frequently to protect the child from badgering, compared to judges who had not received education packages (20 versus 40 interventions), or to support the child (4 versus 46 interventions) (Cashmore & Trimboli, 2006: 52), suggesting that the education received by judges had little or no impact on their control of proceedings.

A similar judicial reluctance to intervene to protect child witnesses was found by Davies et al. (2010) in a study of NZ cross-examination transcripts.

In a study of 120 transcripts of complainant's evidence of CSA, Powell et al. (2016: 236) found that although judges intervened more often than prosecutors, the number of interventions by judges and prosecutors, in either evidence-in-chief or cross-examination did not differ according to the complainant's age. As well, 'the reasons for judges' and prosecutors' interventions did not differ according to complainant age' while 'judges and prosecutors intervened more about question form, followed by giving directions or asking questions, matters of law, complainant care and question manner' (ibid.: 237).

Overall, the study found that judges were intervening more in cross-examination than in evidence-in-chief, although they were not doing so more with children than with adults despite the comprehension problems that children experience in criminal trials (Powell et al., 2016: 239). While both judges and prosecutors were more likely to intervene in relation to the question form (about 40% of interventions),

> the actual number of interventions for question form (172) was low compared to the total number of complex questions defence lawyers asked (432). This could be due to a range of factors, such as the judge not wanting to appear as though they were favouring the prosecution, or … [because] judges and prosecutors need up-skilling in how to identify the types of questions that are likely to decrease the accuracy of complainants' responses. (ibid.: 239)

The study also found that despite the fact that 'defence lawyers are frequently using questions that are based on stereotypes about complainant behaviour', less than 1% of all interventions were related to question substance (ibid.: 239).

Most recently, an Australian Director of Public Prosecutions also noted the reluctance of judges to intervene:

> judges are more likely to intervene to prevent questions in cross-examination that are misleading or confusing than those that are annoying, harassing, intimidating, offensive, oppressive or insulting. (Royal Commission, 2017b: 85)

He also noted that court personnel 'have a much higher threshold when assessing if a question is harassing or offensive than witnesses' (ibid.).

Could lack of judicial intervention be solved by introducing independent intermediaries or legal representatives who have a duty to the court but are not burdened by the need to protect the rights of the accused? Before examining a number of reform options, this chapter canvasses the following issues:

- to what extent is the right to cross-examine by the defence an absolute right?
- what is the real purpose of cross-examination in the CSA trial?
- how does the 'strange language' of the courtroom produce unreliable evidence?
- what do studies about the impact of cross-examination on children's evidence tell us?
- why have reforms so far been inadequate?
- what reforms could make demonstrable differences to improve the experiences and evidence of children (and sexual assault complainants generally)?

4 Attempts to Improve the Cross-Examination Process for Children

In 2015, the NSW Department of Justice (2015) released a consultation paper entitled, *Children's Champions & Pre-Recording of Evidence*. However, the consultation questions were not unique, in that they had been considered by various government and non-government committees and researchers in both Australia and E&W. Thus, the consultation questions need to be understood within a framework of previous research.

For example, in 2010, the 492-page report of the National Child Sexual Assault Reform Committee (Cossins, 2010a) contained 34 recommendations for reform of the CSA trial. Three of these recommendations concerned the use of intermediaries and were based on the need to elicit the *best evidence* from a child complainant and to reduce the distress or trauma experienced by a child during the trial process.

The National Child Sexual Assault Reform Committee arrived at these recommendations after an in-depth analysis of the processes and procedures in both adversarial and inquisitorial jurisdictions which seek to protect sexual assault complainants from re-traumatisation during the trial process. Its 2010 report identified various ways to ameliorate the impact of the court experience on child witnesses in an adversarial context by:

(i) preventing the complainant from appearing at trial by pre-recording her/his evidence-in-chief and/or cross-examination (now available in NSW and E&W);
(ii) informalising the surroundings in which complainants give evidence (for example, the use of remote witness rooms now used in NSW and Western Australia);
(iii) preventing the defence from putting cross-examination questions directly to the child;
(iv) informalising the cross-examination process by allowing it to take place pre-trial under the control of a third-party examiner, such as an intermediary (see Chapter 9);

(v) introducing specialist child sex offences courts with trained specialist judges and prosecutors and 15 other features to reduce delays and produce cultural change.

Even with some or all of these reforms in place, without a cultural change in the form of a trauma-informed specialist court system (see Chapter 11), the key barrier that prevents children from giving their best evidence is cross-examination which involves the use of leading, confusing and suggestive questions designed to produce inconsistencies in a witness's evidence. It also has the effect of establishing an unequal power relationship between child and examiner and the potential for eliciting inaccurate evidence on which jury decision-making is based.

5 Defence Cross-Examination Versus Forensic Interviews

The development of protocols and interview guidelines to assist forensic investigators when interviewing children turn on the use of 'open-ended questions to elicit a narrative account' and the avoidance of questions and statements that may influence or contaminate that account (Westera, Zydervelt, Kaladelfos, & Zajac, 2017: 17). By contrast, the point of defence cross-examination which uses leading and suggestive questions, is to communicate:

> a story to the jury by manipulating the witness into giving the desired evidence *and* by the advocate ... convey[ing] certain messages to the fact finders during questioning. Traditionally, the advocate's focus ... is not really on the witness's evidence but rather on what perception of it can be created. The witness is the medium but not necessarily the message. (Henderson, 2014: 97; footnotes omitted; emphasis added)

Leading and suggestive questions are known to be the most unreliable method for eliciting information from children (Davies et al., 2010; Lamb, Hershkowitz, Orbach, & Esplin, 2008; Snow & Powell, 2007;

Powell, 2013). Since the basis of cross-examination is to put suggestions to witnesses that contradict their testimony, often using convoluted language and grammatical styles, it is surprising that the adversarial system places so much faith in cross-examination as a reliable way of testing the veracity of a witness, particularly child witnesses. Cross-examination of children highlights one of the great inconsistencies in the adversarial system since the type of suggestive and leading questions that would make a child's forensic interview inadmissible on the grounds of unreliability is the very type of questioning adopted by the cross-examiner.

While it is widely accepted that the purpose of cross-examination is to elicit evidence favourable to the defence by testing the accuracy of the witness's evidence and their credibility (Caruso, 2012; Henderson, 2014), the process is akin to an interrogation where one party seeks to undermine the witness at any cost, with facts being secondary to the desired aim, and leading questions used to state the defence case:

> a leading question is not a question at all. It is a statement or suggestion, with an inquisitorial sentiment tacked to the end. ... Leading is a euphemism for story-telling. It permits 'editorial' comments to be put in the form of questions. That style generally means the witness cannot properly respond to the comments. (Caruso, 2012: 217–218)

Because leading questions are the defence's way of 'communicating with the jury', this results in questions 'which confuse and unsettle the witness, since questioning is not designed with their understanding or even participation in mind' (Caruso, 2012: 218). Even if a witness disagrees with a cross-examiner's statement ('You were drunk, weren't you?'), the idea has been conveyed to the fact-finder without the fact-finder realising the statement may be nothing more than supposition based on rumour or stereotype. Such tactics are particularly destructive with a child or other vulnerable witness, as discussed further below.

The more unsettled the witness, the more likely the fact-finder will make a negative judgement of her/his credibility. Even Wigmore, who is often quoted for his famous phrase about the truth-seeking qualities of cross-examination, acknowledged that '[a] lawyer can do anything with a cross-examination ... He may ... do more than he ought to do ... [he] may make the truth appear like falsehood' (Wigmore, 1974: 32; cited in Bowden et al., 2014: 560).

In a study of transcripts of CSA trials in New Zealand, Davies et al. (2010: 352) found that, on average, 84% of cross-examination questions put to children were closed or leading. Also of concern was question complexity—'nearly one in five questions ... contained complex vocabulary (18%) and more than one in four contained two or more embedded clauses (27%)', leading to clear incidences of miscommunication between child and lawyer, although sometimes children do not realise 'they have misunderstood a complex question' (ibid.).

Defence cross-examiners are, generally, not trained in the methods to elicit a child's best evidence (compared to the training received by forensic interviewers). Indeed, defence counsel are unlikely to be interested in such methods since obtaining a child's recantation of their allegations assists the defence case, as does obtaining inconsistencies and confusion. For example, cross-examiners are advised to frame questions 'in such a way that they elicit either a "yes" or a "no". A child will probably answer "yes" to a question that suggests a yes answer and "no" to one that suggests a no answer' (Salhany, 2006: 103).

Indeed, empirical research (discussed below) shows that inconsistencies, recantations and confusions are the product of leading and suggestive questions during cross-examination because of the developmental inability of children to understand and answer such questions. Such research undermines the belief that cross-examination-style questions are effective in revealing when a witness is lying or mistaken since a leading question is not a method for eliciting the truth:

> the truth being expressed is that believed ... by the cross-examiner, rather than inquiry into the truth believed by the witness. ... Leading questions advance the defence case through a technique which involves subterfuge and psychologically deleterious effects on a witness's recall. (Caruso, 2012: 224)

A number of untested assumptions underlie the practice and role of cross-examination since there is no evidence to show that particular styles of cross-examination are effective at flushing out the dishonest (as opposed to the confused) child or adult witness. When it comes to children, 'there is no simple "Pinocchio" test' for determining whether a child is lying or telling the truth (Goodman & Melinder, 2007: 9). In fact, there is 'no widely accepted criteria to differentiate true from false memory' in the psychological literature (ibid.) while inconsistencies in details are not a reliable predictor of lack of veracity (Fisher, Vrij, & Leins, 2013).

6 The Right to Cross-Examine: An Absolute Right?

6.1 The Position in E&W

Because cross-examination is considered to be 'the primary evidentiary safeguard of the adversary trial process' (Ellison, 1999: 35), it is widely accepted that a defendant's inability to effectively test the prosecution's case will infringe the fair trial principle (Hoyano, 2014).[11] Yet commentators are rarely able to articulate how that right would be affected if cross-examination was more tightly regulated.

In E&W, the overriding objective of the Criminal Procedure Rules 2015 is to ensure that criminal cases are dealt with justly which includes recognising a defendant's rights under Article 6 of the European Convention on Human Rights (ECHR) (see Rules 1.1 and 1.2). Article 6 states that 'everyone is entitled to a fair and public hearing within a reasonable time by an independent and impartial tribunal established by law', and lists the minimum rights for a defendant, including the right:

> to examine or have examined witnesses against him and to obtain the attendance and examination of witnesses on his behalf under the same conditions as witnesses against him.

---

[11] *S v The Queen* (1989) 168 CLR 266; *Dietrich v R* (1992) 177 CLR 292; *R v McHardie and Danielson* [1983] 2 NSWLR 733; *R v McLennan* [1999] 2 Qd R 297; *R v Khan* [2003] NSWSC 849; *Stack v State of WA* [2004] WASCA 300.

Hoyano (2014: 4; footnotes omitted) is one of many critics of inroads into the fair trial principle on the grounds that:

> The right to a fair trial embedded in the common law and the … [ECHR] art.6 is pre-eminent because it provides the platform for the vindication of all other legal rights. It is often described in absolutist terms, as 'the birthright of every British citizen', 'fundamental and absolute', and 'axiomatic'. … Over the past decade, British and Strasbourg courts alike have lost sight of this premise. We have reached the point where a criminal trial held to have been unfair as a whole nonetheless can generate a 'safe' verdict under English law.

However, what principle or authority justifies the production of inaccurate evidence in a criminal trial? The production of inaccurate evidence using well-known cross-examination techniques does not constitute one of the rights of the accused as the fair trial principle is understood. Thus, judicial control over cross-examination is required to prevent the manufacture of inaccurate evidence during criminal trials, something that has been recognised by the Court of Appeal (EWCA) in a series of cases. As Rook and Ward (2016: 1556) acknowledge:

> [t]he Court of Appeal has stated in the plainest of terms that the approach to cross-examination of children and vulnerable witnesses should be markedly different from the approach to non-vulnerable adults. … [T]he advocate must now adapt their cross-examination to the witness … to obtain reliable evidence whilst remaining fair to the defendant.

Despite the absolutist notion of the fair trial principle, when it comes to the examination of witnesses, a court has the express power to limit '(i) the examination, cross-examination or re-examination of a witness, and (ii) the duration of any stage of the hearing' under Rule 3.11(d) of the Criminal Procedure Rules 2015. In a number of cases, the EWCA has held that a court's power to limit cross-examination under Rule 3.11(d) is compatible with Article 6 of the ECHR. While a fearless presentation of the defence case is very important, there is always a balance between rights and court resources so that counsel must avoid:

> wasted time, repetition and prolixity. It is no part of the duty of counsel to put every point of the defendant's case … to a witness or to embark on lengthy cross-examination on matters which are not really in issue. It is the duty of counsel to discriminate between important and relevant features of a defence case … and minor and/or unnecessary matters … We are not saying that it should become a routine feature … that judges should impose time limits for evidence in chief or cross-examination of witnesses. … But where … counsel indulges in prolix and repetitious questioning, judges are fully entitled, and … obliged, to impose reasonable time limits. (*R v Butt* (2005) EWCA Crim 805, [10], Dyson LJ)

In *R v Chaaban*, Judge LJ also considered the balance between a fair trial, limited court resources and the needs of others:

> [t]he entitlement to a fair trial is not inconsistent with proper judicial control over the use of time … [since] every trial which takes longer than it reasonably should is wasteful of limited resources. It also results in delays to justice in cases still waiting to be tried, adding to the tension and distress of victims, defendants, particularly those in custody awaiting trial, and witnesses. ([2003] EWCA Crim 1012, [37])

Control over cross-examination is even more necessary in relation to child witnesses, a fact well-recognised by the EWCA in the specially convened Court in *R v Barker* [2010] EWCA Crim 4. The following extract is worth quoting in full as it describes the ease with which counsel could adapt their cross-examination questioning for children:

> When the issue is whether the child is lying or mistaken …, it should not be over-problematic for the advocate to formulate short, simple questions which put the … the defendant's case to the witness … . Aspects of evidence which … are believed to undermine the child's credibility must, of course, be revealed to the jury, but it is not necessarily appropriate for them to form the subject matter of detailed cross-examination of the child and the advocate may have to forego … cross-examination which consists of no more than comment on matters which will be before the jury … from different sources. … [W]hen … the witness … is a child, … it should not take very lengthy cross-examination to demonstrate, when

> it is the case, that the child may indeed be fabricating, or fantasising, or imagining, or reciting a well rehearsed untruthful script, learned by rote, or simply just suggestible, or contaminated by or in collusion with others to make false allegations, or making assertions in language which is beyond his or her level of comprehension, and therefore likely to be derived from another source.[12]

This means that in E&W, wide-ranging, cross-examination has been limited in cases involving child complainants so that one senior advocate has advised colleagues that trial practices have changed to such an extent that it is '[n]o good resorting to old fashioned "rights," [arguments]' because judges are now trained in the matters affecting children's evidence so that it is 'best to focus on [the] most effective forensic approach in difficult circumstances' (Dein, 2015, n.p.).

Furthermore, in *R v Lubemba; R v JP* [2014] EWCA Crim 2064, the EWCA observed how much criminal trial processes had changed in relation to vulnerable witnesses and commended 'Toolkits on how to treat vulnerable witnesses fairly and to get the best from them'.[13] In fact, these Toolkits (which are available online at the advocates gateway[14]) 'have been endorsed by the Lord Chief Justice in the Criminal Practice Directions Amendment No2 as best practice'[15] and include the following principles:

> All witnesses ... should be enabled to give the best evidence they can. In relation to young and/or vulnerable people, this may mean departing radically from traditional cross-examination. ... [T]he court may ... impose restrictions on the advocate 'putting his case' where there is a risk of a young or otherwise vulnerable witness failing to understand, becoming distressed or acquiescing to leading questions. ... If the advocate fails to comply with the limitations, the judge should give relevant directions to the jury when that occurs and prevent further questioning that does not comply with the ground rules settled upon in advance.[16]

[12] [2010] EWCA Crim 4, [42].

[13] [2014] EWCA Crim 2064, [40].

[14] https://www.theadvocatesgateway.org/toolkits.

[15] [2014] EWCA Crim 2064, [40].

[16] Ibid.

In *R v JP* [2014] EWCA Crim 2064, for example, the trial judge took unusual steps to prevent the cross-examination of a child complainant by defence counsel, steps that would be unprecedented in Australian jurisdictions and were not subsequently endorsed by the EWCA.

After visiting the nine-year-old complainant in a child witness waiting room, the judge announced to the court that 'the child could not participate in cross-examination, however sensitively done'[17] even though he had not undertaken a competency inquiry. Both counsel, who had also visited the child, protested, with defence counsel reminding the judge of the defendant's right to a fair trial under Article 6 of the ECHR and 'urg[ing] the judge to let him at least try and ask a few questions to see whether the witness could communicate'.[18] The judge refused this request but allowed defence counsel 'to prepare a document to be placed before the jury, containing any points the defence would have wished to have made to the witness'.[19]

Thus, the only evidence presented to the jury from the complainant was her video-recorded Achieving Best Evidence (ABE) interview. The defendant appealed on the grounds 'that the judge erred in preventing cross-examination of the complainant so that the applicant did not have a fair trial and his convictions are unsafe'.[20] In particular, he argued that it had been unjust for the defence to have been prevented from cross-examining and testing the Crown's chief witness, particularly since the complainant showed no vulnerability apart from her age.

The prosecution conceded that the trial judge had made various procedural errors, including the requirement under s 27 of the *Youth Justice and Criminal Evidence Act 1999* (YJCE) for a witness to be called for cross-examination where the recording of his/her ABE evidence is admitted as evidence-in-chief unless a special measures direction allowed cross-examination to be given 'otherwise than by testimony in court'. The trial judge also failed to consider ss 53 and 54 of the YJCE Act which required him to test the complainant's competency as a witness

---

17 [2014] EWCA Crim 2064, [13] (Hallett, LJ).

18 Ibid.

19 Ibid., [14].

20 Ibid., [17].

and to consider whether she would benefit from the appointment of an intermediary.[21]

In dealing with these procedural errors, the EWCA in *JP* emphasised the non-absolutist nature of the defendant's right to cross-examine a vulnerable witness:

> It is now generally accepted that if justice is to be done to the vulnerable witness and also to the accused, a radical departure from the traditional style of advocacy will be necessary. Advocates must adapt to the witness, not the other way round. They cannot insist upon any supposed right 'to put one's case' or previous inconsistent statements to a vulnerable witness. If there is a right to 'put one's case' (about which we have our doubts) it must be modified for young or vulnerable witnesses. It is perfectly possible to ensure the jury are made aware of the defence case and of significant inconsistencies without intimidation or distressing a witness.[22]

Despite this radically new approach to the cross-examination of vulnerable witnesses, the EWCA in *JP* held that the trial judge had been wrong to disallow cross-examination of the complainant without undertaking a proper competency assessment conducted in the presence of both parties and without considering whether an intermediary would have assisted the complainant to give further evidence.[23]

The EWCA also held that:

- reasonable time limits imposed by a trial judge do not infringe a defendant's right to a fair trial;
- there is no obligation on a trial judge to allow the defence to put their case in full to a vulnerable witness; and
- a judge is duty-bound to intervene when questions are inappropriate.[24]

---

[21] Ibid., [24].

[22] Ibid., [45]. See also *R v E* [2012] EWCA Crim 563; *R v W and M* [2010] EWCA Crim 1926; *R v Wills* [2011] EWCA Crim 1938.

[23] Ibid., [48].

[24] Ibid., [51]–[52].

Thus, in balancing the rights of a defendant to examine prosecution witnesses, and the need to protect vulnerable witnesses from the rigours of the adversarial system, the EWCA has shown that there is no absolute right to cross-examine using traditional, suggestive methods of cross-examination, or to cross-examination for as long an advocate may wish. This appears to reflect the position of the House of Lords that:

> There must be fairness to all sides. In a criminal case this requires the court to consider a triangulation of interests. It involves taking into account the position of the accused, the victim and his or her family, and the public.[25]

Overall, there has been 'a powerful push by successive Chief Justices to reform the management of child witnesses before and during the trial' which has included a 'series of judgments imposing judicial controls on cross-examination' (Hoyano, 2015: 108–109) and 'redefin[ing] the conventional understanding of the rules for cross-examining vulnerable people in criminal trials and deliver[ing] an exceptionally strong direction to advocates to improve their practice' (Henderson, 2014: 94).

The decisions in the above EWCA cases reflect a number of policies regarding the treatment of vulnerable witnesses which have found expression in the *Equal Treatment Benchbook 2013*, the Criminal Procedure Rules 2015 and Criminal Practice Directions.[26] In fact, Henderson (2014: 95) describes the EWCA as an 'unlikely champion of reform' which 'challenges any pessimism about the willingness of the courts to tackle the unfairness latent in the heart of our fair trial protections'.

---

[25] *Attorney General's Reference (No 3 of 1999)* [2001] 2 AC 91, 118, Lord Steyn. See also *R v A (No 2)* [2002] 1 AC 45, 65, Lord Steyn; *R v H* [2004] 2 AC 134, 146, Lord Bingham.

[26] See Criminal Practice Directions 2015, CPD I General Matters 3D Vulnerable people in the Courts; 3E Ground rules hearings to plan the questioning of a vulnerable witness or defendant; 3F Intermediaries (https://www.judiciary.uk/wp-content/uploads/2015/09/crim-pd-2015.pdf; accessed 4 July 2018). The Criminal Practice Directions 2015 at para 3E.4 adopt the position of the EWCA in *Lubemba* [2014] EWCA 2064, stating that in order to promote the giving of best evidence by young and vulnerable witnesses 'this may mean departing radically from traditional cross-examination', including preventing an advocate from putting their case to the witness and preventing further questioning where an advocate does not obey the ground rules for questioning.

Henderson (2014: 95) has identified three restrictions now placed on conventional cross-examination of vulnerable witnesses by the EWCA:

(i) 'miscommunication through the use of developmentally inappropriate language';
(ii) the use of suggestive questions resulting in unreliable answers; and
(iii) confronting the witness with the defence's version of events.

In addition, Rook and Ward (2016: 1556) have identified a fourth restriction, that is, to prevent:

(iv) 'cross-examination on the same topic by multiple advocates'.

The effect of this level of control by courts in E&W 'is a real challenge to the conventional [cross-examination] approach ... since [i]t repositions the witness as a valued participant in a dialogue rather than a puppet in the lawyers' presentation' (Henderson, 2014: 97). Overall, the case law together with judicial training programmes have:

> achieved improvements in an area so long resistant to change that some ... had all but given up on the idea that reform was achievable whilst lawyers remained in the picture:
>
> *Barker* has been a turning point of the whole thing. ... Then Lord Justice Thomas and Lady Justice Hallet have come to training and said "get in there." The sea change isn't in the last ten years but in the last five years and *Barker* is the reason because that gave permission to everyone to behave differently. (Henderson, 2015: 201; citing a judge)

Henderson's (2015: 202) interviews of judges, advocates and intermediaries concluded that greater judicial management has resulted in:

> probably the most successful attempt to reform the culture of advocacy ever—but passive or even active resistance from an unconvinced frontline still poses a lingering threat to its long-term success.

Nonetheless, the EWCA's control over cross-examination is in tension with what the ECHR said in *Al-Khawaja and Tahery v United Kingdom* [2011] ECHR 212:

> Trial proceedings must ensure that a defendant's Article 6 rights are not unacceptably restricted … [T]he Court has consistently assessed the impact that the defendant's inability to examine a witness has had on the overall fairness of his trial … in order to determine whether the defendant's rights have been unacceptably restricted … by having regard to such factors as the way in which statutory safeguards have been applied, the extent to which procedural opportunities were afforded to the defence to counter handicaps that it laboured under and the manner in which the proceedings as a whole have been conducted by the trial judge.[27]

Like the House of Lords, the ECHR has also acknowledged the triangulation of interests in assessing the fairness of a criminal trial:

> when reviewing questions of fairness, … the traditional way in which the Court approaches the issue of the overall fairness of the proceedings … [is] to weigh in the balance the competing interests of the defence, the victim, and witnesses, and the public interest in the effective administration of justice. (*Al-Khawaja* [2011] ECHR 212, [146])

Greater control over suggestive questioning lessens the control that the cross-examiner has over the witness and hence the message they wish to send to the jury (Henderson, 2014: 98). Since manipulation of a witness is the goal of the cross-examiner, that alone justifies questioning the exact extent of the 'right' to cross-examine a witness for the sole purpose of changing a witness's evidence to suit the defence case. Because of the suggestive nature of cross-examination, that right ought to be curtailed in relation to vulnerable witnesses in order to avoid unreliable evidence being given and to promote justice. Although 'conventional cross-examination is not conceived of as a forensic examination' for eliciting the truth, '[t]he startling aspect … is that it begins to look as if the Court of Appeal thinks that it should be' (Henderson, 2014: 99).

[27] [2011] ECHR 212, [142]–[143].

Thus, changes endorsed by the EWCA to cross-examination mean that if cross-examination prompts changes to a complainant's evidence, it must give a 'guarantee of ... reliability' so as to produce reliable answers by vulnerable witnesses (Henderson, 2014: 101).

It is also important to consider criticisms of this greater level of control by the EWCA over cross-examination. In relation to the idea that defence advocates should be excluded from cross-examination, Hoyano (2015: 111) has observed that there is an assumption that 'replacement cross-examiners ... [are] capable of performing a more competent and fair cross-examination than the most highly trained barrister under close judicial supervision'. However, this chapter shows that cross-examination is far from a fair process for children and there is little competence associated with asking children confusing, suggestive and age-inappropriate questions.

The most fundamental aspect of cross-examination is the ability to put the defence's case to a witness, often with the concomitant implication that the witness is lying. In particular, the rule in *Browne v Dunn* (1897) 6 R 67 requires cross-examiners to put any challenges to a witness's evidence, in the interests of fairness, to enable the witness to respond to that challenge.[28] However, the traditional style of challenging a vulnerable witness's evidence is likely to give rise to confusion and manufactured inconsistencies. So how appropriate is this rule with a child? While we assume that an adult:

> has the cognition, and the independence of will, to reject questions which contain a suggestion or assertion of the existence (or non-existence) of a particular fact ... [s]uch assumptions cannot be made in the case of a child witness. ... [A] child's vulnerability and the likelihood that they will assent to suggestive questions increase the risk that the child will give answers that are contradictory [to their previous evidence] ... [F]airness dictates that counsel should only ask questions in a form that is appropriate to the age of the child.[29]

---

[28] *R v Morrow* [2009] VSCA 291, [47] (Redlich JA).

[29] *Ward* [2017] VSCA 37, [121]; [124]; [125] (Maxwell P and Redlich JA).

All in all, the EWCA has effectively abrogated the rule in *Browne v Dunn* (1897) 6 R 67 since, as discussed above, in *Barker* and *Lubemba* the EWCA accepted that a court can impose restrictions on the defence putting its case to a vulnerable witness in order to avoid misunderstandings, acquiescence to leading questions or distress to the witness. For example, in *R v E* [2011] EWCA Crim 3028, the EWCA stated that even though counsel had not been permitted to directly put the defence case to the child witness (such as asking, 'You were never punched, hit, kicked as you have suggested, were you?'), this did not infringe the defendant's right to a fair trial.[30]

The alternative to putting the defence case directly to a vulnerable witness is the practice of defence counsel making a statement to the jury about the matters the defence 'would have put if the witness were not vulnerable', coupled with a judicial explanation to the jury about the reasons for restrictions on cross-examination (Rook & Ward, 2016: 1562). Thus, alternative methods for presenting the defence's case have been developed.

Overall, it appears that the fair trial principle has not been undermined by preventing cross-examiners from manipulating a child witness using unreliable methods such as leading and suggestive questions for the sole purpose of producing evidence that is compatible with the defence case. By focusing on the methods and reliability of cross-examination, the EWCA has raised the bar not only in terms of the quality and reliability of the evidence that is elicited from child witnesses but also the reliability of those methods.

At the same time, the EWCA has been at pains to emphasise the inviolability of a defendant's rights under the fair trial principle.[31] This means that the traditional, age-old methods of defence cross-examination have now been put under the microscope in terms of their reliability and have been found wanting.

[30] [2011] EWCA Crim 3028, [28].

[31] See *Barker* [2010] EWCA Crim 4, [42]; *E* [2011] EWCA Crim 3028, [26].

6.2 The Position in Australia

Compared to E&W, Australia is a federal system, comprised of states and territories, with a Federal Government elected under the Australian Constitution to deal with Federal issues. Unlike E&W, Australia, does not have a Federal Bill of Rights so that Article 6 of the ECHR is not part of Federal law. Only three jurisdictions, Victoria, the Australian Capital Territory (ACT) and Queensland, have enacted Bills of Rights (*Charter of Human Rights and Responsibilities Act 2006* [Vic]; *Human Rights Act 2004* [ACT]; *Human Rights Act 2019* [Qld]). All three contain wording that is similar to Article 6 of the ECHR.

For example, under s 25(2)(g) of the Victorian Act, a defendant in criminal proceedings has the right 'to examine, or have examined, witnesses against him or her, unless otherwise provided for by law', which amounts to a qualified right to examine prosecution witnesses but does not stipulate how that examination can be conducted.

Similarly, under s 22(2)(g) of the ACT Act, a defendant has a right 'to examine prosecution witnesses, or have them examined', although this right is not similarly qualified. While this provision also does not stipulate how that examination can be conducted, unrepresented defendants are not permitted to personally cross-examine a sexual assault complainant in the ACT, as discussed further below.

Despite the lack of a Federal Bill of Rights, it is clear from Australian common law that the rights of an accused under the fair trial principle are not absolute and are subject to 'the interests of the Crown acting on behalf of the community'.[32] Indeed, the concept of fairness is not fixed and immutable and 'may vary with changing social standards and circumstances',[33] such that it is inextricably 'bound up with prevailing

[32] *Dietrich v R* (1992) 177 CLR 292, 335, Deane J; quoting *Barton* v *R* (1980) 147 CLR 75, 101, Gibbs ACJ and Mason J. See also *Jago v District Court of New South Wales* (1989) 168 CLR 23, 33 Mason CJ, 49–50; 54, Brennan J; *R v Lodhi* (2006) 199 FLR 250, [54]–[57], Whealy J.

[33] *Dietrich* (1992) 177 CLR 292, 328 (Deane J) (citations omitted). See also *McKinney v R* (1991) 171 CLR 468, 478 (Mason CJ, Deane, Gaudron and McHugh JJ).

social values'.[34] The concept of fairness can take into account the interests of the victim,[35] including the desirable goal of encouraging victims to report sexual offences to the police, as well as minimising the re-traumatisation experienced by sexual assault complainants during the trial process and achieving best evidence. Thus, protecting complainants from re-traumatisation does not necessarily result in a reduction in the rights of an accused, rather the introduction of a fairer system of justice for all concerned, which is 'more conducive to eliciting the truth' (Hoyano, 2015: 107).

In recent times, parliaments and other bodies have begun to accept that the right to cross-examination by the defendant is not an absolute right. For example, since September 2000 in E&W, s 34 of the YJCE Act has prohibited a defendant charged with a sexual offence from personally cross-examining a complainant.[36] Similarly, s 35 prohibits a defendant charged with certain sexual offences, kidnapping, false imprisonment, abduction, slavery, human trafficking or child cruelty from personally cross-examining a *child* witness. In fact, the inroads into personal cross-examination by a defendant can be extended by a court in relation to other witnesses who might be affected by personal cross-examination under s 36 of the YJCE Act. Instead of personal cross-examination, s 38 allows the court to appoint a representative of an unrepresented defendant to undertake the cross-examination (see also Criminal Procedure Rules 2015, Part 23).

In most Australian jurisdictions the right to cross-examine has also been modified where a defendant is unrepresented so that a defendant is unable to directly cross-examine a complainant in a sexual assault trial.[37] In NSW, this modification was introduced in response to a gang rape

---

[34] *Dietrich v R* (1992) 177 CLR 292, 364, Gaudron J.

[35] *Dietrich v R* (1992) 177 CLR 292, 357, Toohey J.

[36] See also *Sexual Offences (Procedure and Evidence) (Scotland) Act 2002.*

[37] See *Crimes Act 1914* (Cth), s 15YF-15YG; *Evidence (Miscellaneous Provisions) Act 1991* (ACT), s 38D; *Criminal Procedure Act 1986* (NSW), s 294A; *Sexual Offences (Evidence and Procedure) Act 1993* (NT), s 5; *Evidence Act 1977* (Qld), ss 21 N-21O; *Evidence Act 1929* (SA), s 13B(1)(a); *Criminal Procedure Act 2009* (Vic), ss 356–357; *Evidence Act 1906* (WA), s 106G(1). For example in NSW, the complainant can only be cross-examined by a person appointed by the court (not necessarily a lawyer) who will ask the complainant questions requested by the accused: *Criminal Procedure Act 1986* (NSW), ss 294A(2)–(3).

trial in which the defendants had rejected legal representation.[38] Before this case was set down for trial, the modification had been the subject of a reference to the NSW Law Reform Commission (NSWLRC) (2003) which discussed the balance between the rights of the accused and other public interests:

> the public interest in ... the accused [being] fairly tried ... does not mean ... that the *interests* of the accused take priority over all other interests ... There is a substantial public interest in ensuring that ... potential witnesses are not bullied into giving untrue or inaccurate evidence, ... [which would] undermine public confidence in the administration of justice. Without these protections ..., the court would be an instrument of injustice ... [T]o accommodate the accused's wish to cross-examine the complainant personally is to confer an inappropriate advantage on the accused ... by virtue of the intense character of direct personal confrontation. This advantage has never been part of the function of a trial or an element of fairness ... [T]he benefit to complainants and to the community in general outweighs any perceived detriment to accused persons. (NSWLRC, 2003: 45–48; emphasis in original)

In this way, the legitimate expectations of an accused under the fair trial principle are balanced against the needs of sexual assault complainants and the benefits to the community at large. This means that the right to cross-examine prosecution witnesses is not necessarily absolute and can be subject to controls where necessary, a view expressed by a former Chief Justice of the NSW Supreme Court:

> [t]he difficulties encountered by complainants in sexual assault cases ... has been a focus of concern for several decades. Judges play an important role in protecting complainants from unnecessary, inappropriate and irrelevant questioning by or on behalf of an accused. That role is perfectly consistent with the requirements of a fair trial, which requirements do not involve treating the criminal justice system as if it were a forensic game in which every accused is entitled to some kind of sporting chance. ... In a sexual assault matter, it is appropriate for the Court to consider the

[38]The validity of s 294A, *Criminal Procedure Act* 1986 was upheld by the NSW Court of Criminal Appeal in *R v MSK and MAK* [2004] NSWCCA 308.

> effect of cross-examination and of the trial experience upon a complainant when deciding whether cross-examination is unduly harassing, offensive or oppressive.[39]

Certain types of questions are unfair to witnesses such that part of 'the duty to avoid questions which are misleading, confusing or harassing is the *general prohibition* on the use of compound questions'.[40] In *Libke v R* [2007] HCA 30, Heydon J described the problems with compound questions:

> A compound question simultaneously poses more than one inquiry and calls for more than one answer. Such a question presents two problems. First, the question may be ambiguous because of its multiple facets and complexity. Secondly, any answer may be confusing because of uncertainty as to which part of the compound question the witness intended to address. But compound questions have additional vices. It is unfair to force a witness into the position of having to choose which questions in a compound question to answer and in which order. ... To place witnesses in the position of having to reformulate a compound question and answer its component parts bit by bit is unfair to them in the sense that it prevents them from doing justice to themselves.[41]

There is, however, no way of knowing the extent to which judges in lower courts enforce this 'general prohibition' on compound questions. Indeed, the NSWCCA has said that 'an occasional objectionable question in the course of a lengthy cross-examination rarely, if ever, gives rise to a miscarriage of justice'.[42]

Recently, the Victorian Court of Appeal has said that trial judges have 'an obligation that the cross-examination is fair to the witness'[43] in light of judges' powers under s 41 of the Uniform Evidence Laws

[39] *R v TA* (2003) 57 NSWLR 444, 446 (Spigelman CJ).

[40] *Skelton* [2015] NSWCCA 320, [38] (Beazley P and Davis J; emphasis added).

[41] [2007] HCA 30, [127].

[42] *Skelton* [2015] NSWCCA 320, [58] (Beazley P and Davis J).

[43] *Ward* [2017] VSCA 37, [16] (Maxwell P; Redlich JA).

which operate in six Australian jurisdictions including NSW.[44] It can be expected, however, unless specific legislation is enacted, the balance between inappropriate cross-examination of sexual assault complainants and the rights of the accused will favour the accused, as the *Ward* case, below, demonstrates.

Before considering whether or not the right to cross-examine ought to be subject to specific controls in child and adult sexual assault trials, it is necessary to examine the extent to which cross-examination is used as an oppressive tool for intimidation and confusion, rather than a forensic tool for exposing a dishonest witness. In other words, what is the extent of the problem and are reforms really necessary?

7 Juror Beliefs and Biases: The Impact of Rape Myths and Stereotypes During Cross-Examination

While each sexual assault trial will be unique, because of the particular facts of the case, the nature of the evidence, the complainant's age and sex, the relationship between the complainant and the accused, and the complainant's performance as a witness in the 'theatre of the trial', a fact-finder's decision-making takes place within a cultural framework of gender relations that is reproduced by specific patterns of cross-examination. Where these patterns have the effect of constructing the complainant as an unreliable witness by tapping into common myths and stereotypes about the reliability of women and children, this may mean that a jury is more likely to acquit the accused.

Because jurors are drawn from the general community, the studies discussed in Chapters 4 and 5 mean that we cannot discount the effect of pre-existing juror attitudes on their decision-making:

> [j]uror beliefs and attitudes about what a sexual assault case looks like and how a victim of sexual assault would behave therefore become critical to

---

[44] *Evidence Act 1995* (Cth); *Evidence Act 1995* (NSW); *Evidence Act 2001* (Tas); *Evidence Act 2008* (Vic); *Evidence Act 2011* (ACT); *Evidence (National Uniform Legislation) Act 2011* (NT).

understanding why complainants may or may not be believed by jurors, and whether a particular sexual assault case is likely to achieve a guilty verdict. (Taylor, 2007: 2)

Cross-examination is likely to play a central role in confirming pre-existing attitudes and beliefs of jurors since:

[t]here is considerable evidence that people, including professionals … tend to be biased towards information that confirms their initial beliefs and to reject information that challenges their established views … [so that] once formed, impressions and beliefs can be resistant to contradictory evidence. (Goodman & Melinder, 2007: 1)

A perusal of the trial transcripts of the cross-examination of sexual assault complainants, whether adult or child, shows that defence counsel construct scenarios that mirror the commonly believed rape myths and stereotypes, arguably creating 'a confirmation bias that may result in faulty perception and incorrect interpretation' (Goodman & Melinder, 2007: 2) on the part of the jury. Unfortunately, the jury system 'is based on the assumption that jurors are able to judge and evaluate the evidence and to make rational decisions based on information presented in court' (ibid.). Yet the literature reviews in Chapters 4 and 5 suggest that jury decision-making is affected by 'the tendency to deal with information [such as evidence presented in court] by incorporating it within an existing schematic framework' (ibid.: 5).

A useful example of the ways in which defence counsel construct particular stories containing elements of the myths that are commonly associated with sexual assault is the published cross-examination of Tegan Wagner who was gang-raped by three brothers (known as MSK, MAK and MMK) at the age of fourteen. Although this case is more than 10 years old, there is still no legislation in NSW or any other Australian jurisdiction that restricts cross-examination based on commonly held myths about sexual assault.

When she was seventeen, Tegan faced almost 2000 questions over three days during her cross-examination by the three defendants' counsel who were described as 'three barristers operating as a hunting pack'

(Sheehan, 2006: 218–219) with 'little intervention by the judge or the Crown' (ibid.: 216).

The first cross-examination by counsel for MSK focused on Tegan's consumption of alcohol, supposedly for the purposes of releasing her inhibitions and seducing one of the brothers. While it may be necessary for defence lawyers to put their client's version of events to the complainant, the content of the questions reflected common rape myths because they created an entirely *passive* male and an entirely *sexually active* female 'aggressor' (who was a virgin at the time), yet apparently cried 'rape' because of fears of pregnancy. Some of the suggestions used to create this story (all of which were refuted by Tegan) are set out below (ibid.: 219–228):

> And I suggest to you that you continued to pour yourself drinks … during the course of the evening. What do you say to that?
>
> And that you didn't want people to think … that you were excited about drinking vodka this evening. That's the truth, isn't it?
>
> I suggest that you … went and sat next to him and you placed your hand on his leg?
>
> You put your right hand on his left thigh and began to stroke it?
>
> And I suggest to you that you moved your hand to his crotch area?
>
> He put his hand on your hand and removed it from his crotch area. And you said to him: 'Let's go to your bedroom'. Correct?
>
> And you said to him, 'I want to do it 69 style'?
>
> And he said: 'I can't do that', and you said, 'Can I suck your dick'?
>
> [A]nd that's what you did. You started sucking his penis. Is that correct?
>
> You then lay back down on the bed and produced a condom. Correct?
>
> And when you took the condom off the floor where he'd placed it, it appeared that it was broken … .
>
> You went from passionate, willingness, wanting, to hysterical crying because you thought, 'My God, I could get pregnant!' Correct?

For reasons of space it is not possible to include the cross-examination by the other two barristers (see ibid.: 231–234). At no stage did Tegan veer from her version of events. Despite the attempts to portray her as the sexual aggressor who became deliberately drunk in order to overcome her inhibitions and then cried rape due to fears of pregnancy, it appears that her credibility remained intact because of her consistency in giving evidence, her immediate report to the police, the medical evidence presented in court and the bizarre and disruptive behaviour of the three accused during the trial (Sheehan, 2006).

Although the above cross-examination did not achieve its desired effect, the type of questions asked of Tegan are likely to confirm juror beliefs and prejudices where the complainant becomes confused, changes her testimony or retracts her complaint, or where issues, such as drunkenness and flirtatiousness, are not able to be denied.

8 The 'Strange Language' of the Courtroom: Are Leading Questions and Confusion the Way to the Truth?

The impairment of a child's ability to give her or his best evidence can occur in a number of ways. For example, Brennan (1995: 74) has described the features of the 'strange language' of the courtroom, by categorising the types of questions used in cross-examination to exploit children's developmental vulnerability:

- *Tagging*: a statement with a question tagged on at the end which encourages the witness's agreement with the tag, such as 'it wasn't him, was it?' The tag encourages the answer 'no' but in order to disagree, the child would need to have the cognitive ability to understand it would be necessary to reply, 'It was him'.
- *negative tagging* such as, 'Now this happened on a Friday, was it not?' and the *negative rhetorical* question, such as 'Now you had a bruise, did you not, near one of your breasts, do you remember this?' (Brennan, 1995: 88; 75) are statements with a negative which creates a question. Both types are suggestive, although they 'create the illusion of choice' (Brennan, 1995: 75) by asking the witness to agree. The

child must have the cognitive ability to dissect the question to be able to disagree with it.

- the *multi-faceted or compound question* contains more than one proposition so that it is not clear which question should be answered. For example, 'Did he take hold of you and make you do anything? Did he grab hold of your hand or do anything with your hand?' (Brennan, 1995: 76). Where a child assents, 'the control to interpret which sub question it most easily serves remains with the cross-examiner' (Brennan, 1995: 76).
- a question that lacks a *grammatical and/or semantic connection.* For example, 'At any stage whilst you were in the bathroom did he ever enter the bathroom that previous week?' The form of delivery implies the question makes sense, although '[t]he responsibility for finding sense in nonsense is shifted to the witness, and as the child does not recognise that this doesn't make sense to adults either, they assume their own inadequacy and failure' (Brennan, 1995: 77).
- *juxtaposition of topics*: '[t]opics of unequal significance with no obvious sequential ties are placed alongside one another' (Brennan, 1995: 78). For example: 'Q: On that occasion when Mum went to, being that night that Mum [went] to Youth Group, you were at Clareville? . Q: You did not see the defendant at any time when he put his penis in your bottom, did you?' (Brennan, 1995: 78). Although meanings between topics are not connected, they appear to be 'of equal importance' and serve 'to create a "linguistic fog"' (Brennan, 1995: 79), creating confusion and the risk that the child merely agrees with the suggestions put to them.

If these types of questions describe the linguistic realities of cross-examination for child complainants, then it is not surprising that 'children six to fifteen years of age fail to hear as sensible language around half of what is addressed to them during cross-examination' (Brennan, 1995: 71), the more so if they are re-experiencing any of the symptoms of trauma discussed in Chapter 11.

Although Brennan's (1995) work is now more than 20 years old, subsequent studies and case law have confirmed the lack of linguistic match between cross-examiner and child complainants, as well as between cross-examiner and adult complainants (Andrews, Lamb, & Lyon, 2014; Bettenay, Ridley, Henry, & Crane, 2014; Cashmore & Trimboli, 2005; Hanna et al., 2012; Kebbell, Deprez, & Wagstaff, 2003; O'Neill & Zajac, 2013a, 2013b; Plotnikoff & Woolfson, 2012; Powell et al., 2016; Righarts, Jack, Zajac, & Hayne, 2014; Valentine & Mara, 2011; Westera et al., 2017; Zajac & Cannan, 2009; Zajac & Hayne, 2006; Zajac, O'Neill, & Hayne, 2012; Zajac et al., 2003).

For example, Davies et al. (2010) found that, on average, 84% of cross-examination questions in actual CSA trials in NZ were closed or leading, almost one-fifth of questions contained complex vocabulary, over a quarter contained two or more embedded clauses and defence counsel used significantly more double negatives than prosecutors.

When Powell et al. (2016) analysed transcripts of the evidence given by 63 complainants of CSA from three age groups (children, adolescents and adults) in three jurisdictions (NSW, Victoria and WA), they reported the following results (ibid.: 190–194):

- defence lawyers did not adapt the number of questions asked to compensate for differences in age group (they used an average of more than 300 questions for each complainant);
- prosecutors and police varied the number of questions according to the complainant's age (an average of less than 100 for children/adolescents, compared to 300 for adults);
- the types of questions varied as a function of the questioner;
- prosecutors tended to ask closed questions and used leading questions as much as they used open questions. They used complex language in about a third of all questions, but they seldom used complex sense and repeat questions;
- while prosecutors asked children and adolescents fewer open questions and more complex questions than they asked adults, they asked children and adolescents fewer repeated questions and gave more instructions than they did to adults;
- more than 60% of defence lawyers' questions were leading, less than 10% were open while 44% involved complex language;

- judges tended to give instructions with closed questions, with leading questions being used in nearly one-fifth of all questions, while open questions were seldom used.
- Judges used complex language in just over one-third of all questions, although they varied the types of questions they asked according to age. They asked children fewer leading questions than they asked adults, and more open questions than they asked adolescents and adults and gave fewer instructions than they did to adults.

Recent research also shows that young children have particular difficulty with indirect speech questions, beginning with 'Do you know?' which is a type of yes/no question. Children tend to answer yes or no but fail to elaborate on their answers, and, as a result, may be viewed as 'an uncooperative conversational partner' (Evans, Stolzenberg, Lee, & Lyon, 2014).

Other defence tactics involve the use of repetitive questions which may induce a child to give inconsistent evidence 'because they believe that the first answer was wrong or somehow unsatisfactory' (VLRC, 2004: 313). Manuals on advocacy advise lawyers to use strategies to produce inconsistencies, including 'switching rapidly from one topic to another ... as a way of discovering whether the child has memorised his or her testimony', a tactic observed in 12 out of 16 cross-examinations by Davies et al. (2010: 353). Judges and laypeople with no knowledge of the impact of leading and age-inappropriate questions on a child's testimony may be beguiled by the fact that the child *continues* to give answers of some kind, even though they may not understand what is being asked of them (QLRC, 2000: 264). Another tactic, rarely discussed, is described below by a prosecutor interviewed by Powell, Bowden, and Mattison (2014: 504):

> The most devastating cross-examinations of children are by clever barristers who do the 'I'm your friend' routine ... [that is, a barrister] who is not overtly attacking the child, who is asking questions in a befriending manner but still using forms of questions that are apt to mislead or trick the child ... In these cases, the questions are destructive but there is nothing ostensibly improper about them.

Furthermore, the nature of cross-examination is such that there is no way for judges and juries to tell when a child's testimony is affected by the effects of trauma and the instinctive compliance of trauma survivors with authority figures, especially when being questioned in a strange environment using leading questions.

There is a distinction between errors of reporting due to internal factors, such as memory changes, and errors of reporting due to external or social forces (Goodman & Melinder, 2007). For example, an assent to a negative tag or negative rhetorical question does not necessarily mean the child agrees with the statement but may mean s/he does not have the developmental understanding to refute it. Yet the adversarial system has no method for ascertaining whether a child understood the question to which s/he has agreed and, therefore, no way of ascertaining the reliability of answers given in cross-examination.

It is also assumed that the dishonest witness will betray him or herself by their demeanour (Cashmore & Trimboli, 2006), especially under cross-examination. However, a number of psychological studies show that facial and behavioural expressions are an unreliable indicator of veracity and that untrained professionals (including judges and police officers) are no better than laypersons at predicting veracity through observing a person's demeanour such that *both* groups misinterpret behavioural cues at or below chance levels, that is, at or below 50% accuracy (Ekman, O'Sullivan, & Frank, 1999; Porter, Woodworth, & Birt, 2000; Vrij, Granhag, & Porter, 2010). Although Ekman et al. (1999: 265) found that some professionals, such as law enforcement officials and judges, have high levels of accuracy in lie detection, even in these groups there was 'a substantial number who performed at or below chance'.

Cross-examination can also exploit the difficulties that children have in relation to identifying specific times and dates. These difficulties are 'particularly problematic for younger children who have not yet learned to tell time on a clock, who may confuse calendar dates or who have trouble reporting events in exact chronological order' (ALRC and the HREOC, 1997: 307). If children report events out of sequence or if they are unable to give a particular date or time in relation to the alleged abuse, this can be exploited by the defence as bearing on the accuracy of the child's complaint, even though the inability to give such details has been shown not to have any bearing on the accuracy of the allegation (Saywitz, 1995; Spencer & Flin, 1993).

Leading and suggestive questions are known to be the most unreliable method for eliciting information from children (Home Office, 2011; Kuehnle & Connell, 2009; Lamb, La Rooy, Malloy, & Katz, 2011; Lamb et al., 2008; Snow & Powell, 2007). As a result, 'researchers ... have identified ways of interviewing children that maximize their accuracy and decrease their levels of stress while testifying' (Zajac & Hayne, 2003: 187).

In particular, interviewing protocols emphasise the use of non-leading, open-ended questions in order to ensure the accuracy of children's reports and have been endorsed by various professional organisations (Goodman & Melinder, 2007; Judicial College, 2018; Judicial Commission of NSW, 2006–2017; Lamb et al., 2008; Lamb et al., 2011; Plotnikoff & Woolfson, 2009, 2012) since they are associated with the highest rates of accuracy. Many training manuals (see Advocacy Training Council, 2011[45]; Ministry of Justice, 2011) and bench books now include practical guidance for questioning children. For example, the *Benchbook for Children Giving Evidence in Australian Courts* (Australasian Institute of Judicial Administration, 2014: 84–85) lists good practices for questioning children.

- Phrase questions positively rather than negatively.
- Use an active voice rather than a passive voice.
- Separate questions on separate topics. Do not mix topics, or switch back and forth between topics.
- Children's conceptualisation of time, frequency and ordering of events is gradually acquired. ... [P]rovide concrete anchor points, using times or events that are relevant to the child.
- [U]se the child's words to describe people, actions and objects.
- Avoid 'front loading' questions that use a number of qualifying phrases before asking the crucial part of the question.
- Use signposting. ... Example: 'I want to ask you some questions about your father'.

---

[45]Now known as the Inns of Court College of Advocacy.

- Discuss events in logical sequence.
- Ask questions with the child's point of view in mind.
- Include only one query in each question.
- Avoid questions that may be taken too literally.

In order to prevent misunderstandings by a witness, the Advocacy Training Council (2011: 37) recommends that advocates should:

- identify vulnerabilities and witness limitations at the earliest possible stage;
- carefully analyse the material that needs to be put to the witness/defendant;
- use short questions and simple language, allowing adequate time for comprehension;
- use a normal, non-aggressive tone;
- avoid tag questions, double negatives and confusing or complex phrasing;
- be aware of limitations in the witness's/defendant's grasp of abstract concepts such as time and the sequence of events;
- identify areas that can be better put to other witnesses; and
- identify areas of evidence that may be best dealt with not with the witness but by the parties putting before the jury agreed evidence from third parties (such as Social Services' records).

While these guidelines are designed to achieve best evidence, they conflict with the practices of cross-examination. Although researchers warn against the use of multiple interviews of children, leading questions, tag questions and other complex questions because they increase the likelihood that a child will agree with an examiner's suggestions or change their answers to please the interviewer (Goodman & Melinder, 2007; Lamb et al., 2008; Saywitz, Camparo, & Romanoff, 2010; Snow & Powell, 2007), in the adversarial trial, repetitive cross-examination and multiple cross-examination (where there is more than one defendant) is permitted, and leading questions are the order of the day in most Australian jurisdictions.

In Australia, there has been a move towards using a child's investigative interview as his/her evidence-in-chief[46] in order to improve the direct examination process but little or no real change has been made to counter the effect of cross-examination on children's evidence, compared to the more radical, interventionist approach of judges in E&W, discussed above.

There is considerable tension between the attitudes of defence lawyers and efforts to protect children from suggestive and intimidating cross-examination. Care must be taken that in the desire to preserve adversarialism we do not sacrifice the welfare of children. Cross-examiners are aware, strategically, that cross-examination is not a method for the elicitation of the truth since 'defence lawyers will admit that if it is necessary to break a child down, they are willing to do that in the interests of their client' (NSWSCLJ, 2002: 63). For example, the following opinion is an instructive insight into the adversarial model of justice:

> You've got to get around the idea that the criminal justice [system] is about the child. It shouldn't be about the child, and hopefully will never be about the child. ... [I]f I am defending a bloke I want to make life difficult for witnesses. ... I'm not there to find the truth ... no-one's there to find the truth. (Eastwood & Patton, 2002: 76; quoting an unnamed defence lawyer)

In other words, with children, the technique is to extend cross-examination to make 'them sweat a bit' and 'to put them under as much pressure as possible' to make them 'crack' (Henderson, 2002: 279).

In 2018, a Melbourne defence lawyer admitted on Australian national television with tears in his eyes that he would not advise his own daughter to give evidence as a complainant in a sexual assault trial because of aggressive defence lawyers like himself.[47] But aggression is not even

---

[46] See *Crimes Act 1914* (Cth), s 15YM(1); *Evidence (Miscellaneous Provisions) Act* 1991 (ACT), s 40F; *Criminal Procedure Act 1986* (NSW), s 306U; *Evidence Act 1977* (Qld), s 93A; *Evidence Act 1929* (SA), s 34BA; *Evidence (Children and Special Witnesses) Act 2001* (Tas), s 5; *Criminal Procedure Act 2009* (Vic), s 367; *Evidence Act 1906* (WA), ss 106H–106HB; *Youth Justice and Criminal Evidence Act 1999* (UK), s 27.

[47] *Insight*, SBS Television, 27 February 2018.

necessary in order to change the evidence of a child as the *Ward* case [2017] VSCA 37 illustrates below.

8.1 A Case Study of the Cross-Examination Effect: What Price Fairness?

At the age of 68 years, Mr Ward (a pseudonym) was convicted of six counts of sexual assault against J who was between six and seven years of age at the time of the offences. These offences included showing J pornographic videos, exposure, inciting a child to commit indecent acts and various acts of sexual penetration. Ward had befriended J's family after they emigrated to Australia in 2013 and leased two rooms in his house to the family. Ward was frequently J's baby-sitter while her parents worked on Sundays.

On appeal, Ward argued that each verdict of guilty was 'unsafe and unsatisfactory' because of the inconsistencies between J's recorded police interview (known in Victoria as Visual and Audio Recording of Evidence or VARE) and her answers during a special hearing for cross-examination. In a detailed and well-researched judgment, the Victorian Court of Appeal (VSCA) concluded that 'none of the apparent inconsistencies were such as to preclude the jury from being satisfied beyond reasonable doubt that J was a witness of truth'.[48]

J's VARE interview, which was clear and concise in response to open-ended questions by the interviewer, described 'sexing' videos in which Ward 'showed me a lot of girls eating his penis' and 'he always want me to do whatever the girls in the [video]'.[49] During her cross-examination, which took place over two days and eight months after her VARE interview, J gave some of her answers in English and some through an interpreter. She had viewed her VARE before being cross-examined.

It is possible that having English as a second language exacerbated the cross-examination effect since J appeared to contradict herself when it

[48] *Ward* [2017] VSCA 37, [5] (Maxwell P and Redlich JA).

[49] Ibid., [31]; [32].

was put to her in 'a series of propositions' in the form of '[RW] never touched you' since each time she answered 'No'.[50]

This type of statement, 'X never did Y', is usually followed by tagging, that is, a question tagged to the end which encourages the witness to agree with the tag, such as 'did he?' Tagged questions are highly suggestive and seek to admit into evidence the case for the accused without proof of the statement other than the authority of the examiner. In the face of tagged questions, there is:

> a danger of a child witness wishing simply to please. There is undoubtedly a danger of a child witness seeing that to assent to what is put may bring the questioning process to a speedier conclusion than to disagree.[51]

In *Ward*, the confusing effect of tagged statements, which drew agreement from J, can be contrasted with a subsequent part of J's cross-examination where she was able to affirm what Ward had done to her when she was asked an open-ended question (ibid.: [35]). In the extract, below, J is asked a negative, tagged question, which encourages a 'no' in reply but J needed to have the cognitive development to disagree with the statement by saying, 'Yes he did'. J's affirmative answer could mean agreement or disagreement. By contrast, it is followed by an open-ended question and a detailed answer:

> [RW] never showed you rude things on his phone, [did he]?
> Yes.
> Okay. What did he show you on his phone?
> Naked women and naked men.

The *Ward* case also reveals another defence strategy which is to jump from one topic to another to test for inconsistences which elicited 'I don't remember' responses from J[52]:

---

[50] Ibid., [35].

[51] *R v W and M* 80 [2010] EWCA Crim 1926, [30] (Hughes LJ). In *R v W and M*, the two child appellants, convicted of raping an eight-year-old girl, appealed on the grounds that the complainant had retracted her complaints of rape during cross-examination. The EWCA dismissed the appeal.

[52] *Ward* [2017] VSCA 37, [35] (Maxwell P and Redlich JA).

And how long did you look at the video for?
Just one hour.
An hour, okay?
Yes.
Where were your mum and dad?
I don't remember.
Okay. Was your sister at home?
No.
What was happening on the video?
I don't remember.

Even though the police had seized Ward's phone which revealed the existence of the pornographic videos that J had described in detail in her police interview, the effect of cross-examination questions on her evidence is evident in her 'I don't remember' answers and in the next excerpt:

Can you remember if people were doing anything on the video?
No.

Defence counsel mostly used leading, yes/no questions,[53] with various levels of complexity, such as negative tagging and negative rhetorical questions which require the cognitive ability to dissect the question in order to understand the impact of answering 'no', as illustrated below:

Did [RW] ever touch you?
Only hug me.
Only cuddling, okay. So [RW] never touched you on your pee pee? [negative rhetorical]
No.
You never touched [RW's] pee pee, did you? [negative tagging]
No.
Did [RW] ever touch you on the bum?
No.
Did you ever see [his] penis?
Yes.

[53] Ibid., [48]–[49].

> And was that when he was outside having a pee?
> No, in his bedroom.
> Okay. And did [RW] ever put his penis near your pee pee?
> No.
> ...
> Did you ever touch his penis?
> No.
> Are you're sure about that?
> Yes.

Despite these apparent inconsistencies in J's evidence, the VSCA recognised that:

> the nature of the questions and their context can affect the significance to be attached to the answer. ... As the Crown submitted, it is entirely plausible that a child of eight years old, being questioned through ... an interpreter, did not think that, when RW placed her hands on his penis, she was 'touching' him. It was, afterall, his action, not hers. He was forcing her to do something she did not want to do.[54]

However, the answer is probably more complex since the cross-examination effect, discussed below has been shown in several studies to change the accuracy of children's evidence. This phenomenon would explain J's impaired 'ability to comprehend the questions asked over a lengthy period of cross-examination'.[55]

Lack of comprehension is demonstrated in other parts of the cross-examination where J gives a negative answer to one leading question which, when phrased differently, produced an affirmative answer[56]:

> Did [RW] ever touch you on the bum?
> No.
> [Did RW ever put his pee pee near your bottom[57]]?
> Yes.

[54]Ibid., [50]; [54].

[55]Ibid., [59].

[56]Ibid., [64].

[57]This question was paraphrased by the Court; ibid., [64].

By contrast, J ably answered open-ended questions about the same topic (through an interpreter):

> Can you tell me where you were when this happened?
> In his bedroom.
> Where was he?
> On the bed.
> Okay. What were you wearing?
> Pyjamas.
> Okay. And what did he do with his penis?
> He took my pyjamas off and put it inside.
> Put it inside where?
> My bum.

Later in the cross-examination, however, J's non-comprehension is again evident in response to negative tagging and negative rhetorical questions (through an interpreter)[58]:

> [H]is penis didn't go in your bum, did it? [negative tagging]
> I don't remember.
> ...
> So he never put his penis in your bum again, you say? [negative rhetorical]
> No.
> ...
> And ... granddad has never put his penis in your bum? [negative rhetorical]
> Only once.

More confusion and comprehension difficulties are seen in the following excerpt with negative rhetorical questions (through an interpreter)[59]:

> So was that the only time you say that [RW] put his penis in your vagina?
> Yes.
> Are you sure he put his penis in your vagina ... ?

58 Ibid., [65]–[67].

59 Ibid., [68].

> Yes.
> So if I said to you he didn't put his penis in your vagina, would I be wrong? [negative rhetorical]
> I don't remember.
> Okay. Can you ever remember a time where [RW] touched your bum?
> No.
> So he never put his finger in your bum? [negative rhetorical]
> I don't think so.

As the VSCA recognised,[60] these questions jump from topics about J's vagina to questions about RW touching J's bottom, with most questions containing either negatives or double negatives, with inherent comprehension difficulties for an eight-year-old child (see Sas, 2002).

At times, defence counsel took advantage of J's comprehension difficulties by asking repetitive questions about one offence (oral penetration) and then jumping to a question about digital penetration, using negative rhetorical questions:

> [G]randdad has never asked you to eat his pee pee, has he?
> No.
> And [RW] or granddad has never put his penis in your bum?
> Only once.
> ...
> And granddad has never put his penis in your mouth?
> INTERPRETER: I think she said 'only once, 'no only once'.
> Okay. When did he put his penis in your mouth?
> When I was in my room.
> In your room. And what happened?
> He came in my room.
> Yes.
> INTERPRETER: I am just asking her to tell me in [language], sorry.
> Yes?
> I don't remember.
> Okay. So you don't remember him putting his penis in your mouth?
> I don't remember.

60 Ibid., [69].

The VSCA noted that '[a]t this stage of the cross-examination it had been some time since J had had a break. It appeared that she was relatively restless'[61] which suggests J had lost concentration. During the trial, it also appears that there was little or no intervention from the trial judge regarding the inappropriateness of the questions put to J and no recognition of the effect of the cross-examination on her emotional state.

Although J had initially answered that RW had put his penis in her mouth, it appears that J changed her answers due to the repetitive nature of the questions about the topic, a well-documented phenomenon in the literature (as discussed below) since her VARE interview described in detail how she was shown a pornographic video of women 'eating' men's penises and that RW had asked her to do the same to him. Indeed, how else would J know about the video and why would someone show a child such a video?

Later, further negative tagging and negative rhetorical questions elicited the defence's desired responses from J:

> [O]n the day that you got shown the video … he didn't put his penis in your mouth, did he?
>
> No.
>
> He's never put his penis in your mouth?
>
> No.

The VSCA identified the comprehension difficulties with this sequence of questions which moved from:

> this specific incident to a general question. … [I]t is unrealistic to suggest that she should have appreciated that counsel had moved away from [the video] occasion and was now putting to her that RW had never, on any occasion, placed his penis in his mouth. … [With submissions from the prosecutor], the jury were alive to the view that some answers were no more than inaccurate contradictions, resulting from misunderstanding or a willingness to agree with suggestions. Only non-leading questions …

[61] Ibid., [83].

> would have eliminated the risk that apparent inconsistencies would be seen by the jury as inconsequential or inaccurate.[62]

While the VSCA dismissed Ward's appeal, the Court questioned the application of the rule in *Browne v Dunn* (1897) 6 R 67 when the witness is a child, and concluded that the application of the rule in the cross-examination of a child would create unfairness because of the suggestive nature of *Browne v Dunn* challenges.

Ward is a very recent case that was heard in Victoria, an Australian jurisdiction that has all the latest procedures and technology for improving the experiences of, and reducing the trauma for, children giving evidence such as:

(i) abolition of the requirement for children to give evidence in committal proceedings;
(ii) use of the initial police interview as the child's evidence-in-chief in court (to avoid repeated interviews of children);
(iii) pre-trial pre-recording of the child's cross-examination at a special hearing;
(iv) presence of a support person; and
(v) allowing the child to view their police interview before being cross-examined.

It is clear, however, that these reforms, as important as they are, have not addressed the central problem in CSA trials—the cross-examination effect which is discussed below.

The mismatch between the 'strange language' of the courtroom (Brennan, 1995) and the cognitive abilities of children reveal that defence counsel deliberately use strategies to take advantage of a child's lack of comprehension in order to manufacture inaccuracies and inconsistencies in a child's evidence. The inequality between cross-examiner and child due to this mismatch gives rise to profound unfairness within the CSA trial.

---

[62] Ibid., [84]–[85].

The fact that barristers and judges are aware that the adversarial system is not about the truth and is designed to make life difficult for witnesses, no matter how psychologically vulnerable, should ring alarm bells for the administration of justice and the welfare of children. Nonetheless, it is important to engage with the research literature to better inform the criminal justice reform agenda, in terms of measures that might reduce or eliminate the cross-examination effect on sexual assault complainants' evidence.

Although jurors are aware of some of the difficulties faced by children during cross-examination, jurors' verdicts are influenced by the consistency of evidence and the complainant's credibility, both of which are the subject of attack during cross-examination (Cashmore & Trimboli, 2006). In a study of actual jurors, despite jurors' awareness of age-inappropriate questioning and children's comprehension difficulties, there was a positive correlation between their perceptions of consistency and credibility, so that children who gave consistent testimony were rated as more credible. Jurors 'focused on inconsistency and lack of detail, referring to clothing, times and dates' when rating a child's testimony as 'not at all convincing', while '[c]redibility was also strongly correlated with the child's perceived confidence in answering' both prosecutor and defence questions (ibid.: 9). These findings suggest that deliberate questions about detail and weakening a child's confidence through various cross-examination tactics is likely to contribute to decreased perceptions of credibility by jurors:

> both the perceived consistency and credibility of the child complainant were significantly associated with the verdict. Juries which returned a guilty verdict on some or all charges rated the child complainant as significantly more consistent and more credible than those which acquitted the defendant. (ibid.: 9)

Overall, this study provides empirical evidence to confirm what has long been suspected—that there is a positive correlation between jurors' perceptions of complainant consistency, credibility and verdict. More recently, a study by Pichler et al. (2019) confirmed that inconsistencies in evidence are associated with acquittals and case attrition in CSA trials.

There is, however, a distinct mismatch between what lawyers and jurors believe children's inconsistency indicates (unreliability and lack of veracity) and the research literature. In other words, 'the emphasis on consistency may be misplaced' since inconsistencies in 'children's accounts of sexual abuse do not indicate that their claims are false' (Cashmore & Trimboli, 2006: 14), particularly in a context where CSA trials permit the very types of questions that forensic interviewers are trained to avoid.

While jurors may believe that consistency and reliability are intertwined they will have little understanding of the *ways* in which inconsistencies are deliberately created by skilful cross-examiners who exploit children's vulnerability using questions that are deliberately crafted to create confusion and inconsistent answers.

While courtroom questioning styles in sexual assault trials are premised on the historical view that the evidence of children, and sexual assault complainants generally, is inherently unreliable (ALRC & HREOC, 1997), appeal courts in Australia and E&W have begun to accept that children's evidence is no more unreliable than that of adults (Judicial College, 2018).[63]

Nonetheless, the majority of CSA trials in Australia are conducted without intermediaries (discussed in the next chapter) to bring about cultural change in the form of monitoring the age- and developmental appropriateness of cross-examination by defence counsel. As well, adversarial trials are not trauma-informed, as discussed in Chapter 11, such that the cross-examination of children would be categorised as emotionally abusive in any other context.

More importantly, the lack of regulation of cross-examination leads to an inequality of comprehension and resources between child and cross-examiner whose aim is to create inconsistencies in the child's evidence. Defence counsel then argue that any inconsistencies in a child's evidence indicate the unreliability of her/his evidence. More likely, however, these inconsistencies arise from the use of the strange language of the courtroom and an environment of intimidation which creates 'confusion; lack

[63]See, e.g., *Ward* [2017] VSCA 37; *Martin v R* (2013) 46 VR 537; *JJB v R* [2006] NSWCCA 126; *Barker* [2010] EWCA Crim 4.

of understanding …; [an] inability to process what is being put; acquiescence; and an overwillingness to agree with suggestions'.[64] Overall, CSA trials are inherently unfair to child witnesses (Judicial College, 2018).

Even though children are more likely to give evidence using special measures to protect them from the rigours of adversarial processes, the adversarial trial is rigorous *because* of cross-examination which may go on for hours or days and may be 'searching, aggressive or intimidating',[65] or overtly abusive, with defence counsel using whatever methods are permitted by the trial judge.

9 Studies on the Types of Questions Used in the Cross-Examination of Children

Ward's case illustrates why it is important to understand the cross-examination effect on children's evidence and the effects of trauma on a child's ability to give his/her best evidence.

Several empirical studies from the last two decades are relevant to informing the reform agenda in relation to the cross-examination of children. While cross-examination is an integral aspect of adversarial trial practices, it is based on the logically flawed assumption that its methods will uncover an untruthful witness and will have no affect on the evidence of a truthful witness. For example, various studies of question type have found that cross-examiners use questions that are known to restrict a witness's answers, interfere with their concentration and memory and to confuse their understanding of what is being asked. Such questions include closed, leading and yes/no questions, as well as those containing negatives and multiple questions, as seen in the *Ward* case above.

In a study of six rape trials, Kebbell et al. (2003: 54) found that open questions were rare, 'closed [and leading] questions were more frequent, and yes/no questions were most frequent of all'. Since most questions were yes/no questions, witnesses had no choice but to comply with the

---

[64] *Ward* [2017] VSCA 37, [109].

[65] Ibid., [99].

constraints imposed by these questions. Their suggestive nature meant that there was no way of knowing whether a witness's answers to those questions were the truth or the result of suggestion.

Indeed, if a witness's particular recollection of events 'does not further the lawyer's cause ... [then] lawyers are not necessarily interested in eliciting complete, accurate recollections' (Kebbell et al., 2003: 56). They are more interested in promoting their client's case, with little or no incentive to reduce the adversarial nature of their cross-examination unless mandatory controls are introduced. In other words, '[b]y controlling the evidence [produced] ..., the lawyer becomes the narrator with the witness relegated to agreeing or disagreeing ... [so that] cross-examination is a speech, just like an opening or closing' (Hanna et al., 2012: 53).

In order to compare the questioning styles of defence lawyers and prosecutors, Zajac et al. (2003) made a surprising finding when they undertook an analysis of 600 examination-in-chief and re-examination questions and 2935 cross-examination questions involving child complainants in NZ between the ages of 5–13 years old (Zajac et al., 2003: 201).

When assessing whether the styles of questioning used by prosecutors and defence lawyers 'differed as a function of the child's age', they found that defence lawyers asked a higher proportion of complex, grammatically confusing, credibility-challenging, leading and closed questions compared to prosecutors (Zajac et al., 2003: 202; 203).

When the authors assessed children's responses to the questions, they found that responses varied as a function of the type of lawyer (prosecutor or defence), including more uncertainty, misunderstandings, compliance to leading or closed questions and changes to earlier testimony in response to defence questions. Not only did children exhibit 'high rates of misunderstanding and compliance with leading and closed questions, ... [there was also] a low rate of clarification seeking' (ibid.: 206) In particular:

> 76% of children ... made changes to one or more of their earlier statements under cross-examination. ... Ninety-five per cent of changes

> … were made in response to leading questions, credibility-challenging questions, or combinations of both. (ibid.: 204)

Yet these types of inconsistencies in a child's evidence can have significant ramifications for the prosecution's case since:

> children who make one or more changes to peripheral details … yet still allege abuse may be perceived as unreliable in the eyes of the jury, … [resulting] in a not guilty verdict. … [Additionally], witnesses who make substantial changes or recant altogether may lead a case to be dismissed. In either case, if the child has actually been abused, justice has not been served and the child remains vulnerable to further abuse. (ibid.: 188)

Overall, the results reported by Zajac et al. (2003) confirm that there is 'a clear mismatch between courtroom language and the language capabilities of the children being questioned'. This was particularly so for children under the age of 10 years who were less likely than older children to seek clarification to complex, confusing or ambiguous questions, possibly because 'children below the age of 8 years cannot reliably detect [their own] non-comprehension' (ibid.: 207). Yet the age of the child was found to have had no effect on the types of questions asked by defence lawyers, indicating that they did not 'make allowances for the child witness's developmental level' (ibid.: 206).

Children's responses depended on the questioning style of the lawyers and the types of questions asked which was encouraging because 'it suggests that cross-examination can be made more appropriate for children merely by changing the types of questions deployed' (ibid.: 207–208).

A further study by Zajac and Hayne (2006) showed that older children were also not immune from the negative consequences of cross-examination style questions. The authors reported that 'the cross-examination interview significantly decreased the accuracy of 9- and 10-year-old witnesses who were initially highly accurate', with over 40% changing their initial correct responses about a staged event.

Six years later, a study of NZ court transcripts of the evidence given by 18 children (aged 8–15 years) in relation to physical and/or sexual assault, found that children were still frequently asked questions that 'cause comprehension problems ... namely, multiple subordinate clauses, verbs in the passive voice, complex or legalese vocabulary, double negative, and difficult concepts' (Hanna et al., 2012: 532). Specifically, '84% of questions posed during cross-examination were closed or leading, compared to 26% of forensic interviewers' utterances, and 52% of prosecutors' (ibid.: 535). Examples of the complexity of cross-examination questions included those with negatives, double negatives, complex vocabulary and multi-faceted propositions:

> If he told the Police that that was what he thought you wanted to do, are you saying that you don't think he could have thought that? [to a 16-year-old witness]
>
> I'll put it to you that he at *no* time told you *not* to say anything to anyone. [age not specified]. (ibid.: 535–538)

When Stolzenberg and Lyon (2014: 22) analysed 1680 defence and 1707 prosecution questions from CSA trials in California they found that defence attorneys asked more leading questions than prosecutors and that:

> [c]hildren were more likely to give elaborate responses (more than merely assenting, dissenting, or picking an option to a forced choice question) to prosecutors, and more likely to give unelaborated yes-no responses to the defense.

In a study of the transcripts of the cross-examinations of 120 complainants in three Australian jurisdictions, Powell et al. (2016: 205–209) reported that the main cross-examination strategies involved attacks on:

- the complainant's credibility, such as accusations of lying, false allegations and previous dishonesty;
- the complainant's reliability, such as accuracy of evidence;
- the plausibility of the allegations, often based on myths around sexual assault such as absence of resistance, or delayed complaint; and

- the complainant's consistency by raising evidence of inconsistencies (often about minor details).

The authors also reported that the raising of inconsistencies with complainants was frequent but that defence counsel raised complainant inconsistencies with peripheral matters more frequently than inconsistencies regarding issues central to proving the offence (98.4% vs 72.4%) (Powell et al., 2016: 226). For complainants under the age of 18 years, 'as the number of questions asked by police in the pre-recorded interview increased, so did the lines of questioning on inconsistencies in cross-examination' (ibid.: 230). Better quality police interviews resulted in fewer inconsistencies being raised at trial (ibid.: 231).

As listed in Table 1, a number of studies of trial transcripts have found that cross-examination is dominated by leading and/or closed questions of varying complexity in both child and adult sexual assault trials.

The implication of the above studies is that cross-examination is likely to result in less accurate evidence given by a witness in a sexual assault trial compared to their evidence-in-chief. In fact, several studies have specifically analysed the phenomenon of inconsistent evidence given by both adults and children in response to cross-examination style questions. These studies show that there are 'three aspects of cross-examination [that] are likely to pose considerable problems for children', in particular, (Zajac & Cannan, 2009: S37) and may also cause problems for some vulnerable adult complainants:

(i) declaratory and suggestive questions that require a yes or no answer;
(ii) questions that are beyond children's developmental abilities; and
(iii) questions that prevent the ability to put alternative versions of events.

Table 1 Frequency of leading and closed questions during cross-examination by different examiners

Question type	Prosecutors (%)	Defence counsel (%)	Forensic interviewers (%)	Study
Leading/closed	n/a	av. 78.5	n/a	Davies and Seymour (1998) (NZ)
	n/a	65	n/a	Zajac et al. (2003) (NZ)
Closed Yes/no leading Other leading	n/a	10.3 81.8 41.2	n/a	Kebbell et al. (2003) (England)
Leading/closed	n/a	89	n/a	Zajac and Cannan (2009) (NZ)
Leading/closed	52	84	26	Hanna et al. (2012) (NZ)
Closed Leading	52 15	44 39		Stolzenberg and Lyon (2014) (Calif, USA)
Closed Leading	44 24	28 >60		Powell et al. (2016) (Aust)
1950s trials Closed Leading	n/a	 30[a] 65[a]	n/a	Westera et al. (2017) (Aust)
Twenty-first-century trials Closed Leading	n/a	 25[a] 70[a]	n/a	Westera et al. (2017) (NZ)

Note
[a]Approximate figures

10 Studies on the Impact of the Cross-Examination Effect on Children's Evidence: Inconsistent Evidence or False Inaccuracies?

The fact that 76% of children changed their testimony during cross-examination in the study by Zajac et al. (2003), discussed above, led the authors to ask whether or not the changes made by children constituted a change *towards* the truth or *away* from the truth. To answer this, they examined the effect of cross-examination on five- and six-year-olds' reports of a contrived event in which the children actually participated.[66]

After the event but before the first interview, some of the children were exposed to misleading information in order to attempt to mimic the situation where a child has been misled or coached prior to testifying (Zajac & Hayne, 2003: 188). All 46 children were interviewed six weeks after the event using open-ended questions and then more specific questions about two actual things that had happened (photo taken, police car) and questions about two things that did not happen (trying on handcuffs, report of a stolen bike). Eight months[67] after this direct examination, they were interviewed by a different interviewer using cross-examination style questions and language in order to persuade the children to change their accounts of what happened at the police station.

Zajac and Hayne (2003: 190) reported that 85% of children 'changed at least one of their original responses during cross-examination and one-third … changed all of their original responses', with no significant differences in the number of changes made between the control group and the misled group.

When comparing their accuracy, the misled group was significantly less accurate during direct examination than the control group yet 'the errors made by children in the misled group were largely restricted to the

[66]The event involved a tour of a NZ police station during which the children had their thumbprint recorded and 'mug shot' taken. They were also shown a jail cell and a police car with the lights and siren turned on.

[67]The eight-month period was the average delay in NZ between when a child first reports and the matter goes to trial.

false events ... [which] suggests that the effect of prior misinformation was highly specific to those events' (ibid.: 190). In other words, the children in the misled group were as accurate as children in the control group when asked, during direct examination, about events that had actually happened (Zajac & Hayne, 2003: 191).

The next question that Zajac and Hayne (2003) addressed is whether the changes made by 85% of the children during cross-examination had corrected earlier mistakes, or did the children make changes to answers that were originally correct? While the children's overall accuracy during direct examination differed according to whether they had been misled or not, after cross-examination, the children's accuracy scores did not differ as a function of group:

> [f]or children in the misled group, their accuracy after cross-examination was not significantly different from the low level that was seen during direct examination [about false events] ... . For children in the control group, on the other hand, *their accuracy actually declined* after the cross-examination interview. (ibid.: 190; emphasis added)

In addition, 'children were just as likely to change a correct answer under cross-examination ... as they were to change an answer that had initially been incorrect' (ibid.: 191). As well, the misled group's prior exposure to misinformation did not make them more susceptible to probing cross-examination. This means that children who had given accurate answers were persuaded during cross-examination to change their previous accurate accounts of what had happened at the police station. This may have been due to either a weakened memory of the event and greater susceptibility to suggestion (since cross-examination occurred 9.5 months later) and/or because of 'compliance with suggestions' that the children knew to be incorrect (ibid.: 192). Thus, 'cross-examination not only proved to be unsuccessful in discrediting ... misled children questioned about false events ..., it also decreased the accuracy of children who were initially correct' (ibid.: 191).

In addition, the children's performance during cross-examination was associated with their levels of self-confidence, self-esteem and assertiveness—children who were low on these three measures made more changes and changed a greater proportion of their correct responses (Zajac et al., 2009). This finding has implications for sexually abused children who, compared to other children, are more likely to display low self-confidence, self-esteem and assertiveness (Zajac et al., 2009). Because of these characteristics and the trauma they have suffered they are more likely to be more vulnerable to the manipulative effects of cross-examination. Indeed:

> the same characteristics that may serve as risk factors for being [sexually] abused would be the same characteristics that are associated with poor courtroom performance. (ibid.: 931)

Because of limitations in the studies by Zajac and colleagues, such as children's participation in events that had no consequences for them or anyone else if reported, Fogliati and Bussey (2014) undertook a study that tested children's accuracy in reporting a minor transgressive event to determine the ability of cross-examination to uncover children's attempts to conceal the transgression. Nonetheless, unlike CSA, the transgression did not involve any wrongdoing committed against the children.

After participation in a healthy eating lesson in which the teacher accidentally tore a poster, two groups of children (aged 5–6 and 7–8 years) were interviewed twice, with the second interview being either another direct examination or a cross-examination. There was no delay between the first and second interviews. The authors found that both younger and older cross-examined children were significantly less accurate and made 'a higher proportion of incorrect changes' than those who underwent a second examination since cross-examined children changed more of their initial responses (Fogliati & Bussey, 2014: 306; 307; see also O'Neill & Zajac, 2013a, 2013b). The authors concluded that children's changes were due to the types of questions asked, rather than 'the effects of a repeated interview' (ibid.: 309).

In relation to the witnessed transgression, 'an equal number of children disclosed the transgression' during both cross-examination and direct examination (ibid.: 310). While cross-examined children were more likely to 'change from an initial non-disclosure to a truthful disclosure ... they were also more likely to change from a truthful disclosure to a non-disclosure' (ibid.).

However, the transgression used in this study was quite different to a positive report of CSA since the study focused on whether children would *disclose* a transgression which differs from the aim of cross-examination in a CSA trial which is to persuade a child to *retract* their allegations. Nonetheless, the study highlights the possibility that children who retract their CSA allegations under cross-examination may do so because of the suggestibility of cross-examination rather than because of the truth, as demonstrated in the *Ward* case above. Thus, '[s]trategies that adequately test children's evidence, without compromising their accuracy and truthfulness, need to be identified to increase opportunities for justice' in CSA cases (ibid.: 312).

The cross-examination effect may be amplified in relation to children with intellectual disabilities. With poorer cognitive abilities, children with an intellectual disability are more susceptible than other children to the suggestibility inherent in cross-examination (Bettenay et al., 2014 and references therein) and may also be more susceptible to the power dynamics between cross-examiner and witness.

After participation in an interactive magic show, Bettenay et al. (2014) found that 100% of 98 children aged 4–11 years with mild to serious intellectual disabilities changed at least one of their responses from their initial interview as a result of cross-examination. However, 96.7% of a control group of typically developing children also changed at least one of their initial responses under cross-examination. Overall, '[c]hildren with ... poorer memory for event details ... were more likely to cede during cross-examination challenges' (Bettenay et al., 2014: 210). This meant that there was no significant difference between children as a function of cognitive ability, even though all children viewed the 'videotape of their initial interview' before being cross-examined which is standard practice in E&W and in some Australian jurisdictions.

Table 2 documents the cross-examination effect by summarising the extent to which children changed their original interview evidence after being subject to cross-examination.

Table 2 The cross-examination effect: degree of changes to evidence by children subject to cross-examination-type questions

Children's cognitive abilities	Age (years)	One or more changes under x-examination (%)	Event	Delay between interview & x-examination	Study
TD	5–13	76	Court transcripts	N/A	Zajac et al. (2003)
TD	5–6	85 (33% changed all original evidence)	Participation in staged, neutral event	8 months	Zajac and Hayne (2003)
TD	9–10	70 (43% changed correct responses)	Participation in staged, neutral event	8 months	Zajac and Hayne (2006)
TD	5–12	93	Court transcripts	N/A	Zajac et al. (2009)
TD	5–6 9–10	66[a] 42[b]	Participation in staged, neutral event	1 week 6 months	O'Neill and Zajac (2013a, 2013b)
TD	4–11	96.7	Staged, neutral event	10 months	Bettenay et al. (2014)
ID & BID	4–11	100	Participation in staged, neutral event	10 months	Bettenay et al. (2014)
TD	 9–11 14–16	Mean changes in evidence[#]: 3.33 2.98	Observed film clip: non-violent crime	8 months	Jack and Zajac (2014)
TD	6 & 8	Mean changes in evidence[#]: 1.44	Participation in staged, transgressive event	No delay	Fogliati and Bussey (2014)
TD	5 & 6	78	Participation in staged, neutral event	Short delay: 1–3 days Long delay: 8 months	Righarts et al. (2014)

Notes
[a]Children underwent either a cross-examination or a second examination as their second interview; these were changes made as the result of the second interview, although cross-examined children made more changes and more inaccurate changes compared to children who underwent a second examination
[b]As above
[#]No percentages reported
TD: Typically developing
ID: Mild to moderate intellectually disabled
BID: Borderline intellectually disabled

Thus, studies show that cross-examination, ostensibly designed to flush out the dishonest witness, is incapable of achieving that task with children. For example, in their study of five- and six-year-old children who visited a police station, Righarts et al. (2014: 282) found that:

> Responses to questions about the true events were just as likely to be changed (33%) during cross-examination as responses about the false events (42%) ... [while] [a]ttempts to talk a child out of an event (36%) during cross-examination were just as successful as attempts to talk them into an event (38%).

Instead, cross-examination achieves what has long been thought to be its main aim in CSA trials—producing inaccurate inconsistencies or retractions. Cross-examination is not able to discriminate between true and false testimony and produces inaccuracies in children who had previously given accurate accounts.

The question is whether these inaccuracies are produced within the actual courtroom. Since the cross-examination questions used in the above studies were based on the questioning styles used by defence counsel in CSA trials, and because children in court are cross-examined under much more intimidating conditions than those used in the above studies in a public forum by people unknown to them and for considerably longer periods of time, it is highly likely that cross-examination will produce similar inaccuracies during CSA trials, as illustrated by the cross-examination of the eight-year-old child in *Ward*, above.

Indeed, Bettenay et al. (2014: 211) reported 'higher rates of changed responses than those reported in previous research ... possibly due to the use of trained legal professionals rather than researchers to conduct interviews'. Thus, children of various age groups do not appear to give their best evidence when faced with cross-examination style questions, suggesting that children should be exempted from this type of questioning. What then would replace it?

An inherent assumption about the truth-finding effectiveness of cross-examination is that *any* change to a witness's testimony is a change from a lie or mistake to the truth. However, in an actual trial, lawyers and juries have no way of knowing whether that is the case.

For example, Fogliati and Bussey (2014: 309) investigated 'the claim that cross-examination promotes true reporting of neutral and transgressive events' in a study with 119 male children aged 6 and 8 years. During a healthy eating lesson, they witnessed their instructor commit a staged, minor transgression and heard her say that she hoped her mistake would not be found out, although she did not ask the children to keep her secret. The children were divided into two groups and subject to two direct examinations or to a direct examination followed by a cross-examination.

During their initial open-ended narratives, only 10 children (8.40%) 'spontaneously reported the transgression' (ibid.: 305) after they were given two prompts, 'Tell me everything that happened during the healthy eating lesson' and 'Tell me more about what happened' (ibid.: 301). While there was no difference in the accuracy of children's reports after the initial interview (with six-year-olds being 'as accurate as older children, when asked non-misleading direct questions': ibid.: 309), in line with other studies, children who underwent cross-examination were significantly less accurate than those who underwent a second direct examination since they changed more of their original responses during cross-examination (ibid.: 306). Irrespective of age, children subject to cross-examination 'made a higher proportion of incorrect changes' compared to those subject to a second examination (ibid.: 307).

While there was no difference in the number of children who disclosed the transgression after a second examination for both six- and eight-year-olds (ibid.: 308), it might have been expected that cross-examination would elicit more disclosures of the teacher's transgression. However, 'the number of kindergarten children who disclosed the transgression did not differ' between their first and second interviews while *fewer* eight-year-olds disclosed the transgression after cross-examination compared to direct examination (ibid.: 308). Thus, 'cross-examination did not promote truthful disclosure for kindergarten children, and actually reduced the number of older children who provided truthful disclosures' (ibid.: 309).

Although children subject to cross-examination were more likely 'to change from an initial non-disclosure to a truthful disclosure ... they were also more likely to change from a truthful disclosure to a non-disclosure than … to make no disclosure change'. This means that cross-examination encouraged some children to disclose the transgression but also persuaded others to retract their initial report of the teacher's transgression (ibid.: 310). While some would argue that cross-examination is, therefore, essential to reveal the child who is lying or mistaken about being sexually abused, cross-examination in court is not about getting children to *disclose* abuse but to *retract* allegations of abuse. In other words, cross-examination is used by defence barristers to elicit retractions not to elicit disclosures.

Overall, this study confirms the findings from other studies that have shown that 'the detrimental effect of cross-examination [is] due to the types of questions asked during cross-examination, not to the effects of a repeated interview' (ibid.). It also confirms that children should not be subject to cross-examination style questions.

Whether children should be subject to a *second direct examination* is also questionable since Fogliati and Bussey (2014: 310) found that six-year-olds made a higher proportion of incorrect changes when subject to a second direct examination, compared to eight-year-olds. This finding is consistent with previous research that 'demonstrated that younger children had a greater tendency than their older counterparts to change their initial accurate response towards an inaccurate one across repeated interview'. It is possible that the incorrect changes by younger children were due to social pressure in that they assumed that their first answers were incorrect and made adjustments to please adult interviewers.

A series of studies have investigated the effect of coaching on children's ability to give truthful evidence and the effect of cross-examination on persuading coached children to change their evidence. The first study was conducted by Zajac et al. (2003), discussed above, who found that misled or coached five- and six-year-old children were no more susceptible to the cross-examination effect than a control group of non-coached children. Thus, cross-examination proved unsuccessful in discriminating between coached and non-coached children.

Zajac and Hayne (2006: 12) found that when nine- and 10-year-old children were given misinformation before being cross-examined they were 'significantly more accurate' compared to five- and six-year-olds and did not differ from non-coached nine- and 10-year-olds after direct examination.

More recently, Fogliati and Bussey (2015) conducted a study in which children were coached to lie, resulting in three experimental conditions: (i) those who were coached to say that a transgression had occurred during a healthy eating lesson; (ii) those who were coached to deny that an actual transgression had occurred and (iii) those who were not coached.

Cross-examination of the two groups of coached children was found to be more effective than neutral, examination-style questions at eliciting accurate accounts of what the children had witnessed. However, cross-examination of the non-coached children produced more inaccuracies compared to neutral questioning, in line with previous research. Nonetheless, the limitations of this study must be noted, since the children were coached by a stranger about events that did not happen to them personally. Although the coached children readily fabricated events when examined, they did so about neutral events that had not happened to them and that were non-abusive in nature. Thus, the question arises, are children just as easily coached in relation to sexual acts which are beyond their actual lived experiences?

Indeed, in a CSA trial, there is rarely actual evidence to prove that a child complainant has been coached so that lawyers and fact-finders have no measure for determining whether a child's change to her/his evidence, in the form of a retraction, is a change towards, or away from, the truth.

In order to determine how well cross-examination can discriminate between truthful and untruthful children, Zajac, Irvine, Ingram, and Jack (2016) conducted a study to determine the effectiveness of cross-examination on children aged 6–11 years who had been coached by a parent (who acted as a confederate), rather than a stranger, during a staged computer game, compared with a group of non-coached children. They found that 32 out of 33 out of the latter group 'gave highly accurate' evidence about two events while all 32 coached children 'told at least one lie' (Zajac et al., 2016: 168). After cross-examination, the coached children significantly increased their accuracy compared to the non-coached children whose accuracy decreased significantly. However, this study does not prove that cross-examined children in CSA trials necessarily change their evidence towards the truth since a 'changed answer in response to a cross-examination-style challenge was not diagnostic of accuracy beyond the level of chance' (Zajac et al., 2016: 172). Both neutral and cross-examination questions were found to be 'poor discriminants' in eliciting the truth (ibid.).

The above study was limited by the fact that parental coaching was designed to prevent a child from revealing that the parent had disobeyed researchers' instructions in relation to a computer game, rather than coaching children about sexually abusive matters that had not occurred. Thus, the likely rationale for lying by the coached children was to protect their parents from the consequences of their parents' disobedience, something that is emotionally and socially quite different to lying about sexual abuse in the face of police and prosecutorial questioning, and in the authoritarian and intimidating setting of a courtroom where children are generally required to take an oath before giving evidence.

Overall, since 2003 studies have shown that:

(i) cross-examination questions significantly affect children's accuracy about events they have witnessed or participated in (Bettenay et al., 2014; Fogliati & Bussey, 2015; O'Neill & Zajac, 2013a, 2013b; Righarts et al., 2014; Zajac & Hayne, 2003; Zajac, Jury, & O'Neill, 2009);
(ii) the accuracy of both younger (5 and 6-year olds: Zajac & Hayne, 2003) and older children is similarly affected (9 and 10 years olds: Zajac & Hayne, 2006);
(iii) participation in an event is no safeguard against the manipulative effects of cross-examination (Zajac & Hayne, 2003, 2006; Zajac et al., 2003);
(iv) the cross-examination effect has been seen when children are cross-examined soon after an event (1 week: Righarts et al., 2014) and several months after an event (8 months: Zajac & Hayne, 2003; 6 months: O'Neill & Zajac, 2013a, 2013b);
(v) particular characteristics of children increase the cross-examination effect, including low self-esteem, low self-confidence and low assertiveness (Zajac et al., 2009);

(vi) the cross-examination effect for younger children (5–6 years) is compounded by long delays between the initial interview and cross-examination compared to older children (9–10 years) (O'Neill & Zajac, 2013a, 2013b);

(vii) accuracy changes appear to be due to social factors (such as pressure from authority figures) rather than memory loss since the type of interview influences accuracy changes—re-examination soon after cross-examination restores accuracy (Righarts et al., 2014);

(viii) while children make changes when subject to any type of second interview, children make *more* changes and more inaccurate changes when they are subject to a second interview in the form of cross-examination compared to a re-examination (O'Neill & Zajac, 2013a, 2013b);

(ix) practice at answering cross-examination questions reduces the cross-examination effect but only after a one-week delay before cross-examination compared to a one-month delay (O'Neill & Zajac, 2013a, 2013b; Righarts, O'Neill, & Zajac, 2013).

We also know that mental abuse, intimidation and humiliation by defence lawyers are relatively common occurrences in CSA trials and that defence counsel deliberately use complex and leading questions to produce inaccuracies and inconsistencies in children's testimony. In fact, the research shows that 'narrowing children's response options [through the use of leading yes/no questions] makes them more susceptible to errors', compared to open questions which broaden their range of response options since they are more likely to guess the answer to yes/no questions (Sharman & Powell, 2012: 48).

11 The Effect of Cross-Examination on the Evidence of Adults

Most of the research on the effect of cross-examination has focused on children because of the mismatch, in terms of power and language, between a cognitively undeveloped child and a trained adult lawyer.

What do we know about the effect of cross-examination on the evidence of adult complainants?

When Westera et al. (2017: 28) undertook a comparison of courtroom questioning in adult sexual assault cases in the 1950s and the 2000s they found that complainants in contemporary cases were asked more questions overall compared to complainants in the 1950s, including '34% more questions during cross-examination'. In both time periods, lawyers spoke 'considerably more words than complainants' during cross-examination although more words were uttered by lawyers during contemporary cross-examination (ibid.: 23). In fact, 'the length of cross-examination was independently driven by the number of words uttered by the [prosecutor]' (ibid.: 27).

There was evidence that questioning during evidence-in-chief had improved over the years with 'proportionately more open questions, ... fewer closed questions, ... and marginally fewer leading questions' in contemporary cases, although most prosecutors' questions were still closed and leading (ibid.: 24; 27). However, 'the proportions of open, closed, and leading questions' remained the same during cross-examination in both time periods (ibid.), with most being leading.

Do adults, like children, have difficulties in understanding the types of complex questions used in cross-examination? Westera et al. (2017: 28) found that in the longer cross-examinations in the 2000s cases, contemporary complainants used various 'adaptive strategies' such as clarification-seeking compared to historical complainants. When complainants' responses were examined for levels of uncertainty, 'complainant uncertainty was more common during cross-examination than during evidence-in-chief' in both time periods, as were inconsistencies in evidence (ibid.: 26; 28).

The vast majority of complainants also made at least one change to their earlier testimony during cross-examination (100%, historical; 95%, contemporary). While the authors had no way of knowing whether these were changes towards or away from the truth, they found 'a high rate of compliance with leading questions'. Critically, however, the number of changes to earlier testimony 'was positively associated with the number of questions asked' (ibid.: 26) which suggests that if a questioner repeats a particular question they will eventually get the answer they want.

Overall, the research shows that adults struggle to understand linguistically complex questions and are susceptible to leading questions and social pressures to conform (see review in Zajac & Cannan, 2009), with adults' accuracy decreasing significantly in the face of cross-examination style questions.

To determine the effect of cross-examination as a function of age, Zajac and Cannan (2009) analysed 30 transcripts of sexual assault proceedings involving children aged 5–12 years and adults aged 18–35 years. As expected, defence lawyers asked more leading questions of both children and adults than prosecutors. They also asked a higher proportion of questions with complex vocabulary or language structure, and questions that suggested poor memory, confusion or lying, than did prosecutors. However, adults were more likely than children to be accused of lying by defence counsel (Zajac & Cannan, 2009: S44).

In terms of the cross-examination effect, 'complainants were more likely to change their story when questioned by defence lawyers' so much so that 100% of the adults and 93% of the children made at least one change to their original evidence during cross-examination (ibid.), although the authors could not determine if these were changes towards or away from the truth. In addition, '[t]he more cross-examination questions that complainants were asked, the more changes they made' with these changes occurring at higher than chance levels (ibid.: S45; S46). The questions that challenged a complainant's credibility were 'predictive of changes' made by complainants and when there was a change in story, 'lawyers were more likely than chance to follow up … with a credibility challenging question', revealing the specific strategies that lawyers employ (ibid.: S47). These results suggest that social pressure, rather than lack of veracity, explains some of the changes made under cross-examination.

Lawyers used specific strategies when complainants resisted a question, in that 'resistance was [also] predictive of a subsequent credibility-challenging question … [and] … predictive of a subsequent closed question for children' (ibid.: S47). Remarkably, when a complainant sought clarification, the 'subsequent question was more likely than chance to be complex' for both adults and children, although prosecutors were also more likely to do this for adults (ibid.). However, clarification seeking was low for both adults and children while 'clear misunderstandings' of questions was evident (ibid.: S49).

Overall, defence lawyers 'were more likely to ask credibility-challenging questions suggesting that the complainant was purposefully untruthful ... than ... to ask questions that merely suggested' confusion or mistake (ibid.: S48). Such a strategy aims to create reasonable doubt in the minds of the fact-finders since suggestions of lying are probably more likely to trigger jurors' own RMA and gender biases than suggestions that the complainant has made a mistake.

There were also differences in responses between children and adults undergoing cross-examination in that children were more likely to comply, and less likely to disagree with lawyers' suggestions, as well as less likely to clarify their responses with additional information (ibid.: S49). Surprisingly, adults were more likely to display clear misunderstandings of lawyers' questions than children (ibid.: S45).

Valentine and Maras (2011) also investigated the effect of cross-examination on the evidence of adult eyewitnesses who watched a simulated crime event. After cross-examination, almost three-quarters (73%) changed one answer from their original statement, with more than a third (37%) changing two or more answers, although the witnesses' memories 'did not become more accurate as a result of cross-examination'. This study also illustrates the manipulative effect of cross-examination, with 84% of witnesses accepting 'at least once that they may be mistaken' (ibid.: 559), a finding that was not surprising since cross-examiners 'made extensive use of social pressure (e.g. negative feedback ...) and leading questions' (ibid.: 559).

Sharman and Powell (2012: 50) conducted a study of adults' responses to four different question structures:

(i) closed ('Did Eric have a company logo on his van?');
(ii) closed specific ('Did Eric have a company logo in large black letters on his van?');
(iii) closed presumptive or suggestive ('Eric had a company logo on his van, didn't he?'); and

(iv) open presumptive or suggestive ('Tell me about the company logo on Eric's van?'),

They found that participants (aged 18–60 years) were more likely to be misled when asked closed specific and open presumptive questions: '[t]hey incorrectly agreed with more misleading suggestions when these suggestions were delivered in closed specific and open presumptive questions (37.8%) than closed and closed presumptive questions (24.2%)' (ibid.).

This study also supports the proposition that adults are susceptible to agreeing with suggestions that they do not themselves believe to be true. The authors reported that participants:

> were more misled when previously exposed to misleading information in closed specific and open presumptive questions than when exposed to this information in closed and closed presumptive interview questions. Not only did the closed specific and open presumptive questions encourage people to agree with the misleading questions during the initial interview but also these questions decreased the accuracy of participants' memories during the later recognition test. … These findings fit with earlier research demonstrating that the way in which interview questions are worded affects witnesses' memories. (Sharman & Powell, 2012: 52)

In a study of three age groups (45 children aged 9–11 years, 41 adolescents aged 14–16 years and 42 adults aged 25–60 years), Jack and Zajac (2014) found that participants in all age groups were more likely to change responses in their initial interview under cross-examination compared with a second examination. However, children and adolescents were more vulnerable to the cross-examination effect than adults while 'the common practice of playing children a recording of their evidential interview prior to appearing in court provides no buffer against this effect' (Jack & Zajac, 2014: 5). There was also a decrease in accuracy between the first and second interview which was 'significantly greater for peripheral details than for central details' (ibid.: 4).

Most recently, Westera et al. (2017) conducted a historical comparison of the questioning of sexual assault complainants in the 1950s and the 2000s, in order to determine whether questioning practices had evolved over the past 50 years, with the two time periods representing conservative and more liberal sexual and social views about women, respectively.

After examining 42 transcripts of the evidence of complainants aged 16 years or older (of which 50% were historical), Westera et al. (2017: 22) found that complainants were asked more questions in cross-examination than in evidence-in-chief and also more questions in contemporary compared to historical cases. Matching this latter finding was the fact that defence lawyers spoke considerably more words than complainants.

In terms of the cross-examination effect, more complainants made at least one change during cross-examination than during evidence-in-chief; that is, 100% (historical) and 95% (contemporary) compared with 29% (historical) and 43% (contemporary) during evidence-in-chief.

Possibly reflecting current modern approaches, prosecutors in contemporary cases 'asked complainants a higher proportion of open-ended questions … than in historical cases' but 'the fact remains that the bulk of prosecutors' questions are still closed and leading' (ibid.: 26; 27). In contrast, 'the format of cross-examination questions has remained remarkably consistent over time', with leading questions still making up the bulk of questions, although contemporary cross-examinations 'are significantly longer' than in the 1950s (ibid.: 28; 29). As a result, contemporary complainants spent more time giving and seeking clarification than historical complainants. What had not changed was 'a high rate of compliance with leading questions', as well as uncertainty and inconsistency during cross-examination compared to evidence-in-chief (ibid.).

In a follow-up study to that of Westera et al. (2017) and Zydervelt, Zajac, Kaladelfos, and Westera (2017) explored the *content* of cross-examiners' questions to determine the strategies used to discredit complainants in the 1950s compared with the 2000s. Because of the rules of evidence that applied in the 1950s, '[c]omplainants were routinely asked humiliating questions about their sexual morals and respectability, including … sexual history, sexual reputation, sexual desires and modes of dress' (ibid.: 552). But with the introduction of rape shield laws which restrict the scope of cross-examination on sexual history and reputation, is the content of questions still the same?[68]

Zydervelt et al. (2017: 560) found that '[l]awyers conducting contemporary cross-examinations used a significantly larger number of specific tactics' with complainants than in historical cross-examinations. In both time periods, strategies targeted 'reliability, consistency with other evidence, credibility and the plausibility of the allegation' (ibid.), although defence counsel mostly challenged plausibility. Like the *Lazarus* case discussed in Chapter 7, contemporary lawyers commonly challenged plausibility by referring to the complainant's behaviour 'immediately before the offence … or immediately afterwards' (ibid.: 561). Delays in reporting, lack of resistance and continued relationship with the defendant were less common tactics.

The most common credibility tactics were about 'the complainant's personal traits or potential ulterior motives for making the allegation' (ibid.: 563). Despite rape shield laws, questions about the complainant's sexual history with other people was more common than in historical cases (ibid.: 563–564). Questions about reliability were more likely in contemporary cases and included issues around intoxication, memory and perception fallibility.

Overall, the tactics of defence lawyers have changed little over 50 years—they are 'pursuing the same goals in slightly different ways' with tactics based on rape myths being common (ibid.: 565). Complainant behaviour was used in more than 85% of cases to infer consent (and hence the falsity of the allegation) while a complainant's personal attributes were used to make her appear less credible in about 60% of cases (ibid.).

As discussed in Chapters 4 and 5, one of the aims of defence cross-examination is to paint the adult complainant as someone who is morally questionable by focusing on rape myths about her behaviour and habits, thereby raising doubts about the veracity of her complaint. The studies

[68]In E&W, for example, the Ministry of Justice (2018) reported that, after an analysis by the CPS of 309 sexual assault cases (finalised in 2016) to determine the frequency of applications to admit sexual history evidence under s 41 of the YJCE Act (1999), the trial judge refused to allow sexual history evidence in 92% of cases and such applications were only made in 13% of cases.

above not only confirm this time-honoured strategy but highlight the fact that adult complainants' accuracy in actual cases also decreases with changes to testimony under cross-examination and that longer cross-examinations will produce more inaccurate evidence.

As discussed in Chapter 11, the lack of a trauma-informed court environment means that the adversarial trial tends to ignore the effect of trauma on adult rape complainants' ability to give evidence and the cross-examination effect on adults' testimony. The above study by Westera et al. (2017) suggests that the length of cross-examination, the style of cross-examination questions, as well as who the questioner is, are key reform issues for the sexual assault trial. These reform issues are discussed in the next chapters.

References

Advocacy Training Council. (2011). *Raising the bar: The handling of vulnerable witnesses, victims and defendants in court*. London: The Advocacy Training Council. https://www.icca.ac.uk/wp-content/uploads/2019/07/Raising-the-Bar.pdf.

Andrews, S. J., Lamb, M. E., & Lyon, T. D. (2014). Question types, responsiveness and self-contradictions when prosecutors and defense attorneys question alleged victims of child sexual abuse. *Applied Cognitive Psychology, 25*, 253–261.

Australasian Institute of Judicial Administration Committee (AIJA). (2014). *Bench book for children giving evidence in Australian courts*. Melbourne: AIJA.

Australian Law Reform Commission and Human Rights and Equal Opportunity Commission. (1997). *Seen and heard: Priority for children in the legal process* (ALRC Report No. 84). Sydney: ALRC.

Bettenay, C., Ridley, A. M., Henry, L. A., & Crane, L. (2014). Cross-examination: The testimony of children with and without intellectual disabilities. *Applied Cognitive Psychology, 28*, 204–214.

Boniface, D. J. (1994). Ruining a good boy for the sake of a bad girl: False accusation theory in sexual offences, and New South Wales Limitations Periods—Gone but not forgotten. *Current Issues in Criminal Justice, 6*, 54–75.

Brennan, M. (1995). The discourse of denial: Cross-examining child victim witnesses. *Journal of Pragmatics, 23,* 71–91.

Caruso, D. (2012). Proposed reforms for the cross-examination of child witnesses and the reception and treatment of their evidence. *Journal of Judicial Administration, 21,* 191–236.

Cashmore, J., & Trimboli, L. (2005). *An evaluation of the NSW child sexual assault specialist jurisdiction.* Sydney: NSW Bureau of Crime Statistics and Research.

Cashmore, J., & Trimboli, L. (2006). Child sexual assault trials: A survey of juror perceptions. *Crime and Justice Bulletin, 102,* 1–20.

Cossins, A. (2000). *Masculinities, sexualities and child sexual abuse.* The Hague: Kluwer Law International.

Cossins, A. (2009). Cross-examination in child sexual assault trials: Evidentiary safeguard or an opportunity to confuse? *Melbourne University Law Review, 33,* 68–104.

Cossins, A. (2010a). *Alternative models for prosecuting child sex offences in Australia.* Sydney: National Child Sexual Assault Reform Committee, UNSW.

Coyle, I. R., Field, D., Wilson, P., Cuthbert, C., & Miller, G. (2009). Out of the mouths of babes: The case for an increased use of expert evidence in rebuttal of sexual abuse allegations by child witnesses. *Criminal Law Journal, 33,* 139–164.

Criminal Justice and Sexual Offences Taskforce. (2006). *Responding to sexual assault: The way forward.* Sydney: Attorney-General's Department.

Davies, E., Henderson, E., & Hanna, K. (2010). Facilitating children to give best evidence: Are there better ways to challenge children's testimony? *Criminal Law Journal, 34,* 347–362.

Davies, E., Henderson, E., & Seymour, F. W. (1997). In the interests of justice? The cross-examination of child complainants of sexual abuse in criminal proceedings. *Psychiatry, Psychology and Law, 4,* 217–229.

Davies, E., & Seymour, F. W. (1998). Questioning child complainants of sexual abuse: Analysis of criminal court transcripts in New Zealand. *Psychiatry, Psychology and Law, 5,* 47–61.

Dein, J. (2015, September). *Crown Court trial in 2015: A practical update.* https://www.25bedfordrow.com/cms/document/Madrid__edited_pdf.

Dulcan, M. K., & Wiener, J. M. (2006). *Essentials of child and adolescent psychiatry.* Arlington, VA: American Psychiatric Publishing.

Eastwood, C., & Patton, W. (2002). *The experiences of child complainants of sexual abuse in the criminal justice system.* Brisbane: Queensland University of Technology. http://www.criminologyresearchcouncil.gov.au/reports/eastwood.pdf.

Eastwood, C., Kift, S., & Grace, R. (2006). Attrition in child sexual assault cases: Why Lord Chief Justice Hale got it wrong. *Journal of Judicial Administration, 16,* 81–91.

Ekman, P., O'Sullivan, M., & Frank, M. G. (1999). A few can catch a liar. *Psychological Science, 10,* 263–266.

Ellison, L. (1999). The protection of vulnerable witnesses in court: An Anglo-Dutch comparison. *International Journal of Evidence and Proof, 3,* 29–43.

Evans, A. D., Stolzenberg, S. N., Lee, K., & Lyon, T. D. (2014). Children's difficulty with indirect speech acts: Implications for questioning child witnesses. *Behavioral Sciences & the Law, 32,* 775–788.

Fisher, R. P., Vrij, A., & Leins, D. A. (2013). Does testimonial inconsistency indicate memory inaccuracy and deception? Beliefs, empirical research, and theory. In B. S. Cooper, D. Griesel, & M. Ternes (Eds.), *Applied issues in investigative interviewing, eyewitness memory, and credibility assessment* (pp. 173–189). New York: Springer.

Fogliati, R., & Bussey, K. (2014). The effects of cross-examination on children's reports of neutral and transgressive events. *Legal & Criminological Psychology, 19,* 296–315.

Fogliati, R., & Bussey, K. (2015). The effects of cross-examination on children's coached reports. *Psychology, Public Policy, and Law, 21,* 10–23.

Goodman, G. S., & Melinder, A. (2007). Child witness research and forensic interviews of young children: A review. *Legal and Criminological Psychology, 12,* 1–19.

Hale, M. (1736/1971). *Historia Placitorum Coronae* (P. R. Glazebrook, Ed., Vol. 1). London: Professional Books.

Hanna, K., Davies, E., Crothers, C., & Henderson, E. (2012). Questioning child witnesses in New Zealand's criminal justice system: Is cross-examination fair? *Psychiatry, Psychology and Law, 19,* 530–546.

Henderson, E. (2002). Persuading and controlling: The theory of cross-examination in relation to children. In H. Westcott, G. Davies, & R. Bull (Eds.), *Children's testimony: A handbook of psychological research and forensic practice* (pp. 279–293). Chicester: Wiley.

Henderson, E. (2014). All the proper protections—The Court of Appeal rewrites the rules of the cross-examination of vulnerable witnesses. *Criminal Law Review, 2,* 93–108.

Henderson, E. (2015). Taking control of cross-examination: Judges, advocates and intermediaries discuss judicial management of the cross-examination of vulnerable people. *Criminal Law Review, 3,* 181–205.

Henning, T. (2006) Control of cross-examination—A snowflake's chance in hell? *Criminal Law Journal, 30,* 133–137.

Home Office. (2011). *Achieving best evidence: Guidance on interviewing victims and witnesses.* London: Home Office.

Hopkins, A., & Boyd, R. (2010). Cross-examination of child sexual assault complainants: Concerns about the application of s 41 of the Evidence Act. *Criminal Law Journal, 34*, 149–166.

Hoyano, L. (2014). What is balanced on the scales of justice? In search of the essence of the right to a fair trial. *Criminal Law Review, 1,* 4–29.

Hoyano, L. (2015). Reforming the adversarial trial for vulnerable witnesses. *Criminal Law Review, 2,* 107–129.

Jack, F., & Zajac, R. (2014). The effect of age and reminders on witnesses' responses to cross-examination-style questioning. *Journal of Applied Research in Memory and Cognition, 3,* 1–6.

Judicial College. (2013–2019). *Equal treatment bench book.* https://www.judiciary.uk/wp-content/uploads/2018/02/equal-treatment-bench-book-february2018-v5-02mar18.pdf.

Judicial Commission of NSW. (2006–2017). *Equality before the law bench book.* Sydney: Judicial Commission of NSW. https://www.judcom.nsw.gov.au/wp-content/uploads/2016/07/Equality_before_the_Law_Bench_Book.pdf.

Judicial Commission of NSW. (2017, Update). *Criminal trial courts bench-book.* https://www.judcom.nsw.gov.au/publications/benchbks/criminal/index.html.

Kebbell, M. R., Deprez, S., & Wagstaff, G. F. (2003). The direct and cross-examination of complainants and defendants in rape trials: A quantitative analysis of question type. *Psychology, Crime & Law, 9,* 49–59.

Klemfuss, J. Z., Quas, J. A., & Lyon, T. D. (2014). Attorneys' questions and children's productivity in child sexual abuse criminal trials. *Applied Cognitive Psychology, 28,* 780–788.

Kuehnle, K., & Connell, M. (2009). *The evaluation of child sexual abuse allegations: A comprehensive guide to assessment and testimony.* Hoboken, NJ: Wiley.

Lamb, M. E., Hershkowitz, I., Orbach, Y., & Esplin, P. W. (2008). *Tell me what happened: Structured investigative interviews of child victims and witnesses.* Hoboken, NJ: Wiley-Blackwell.

Lamb, M. E., La Rooy, D. J., Malloy, L. C., & Katz, C. (2011). *Children's testimony: A handbook of psychological research and forensic practice*. Oxford: Wiley-Blackwell.

Langbein, J. H. (2003). *The origin of adversary criminal trial*. Oxford: Oxford University Press.

Ministry of Justice. (2011). *Achieving best evidence in criminal proceedings: Guidance on interviewing victims and witnesses, and guidance on using special measures*. London: Ministry of Justice.

Mugno, A. P., Klemfuss, J. Z., & Lyon, T. D. (2016). Attorney questions predict jury-eligible adult assessments of attorneys, child witnesses, and defendant guilt. *Behavioral Sciences & the Law, 34,* 178–199.

NSW Department for Women. (1996). *Heroines of fortitude: The experiences of women in court as victims of sexual assault*. Sydney: New South Wales Government.

NSW Department of Justice. (2015). *Children's champions & pre-recording of evidence*. Sydney: Department of Justice.

NSW Law Reform Commission. (2003). *Questioning of complainants by unrepresented accused in sexual offence trials* (Report No. 101). Sydney: NSW Law Reform Commission.

NSW Standing Committee on Law and Justice. (2002). *Report on child sexual assault prosecutions* (Parliamentary Paper No. 208; Report No. 22). Sydney: Parliament of NSW.

O'Neill, S., & Zajac, R. (2013a). Preparing children for cross-examination: How does intervention timing influence efficacy? *Pyschology, Public Policy, and Law, 19,* 307–320.

O'Neill, S., & Zajac, R. (2013b). The role of repeated interviewing in children's responses to cross-examination-style questioning. *British Journal of Psychology, 104,* 14–38.

Pichler, A. S., Sharman, S. J., Powell, M., Westera, N., & Goodman-Delahunty, J. (2019). Association between interview quality and child sexual abuse trial outcome. *Journal of Family Violence*, online, 1–9. https://link.springer.com/article/10.1007/s10896-019-00051-5.

Plotnikoff, J., & Woolfson, R. (2009). *Measuring up? Evaluating implementation of government commitments to young witnesses in criminal proceedings*. London: NPSCC & Nuffield Foundation.

Plotnikoff, J., & Woolfson, R. (2012). 'Kicking and screaming': The slow road to best evidence. In J. R. Spencer & M. E. Lamb (Eds.), *Children and cross-examination: Time to change the rules* (pp. 21–41). Oxford: Hart Publishing.

Porter, S., Woodworth, M., & Birt, A. R. (2000). Truth, lies, and videotape: An investigation of the ability of federal parole officers to detect deception. *Law and Human Behavior, 24,* 643–658.

Powell, M. B. (2013). An overview of current initiatives to improve child witness interviews about sexual abuse. *Current Issues in Criminal Justice, 25,* 711–720.

Powell, M. B., Bowden, P., & Mattison, M. (2014). Stakeholders' perceptions of the benefit of introducing an Australian intermediary system for vulnerable witnesses. *Australian & New Zealand Journal of Criminology, 48,* 498–512.

Powell, M. B., Westera, N. J., Goodman-Delahunty, J., & Pichler, A. S. (2016). *An evaluation of how evidence is elicited from complainants of child sexual abuse.* Sydney: Royal Commission into Institutional Responses to Child Sexual Abuse.

Queensland Law Reform Commission. (2000). *The receipt of evidence by Queensland courts: The evidence of children* (Report No. 55; Part 2). Brisbane: Queensland Law Reform Commission.

Righarts, S., O'Neill, S., & Zajac, R. (2013). Addressing the negative effect of cross-examination questioning on children's accuracy: Can we intervene? *Law and Human Behavior, 37,* 354–365.

Righarts, S., Jack, F., Zajac, R., & Hayne, H. (2014). Young children's responses to cross-examination style questioning: The effects of delay and subsequent questioning. *Psychology, Crime & Law, 21,* 274–296.

Rook, P., & Ward, R. (2016). *Rook & Ward on sexual offences: Law & practice* (5th ed.). London: Sweet & Maxwell.

Royal Commission into Institutional Responses to Child Sexual Abuse. (2017a). *Final report: Nature and cause* (Vol. 2). Sydney: Royal Commission into Institutional Responses to Child Sexual Abuse.

Royal Commission into Institutional Responses to Child Sexual Abuse. (2017b). *Criminal justice report* (Executive Summary and Parts I–II). Sydney: Royal Commission into Institutional Responses to Child Sexual Abuse.

Royal Commission into Institutional Responses to Child Sexual Abuse. (2017c). *Criminal justice report* (Parts VII–X and Appendices). Sydney: Royal Commission into Institutional Responses to Child Sexual Abuse.

Salhany, R. E. (2006). *Cross-examination: The art of the advocate.* Sydney: LexisNexis.

Sas, L. (2002). *The interaction between children's developmental capabilities and the courtroom environment: The impact on testimonial competency*. Ottawa, ON: Department of Justice.

Saywitz, K. J. (1995). Improving children's testimony: The question, the answer and the environment. In M. Zaragoza, J. R. Graham, G. C. N. Hall, R. Hirschman, & Y. S. Ben-Porat (Eds.), *Memory and testimony in the child witness* (pp. 113–140). Thousand Oaks: Sage.

Saywitz, K., Camparo, L. B., & Romanoff, A. (2010). Interviewing children in custody cases: Implications of research and policy for practice. *Behavioral Sciences & the Law, 24*, 542–562.

Scottish Executive Central Research Unit. (2002). *Vulnerable and Intimidated witnesses: Review of provisions in other jurisdictions*. Edinburgh: Scottish Executive.

Sharman, S. J., & Powell, M. B. (2012). A comparison of adult witnesses' suggestibility across various types of leading questions. *Applied Cognitive Psychology, 26*, 48–53.

Sheehan, P. (2006). *Girls like you: Four young girls, six brothers and a cultural timebomb*. Sydney: Pan Macmillan Australia.

Smart, C. (1990). Law's truth/women's experiences. In R. Graycar (Ed.), *Dissenting opinions: Feminist explorations in law and society* (pp. 1–20). Sydney: Allen & Unwin.

Snow, P. C., & Powell, M. B. (2007) *Getting the story in forensic interviews with child witnesses: Applying a story grammar framework* (Report to the Criminology Research Council Grant: CRC 04/04-05). https://www.criminologyresearchcouncil.gov.au/reports/200405-04.pdf.

Spencer, J. R., & Flin, R. (1993). *The evidence of children: The law and the psychology* (pp. 289–291). London: Blackstone Press.

Spencer, J. R., & Lamb, M. (2012). *Children and cross-examination: Time to change the rules?*. Oxford: Hart Publishing.

Stolzenberg, S. N., & Lyon, T. D. (2014). How attorneys question children about the dynamics of sexual abuse and disclosure in criminal trials. *Psychology, Public Policy and Law, 20*, 19–30.

Taylor, N. (2007). *Juror attitudes and biases in sexual assault cases* (Trends and Issues in Crime and Criminal Justice, No. 344). Canberra: Australian Institute of Criminology.

Valentine, T., & Maras, K. (2011). The effect of cross-examination on the accuracy of adult eyewitness testimony. *Applied Cognitive Psychology, 25*, 554–561.

Victorian Law Reform Commission. (2004). *Sexual offences* (Final Report). Melbourne: Victorian Law Reform Commission.

Vrij, A., Granhag, P., & Porter, S. (2010). Pitfalls and opportunities in nonverbal and verbal lie detection. *Psychological Science in the Public Interest, 11,* 89–121.

Westcott, H. L., & Page, M. (2002). Cross-examination, sexual abuse and child witness identity. *Child Abuse Review, 11,* 137–152.

Westera, N., Zydervelt, S., Kaladelfos, A., & Zajac, R. (2017). Sexual assault complainants on the stand: A historical comparison of courtroom questioning. *Psychology, Crime & Law, 23,* 15–31.

Wigmore, J. H. (1974). *Evidence in Trials at Common Law (Volume 5).* Boston: Little Brown.

Zajac, R., & Cannan, P. (2009). Cross-examination of sexual assault complainants: A developmental comparison. *Psychiatry, Psychology and Law, 16,* S36–S54.

Zajac, R., & Hayne, H. (2003). I Don't Think That's What Really Happened: The effect of cross-examination on the accuracy of children's reports. *Journal of Experimental Psychology, 9,* 187–195.

Zajac, R., & Hayne, H. (2006). The negative effect of cross-examination style questioning on children's accuracy: Older children not immune. *Applied Cognitive Psychology, 20,* 3–16.

Zajac, R., Irvine, B., Ingram, J. M., & Jack, F. (2016). The diagnostic value of children's responses to cross-examination questions. *Behavioral Sciences & the Law, 34,* 160–177.

Zajac, R., Gross, J., & Hayne, H. (2003). Asked and Answered: Questioning children in the courtroom. *Psychiatry, Psychology and Law, 10,* 199–209.

Zajac, R., Jury, E., & O'Neill, S. (2009). The role of psychosocial factors in young children's responses to cross-examination style questioning. *Applied Cognitive Psychology, 23,* 918–935.

Zajac, R., O'Neill, S., & Hayne, H. (2012). Disorder in the courtroom? Child witnesses under cross-examination. *Developmental Review, 32,* 181–204.

Zydervelt, S., Zajac, R., Kaladelfos, A., & Westera, N. (2017). Lawyers' strategies for cross-examining rape complainants: Have we moved beyond the 1950s. *British Journal of Criminology, 57,* 551–569.

9

Contemporary Reforms to Cross-Examination

1 Judicial Intervention: The Best Control of Cross-Examination?

The review of the literature in Chapter 8 shows that cross-examination is used, and allowed to be used, as a method for producing inaccurate evidence that favours the defence case. The question is whether it is in the public interest for jurors to make decisions based on manufactured inaccuracies, particularly since studies in Chapters 4 and 6 show that cross-examination which confirms pre-existing beliefs on the part of jurors will influence jury decision-making.

Arguably, a fair trial from the point of view of victims and the community must encompass methods for preventing the contamination of a complainant's evidence. But how can the cross-examination process be reformed at the same time as ensuring a fair trial for the defendant?

It may have been hoped that the introduction of measures allowing sexual assault complainants to pre-record their evidence or give live evidence from a remote room via CCTV would protect them 'from the full rigour of adversarial style-proceedings' (Ellison, 1999: 34). Despite these improvements, a complainant's emotional welfare is not prioritised during cross-examination, as it would be in a trauma-informed system

A. Cossins, *Closing the Justice Gap for Adult and Child Sexual Assault*,
https://doi.org/10.1057/978-1-137-32051-3_9

(discussed in Chapter 11), even if judges have the power to ensure a complainant is not subject to improper forms of cross-examination.

In other words, the trial process has *not* been structured to protect the welfare of sexual assault complainants. Although intermediaries in E&W (see below) would have some awareness of a child's emotional state when they are advising a court on a child's ability to comprehend lawyers' questions, there are no specific court personnel who are responsible for monitoring the welfare of complainants during their court appearance.

While some cultural change has been achieved with a myriad of legislative initiatives such as the introduction of CCTV, remote rooms, pre-recording of evidence and support persons, the style and patterns of cross-examination have remained unchanged in most jurisdictions (Andrews, Lamb, & Lyon, 2014; Cashmore & Trimboli, 2005, 2006; Klemfuss, Quas, & Lyon, 2014; Plotnikoff & Woolfson, 2012; Powell, Westera, Goodman-Delahunty, & Pichler, 2016; Westera, Zydervelt, Kaladelfos, & Zajac, 2017; Zydervelt, Zajac, Kaladelfos, & Westera, 2017), with no evidence to show that complainants' susceptibility to suggestive styles of cross-examination is reduced through vulnerable witness protections.

Although E&W stand out as an exception, these jurisdictions are still in the process of changing the culture of the courtroom for child complainants through the use of intermediaries and mandatory education of judges. Judges who sit on sexual assault trials in E&W must undergo a three-day, residential course (the Serious Sexual Offences Seminar) every three years which has been found to be effective in influencing judicial practice (Rumney & Fenton, 2011).

In E&W, this cultural change has been extended to adults in sexual assault trials since special measures are available to various categories of witnesses, including, in addition to those under the age of 18 years:

- those who suffer from a mental disorder or physical disability/disorder (s 16(2), YJCE Act);
- those in fear or distress about testifying (s 17, YJCE Act);
- adult complainants of sexual offences or trafficking/exploitation offences (s 17(4) YJCE Act); and

- witnesses to serious offences (homicide and other offences involving a firearm or knife).

This means that an adult sexual assault complainant is also eligible for any of the special measures listed in ss 23–30 of the YJCE (such as evidence via video-link), although intermediaries are not routinely used for adult witnesses. However, the *Equal Treatment Benchbook* makes it clear that courts and tribunals also have a responsibility to safeguard the interests of vulnerable adults who are involved in court processes: 'the best interests of the witness are the paramount consideration' such that courts and tribunals 'are expected to adapt normal trial procedure to facilitate the effective participation of witnesses' (Judicial College, 2018: 2–10; 2–11; see also HMCPSI & HMIC, 2012).

The critical question, therefore, is: 'to what extent [should] the normal methods of cross-examination to attack a witness's credit … be restricted to give proper recognition of the [complainant's] particular vulnerability' (Sleight, 2007: 3)? For example, is judicial intervention the best way of preventing the improper cross-examination of complainants?

Judicial officers are often reluctant to intervene to protect witnesses in criminal trials (ALRC & HREOC, 1997: 346; Cashmore & Trimboli, 2005; Hanna, Davies, Crothers, & Henderson, 2012; Henderson, 2015b; NSWSCLJ, 2002: 70–75; Powell et al., 2016) and may tolerate, fail to recognise or perpetuate the abuse experienced by complainants in sexual assault trials. In Australia, judicial intervention in cross-examination is highly variable, with few interventions regarding the well-being of complainants (Powell et al., 2016). The vast majority of interventions in 120 adult and child sexual assault trials, which ranged from 0 to 162 per trial (average = 10.78), were about the form of a question (such as a request for rephrasing) while interventions regarding the substance of a question were rare (Powell et al., 2016: 237). As well, interventions did not differ significantly according to the age of the complainant (ibid.: 237).

However, it is necessary to consider the extent to which judges can be expected to intervene to protect vulnerable witnesses and whether they should be relied upon as the only control on cross-examination in sexual assault trials.

It cannot be assumed that judicial officers are themselves immune to rape myths and misconceptions about adult and child complainants. For example, one study found that Swedish judges were more sceptical about the reliability of children's evidence than Swedish police officers (Granhag, Strömwall, & Hartwig, 2005). Although there are no similar studies in Australia and E&W, such data raise questions about the attitudes and beliefs of judges in relation to the reliability and credibility of complainants as witnesses and the possibility that judges who are sceptical about children's evidence will be unlikely to intervene in cross-examination that confirms their beliefs. In relation to a group of Finnish judges, Korkman, Svanbäck, Finnilä, and Santt (2014) found that 40% of judges believed that it was appropriate to use suggestive techniques for interviewing children, suggesting that they would consider evidence elicited via leading questions to be reliable. The vast majority (90.3%) also believed that it is possible to persuade a child to lie about being abused.

A more robust view of children's evidence was expressed by the EWCA in *R v Barker* [2010] EWCA Crim 4, [40], a case in which the complainant was under the age of 3 years when she first reported sexual abuse by the defendant:

> in our collective experience the age of a witness is not determinative on his or her ability to give truthful and accurate evidence. Like adults some children will provide truthful and accurate testimony, and some will not. However children are not miniature adults, … and [are] to be treated and judged for what they are, not what they will [be] … [N]one of the characteristics of childhood, and none of the special measures which apply to the evidence of children carry with them the implicit stigma that children should be deemed in advance to be somehow less reliable than adults. … If competent, … the child witness starts off on the basis of equality with every other witness.[1]

[1]The essence of this paragraph in *Barker* [2010] EWCA Crim 4 was repeated by the trial judge in a Victorian case (in Australia): *CMG v R* [2011] VSCA 416. On appeal, the Court noted that there could be no valid complaint about this direction to the jury about how to approach the evidence of a child witness.

In *Barker*, the defendant had argued that he had not received a fair trial because his counsel had been unable to effectively cross-examine the complainant due to her young age (four and a half years) and that a conviction based on the evidence of a young child is inherently unsafe. The EWCA did not agree with the age-old arguments about the unreliability of children's evidence:

> what we are being asked to consider is an underlying submission that no such conviction can ever be safe. The short answer is that it is open to a properly directed jury … about the dangers and difficulties of doing so, to reach a safe conclusion on the basis of the evidence of a single competent witness, whatever his or her age, and whatever his or her disability. … [T]he ABE interview shows an utterly guileless child, too naive and innocent for any deficiencies in her evidence to remain undiscovered, speaking in matter of fact terms. She was indeed a compelling as well as a competent witness. On all the evidence, this jury was entitled to conclude that the allegation was proved. *Unless we simply resuscitate the tired and outdated misconceptions about the evidence of children*, there is no justifiable basis for interfering with the verdict. (*R v Barker* [2010] EWCA Crim 4, [51]–[52]; emphasis added)

However, it cannot be expected that these views are shared by all judicial officers. As well, the expected neutrality of judicial officers hinders the extent to which they are willing to intervene in cross-examination since undue interference is likely to lead to an appeal if the defendant is convicted:

> the trial judge's real dilemma is that to halt cross-examination … is a hazardous exercise because the appeal court is very likely to say, 'Well, the accused was not given an adequate and fair trial because this was a relevant line of questioning and counsel for the accused was not given adequate opportunity to pursue it'. (Parliament of Victoria, Crime Prevention Committee, 1995: 188; quoting Judge Waldron)

Even in E&W, where many judges have embraced what is known, post-*Barker*, as the '"best evidence" theory of cross-examination' (Henderson, 2015b: 936), Henderson's (2015b) interviews with judges found that there is still a wide variety of approaches to managing and intervening in cross-examination even in a context where it is widely acknowledged that achieving 'best evidence' from a child should be the goal of the cross-examiner.

While there was no evidence that judges in E&W had become inquisitors post-*Barker* (Henderson, 2015b: 944), it appears that judges still use their powers to intervene idiosyncratically which creates different levels of 'fairness' for vulnerable witnesses and different standards of 'best evidence'. Approaches ranged from asking counsel to rephrase questions, restricting certain questions, asking questions themselves to clarify a witness's evidence, imposing time limits on cross-examiners but in an ad hoc manner with no formal criteria apparent. Advocates 'were more likely to complain that judges are still not interventionist enough rather than that they are too interventionist' (Henderson, 2015b: 945).

However, the 'game' of cross-examination and the will to win by advocates appears to dominate approaches to cross-examination, another difficulty for judicial control, particularly for untrained or non-interventionist judges:

> a number of respondents described opportunistic advocates taking advantage of any loophole or weakness in the judge's conduct of the trial, such as a failure to set explicit pre-trial directions. A silk described a case in which: 'There was a pretty weak judge who never set any ground rules … [and] didn't enforce them. I was asked to give a list of questions but I thought of them as examples and in court pretty much abandoned them.' … The continuation of this thinking should be a warning to reformers. (Henderson, 2015b: 947)

All in all, Henderson (2015c: 676) concluded from her interviews of advocates that the majority 'are not sufficiently skilled' when cross-examining vulnerable witnesses, with 'a small group of advocates who are especially poor and often aggressive cross-examiners'.

Unless judges who sit on sexual assault trials receive specific training about the cross-examination effect, judicial intervention to protect complainants is likely to remain an unreliable and ad hoc method of preventing the manipulation of complainant evidence by defence counsel. Even with intervention, defence counsel can refuse to be controlled all of which leads to the conclusion that legislation which requires judges to control cross-examination will not necessarily work.

However, Henderson (2015c: 676–677) criticised my early proposals for legislative reform to control cross-examination:

> Many cross-examination reform proposals circulating at present tend to look to the legislature to either set specific standards for questioning [citing Cossins, 2012] or to take the questioning of vulnerable people out of the hands of lawyers altogether. However, the latter would require a drastic and costly restructuring of the criminal justice system while the former are not only repetitive (since there are already ample common law and statutory rules on cross-examination), but the fact that we so often ignore the existing rules makes it easy to predict the fate of any others we might enact. It is practitioners, and not the legislature, who govern what happens in cross-examination. (footnotes omitted)

Instead, Henderson (2015c: 677) considers that 'the English experience suggests that the more effective way to achieve reform is for the senior judiciary to take the lead role'. However, Henderson (2015c) did not acknowledge the fact that existing controls over cross-examination are weak, piecemeal and generalist and that my suggestions for legislative reform were targeted towards the cross-examination of children specifically and were proposed in a framework which would involve increasing the role of intermediaries to ensure the implementation of such reforms (see Chapters 10 and 11). If it were possible for the senior judiciary to step up that would enhance such an implementation but reliance on the judiciary alone is unlikely to see any significant changes in other countries since it very much relies on the idiosyncratic values of existing judges, as seen below, in relation to the positive duty on judges in NSW to prevent improper questions.

2 Contemporary Reforms to Cross-Examination

Although more accurate evidence is elicited from both adults and children via open-ended questions, such questions may not always be practical during the constraints of a criminal trial. How then can courts maximise changes towards the truth during a complainant's cross-examination by a defence lawyer?

2.1 Controlling Improper Questions

Recommendations for reform of cross-examination have tended to focus on educating judges, with the expectation they will become more interventionist, and amending professional conduct rules in the hope that lawyers will obey them (ALRC & HREOC, 1997; Boyd & Hopkins, 2010; Caruso, 2012).

In 2002, the NSW government considered that these controls were insufficient to control improper cross-examination. As a result, s 275A of the *Criminal Procedure Act* 1986 (NSW) was enacted, which for the first time in Australia, imposed a *positive* duty on judges to intervene in relation to a range of improper questions, irrespective of whether or not the prosecution or defence raises an objection.

This reform was later adopted under s 41 of the Australian Uniform Evidence Legislation (UEL) to 'ensure that best evidence is received by the courts' from vulnerable witnesses (ALRC, NSWLRC, & VLRC, 2005: 153). It was considered that this type of duty would be necessary to overcome judges' long-standing reluctance to intervene in cross-examination.

The general applicability of s 41 to all witnesses, not just vulnerable ones under the NSW version of the UEL (*Evidence Act 1995*), was based on the belief that it would be difficult for trial judges to determine the mental, physical or other vulnerability of a particular witness and that lengthy argument might ensue about that vulnerability. This mandatory provision has since been adopted in five other Australian jurisdictions, although in Victoria and the Northern Territory the provision only applies to vulnerable witnesses.[2]

Section 41 has expanded the type of improper questions to be disallowed, taking into account the tone and manner of the cross-examiner and the use of particular stereotypes. As set out below, the power under s 41, as it applies in NSW, is extensive and enables judges to prevent improper questions irrespective of whether a party to proceedings objects:

1. The court must disallow a question put to a witness in cross-examination, or inform the witness that it need not be answered, if the court is of the opinion that the question (referred to as a disallowable question):

   (a) is misleading or confusing;
   (b) is unduly annoying, harassing, intimidating, offensive, oppressive, humiliating or repetitive;
   (c) is put to the witness in a manner or tone that is belittling, insulting or otherwise inappropriate; or
   (d) has no basis other than a stereotype (for example, a stereotype based on the witness's sex, race, culture, ethnicity, age or mental, intellectual or physical disability).

2. Without limiting the matters the court may take into account for the purposes of subsection (1), it is to take into account:

   (a) any relevant condition or characteristic of the witness of which the court is, or is made, aware, including age, education, ethnic and cultural background, gender, language background and skills, level of maturity and understanding and personality;

[2]These jurisdictions are known as the Uniform Evidence Legislation jurisdictions: see *Evidence Act 1995* (Cth), s 41; *Evidence Act 2011* (ACT), s 41; *Evidence (National Uniform Legislation) Act 2013* (NT), s 41; *Evidence Act 2008* (Vic), s 41; *Evidence Act 2001* (Tas), 41. See also *Evidence Act 1929* (SA), s 25. In NSW, new Bar Association Rules were gazetted to prevent barristers asking sexual assault complainants improper questions and to encourage them to take into account 'any particular vulnerability of the witness' in the way questions are put (Rules 35A and 35B were gazetted on 30 May 2008).

(b) any mental, intellectual or physical disability of which the court is, or is made, aware and to which the witness is, or appears to be, subject;

(c) the context in which the question is put, including:

(i) the nature of the proceeding;

(ii) in a criminal proceeding—the nature of the offence to which the proceeding relates; and

(iii) the relationship (if any) between the witness and any other party to the proceeding.

3. A question is not a disallowable question merely because:

(a) the question challenges the truthfulness of the witness or the consistency or accuracy of any statement made by the witness; or

(b) the question requires the witness to discuss a subject that could be considered distasteful to, or private by, the witness.

4. A party may object to a question put to a witness on the ground that it is a disallowable question.
5. However, the duty imposed on the court by this section applies whether or not an objection is raised to a particular question.
6. A failure by the court to disallow a question under this section, or to inform the witness that it need not be answered, does not affect the admissibility in evidence of any answer given by the witness in response to the question.

A large degree of discretion still remains under the above provision because it is a subjective judgement as to whether a question *is* misleading or confusing; whether a question is put to a witness in a manner or tone that is belittling, insulting or otherwise inappropriate, or whether a question is based on stereotype. Questions that are annoying, harassing, intimidating, offensive, oppressive, humiliating or repetitive have to be *unduly* so, requiring another value judgement by the trial judge. Boyd and Hopkins (2010: 150) concluded from the interviews of six prosecutors and defence lawyers that 'drawing the line between acceptable and unacceptable cross examination is not simply a matter of legislative definition … it is a question of perspective'.

After the enactment of this positive duty on trial judges to disallow improper questions, interviewees considered that rates of judicial intervention to control cross-examination had not increased 'either at the request of the prosecutor or of the court's own motion'. While '[o]ne prosecutor said that there had been a slight increase …. this had "tapered off". Overall, all practitioners felt there had been no lasting change' (Boyd & Hopkins, 2010: 161).

While the four defence interviewees 'asserted no change to their own overall style and approach to cross-examining children' since the enactment of the positive duty, prosecutors perceived some change in the approach of the defence lawyers they had encountered in day to day trials. Nonetheless, they thought the changes were not specifically due to the mandatory duty but greater awareness of 'the trauma that victims/witnesses endure in the trial process' (Boyd & Hopkins, 2010: 161). The study concluded that:

> with no reported change in the frequency of judicial intervention and little if any reported change in conduct of cross-examination, … [the mandatory duty] failed to achieve the purpose for which it was enacted. Far from setting a new standard in cross-examination, [it] did not provide any additional protection for child sexual assault complainants from the trauma of being questioned by the defendant's lawyer. (Boyd & Hopkins, 2010: 162)

Because the interviewees considered that improper questions were generally not asked of children by defence counsel, the authors concluded that there was a clear disconnect between interviewees' perceptions of an improper question, the empirical research and the trauma experienced by children undergoing cross-examination which amounted to 'a discord between a trial-centred and child-centred interpretations of improper questioning'. Not surprisingly, lawyers taking a 'trial-centred' approach considered that:

> if a question is required in order to robustly challenge a witness it will not be improper, regardless of its traumatic effect. Accordingly, the conflict between the wellbeing of the child and the dictates of the principle of fair trial is to some extent intractable. (Boyd & Hopkins, 2010: 163)

In fact, interviewees and the authors endorsed the view that the mandatory duty preventing improper questions was:

> drafted such that the likelihood that a question will produce trauma for the child does not, of itself, demonstrate its impropriety. ... Indeed, there is nothing in the drafting of [s 41] to support a presumption that a question is improper if it is likely to produce trauma'. (ibid.: 163–164)

The alternative—a child-centred approach—requires more than the occasional intervention by trial judges in an otherwise uncontrolled defence cross-examination. As discussed in Chapter 11, the questioning of traumatised sexual assault complainants requires a trauma-informed approach to the adversarial system since the study by Boyd and Hopkins (2010), as well as numerous inquiries and cases, reveal that judges and trial counsel have a profound lack of awareness of the vulnerability of child complainants of sexual abuse and the effect of the trial process on their ability to comprehend and answer questions asked of them:

> Such a failure ... is explicable on the basis that legal participants to a trial have lived, breathed and absorbed the norms of the adversarial system. Their roles have been defined by it, and they are so long practised in the arena that their lens has become the adversarial lens, to the virtual exclusion of other perspectives. (Boyd & Hopkins, 2010: 164)

By contrast, as Chapter 11 explains, a trauma-informed system recognises that its clients or participants are psychologically vulnerable, so that root and branch cultural change is required in relation to the provision of services or the treatment of clients within a system, be it a system delivering psychological services or a criminal justice system.

The main problem with enacting a mandatory duty to disallow improper questions is that it is, largely, unenforceable. If a judge fails to disallow an improper question, the decision is not open to appeal, unless the failure occurs in a pre-trial hearing where an interlocutory appeal can be made by the prosecution.[3] At trial, however, there are no consequences for judges if the obligation to disallow is ignored. Unless judges are aware of the consequences of allowing improper questions to be asked of vulnerable witnesses, non-interventionist judges are likely to remain so: '[t]he adversarial nature of the system will disincline a judge to intervene, regardless of the how much power is bestowed on them to do so' (Caruso, 2012: 204).[4]

Based on the case law to date, it appears that s 41 is more likely to be used against prosecutors than defence counsel. In *Skelton v R* [2015] NSWCCA 320, the defendant appealed on the grounds that '[t]hat a miscarriage of justice was occasioned by the manner in which the Crown Prosecutor cross-examined the appellant'[5] who was apparently 'suffering from schizophrenia, was taking antipsychotic medication and was affected by drowsiness as a side-effect of the medication'.[6]

The appellant argued that given his mental state, 'the Crown Prosecutor was required, in accordance with the requirements of … s 41, to cross-examine him with an appropriate degree of caution and restraint' including:

> fram[ing] the questions put in cross-examination clearly and unambiguously so as not to cause avoidable confusion; refrain[ing] from unduly repetitive or aggressive questioning and refrain[ing] from sarcastic or ridiculing comment; refrain[ing] from asking questions with inadequate or inaccurate factual foundations; and avoid[ing] compound questions and argumentative questions or comments.[7]

Nonetheless, none of the objectionable questions used by the prosecutor were considered by the NSWCCA to amount to a miscarriage of justice.

---

[3]For example, an appeal under s 5F(2) of the *Criminal Appeal Act 1912* (NSW).

[4]The need for cultural change within the adversarial trial is discussed in Chapter 11 in the context of trauma-informed systems.

[5][2015] NSWCCA 320, [35] (Beazley P and Davis J).

[6]Ibid., [39].

[7]Ibid.

Because it appears this mandatory judicial duty is exercised sparingly and varies from judge to judge (Boyd & Hopkins, 2010), relying on judicial discretion is not the most effective way to create a non-traumatising system for sexual assault complainants. For example, children's developmental and cognitive abilities, as well as their vulnerability to suggestion and confusion and the effects of PTSD on a complainant's performance in the witness box (discussed in Chapter 11), is specialised knowledge of which few judges and prosecutors will be aware.

Reform of the cross-examination process ought to be guided by the public interest in ensuring verdicts are based on a complainant's best evidence, such that any discretionary approach to disallowing improper questions needs to be discarded. For example, the Judicial College (2018: 2–2) in E&W observes that:

> Accommodating a vulnerable person's needs (as required by case law, the Equality Act 2010, the European Convention on Human Rights, the UN Convention on the Rights of the Child, the UN Convention on the Rights of Persons with Disabilities) requires the court or tribunal to adopt a flexible approach in order to deal with cases justly. Child witnesses … have been shown to experience much higher levels of communication difficulty in the justice system than was previously recognised. This is also likely to be the case for vulnerable adult witnesses and the elderly. … Children and vulnerable adults under stress can function at a lower level, making it harder for them to remember accurately and think clearly.

Furthermore:

> If justice is to be done to the vulnerable witness … a radical departure from the traditional style of advocacy may be necessary. There is strong support from the higher courts for detailed constraints on the length, tone and wording of cross-examination where required. (Judicial College, 2018: 2–4)

If, as the research literature indicates, oral evidence can become inconsistent, skewed or inaccurate because of the *method* used to elicit that evidence during cross-examination, then the legitimate public interest in the goals of justice in relation to sexual assault are undermined.

According to the trauma-informed principles discussed in Chapter 11, improvements to the cross-examination process are also required to preserve a complainant's emotional and mental health, as well as to improve the community's perceptions of the fairness of the trial, the willingness to report and the complainant's overall participation in the trial process.

At the heart of the problem, is how best to change the traumatic culture of the adversarial system. It appears that judges require in-court assistance in order to recognise the vulnerability of witnesses and the improper nature of questions put to such witnesses. For example, as discussed below, intermediaries have been introduced in South Africa, E&W, Northern Ireland and in two Australian jurisdictions, NSW and Victoria, although other jurisdictions have less formal options for witness assistance. In Norway's inquisitorial system, independent experts conduct the entire examination of vulnerable witnesses. In several adversarial jurisdictions, including NSW and E&W, trained interviewers conduct the initial forensic interview which is then played to the court as the vulnerable witness's evidence-in-chief.[8]

There is also a scheme for intermediaries in Canada although it appears to be limited to witnesses with speech and language disabilities and is run by a not-for-profit charity called Communication Disabilities Access Canada.[9]

Below I discuss those jurisdictions where intermediaries have been introduced as part of a pilot scheme subject to evaluation. They are all similar in terms of their role and function since the schemes in NSW and Northern Ireland are based on the scheme that operates in E&W. However, the Northern Ireland scheme is the broadest since it applies to both vulnerable witnesses and suspects/defendants, while the NSW scheme only applies to child witnesses.

[8]See *Criminal Procedure Act 1986* (NSW), ss 306R, 306U; YJCE Act, s 27.

[9]See www.access-to-justice-org; accessed 3 September 2018.

2.2 Intermediaries: E&W

Provision for the use of intermediaries is set out under the YJCE Act, c 23, ss 16–17, 29, which gives a court the power to order the examination of vulnerable witnesses using an intermediary during live or pre-recorded evidence-in-chief, cross-examination and re-examination. Either the police or the Crown Prosecution Service (CPS) will seek the services of a registered intermediary from the register of intermediaries managed by the Witness Intermediary Team.[10]

Examination by an intermediary is one of the various special measures[11] that are available under the YJCE Act to vulnerable witnesses, the categories of which are outlined above. The intermediary service was established between February 2004 and June 2005 in six pathfinder areas in E&W. After a positive evaluation of the impact of intermediaries within the criminal justice system (Plotnikoff & Woolfson, 2007), the Home Office Minister formally announced a national roll-out of the service, although a type of intermediary (called an interlocutor) had been recommended as far back as 1989 in the Pigot Report (Home Office, 1989) which considered the treatment of vulnerable witnesses in the criminal justice system and again in 1998 in the *Speaking Up for Justice Report* (Home Office, 1998).

With the intermediary scheme covering all 43 police and prosecution areas in E&W, by 2007 there was a national register of 150 intermediaries with a wide range of communication skills. By 2016, there were 'approximately 200 Registered Intermediaries' while requests for intermediaries were averaging 530 per month, with two-thirds of those requests concerning a complainant in a sex offence case (Cooper & Mattison, 2017: 355). In 2018, the Government had made a commitment to increase the number of Registered Intermediaries by 25% (HM Government, 2018: 31).

---

[10]www.theadvocatesgateway.org/intermediaries; accessed 26 February 2018.

[11]Under ss 23–41 of the YJCE Act, these special measures include: screens, evidence by live link, evidence given in private, removal of wigs and gowns (s 26), video-recorded evidence-in-chief, video-recorded cross-examination and re-examination, examination of a witness through an intermediary, aids to communication, protection of witnesses from cross-examination by the accused in person, restriction on evidence and questions about a complainant's sexual behaviour.

The backgrounds of most intermediaries include speech and language therapists, psychologists, occupational therapists and those involved in the disciplines of health and education (Plotnikoff & Woolfson, 2007: 3). Within the criminal justice system, they are trained to be a 'communication specialist whose primary responsibility is to enable complete, coherent and accurate communication' on the part of the vulnerable witness by advising the judicial officer about the witness's communications vulnerabilities and needs, as well as intervening during questioning to 'prevent miscommunication' (Judicial College, 2018: 2–22). The duties of an intermediary are to the court and they do not act on behalf of witnesses, the prosecution or the defence. The intermediary must make a declaration of faithful performance and, under s 29(7) of the YJCE Act, *the Perjury Act* applies to a person acting as an intermediary in the same way that the Act applies to someone acting as an interpreter in a proceeding.

Although s 29(2) of the YJCE Act envisages that an intermediary will communicate with the vulnerable witness on behalf of the court by interpreting 'questions put to the witness, and to any persons asking such questions, the answers given by the witness in reply to them, and to explain such questions or answers so far as necessary to enable them to be understood by the witness or person in question', in practice, intermediaries have an advisory role only (Cooper & Mattison, 2017). Interestingly, '[m]ost of what an intermediary does in a case has evolved through their training and the development of good practice. Only a small part is found in statute' (ibid.: 355).

Once an intermediary is appointed, a ground rules hearing will determine the manner of questioning of the vulnerable witness and any limits on cross-examination (Judicial College, 2018: 2–26), with rules of the court requiring the presence of the intermediary at the hearing (Criminal Procedure Rules 2015, 3.9(7)(a)). This amendment arose after evidence that some hearings were '"perfunctory" or … treated by the court as a mere "tick box" exercise' (Cooper & Mattison, 2017: 364).

In *Lubemba* [2014] EWCA 2064, the EWCA observed that courts are now:

> required to take every reasonable step to encourage and facilitate the [participation] of vulnerable witnesses … in the trial process. … [I]t is best practice to hold hearings in advance of the trial to ensure the smooth running of the trial, to give any special measures directions and to set the ground rules for the treatment of a vulnerable witness. We would expect a ground rules hearing in every case involving a vulnerable witness … [which] should cover … the general care of the witness, if, when and where the witness is to be shown their video interview, when, where and how the parties (and the judge …) intend to introduce themselves to the witness, the length of questioning and frequency of breaks and the nature of the questions to be asked. So as to avoid any unfortunate misunderstanding at trial, it would be an entirely reasonable step for a judge … to invite defence advocates to reduce their questions to writing in advance.[12]

Thus, rule 3.9(7) of the Criminal Procedure Rules 2015 now requires a court to invite representations from the parties and the intermediary. The court must set ground rules for the conduct of questioning although judges are at liberty to choose procedures appropriate to the case, such as the manner and duration of questioning, questions that may or may not be asked, restrictions on multiple advocates and the use of communication aids.

A ground rules checklist, below, has been created by the Courts and Tribunal Judiciary website[13] which requires both the prosecution and the defence to consider a number of issues pre-trial:

Directions to both advocates at 'ground rules' discussions

- Adapt questions to the child's developmental stage, enabling *this* child's 'best evidence'
- Ask short, simple questions (one idea at a time)
- Follow a logical sequence
- Speak slowly, pause and allow the child enough time to process questions (for younger children, almost twice as much)
- Allow full opportunity to answer

---

[12] [2014] EWCA 2064, [42]–[43].

[13] *Judicial College Bench Checklist: Young Witness Cases*, January 2012 (https://www.judiciary.uk/publications/jc-bench-checklist-young-wit-cases/; accessed 21 June 2018).

- Avoid question types which may produce unreliable answers. 'Tag' questions (e.g. 'He didn't touch you, did he?') are particularly complex. Put more directly e.g. 'Did Jim touch you?' (and if the answer is 'yes') 'How did Jim touch you?' (Use name not pronoun)
- Avoid allegations of misconduct without reasonable grounds. Being accused of lying, particularly if repeated, may cause a child to give inaccurate answers or to agree simply to bring questioning to an end
- Do not ask children to give their address aloud unless for a specific reason
- Do not ask children to demonstrate intimate touching on their body. Use a body diagram
- How the child is to be questioned about matters arising from third-party disclosure
- How defence case is to be put. For younger children, inform jury of evidence believed to undermine credibility, but do not necessarily address in detailed cross-examination. (see *R v Barker* [2010] EWCA Crim 4)

The intermediary can be involved at both stages of witness questioning: the police interview (known as the Achieving Best Evidence [ABE] interview) and then examination in court (Home Office, 2011; Plotnikoff & Woolfson, 2015). In order to comply with the principles of Achieving Best Evidence, the ABE interview has six main stages (Home Office, 2011: 70–77):

1. rapport building using neutral topics;
2. explanation of the purpose of the interview and how it will be conducted;
3. after 'ground rules have been explained … the interviewer should advise the witness to give a truthful and accurate account of any incident they describe';
4. initiation of 'an uninterrupted free narrative account of the incident/event(s) from the witness by means of an open-ended invitation';
5. questioning using open-ended or specific closed questions based upon what the witness has already narrated, dividing this phase into manageable topics; and
6. closure.

The intermediary is not a joint interviewer but may play 'an active part to facilitate communication, speaking alongside the interviewer' if the child is very young or developmentally delayed (Plotnikoff & Woolfson, 2015: 86). The intermediary will assess the vulnerable witness's communication abilities and needs before producing a report for the court which 'provide[s] detailed recommendations … on what to say and do when communicating with the witness' (Ministry of Justice, 2015a: 53), although the assessment 'must not involve any discussion about the case or the evidence' (Cooper & Mattison, 2017: 358). In addition, the report may contain 'recommendations about managing the vulnerable person's emotions' (ibid.: 359). This report will then form the basis for a subsequent application by the CPS for a Special Measures Direction[14] which seeks the court's approval for the use of an intermediary during witness questioning.

This means that intermediaries are not mandated for vulnerable witnesses since the CPS must make an application for the appointment of an intermediary.[15] In E&W, this has led to:

> poor levels of awareness about the benefits of intermediary use. For example, intermediaries appointed post-interview often find that a written statement has been taken from witnesses who do not understand them and cannot read them. (Judicial College, 2018: 2–23)

The lack of a mandated intermediary in court has also led to CPS decisions that an intermediary is not needed, only to see the vulnerable witness unable to cope with cross-examination and unable to continue with giving evidence (Plotnikoff & Woolfson, 2015).

If the use of an intermediary is approved by the court, the intermediary will attend 'the witness's court familiarisation visit to assist with communication' and will advise the Witness Service on any issues concerning the witness's welfare. In addition, ground rules hearings

---

[14]See Application for a Special Measures Direction under the Criminal Procedure Rules, rule 29.3 and 29.10; http://www.justice.gov.uk/courts/procedure-rules/criminal/docs/crim-pr-form-part29-application-for-special-measures.pdf; accessed 26 February 2018.

[15]This is also the case in South Africa under s 170A(1) and (7) of the *Criminal Procedure Act 1977*.

'are now a requirement in intermediary cases' and even in cases with vulnerable witnesses that do not involve intermediaries (Plotnikoff & Woolfson, 2015: 109; citing *R v Lubemba* [2014] EWCA Crim 2064 [42]):

> 'Ground rules' for questioning must be discussed between the court, the advocates and the intermediary before the witness gives evidence, to establish (a) how questions should be put to help the witness understand them, and (b) how the proposed intermediary will alert the court if the witness has not understood, or needs a break.[16]

In addition, the judge might include a vetting procedure, in that the intermediary is given the task of reviewing the cross-examination questions prior to cross-examination taking place. As Cooper and Mattison (2017: 359) acknowledge, '[t]his practice enables questions to be prepared and framed according to the communication needs and abilities of the [witness], and minimises the extent to which the intermediary is likely to need to intervene during cross-examination'. Hoyano (2015: 115) criticised just such a suggestion made by this author as 'hopelessly impractical and cumbersome for live testimony'. In a 2009 article, I had recommended the following for Australian courts:

> a court-appointed intermediary … trained in child cognition, language, and development to assess defence questions during the cross-examination of a child complainant. The role of this intermediary would be to advise the trial judge on whether or not each question put in cross-examination is age-inappropriate, suggestive in content, misleading, confusing, oppressive, intimidating, humiliating, repetitive, or unable to be understood by a child of the particular complainant's age (the intermediary's training providing an objective basis for this advice). In addition, the intermediary would be able to advise the court about how to rephrase a particular question so that the child can understand it. (Cossins, 2009: 101–102)

[16]See Application for a Special Measures Direction under the Criminal Procedure Rules, Rules 29.3 and 29.10; http://www.justice.gov.uk/courts/procedure-rules/criminal/docs/crim-pr-form-part29-application-for-special-measures.pdf; accessed 26 February 2018; Rule 3.9(7) sets out the agenda for the hearing.

Hoyano (2015: 115) also stated that 'there is no reason for an intermediary to usurp the function of the court in determining whether a question is "improper" as defined by Cossins' even though, without appropriate training, judges are unable to determine the effect of particular questions on the cognitive abilities of vulnerable witnesses, compared to trained and experienced intermediaries. Nevertheless, there is a legitimate question about 'how far such measures can be taken within an adversarial trial system and fairness be maintained' (Elliott, 2015).

Nonetheless, the EWCA has endorsed the practice of lawyers providing their questions in advance in order to seek advice from an intermediary. In *Lubemba* [2014] EWCA Crim 2064, the EWCA stated: '[s]o as to avoid any unfortunate misunderstanding at trial, it would be an entirely reasonable step for a judge at the ground rules hearing to invite defence advocates to reduce their questions to writing in advance'.[17]

For example, had the following questions been vetted at a ground rules hearing, counsel, the intermediary, the judge, the jury and the child witness, a 7-year-old, would have been saved time and possible confusion in relation to the defence counsel's observations of the defendant's behaviour with another child (Plotnikoff & Woolfson, 2015: 195–196):

> *Barrister*: 'I put it to you that because of the absence of light in the room, it was not possible for you to have seen what you say you saw, was it?'
> *Intermediary*: 'Your Honour, that's a long and complex question.'
> *Judge*: 'Counsel, please rephrase.'
> *Barrister*: 'I put it to you that you did not see John do any of those things, did you?'
> *Intermediary*: 'Your Honour, that's a negative and a tagged question.'
> *Judge*: 'Counsel, please rephrase.'
> *Barrister*: 'Did you see John doing those things?'
> *Witness*: 'John was doing those things. I did know.'
> *Barrister*: 'But if as you say it was dark outside, and if as you say there was no light on in the room, it would not have been possible for you to see what was happening on the bottom bunk, would it?'
> *Judge*: 'Counsel, you must ask one question at a time.'

[17] [2014] EWCA Crim 2064, [43].

Barrister: 'If it was dark, you could not see what John was doing, could you?'
Intermediary: 'Your Honour, that's a negative tagged question.'
Judge: 'Counsel, you must make your questions simple and untagged.'
Barrister: 'How did you know what John was doing?'
Witness: 'Well, John was doing the willy in the private thing to her, so the bunk beds were going like this' [shows with hands, up and down and side to side]. Jigging.' (Plotnikoff & Woolfson, 2015: 195–196)

To avoid the problem illustrated above, counsel for the defendant submitted his list of cross-examination questions in *Re RL* [2015] EWCA Crim 1215 which allowed the trial judge, with the assistance of an intermediary, to rule that various questions could not be asked 'because they were either unnecessary or repetitious' or because they were 'inappropriate having regard to the age' of the two child witnesses.[18] A number of other questions were amended to avoid tagged questions being asked.

The defence made no objection since it was accepted that 'the trial judge has a discretion to prevent cross-examination which he regards as unnecessary, improper or oppressive'.[19] To deal with any perceived unfairness to the defendant, the trial judge also 'gave an entirely sufficient and proper direction to the jury, to the effect that cross-examination of a child witness necessarily differs from cross-examination of an adult witness and that counsel had accordingly been limited in the questions he could ask'.[20]

On appeal, the appellant argued that the combined effect of the rulings on cross-examination questions 'went beyond the legitimate protection of young witnesses and restricted permissible cross-examination to such a draconian extent that the [defendant] was unfairly disadvantaged and prevented from having a fair trial'.[21] The defence drew a comparison between the lengthy recorded ABE interviews of both boys and the much shorter cross-examinations due to the restrictions imposed.

---

[18] [2015] EWCA Crim 1215, [7].
[19] Ibid., [10].
[20] Ibid.
[21] Ibid., [11].

The EWCA was not persuaded by these arguments on the grounds that Rules 3.9(3) and 3.9(6) of the Criminal Procedure Rules 2015 require courts to take every reasonable step to facilitate the participation of witnesses which includes directions regarding the questioning of vulnerable witnesses:

> The practice of the court imposing restrictions upon the scope and content of cross-examination of children and other vulnerable witnesses is well established [so that] '[a]dvocates must adapt to the witness, not the other way round. They cannot insist upon any supposed right "to put one's case" … If there is a right to "put one's case" (about which we have our doubts) it must be modified for young or vulnerable witnesses. It is perfectly possible to ensure the jury are made aware of the defence case and of significant inconsistencies without intimidating or distressing a witness'.[22]

The EWCA also noted that the appellant had 'not sought to identify a specific example of a question which he says he should have been permitted to ask but was not allowed to do' and noted that defence counsel was able to 'to make his forensic points' in his closing address to the jury[23] which was enhanced by the trial judge's direction regarding the restricted cross-examination. In another case where cross-examination questions were reviewed in advance by an intermediary, the EWCA again noted that vetting of questions involved teamwork between the prosecutor, the intermediary and defence counsel which served the interests of justice not only for the complainant but also for the defendant.[24]

Whether the task of an intermediary should extend beyond being a communication specialist was considered in relation to an adult complainant who had 'a history of self-harm, suicidal thoughts and repeated admissions to hospital as a result of overdoses and mental health problems'.[25] When the complainant became very distressed while viewing her ABE video, the intermediary put her arm around her and

[22] Ibid., [15], citing *Lubemba* [2014] EWCA Crim 2064, [45].
[23] Ibid., [17].
[24] *Re FA* [2015] EWCA Crim 209, [13].
[25] *R v Christian* [2015] EWCA 1582, [3].

'worked hard to keep KC calm' since the intermediary considered that KC would not be 'able to cope without physical support'.[26] This support continued during cross-examination.

On appeal, the appellant argued that the intermediary had gone far beyond her role as a communication facilitator between the witness and the court and that the trial judge had 'failed in summing up to deal with the intermediary's conduct in any adequate way' (ibid.: [36]).[27] While the EWCA said that the Ministry of Justice's Registered Intermediary Procedure Guidance Manual makes it clear that an intermediary 'is not a witness supporter',[28] the Court did not consider that:

> the fact [KC] received physical support … [from the intermediary] will have been particularly surprising or impactful upon the jury. The experienced judge appears to have taken the view that the support given enabled KC to proceed at a time when she was very distressed. … [T]he relevant consideration … is not whether the intermediary overstepped the guidance given … as much as whether there was any serious risk of unfairness … to this appellant. We do not think that in the circumstances there was any sensible prospect of unfairness. … [B]oth counsel had addressed the jury on the need for an objective examination of the evidence untrammelled by sympathy, and the judge had reinforced this matter in effective terms in the direction which we have already cited.[29]

In fact, intermediaries have spoken about the wider nature of their role; for example, one UK intermediary stated:

> I also monitor and carefully watch the child or the vulnerable adult's anxiety and concentration and, where appropriate, I may suggest that the person needs a break or we need to think about strategies to help that person remain calm and focused. (Royal Commission into Institutional Responses to Child Sexual Abuse, 2017b: 46; citing Dr Mattison)

[26] Ibid., [29].

[27] Ibid., [36].

[28] Ibid, [34].

[29] Ibid., [39]–[41].

2.3 Evaluation of the Role of Intermediaries

An evaluation of 140 referrals for intermediaries in E&W was completed in 2007. Eighty-nine percent of those referrals had been made by police and intermediaries were mostly used for witnesses with physical or cognitive impairments (86%), rather than for children (14%), in relation to a range of offences. The perceived benefits were found to be numerous and wide ranging (Plotnikoff & Woolfson, 2007: 4):

- witnesses and their carers were 'uniformly enthusiastic', with intermediaries not only facilitating communication but also helping witnesses cope with the stress of giving evidence;
- the judiciary and other criminal justice personnel were 'almost unanimous' in their appreciation of the role of intermediaries;
- participants estimated that at least half of the 12 trial cases would not have reached the trial stage without an intermediary's involvement;
- participants considered that the use of intermediaries saved court time by keeping witnesses focused, thus reducing the time needed to question them;
- intermediaries were able to identify low levels of witness comprehension, assist in planning of interviews, assist witnesses during identification procedures and help prosecutors determine a witness's potential for suggestibility and their ability to cope with cross-examination;
- the use of intermediaries resulted in improved witness comprehension at trial through appropriate explanations and instructions.

Nonetheless, it was not possible to determine the influence, if any, of the use of intermediaries on case outcomes (ibid.: 2). The evaluation also identified several challenges associated with the implementation of a national intermediary scheme in E&W. These included correcting misunderstandings about the role of intermediaries, the need for sufficient planning to enable an intermediary to assess a witness's capacities and lack of funding which would 'result in intermediaries being denied to many eligible witnesses and restricted to only the most extreme cases' (ibid.: 6). Probably the greatest challenge, however, was the need for significant cultural change to increase the awareness and receptivity of legal practitioners to using intermediaries, particularly for children given the low referral rate of intermediaries for people under the age of 17 years in the 140 cases evaluated (ibid.).

The evaluation also identified a key disadvantage associated with the role and powers of intermediaries—their inability to intervene to prevent improper questioning at trial, and the concomitant discovery that 'judges and prosecutors said they would be less likely to intervene in inappropriate questioning where an intermediary was present' (ibid.: 5). This finding suggests that a wider role for intermediaries is required, as envisaged under the recommendations in Chapter 12, to work in conjunction with trial judges to prevent the improper cross-examination of children.

Since the evaluation, the use of intermediaries has increased over the years in E&W:

> Since July 2010, there has been a steady increase in the number of advice inquiries and requests ... for Registered Intermediaries. In July 2010, there were 111 and in May 2017 there were 540 ... [with] a steady increase in the monthly average for referrals. ... Referrals for April and May of 2017 were 498 and 540 respectively. (Tasmania Law Reform Institute, 2018: 53; footnotes omitted)

In the period, 1 April 2015–31 March 2016, 'there were a total of 5,772 requests for ... Registered Intermediaries, of which 3,994 (69%) were for children' (Cooper & Mattison, 2017: 360).

Other feedback on the performance of intermediaries comes from the National Crime Agency (NCA) which manages the appointment of registered intermediaries when they are requested. Comments submitted to the NCA by the police and the CPS reveal that '[b]etween August 2009 and June 2014 the Agency received over 2,000 comments' with 99% of feedback being positive' (Plotnikoff & Woolfson, 2015: 282). Police officers, advocates and judges have all acknowledged that their practices have changed as a result of the intermediary scheme:

> It is striking that two-thirds of judges say that working with intermediaries has changed their own practice. They refer to greater awareness that questioning needs to be 'simple, short, with just one concept' and 'to the point and no waffle'. Intermediaries have helped them to 'manage

> cross-examination more firmly'; 'take the initiative'; 'be more active with counsel, limiting their questions'. (Plotnikoff & Woolfson, 2015: 283)

According to one judge, the intermediary's report on the vulnerable witness's communication issues typically:

> provides detailed and helpful information about a witness that the judge would not know about and would have to ascertain. This saves judicial time and distress to the witness as questioning is more sensitive to their particular circumstances. (Plotnikoff & Woolfson, 2015: 284)

A small number of judges complained that intermediaries intervene in cross-examination too much while 'a similar number say they do not intervene enough' (Plotnikoff & Woolfson, 2015: 285). Another problem identified is that the quality of intermediaries varies: while the '"Good ones are very good; the poor ones are awful"' (Plotnikoff & Woolfson, 2015: 285). Defence counsel, in particular, resent the intervention of intermediaries in cross-examination because of the perception it hampers their ability to put the defendant's case to the witness. Nonetheless, intervention appears to have enacted cultural change so that some barristers are much more aware of asking age-inappropriate questions, such as tagged questions (Plotnikoff & Woolfson, 2015: 285). Indeed, Wurtzel and Marchant (2017) consider that the intermediary scheme has, more than any other reform, produced a cultural change within the criminal justice system in relation to vulnerable witnesses. In interviews with judges, lawyers and intermediaries, Henderson (2015a, 2015b) also found that the intermediary scheme in E&W was highly successful. However, Henderson (2014: 94; footnotes omitted) notes that:

> While intermediaries are a remarkable and … highly effective tool for improving the quality of communication in the courtroom they are only generally used in a very few, difficult cases. Unfortunately, the bulk of vulnerable, linguistically challenged witnesses are cross-examined by advocates working without any expert assistance.

2.4 Intermediaries: Europe and Elsewhere

In 2013, a pilot scheme was introduced into the Northern Ireland Crown Courts which closely matches the intermediary scheme in E&W for vulnerable witnesses although a pilot scheme for vulnerable defendants was introduced at the same time (Cooper & Mattison, 2017: 356). After a positive report on both schemes by the Department of Justice (2015), the schemes were extended to all criminal courts from April 2017.[30]

In the Republic of South Africa, intermediaries have been utilised in courts since 1993, although the effectiveness of this reform has suffered from inadequate training and lack of resources (Matthias & Zaal, 2011). Intermediaries in South Africa have a broader role than in E&W in that they communicate questions to the child witness and then communicate the witness's answers back to the questioner (Matthias & Zaal, 2011) while both are located in a room outside of the court. In a country where several different languages are spoken, the intermediary's role is designed to eliminate misunderstandings due to miscommunication (ibid.). Section 170A of the *Criminal Procedure Act 1977* (RSA) states:

1. Whenever criminal proceedings are pending before any court and it appears to such court that it would expose any witness under the biological or mental age of eighteen years to undue mental stress or suffering if he or she testifies at such proceedings, the court may … appoint a competent person as an intermediary in order to enable such witness to give his or her evidence through that intermediary.
2. (a) No examination, cross-examination or re-examination of any witness in respect of whom a court has appointed an intermediary under subsection (1), except examination by the court, shall take place in any manner other than through that intermediary.
   (b) The said intermediary may, unless the court directs otherwise, convey the general purport of any question to the relevant witness.

[30] https://www.justice-ni.gov.uk/ri; accessed 8 November 2018.

Similarly, in Israel, specialist intermediaries, known as 'youth investigators', have much more power than intermediaries in E&W in that they control child victims' 'entire interaction with the judicial system' (Robinson, 2015: 172) under the *Law of Evidence Revision (Protection of Children) 1955* (Israel).

Under s 9 of the *Law of Evidence Revision (Protection of Children) 1955*, children under the age of 14 years are not subject to cross-examination, with intermediaries relaying the child's evidence to the court (ibid.), a form of hearsay, unless the child chooses to give evidence in court. Overall, youth investigators have the power to decide:

- the child's competence as a witness; and
- special measures to protect the child;

As a result, it appears that few children testify as witnesses but there are also few prosecutions involving child witnesses since a child's evidence requires corroboration if under the age of 12 years (ibid.).

In Norway, children under the age of 14 years have their entire evidence recorded by an independent, qualified expert, typically a police officer (Myklebust, 2012; see s 239, *Criminal Procedure Act* [Norway]).[31] The expert's questioning remains under the control of the judge, while the judge, prosecutor and the defendant's lawyer are able to observe the child's examination via CCTV. During the interview, all three can ask the interviewer to put further matters to the child, with appropriate questions being devised by the interviewer (Myklebust, 2012: 158). The video of the completed interview then constitutes the complete examination of the child, with no cross-examination by the defendant. Unlike the situation in adversarial systems, where defence counsel utilise leading questions to communicate the defence case, Norway's interviewers control how the child gives evidence, with the aim of eliciting accurate and reliable evidence which does not exploit their vulnerability.

---

[31] Such a procedure also occurs in NSW, for example, where Joint Investigative Response Teams (JIRT) (comprised of interviewers from the police and Department of Family and Community Services) interview child complainants of sexual abuse, with the video-recorded interviews constituting the child's examination-in-chief at trial. Nonetheless, the JIRT interview does not substitute for formal cross-examination during any subsequent trial.

As a result, several academics are enthusiastic about the Norwegian system for questioning child witnesses (Hoyano, 2015: 112; see Bowden & Plater, 2014; Hanna, Davies, Henderson, & Hand, 2013) which Myklebust (2012) has described in detail.

Bowden and Plater (2014: 581) note that because the Norwegian system 'avoids the problems generated by traditional cross-examination, there is no need for interviewers to assume differing stances or roles (pro-prosecution or pro-defence) during questioning'. As a result, they suggest the Norwegian approach for the examination and cross-examination of vulnerable witnesses could be introduced into an adversarial system because it would 'satisfy the legitimate goals that cross-examination is designed to achieve', that is, to allow the defendant 'to challenge the content and credibility of prosecution witnesses' testimony' even though the defendant's lawyer does not do so directly:

> It is for this reason that the European Court of Human Rights has ruled that a similar Swedish procedure does not violate a defendant's right to examine a witness and is consistent with a fair trial. (see *SN v Sweden* (2004) 39 EHRR 13) (Bowden & Plater, 2014: 582)

Hoyano (2015: 112) considers that '[t]o a lawyer from an adversarial system it is incongruous to have all questioning conducted, not by a neutral party, but by a police investigator allied to the prosecution'. This is unlikely to be a cause for concern if conducted under the control of the trial judge although it appears that Norwegian police officers are just as likely to use leading and suggestive questions during the examination process (Myklebust, 2012).

Nonetheless, as discussed further below, to fall back onto defence lawyers as the only personnel who are competent to cross-examine sexual assault complainants is to ignore nearly two decades of research on the damaging impact of defence cross-examination on the accuracy of complainants' cross-examination answers.

2.5 Intermediaries: Australia

The idea of intermediaries in Australia was first raised as a reform issue by the National Child Sexual Assault Reform Committee (Cossins, 2010a) which was the first body in Australia to research, and propose reforms to the child sexual assault trial as a whole. In particular, the Committee considered the adoption of certain features of inquisitorial systems since such jurisdictions have developed unique methods which could be adopted in order to reduce the secondary traumatisation that may be experienced by a child complainant in a CSA trial, at the same time as improving the best evidence given by the child. The principal advantages for sexual assault complainants from inquisitorial systems include the following:

- complainants are rarely required to testify at trial;
- the informal atmosphere of the examining magistrate's office in which the complainant gives evidence at a pre-trial hearing seated at an ordinary desk, rather than from a witness box;
- control of examination and questioning by the examining magistrate (pre-trial) and the presiding judge (at trial);
- the ability of witnesses to give evidence in a narrative form rather than by way of responsive answers to prosecution questions;
- the general tolerance of hearsay evidence;
- the lack of concern by a neutral examining magistrate with issues of admissibility (while the complainant and other witnesses give evidence) or the complainant's oral performance (demeanour);
- privacy of the pre-trial hearing so that evidence is not given in public and is given in the absence of the accused;
- complainant's right to legal representation;
- the absence of cross-examination; and
- regular intervention to prevent defence counsel from asking questions that are harmful or degrading.

Within an adversarial trial, the above list suggests that there are various ways to ameliorate the impact of the court experience on child witnesses:

i. preventing the complainant from appearing at trial by pre-recording the complainant's evidence-in-chief and cross-examination (already in place in E&W and NSW);
ii. informalising the surroundings in which complainants give evidence, such as the use of remote witness rooms (already in place in NSW);
iii. preventing the defence from putting cross-examination questions directly to the child;
iv. informalising the cross-examination process by allowing it to take place pre-trial under the control of a third-party examiner; and/or
v. providing the complainant with legal representation.

Placing cross-examination under the control of an independent third-party examiner could involve either of the following:

i. the use of a court-appointed intermediary to assess cross-examination questions to ensure that they are not improper and are able to be understood by the child complainant with regard to her/his age and cognitive development (now in place in E&W and NSW);
ii. the communication of pre-prepared questions by the defence via a court-appointed and trained intermediary who would then put the questions to the child in age-appropriate language (as occurs in South Africa and Norway). This would involve decisions as to the admissibility of the pre-prepared questions by the trial judge by reference to the provisions in each jurisdiction which disallow improper questions;
iii. right of appearance of a complainant's legal representative who would have the right to vet and to object to improper and age-inappropriate questions; or
iv. placing control of the conduct of cross-examination in the trial judge using an inquisitorial model.

Overall, in Australia, four jurisdictions (NSW, Victoria, South Australia and Western Australia) have introduced communication assistants although they are not all part of a registered intermediary scheme.

It appears that the first legislative scheme for a communicator or intermediary was enacted in Western Australia in 1991 (Jackson, 2012).

Under s 106F(1)–(2) of the *Evidence Act 1906* (WA) a person may be appointed by the court to communicate and explain the questions put to a child and to explain the evidence given by a child to the court. But it is an option rarely used, possibly because it was never the subject of a pilot scheme and evaluation and did not give rise to a state-wide, formal intermediary scheme.

Similarly, in South Australia communication partners have been available under s 14A of the *Evidence Act 1929* for witnesses and defendants with communication needs since 1 July 2016. A communication partner is defined under the Act as 'a person, or a person of a class, approved by the Minister for the purposes of providing assistance in proceedings to a witness with complex communication needs'.

These partners are part of the state's Disability Justice Plan which 'aim[s] to ensure that people with disability, whether as victims, witnesses, suspects or defendants, are better served by the justice system'.[32] Unlike a registered intermediary scheme, communication partners are volunteers who must be approved by the court and who receive training with an NGO called Uniting Communities. While they must take an oath or affirmation that they 'will communicate accurately with both the witness and the court' (*Evidence Act 1929*, s 14A(4)), they owe no duties to the court and are not members of a professional body.

In recent years, the idea of an intermediary scheme has gathered momentum for jurisdictions other than NSW. In its review of the needs and rights of victims of crime, in Victoria, the VLRC (2016) recommended the mandatory appointment of intermediaries for children under 16 years of age and complainants who have a particular disability that is likely to affect their ability to give evidence (Recommendations 30 and 31) based on the Witness Intermediary Scheme in E&W. An intermediary pilot programme subsequently commenced on 1 July 2018 and is due to finish on 30 June 2020 under Part 8.2A of the *Criminal Procedure Act 2009*.[33] In 2018, the Tasmania Law Reform Institute (2018)

---

[32]See https://www.agd.sa.gov.au/projects-and-consultations/disability-justice-plan; *Statutes Amendment (Vulnerable Witnesses) Act 2015*.

[33]*Multi-Jurisdictional Court Guide for the Intermediary Pilot Program: Intermediaries and Ground Rules Hearings*; https://www.countycourt.vic.gov.au/files/documents/2019-10/multi-jurisdictional-court-guide-intermediary-pilot-program.pdf; as at 28 June 2018.

recommended an intermediary scheme for Tasmania, although at the time of writing this had not been introduced.

In its criminal justice report, the Royal Commission into Institutional Responses to Child Sexual Abuse (2017) recommended the introduction of intermediaries for children in all Australian jurisdictions for both police interviews and while giving evidence in court.

In the fourth jurisdiction, a pilot intermediary scheme began operating in NSW in April 2016.[34] Cooper and Mattison (2017) state that the NSW scheme was recommended by Watts (2014) after a study tour of international intermediary schemes. However, history needs to reflect that many others were involved in the conception of this reform. In 2010, the National Child Sexual Assault Reform Committee (Cossins, 2010a), recommended the appointment of intermediaries in all CSA trials conducted in Australia, along with specialist sex offences courts. The National Committee also recommended that a national register of intermediaries be established, along with a code of practice and a code of ethics to be overseen by an Intermediary Registration Board.

Based on these recommendations, in 2011, the then NSW Labor Government had promised that specialist sex offences courts would be introduced into NSW, including an intermediary scheme. After the Labor Government failed to be re-elected, this author lobbied the new government and recommended specialist judges, specialist courts and an intermediary scheme in a series of meetings with a new Liberal Government in 2015.

In the 2014 report of the Joint Select Committee on Sentencing of Child Sexual Assault Offenders of the NSW Parliament (2014), 19 pages of the National Committee's report on alternative models for prosecuting sex offences were quoted which formed the basis of the Joint Select Committee's recommendations that a specialist sex offences court be established in NSW, including an intermediary scheme.

Under Schedule 2, Part 29 of the *Criminal Procedure Act 1986* (NSW), a pilot scheme was established in two NSW District Court registries to run from March 2016 to March 2019 based on the Witness

[34] *Criminal Procedure Amendment (Child Sexual Offence Evidence Pilot) Act 2015* (NSW). This Act amended Sch 2 of the *Criminal Procedure Act 1986* (NSW).

Intermediary Scheme in E&W, discussed above. In NSW, intermediaries are those who have a 'tertiary qualification in Psychology, Social Work, Speech Pathology, Teaching or Occupational Therapy or such other qualifications, training, experience or skills as may be prescribed by the regulations' (cl 89(2)) and are recruited, registered and trained by Victims Services NSW.[35] As of 28 April 2018, there were 41 registered intermediaries in NSW.

Intermediaries in NSW may be involved at the police interview, or in trial proceedings, or both. After an assessment of the child's communication needs before a police interview, the intermediary will prepare a written or oral preliminary report for the interviewing officer who is likely to have been present at the intermediary's assessment.

In the 14-month period, 4 April 2016–31 May 2017, there had been 751 requests for intermediaries. As of 28 April 2018, the police had made 1373 referrals for intermediaries with 92% being successfully matched to a witness intermediary although there were another '109 out-of-pilot referrals from both Police and Courts at various locations throughout NSW'. Court referrals for intermediaries numbered 142 as of April 2018, according to the Victims Services NSW website.

For court proceedings under the pilot scheme, the evidence of all children under the age of 16 years (at the time the defendant was committed for trial) must be given in a 'pre-recorded evidence hearing'. Before this hearing, the intermediary provides a report to the trial judge on the child's needs, such as simple language, the use of dolls or visual memory aids in order to facilitate communication.

As an 'officer of the court', an intermediary is bound by a Code of Practice (Victims Services, NSW Department of Justice, 2016) and 'has a duty to impartially facilitate the communication of, and with, the witness so the witness can provide the witness's best evidence' (cl 88(2)). Before doing so, they are required to take an oath or affirmation, like an interpreter, under s 22 of the *Evidence Act 1995*.

A court must appoint an intermediary for a child under 16 years, and may do so on its own motion for a child over that age, unless an intermediary is not available to meet the needs of the child, if it is impractical,

[35] See https://www.victimsservices.justice.nsw.gov.au/.

unnecessary, inappropriate or not in the interests of justice to do so (cl 89(4)).

In trial proceedings, the role of NSW witness intermediaries is to communicate questions put to the witness and then provide to the questioner the witness's answers, as well as 'to explain such questions or answers so far as necessary to enable them to be understood by the witness or person in question' (cl 88(1)).[36] In practice, however it appears this occurs infrequently. Rather, under a procedure guidance manual which sets out intermediaries' roles and duties in detail, the manual advises that '[t]he advocate should be given an opportunity to rephrase the question before the [intermediary] is asked to phrase it differently' (Victims Services, NSW Department of Justice, 2016: 25).

In fact, there is a contradiction between the legislation and the guidance manual for intermediaries in NSW. Although the legislation describes the in-court role of intermediaries, such as putting questions to child witnesses (cl 88(1)), the guidance manual states that they should intervene 'only as necessary, in line with their statutory role and in accordance with any pre-trial directions made by the court' (Victims Services, NSW Department of Justice, 2016: 17) and that their role is *not* to put questions directly to the child witness. Ultimately, it is the judge's decision to accept the intermediary's recommendations during an intervention.

If involved in court proceedings, the intermediary must write a detailed assessment report for the court to be considered in a pre-trial hearing. The report will 'advise the prosecution and defence (in particular the advocates) and the judge about how best to communicate with the witness at the trial', including the types of questions and language to avoid (Victims Services, NSW Department of Justice, 2016: 20; 24). In order to 'help shape the pre-trial discussions about how best to adapt the trial to ensure the witness has an opportunity to give their best evidence' (ibid.: 20), the report will also provide:

[36]The description of the role of the intermediary in NSW matches that under s 29 (2) of the YJCE Act.

> detailed recommendations as to how questions should be put to the witness … [and] on: pace of questioning, prefacing questions with the name of the witness, allowing the witness to process the question and formulate their answer, chronology of topics, whether questions about certain times should be linked to events, length of questions, avoiding inferences and double negatives. (ibid.: 24)

After a process evaluation 'to assess the barriers and facilitating factors to successful implementation of the Pilot', Cashmore, Taylor, and Parkinson (2017: 6) reported that, overall, there was 'unanimous support for the objectives of the Pilot from stakeholders' with a number of 'key themes' being identified:

- Witness intermediaries are fulfilling their intended role of acting in the interests of the court, not as advocates or experts.
- Some stakeholders were initially hesitant about the Pilot, but these hesitations have largely been overcome.
- All aspects of the Pilot design and implementation were described by participants as effective and valuable.

2.6 Comparisons of Different Intermediary Schemes

It is far too early to compare the effectiveness of the intermediary scheme in E&W with that of NSW since NSW has only had its intermediary scheme running for just over three years, with the transition from a pilot programme to a permanent programme occurring on 1 April 2019 in only two court registries (Newcastle District Court and Sydney District Court [Downing Centre]).

Nonetheless, the eligibility criteria in E&W are much broader with a focus on vulnerable witnesses who are entitled to intermediary assistance because of age or incapacity, such as someone suffering from a mental disorder. In NSW, only child complainants in sexual assault trials are entitled to an intermediary which means that child witnesses in other criminal trials, and adults who are vulnerable because of pre-existing mental health issues, such as trauma-induced post-traumatic stress disorder (relatively common among sexual assault victims), remain vulnerable in NSW courts to abusive questioning strategies when giving evidence. Unlike Northern Ireland, neither schemes apply to defendants or suspects.[37]

When 25 Australian professionals with extensive experience in working with vulnerable people were interviewed to assess the degree of support for introducing an intermediary system in Australia, views were mixed although:

> [o]verall, concerns about the introduction of an intermediary scheme focused around two key themes; the need for improved use and effectiveness of current measures and concern about adding further complication to the system. (Powell, Bowden, & Mattison, 2014: 503)

2.7 Research on the Effectiveness of Intermediaries

Cooper and Mattison (2017: 364–365) discuss the fact that there is a lack of empirical research into intermediary assessments about witnesses' communication needs, including evaluation of their assessments, that is, 'whether or not they are addressing factors pertinent to an individual's need and abilities to communicate their best evidence'. As well, it is unknown whether or not the presence of an intermediary, who sits or stands next to the vulnerable witness and may intervene during cross-examination, affects actual jurors' perceptions of witness credibility and jury outcomes.

Although there is anecdotal evidence about the effectiveness of intermediaries (Plotnikoff & Woolfson, 2015), research has begun on studying the impact of intermediaries in both interview and court situations.

A study by Hanna et al. (2013) investigated the utility of three intermediary models through lawyers' perceptions of mock examinations of a child witness. The first was the 'full' intermediary model whereby '[t]he

[37]The case for extension of intermediary schemes to defendants/suspects is beyond the scope of this book but see Hoyano (2015).

intermediary prepares appropriate questions to probe the child's evidence as instructed' by the prosecutor and defence and then puts these questions to the child on behalf of each counsel, thus 'taking responsibility for determining how questions are phrased and the order in which they are put' (Hanna et al., 2013: 530).

The second model, the 'question-by-question model', mimicked the South African system and involved counsel posing questions to the intermediary 'who then translates each question into a developmentally appropriate form for the child' (ibid.: 531). Under the third model, the 'topic-by-topic model', the prosecution and the defence 'identify the distinct topics they want to question the child on' (ibid.). A list of topics is given to the intermediary along with relevant questions for the child. The intermediary then questions the child on each topic, receives further instructions if necessary, then moves to the next topic.

The authors reported that '[p]articipants perceived the cross-examination under the topic-by-topic model to be more effective than that observed under the other models' (ibid.: 536). One defence lawyer found that '[h]aving an agreed script … contributed to … [his experiences of] cross-examination as less stressful than ordinary cross-examination' (ibid.: 536):

> it was very relaxing, I must admit, because I'm not having to ask the questions. It's a less stressful experience because you've written the script and, subject to the answers, you can revise it as you go.

This particular defence counsel compensated for the loss of control over cross-examination by making 'a strategic decision to shift the focus from putting allegations strongly to the child, to commenting on the child's evidence during his closing speech to the jury' which is the approach of counsel in E&W, post-*Barker*, as discussed above.

Henry et al. (2017: 2348) carried out a study to 'explore whether three promising investigative interview interventions … would increase the amount of information recalled about a witnessed event … by child witnesses with and without autism spectrum disorder (ASD)'. These interventions included 'Verbal Labels', 'Sketch Reinstatement of Context' or 'Registered Intermediary' interviews.

The authors compared all three interventions to 'an interview carried out according to usual police best practice in England and Wales' with 71 children with ASD and 199 typically developing (TD) children, aged 6–11 years. For children with ASD, neither the presence of an intermediary or the other 'interview interventions significantly improved overall number of correct details recalled, type of details recalled, or error rates compared to a Best-Practice interview' (ibid.: 2356).

By comparison, the presence of an intermediary for TD children 'increased the number of correct details recalled compared to a Best-Practice interview', with intermediary interviews showing the most increase (ibid.: 2362). In addition, intermediary interviews 'increased the number of people, actions, objects and general details recalled' compared to the other interventions (ibid.).

When mock jurors, police officers and barristers read a written transcript with an intermediary (who intervened five times during a child's testimony), or without the presence of an intermediary, Ridley, van Rheede, and Wilcock (2015) found no difference in participants' perceptions of the child, possibly because of a lack of ecological validity with the use of written transcripts.

Collins, Harker, and Antonopoulos (2017) undertook research with mock jurors in order to investigate the impact of intermediaries on jurors' perceptions of children (aged either 4 years or 13 years) undergoing cross-examination. In the condition with the presence of an intermediary, the intermediary made five interventions to correct inappropriate questions so that they could be rephrased. Children with an intermediary present were rated as significantly more truthful, more credible, more believable, more cooperative, more responsive, less vulnerable and less suggestible than children without an intermediary. Participants also considered that the child was significantly more comfortable and confident and less stressed with the presence of an intermediary than without. The age of the child had no effect on these perceptions.

In addition, the cross-examination itself was perceived as being significantly more child appropriate when an intermediary was present. Overall, the authors concluded that the presence of an intermediary was not detrimental to perceptions of the child or of the quality of the cross-examination.

Nonetheless, none of these studies investigated the extent to which a child's evidence is improved by the presence of an intermediary during cross-examination.

2.8 Conclusion: Should the Intermediary Adopt the Role of Cross-Examiner?

As discussed in this chapter, the research literature tells us that techniques of cross-examination are used by defence counsel to change the accuracy of children's evidence which ultimately influences a jury's decision as to the guilt or innocence of the accused.

Empirical evidence shows that there is a positive correlation between actual jurors' perceptions of consistency, credibility and verdict (Cashmore & Trimboli, 2006). The effect between inconsistencies, low credibility ratings and verdicts has also been seen with jury-eligible mock jurors (Malloy & Lamb 2010; Molinaro & Malloy, 2016; Redlich, Ghetti, & Quas, 2008; Zajac & Cannan, 2009) while some mock jurors have interpreted inconsistent evidence by children as evidence of fabrication (Cossins, Goodman-Delahunty, & O'Brien, 2009; Morison & Greene, 1992; Quas, Thompson, & Clarke-Stewart, 2005). Feeding into beliefs about inconsistencies are actual beliefs or uncertainty that 'Children sometimes make up stories about being sexually abused when they actually have not' and 'Children who retract their reports have fabricated' (Cossins et al., 2009; Morison & Greene, 1992; Quas et al., 2005; see Table 3, Chapter 5).

It appears that in E&W:

> It is now generally accepted that if justice is to be done to the vulnerable witness and also to the accused, a radical departure from the traditional style of advocacy will be necessary. Advocates must adapt to the witness, not the other way round. (*R v Lubemba* [2014] EWCA Crim 2064, [45]

But as Henderson (2014: 107–108) observes, issues remain unaddressed by the EWCA:

- endorsement of questions and techniques that are likely to produce unreliable evidence;
- problematic tactics, 'including misleading question sequences, rapid questioning or rapid subject changes';
- failure to criticise the non-appointment of a Registered Intermediary in cases where the child complainants were very young (e.g. *Barker* and *E*) 'to assess the children's communication abilities' and advise on appropriate questions; and
- apart from suggestive and tagged questions, the Court has not identified 'the extent to which other less obvious but more pervasive ways of leading witnesses remain acceptable'.

Henderson (2014: 107) gives the example of the defence's approach to cross-examination of a six-year-old child in *E* [2011] EWCA Crim 3028 which was described by the EWCA as 'the clearest of approaches'. The child was told by counsel that he had 'ten areas to question her upon', and enumerated them, one by one' and at one point says, '"Good, okay. We're still on number three. All right?"'. Henderson (2014: 107) observes:

> It is very hard to imagine that the six-year-old complainant derived any assistance from this whatsoever. The Court goes on to quote with apparent approval counsel's use of questions containing multiple embedded clauses, questions ending in highly suggestive tags and the putting of several distinct questions in one utterance.

In jurisdictions and courts without the benefits of the cultural change wrought by intermediaries, all the dangers of cross-examination remain with controls over cross-examination being entirely dependent on the trial judge within a culture of adversarialism. As the *Ward* case discussed above, demonstrates, on a daily basis, aggressive, confusing, intimidating and/or repetitive styles of cross-examination are commonly used in CSA trials throughout Australia, including the use of age-inappropriate language, sentence structure and grammatical styles to exploit children's age and developmental vulnerability.

In order to produce real change to the cross-examination process, reforms will need to go further than a judicial duty to disallow improper questions, given the subjectivity that is inherent in provisions that require a judge to assess whether questions are *unduly* annoying, harassing, intimidating, offensive, oppressive, humiliating or repetitive. In other words, 'where cross-examination will cross the line from *due* intimidation (whatever that is) to … *undue* intimidation … is anybody's guess' (Henning, 2006: 136). As well, the expected neutrality of judicial officers hinders the extent to which they are capable of intervening in cross-examination, while defence counsel do not always comply with judicial interventions.

While Henderson (2015a: 181) considers that 'the single most important factor in achieving any sort of change in trial practice is not legislation or governmental policy declarations but the attitude of the judiciary and the legal profession', waiting for this to happen can be a futile exercise with cultural change within the courtroom taking decades, not just months or years to achieve. Indeed, 'examples of the legal profession's ability to "subvert" both legislative and judiciary-led reform of legal practice are legion' (ibid.; footnotes omitted).

Unless the sexual assault trial develops into a trauma-informed system, as discussed in Chapter 11, with trauma-informed protections for complainants of sexual assault, judicial education is also unlikely to provide a comprehensive solution to the problems of protecting complainants from the rigours of cross-examination since there are no consequences for judges if they do not intervene to protect vulnerable witnesses. As well, lawyers and judges who are untrained in child development will not necessarily recognise that a child or adult is stressed or confused or is responding to questions they do not understand. In particular:

> children's evidence requires specialist knowledge and skills that judges and lawyers may not have the time to acquire … Some also believe that communicating with their own children and grandchildren … qualifies them to communicate effectively in forensic contexts. However, … this belief is mistaken. … Recent scholarship in the field of first-language acquisition has demonstrated that significant growth occurs

> during adolescence and into early adulthood in several areas of language acquisition including grammar, semantics and pragmatics. Hence, care should not only be taken when questioning very young children, but also adolescents, who may not comprehend language that highly literate adults take for granted. (Davies, Henderson, & Hanna, 2010: 354; reference omitted)

Indeed, a judge interviewed by Powell et al. (2014: 505) observed:

> Judges will think 'well I can understand these questions and I'm a person of the world and I know kids, I've brought up my own and I've done that wonderfully well and I know what's happening.' Often they overestimate their ability to detect an inappropriate question because they have led a sheltered and privileged life.

Powell et al.'s (2014: 505) interviews of professionals working with vulnerable witnesses also identified the considerable '[i]nconsistency in judicial monitoring and knowledge of appropriate questioning was a particular source of frustration'. It was apparent from interviews that despite best-practice guidelines, non-leading, open-ended questions were not standard practice, mainly because of inadequate training (Powell et al., 2014: 504):

> Professionals emphasised that if best-practice questioning standards in investigative and evidential interviewing were adhered to, then the concerns underpinning the need for intermediaries would be substantially reduced. Without addressing the underlying problem of poor questioning, the intermediary scheme was merely perceived as a Band-Aid reform for a deeply dysfunctional justice system.

However, the poor questioning of children arises from the inherent culture of adversarialism which is to beat one's opponent, such that tactics designed to confuse and/or trap a witness into giving inconsistent evidence are long-accepted traditions. Half of the participants in Powell et al.'s (2014: 504) study observed that 'cross examination can be confusing even with the use of well crafted, non-aggressive and simply phrased questions. As such, participants doubted whether an intermediary (focused on ensuring the use of developmentally appropriate questions) could limit suggestibility arising from inappropriate questions phrased by defence'.

Similarly, Henderson's (2015a: 202) interviews of judges, advocates and intermediaries in E&W found that in court:

> there were clear signs that actual interventions may in fact remain low. In particular, there were indications that even judges who were happy to intervene in theory might simply not have enough knowledge to recognise problems when they arose. … [M]any judges found intervention philosophically problematic and technically difficult …, would … prefer not to have to intervene, [and would] … prefer to keep any interventions as minimal as possible.

Since it is not the goal of a cross-examiner to ask age-appropriate questions, this requirement ought to be mandatory within CSA trials, given the complexities of children's language development at different ages and the inability of children to understand adult language until the ages of 10–12 years (Sas, 2002: 26).[38] In E&W, the Inns of Court College of Advocacy (ICCA) has developed a training course for lawyers who deal with cases involving vulnerable witnesses. Training is 'mandatory for any advocate wishing to undertake publicly funded work in serious sexual offence cases involving vulnerable witnesses'.[39] As Cooper and Mattison (2017: 364) observe:

> [t]here is a growing body of evidence which suggests that with appropriate preparation and questioning, quality evidence can be (and has been) gathered from children as young as 22 months (Marchant, 2016). Advocates require training about the capabilities of very vulnerable witnesses when communication is supported by an intermediary.

As discussed above, in *Barker* [2010] EWCA Crim 4, the EWCA considered that normal, lengthy cross-examination of a child was unnecessary

[38]See report by Sas (2002) about the importance of understanding language development in children.

[39]https://icca.ac.uk/advocacy-the-vulnerable/national-training-programme-2016-18; accessed 21 June 2018.

in order to reveal that a child might be lying, mistaken or suggestible. However, restricting the length and type of cross-examination through the use of intermediaries and greater judicial control is likely to give rise to arguments from defence counsel that a defendant's right to a fair trial will be compromised. But, as the EWCA observed in *E* [2011] EWCA Crim 3028, 'we struggle to understand how the defendant's right to a fair trial was in any way compromised simply because [defence counsel] was not allowed to ask' a leading, tagged question of a five-year-old child.[40]

One solution would be for the intermediary's role to be extended to not only vetting prosecution and defence questions to ensure their age appropriateness, a practice that has been adopted in some E&W courts, but to become the neutral party interviewer at pre-trial examinations of all child complainants, as per the system in Norway. As a reform measure, it would involve a second examination using age-appropriate, non-suggestive, non-leading and non-repetitive questions according to the case that the defence wishes to present. Such a reform measure is based on the research discussed above.

This book also advocates that neutral third-party cross-examination should be available for adult complainants when it is clear, after an intermediary's assessment, that an adult would be vulnerable to the cross-examination effect. Hoyano (2015: 113), however, considers that:

> [a]n intermediary, at least as currently conceived, cannot be entrusted with this role. Typically speech and language therapists, they have a limited perspective on the criminal justice system: they are not trained in criminal and evidence law … They are not trained to develop a line of questioning, but only to evaluate, and if necessary reword, the formulation of others. … In short, intermediaries are not advocates.

While Hoyano (2015) raises important points in the above quote, she fails to grasp the dangers of defence counsel cross-examining vulnerable witnesses and that, as much as lawyers are trained in criminal and evidence law, they are imbued with adversarial modes of interacting with witnesses, something that does not apply to speech therapists, social

---

[40][2011] EWCA Crim 3028, [28].

workers and other professionals employed as intermediaries. As stated above, to establish this 'shift in professional roles' (Hoyano, 2015: 113), intermediaries would need to act on instructions from the defence in terms of the general content of questions but at the same time undertake vetting to eliminate age-inappropriate questions.

While Hoyano (2015: 115) describes vetting of questions by intermediaries as hopelessly impractical, that is what now happens in some courts in E&W and in NSW before pre-recording takes place.

However, the cultural change that has been wrought by judges in the courts of E&W, along with the intermediary scheme, was introduced without the recognition that sexual assault trials, in particular, are most likely to be dealing with adult and child witnesses who are suffering from the effects of trauma. Thus, this cultural change has occurred without integration of the principles of trauma-informed care.

In light of the discussion in this chapter, Chapter 11 canvasses the possibility of transforming the adversarial trial into a trauma-informed system, along with the introduction of reforms that are informed by trauma-informed principles. It also considers the reforms that would be necessary to overcome the cross-examination effect (as documented in this chapter) to enable both adults and children to give their best evidence as complainants in sexual assault trials. Those reforms will be considered in the context of using trauma-informed theory to transform the sexual assault trial into a trauma-informed system.

References

Andrews, S. J., Lamb, M. E., & Lyon, T. D. (2014). Question types, responsiveness and self-contradictions when prosecutors and defense attorneys question alleged victims of child sexual abuse. *Applied Cognitive Psychology, 25*, 253–261.

Australian Law Reform Commission and Human Rights and Equal Opportunity Commission. (1997). *Seen and heard: Priority for children in the legal process* (ALRC Report No. 84). Sydney: ALRC.

Australian Law Reform Commission, NSW Law Reform Commission and Victorian Law Reform Commission. (2005). *Uniform evidence law report*

(ALRC Report No. 102; NSWLRC Report No. 112; VLRC Final Report). Sydney: ALRC.

Bowden, P., Henning, T., & Plater, D. (2014). Balancing fairness to victims, society and defendants in the cross-examination of vulnerable witnesses: An impossible triangulation, *Melbourne University Law Review*, *37*, 539–584.

Boyd, R., & Hopkins, A. (2010). Cross-examination of child sexual assault complainants: Concerns about the application of s 41 of the Evidence Act. *Criminal Law Journal, 34,* 149–166.

Caruso, D. (2012). Proposed reforms for the cross-examination of child witnesses and the reception and treatment of their evidence. *Journal of Judicial Administration, 21*, 191–236.

Cashmore, J., & Trimboli, L. (2005). *An evaluation of the NSW child sexual assault specialist jurisdiction.* Sydney: NSW Bureau of Crime Statistics and Research.

Cashmore, J., & Trimboli, L. (2006). Child sexual assault trials: A survey of juror perceptions. *Crime and Justice Bulletin, 102,* 1–20.

Cashmore, J., Taylor, A., & Parkinson, P. (2017). The characteristics of reports to the police of child sexual abuse and the likelihood of cases proceeding to prosecution after delays in reporting. *Child Sexual Abuse & Neglect, 74,* 49–61.

Collins, K., Harker, N., & Antonopoulos, G. A. (2017). The impact of the registered intermediary on adults' perceptions of child witnesses: Evidence from a mock cross-examination. *European Journal of Criminal Policy and Research, 23,* 211–225.

Cooper, P., & Mattison, M. (2017). Intermediaries, vulnerable people and the quality of evidence: An international comparison of three versions of the English intermediary model. *The International Journal of Evidence & Proof, 21,* 351–370.

Cossins, A. (2009). Cross-examination in child sexual assault trials: Evidentiary safeguard or an opportunity to confuse? *Melbourne University Law Review, 33,* 68–104.

Cossins, A. (2010a). *Alternative models for prosecuting child sex offences in Australia.* Sydney: National Child Sexual Assault Reform Committee, UNSW.

Cossins, A., Goodman-Delahunty, J., & O'Brien, K. (2009). Uncertainty and misconceptions about child sexual abuse: Implications for the criminal justice system. *Psychiatry, Psychology & Law, 16,* 435–452.

Davies, E., Henderson, E., & Hanna, K. (2010). Facilitating children to give best evidence: Are there better ways to challenge children's testimony? *Criminal Law Journal, 34,* 347–362.

Department of Justice. (2015). *Northern Ireland registered intermediaries schemes pilot project: Post project review.* https://www.justice-ni.gov.uk/sites/default/files/publications/doj/ri-post-project-reviewfeb15.pdf.

Elliott, S. (2015). The new regime for vulnerable witnesses. *The Criminal Appeals Bulletin,* Issue 3. http://doughty-street-chambers.newsweaver.com/Appeals/5z2g7ifzdun?a=2&p=698889&t=174048.

Ellison, L. (1999). The protection of vulnerable witnesses in court: An Anglo-Dutch comparison. *International Journal of Evidence and Proof, 3,* 29–43.

Granhag, P. A., Strömwall, L. A., & Hartwig, M. (2005). Eyewitness testimony: Tracing the beliefs of Swedish legal professionals. *Behavioral Sciences & the Law, 23,* 709–727.

Hanna, K., Davies, E., Henderson, E., & Hand, L. (2013). Questioning child witnesses: Exploring the benefits and risks of intermediary models in New Zealand. *Psychiatry, Psychology and Law, 20,* 527–542.

Hanna, K., Davies, E., Crothers, C., & Henderson, E. (2012). Questioning child witnesses in New Zealand's criminal justice system: Is cross-examination fair? *Psychiatry, Psychology and Law, 19,* 530–546.

Henderson, E. (2014). All the proper protections—The Court of Appeal rewrites the rules of the cross-examination of vulnerable witnesses. *Criminal Law Review, 2,* 93–108.

Henderson, E. (2015a). Taking control of cross-examination: Judges, advocates and intermediaries discuss judicial management of the cross-examination of vulnerable people. *Criminal Law Review, 3,* 181–205.

Henderson, E. (2015b). Theoretically speaking: English judges and advocates discuss the changing theory of cross-examination. *Criminal Law Review, 12,* 929–948.

Henderson, E. (2015c). 'Communicative competence? Judges, advocates and intermediaries discuss communication issues in the cross-examination of vulnerable witnesses. *Criminal Law Review, 9,* 659–678.

Henning, T. (2006). Control of cross-examination—A snowflake's chance in hell? *Criminal Law Journal, 30,* 133–137.

Henry, L., Crane, L., Nash, G., Hobson, Z., Kirke-Smith, M., & Wilcock, R. (2017). Verbal, visual, and intermediary support for child witnesses with autism during investigative interviews. *Journal of Autism and Developmental Disorders, 47,* 2348–2362.

HM CPS Inspectorate and HM Inspectorate of Constabulary. (2012). *Joint inspection report on the experience of young victims and witnesses in the CJS*. London: HMIC & HMCPSI.

HM Government. (2018). *Victims strategy*. London: Ministry of Justice.

Home Office. (1989). *Report of the interdepartmental working group on the treatment of vulnerable or intimidated witnesses in the criminal justice system*. London: Home Office.

Home Office. (1998). *Speaking up for justice: Report of the interdepartmental working group on the treatment of vulnerable or intimidated witnesses in the criminal justice system*. London: Home Office.

Home Office. (2011). *Achieving best evidence: Guidance on interviewing victims and witnesses*. London: Home Office.

Hoyano, L. (2015). Reforming the adversarial trial for vulnerable witnesses. *Criminal Law Review, 2*, 107–129.

Jackson, H. (2012). Children's evidence in legal proceedings—The position in Western Australia. In J. R. Spencer & M. E. Lamb (Eds.), *Children and cross-examination: Time to change the rules* (pp. 75–94). Oxford: Hart Publishing.

Joint Select Committee, Parliament of NSW. (2014). *Joint select committee on sentencing of child sexual assault offencers* (Report No. 1/55). Sydney: Parliament of NSW.

Judicial College. (2013–2019). *Equal treatment bench book*. https://www.judiciary.uk/wp-content/uploads/2018/02/equal-treatment-bench-book-february2018-v5-02mar18.pdf.

Klemfuss, J. Z., Quas, J. A., & Lyon, T. D. (2014). Attorneys' questions and children's productivity in child sexual abuse criminal trials. *Applied Cognitive Psychology, 28*, 780–788.

Korkman, J., Svanbäck, J., Finnilä, K., & Santt, P. (2014). Judges' views of child sexual abuse: Evaluating beliefs against research findings in a Finnish sample. *Scandanavian Journal of Psychology, 55*, 497–504.

Malloy, L. C., & Lamb, M. E. (2010). Biases in judging victims and suspects whose statements are inconsistent. *Law and Human Behavior, 34*, 46–48.

Marchant, R. (2016). 'Age is not determinative': The evidence of very young children in the English justice system. *Criminal Law and Justice Weekly, 180*, 12–13.

Matthias, C. R., & Zaal, F. N. (2011). Intermediaries for child witnesses: Old problems, new solutions and judicial differences in South Africa. *International Journal of Children's Rights, 19*, 251–269.

Ministry of Justice. (2015a). *Registered intermediary procedural guidance manual*. London: Ministry of Justice. https://www.zakon.co.uk/admin/

resources/downloads/registered-intermediary-procedural-guidance-manual-2015.pdf.

Molinaro, P. F., & Malloy, L. C. (2016). Statements from youth in legal contexts: Effects of consistency, legal role, and age. *Behavioral Sciences & the Law, 34,* 139–159.

Morison, S., & Greene, E. (1992). Juror and expert knowledge of child sexual abuse. *Child Abuse & Neglect, 16,* 595–613.

Myklebust, T. (2012). The position in Norway. In J. R. Spencer & M. E. Lamb (Eds.), *Children and cross-examination: Time to change the rules?* (pp. 147–170). Oxford: Hart Publishing.

NSW Standing Committee on Law and Justice. (2002). *Report on child sexual assault prosecutions* (Parliamentary Paper No. 208; Report No. 22). Sydney: Parliament of NSW.

Parliament of Victoria, Crime Prevention Committee. (1995). *Combating child sexual assault: An integrated model* (First Report Upon the Inquiry into Sexual Offences Against Children and Adults). Melbourne: Government Printer.

Plotnikoff, J., & Woolfson, R. (2007). *Evaluation of young witness support: Examining the impact on witnesses and the criminal justice system.* London: Ministry of Justice. https://www.lexiconlimited.co.uk/PDF%20files/Young_Witness_Study_Report.pdf.

Plotnikoff, J., & Woolfson, R. (2012). 'Kicking and screaming': The slow road to best evidence. In J. R. Spencer & M. E. Lamb (Eds.), *Children and cross-examination: Time to change the rules* (pp. 21–41). Oxford: Hart Publishing.

Plotnikoff, J., & Woolfson, R. (2015). *Intermediaries in the criminal justice system: Improving communication for vulnerable witnesses and defendants.* Bristol: Policy Press.

Powell, M. B., Bowden, P., & Mattison, M. (2014). Stakeholders' perceptions of the benefit of introducing an Australian intermediary system for vulnerable witnesses. *Australian & New Zealand Journal of Criminology, 48,* 498–512.

Powell, M. B., Westera, N. J., Goodman-Delahunty, J., & Pichler, A. S. (2016). *An evaluation of how evidence is elicited from complainants of child sexual abuse.* Sydney: Royal Commission into Institutional Responses to Child Sexual Abuse.

Quas, J. A., Thompson, W. C., & Clarke-Stewart, K. A. (2005). Do jurors 'know' what isn't so about child witnesses? *Law and Human Behavior, 29,* 425–456.

Redlich, A. D., Ghetti, S., & Quas, J. A. (2008). Perceptions of children during a police interview: A comparison of alleged victims and suspects. *Journal of Applied Social Psychology, 38,* 705–735.

Ridley, A. M., van Rheede, V., & Wilcock, R. (2015). Interviews, intermediaries and witnesses interview. *Investigative Interviewing: Research and Practice, 7,* 21–315.

Robinson, J. (2015). The experience of the child witness: Legal and psychological issue. *International Journal of Law and Psychiatry, 42–43,* 168–176.

Royal Commission into Institutional Responses to Child Sexual Abuse. (2017a). *Final report: Nature and cause* (Vol. 2). Sydney: Royal Commission into Institutional Responses to Child Sexual Abuse.

Royal Commission into Institutional Responses to Child Sexual Abuse. (2017b). *Criminal justice report* (Executive Summary and Parts I–II). Sydney: Royal Commission into Institutional Responses to Child Sexual Abuse.

Royal Commission into Institutional Responses to Child Sexual Abuse. (2017c). *Criminal justice report* (Parts VII–X and Appendices). Sydney: Royal Commission into Institutional Responses to Child Sexual Abuse.

Rumney, P. N., & Fenton, R. A. (2011). Judicial training and rape. *Journal of Criminal Law, 75,* 473–481.

Sas, L. (2002). *The interaction between children's developmental capabilities and the courtroom environment: The impact on testimonial competency.* Ottawa, ON: Department of Justice.

Sleight, K. (2007, June 27–July 1). *Commentary on the video 'A Case for Balance': The issue of judicial control of cross-examination.* Paper presented at the Biennial District and County Court Judges' Conference, Fremantle, Western Australia.

Tasmania Law Reform Institute. (2018). *Facilitating equal access to justice: An intermediary/communication assistance scheme for Tasmania?* (Final Report No. 23). http://www.utas.edu.au/__data/assets/pdf_file/0011/1061858/Intermediaries-Final-Report.pdf.

Victims Services, NSW Department of Justice. (2016). *Children's champion (witness intermediary) procedural guidance manual (2016).* Sydney: NSW Department of Justice. https://www.victimsservices.justice.nsw.gov.au/Documents/child-champ_manual.pdf.

Victorian Law Reform Commission. (2016). *The role of victims of crime in the criminal trial process* (Report No. 34). Melbourne: Victorian Law Reform Commission.

Watts, A. (2014). *To investigate models of Intermediaries for child victim and witnesses in the criminal justice system in England, Ireland, Austria and Norway*. Sydney: The Winston Churchill Memorial Trust of Australia. https://www.churchilltrust.com.au/media/fellows/Watts._Amy_2013.pdf.

Westera, N., Zydervelt, S., Kaladelfos, A., & Zajac, R. (2017). Sexual assault complainants on the stand: A historical comparison of courtroom questioning. *Psychology, Crime & Law, 23,* 15–31.

Wurtzel, D., & Marchant, R. (2017). Intermediaries. In P. Cooper & H. Norton (Eds.), *Vulnerable people and the criminal justice system: A guide to law and practice*. Oxford: Oxford University Press.

Zajac, R., & Cannan, P. (2009). Cross-examination of sexual assault complainants: A developmental comparison. *Psychiatry, Psychology and Law, 16,* S36–S54.

Zydervelt, S., Zajac, R., Kaladelfos, A., & Westera, N. (2017). Lawyers' strategies for cross-examining rape complainants: Have we moved beyond the 1950s. *British Journal of Criminology, 57,* 551–569.

10

The Problems Facing Reformers of the Sexual Assault Trial

1 Introduction: The Problems Facing Reformers of the Sexual Assault Trial

While law reform in the area of sexual assault has traditionally been 'far removed from the values and politics of the women's movement' (Smart, 1989: 164), feminist academics in recent years have had much more input into the process than in earlier decades. However, as discussed in Chapter 1, some believe that 'these significant social, political and legal reforms have resulted in little practical improvement in the operation of the criminal justice system' (Naylor, 2010: 662; see also Daly & Bouhours, 2010; Pether, 2009; Smith & Skinner, 2017). Certainly, low reporting rates, high attrition rates and relatively low conviction rates (see Chapter 1) do not appear to have been affected by legal reforms to the sexual assault trial.

When a former UK Director of Public Prosecutions, Sir Keir Starmer, retired in 2013 he believed that there was much more to be done in relation to the prosecution of sex offences because of inaccurate assumptions:

A. Cossins, *Closing the Justice Gap for Adult and Child Sexual Assault*,
https://doi.org/10.1057/978-1-137-32051-3_10

> about what 'real' victims do: a real victim goes straight to the police; a real victim will give a coherent and consistent account, in chronological order; a real victim would never go back to the perpetrator; a real victim wouldn't dress in a particular way, or drink or take drugs. Over time, those tests or assumptions have ended up ringfencing some of the most vulnerable victims from criminal justice protection. (Williams, 2013)

Indeed, the experience of a juror in a CSA trial in NSW in 2018 highlights the profound inadequacies of jurors in assessing the behaviours of victims:

> [the jury is a] combination of genders, ages, backgrounds, religions and life experiences. What became clear over the three weeks of deliberation that followed a six-week trial is that the general public does not have the ability to do its job properly … [and does] not have the emotional intelligence to understand the psychology of victims and how their responses vary. Many of my fellow jurors found the girls and women unreliable. They could not fathom how the victims continued to place themselves in harm's way. Girls between 10 and 16 years of age at the time of their assault, many of whom had been abused over a number of years, by a man who was either their uncle or foster father. That lack of empathy among so many on the jury undermined the facts of the case and left room for doubt.
>
> Sitting around that table, I realised just how broken the system and society is when it comes to sexual assault. When you hear statements such as, 'two fingers in a vagina wasn't sexual assault in my day' or 'maybe they enjoyed it' you realise we are fighting a battle that cannot be won. People like that, are never going to understand sexual assault and it's impossible to convict a man with a jury that holds that mindset. … If my sister, or a friend or colleague came to me now and confided in me they had been sexually assaulted, I would encourage them not to report it. I realise how … that perpetuates the cycle of abuse, but I could not encourage anyone to go through the process I have just witnessed. (Cole, 2018)

The premise of this book is that juries' verdicts and credibility assessments are influenced by a number of extra-legal factors, including individual jurors' adherence to rape myths, the influence of which is likely to be ameliorated or exaggerated based on the extent to which rape myths are reproduced within the trial process, with various points within the trial that activate jurors' heuristic reasoning (that is, reasoning based on intuitive 'short cuts', such as myths and inherent biases), as discussed in Chapter 6.

If complainants of sexual assault do not report or drop out of the criminal justice system because of the arduous nature of being interviewed by police and/or warnings about how they will be treated at trial then:

> [t]he key to making the trial process meaningful to victims is the early acknowledgement of guilt by defendants who are in fact guilty. All of the current features of the trial militate against this. … In a contested trial, the victim will have to testify, running the gauntlet of … rape myths, of women as sexual temptresses and liars and men as hapless automatons. (Naylor, 2010: 663)

Legal reform is rarely informed with reference to the gendered cultural space represented by the sexual assault trial, leading to the question, 'why have the waves of rape law reform … not made a difference to the law's ability to do justice in the case of rape?' (Pether, 2009: 244). In raising this question, however, it is necessary to interrogate the monolith called 'the law' and the meaning of 'justice'.

Historically, rape laws were premised on 'the logic that the law can tell the difference' between consensual sex and sexual assault (Pether, 2009: 244) but this logic was in turn premised on the moral regulation of women (Cossins, 2015)—those worthy of protection and those who were not—which explains why a number of rules of evidence and procedure developed that were unique to the sexual assault trial, including evidence of sexual history and reputation, the delay in complaint rule, and jury warnings about the dangers of convicting in the absence of corroborating evidence (Rumney, 2006). Over the centuries many legal mechanisms were introduced to protect men from false complaints of sexual assault (see e.g. Boniface, 1994; Cossins, 1999, 2001; Kelly, 2010; Quilter, 2015).

Reform of this gendered cultural space is the mammoth task facing law reformers. The cultural context of the sexual assault trial is one of victim blaming with the underlying message that the complainant is responsible for the defendant's sexual behaviour. The moral regulation of women's and girls' behaviours and reputations, historically, promoted the sexual access of men to women and reinforced the gendered power relations between the sexes. As discussed in Chapter 5, the moral worth of the complainant has always been on trial so that measures of her moral worth—active versus passive resistance, abstemious versus drunken behaviour, demure versus lascivious dress and behaviour—were and still are used to determine the credibility of her allegations.

As a result, female bodies became legally sexed into two categories—the chaste victim (who had no sexual history or reputation, who complained immediately and whose violation could be corroborated) and the unchaste victim (who had an immoral sexual history/reputation, delayed her complaint and whose complaint could not be corroborated), so that the law did not protect the latter from non-consensual sexual relations. The chaste victim's lack of consent is implied while the immoral behaviour and/or reputation of the unchaste victim implies her consent.

In this way, the sexual relationship has been one of the key sites for the social control of women. Historically, men have controlled women's bodies through the legality of physical violence, the criminalisation of abortion, the illegality of contraception, and the lack of recognition of rape in marriage as a crime. The sexual assault trial reflects this historical moral regulation by constructing the complainant as moral or immoral through various rules of evidence, the use of stereotypes and rape myths during cross-examination, measures of credibility and judicial directions.

Thus, the sexual assault trial takes place within an existing set of power relations represented by the power of the state through the police, prosecutorial agencies, judicial authority and the rights accorded to defendants. The complainant is situated within this hierarchical arrangement in a relatively powerless position. While she has no power to instigate a prosecution or to represent herself, she is not just a complainant of a crime, she is a sexed body—sexed according to the values associated with the female body and the behaviours expected of a chaste victim (Cossins, 2003). Only in recent times has the sexual assault complainant been recognised as a possible victim of trauma, a topic covered in Chapter 11.

For example, hearsay evidence of a complainant's recent complaint was only ever relevant to boost a complainant's credibility[1] while evidence of a delayed complaint can still be used to undermine a complainant's credibility (see Chapter 7). Legislative and common law protections for defendants based on delay in complaint and judicial warnings regarding the dangers of delayed complaint constitute forms of moral regulation of complainants. Many children and adults experience sexual abuse that is ongoing, rather than one-off, and is 'frequently accompanied by psychological trauma, threats and other forms of abuse' (Royal Commission in the NSW Police Service, 1997: 613) which ensures that victims will not report to the authorities for months or years (see Chapter 1). In other words, the delay in complaint warning penalised complainants for not responding to sexual assault in atypical ways since, as summarised in Chapter 1, psychological studies reveal that delay is a *typical* response to sexual assault.

Although the crime of rape began to be treated 'as a crime of sexual violation' during the eighteenth century—when a 'woman' was defined as a female over the age of 10 years (Hale, 1736/1971: 628)—this was 'a period in which a number of ... dubious "requirements" ... made their way into the legal category of "rape"' (Quilter, 2015: 104–105). Quilter (2015: 111) found that 'the emphasis on resistance and injury, which has persisted through decades of attempts at statutory erasure, was the product of re-writings of the elements of "rape" from the older marriage and property laws'. Despite the conversion of rape into 'a crime of sexual violation ... requirements drawn from rape's history as a property crime' persisted (Quilter, 2015: 111) because of the status of women in previous centuries who had few political and legal rights and the entrenched moral regulation of women's bodies (Cossins, 2015).

These requirements included:

(i) Proof of the use of force against a woman's will (formerly elements of the offence of rape) (Hale, 1736/1971);
(ii) Proof of physical resistance (originally an element of the offence of rape);

[1] See, for example, the discussion in *R v Papakosmos* (1999) 196 CLR 297.

(iii) Immediate complaint (Hale, 1736/1971) which meant that delay in complaint was relevant to credibility and later became the subject of a judicial warning;
(iv) Evidence of corroboration (resulting in the development of a corroboration warning if lacking);
(v) Evidence of sexual history and sexual reputation; and
(vi) A defence of mistaken belief as to consent in the substantive law of rape (see Chapter 7).

The problem for women was the cultural distinction made between 'common strumpets' (those of 'evil fame') and women whose chastity was worth preserving:

> the party ravished ... is in law a competent witness; but the credibility of her testimony, ... [depends] upon the circumstances ... that concur in that testimony. For instance: if the witness be of good fame; if she presently discovered the offense, and made search for the offender; if the party accused fled for it; ... give greater probability to her evidence. But ... *if she be of evil fame*, and stands unsupported by others; if she concealed the injury for any considerable time after she had opportunity to complain; if the place ... was where it was possible she might have been heard, and she made no outcry; these and the like circumstances carry a strong ... presumption that her testimony is false or feigned. (Blackstone, 1765–1769; emphasis added)

In fact, Blackstone (1765–1769) relays a cautionary tale told by a judge, a comment that has passed down the centuries from judge to judge:

> but it must be remembered, that it is an accusation easy to be made, hard to be proved, but harder to be defended by the party accused, though innocent.

Remarkably, all of the above historical factors for assessing a false complaint are still evident in RMA studies and simulated jury studies of sexual assault trials ('evil fame' or moral worthiness, lack of immediate complaint; failure to cry out or resist and lack of supporting evidence).

For example, when Burgin and Flynn (2019: 297) examined the transcripts of five sexual assault trials in depth, she found that 'the attempts of law reform to date to remove the expectation that victims actively resist a violent attack have not been completely successful'. She reported that these trials revealed the reliance by defence counsel and judges on 'the expectation that women demonstrate or "perform" active resistance … in constructing narratives of consent' (ibid., 304). This occurred despite the enactment of jury directions in Victoria (s 47(3)(d), *Jury Directions Act 2015*), that allows a judge to inform a jury that 'people who do not consent to a sexual act may not protest or physically resist the act' (ibid., 303).

By the beginning of the eighteenth century, case law indicated that the failure to raise a 'hue and cry' had evolved into a presumption of fabrication so that evidence of a speedy complainant was admissible to boost the complainant's credit as a witness (Gobbo, 1970: 245). Rape complainants, thus, became a special category of witness whose credit could be boosted by evidence of recent complaint but the converse was also true—the credit of rape complainants could be undermined by evidence of a delayed complaint, no matter how short.

Because it is common in Western cultures to blame the victim of an alleged sexual assault as a result of her perceived immoral behaviour, or, in the case of children, their supposed propensity for lying or fantasising, the prosecution must also prove the complainant's moral worthiness, a difficult task, according to the jury studies discussed in Chapters 4 and 5.

In no other criminal trial is the moral worthiness of a victim or complainant a de facto fact in issue, in addition to the elements of the charge(s) that the prosecution must prove beyond a reasonable doubt. Since it is likely to remain so for the foreseeable future, the structure of the sexual assault trial requires reform to ameliorate this unfairness to complainants of sexual assault, both adults and children.

But reform of these rules only gets us so far. Even if the rules disappear, the myths behind them linger in the minds of fact-finders and also in modern benchbooks and judicial directions. For example, the UK *Crown Court Compendium* (Judicial College, 2017: 10-4) states:

> Although corroboration in the strict sense is now no longer required in support of … [the evidence of children and sexual assault complainants], circumstances may nevertheless require the judge, as a matter of discretion in summing up, to give a warning to the jury about the need for caution in the absence of supporting evidence.

These circumstances can include the mere fact that there is no supporting evidence (the typical situation for historical sexual assault cases where the complainant has delayed her report to police):

> Where there is no independent supportive evidence, it may be appropriate to remind the jury of that fact, and possibly to suggest that the jury may have wished for such evidence. In that event the jury should also be directed that they may nevertheless rely on the evidence of W if, having taken into account the need for caution and the absence of any independent supportive evidence, they are sure that W is telling the truth. (Judicial College, 2017: 10-7)

Similarly, in NSW, a corroboration warning can still be given despite abrogation of the requirement that it be mandatory.[2]

Any effective reform of the adversarial sexual assault trial must address the relations of power constructed by the sex-specific rules and procedures that have characterised complainants of sexual assault as an unreliable category of witness and which deny the reality of sexual assault—a crime that arises out of institutional, social and cultural relations of inequality and exploitation.

Law reform attempts will be limited unless they address this power imbalance and recognise that the criminal justice system is an institutional site for the reproduction of particular relations of power. Without addressing the gendered context in which sex offences are prosecuted, reforms can be easily ignored (Burgin & Flynn, 2019; Connolly, Coburn, & Chong, 2017) or undermined by old-fashioned reasoning about the unreliability of sexual assault complainants, both adults and children.

Some will argue recent law reforms have fixed the problem of myths and prejudice against sexual assault complainants since they highlight the

---

[2]See s 164, *Evidence Act 1995* (NSW).

modern sensitivity to the unique problems associated with prosecuting sexual assault (Connolly et al., 2017). These reforms include:

- the abrogation of corroboration warnings which are no longer mandatory in relation to the evidence of children and sexual assault complainants;
- the abrogation of delay in complaint warnings;
- the enactment of rape shield laws which prevent admissibility of a complainant's sexual reputation but still permit the admissibility of evidence of her sexual experience (depending on the jurisdiction);
- the enactment of a legal privilege which prevents the admissibility of a complainant's communications to her counsellor; and
- courtroom innovations that enable a complainant to give pre-recorded evidence or evidence via CCTV (Cossins, 2010a).

However, Connolly et al. (2017) argue that it can take several years before such reforms result in changes in practice. When they examined 3035 historical CSA cases from 1986 to 2012, they found that, 17 years after the delay in complaint rule was abrogated in Canada:

> the average length of delays to court began to decrease as did the average age of complainants … The late 1990s to early 2000s also marked the beginning of an increase in guilty pleas, [and] an increase in trial convictions. (Connolly et al., 2017: 172)

For example, the particular adversarial contortions that are required when evidence of a delayed complaint is admitted is evidenced by the extraordinarily long and misleading judicial direction that judges are required to give juries in E&W. Such a direction does everything to highlight the apparent significance of a delayed complaint to a group of laypeople even though there is sound evidence that the majority of complainants of sexual assault delay their complaint (see Chapter 1) and there is no evidence to prove a relationship between delay and fabrication.

The UK Crown Court Compendium (Judicial College, 2017: 10-4) states that '[w]here there has been a substantial delay between the alleged offence(s) and the making of the complaint that led to the current criminal proceedings', the jury should be directed as follows:

(1) The jury should consider the length of and the reasons for the delay in making the complaint and ask whether or not the delay makes the evidence in court of V more difficult to believe.
(2) In a sexual case: the courts have found that victims of sexual offences can react in different ways. Some may complain immediately. Others may feel, for example, afraid, shocked, ashamed, confused or even guilty and may not speak out until some time has passed. There is no typical reaction. Every case is different. …
(3) The jury should not assume that a late complaint is bound to be false, any more than an immediate complaint would definitely be truthful. The jury should consider the circumstances of the particular case.
(4) The matters to be considered are (depending on the evidence and issues in the case):

    (a) Any reason(s) given by V for not having complained earlier.
    (b) Any reasons why V may have been put off from speaking out earlier (about which V did not give evidence) such as:
        (i) V felt afraid of D;
        (ii) V was shocked and/or ashamed and/or confused;
        (iii) V blamed himself;
        (iv) V had mixed feelings for D;
        (v) V was worried that no-one would believe him;
        (vi) V was worried about what would happen to him/D/the family if he spoke out.
    (c) Whether or not D is said to have put pressure on V to keep quiet and if so, how;
    (d) What triggered the eventual making of the complaint.
    (e) The age and degree of maturity and understanding of V at the time/s it is said that the offence/s was/were committed.
    (f) The difference in age and the relationship (if any) between V and D.

(g) The physical and/or emotional situation in which V was living at the time.
(h) Whether V had made earlier complaints that did not lead to criminal proceedings and if so when and, briefly, if relevant why they were not proceeded with.
(i) Any reasons for the delay suggested by or on behalf of D.

(5) It is for the jury alone to weigh up all these matters when deciding whether they are sure that V has given truthful and reliable evidence.

The question raised by the above analysis is, what is the reason for the entrenched relationship between delay, lack of corroboration and credibility? Clearly the issue is cultural and based on historical gendered power relations. As the above judicial direction states, if everyone reacts differently to sexual assault and a delayed complaint is not bound to be false just as an immediate complaint is not bound to be true, then why allow evidence of delay to be adduced at trial? How can delay be relevant to the facts in issue in a sexual assault trial, and why should a complainant be required to explain her reasons for delay, when the most common reaction to sexual assault is delayed complaint (see Chapter 1)?

A case study, *TJ v R*,[3] illustrates how important reforms can be undermined in practice since 'legal and attitudinal changes to CSA prosecutions … may take decades to observe real and substantial change' (Connolly et al., 2017: 173). As happened in Canada (see Connolly et al., 2017), it may take an appeal case delivered some years later to endorse a particular legal reform and result in a change to prosecutorial and judicial practice.

TJ was a joint trial involving allegations of child sexual assault by two complainants, KB and PD. KB was first sexually abused at the age of 6 years. The case included a typical, lengthy direction to the jury about the 'significance' of delay in complaint, as well as lack of corroboration, which was worded in such a way that it could have been interpreted as a message to acquit:

[3] [2009] NSWCCA 257.

> There is no independent, objective evidence confirming the relevant complainant's testimony ... Therefore, in relation to each charge you should scrutinise the evidence of the complainant, KB or PD, very carefully before determining whether you are prepared to accept her evidence ... .
>
> You should consider the delay between the alleged events and the first complaints ... [and] whether any of those delays may have meant that the recollection of K ... could in any way be flawed and therefore unreliable ... [since] human recollection is often inaccurate and the likelihood of inaccuracy increases as time passes. That is something you need to consider in terms of whether recollection was an honest but mistaken recollection.
>
> Because of the delay in the accused learning of these allegations, he has been prejudiced in the conduct of his defence. I therefore caution you that it may be wrong for you to convict on either complainant's evidence, unless, after scrutinising her evidence very carefully indeed, you are well satisfied that her evidence was both truthful and accurate.[4]

At the time of the joint trial involving KB and PD, which began in August 2007, the mandatory corroboration warning requirement had been abrogated and s 294 of the *Criminal Procedure Act* 1986 (NSW) was applicable, a provision that deals with delayed complaints. It was enacted to overcome the common law presumption that a delayed complaint could be used by the jury for its credibility purpose, that is, as evidence of false complaint.[5]

Where a question is asked of a witness that tends to suggest delay in, or an absence of, complaint, trial judges are required to give a s 294(2) warning juries in sexual assault trials in NSW, although in *TJ*, the trial judge ignored that requirement:

---

[4] *TJ* [2009] NSWCCA 257, [29]–[31] (quoting Murrell DCJ); emphasis added. The warning about delay in complaint is based on what is known in Australia as the *Longman* warning, after a High Court case in which the Court stated: 'The jury should have been told that, as the evidence of the complainant could not be adequately tested after the passage of more than 20 years, it would be dangerous to convict on that evidence alone unless the jury, scrutinising the evidence with great care, considering the circumstances relevant to its evaluation and paying heed to the warning, were satisfied of its truth and accuracy' *Longman v R* (1989) 168 CLR 79, [91] (Brennan, Dawson and Toohey JJ).

[5] *Jarrett v R* [2014] NSWCCA 140, [34] (Basten JA).

(a) … that absence of complaint or delay in complaining does not necessarily indicate that the allegation that the offence was committed is false, and
(b) … that there may be good reasons why a victim of a sexual assault may hesitate in making, or may refrain from making, a complaint about the assault.

This and other cases discussed in Chapter 7 reveal the limitations of law reform in the gendered context of the sexual assault trial where entrenched suspicions of the evidence of sexual assault complainants have existed for centuries. One only has to consider the realities of CSA in the *TJ* case: how likely is it that an offender would sexually abuse a six-year-old (the age of KB at the time) in front of witnesses? How likely is that a six-year-old would head down to her local police station and report the sexual abuse or even know that what had been done to her was a crime?

Indeed, it is one of the peculiarities of the criminal justice system that the innate vulnerability of children and the strategies used by sex offenders to groom victims and maintain their silence (O'Leary, Koh, & Dare, 2017) remain largely unrecognised so that this silence is allowed to be used as 'evidence' of the unreliability of the evidence given by child complainants.

On appeal, it is the habit of defence counsel to argue that the strength of the warning given in relation to a delayed complaint is too weak. Such an argument formed one of the grounds of appeal in *TJ* which resulted in a discussion of semantics by the appeal judges, that is, whether or not 'caution' was a synonym for the word, 'warning', a discussion that misses the point.[6] The question is, why does a sexual assault complainant's evidence require *any* warning in circumstances of delay or lack of corroboration when there is no evidence to prove that delay is indicative of fabrication, or that lack of corroboration is proof of unreliability? Some elucidation comes from McCallum J in *TJ* who said about warnings in general:

[6]See, e.g. *TJ* [2009] NSWCCA 257, [71]–[72] (McClellan CJ at CL).

> The essence of the distinction between … a caution and a direction framed as a warning lies in the requirement for a warning to identify and explain the risk or danger inherent in the trial as one the recognition of which derives from *the Court's specialised or accumulated experience*.[7]

But individual judges' experiences are anecdotal only, rather than specialised knowledge, and do not amount to research that would enable them to make any conclusions about the meaning of delay, generally, or in a particular case. In fact, judges rarely refer to the psychological literature which reveals that delay is a typical, not aberrant, feature of sexual assault, as discussed in Chapter 1.

Because of the ignorance within the criminal justice system about the phenomenon of sexual assault as a power-based crime which, typically, is not accompanied by corroborating evidence (such as eyewitnesses) and results in trauma-like symptoms, leading to underreporting and delayed complaints, the context for considering the reform measures in this chapter and the next is trauma-informed care of the complainant from the time her case is set down for prosecution.

The legacy of powerlessness for victims of trauma is repeated within the sexual assault trial since the complainant is a mere witness with no legal representation, and no other professional to monitor the effects of re-traumatisation on her ability to give her best evidence. Typically, the complainant is subject to traps set by defence counsel during the cross-examination process in order to produce confusion and inconsistencies in her evidence, and is subject to rape myths about her moral worth. Few complainants are prepared for the fact that their moral worth is on trial and that fact-finders' assessments of her moral worth will likely determine the defendant's guilt or innocence.

As discussed in this chapter, studies show that the use of gender and victim stereotypes within sexual assault scenarios can negatively influence perceptions of complainant credibility (Masser, Lee, & McKimmie, 2010; McKimmie, Masser, & Bongiorno, 2014; Schuller, McKimmie, Masser, & Klippenstine, 2010). One study found that '92 per cent of defence counsel … utilised one or more of the misconceptions

[7]Ibid., [102]; emphasis added.

about child sexual assault as the platform for the defence case during cross-examination of the child complainant and in opening or closing addresses to the jury' (Blackwell, 2008: 15). Similarly, when 120 transcripts of complainant evidence from 94 child sexual abuse cases were analysed, Powell, Westera, Goodman-Delahunty, and Pichler (2016: 198, 202; footnotes omitted) found that:

> defence lawyers used strategies that were inconsistent with the three key robust findings from psychological research, namely that:
>
> - children are capable of giving reliable evidence
> - errors about minor details do not indicate the central allegation is wrong
> - victims respond to abuse in many ways. …
>
> Of greatest concern were questions implying poor complainant reliability or credibility based on incorrect and antiquated concepts of human memory and reactions to sexual abuse.

By focusing on the traumatic nature of sexual assault, the next chapter aims to shift understandings of sexual assault from a crime defined by rape myths to a historical cultural phenomenon with profound psychological consequences for victims. Unless the court environment is trauma-informed, a trauma survivor is likely to respond to triggers which re-enact her original experiences of trauma, thus setting off a range of emotions that can interfere with the ability to remember events and provide consistent answers. The sexual assault trial requires an understanding of justice from a trauma-informed perspective, which requires reform of the *status* of a complainant within a sexual assault trial. Only by recognising the gendered relations of power within the sexual assault trial, is it possible to explain why the evidence given by children and adults who have been sexually assaulted (who are often vulnerable as a result of age, social disadvantage and/or trauma symptoms) is treated as inherently suspicious. Reform options will be considered from these perspectives.

2 Special Measures for the Protection of Vulnerable Witnesses

While there has never been a better time for complainants of sexual assault, given the range of protective strategies that have been implemented in E&W and various Australian jurisdictions, their behaviours and credibility are still filtered through the misconceptions of laypeople.

The jury is the metaphorical elephant in the room that seems to be an intractable problem that is not able to be reformed. Paradoxically, the myths and misconceptions of jurors are allowed to sit side-by-side the many reforms in Australia and E&W that have focused on defining children and sexual assault complainants as 'vulnerable witnesses', thus providing a range of protective measures to ameliorate the traumatic nature of the sexual assault trial by facilitating the reception of their evidence in ways that aim to minimise re-traumatisation.

Although this chapter is not about already existing special measures to protect vulnerable witnesses since they are adequately dealt with elsewhere (Baverstock, 2016; Bowden, Henning, & Plater, 2014; Charles, 2012; Cossins, 2006, 2010a; HM Government, 2018; Ministry of Justice, 2012; Spencer & Lamb, 2012; Royal Commission into Institutional Responses to Child Sexual Abuse, 2017b, 2017c), a summary of the measures to improve complainants' experiences in court reveals the legislative changes that have been designed to lessen the trauma of giving evidence of sexual assault. The availability of these measures varies from jurisdiction to jurisdiction, depending on eligibility requirements (such as age or disability). These measures include:

- *Video-recorded police interviews* as the complainant's evidence-in-chief in court which is then played at trial so the complainant is not required to give evidence in court[8]; or
- *Pre-recording* of the complainant's evidence-in-chief at a pre-trial hearing[9];

[8]For example, YJCE Act, s 27(1); *Criminal Procedure Act 1986* (NSW), ss 306S, 306U.

[9]For example, *Criminal Procedure Amendment (Child Sexual Offence Evidence Pilot) Act 2015*; *Criminal Procedure Act 1986*, Part 29, Schedule 2.

- *Pre-recording* of cross-examination in a pre-trial hearing[10]; or
- *CCTV and remote rooms* (outside of the courtroom) for streaming the complainant's 'live' evidence into the court[11];
- *Screens* between the complainant and defendant if the complainant chooses to give evidence in court[12];
- *A support person* for the complainant while she gives evidence;
- The conduct of sexual assault trials *in camera*[13];
- *Non-publication* of the name(s) of complainant(s) and other identifying information[14];
- *Mandatory obligations* on judges to disallow improper questions by counsel, with legislation in NSW defining an improper question to include the manner or tone in which a question is asked[15];
- *Enactment of provisions* that prevent general judicial comments being made about the reliability of the evidence of sexual assault complainants and children[16];
- *Preventing unrepresented defendants* from personally cross-examining complainants[17];
- *Removal of wigs and gowns* by court personnel[18];

[10]For example, YJCE Act, s 28(1). In Australia, Western Australia was the first jurisdiction to introduce pre-recording of cross-examination: *Evidence Act* 1906, s 106K, 106I.

[11]For example, *Criminal Procedure Act 1986* (NSW), s 294B-C. In E&W, more than 2000 operational video links exist in Magistrates' and Crown Courts that enable complainants to give evidence outside of the courtroom. Some studies have shown that there is no difference in real jurors' and mock jurors' perceptions of complainants when comparing CCTV versus in-court testimony (Cashmore & Trimboli, 2006; Ellison & Munro, 2014; Taylor & Joudo, 2005), while other studies have shown that jurors view children's evidence more favourably when they observe children in court compared to evidence given via CCTV (Landström & Granhag, 2010). A review by Hoyano and Keenan (2010) concluded that there is no significant difference in conviction rates when witnesses give evidence via live links into the courtroom, compared to in-court evidence. For an alternative view, see McAuliff and Kovera (2012).

[12]*Criminal Procedure Act 1986* (NSW), s 294B-C.

[13]For example, *Children (Criminal Procedure Act)* 1987 (NSW), s 10.

[14]For example, YJCE Act, ss 44; 46; *Criminal Procedure Act 1986* (NSW), s 291.

[15]See for example, *Evidence Act 1995* (NSW), s 41.

[16]See, for example, *Evidence Act 1995* (NSW), ss 165(6) and 165A; *Criminal Procedure Act 1986* (NSW), s 294AA.

[17]For example, YJCE Act, ss 34, 35.

[18]For example, YJCE Act, s 26.

- *Use of intermediaries* at the police interview stage and at trial (see Chapter 9);
- *Training* of specialist prosecutors and judges.

Other interventions such as court dogs which are relatively common in US states (Caprioli & Crenshaw, 2017; Courthouse Dogs Foundation, 2015; Crenshaw, Stella, O'Neill-Stephens, & Walsen, 2016; Gerkey, 2016) are becoming more common in Australia (Royal Commission, 2017b). However, such interventions, which are designed to ameliorate the emotionally abusive nature of the adversarial system, do not take place within a trauma-informed system. While Crenshaw et al. (2016), for example, recognise the 'inhospitable' court environment in the USA in which children are required to give evidence in their discussion of the need for court dogs, they do not canvass trauma-informed principles and their application to the adversarial trial.

In fact, the introduction of special measures for protecting vulnerable witnesses implicitly condones the traumatising impact of the adversarial system, resulting in the paradoxical situation whereby a complainant may be allowed a court dog, support person or other measures to reduce her stress and re-traumatisation within a system that is designed to traumatise her and prevent her from giving her best evidence. Indeed, the VLRC (2016) recently recognised this trauma in its one of its recommendations for greater protection of vulnerable witnesses:

> Recommendation 37 (emphases added)
>
> The *Criminal Procedure Act 2009* (Vic) should be amended to include a definition of protected victim. A protected victim should be defined as a victim *who is likely to suffer severe emotional trauma* or be *so intimidated or distressed* as to be unable to give evidence or give evidence fairly.

As argued below, all sexual assault complainants ought to be treated as vulnerable or protected witnesses. But with no recognition of the need for trauma-informed principles within the sexual assault trial, definitions such as the above are mere words on paper. In the absence of specific reforms to prevent re-traumatisation, reforms to date are limited in preventing a complainant from 'suffer[ing] severe emotional trauma or be so intimidated or distressed as to be unable to give evidence' (as per Recommendation 37 above).

Generally, the approach of reformers is to institute reforms that are based on *ameliorating* the effects of the adversarial trial rather than *changing* the adversarial system to prevent harm to vulnerable victims. For example, Caprioli and Crenshaw (2017) recommended that children should be exposed to aggressive and hostile questioning to practice their responses in order to prepare them for trial. But how appropriate is it to emotionally abuse a child in order to prepare her or him for the emotional abuse s/he will experience during a criminal trial?

In another example, the Home Affairs Select Committee (2013) in E&W argued for reforms to ensure that traumatised child victims are able to give their best evidence in court. It made a number of recommendations (2013: 62–70) including that all victims of child sexual exploitation be offered the services of a trained Independent Sexual Violence Advisor (ISVA) (prior to the child's ABE interview), as well as support services in the form of pre-trial therapy, a pre-court familiarisation visit and a meeting with the prosecutor in the presence of the ISVA. The aim was to ensure that a child would be supported by the same ISVA throughout the trial process.

There was also a view that 'the balance is skewed too strongly in favour of protecting the defendant's rights as opposed to the very vulnerable witnesses in cases of child sexual exploitation' (Home Affairs Select Committee, 2013: 45). The Committee stated that reforms were needed to ensure that a child witness is capable of giving clear and effective evidence in court, such as immediate implementation of pre-recorded cross-examination and re-examination of a child witness and a nominated person in each court with responsibility for ensuring that these and other special measures were implemented as required.

Training was recommended to educate the judiciary about the effects of cross-examination on child witnesses, in particular the problem of cross-examination by multiple defence counsel in cases with multiple defendants and how judges might allocate issues between counsel, and impose time limits.

Since then the British Government has adopted further reforms, including the piloting of a 'Child House' to improve support services for

CSA victims. The Child House pilot will be tested in London over a two-year period by 'bring[ing] multiple services together in a child-friendly environment to minimise' trauma for victims (HM Government, 2018: 24). But nowhere in the British Government's *Victims Strategy* document of 2018 was there a mention of trauma-informed services and specialist courtroom processes for vulnerable witnesses, despite acknowledgement of the need for enhanced services and support for victims prior to court.

On a broader perspective, the House of Commons, Committee of Public Accounts (2016: 3, 5) said that the British criminal justice system:

> is close to breaking point. Lack of shared accountability and resource pressures mean that costs are being shunted from one part of the system to another and the system suffers from too many delays and inefficiencies. There is insufficient focus on victims, who face a postcode lottery in their access to justice due to the significant variations in performance in different areas of the country. ... The Government is implementing reforms to improve the system but we are concerned that users of the system won't see the full benefit for another four years. ... Around two-thirds of trials in the Crown Court are delayed or do not go ahead at all.

If 45% of the victims and witnesses who gave evidence said they would not be prepared to give evidence again (House of Commons, Committee of Public Accounts, 2016: 5) and if 'the court environment can be challenging' for vulnerable witnesses, it is time to challenge the appropriateness of that environment for giving evidence and consider reforms *beyond* special measures and refurbishment of court buildings so that victims/witnesses will not encounter the defendant (HM Government, 2018: 34, 35).

The aim of this book is not to review all of these above innovations, many of which have been introduced on an ad hoc basis over many years in the genuine hope of improving the experiences of sexual assault complainants in court. This book endorses these attempts at genuine goodwill towards victims but considers whether reform has gone far enough. The key question is: is it time to change the adversarial system to cater for the needs of vulnerable witnesses?

Like inquiries in Australia (for example, NSW Joint Select Committee on Sentencing of Child Sexual Assault Offenders, 2014; NSW Standing Committee on Law and Justice, 2002), the Home Affairs Select Committee (2013) also recommended that specialist courts be introduced to prosecute CSA or all sexual offences, including designated courtrooms with the most up-to-date technology and appropriate access and waiting facilities. In order to ensure the most serious cases would be guaranteed the most experienced court team delivering best practice, it was recommended that the specialist court should have a team of specialist child sexual exploitation judges, prosecutors, police, witness support and ushers who are trained and linked into local Multi-Agency Safeguarding Hubs which house a range of professionals and services for victims.

The implementation of specialist courts was to be reviewed at the end of 2014, however, the Ministry of Justice (2014) did not see the need for specialist courts in light of other reforms, even though it acknowledged:

> One of the potential benefits of 'specialist courts' for child sexual abuse cases or for all sexual violence cases, would be the ability to join everything up and provide a wrap-around service strongly oriented around the victim and witnesses. (Ministry of Justice, 2014a: 14)

Although specialist domestic violence courts are in existence in E&W, the Ministry believed that an alternative approach based on case management would suffice 'to ensure that [sexual assault cases] are progressed and actively managed through all stages of the criminal justice system and by people who are specialised' (ibid., 15). Such an approach ignores the fact that case management is entirely different to the traumatising practices of the courtroom which involve the cross-examination effect and the unregulated use of rape myths to gain acquittals.

By and large, special measures for vulnerable witnesses do not directly address the cross-examination effect since the same type of 'inappropriate questioning occurs regardless of the mode of evidence-giving' (Smith, 2017: 3) unless innovations like intermediaries are used, as discussed in Chapter 9, or judges are trained to recognise and actively intervene to prevent improper and age-inappropriate questions, thus producing cultural change. The fact that cross-examination is the key cultural site for creating unfairness to complainants in a sexual assault trial is reinforced by the Royal Commission's (2017b: 27) observation that if the videotaped police investigative interview is:

> not well conducted ... it may adversely affect the jury's view of the complainant's reliability and credibility. This is particularly a problem if the interview includes many peripheral details which lead to extensive cross-examination on inconsistencies that are not central to the offences charged.

Although some special measures fall within the concept of therapeutic jurisprudence (King, Freiberg, Batagol, & Hyams, 2014) since they have been introduced to prevent the re-traumatisation of complainants, no evidence-base in terms of their effects on reducing trauma informed their introduction with few, if any, evaluations of most of these measures. Thus, the mere existence of special measures does make criminal courts in E&W or Australia trauma-informed systems. Although there is evidence from E&W (Hamlyn, Phelps, Turtle, & Sattar, 2004) that some measures improve satisfaction rates of complainants, there is no evidence that these reforms ameliorate the cross-examination effect, or reduce fact-finders' reliance on myths and misconceptions or improve actual trial outcomes.

3 Victims' Rights: A Panacea to the Adversarial Trial?

Even if a conviction is the outcome in a sexual assault trial, the costs and benefits to the complainant need to be taken into account in terms of the degree of re-traumatisation she has suffered as a result of the hostile environment of the courtroom. In other words, what constitutes complainants' justice interests?

The rights of victims might be conceptualised in a document setting out victims' rights, such as the NSW Charter of Rights of Victims of Crime (Appendix 2) enacted under the *Victims Rights and Support*

Act 2013 (NSW) and the UK Code of Practice for Victims of Crime (Appendix 3) (see Ministry of Justice, 2015b).

Probably the most detailed charter is the Canadian *Victims Bill of Rights* enacted in 2015 (Appendix 1). A perusal of this statute reveals that every victim has a right to certain information (ss 6–8) such as 'the status and outcome of the investigation into the offence; and the location of proceedings in relation to the offence, when they will take place and their progress and outcome' (s 7). Victims also have rights to (ss 10–13):

- protection from intimidation and retaliation;
- privacy;
- identity protection; and
- request testimonial aids.

Victims have a right to put their views about decisions that will affect their rights under the Canadian Victims Bill of Rights and to have them considered by appropriate authorities (s 14) which does not seem to amount to much more than lip-service to victim consultation. Victims also have the right to present a victim impact statement and to have it considered (s 15). In relation to compensation, a victim can apply to a court for a restitution order against the offender (s 16) presumably after the offender is found guilty.

Certain remedies are available to protect the above rights. If a victim wishes to complain that any of their rights 'have been infringed or denied by a federal department, agency or body', they have the right to file a complaint (s 25) under the 'complaints mechanism' (s 25(3)) that every department, agency or body involved in the criminal justice system must establish. However, this complaints mechanism is qualified by the fact that victims do not have a cause of action or a right to damages if a right has been infringed or denied (s 28) and they cannot appeal a decision or order that has infringed or denied one of their rights (s 29).

Victims' rights are similar in other jurisdictions. In NSW the Charter of Victims' Rights (Appendix 2) was enacted under the *Victims Rights and Support Act 2013* and applies to all NSW government agencies who deal with victims of crime. Like Canada, the NSW Charter of Victims'

Rights mostly deals with rights to information but there is little recourse for victims if an agency infringes or denies one of their rights other than a complaint, although there is no legislated complaint mechanism for filing a complaint.

In E&W, victims' rights are set out in a statutory Code of Practice for Victims of Crime (Appendix 3). The requirement for such a code was enacted under s 32 of the *Domestic Violence Crime and Victims Act 2004*, with the Secretary of State for Justice under a duty to 'issue a code of practice as to the services to be provided to a victim of criminal conduct'. The Code is set out in a 104-page document (Ministry of Justice, 2014a). Like the case in Canada and NSW, a failure to uphold the Code or perform a duty imposed by the Code does not give rise to criminal or civil proceedings. However, a failure to comply with the Code may be admissible in civil proceedings in relation to any of the facts in issue; for example, if a complainant seeks redress against the police or the CPS.

Furthermore, the Ministry of Justice provides updates for victims about what the government has achieved and plans for further assistance. For example, in 2014 the Ministry of Justice (2014b: 10) reported that it had achieved the following:

- published a new Victims' Code which gives victims of crime clearer entitlements from criminal justice agencies and better tailors services to individual need so they get the right support at the right time;
- published a revised Witness Charter, which sets out the standards of service all witnesses should receive, from the time of reporting a crime through to trial;
- improved the complaints process for victims and witnesses so that they know who to contact and what to expect if things go wrong;
- begun piloting pre-trial recorded cross-examination to help vulnerable witnesses give their best possible evidence—without subjecting them to the full atmosphere of the courtroom. The first such cross-examination took place in Liverpool on 28 April 2014;
- opened 13 new rape support centres since 2010; …
- created a Victims' Panel, which met for the first time on 7 May 2014, so that Ministers can hear first-hand from victims about what we can

do better to help them come to terms with and recover from the traumatic effects of crime; and

- adopted the TrackMyCrime IT system … which enables victims to view information about the progress of their case, and exchange messages with the investigating officer.

Clearly, the above victim rights and services are not equivalent to the rights conferred by either statute or the common law on defendants (such as a right to legal representation, the presumption of innocence and the right to silence) because the defendant is the person on trial who, if his/her rights are not protected, may end up being wrongly convicted. But as Chapter 5 clearly showed, the complainant is also 'on trial' in a sexual assault case. While she cannot be convicted of an offence, she can have her experience completely undermined by defence counsel, and her reputation shredded through accusations of lying and promiscuity, leading to emotional trauma both during and after the trial. If the defendant is acquitted, the complainant has no appeal rights, even if lies were told about her or inculpatory evidence about the defendant was deemed inadmissible.

Broadly, victims' rights charters are designed to provide information to victims about the progress of their case and contain various 'motherhood' statements about being treated with courtesy, respect and compassion. But what does it say about our criminal justice systems that personnel need to be reminded about common human decency towards victims? Apart from these issues, charters of victims' rights do not extend to the trial itself since there is no such code or charter for the treatment of victims/complainants *in court* so that victims remain subject to all the rules and procedures of the criminal trial with no rights to protect them from defence attacks, the cross-examination effect or the myths and misconceptions of fact-finders. In Australian and E&W, they also have no rights to legal representation (as discussed below).

While victims' charters or codes of practice might ensure that complainants are provided with information about the court process, they do not guarantee fair treatment within the trial itself, that is, treatment free of gender and victim stereotypes, free of bias and free of re-traumatisation. They do not inform victims that they are likely to have their experiences and behaviours compared with the mythical 'real' rape scenario and that they will be judged negatively if their behaviours do not match those of the 'chaste' rape complainant. They do not provide for mechanisms to complain about unfair treatment such as bullying, sexism, racism and other forms of bias and prejudice within the trial process.

In E&W, the Code of Practice for Victims has been criticised on the grounds that the Code is not delivering entitlements to victims (Victims' Commissioner Office, 2017a, 2017b; see also Burton, Evan, & Sanders, 2007; Payne, 2009). For example, after 12 young victims (and in some cases their families) were interviewed about whether they had been informed about, and received their entitlements under the Victims' Code, the Victims' Commissioner Office (2017b: 6) found:

> a mixture of experiences ... There were some examples of good practice ... but on the whole the young victims who were interviewed were not informed about or did not receive all of their entitlements under the [Victims'] Code. Many ... did not feel that they were treated with dignity and respect by criminal justice agencies, with some feeling that they were not believed nor taken seriously because of their age. ... In particular the children, young people and their families expressed confusion and frustration because of a lack of accurate and timely information and communication. Some children and young people reported a perceived lack of procedural justice in which they were made to feel like criminals themselves. ... This review concluded that the provision of a professional victims' advocate service would help alleviate many of the frustrations and difficulties that children, young people and their families reported in this review.

Overall, victims' rights are limited and do not address the gendered power relations of the adversarial trial in that they offer no substantive rights to protect complainants from gendered assumptions about their behaviour and character. In essence, they do not protect complainants' moral worth from being on trial.

If there is a failure to uphold any of the victims' rights, or there is a breach, denial or infringement of one of those rights, there is no civil or criminal redress by the victim. None of these rights amount to the legal rights which would grant a complainant in a sexual assault trial legal personhood.

By contrast, limited substantive rights in relation to the criminal trial for victims exist in Canada and Ireland. A right to legal representation in Canada arises if an accused seeks access to a 'record' relating to a complainant, that is:

> any form of record that contains personal information for which there is a reasonable expectation of privacy and includes, … medical, psychiatric, therapeutic, counselling, education, employment, child welfare, adoption and social services records, personal journals and diaries, and records containing personal information the production or disclosure of which is protected by any other Act of Parliament or a provincial legislature, but does not include records made by persons responsible for the investigation or prosecution of the offence. (Criminal Code of Canada, s 278.1)

Under s 278.4(2) of the Criminal Code of Canada, 'The person who has possession or control of the record, the complainant or witness, as the case may be, and any other person to whom the record relates may appear and make submissions at the hearing'. Under s 278.4(2.1), 'The judge shall, as soon as feasible, inform any person referred to in subsection (2) who participates in the hearing of their right to be represented by counsel'.

The enactment of a similar right was recommended in Australia by the VLRC (2016: xxiv) in relation to challenging a defence subpoena seeking access to a complainant's confidential communications (usually with their counsellor) (Recommendation 25). Thus, amendments were recommended to Division 2A of Part 2 of the *Evidence (Miscellaneous Provisions) Act 1958* (Vic) as follows:

(a) requiring the prosecution to notify the victim of their right to appear and the availability of legal assistance in relation to an application to subpoena, access and use their confidential communications;
(b) requiring the court to be satisfied that the victim is aware of the application and has had an opportunity to obtain legal advice;

(c) prohibiting the court from waiving the notice requirements except where the victim cannot be located after reasonable attempts or the victim has provided informed consent to the waiver;
(d) providing victims with standing to appear;
(e) permitting victims to provide a confidential sworn or affirmed statement to the court specifying the harm the victim is likely to suffer if the application is granted.

Nonetheless, this recommendation would not affect the trial process since it pertains to a pre-trial hearing in which the prosecution challenges the terms of the subpoena seeking access to confidential communications. In any case, the Victorian Government did not subsequently enact this recommendation.[19]

In Ireland, a right to legal representation for the complainant arises when a defendant seeks leave to adduce evidence or cross-examine a complainant 'about any sexual experience of [the] complainant with a person other than that accused' (Criminal Law (Rape) Act 1981, ss 3 and 4A).

Is there an inequality of arms for victims, as proposed by the Ministry of Justice (2014a)? Hoyano (2015: 116) describes such a proposition as a fallacy and criticised the Ministry of Justice for its consideration of the idea of legal representation for victims. Various arguments have been made over the years in favour of legal representation for both adult and child witnesses in sexual assault trials (Braun, 2013; Cossins, 2004, 2010a; Kirchengast, 2013; Raitt, 2010; Shapland & Hall, 2010; Spencer, 2012; *cf* Royal Commission into Institutional Responses to Child Sexual Abuse, 2017b, 2017c; VLRC, 2016). The idea of representation for complainants comes from civil jurisdictions in Western Europe in which some or all victims of crime have a right to legal representation at the time of complaint and trial.

[19] See https://www.lawreform.vic.gov.au/all-projects/victims-crime-criminal-trial-process, accessed 18 March 2019.

One of the main reasons for proposing representation for complainants in an adversarial context is to protect them, particularly during the cross-examination stage of the trial. In a review of the role of victims' lawyers, Kirchengast (2013: 572) writes that they:

> may now present for certain pretrial matters for federal offenses in the United States … and to a more limited extent, for family members of homicide victims in the Crown Court in England and Wales, and rape or sexual assault victims in [NSW in order to challenge defence access to confidential counselling notes]. Such reforms have proven controversial, however, and debate abounds about the extent such lawyers may jeopardize the state's control of the prosecution process, or otherwise jeopardize a defendant's right to challenge the state case … Further concern resides in the integration of a 'third party' into an otherwise two-party process. Although it is commonly agreed that various parts of the criminal trial process … may significantly impact upon the victim and their family, the extent to which the victim ought to contribute to decision-making processes or contest substantive principles of law remains uncertain.

There is a strong belief that the introduction of legal representation for complainants would undermine 'the accused's right to a fair trial and the impartial and independent conduct of prosecutions' (Royal Commission into Institutional Responses to Child Sexual Abuse, 2017b: 226, 228; see also Hoyano, 2015). While I do not subscribe to this view, I believe that, because of cost, governments would not be prepared to provide legal aid to fund the legal representation of all complainants both pre-trial and during trial proceedings. An alternative, conferring a right to *self*-funded legal representation, would be unjust in that it would create a two-tier system of justice for victims of sexual assault—those with and without the means to afford a lawyer.

Even if complainants had a right to legal representation, the fundamental structure of the adversarial system would remain unchanged. Thus, I believe that more radical reform of the sexual assault trial is required to address its inherent gendered power imbalance and to change the status of a complainant from a morally unworthy subject to a person who is vulnerable and requires protection from re-traumatisation.

I now turn to the issue of trauma and its effects on those who must battle trauma-like symptoms, including memory recall, at the same time as defending their moral worth in a hostile court environment. This discussion raises the issue that we have created a morally flawed system, which permits the use of myths, biases and prejudice, to undermine the evidence of traumatised individuals.

4 The Effect of Trauma on Memory Recall: The Myths and the Evidence

There is a considerable amount of psychological research on eyewitness memory, including:

(i) The effect of emotional arousal;
(ii) Rates of forgetting;
(iii) The misinformation effect; and
(iv) Trauma and memory (ALRC, NSWLRC & VLRC, 2005: [8.86]–[8.112]; see also The British Psychological Society Research Board, 2010).

For the purposes of this and the next chapter, it is important to consider the effects of trauma on the memory recall of complainants of sexual assault, given the fact that CSA and sexual assault are known to cause PTSD or trauma-like symptoms, although these effects are rarely taken into account when a complainant is giving evidence.

In fact, Hohl and Conway (2017: 249) consider that a 'significant proportion' of reports to police that do not proceed to court 'may be wrongly dismissed because the criteria criminal justice agents use to judge the reliability and veracity of a victim's complaint of rape are, from a memory research perspective, flawed'.

As discussed previously, both jurors and mock jurors distrust the evidence of witnesses that reveals inconsistencies or inaccuracies or where the witness cannot recall particular details, however peripheral they are to the events in question (Cashmore & Trimboli, 2006; Hohl & Conway,

2017). Several studies that have surveyed lawyers, judges, jury-eligible citizens and law enforcement personnel about how memory works reveal clear inconsistencies between people's common knowledge and scientific understandings of the nature of human memory.

For example, there is a widespread belief that human memories are akin to a video-recording (Houston, Hope, Memon, & Read, 2013) while jurors, judges and police officers have a poor understanding of eyewitness memories. When Benton, Ross, Bradshaw, Thomas, and Bradshaw (2006: 125) were the first to compare the knowledge level of these three groups with that of experts, they found that there was:

- only 13% correspondence between jurors and experts about eyewitness evidence; and
- 40% correspondence between judges and experts, and between police officers and experts.

Research shows that inconsistencies in evidence are associated with acquittals and case attrition (Cashmore & Trimboli, 2006; Kelly, Lovett, & Regan, 2005; Pichler, Sharman, Powell, Westera, & Goodman-Delahunty, 2019) which means that the 'internal consistency' of a complainant's story of sexual assault as well as the amount of 'often insignificant peripheral detail … are key criteria the police and prosecution use to assess the veracity of a complaint' (Hohl & Conway, 2017: 249).

For example, in their study of 2284 cases reported to police, Kelly et al. (2005) found an association between the presence of inconsistencies and case attrition. Of the 30 cases that had been classified as false allegations and dropped by police, all were characterised by inconsistencies in evidence, according to the police (ibid., 49). Most recently, a study of 69 trial transcripts found that the greater the number of inconsistencies within a child complainant's police interview or between that interview and other statements, the more likely the case resulted in an acquittal (Pichler et al., 2019: 1).

While there is 'no research on the amount and nature of inconsistencies … that is likely to put the complaint below the credibility threshold and into danger of attrition' (Hohl & Conway, 2017: 261), in a study of all rape complaints reported to the London Metropolitan Police Service (MPS) during April and May 2012 ($N = 679$), Hohl and Conway (2017: 259–260) found that 'attrition through police and CPS decisions to drop the case is significantly higher when inconsistencies are noted in the case file'. In other words, only 'half as many cases with inconsistencies are referred to the CPS'. They also found an interaction effect between complainant consumption of alcohol and inconsistencies: 'the odds of the case being no-crimed increase[d] from 2.5 if the victim [was] not intoxicated to 13.9 if the victim had consumed alcohol prior to the attack' (ibid., 260; see further Chapters 4 and 7).

Of all the cases referred to the CPS, 'no complaint with an inconsistent victim account resulted in a prosecution' whereas more than 50% of referred cases with no inconsistencies resulted in a prosecution. However, the authors had no way of knowing whether the inconsistencies noted by police were due to errors of recall by the complainant, deliberate omissions, a result of '[p]oor rapport between the interviewing officer and the complainant', poor interviewing techniques (Hohl & Conway, 2017: 261), or, something not considered by the authors, the result of trauma-like symptoms affecting complainant recall.

Hohl and Conway (2017: 250) discuss the fundamental flaw in the criminal justice system when it comes to witness memory—the lack of awareness of how human memory works. Even without trauma, memory recall is imperfect. Memories are 'fragmented remnants of what happened in the past, pieced together in a "sensible" manner according to the rememberer's current world view' (Howe, 2013: 869), rather than a complete, literal record of events and experience:

> The consistent, detailed narratives that are considered 'good' evidence … are at odds with the nature of human memory – memories are always fragmentary, time-compressed and prone to errors of omission and commission. While inconsistencies, lack of detail, errors and omissions … undermine [the credibility of a complainant] … and put the complaint at risk of attrition, the modern view of human memory considers all of these [to be] typical features of a normal memory. (Hohl & Conway, 2017: 261)

Because memory is the brain's re-construction of an event, it is subject to both internal and external influences which can cause gaps in memory, distortion and error. These influences include: psychological distress, the use of alcohol and drugs both before and after an event, ageing and mental illness. In addition the memory of a person who has suffered a traumatic event, such as sexual assault, is likely to be 'fragmented into several key "hotspot" moments … [which] are typically the 'worst moments' for the person during the trauma, and are also those points that tend to come back, as intrusive memories' (The British Psychological Society Research Board, 2010: 25).

While 'hotspots' are generally 'very vivid and clear', they may be recalled randomly, rather than sequentially, while the intrusiveness and longevity of hotspot memories means that 'other parts of the trauma can be more difficult to recall (e.g. details that were less important to the person at the time)' (ibid.), inevitably leading to gaps in memory.

Because inconsistencies and lack of detail are typical features of *all* witness memories, they are 'poor indicators of reliable memory or any sort of intention to deceive' (Hohl & Conway, 2017: 254). Indeed, The British Psychological Society Research Board (2010: 2) emphasises that gaps in memory are a normal part of all human memory because of their reconstructed nature:

> Memories for experienced events are always incomplete. … Any account of a memory will feature forgotten details and gaps, and this must not be taken as any sort of indicator of accuracy.

This is a critical issue in a sexual assault trial where the child or adult complainant is the prosecution's chief, and often only, witness, and where there is little or no corroborating evidence. One of the main defence tactics, therefore, is to discredit the complainant by focusing on apparent gaps or flaws in her memory, including every apparent inconsistency about even the most minor details.

For example, a study of 94 CSA trials 'found that defence lawyers used strategies which questioned robust findings from [the] psychological research' including:

- children are capable of giving reliable evidence;
- errors about minor details do not indicate the central allegation is wrong;
- victims respond to abuse in many ways. (Royal Commission, 2017b: 136; citing Powell et al., 2016: 198)

Powell et al. (2016: 201–202) found that suggestions of impaired memory and inconsistencies were routinely used by defence counsel to undermine child complainants' sexual abuse allegations. In particular, inconsistencies relating to peripheral details were raised more frequently than inconsistencies about matters central to proving the offence (98.4% vs 72.4% of complainants). Defence counsel also exploited common misconceptions held by laypeople that suggest an allegation is false, including lack of resistance, delayed complaint, lack of emotional display by a complainant and a complainant's continued relationship with the defendant. As Hohl and Conway (2017: 262) ask, '[w]hy are the criteria criminal justice agents use to judge the credibility of victim memory – such as consistency and rich detail – so at odds with the scientific understanding of human memory?'

Because the adversarial trial is based on attack and defence, rather than truth-seeking, vulnerable witnesses are most susceptible to the effects of defence strategies around memory. Indeed, because gender stereotypes (the chaste victim vs the unchaste victim) characterise the sexual assault trial so that the moral worth of the complainant is on trial, inconsistencies in evidence 'confirm', for the layperson, the gender stereotype that is constructed by the defence because of the link made between inconsistencies in evidence with lying and moral unworthiness.

Another relevant question is why the criminal justice system permits a complainant's credibility to be judged against common rape myths, given their clear inconsistencies with the documented effects of sexual assault on human behaviour, such as the belief that a 'real' victim will resist her attacker versus psychological evidence of the freeze response (see Chapter 4, Table 1).

In light of what we know from the literature, is 'the nature of human memory evidence … fundamentally incompatible with the evidentiary demands of the criminal justice system' (Hohl & Conway, 2017: 262)? More particularly, is the nature of human memory fundamentally incompatible with the evidentiary demands of the criminal standard of proof in a sexual assault trial because of the insidious influence of cultural beliefs about 'chaste' and 'unchaste' victims of sexual assault? Would a system that recognises the vulnerabilities of traumatised complainants ameliorate the worst aspects of adversarialism as played out in the sexual assault trial? Why do we tolerate the questioning of vulnerable and traumatised witnesses in a way that is incompatible with the nature of human memory?

The focus of the criminal justice system is on the management and control of defendants who are brought to trial, a culture that extends to witnesses but is in conflict with the principles of trauma-informed care (discussed in the next chapter), leaving witnesses open to various forms of emotional abuse that would not be condoned in the workplace or in public. For complainants in sexual assault trials there is little or no recognition of the basic principles of trauma-informed care which informs the treatment of trauma survivors.

In the next chapter, I consider the efficacy of trauma-informed theory for the development of trauma-informed criminal justice processes, such as specialist sex offences courts and restorative justice.

Appendix 1

Canadian Victims Bill of Rights

S.C. 2015, c. 13, s. 2

Assented to 23 April 2015

An Act for the Recognition of Victims Rights

[Enacted by section 2 of chapter 13 of the Statutes of Canada, 2015, in force July 23, 2015]

Preamble

Whereas crime has a harmful impact on victims and on society;

Whereas victims of crime and their families deserve to be treated with courtesy, compassion and respect, including respect for their dignity;

Whereas it is important that victims' rights be considered throughout the criminal justice system;

Whereas victims of crime have rights that are guaranteed by the *Canadian Charter of Rights and Freedoms*;

Whereas consideration of the rights of victims of crime is in the interest of the proper administration of justice;

Whereas the federal, provincial and territorial governments share responsibility for criminal justice;

Whereas, in 1988, the federal, provincial and territorial governments endorsed the *Canadian Statement of Basic Principles of Justice for Victims of Crime* and, in 2003, the *Canadian Statement of Basic Principles of Justice for Victims of Crime, 2003*;

Now, therefore, Her Majesty, by and with the advice and consent of the Senate and House of Commons of Canada, enacts as follows:

Short Title

Marginal note: Short title

1. This Act may be cited as the *Canadian Victims Bill of Rights*.

Interpretation

Marginal note: Definitions

2. The following definitions apply in this Act.

offence means an offence under the *Criminal Code*, the *Youth Criminal Justice Act* or the *Crimes Against Humanity and War Crimes Act*, a designated substance offence as defined in subsection 2(1) of the *Controlled Drugs and Substances Act* or an offence under section 91 or Part 3 of the *Immigration and Refugee Protection Act*. (*infraction*)

victim means an individual who has suffered physical or emotional harm, property damage or economic loss as the result of the commission or alleged commission of an offence. (*victime*)

Marginal note: Acting on victim's behalf

3. Any of the following individuals may exercise a victim's rights under this Act if the victim is dead or incapable of acting on their own behalf:

- **(a)** the victim's spouse or the individual who was at the time of the victim's death their spouse;
- **(b)** the individual who is or was at the time of the victim's death, cohabiting with them in a conjugal relationship, having so cohabited for a period of at least one year;
- **(c)** a relative or dependant of the victim;
- **(d)** an individual who has in law or fact custody, or is responsible for the care or support, of the victim;
- **(e)** an individual who has in law or fact custody, or is responsible for the care or support, of a dependant of the victim.

Marginal note: Exception

4. An individual is not a victim in relation to an offence, or entitled to exercise a victim's rights under this Act, if the individual is charged with the offence, found guilty of the offence or found not criminally responsible on account of mental disorder or unfit to stand trial in respect of the offence.

Marginal note: Criminal justice system

5. For the purpose of this Act, the criminal justice system consists of

- **(a)** the investigation and prosecution of offences in Canada;
- **(b)** the corrections process and the conditional release process in Canada; and
- **(c)** the proceedings of courts and Review Boards, as those terms are defined in subsection 672.1(1) of the *Criminal Code*, in respect of accused who are found not criminally responsible on account of mental disorder or unfit to stand trial.

Rights

Information

Marginal note: General information

6. Every victim has the right, on request, to information about

- **(a)** the criminal justice system and the role of victims in it;

- **(b)** the services and programs available to them as a victim, including restorative justice programs; and
- **(c)** their right to file a complaint for an infringement or denial of any of their rights under this Act.

Marginal note: Investigation and proceedings
7. Every victim has the right, on request, to information about

- **(a)** the status and outcome of the investigation into the offence; and
- **(b)** the location of proceedings in relation to the offence, when they will take place and their progress and outcome.

Marginal note: Information about offender or accused
8. Every victim has the right, on request, to information about

- **(a)** reviews under the *Corrections and Conditional Release Act* relating to the offender's conditional release and the timing and conditions of that release; and
- **(b)** hearings held for the purpose of making dispositions, as defined in subsection 672.1(1) of the *Criminal Code*, in relation to the accused, if the accused is found not criminally responsible on account of mental disorder or unfit to stand trial, and the dispositions made at those hearings.

Protection

Marginal note: Security
9 Every victim has the right to have their security considered by the appropriate authorities in the criminal justice system.
Marginal note: Protection from intimidation and retaliation
10. Every victim has the right to have reasonable and necessary measures taken by the appropriate authorities in the criminal justice system to protect the victim from intimidation and retaliation.
Marginal note: Privacy
11. Every victim has the right to have their privacy considered by the appropriate authorities in the criminal justice system.

Marginal note: Identity protection

12. Every victim has the right to request that their identity be protected if they are a complainant to the offence or a witness in proceedings relating to the offence.

Marginal note: Testimonial aids

13. Every victim has the right to request testimonial aids when appearing as a witness in proceedings relating to the offence.

Participation

Marginal note: Views to be considered

14. Every victim has the right to convey their views about decisions to be made by appropriate authorities in the criminal justice system that affect the victim's rights under this Act and to have those views considered.

Marginal note: Victim impact statement

15. Every victim has the right to present a victim impact statement to the appropriate authorities in the criminal justice system and to have it considered.

Restitution

Marginal note: Restitution order

16. Every victim has the right to have the court consider making a restitution order against the offender.

Marginal note: Enforcement

17. Every victim in whose favour a restitution order is made has the right, if they are not paid, to have the order entered as a civil court judgment that is enforceable against the offender.

General Provisions

Marginal note: Application

- **18 (1)** This Act applies in respect of a victim of an offence in their interactions with the criminal justice system

  (a) while the offence is investigated or prosecuted;
  (b) while the offender is subject to the corrections process or the conditional release process in relation to the offence; and

(**c**) while the accused is, in relation to the offence, under the jurisdiction of a court or a Review Board, as those terms are defined in subsection 672.1(1) of the *Criminal Code*, if they are found not criminally responsible on account of mental disorder or unfit to stand trial.

- **Marginal note: Reporting of offence**
  (**2**) For the purpose of subsection (1), if an offence is reported to the appropriate authorities in the criminal justice system, the investigation of the offence is deemed to begin at the time of the reporting.
- **Marginal note: *National Defence Act***
  (**3**) This Act does not apply in respect of offences that are service offences, as defined in subsection 2(1) of the *National Defence Act*, that are investigated or proceeded with under that Act.

Marginal note: Exercise of rights

- **19** (**1**) The rights of victims under this Act are to be exercised through the mechanisms provided by law.
- **Marginal note: Connection to Canada**
  (**2**) A victim is entitled to exercise their rights under this Act only if they are present in Canada or they are a Canadian citizen or a permanent resident within the meaning of subsection 2(1) of the *Immigration and Refugee Protection Act*.

Marginal note: Interpretation of this Act

20. This Act is to be construed and applied in a manner that is reasonable in the circumstances, and in a manner that is not likely to

- (**a**) interfere with the proper administration of justice, including

  (**i**) by causing interference with police discretion or causing excessive delay in, or compromising or hindering, the investigation of any offence, and
  (**ii**) by causing interference with prosecutorial discretion or causing excessive delay in, or compromising or hindering, the prosecution of any offence;

- **(b)** interfere with ministerial discretion;
- **(c)** interfere with the discretion that may be exercised by any person or body authorized to release an offender into the community;
- **(d)** endanger the life or safety of any individual; or
- **(e)** cause injury to international relations or national defence or national security.

Marginal note: Interpretation of other Acts, regulations, etc.

21. To the extent that it is possible to do so, every Act of Parliament enacted—and every order, rule or regulation made under such an Act—before, on or after the day on which this Act comes into force must be construed and applied in a manner that is compatible with the rights under this Act.

Marginal note: Primacy in event of inconsistency

- **22 (1)** If, after the application of sections 20 and 21, there is any inconsistency between any provision of this Act and any provision of any Act, order, rule or regulation referred to in section 21, the provision of this Act prevails to the extent of the inconsistency.
- **Marginal note: Exception—Acts and regulations, etc.**

  (2) Subsection (1) does not apply in respect of the *Canadian Bill of Rights*, the *Canadian Human Rights Act*, the *Official Languages Act*, the *Access to Information Act* and the *Privacy Act* and orders, rules and regulations made under any of those Acts.

Marginal note: No adverse inference

23. No adverse inference is to be drawn against a person who is charged with an offence from the fact that an individual has been identified as a victim in relation to the offence.

Marginal note: Entering or remaining in Canada

24. Nothing in this Act is to be construed so as to permit any individual to

- **(a)** enter Canada or to remain in Canada beyond the end of the period for which they are authorized to so remain;
- **(b)** delay any removal proceedings or prevent the enforcement of any removal order; or
- **(c)** delay any extradition proceedings or prevent the extradition of any person to or from Canada.

Remedies

Marginal note: Complaint—federal entity

- **25 (1)** Every victim who is of the opinion that any of their rights under this Act have been infringed or denied by a federal department, agency or body has the right to file a complaint in accordance with its complaints mechanism.
- **Marginal note: Complaint to authority**

  (2) Every victim who has exhausted their recourse under the complaints mechanism and who is not satisfied with the response of the federal department, agency or body may file a complaint with any authority that has jurisdiction to review complaints in relation to that department, agency or body.
- **Marginal note: Complaints mechanism**

  (3) Every federal department, agency or body that is involved in the criminal justice system must have a complaints mechanism that provides for

  - **(a)** a review of complaints involving alleged infringements or denials of rights under this Act;
  - **(b)** the power to make recommendations to remedy such infringements and denials; and
  - **(c)** the obligation to notify victims of the result of those reviews and of the recommendations, if any were made.

Marginal note: Complaint—provincial or territorial entity

26. Every victim who is of the opinion that their rights under this Act have been infringed or denied by a provincial or territorial department, agency or body may file a complaint in accordance with the laws of the province or territory.

Marginal note: Status

27. Nothing in this Act is to be construed as granting to, or removing from, any victim or any individual acting on behalf of a victim the status of party, intervenor or observer in any proceedings.

Marginal note: No cause of action

28. No cause of action or right to damages arises from an infringement or denial of a right under this Act.

Marginal note: No appeal

29. No appeal lies from any decision or order solely on the grounds that a right under this Act has been infringed or denied.

RELATED PROVISIONS

- **—2015, c. 13, s. 2.1**

  - **Review of *Canadian Victims Bill of Rights***

    2.1 Five years after section 2 comes into force, a committee of Parliament is to be designated or established for the purpose of reviewing the *Canadian Victims Bill of Rights* enacted by that section.

Appendix 2

NSW Charter of Rights of Victims of Crime
(*Victims Rights and Support Act 2013* (NSW), s 6)

Number	Victims' rights
6.1	Courtesy, compassion and respect A victim will be treated with courtesy, compassion, cultural sensitivity and respect for the victim's rights and dignity
6.2	Information about services and remedies A victim will be informed at the earliest practical opportunity, by relevant agencies and officials, of the services and remedies available to the victim
6.3	Access to services A victim will have access where necessary to available welfare, health, counselling and legal assistance responsive to the victim's needs
6.4	Information about investigation of the crime A victim will, on request, be informed of the progress of the investigation of the crime, unless the disclosure might jeopardise the investigation. In that case, the victim will be informed accordingly
6.5	Information about prosecution of accused (1) A victim will be informed in a timely manner of the following: (a) the charges laid against the accused or the reasons for not laying charges, (b) any decision of the prosecution to modify or not to proceed with charges laid against the accused, including any decision to accept a plea of guilty by the accused to a less serious charge in return for a full discharge with respect to the other charges, (c) the date and place of hearing of any charge laid against the accused, (d) the outcome of the criminal proceedings against the accused (including proceedings on appeal) and the sentence (if any) imposed (2) A victim will be consulted before a decision referred to in paragraph (b) above is taken if the accused has been charged with a serious crime that involves sexual violence or that results in actual bodily harm or psychological or psychiatric harm to the victim, unless: (a) the victim has indicated that he or she does not wish to be so consulted, (b) the whereabouts of the victim cannot be ascertained after reasonable inquiry

(continued)

(continued)

Number	Victims' rights
6.6	Information about trial process and role as witness A victim who is a witness in the trial for the crime will be informed about the trial process and the role of the victim as a witness in the prosecution of the accused
6.7	Protection from contact with accused A victim will be protected from unnecessary contact with the accused and defence witnesses during the course of court proceedings
6.8	Protection of identity of victim A victim's residential address and telephone number will not be disclosed unless a court otherwise directs
6.9	Attendance at preliminary hearings A victim will be relieved from appearing at preliminary hearings or committal hearings unless the court otherwise directs
6.10	Return of property of victim held by State If any property of a victim is held by the State for the purpose of investigation or evidence, the inconvenience to the victim will be minimised and the property returned promptly
6.11	Protection from accused A victim's need or perceived need for protection will be put before a bail authority by the prosecutor in any bail application by the accused
6.12	Information about special bail conditions A victim will be informed about any special bail conditions imposed on the accused that are designed to protect the victim or the victim's family
6.13	Information about outcome of bail application A victim will be informed of the outcome of a bail application if the accused has been charged with sexual assault or other serious personal violence
6.14	Victim impact statement A relevant victim will have access to information and assistance for the preparation of any victim impact statement authorised by law to ensure that the full effect of the crime on the victim is placed before the court
6.15	Information about impending release, escape or eligibility for absence from custody. A victim will, on request, be kept informed of the offender's impending release or escape from custody, or of any change in security classification that results in the offender being eligible for unescorted absence from custody

(continued)

(continued)

Number	Victims' rights
6.16	Submissions on parole and eligibility for absence from custody of serious offenders A victim will, on request, be provided with the opportunity to make submissions concerning the granting of parole to a serious offender or any change in security classification that would result in a serious offender being eligible for unescorted absence from custody
6.17	Financial assistance for victims of personal violence A victim of a crime involving sexual or other serious personal violence is entitled to make a claim under the Victims Support Scheme
6.18	Information about complaint procedure where Charter is breached A victim may make a complaint about a breach of the Charter and will, on request, be provided with information on the procedure for making such a complaint

Appendix 3

UK Code of Practice for Victims of Crime

(Ministry of Justice, 2014a)

The key entitlements under the Code are as follows:

- A written acknowledgement that you have reported a crime, including the basic details of the offence;
- An enhanced service if you are a victim of serious crime, a persistently targeted victim or a vulnerable or intimidated victim;
- A needs assessment to help work out what support you need;
- Information on what to expect from the criminal justice system;
- Be referred to organisations supporting victims of crime;
- Be informed about the police investigation, such as if a suspect is arrested and charged and any bail conditions imposed;
- Make a Victim Personal Statement (VPS) to explain how the crime affected you;
- Read your VPS aloud or have it read aloud on your behalf, subject to the views of the court, if a defendant is found guilty;

- Be informed if the suspect is to be prosecuted or not or given an out of court disposal;
- Seek a review of the police or CPS's decision not to prosecute in accordance with the National Police Chiefs Council (NPCC) and CPS Victims' Right to Review schemes;
- Be informed of the time, date and location and outcome of any court hearings;
- Be informed if you need to give evidence in court, what to expect and discuss what help and support you might need with the Witness Care Unit;
- Arrange a court familiarisation visit and enter the court through a different entrance from the suspect and sit in a separate waiting area where possible;
- Meet the CPS advocate and ask him or her questions about the court process where circumstances permit;
- Be informed of any appeal against the offender's conviction or sentence;
- To opt into the Victim Contact Scheme (VCS) if the offender is sentenced to 12 months or more for a specified violent or sexual offence;
- If you opt into the VCS to:
- make a VPS for consideration by the Parole Board if the offender is considered for release or transfer and apply to the Parole Board to read it out at the hearing;
- make representations about the conditions attached to the offender's licence on release and be informed about any licence conditions relating to you;
- Apply for compensation under the Criminal Injuries Compensation Scheme;
- Receive information about Restorative Justice and how you can take part;
- Make a complaint if you do not receive the information and services you are entitled to, and to receive a full response from the relevant service provider.

References

Australian Law Reform Commission, NSW Law Reform Commission and Victorian Law Reform Commission. (2005). *Uniform evidence law report* (ALRC Report No. 102; NSWLRC Report No. 112; VLRC Final Report). Sydney: ALRC.

Baverstock, J. (2016). *Process evaluation of pre-recorded cross-examination scheme* (Section 28). London: Ministry of Justice. https://www.gov.uk/government/publications/process-evaluation-of-pre-recorded-cross-examination-pilot-section-28.

Benton, T. R., Ross, D. F., Bradshaw, E., Thomas, W. N., & Bradshaw, G. S. (2006). Eyewitness memory is still not common sense: Comparing jurors, judges and law enforcement to eyewitness experts. *Applied Cognitive Psychology, 20,* 115–129.

Blackstone, W. (1765–1769). *Commentaries on the laws of England* (Book 4, Chapter 15 of Offenses Against the Persons of Individuals). Oxford: The Clarendon Press.

Blackwell, S. (2008, November). *Child sexual abuse on trial in New Zealand*. Paper presented at the Criminal Law Symposium, Auckland, New Zealand.

Boniface, D. J. (1994). Ruining a good boy for the sake of a bad girl: False accusation theory in sexual offences, and New South Wales Limitations Periods—Gone but not forgotten. *Current Issues in Criminal Justice, 6,* 54–75.

Bowden, P., Henning, T., & Plater, D. (2014). Balancing fairness to victims, society and defendants in the cross-examination of vulnerable witnesses: An impossible triangulation, *Melbourne University Law Review, 37*, 539–584.

Braun, K. (2013). Legal representation for sexual assault victims—Possibilities for law reform. *Current Issues Criminal Justice, 25,* 819–837.

Burgin, R., & Flynn, A. (2019). Women's behavior as implied consent: Male "reasonableness" in Australian rape law. *Criminology & Criminal Justice,* online. https://doi.org/10.1177/1748895819880953.

Burton, M., Evans, R., & Sanders, A. (2007). Vulnerable and intimated witnesses and the adversarial process in England and Wales. *International Journal of Evidence and Proof, 11,* 1–23.

Caprioli, S., & Crenshaw, D. A. (2017). The culture of silencing child victims of sexual abuse: Implications for child witnesses in court. *Journal of Humanistic Psychology, 57,* 190–209.

Cashmore, J., & Trimboli, L. (2006). Child sexual assault trials: A survey of juror perceptions. *Crime and Justice Bulletin, 102,* 1–20.

Charles, C. (2012). *Special measures for vulnerable and intimidated witnesses: Research exploring the decisions and actions taken by prosecutors in a sample of CPS case files.* London: Crown Prosecution Service.

Cole, E. (2018, January 8). Can juries deliver justice to sexual assault victims? *The Sydney Morning Herald.* http://www.smh.com.au/comment/can-juries-deliver-justice-to-sexual-assault-victims-20171220-h0870m.html. Accessed 16 January 2018.

Connolly, D. A., Coburn, P. I., & Chong, K. (2017). Twenty-six years prosecuting historical child sexual abuse cases: Has anything changed? *Psychology, Public Policy, and Law, 23,* 166–177.

Cossins, A. (1999). Defying reality: Child sexual assault and the delay in complaint rule. *Current Issues in Criminal Justice, 11,* 17–34.

Cossins, A. (2001). Complaints of child sexual abuse: Too easy to make or too difficult to prove? *Australian and New Zealand Journal of Criminology, 34,* 149–168.

Cossins, A. (2003). Saints, sluts and sexual assault: Rethinking the relationship between sex, race and gender. *Social and Legal Studies, 12,* 77–103.

Cossins, A. (2006). Prosecuting child sexual assault cases: Are vulnerable witness protections enough? *Current Issues in Criminal Justice, 18,* 299–317.

Cossins, A. (2010a). *Alternative models for prosecuting child sex offences in Australia.* Sydney: National Child Sexual Assault Reform Committee, UNSW.

Cossins, A. (2015). *Female Criminality: Infanticide, Moral Panics and the Female Body.* Basingstoke, UK: Palgrave Macmillan.

Courthouse Dogs Foundation. (2015). *Facility dogs at Children's Advocacy Centers and in legal proceedings: Best practice.* Courthouse Dogs Foundation, Western Legal Advocacy Center and Office of Juvenile Justice and Delinquency Prevention.

Crenshaw, D. A., Stella, L., O'Neill-Stephens, E., & Walsen, C. (2016). Developmentally and trauma-sensitive courtrooms. *Journal of Humanistic Psychology*, online, 1–7. https://doi.org/10.1177/0022167816641854.

Daly, K., & Bouhours, B. (2010). Rape and attrition in the legal process: A comparative analysis of five countries. In M. Tonry (Ed.), *Crime and justice: A review of research.* Chicago: University of Chicago Press.

Ellison, L., & Munro, V. E. (2014). A 'special' delivery? Exploring the impact of screens, live-links and video-recorded evidence on mock juror deliberation in rape trials. *Social & Legal Studies, 23,* 3–29.

Gerkey, L. (2016). Legal beagles, a silent minority: Therapeutic effects of facility dogs in the courtroom. *International Journal of Therapeutic Jurisprudence, 1,* 405–431.

Gobbo, J. A. (1970). *Cross on Evidence*. Sydney: Butterworths.

Hale, M. (1736/1971). *Historia Placitorum Coronae* (P. R. Glazebrook, Ed., Vol. 1). London: Professional Books.

Hamlyn, B., Phelps, A., Turtle, J., & Sattar, G. (2004). *Are special measures working? Evidence from surveys of vulnerable and intimidated witnesses* (Home Office Research Study 283). London: Home Office.

HM Government. (2018). *Victims strategy*. London: Ministry of Justice.

Hohl, K., & Conway, M. A. (2017). Memory as evidence: How normal features of victim memory lead to the attrition of rape complaints. *Criminology & Criminal Justice, 17,* 248–265.

House of Commons, Home Affairs Select Committee. (2013). *Child exploitation and the response to localised grooming: Second report of session 2013–14*. London: The Stationery Office Ltd.

House of Commons, Committee of Public Accounts. (2016). *Efficiency in the criminal justice system: First report of session 2016–17*. London: House of Commons.

Houston, K. A., Hope, L., Memon, A., & Read, J. D. (2013). Expert testimony on eyewitness evidence: In search of common sense. *Behavioral Sciences & the Law, 31,* 637–651.

Howe, M. L. (2013). Memory development: Implications for adults recalling childhood experiences in the courtroom. *Nature Reviews Neuroscience, 14,* 869–876.

Hoyano, L. (2015). Reforming the adversarial trial for vulnerable witnesses. *Criminal Law Review, 2,* 107–129.

Hoyano, L., & Keenan, (2010). *Child abuse: Law and policy across boundaries*. Oxford: Oxford University Press.

Judicial College. (2017). *The Crown Court Compendium: Part 1: Jury and trial management and summing up*. www.judiciary.gov.uk/wp-content/uploads/2016/06/crown-court-compendium-pt1-jury-and-trial-management-and-summing-up-feb2017.pdf. Accessed 24 May 2017.

Kelly, L. (2010). The (in)credible words of women: False allegations in European rape research. *Violence Against Women, 16,* 1345–1355.

Kelly, L., Lovett, J., & Regan, L. (2005). *A gap or a chasm? Attrition in reported rape cases* (Home Office Research Study No. 293). London: Home Office. https://webarchive.nationalarchives.gov.uk/20110218141141/http://rds.homeoffice.gov.uk/rds/pdfs05/hors293.pdf.

King, M., Freiberg, A., Batagol, B., & Hyams, R. (2014). *Non-Adversarial Justice*. Sydney: Federation Press.

Kirchengast, T. (2013). Victim lawyers, victim advocates, and the adversarial criminal trial. *New Criminal Law Review: an International and Interdisciplinary Journal, 16,* 568–594.

Landström, S., & Granhag, P. A. (2010). In-court versus out-of-court testimonies: Children's experiences and adults' assessments. *Applied Cognitive Psychology, 24,* 941–955.

Masser, B. M., Lee, K., & McKimmie, B. M. (2010). Bad woman, bad victim? Disentangling the effects of victim stereotypicality, gender stereotypicality and benevolent sexism on acquaintance rape victim blame. *Sex Roles, 62,* 494–504.

McAuliff, B. D., & Kovera, M. B. (2012a). When will a child be believed? The impact of the victim's age and juror's gender on children's credibility and verdict in sexual-abuse cases. *Child Abuse & Neglect, 25,* 523–539.

McAuliff, B. D., & Kovera, M. B. (2012b). Do jurors get what they expect? Traditional versus alternative forms of children's testimony. *Psychology, Crime & Law, 18,* 27–47.

McKimmie, B. M., Masser, B. M., & Bongiorno, R. (2014). What counts as rape? The effect of offense prototypes, victim stereotypes, and participant gender on how the complainant and defendant are perceived. *Journal of Interpersonal Violence, 29,* 2273–2303.

Ministry of Justice. (2012). *Swift and sure justice: The government's plans for reform of the criminal justice system.* London: Ministry of Justice.

Ministry of Justice. (2014a). *Report on review of ways to reduce distress of victims in trials of sexual violence*. London: Ministry of Justice.

Ministry of Justice. (2014b). *Transforming the criminal justice system strategy and action plan—Implementation update*. London: Ministry of Justice.

Ministry of Justice. (2015a). *Code of practice for victims of crime presented to Parliament pursuant to section 33 of the Domestic Violence, Crime and Victims Act 2004*. London: Ministry of Justice.

Ministry of Justice. (2015b). *Code of practice for victims of crime*. London: Ministry of Justice.

Naylor, B. (2010). Effective justice for victims of sexual assault: Taking up the debate on alternative pathways. *University of New South Wales Law Journal, 33,* 662–684.

NSW Joint Select Committee on Sentencing of Child Sexual Assault Offenders. (2014). *Every sentence tells a story—Report on sentencing of child sexual assault offenders* (Report No. 1/55). Sydney: Parliament of NSW.

NSW Standing Committee on Law and Justice. (2002). *Report on child sexual assault prosecutions* (Parliamentary Paper No. 208; Report No. 22). Sydney: Parliament of NSW.

O'Leary, P., Koh, E., & Dare, A. (2017). *Grooming and child sexual abuse in institutional contexts*. Sydney: Royal Commission into Institutional Responses to Child Sexual Abuse.

Payne, S. (2009). *Rape: The victim experience review*. London: Home Office.

Pether, P. (2009). What is due to others: Speaking and signifying subject(s) of rape law. *Griffith Law Review, 18*, 237–258.

Pichler, A. S., Sharman, S. J., Powell, M., Westera, N., & Goodman-Delahunty, J. (2019). Association between interview quality and child sexual abuse trial outcome. *Journal of Family Violence*, online, 1–9. https://link.springer.com/article/10.1007/s10896-019-00051-5.

Powell, M. B., Westera, N. J., Goodman-Delahunty, J., & Pichler, A. S. (2016). *An evaluation of how evidence is elicited from complainants of child sexual abuse*. Sydney: Royal Commission into Institutional Responses to Child Sexual Abuse.

Quilter, J. (2015). From raptus to rape: A history of the requirements of resistance and injury. *Law & History, 2*, 89–113.

Raitt, F. E. (2010). Independent legal representation for complainants in rape trials. In C. McGlynn & V. E. Munro (Eds.), *Rethinking rape law: International and comparative perspectives*. Abingdon: Routledge.

Royal Commission into Institutional Responses to Child Sexual Abuse. (2017a). *Final report: Nature and cause* (Vol. 2). Sydney: Royal Commission into Institutional Responses to Child Sexual Abuse.

Royal Commission into Institutional Responses to Child Sexual Abuse. (2017b). *Criminal justice report* (Executive Summary and Parts I–II). Sydney: Royal Commission into Institutional Responses to Child Sexual Abuse.

Royal Commission into Institutional Responses to Child Sexual Abuse. (2017c). *Criminal justice report* (Parts VII–X and Appendices). Sydney: Royal Commission into Institutional Responses to Child Sexual Abuse.

Royal Commission into the New South Wales Police Service. (1997). *The paedophile inquiry* (Vol. 5, Final Report). Sydney: The Government of the State of New South Wales.

Rumney, P. N. (2006). False allegations of rape. *The Cambridge Law Journal, 65*, 128–158.

Schuller, R. A., McKimmie, B. M., Masser, B. M., & Klippenstine, M. A. (2010). Judgments of sexual assault: The impact of complainant emotional demeanor, gender and victim stereotypes. *New Criminal Law Review, 13,* 759–780.

Shapland, J., & Hall, M. (2011). Victims at court: Necessary accessories or principal players at centre state? In A. Bottoms & J. Roberts (Eds.), *Hearing the victim: Adversarial justice, crime victims and the state.* London: Willan Publishing, Routledge.

Smart, C. (1989). *Feminism and the power of the law.* London: Routledge.

Smith, O. (2017). The practicalities of English and Welsh rape trials: Observations and avenues for improvement. *Criminology & Criminal Justice, 18,* 332–348.

Smith, O., & Skinner, T. (2017). How rape myths are used and challenged in rape and sexual assault trials. *Social & Legal Studies, 26,* 441–466.

Spencer, J. R. (2012). Conclusions. In J. R. Spencer & M. Lamb (Eds.), *Children and cross-examination: Time to change the rules?* (pp. 171–202). Oxford: Hart Publishing.

Spencer, J. R., & Lamb, M. (2012). *Children and cross-examination: Time to change the rules?*. Oxford: Hart Publishing.

Taylor, N., & Joudo, J. (2005) *The impact of pre-recorded video and closed circuit television testimony by adult sexual assault complainants on jury decision-making: An experimental study* (Research and Public Policy Series No. 68). Canberra: Australian Institute of Criminology.

The British Psychological Society Research Board. (2010). *Guidelines from memory and the law: Recommendations from the scientific study of human memory.* Leicester: British Psychological Society.

Victims' Commissioner Office. (2017a). *Victims code is not delivering entitlements to victims.* http://victimscommissioner.org.uk/victims-code-is-not-delivering-entitlements-for-victims/.

Victims' Commissioner Office. (2017b). *Are we getting it right for young victims of crime? A review of children's entitlement in the victims' code.* https://s3-eu-west-2.amazonaws.com/victcomm2-prod-storage-119w3o4kq2z48/uploads/2019/02/VC-Young-victims-of-crime-Review-2017.pdf.

Victorian Law Reform Commission. (2016). *The Role of Victims of Crime in the Criminal Trial Process (Report No. 34).* Melbourne: Victorian Law Reform Commission.

Williams, Z. (2013, October 19). Keir Starmer: 'The potential for change in our criminal justice system is huge'. *The Guardian.* https://www.theguardian.com/theguardian/2013/oct/18/keir-starmer-potential-change-criminal-justice.

11

Achieving Best Evidence for Vulnerable Witnesses: The Use of Trauma-Informed Theory to Reform the Sexual Assault Trial

1 Introduction

The aim of this chapter is to consider measures to transform the adversarial trial process into a trauma-informed system that recognises the triggers for re-traumatisation within the criminal justice system and the measures needed to eliminate shaming, humiliation and blame of the complainant. In doing so, I will document the environmental trauma triggers that exist within the sexual assault trial and have the potential to undermine a complainant's ability to give her best evidence. In so doing, I consider the extent to which these triggers can be ameliorated by a system of trauma-informed care.

For example, 'children with a disability are disproportionately targeted as victims of CSA' (Royal Commission, 2017a: 97), although the adversarial nature of the criminal trial means that such children are essentially prevented from giving their best evidence and even from participating as witnesses. However, by '[i]mproving the quality of evidence provided – and in some cases, providing reliable evidence where at present none can be given – [this] is consistent with the aims of making the criminal justice system accessible' (ibid.).

A. Cossins, *Closing the Justice Gap for Adult and Child Sexual Assault*,
https://doi.org/10.1057/978-1-137-32051-3_11

The reality of giving evidence in a sexual assault trial was revealed in a recent current affairs programme shown on Australian national television,[1] where an adult complainant of CSA ('Veronique') spoke of the trauma of giving evidence in front of a room full of strangers. During her courtroom appearance, she 'had to fight … to be believed' after many years of not being believed as a child, describing her experience as one where she was 'completely dispossessed of [her] own story' in the adversarial trial. She came out of that experience feeling traumatised and disempowered.

In the same programme, a 14-year-old complainant, 'Amy', who alleged she had been gang-raped by three men, had been warned by prosecutors about the gruelling cross-examination process she could expect from the defendants' three defence barristers. She was also warned that this process was not about the truth, but about confusing and discrediting her in the 'theatre of the trial'. Ultimately, Amy withdrew her complaint after receiving psychological advice that the court process could be worse than the gang-rape.

When an adult complainant of CSA (FAB) gave evidence to the Royal Commission into Institutional Responses to Child Sexual Abuse (2017a: 17) about his experiences of giving evidence in court, he revealed the trauma of giving evidence:

> I gave evidence over two days at the trial. It was a pretty gruelling experience. … [N]o-one told me the level of details that I was required to go into … I was asked questions about the nitty-gritty of each particular incident, such as, … whether it happened in the morning or the afternoon or the colour of [the defendant's] pubic hair. … [The defendant's] lawyers absolutely tore me to shreds when they cross-examined me … [and] I became very upset. … They said that the inconsistencies [between two different statements] showed that I was able to make up the abuse in order to get compensation from the Catholic Church. They made me feel like a real piece of crap.

This style of cross-examination worked since the judge, as fact-finder, acquitted the defendant but noted, paradoxically: 'I am well satisfied

[1] *Insight*, SBS Television, 27 February 2018.

that the accused did sexually abuse the complainant … and I reject his blanket denial as a reasonable possibility' (ibid., 17).

A recent British case study confirms the above experiences, with children reporting that they were under 'extreme pressure to remember events accurately' and that defence questions were 'repetitive, rapid, confusing, and focused on secondary content rather than the central criminal acts' (Ahern, Kowalski, & Lamb, 2018: 321).

Although the culture of the courtroom is in the hands of the trial judge who has the power to control proceedings to protect a complainant by disallowing improper questions and implementing measures to address a complainant's distress, is adversarialism the best we can offer child and adult complainants of sexual assault?

While the above accounts provide anecdotal evidence of the psychological distress that can be experienced by CSA complainants, a number of studies discussed below have documented the psychological impacts of testifying on children (see Table 1).

Despite the empirical evidence listed in Table 1, which reveals that a majority of children who testify in court suffer mental health problems prior to, during and/or post-trial, recovery from trauma is not a goal of the criminal trial. A trial is of relatively short duration and only requires the presence of witnesses for short periods. By contrast, the rationale for the introduction of trauma-informed care within mental health facilities is based on the goal of achieving recovery from trauma for clients who will be typically receiving ongoing services for a period of time (Harris & Fallot, 2001).

Unlike systems that may be trauma-informed, such as correctional or psychiatric facilities, the criminal trial is not an intervention system; rather it is a forum for the adjudication of criminal charges. As such, child welfare agencies are not involved in criminal trial processes even if a child is called as a witness, nor does the criminal trial provide public health services to witnesses, although it may coordinate the provision of services to convicted *defendants* by other agencies at a sentencing hearing after adjudication of the criminal charges (see, for example, Drabble, Jones, & Brown, 2013).

Table 1 Studies on the impact of testifying in court on children in CSA cases[a]

Study	Age of children (years)	Testifiers (*N*)	Comparison group	Impact of testifying
Oates and Tong (1987)	5–19	21	Non-testifying children (*N* = 25)	• 18 out of 21 parents said their child had been very upset or extremely upset after testifying • 12 out of 21 parents said their child was still upset 2.5 years later • 12 out of 21 testifiers had persisting behavioural problems and of those who repeated a year of school, 7 out of 8 were testifiers • 15 out of 46 children had developed behavioural problems at school which were still present at the time of study, including aggression, truancy and attention-seeking behaviour • Waiting for the trial had an adverse effect on all children
Whitcomb et al. (1991)	4–17	65	Non-testifying children (*N* = 224)	• Testifying once, and long and/or harsh cross-examination has significant adverse effects for children less than 8 years of age
Sas et al. (1993)	5–17 8–20	71 39		• No significant relationship between testifying and mental health for children who participated in a court preparation programme before testifying, initially or 3 years later • Poorer adjustment for children in acquittal cases *cf* guilty verdicts
Goodman et al. (1992)	4–17	63	Non-testifying children	• No improvement in behavioural problems several months after the case ended *cf* non-testifiers • Testifiers in cases without corroborative evidence and without maternal support at greatest risk of adverse mental health outcomes • Older children more anxious about testifying and more emotional in court compared to younger children

(continued)

Table 1 (continued)

Study	Age of children (years)	Testifiers (*N*)	Comparison group	Impact of testifying
Berliner and Conte (1995)	10–15	12		• The anticipation of testifying in addition to, or instead of, testifying itself predicts increased distress
Henry (1997)	9–19	30	Non-testifying children ($N = 60$)	• No significant relationship between testifying and mental health outcomes • Nonetheless, 34% of testifiers said it was harmful • A majority of testifiers said they were either scared or felt like they were on trial • 90% of testifiers said it was frightening being in the presence of the defendant • The more interviews, the greater a child's level of trauma
Quas et al. (2005)	15–29	63	Non-testifying children from the Goodman et al. (1992) study	• Testifiers followed up 12 years later had higher levels of defensive avoidance, and internalising symptoms • Repeated testifying in childhood predicted poorer current functioning • Being more distressed in court was associated with later adverse outcomes and with more negative feelings about the effect of the case on their lives • Young age was associated with poorer later adjustment • 7–11-year-olds (50%) and 12–17-year-olds (30%) had more negative feelings about court *cf* 4–6-year-olds (0%) and were more likely to cry while testifying • The above findings correlated with longer questioning *and* lawyers' lower support for older children

(continued)

Table 1 (continued)

Study	Age of children (years)	Testifiers (*N*)	Comparison group	Impact of testifying
Hayes and Bunting (2013)	Young people less than 18	37	N/A	• 83.8% were very anxious pre-trial • 78.4% very nervous or upset while waiting to give evidence on the day of trial • While 88.6% gave evidence via CCTV, a majority were nervous: 48.6% were upset, scared or shaky, 25.8% were confused, 14.3% felt physically sick • A majority had problems with defence questions: 42.9% did not understand them, 77.1% said they were repetitive, 45.7% said they were too long/complicated, 34.3% said they jumped around in time, 31.4% said they placed unrealistic demands on their memory • 77.1% were unhappy with how defence behaved towards them • 54.1% were still upset, scared and/or worried at the time of study • 51.4% said there was nothing positive about being a witness
Hobbs et al. (2014)	7–10	52	Non-testifying children	• CSA victims were more distressed about seeing defendants in court than victims of other child abuse • Older age and abuse severity predicted degree of negative feelings about answering questions • Girls expressed greater negativity than boys about seeing defendants in court

(continued)

Table 1 (continued)

Study	Age of children (years)	Testifiers (*N*)	Comparison group	Impact of testifying
Elmi, Daignault, and Hébert (2018)	6–14	130	Non-testifying children (*N* = 214)	• The higher the number of stressors on a child, the higher the probability of experiencing problems • Several factors affected testifiers' mental health including: individual characteristics, parental support, corroborative evidence • Those who testified more than once showed higher levels of emotional distress 2 years later including depression, anxiety, PTSD, hypervigilance and avoidance

[a]Based on studies cited in Quas and Goodman (2012) and updated research

Nonetheless, the criminal trial is likely to have an impact on a complainant's mental health because of the phenomenon of re-traumatisation, since there is overwhelming evidence that, compared to non-sexual assault survivors, sexual assault survivors are at increased life-time risk of developing a range of mental health issues and behavioural disorders including major depression, anxiety disorder, post-traumatic stress disorder or injury (PTSD or PTSI), anti-social personality disorder, addictions such as alcohol and drug dependence, eating disorders, suicidal ideation and suicide attempts (Chen et al., 2010; Fergusson, Boden, & Horwood, 2008; Fergusson, McLeod, & Horwood, 2013; Hillberg, Hamilton-Giachritsis, & Dixon, 2011; Maniglio, 2009, 2013; Wilson, 2010).

Yet more than 20 years ago, Henry's (1997: 509) study found that if testifying children have a relationship with a trusted professional this helps to ameliorate the fear and emotional consequences of giving evidence: '[t]he establishment of trust as a primary goal of societal system intervention is crucial in minimizing potential trauma to sexually abused children'.

Arguably, there is a need for trauma-informed services within the criminal trial, not for the purposes of dealing with the mental health needs of trauma survivors but to do *no further harm* in order to allow survivors to give their best evidence. In other words, the criminal trial provides the best evidence to fact-finders (jurors or judges) when a witness's memory works at its optimum level of recall, something that is impeded when the emotional memories of the original trauma are re-triggered, as discussed below. For example, Boyd and Hopkins' (2010: 164) study of lawyers found that 'those responsible for asking the questions, objecting to them or disallowing them were unaware of the level of confusion and trauma being experienced by children in the witness stand'.

Unsurprisingly, the introduction of trauma-informed care within an organisation is typically framed within a public health paradigm (see, for example, Ford & Blaustein, 2013; Hodgdon, Kinniburgh, Gabowitz, Blaustein, & Spinazzola, 2013). Because the criminal trial is not analogous to organisations that provide trauma-informed care, there is a need to distinguish between trauma-*informed* services and trauma-*specific* services (Harris & Fallot, 2001) although both employ trauma-informed principles and are framed within a public health paradigm. Trauma-specific services are defined as 'those whose primary task is to address the impact of trauma and to facilitate trauma recovery', while trauma-informed services include organisations that have 'incorporated an understanding of trauma, including its consequences and the conditions that enhance healing, in all aspects of service delivery' (Fallot & Harris, 2008: 6).

Trauma-informed care is a philosophy of care from the psychological literature on the treatment of patients with a history of psychological trauma. A useful definition comes from the US-based Substance Abuse and Mental Health Services Administration (SAMHSA) (SAMHSA, 2013a: 3):

> trauma-informed care is a philosophy for reorganizing service environments to meet the unique needs of survivors and to avoid inadvertent re-traumatization.... In trauma-informed settings, everyone is educated about trauma and its consequences, and ... the need to make the environment more healing and less re-traumatizing for both program participants and staff.

As discussed below, the pathway to becoming trauma-informed involves organisational cultural change, including 'multi-level changes across many domains ... with administrative resolve to ensure the availability of resources for disseminating information' (Butler, Critelli, & Rinfrette, 2011: 181) in order to respond to the needs of trauma survivors. In the USA, for example, trauma-informed care is promoted through the National Center for Trauma-Informed Care (NCTIC) and the National Child Traumatic Stress Network (NCTSN).[2]

This chapter considers how principles derived under a public health paradigm can translate to a different paradigm, that is, a criminal justice framework for achieving best evidence. Since there is a strong association between experiences of sexual abuse and the development of PTSD and related trauma symptoms, rates of PTSD among children and adults giving evidence in sexual assault trials are likely to be relatively high, compared to the general population (see below).

Even though the issue of trauma is not central to the sexual assault trial, because of the adversarial and authoritarian nature of the criminal trial, the courtroom environment has the potential to re-traumatise children and adults and undermine their ability to give their best evidence.

Despite special measures in some jurisdictions that have been designed to improve the court experience for sexual assault complainants (see Chapter 10), the criminal trial has limited means or imagination for dealing with a child or adult suffering from PTSD who is required to give evidence in court about allegations of sexual assault. Although support persons are available in most Australian jurisdictions and in E&W while children and adults give their evidence, courts do not employ therapists who can provide psychological support to the complainant before, during or after giving evidence.

By contrast, the goals of trauma-informed care include staff training about the impact of trauma on behaviour and memory, identification of trauma-based symptoms, minimisation of re-traumatisation and identification of the ways in which institutions re-enact the dynamics of

[2] www.nasmhpd.org/content/national-center-trauma-informed-care-nctic-0; www.nctsn.org/; accessed 6 February 2017.

trauma. Thus, it is necessary to explore both the promises and challenges of trauma-informed care and its principles to consider the possibility of transforming the sexual assault trial into a trauma-informed system, not for the purposes of providing trauma-specific services, but to create *trauma-informed interactions* between court personnel and complainants.

Since sexual assault trials are likely to deal with children and adults with histories of psychological trauma, the broad questions are: is it possible to design criminal justice processes that are trauma-informed? How would trauma-informed principles inform and influence the processes and procedures of an adversarial trial system? Or is the concept of trauma-informed systems so alien to, and incompatible with, the adversarial trial model (its principles and objectives) that the concepts are mutually exclusive, particularly since the criminal trial is a system of adjudication, not a system of intervention or for the provision of services.

In order to answer these questions, it is necessary to:

(i) identify the reasons for introducing trauma-informed principles into the sexual assault trial;
(ii) define the principles and philosophy of trauma-informed care;
(iii) consider the compatibility of trauma-informed principles within the adversarial system; and
(iv) envisage a trauma-informed system within the criminal trial with a specific focus on the sexual assault trial.

2 The Need for Trauma-Informed Care Within the Sexual Assault Trial: Balancing Competing Goals

The need for trauma-informed care within the sexual assault trial arises because of the documented effects of sexual abuse on mental health which leads to imbalances of power between court personnel and witnesses. For example:

> Even before a legal case ensues, the trauma associated with the crime that led to legal involvement—the most common being child maltreatment— already places children at risk for numerous adverse outcomes ... including poor mental health, low academic achievement, insecure attachment, and relationship problems, to name a few. (Quas & Goodman, 2012: 395)

Because of the public order focus of criminal justice agencies, it is likely that most lawyers and judges working within criminal jurisdictions are unaware that rates of PTSD among victims of sexual assault are considerably higher than among the general population: the 'highest rates [of PTSD] (ranging from one-third to more than one-half ...) [are] found among survivors of rape, military combat and captivity, and ... genocide' (American Psychiatric Association, 2013).

Rates of PTSD among those exposed to traumatic events in childhood vary from study to study—in a nationally representative study of 1848 American children (who had been involved in a child welfare investigation), Kolko et al. (2010) reported that 11.7% displayed clinically significant PTSD symptoms (compared to 2.2% of the general population: Copeland, Keeler, Angold, & Costello, 2007), although the rate was higher in children in out-of-home care (19.2%). This compares to PTSD rates of between 20 and 63% for survivors of child maltreatment in a review by Gabbay, Oatis, Silva, and Hirsch (2004).

Sexually abused children and teenagers are also vulnerable to being sexually assaulted as adults. For example, women who suffer from a severe mental illness as adults 'have rates of lifetime physical or sexual assault ranging from 51% to 97%, with a significant number experiencing multiple victimizations' (Butler et al., 2011: 179), many of which begin in childhood. Complicating matters for trauma survivors is the fact that the presence of PTSD increases the risk of a person engaging in substance abuse (Najavits, Weiss, & Shaw, 1997; Ouimette & Brown, 2003) and other risky behaviours which may exacerbate already existing trauma symptoms.

Despite these findings, the criminal trial has a limited understanding of the pervasive 'sensory and environmental trauma triggers' (Miller & Najavits, 2012: 17246/1) that can pose a threat to a complainant's mental stability and their ability to give evidence, as well as having few processes to prevent re-traumatisation. Because it is unlikely that a complainant will be able to give their best evidence when they cannot regulate the effects of trauma (Miragoli, Procaccia, & Di Blasio, 2014; Miragoli, Camisasca, & Di Blasio, 2017, 2019), fact-finders are likely to interpret the type of evidence and emotions associated with re-traumatisation negatively, particularly where inconsistencies and confusion arise out of trauma and poor recall, as discussed in Chapter 10.

Overall, the most pervasive 'impact of complex trauma is the dysregulation of emotions and impulses' (Bath, 2008: 20) since trauma is 'a defining and organizing experience that forms the core of an individual's identity' (Harris & Fallot, 2001: 12). The symptoms of PTSD include:

> repeated, cue-triggered, involuntary re-experiencing of the terror and helplessness (often through nightmares and flashbacks); … avoid[ance] of cues that might be reminders of the trauma; hyperarousal and hypervigilance; problems with concentration and focus; and an exaggerated startle response. (NCTSN, 2017: 1)

However, not all PTSD sufferers experience the same symptoms or range of symptoms, since the manifestation of PTSD symptoms varies from person to person, while '[m]any trauma survivors will not meet the criteria for a PTSD diagnosis but will experience significant trauma-related impairment in daily living' (NCTSN, 2017: 1; see Table 1, above).

Children, for example, face two types of stress or anxiety in relation to participating in the court process as a witness. First, the phenomenon of anticipatory stress (Grogan & Murphy, 2011) means that a child will suffer varying degrees of anxiety while awaiting the trial (see Table 1, above), leading to an exacerbation of any existing trauma symptoms. Second, testifying itself may be accompanied by a range of possible triggers of the original trauma, including the strangeness of the court environment, dealing with strangers, seeing the defendant, as well as being questioned, harassed or intimidated by counsel. Delays, adjournments and appeals can mean that children remain in a high anxiety state for long periods:

> Lack of caregiver support, a greater number of interviews, long delays, repeated continuances, and a lenient outcome for the defendant have similarly been linked to poorer mental health following legal involvement. (Quas & Goodman, 2012: 403)

Should children testify in court at all? Overall, traumatised children have impaired memory recall, impaired ability to concentrate and process information, are more likely to provide inaccurate answers to questions, and provide less coherence and content in relation to events. The studies in Table 1, above reveal that giving evidence in court is harmful to children's mental health, although testifying can be beneficial in certain circumstances (Quas & Goodman, 2012).

Even if beneficial, the key issue for the CSA trial is the extent to which the cross-examination effect, together with the effects of trauma, prevent children from giving their best evidence, and the reliance by the fact-finder on less than best evidence to reach a verdict.

Compared to adults, research shows that child abuse and neglect adversely affects brain development, 'the nervous, and endocrine systems and ... impair[s] psychosocial development, including the acquisition of social skills, emotional regulation, and respect for societal institutions' (NCTSN, 2009: 1; see Porges, 2011; van der Kolk, 2006, 2015). While the frequency of CSA increases the risk of a complainant suffering from complex trauma and PTSD (van der Kolk, 2005), the symptoms of post-traumatic stress 'may manifest differently in children of different ages' (NCTSN, 2009: 1). It is useful to consider the PTSD reactions that may be exhibited by traumatised children as set out in Table 2.

While many of the reactions listed in Table 2 are also indicative of different stages of child development, such as aggressive outbursts, the difference between the behaviour of a traumatised child and normal child development is the severity and chronicity of the reaction (Denham, 1998; Kochanska, 2003; Schore, 2016). For traumatised children, the 'most significant consequence of early relational trauma is the loss of the ability to regulate the intensity and duration of effects' (Schore, 2003: 141) especially during high-stress experiences, such as giving evidence in court. In fact, many of the reactions listed in Table 2 are antithetical to giving best evidence because of their impact on memory access and

Table 2 Post-traumatic stress reactions for children according to age[a]

Age group	Common post-traumatic stress reactions
Young children (0–5 years)	• Withdrawal and passivity • Exaggerated startle response • Aggressive outbursts • Sleep difficulties (including night terrors) • Separation anxiety • Fear of new situations • Difficulty assessing threats and finding protection • Regression to previous behaviours (e.g. baby talk, bed-wetting, crying)
School age (6–12 years)	• Abrupt and unpredictable shifts between withdrawn and aggressive behaviours • Social isolation and withdrawal • Sleep disturbances that interfere with daytime concentration and attention • Preoccupation with the traumatic experience(s) • Intense, specific fears related to the traumatic event(s)
Adolescents (13–18 years)	• Increased risk-taking (substance abuse, truancy, risky sexual behaviours) • Heightened sensitivity to perceived threats • Social isolation • Withdrawal and emotional numbing • Low self-esteem

[a]Adapted from National Child Traumatic Stress Network (2009)

communication skills. As Perry (2009: 241) explains, childhood trauma disrupts normal neural development:

> trauma, neglect, and related experiences of maltreatment … all influence the developing brain. These adverse experiences interfere with normal patterns of experience-guided neurodevelopment by creating extreme and abnormal patterns of neural and neurohormonal activity. … [F]rom speech to motor functioning to social, emotional, or behavioral regulation—developmental trauma and maltreatment increase risk of dysfunction.

When a person is reminded of the trauma (via triggers that mimic the original traumatic experiences) there is involuntary 'increased activity in areas of the brain that support intense emotions and a simultaneous decrease in regions that govern speech and communication' (Crenshaw & Caprioli, 2017: 198 citing van der Kolk, 2006, 2015). Thus, the type of skills necessary to give evidence in court—concentration, comprehension of questions asked, memory recall, accuracy and clear communication—are likely to be impaired in the traumatised child, especially during lengthy and age-inappropriate cross-examination, thus exacerbating the cross-examination effect. Paradoxically, the involuntary symptoms of trauma can then be exploited by defence counsel and misinterpreted by the fact-finder as evidence of lack of veracity.

3 The Principles and Philosophy of Trauma-Informed Care

Within a treatment context, trauma-informed care and trauma-informed systems facilitate a client's recovery from trauma. Although this is not the role of a criminal trial, this section will outline the principles of trauma-informed care in order to envisage a trauma-informed court environment, not to provide trauma-informed services, but to facilitate the goals of doing no further harm and the achievement of best evidence.

Trauma-informed care involves the identification of a client's trauma-induced symptoms along with processes that are designed to minimise her or his re-experiences of these symptoms. This 'do no harm' approach requires training of all organisational staff about the institutional behaviours and processes that mimic the dynamics likely to trigger re-traumatisation—staff must be able to identify 'inadvertent re-traumatisation when a service system's usual operating procedures trigger a re-emergence or an exacerbation of trauma symptoms' (Harris & Fallot, 2001: 3).

Essentially, to be trauma-informed is 'to know the history of past and current abuse in the [client's] life' in order to 'design service systems that accommodate the vulnerabilities of trauma survivors' (Harris & Fallot, 2001: 4). Such an approach 'perceives trauma not simply as a past event but as a formative one that continues to contribute to a client's emotional state and coping strategies' (Butler et al., 2011: 178), as explained by theories of PTSD (Brewin et al., 2002; Ehlers & Clark, 2000; Ehlers, Clark, Hackmann, McManus, & Fennell, 2005; Steil, Dyer, Priebe, Kleindienst, & Bohus, 2011).

However, not all trauma-informed services are designed to treat the actual symptoms of sexual abuse: 'regardless of their primary mission … their commitment is to provide services in a manner that is … appropriate to the special needs of trauma survivors' (Harris & Fallot, 2001: 5), compared to trauma-specific services which expressly 'treat the symptoms and syndromes related to current or past trauma' (Butler et al., 2011: 179).

It may be more appropriate to talk about trauma-informed *interactions* since not all trauma-informed systems will be delivering clinical services. In order to achieve trauma-informed interactions with a legal context, relevant principles of trauma-informed care would ideally inform reforms of various legal processes from the first report to the police through to trial and sentencing. But what are these principles?

Harris and Fallot (2001) are credited with clarifying 'the conceptualization of trauma-informed care' (Butler et al., 2011: 180) which is underpinned by three core pillars—safety, healing relationships and self-management of emotions (Bath, 2008: 18). These core pillars underpin the 10 principles that define an organisation which specifically provides trauma-informed services as set out in Table 3 (taken from Elliott, Bjelajac, Fallot, Markoff, & Reed, 2005).

The above ten principles, which have been developed in the field of mental health services to increase the accessibility and effectiveness of these services, are explained below in order to explain their suitability, or otherwise, within the criminal trial with quotes from Elliott et al. (2005: 464–468).

The first principle identifies that childhood abuse or interpersonal violence are rarely one-off events. Survivors may have difficulty regulating their emotions and relating to authority figures since their survival/coping strategies were developed as adaptations to traumatic events (Ehlers & Clark, 2000; Elliott et al., 2005; NCTSN, 2009;

Table 3 The ten principles of trauma-informed services

1. Recognise the long-term impact of violence and victimisation on development and coping strategies (S)
2. Make recovery from trauma the primary goal
3. Employ an empowerment model (S)
4. Maximise a client's choices and control over recovery from trauma (*)
5. Create a therapeutic relationship that is collaborative, empowering and safe (*)
6. Create an environment that provides safety, respect and acceptance (S)
7. Emphasise a client's strengths
8. Minimise re-traumatisation (S)
9. Culturally competent (S)
10. Solicit consumer input in designing and evaluating services

Notes
(S) Represents those principles that would be appropriate for trauma-informed systems *not* delivering trauma-specific services
(*) Survivor choice and collaboration could be added to the above list, depending on what a particular trauma-informed system offers

van der Kolk, 2015). This principle is needed to inform both trauma-specific services delivering trauma-informed care and trauma-informed systems. In the legal context, a trauma-informed system would mean understanding the impact of sexual assault on the ability of adults and children to participate in, and engage with, the legal process after they make a report to authorities, as well as to cope with intense courtroom questioning.

Recovery from trauma as the primary goal (the second principle) involves 'specialized services ... or integrat[ion of] a client's care with an agency that does provide those services' for trauma-specific services *only*.

Employment of an empowerment model (the third principle) facilitates a person's ability to 'have conscious choice and control over her actions' in order to counteract 'the overwhelming fear and helplessness that is the legacy of victimization'. Thus, organisations that interact with trauma survivors are in a collaborative partnership which builds on a client's existing strengths rather than a relationship characterised by authority and control such that this principle is applicable to both trauma-specific services and trauma-informed systems.

Maximisation of a client's choices and control over recovery from trauma (the fourth principle) is aimed at counteracting clients' experiences of powerlessness within trauma-specific services. This will be possible under the creation of a therapeutic relationship that is collaborative, empowering, safe and 'the opposite of traumatizing' (the fifth principle). Safe relationships are 'consistent, predictable, nonviolent, nonshaming, and nonblaming' and because of an 'inherent power imbalance in the helper-helped relationship' there is a need to 'flatten the hierarchy'.

Closely linked is the sixth principle, the creation of an environment that provides safety, respect and acceptance. Because the original trauma occurred in an unsafe environment, the physical setting must create a welcoming and safe space for survivors in order to remove possible obstacles to treatment and recovery such as suspicion, avoidance or hostility. Safe, non-hierarchical relationships require appropriate trauma-informed interactions by all personnel which is particularly pertinent to the criminal trial context in order to promote the best evidence.

Emphasis of a client's strengths (the seventh principle) recognises that rather than something being wrong with a client, 'something wrong was done to that person' and that a client's symptoms constitute adaptations to the original traumatic events. This, coupled with the eighth principle, the minimisation of re-traumatisation are essential features of both trauma-specific services and trauma-informed systems. Since all forms of victimisation involve abuses of power, 'the power differential' between the client and service provider may re-trigger traumatic experiences. Thus, re-traumatisation prevention processes are needed to manage 'the posttraumatic stress symptoms of hyperarousal or avoidance'.

A client's problems need to be understood with respect to her/his cultural background, that is, with an awareness of cultural competence (the ninth principle) another important concept for legal personnel within the criminal trial in order to understand a complainant's reactions to the court environment. Finally, the tenth principle means that consumer input in designing and evaluating services is solicited in that trauma-informed services actively seek the input of clients in designing a trauma-informed system.

All of the above principles characterise the provision of services that are trauma-informed which would, typically, involve clinical services to a client base within a public health framework with public health goals.

Since the goals of the criminal trial are entirely different, as discussed above, it is better to conceive of the criminal trial as engaging in a series of interactions, rather than services, particularly since witnesses and defendants are subject to the coercive powers of the court, powers that are largely antithetical to the principles of trauma-informed care. By contrast, the principles underpinning the evolution of the contemporary criminal trial can be understood within a public order framework which, in turn, is underpinned by the governmental power of the state. That power is ameliorated through the fair trial principle (to prevent wrongful convictions) which in recent years has been extended to cover witnesses, as discussed in Chapter 8, notably sexual assault complainants whose unfair treatment has been well-documented.

In summary, Fallot and Harris (2008: 6) have 'distilled five core principles to guide agency self-assessment and planning: safety, trustworthiness, choice, collaboration, and empowerment' to which I would add recognition and cultural competence.

4 The Compatibility of Trauma-Informed Care with the Adversarial System

Many institutions that are part of the criminal justice system, such as prisons and juvenile detention centres, are 'full of unavoidable triggers, such as pat downs and strip searches, frequent discipline from authority figures, and restricted movement' (Miller & Najavits, 2012: 17246/2). For many CSA and sexual assault survivors, these triggers closely mimic the intrusive and abusive behaviours they suffered.

However, different parts of the criminal justice system are unique in terms of their internal cultures, goals, systems, practices and unavoidable triggers since some parts are specialised in their approach, such as specialist police investigation units for CSA (for a review of the efficacy of specialist police squads in responding to CSA, see Westera, Darwinkel,

& Powell, 2016),[3] while most jurisdictions employ non-specialised prosecutorial services and court processes.

Within the adversarial criminal trial, there will also be a number of unavoidable triggers as a result of the court environment, and the types of interactions between witnesses and legal personnel (who typically have no training about trauma-inducing triggers) which are based on authority structures. Witnesses, generally, have a lack of control over the court environment, the trial process and their treatment by judges and counsel. This lack of control arises from the inherent power imbalance between court personnel and witnesses, an imbalance which is easily and readily exploited by defence counsel who may threaten, cajole, badger, interrogate, insult, confuse, ridicule and/or intimidate witnesses with little or no judicial intervention.

Arguably, the type of intimidation and control that characterises the cross-examination of complainants is a form of emotional abuse which is defined as the communication of hurtful or insulting comments and includes threatening or intimidating behaviours (Haferkamp, Bebermeier, Möllering, & Neuner, 2015; Spertus, Yehuda, Wong, Halligan, & Seremitis, 2003). In a recent study, Cecil, Viding, Fearon, Glaser, and McCrory (2017: 106) found that emotional abuse, compared to all other forms of child abuse, 'emerged as the main independent predictor of psychiatric symptomatology', that is, as a robust and independent predictor of mental health difficulties.

If a complainant experiences any of the trauma symptoms listed in Tables 1 and 2, these are likely to affect her ability to cope with being interviewed and giving evidence in court (Quas & Goodman, 2012). For example, '[t]he insidious effects of constantly elevated stress hormones include memory and attention problems' (van der Kolk, 2015: 46). If a complainant 'cannot control her dissociative symptoms in the face of multiple triggers' (Miller & Najavits, 2012: 17246/2), such as the

[3]For example, the Sexual Offences and Child Abuse Investigation Team in Victoria (https://www.chiefexaminer.vic.gov.au/content.asp?document_id=36448; accessed 28 June 2020); the Sex Crimes Squad and the Joint Investigation Response Squad in NSW (See https://www.police.nsw.gov.au/crime/sex_crimes/child_abuse) and the Sexual Offences Exploitation and Child Abuse Unit in the London Metropolitan Police.

types of questions used in cross-examination to exploit children's developmental vulnerability, this may result in inconsistencies in evidence, confusion, retraction of evidence, misinterpretation of questions and/or agreement with misunderstood questions, all of which is likely to have a negative impact on credibility assessments of the complainant by fact-finders.

Fortunately, the concept of trauma-informed care is not new to the legal system so that 'legal professionals who work with children and youth in the [US] child welfare and juvenile justice systems' are becoming aware of the negative effects of trauma and trauma-informed practices (American Bar Association, 2014: 3), not on public health grounds but in order to achieve optimum representation through the lawyer–client relationship.

Trauma-informed legal practice is recommended by the US NCTSN for lawyers representing children and families in the welfare system, since knowledge about the effects of trauma on clients informs this important lawyer–client relationship. In the USA, the Attorney General's National Task Force on Children Exposed to Violence (2012) recommended that:

> all professionals serving children exposed to violence and psychological trauma learn about and provide for trauma-informed care and trauma-focused services. Similarly, the American Bar Association has called for integrating trauma knowledge into daily legal practice and integrating and sustaining trauma awareness and skills in practice and policies. (NCTSN, 2017: 4)

In 2014, the American Bar Association (2014: 1) urged:

> the development of trauma-informed, evidence-based approaches and practices on behalf of justice system-involved children and youth who have been exposed to violence ... by ... [r]esponding to child traumatic stress through legal representation that reflects awareness of trauma's adverse impacts on children and youth who have contact with the legal system.

One example comes from Ohio in the USA which has trauma-informed courts to provide appropriate services for traumatised children and youth who are involved in child welfare and juvenile justice cases:

> [i]n the Stark County Family Court in Ohio … the court provides trauma training for judges and staff. The court also utilizes a screening tool during the intake process to identify children and youth who have experienced trauma. (American Bar Association, 2014: 11)

Similarly, the New York State Child Welfare Court Improvement Project has published a guide for lawyers on interviewing traumatised children and youth (American Bar Association, 2014; Reitman, 2011).

In California, Family Drug Treatment Courts (FDTC) are non-adversarial settings which operate within the child protection system to determine the treatment needs of substance-abusing parents whose children are in care (Drabble et al., 2013). On the basis that many such parents have a reported lifetime exposure to trauma-inducing events, and the potential for re-traumatisation of these parents within the court process, Drabble and colleagues undertook a qualitative study of key personnel associated with the FDTCs to assess the success of trauma-informed systems changes with the FDTCs. They found that personnel reported both benefits and barriers, with the main benefits including increased understanding of their clients, their client's histories and 'their ability to parent and connect with their children' (Drabble et al., 2013: 100). Barriers to implementing trauma-informed change included the 'physical, functional and social environment of courts', in particular the adversarial nature of the court, the imposing architecture of courts and their location, the foreign environment populated by strangers and the presence of security personnel such as security guards and police (Drabble et al., 2013: 101).

It is also equally important for lawyers and judges to be aware of the negative effects of trauma on adults who participate in adversarial criminal trials as witnesses since adult sexual assault survivors are also at risk of developing PTSD or trauma symptoms. Within the legal system, a 'systems-wide approach' would require training of all personnel who have contact or interactions with traumatised complainants, such as judges, lawyers, witness assistance service providers and other court and prosecutorial staff with the aim of ensuring the physical and psychological well-being of complainants and avoiding administrative and legal practices that could result in re-traumatisation in order to achieve best evidence.

The American Bar Association (2014: 1), for example, has urged all other federal, state, local, tribal and territorial bar associations 'to develop and implement training programs for judges, child welfare attorneys, prosecutors, defense counsel, and law students ... to integrate trauma knowledge into daily legal practice and ... policies' and 'to develop positive strategies for addressing secondary trauma among those involved with children and youth in the justice system'.

5 What Are the Triggers for Traumatised Victims Within the Adversarial Criminal Trial?

Research shows that traumatic experiences, such as child abuse and sexual assault, are likely to influence 'how the brain assesses threat', and a person's response to any 'trigger' that reminds them of the original trauma and danger (NCTSN, 2017: 5; see also Feinstein, Adolphs, Damasio, & Tranel, 2011; Shin, Rauch, & Pitman, 2006; van der Kolk, 2015; Williams et al., 2006). These responses are *involuntary* so that when a person is triggered:

> the brain ... sets off a cascade of immediate physiological changes that prepare one for Fight-Flight-Freeze response in order to stay safe. This is a complex response that involves multiple areas of the brain, including the sympathetic nervous system and the amygdale. (NCTSN, 2017: 5)

After a traumatic event, 'the world is experienced with a different nervous system' and the body 'continues to defend against a threat that belongs to the past' (van der Kolk, 2015: 53). In fact, 'the stress hormones of traumatised people ... take much longer to return to baseline and spike quickly and disproportionately in response to mildly stressful stimuli' (van der Kolk, 2015: 46).

For traumatised children and adults, the court environment is a stressful stimulus with alien and imposing representations of authority and power structures in terms of architecture, layout, furnishings, personnel, legal language and clothing. For example, wigs and gowns are still worn in many Australian courts, compared to E&W where an application for the removal of wigs and gowns can be made in trials involving vulnerable witnesses.[4] While some vulnerable witnesses in some jurisdictions are able to give evidence from a remote room outside of the court precinct (see Chapter 10), others must deal with the imposing environment of a court building and the presence of police, sheriffs and/or security guards.

In many jurisdictions, complainants must also face the ordeal of the trial process which includes the gruelling conditions of indefinite cross-examination, as well as the well-documented cross-examination effect, that is, the phenomenon whereby children, in particular, in the face of age-inappropriate questions, agree with propositions of the cross-examiner, thereby contradicting their original, truthful evidence, although the cross-examination effect also impacts the evidence of adults as discussed in Chapter 8. The trauma-like triggers associated with criminal proceedings mean that children, and to some extent adult complainants, are 'exposed to a powerful culture of silencing .... Indeed, the courtroom environment mirrors in many ways the same factors that keep children silent during the abuse', with age-inappropriate methods of questioning 'shut[ting] down the child witness's ability to communicate' (Caprioli & Crenshaw, 2017: 197).

As stated above, the focus of the trial process is on the management and control of defendants who are brought to trial, a culture that extends to witnesses but is in conflict with the basic principles of trauma-informed care and trauma-informed systems as set out in Table 4. This table contrasts trauma-informed systems with non-trauma-

[4]See Application for a Special Measures Direction under the Criminal Procedure Rules 2015, rule 29.3 and 29.10.

Table 4 Comparison of the cultural environments of the adversarial trial and a trauma-informed system

Cultural Environment: *Adversarial trial*	Potential Triggers within Trial	Cultural Environment: *Trauma-informed system*
Power • **Institutional power** control over defendants and witnesses	**Power differential** between court and witnesses → Disempowerment → Disorientation and alienation	• **Empowerment** of client through the empowerment model • **Strengths** of client developed
Authority and responsibility • Remains with the institution • Imposed via legal mechanisms (e.g. subpoenas;contempt proceedings)	• Witness inability to exercise choice • Methods which emphasise a witness's weaknesses	• **Encourages** client to assume self -responsibility • **Maximises** strengths and individual choice • **Links** past abuse to current coping skills
Language: • Authority and power manifests through the use of legal jargon • Uncontrolled cross-examination which produces confusion and inconsistencies in evidence	*Lack of emotional safety*: • Complainant must give detailed descriptions of sexual assaults • Subject to lengthy cross-examination • Age-inappropriate questions to elicit inconsistencies, confusion and retraction • Allegations of lying, authoritarian body language/tone of voice, interruptions to produce confusion	• **Avoidance** of clinical jargon • **Maximisation** of emotional safety
Goals • Prosecution of criminal offences • Prioritises defendant's rights • Minimal conception of victims' rights • Indifferent to witnesses' psychological health • Promotes avoidable forms of re-traumatisation that would not be tolerated in institutions dealing with traumatised children. • Culturally indifferent.	*Non-victim centred goals*: → Lack of recognition of impact of trauma → Disorientation, alienation → Inability to give best evidence	• **Recognises** long-term impact of trauma • **Recovery** from trauma • **Promotion** of respectand a safe culture for healing • **Culturally** competent

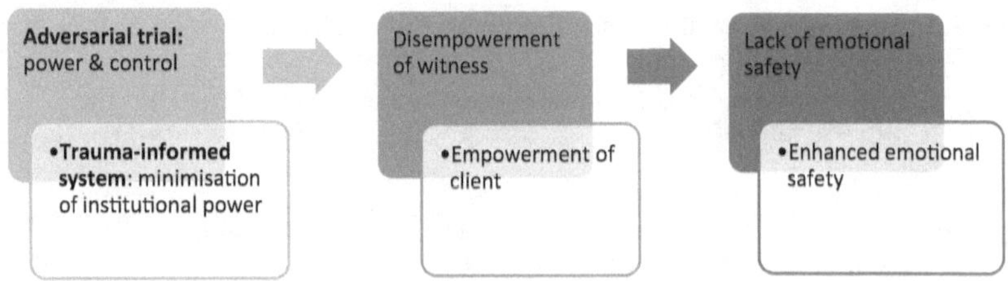

Fig. 1 Comparison of adversarial trial and trauma-informed system

informed systems in order to highlight how the culture of an organisation produces triggers for re-traumatisation.

By way of summary, the triggers embedded in the cultural environment of the adversarial trial result in a lack of emotional safety for those who have experienced trauma, as illustrated by Fig. 1.

As a result of unequal power relationships, '[t]he traditional service relationship replicates some of the most damaging dynamics of childhood trauma' and 'is tragically reminiscent of the [original] abuse dynamic' (Harris & Fallot, 2001: 18; 19). This is also true of the sexual assault trial where a complainant is merely a passive witness in criminal proceedings and has no decision-making capacity other than to participate or withdraw from the process. If she chooses to participate, she must give evidence and have her evidence tested, no matter how damaging to her psychological health, and is unlikely to have an understanding of how re-traumatisation could affect her evidence.

Figure 1 and Table 4 show that, for the sexual assault complainant, engagement in the adversarial trial process is fraught with danger, given the inherent power imbalance between the individual and court authorities and the opportunities for further experiences of disempowerment. In other words, '[u]nacknowledged or untreated trauma and related symptoms' (Elliott et al., 2005: 463) will interfere with the ability of a complainant to fully engage with the requirements of the legal process.

For example, experiences of powerlessness are one of the defining features of sexual assault (Cossins, 2000; Cossins & Plummer, 2016), particularly CSA, while, as per Table 4, the adversarial system is a manifestation of the governmental power of the state, a characteristic that conflicts with the empowerment model (principle three in Table 1). The adversarial system is not in a collaborative relationship with witnesses but a coercive relationship whereby witnesses are required to attend court to give evidence and are subject to the rules of the court. This creates a culture of power and powerlessness.

Possible triggers for traumatised complainants as set out in Table 4 include the authoritarian court environment itself (as a result of a complainant's lack of control over court processes), lack of awareness of, and attention to, a complainant's specific needs, including psychological, cultural and age-related needs, as well as the authoritarian body and verbal language used by lawyers (Andrews & Lamb, 2017; Andrews, Lamb, & Lyon, 2014; Behzadnia & Mehrani, 2017; Cleveland, Quas, & Lyon, 2016; Klemfuss, Quas, & Lyon, 2014; Lamb & Fauchier, 2001; Zajac, O'Neill, & Hayne, 2012).

For example, PTSD places an individual 'into a hypervigilant mode that may cause [them] to be highly sensitive to power differentials, perceived attacks, and a perceived loss of control' (NCTSN, 2017: 6). Thus, post-traumatic stress 'can interfere with the ... [a] client's capacity to trust others, process information, communicate, and respond to stressful situations' within the court environment (NCTSN, 2017: 8; see also van der Kolk, 2015). Furthermore, when a traumatised victim is:

> reminded, either consciously or unconsciously, of a past trauma, that trigger may cause [them] to feel as if [they are] in imminent danger [which may cause them to]... become focused on protecting themselves and avoiding the perceived danger. (NCTSN, 2017: 8)

This means that a complainant may dissociate or freeze, cease processing and answering questions, appear confused even when questions are repeated, look 'spaced-out', become defiant, jumpy or fidgety, exhibit dramatic mood changes, refuse to talk, agree with the (perceived) wishes of the examiner, or, if a child, 'adopt regressive [soothing] behaviours' (NCTSN, 2017: 10; see also Lima et al., 2010; van der Kolk, 2015; Williams, 2007), all of which will impede their ability to give their best evidence. In order to understand the ramifications of trauma on the human brain, it is clear that judges and lawyers need training about trauma symptoms and their impact on a complainant's ability to give evidence, how to avoid re-traumatisation and how to manage the situation when a complainant is triggered.

Although children may have their evidence pre-recorded pre-trial in some jurisdictions (e.g. Western Australia, two court registries in NSW, and E&W) and adults may be able to give their evidence via CCTV from a remote room away from the courtroom (e.g. NSW), many triggers remain. The courtroom environment represents a site of institutional trauma since the very nature of sexual abuse involves the abuse of power. The more an institution relies on authoritative structures, the more likely it will create dynamics in which a traumatised complainant will be re-triggered.

Legal personnel will not have the qualifications or resources to diagnose those suffering from PTSD and other mental illnesses so that best practice would treat all complainants of sexual assault as trauma survivors (Elliott et al., 2005) by introducing common procedures and practices that are non-traumatising in order to 'do no harm', a key element of therapeutic jurisprudence which seeks to minimise negative outcomes on those affected by the law, such as the criminal justice system (King, Freiberg, Batagol, & Hyams, 2014: 25). This might 'result in the universal elimination of certain aggressive practices that most consumers, trauma survivors or not, find frightening and demeaning' (Harris & Fallot, 2001: 10). Such an approach is also important because, in addition to the original trauma, complainants may have a range of other problems such as drug or alcohol addiction, medical issues, homelessness, unemployment, family problems and/or legal issues with other government agencies, any of which can exacerbate the impact of the original trauma.

6 What Are the Requirements for Creating a Trauma-Informed Adversarial System?

Compared to the criminal trial, '[t]he core of the service relationship in a trauma-informed system is open and genuine collaboration between provider and consumer at all phases of the service delivery' (Harris &

Fallot, 2001: 19). The question is whether this is desirable and attainable within the criminal trial context since there is a limit on the extent to which a complainant can be actively involved in criminal proceedings. For example, in adversarial systems of justice, witnesses are, generally, not entitled to legal representation (as discussed in Chapter 10).

Collaborative relationships are possible in relation to pre-trial issues since police and prosecutors can explain the reasons for their decisions (for example, to proceed or not with a prosecution, to call certain witnesses or not), as required under a charter of victims' rights. They can also prepare the complainant for court which is already undertaken in some jurisdictions, such as the Witness Assistance Program in the Office of the Director of Public Prosecutions in NSW, the Citizens Advice Witness Service in E&W and the Crime Victims Specialist Program provided by the New York State Police.[5] But it is the actual trial itself where the relationships of power—between judge and witness, and examiner and witness—replicate the damaging aspects of childhood trauma and sexual assault.

Is it ever possible for these relationships to do no harm? A re-interpretation of the importance of witness evidence in the context of the sexual assault trial would recognise that there is no trial without a complainant who is generally the prosecution's chief witness and must have the mental and physical stamina to participate in the trial process. The interests of justice require a traumatised witness to be able to give their *best* evidence, as recognised in various policy documents (Home Office, 2011; Victims Services, NSW Department of Justice, 2016) rather than evidence that is the product of re-traumatisation as the result of hostile, power relationships created through the adversarial process. For example, '[l]eading and suggestive questions are known to be the most unreliable method for eliciting information from children' (Cossins, 2009: 81; see also Lamb et al., 2008; Lamb & Fouchier, 2001; Powell, Westera, Goodman-Delahunty, & Pichler, 2016), yet are used routinely during the cross-examination of child witnesses, as discussed in Chapter 8.

[5]See www.citizensadvice.org.uk/about-us/citizens-advice-witness-service/about-the-citizens-advice-witness-service/; www.troopers.ny.gov/Crime_Prevention/Violence/Crime_Victims_Specialists.

While protections against improper questions do exist in some jurisdictions (see Chapter 8), both empirical and anecdotal evidence (American Bar Association, 2014; Caruso, 2012; Cashmore & Trimboli, 2005; Cossins, 2009; Powell et al., 2016) show that these protections are infrequently used by judges.

The key component of a complainant's evidence includes the details of the actual sexual assault. Speaking about these experiences potentially exposes her to re-traumatisation as she describes events which may involve extreme boundary violations, betrayal, powerlessness, fear, terror and/or humiliation. While giving evidence, she may display the symptoms associated with re-experiencing the distressing emotions of the time, or the dissociation and lack of emotions experienced at the time.

Moving to a trauma-informed system requires a 'paradigm shift' because it is necessary for the issue of trauma to 'move to the center' of an organisation's interactions with the public (Harris & Fallot, 2001: 21). Trauma-informed systems are 'content specific, time limited and outcome focused', while trauma-informed interactions require a commitment to change by 'integrating knowledge about violence and abuse' into an organisation's practices and procedures (Harris & Fallot, 2001: 16; 5).

In a criminal trial context, this paradigm-shift is not about delivering trauma-specific services (that is, psychological counselling)—rather, the integration of knowledge would involve adoption of the principles of trauma-informed care so as to achieve cultural change. In order to create a trauma-informed adversarial trial, it would be necessary to introduce procedures to prevent the unavoidable triggers of the sexual assault trial. These changes would require a review of all aspects of how complainants are interviewed, before trial, and how they are examined in court in order to envisage a trauma-informed environment.

Specifically, it is necessary to consider the relevance and applicability of the principles listed in Table 1 to the sexual assault trial by identifying those that are relevant to a trauma-informed system not delivering trauma-specific services (Fallot & Harris, 2008) in order to reduce disempowerment, enhance emotional safety and achieve best evidence.

First, training about the long-term impact of trauma of all those who interact with complainants would be needed: police, prosecutorial staff and all court personnel, including security guards, clerks, tipstaff, defence lawyers, judges and sheriffs.[6] Adequate funding to design and conduct trauma-informed training programmes would be the major barrier.

Second, a review of the policies and procedures of the criminal trial would include the identification of practices that 'replicate trauma dynamics', in particular 'dynamics that characterize abusive relationships', such as boundary violations, practices that deny or invalidate a complainant's experiences, or practices that reconstruct reality in a way that 'represent[s] the values and beliefs of the abuser' (Harris & Fallot, 2001: 9).

For example, witness assistance services provided before trial are designed to limit re-traumatisation by familiarising complainants with the court process and preparing them for examination and cross-examination. However, preparing someone for the triggers that may re-traumatise them may not be sufficient to 'do no harm'. As discussed below, a paradigm shift could involve the introduction of non-legal personnel into the legal system who can initiate and oversee cultural change.

Strategies designed to eliminate or reduce unavoidable triggers ought to involve the core principles of empowerment and choice in order to facilitate a collaborative relationship between complainant and prosecutor. Rather than a relationship characterised by authority and control, this would enable the creation of safe relationships to counteract the fear and helplessness of victimisation (Elliott et al., 2005) and to empower the complainant to give her best evidence. Well-funded specialist prosecutorial units which commit to the creation of collaborative relationships with complainants are one solution (American Bar Association, 2014) while legal representation is another. Nonetheless, the latter suggestion faces considerable barriers, such as funding by governments and the belief that legal representation for witnesses is inconsistent with the adversarial trial process, as discussed in Chapter 10.

The creation of an environment that provides safety, respect and acceptance (another core principle of trauma-informed systems) is also necessary because the original trauma of sexual assault occurred in an

[6]For resources for training staff on the impact of trauma, see Elliott (2003) for non-clinicians and Pilnik and Kendall (2012) for lawyers.

unsafe environment. Because the courtroom is configured to represent the authority of the state over defendants and witnesses, a safe court environment would require appropriate trauma-informed behaviour by all legal personnel involved in the court process along with procedures to protect a complainant from re-traumatisation before and during their evidence. This could involve, for example, the reconfiguration of court spaces, in order to equalise the relations between complainants and court personnel, or the use of remote rooms for giving evidence via CCTV (as discussed below) in order to create emotionally safe interactions between court personnel and complainants (see, further, Cossins & Rowden, 2020).

The issue of safety also arises when considering how the criminal trial emphasises a witness's weaknesses rather than their strengths through the use of humiliating, confusing and/or hostile forms of cross-examination. Thus, the trial process fosters the belief that any degree of confusion, inconsistencies in evidence and/or gaps in memory can be used as measures of veracity and credibility rather than being understood as manifestations of the cross-examination effect and/or the symptoms of trauma.

Indeed, some complainants will have engaged in risky and self-destructive behaviours after being sexually assaulted which can also be used by defence counsel to undermine their credibility since rules of evidence still permit admissibility of evidence of a complainant's prior sexual behaviour in some jurisdictions, or evidence or a complainant's prior criminal conduct (such as drug-taking). However:

> An essential component of being trauma-informed is to understand these behaviors not as character flaws or symptoms of mental illness, but as strategies or behavioral adaptations developed to cope with the physical and emotional impact of past trauma. (Najavits et al., 1997: 3)

Both trauma-informed services and systems should seek to be culturally competent, where a person's problems are understood with respect to her cultural background. However, the criminal trial, traditionally, has no mandated mechanisms for implementing cultural competence.

In order to achieve cultural competence as well as oversee cultural change, other court personnel may be required in the shift of a criminal trial towards a trauma-informed system, such as the use of intermediaries, discussed in Chapter 9, which anecdotally appear to have wrought cultural change in courts in E&W, although they were not introduced within the context of a trauma-informed system.

Compared to the process in E&W for the appointment of an intermediary, intermediaries would need to be mandated in a trauma-informed sexual assault trial because of the documented cross-examination effect on vulnerable witnesses. In other words:

> Witnesses must be able to understand the questions and enabled to give answers they believe to be correct. If the witness does not understand the question, the answer will not further the overriding objective [to facilitate best evidence]. ... The manner, tenor, tone, language and duration of questioning should be appropriate to the witness's developmental age and communication abilities. (Plotnikoff & Woolfson, 2007: 5–13)

If intermediaries were compulsory for complainants giving evidence in sexual assault trials, they could also assist a court in becoming more culturally competent in relation to complainants from culturally diverse and non-English speaking backgrounds, as well as Indigenous complainants. Within a trauma-informed system, a wider role for intermediaries could be envisaged in order to remove the power differential between examiner and complainant. This might mean the intermediary becoming an advocate for protecting the complainant from abusive strategies within the adversarial trial or the intermediary becoming the examiner, as discussed in Chapter 9.

An evaluation by Plotnikoff and Woolfson (2007) identified a key disadvantage associated with the role and powers of intermediaries—their inability to intervene to prevent improper questioning at trial, and the concomitant discovery that 'judges and prosecutors said they would be less likely to intervene in inappropriate questioning where an intermediary was present' (Ministry of Justice, 2015a: 5). This finding suggests that a much wider role for intermediaries is required to work in conjunction with trial judges to introduce cultural change to the sexual assault trial.

7 Summary

With reference to the ten principles of trauma-informed care, Table 5 lists the trauma-informed changes to the courtroom that could promote both the physical and psychological safety of complainants.

This discussion has shown that the public health concept of trauma-informed care could be used to enact cultural change in organisations that do not deliver trauma-informed specific services but deal with traumatised individuals, such as victims of sexual assault. The aim of this discussion was to consider if and how the sexual assault trial could be transformed into a trauma-informed system. By undertaking an analysis of trauma-informed systems and trauma-specific services, this discussion identified specific principles that characterise trauma-informed systems not delivering trauma-specific services. These broad principles include:

- recognition of the long-term impact of trauma;
- safety;
- minimisation of re-traumatisation;
- empowerment; and
- cultural competence.

The identification of these principles means that it is possible to examine their compatibility with the adversarial criminal trial by proposing ways they could be introduced to create a trauma-informed trial process, with a specific focus on the sexual assault trial.

The need for trauma-informed processes within the sexual assault trial is based on the existence of relatively high rates of PTSD and trauma-like symptoms among victims of sexual assault, the limited understanding on the part of criminal justice personnel of the pervasive effects of trauma and the types of environmental triggers that exist within the courtroom environment (Tables 4 and 5). Such triggers mean that traumatised complainants, particularly children, are likely to have an impaired ability to cope with giving evidence in court and are vulnerable to defence exploitation and the cross-examination effect, resulting in inconsistencies in evidence, confusion, retraction of evidence, misinterpretation of questions and/or agreement with misunderstood questions, all of which is likely to have a negative impact on credibility assessments by fact-finders.

Table 5 A trauma-informed courtroom environment[a]

Courtroom environment	Possible reaction of trauma survivor	Trauma-informed approach[b]
Disempowerment: • Judge sits at a raised bench to emphasise the authority invested in her/him	• Reaction to an authority figure: isolation, fear, low self-esteem	• Through courtroom reconfiguration, establish a more equal relationship between judge and complainant; lawyers and complainant
Physical & emotional safety (court precinct): • Complainants may have to wait in the same waiting area as the defendant and his supporters • Imposing environment of court precinct	• Fight-flight-freeze response may be triggered	• Use of remote rooms (with CCTV facilities) that are housed in a separate building to the courtroom; or • Construct separate entrances and waiting rooms for complainants
Emotional safety: examination-in-chief • Complainants traditionally give evidence in the courtroom in front of strangers, the defendant and his supporters • Complainant is required to give detailed descriptions of the alleged sexual assaults	• Fear of defendant, courtroom personnel and other strangers • Inability to regulate overwhelming emotions • Impeded ability to understand questions, access memory or communicate clearly • The emotions of the original trauma are re-experienced • Interference with memory of events producing confusion, gaps in memory, inconsistencies	***Strategies to elicit best evidence***: • Witness assistance and psychological services pre-trial • Specialist examiner who ensures questions are age-appropriate • Use of police interview as evidence-in-chief so complainants do not have to give evidence twice • Pre-recording of a complainant's cross-examination; or • Complainant gives live evidence from a remote room via CCTV with a support person present

(continued)

Table 5 (continued)

Courtroom environment	Possible reaction of trauma survivor	Trauma-informed approach[b]
Emotional safety: *cross-examination* • Complainant's out-of-court and in-court statements subject to lengthy forensic cross-examination • Age-inappropriate questions designed to elicit inconsistencies, confusion and retraction • Improper questions such as repetitive, confusing and humiliating statements often accompanied by allegations of lying, authoritarian body language/tone of voice, interruptions to produce confusion	• As above	***Strategies to elicit best evidence***: • Pre-trial hearing: Specialist examiner undertakes the cross-examination of the complainant after vetting of defence questions which are translated into age-appropriate questions • Time-limited cross-examination • No cross-examination by multiple counsel • Judicial direction to the jury that inconsistencies in evidence and gaps in memory are not necessarily indicative of veracity but may be symptoms of trauma

[a]Headings of table adapted from Substance Abuse and Mental Health Services Administration (2013: 8)
[b]Many of these options are already available in a number of Australian jurisdictions, as well as E&W

While a number of organisations in the USA have recommended trauma-informed legal practice for lawyers representing children and families, no one has previously considered whether and how principles of trauma-informed systems could apply in criminal trials where a child is a complainant of sexual abuse, nor in relation to adult complainants of sexual assault.

Because of the inherent power imbalance between a complainant and court authority, there are many triggers in the courtroom environment, as described in Table 4, which compares the cultural environments of the adversarial legal system with trauma-informed systems. The first is centred on the exercise of power over witnesses and defendants, while the second is focused on the empowerment of the trauma-survivor.

In considering the appropriateness of the principles of trauma-informed systems to the sexual assault trial, it is clear that legal personnel will not have the qualifications or resources to diagnose the symptoms of PTSD so that best practice would treat all complainants as trauma survivors by introducing non-traumatising procedures and practices in order to 'do no harm' and achieve best evidence. The reforms that would be necessary to introduce trauma-informed principles into the criminal justice system are discussed in the next chapter.

References

Ahern, E., Kowalski, M., & Lamb, M. E. (2018). A case study perspective: The experiences of young persons testifying to child sexual exploitation in British criminal court. *Journal of Child Sexual Abuse, 27,* 321–334.

American Bar Association. (2014). *ABA policy on trauma-informed advocacy for children and youth.* www.americanbar.org/content/dam/aba/administrative/child_law/ABAPolicyonTrauma-InformedAdvocacy.authcheckdam.pdf. Accessed 8 February 2018.

American Psychiatric Association. (2013). *Diagnostic and statistical manual of mental disorders (DSM-5)* (5th ed.). Arlington, VA: American Psychiatric Publishing.

Andrews, S. J., & Lamb, M. E. (2017). The structural linguistic complexity of lawyers' questions and children's responses in Scottish criminal courts. *Child Abuse and Neglect, 65,* 182–193.

Andrews, S. J., Lamb, M. E., & Lyon, T. D. (2014). Question types, responsiveness and self-contradictions when prosecutors and defense attorneys question alleged victims of child sexual abuse. *Applied Cognitive Psychology, 25,* 253–261.

Attorney General's National Task Force on Children Exposed to Violence. (2012). *Defending childhood: Report of the Attorney General's national task force on children exposed to violence.* Washington, DC: US Department of Justice.

Bath, H. I. (2008). The three pillars of trauma-informed care. *Reclaiming Children and Youth, 17,* 17–21.

Behzadnia, A., & Mehrani, M. B. (2017). Young children's yes bias in response to tag questions. *Early Child Development and Care, 188,* 1663–1672.

Berliner, L., & Conte, J. R. (1995). The effects of disclosure and intervention on sexually abused children. *Child Abuse & Neglect, 19*(3), 371–384.

Boyd, R., & Hopkins, A. (2010). Cross-examination of child sexual assault complainants: Concerns about the application of s 41 of the Evidence Act. *Criminal Law Journal, 34,* 149–166.

Brewin, C. R., Rose, S., Andrews, B., Green, J., Tata, P., McEvedy, C., … Foa, E. B. (2002). Brief screening instrument for post-traumatic stress disorder. *British Journal of Psychiatry, 181,* 158–162.

Butler, L. D., Critelli, F. M., & Rinfrette, E. S. (2011). Trauma-informed care and mental health. *Directions in Psychiatry, 31,* 177–192.

Caprioli, S., & Crenshaw, D. A. (2017). The culture of silencing child victims of sexual abuse: Implications for child witnesses in court. *Journal of Humanistic Psychology, 57,* 190–209.

Caruso, D. (2012). Proposed reforms for the cross-examination of child witnesses and the reception and treatment of their evidence. *Journal of Judicial Administration, 21,* 191–236.

Cashmore, J., & Trimboli, L. (2005). *An evaluation of the NSW child sexual assault specialist jurisdiction.* Sydney: NSW Bureau of Crime Statistics and Research.

Cecil, C. A. M., Viding, E., Fearon, P., Glaser, D., & McCrory, E. J. (2017). Disentangling the mental health impact of childhood abuse and neglect. *Child Abuse and Neglect, 63,* 106–119.

Chen, L. P., Murad, M. H., Paras, M. L., Colbenson, K. M., Sattler, A. L., Goranson, E. N., … Zirakzadeh, A. (2010). Sexual abuse and lifetime diagnosis of psychiatric disorders: Systematic review and meta-analysis. *Mayo Clinic Proceedings, 85,* 618–629.

Cleveland, K. C., Quas, J. A., & Lyon, T. D. (2016). Valence, implicated actor, and children's acquiescence to false suggestions. *Journal of Applied Development Psychology, 43,* 1–7.

Copeland, W., Keeler, G. P., Angold, A., & Costello, E. J. (2007). Traumatic events and posttraumatic stress in childhood. *Archives of General Psychiatry, 64,* 577–584.

Cossins, A. (2000). *Masculinities, sexualities and child sexual abuse.* The Hague: Kluwer Law International.

Cossins, A. (2009). Cross-examination in child sexual assault trials: Evidentiary safeguard or an opportunity to confuse? *Melbourne University Law Review, 33,* 68–104.

Cossins, A., & Plummer, M. (2016). Masculinity and sexual abuse: Explaining the transition from victim to offender. *Men and Masculinities, 21*, 163–188.

Cossins, A., & Rowden, E. (2020). The child sexual assault trial: Redesigning courtroom spaces according to trauma informed principles. In K. Duncanson & E. Henderson (Eds.), *Courthouse design and social justice*. London: Routledge (in press).

Denham, S. A. (1998). *The Guilford series on special and emotional development: Emotional development in young children.* New York: Guilford Press.

Drabble, L. A., Jones, S., & Brown, V. (2013). Advancing trauma-informed systems change in a family drug treatment court context. *Journal of Social Work Practice in the Addictions, 13*, 91–113.

Ehlers, A., & Clark, D. M. (2000). A cognitive model of posttraumatic stress disorder. *Behaviour Research and Therapy, 38*, 319–345.

Ehlers, A., Clark, D. M., Hackmann, A., McManus, F., & Fennell, M. (2005). Cognitive therapy for PTSD: Development and evaluation. *Behaviour Research and Therapy, 43*, 413–431.

Elliott, D. E. (2003). *Difficult conversations: A training curriculum on becoming trauma-informed*. Holyoke, MA: Franklin County Women's Research Project.

Elliott, D. E., Bjelajac, P., Fallot, R. D., Markoff, L. S., & Reed, B. G. (2005). Trauma-informed or trauma-denied: Principles and implementation of trauma-informed services for women. *Journal of Community Psychology, 33*, 461–477.

Elmi, M. H., Daignault, I. V., & Hébert, M. (2018). Child sexual abuse victims as witnesses: The influence of testifying on their recovery. *Child Abuse and Neglect, 86*, 22–32.

Fallot, R. D., & Harris, M. (2008). Trauma-informed approaches to systems to care. *Trauma Psychology Newsletter, 3*, 6–7.

Feinstein, J. S., Adolphs, R., Damasio, A., & Tranel, D. (2011). The human amygdala and the induction and experience of fear. *Current Biology, 21*, 34–38.

Fergusson, D. M., Boden, J. M., & Horwood, L. J. (2008). Exposure to childhood sexual and physical abuse and adjustment in early adulthood. *Child Abuse and Neglect, 32*, 607–619.

Fergusson, D. M., McLeod, G. F. H., & Horwood, L. J. (2013). Childhood sexual abuse and adult developmental outcomes: Findings from a 30-year longitudinal study in New Zealand. *Child Abuse and Neglect, 37*, 664–674.

Ford, J. D., & Blaustein, M. E. (2013). Systemic self-regulation: A framework for trauma-informed services in residential juvenile justice programs. *Journal of Family Violence, 28,* 665–677.

Gabbay, V., Oatis, M. D., Silva, R. R., & Hirsch, G. (2004). Epidemiological aspects of PTSD in children and adolescents. In R. R. Silva (Ed.), *Posttraumatic stress disorder in children and adolescents: Handbook* (pp. 1–17). New York: W. W. Norton.

Goodman, G. S., Taub, E. P., Jones, D. P. H., England, P., Port, L. K., Rudy, L., Prado, L., Myers, J. E. B., & Melton, G. B. (1992). Testifying in criminal court: Emotional effects on child sexual assault victims. *Monographs of the Society for Research in Child Development, 57*, 1–159.

Grogan, S., & Murphy, K. P. (2011). Anticipatory Stress Response in PTSD: Extreme stress in children. *Journal of Child & Adolescent Psychiatric Nursing, 24,* 58–71.

Haferkamp, L., Bebermeier, A., Möllering, A., & Neuner, F. (2015). Dissociation is associated with emotional maltreatment in a sample of traumatized women with a history of child abuse. *Journal of Trauma & Dissociation, 16,* 86–99.

Harris, M., & Fallot, R. D. (2001). Envisioning a trauma-informed service system: A vital paradigm shift. *New Directions for Mental Health Services, 89,* 3–22.

Hayes, D., & Bunting, L. (2013). 'Just be Brave'—The experiences of young witnesses in criminal proceedings in Northern Ireland. *Child Abuse Review, 22,* 419–431.

Henry, J. (1997). System intervention trauma to child sexual abuse victims following disclosure. *Journal of Interpersonal Violence, 12,* 499–512.

Hillberg, T., Hamilton-Giachritsis, C., & Dixon, L. (2011). Review of meta-analyses on the association between child sexual abuse and adult mental health difficulties: A systematic approach. *Trauma, Violence & Abuse, 12,* 38–49.

Hobbs, S., Goodman, G. S., Block, S. D., Oran, D., Quas, J. A., Park, A., … Baumrind, N. (2014). Child maltreatment victims' attitudes about appearing in dependency and criminal courts. *Children and Youth Services Review, 44,* 407–416.

Hodgdon, H., Kinniburgh, K., Gabowitz, D., Blaustein, M. E., & Spinazzola, J. (2013). Development and implementation of trauma-informed programming in youth residential treatment centers using the ARC framework. *Journal of Family Violence, 28,* 679–692.

Home Office. (2011). *Achieving best evidence: Guidance on interviewing victims and witnesses*. London: Home Office.

King, M., Freiberg, A., Batagol, B., & Hyams, R. (2014). *Non-Adversarial Justice*. Sydney: Federation Press.

Klemfuss, J. Z., Quas, J. A., & Lyon, T. D. (2014). Attorneys' questions and children's productivity in child sexual abuse criminal trials. *Applied Cognitive Psychology, 28,* 780–788.

Kochanska, G. (2003). Emotional development in children with different attachment histories: The first three years. *Child Development, 72,* 474–490.

Kolko, D. J., Hurlburt, M. S., Zhang, J., Barth, R. P., Leslie, L. K., & Burns, B. J. (2010). Posttraumatic stress symptoms in children and adolescents referred for child welfare investigation: A national sample of in-home and out-of-home care. *Child Maltreatment, 15,* 48–63.

Lamb, M. E., & Fauchier, A. (2001). The effects of question type on self-contradictions by children in the course of forensic interviews. *Applied Cognitive Psychology, 15,* 483–491.

Lamb, M. E., Hershkowitz, I., Orbach, Y., & Esplin, P. W. (2008). *Tell me what happened: Structured investigative interviews of child victims and witnesses.* Hoboken, NJ: Wiley-Blackwell.

Lima, A. A., Fiszman, A., Marques-Portella, C., Mendlowicz, M., Coutinho, E. S. F., Maia, D. C. B., ... Figueira, I. (2010). The impact of tonic immobility reaction on the prognosis of posttraumatic stress disorder. *Journal of Psychiatric Research, 44,* 224–228.

Maniglio, R. (2009). The impact of child sexual abuse on health: A systematic review of reviews. *Clinical Psychology Review, 29,* 647–657.

Maniglio, R. (2013). Child sexual abuse in the etiology of anxiety disorders: A systematic review of reviews. *Trauma, Violence, & Abuse, 14,* 96–112.

Miller, N. A., & Najavits, L. M. (2012). Creating trauma-informed correctional care: A balance of goals and environment. *European Journal of Psychotraumatology*, *3*, 17246/1–8.

Ministry of Justice. (2015a). *Registered intermediary procedural guidance manual*. London: Ministry of Justice. https://www.zakon.co.uk/admin/resources/downloads/registered-intermediary-procedural-guidance-manual-2015.pdf.

Miragoli, S., Camisasca, E., & Di Blasio, P. (2017). The narrative fragmentation in child sexual abuse: The role of age and posttraumatic stress disorder. *Child Abuse Neglect, 73C,* 106–114.

Miragoli, S., Camisasca, E., & Di Blasio, P. (2019). Investigating linguistic coherence relations in child sexual abuse: A comparison of PTSD and non-PTSD children. *Heliyon, 5,* e01163.

Miragoli, S., Procaccia, R., & Di Blasio, P. (2014). Language use and PTSD symptoms: Content analyses of allegations of child sexual abuse. *Journal of Forensic Psychology Practice, 14,* 355–382.

Najavits, L. M., Weiss, R. D., & Shaw, S. R. (1997). The link between substance abuse and posttraumatic stress disorder in women. *The American Journal on Addictions, 6,* 273–283.

National Child Traumatic Stress Network. (2009). *Helping traumatized children: Tips for judges.* https://www.nctsn.org/sites/default/files/assets/pdfs/JudgesFactSheet.pdf.

National Child Traumatic Stress Network. (2017). *Trauma: What child welfare attorneys should know.* https://www.nctsn.org/sites/default/files/assets/pdfs/attorneyresourceguide.pdf.

Oates, R. K., & Tong, L. (1987). Sexual abuse of children: An area with room for professional reforms. *Medical Journal of Australia, 147,* 544–548.

Ouimette, P., & Brown, P. J. (Eds.). (2003). *Trauma and substance abuse: Causes, Consequences, and treatment of comorbid disorders.* Washington, DC: American Psychological Association.

Perry, B. D. (2009). Examining child maltreatment through a neurodevelopmental lens: Clinical applications of the neurosequential model of therapeutics. *Journal of Loss and Trauma, 14,* 240–255.

Pilnik, L., & Kendall, J. R. (2012). *Identifying polyvictimization and trauma among court-involved children and youth: A checklist and resource guide for attorneys and other court-appointed advocates 2.* Safe Start Center, Office Juvenile Justice and Delinquency Prevention, U.S. Department of Justice.

Plotnikoff, J., & Woolfson, R. (2007). *Evaluation of young witness support: Examining the impact on witnesses and the criminal justice system.* London: Ministry of Justice. https://www.lexiconlimited.co.uk/PDF%20files/Young_Witness_Study_Report.pdf.

Porges, S. W. (2011). *The polyvagal theory: Neurophysiological foundations of emotions, attachment, communication, self-regulation.* New York: W. W. Norton.

Powell, M. B., Westera, N. J., Goodman-Delahunty, J., & Pichler, A. S. (2016). *An evaluation of how evidence is elicited from complainants of child sexual abuse.* Sydney: Royal Commission into Institutional Responses to Child Sexual Abuse.

Quas, J. A., & Goodman, G. S. (2012). Consequences of criminal court involvement for child victims. *Psychology, Public Policy, and Law, 18,* 392–414.

Quas, J. A., Goodman, G. S., Ghetti, S., Alexander, K. W., Edelstein, R., Redlich, A. D., & Jones, D. P. H. (2005). Childhood sexual assault victims: Long-term outcomes after testifying in criminal court. *Monographs of the Society for Research in Child Development, 70*, Serial No. 280.

Reitman, K. A. (2011). *Attorneys for children guide to interviewing clients: Integrating trauma informed care and solution focused strategies*. http://www.nycourts.gov/ip/cwcip/Publications/attorneyGuide.pdf.

Royal Commission into Institutional Responses to Child Sexual Abuse. (2017a). *Final report: Nature and cause* (Vol. 2). Sydney: Royal Commission into Institutional Responses to Child Sexual Abuse.

Sas, L. D., Hatch, A., Malla, S., Dick, T., & Hurley, P. (1993). *Three Years After the Verdict: A Longitudinal Study of the Social and Psychological Adjustment of Child Witnesses Referred to the Child Witness Project*. London, ON: National Criminal Justice Reference Service.

Schore, A. N. (2003). *Affect regulation and repair of the self*. New York: W. W. Norton.

Schore, A. N. (2016). *Affect regulation and the origin of the self: The neurobiology of emotional development*. New York: Routledge.

Shin, L. M., Rauch, S. L., & Pitman, R. K. (2006). Amygdala, medial prefrontal cortex, and hippocampal function in PTSD. *Annals of the New York Academy of Science, 1071*, 67–79.

Spertus, I. L., Yehuda, R., Wong, C. M., Halligan, S., & Seremitis, S. V. (2003). Childhood emotional abuse and neglect as predictors of psychological and physical symptoms in women presenting to a primary care practice. *Child Abuse and Neglect, 27,* 1247–1258.

Steil, R., Dyer, A., Priebe, K., Kleindienst, N., & Bohus, M. (2011). Dialectical behavior therapy for posttraumatic stress disorder related to childhood sexual abuse: A pilot study of an intensive residential treatment program. *Journal of Traumatic Stress, 24,* 102–106.

Substance Abuse and Mental Health Services Administration. (2013a). *Essential components of trauma-informed judicial practice* (pp. 1–12). https://www.nasmhpd.org/sites/default/files/JudgesEssential_5%201%202013finaldraft.pdf.

van der Kolk, B. A. (2005). Developmental trauma disorder: Towards a rational diagnosis for children with complex trauma histories. *Psychiatric Annals, 33,* 401–408.

van der Kolk, B. A. (2006). Clinical implications of neuroscience research in PTSD. *Annals of New York Academy of Sciences, 1071*, 277–293.

van der Kolk, B. A. (2015). *The body keeps the score: Brain, mind, and body in the healing of trauma.* New York: Viking Press.

Victims Services, NSW Department of Justice. (2016). *Children's champion (witness intermediary) procedural guidance manual (2016).* Sydney: NSW Department of Justice. https://www.victimsservices.justice.nsw.gov.au/Documents/child-champ_manual.pdf.

Westera, N., Darwinkel, E., & Powell, M. (2016). *A systematic review of the efficacy of specialist police investigative units in responding to child sexual abuse.* Sydney: Royal Commission into Institutional Responses to Child Sexual Abuse.

Whitcomb, D., Runyan, D. K., De Vos, E., Hunter, W. M., Cross, T. P., Everson, … Cropper, C. (1991). *Child victim as witness project: Final report.* Washington, DC: Office of Juvenile Justice and Delinquency Prevention (U.S. Department of Justice), U.S. Government Printing Office. https://www.ncjrs.gov/pdffiles1/Digitization/149172NCJRS.pdf.

Williams, R. (2007). The psychosocial consequences for children of mass violence, terrorism and disasters. *International Review of Psychiatry, 19*, 263–277.

Williams, L. M., Kemp, A. H., Felmingham, K., Barton, M., Olivieri, G., Peduto, A., … Bryant, R. A. (2006). Trauma modulates amygdala and medial prefrontal responses to consciously attended fear. *Neuroimage, 29*, 347–357.

Wilson, D. R. (2010). Health consequences of childhood sexual abuse. *Perspectives in Psychiatric Care, 46*, 56–64.

Zajac, R., O'Neill, S., & Hayne, H. (2012). Disorder in the courtroom? Child witnesses under cross-examination. *Developmental Review, 32*, 181–204.

12

Reform Measures: The Devil Is in the Detail

1 Introduction

As someone who has been actively involved in law reform of the sexual assault trial for over two decades, it is sad to read the following parental experience which reveals the problems faced by law reformers when they set out a reform agenda:

> The present criminal justice system forces parents of child abuse victims to decide between two options. Parents can either expose their children to the trauma of participating in the criminal justice system in order to achieve justice by putting paedophiles in gaol to prevent harm to further children. Alternatively, parents can allow paedophiles to remain free in order to prevent the criminal justice system from causing further harm to their own child. *In my mind, that will never be a fair and just system.* (Royal Commission, 2017a: 15; quoting CDP, a parent; emphasis added)

Indeed, the needs of parents and children for fairness in the form of a non-traumatising system are fundamentally incompatible with the mindset of lawyers:

A. Cossins, *Closing the Justice Gap for Adult and Child Sexual Assault*,
https://doi.org/10.1057/978-1-137-32051-3_12

> Reform initiatives in criminal justice have a habit of foundering on the rock of lawyerly insularity, the tendency, as one [English senior barrister] … put it, to tell reformers "to piss off" when their plans conflict with practitioners' principles. … [T]he key to creating real and lasting practice reform is not to impose change from outside but to work from within the culture. … Lawyers have good reason to be insular. *They are the guardians of the fair trial*. However … once that fundamental concern to protect fairness is addressed, it is possible to convince them to change. In fact, once convinced their current practices impede fairness, they can become the drivers of reform, or … "revolutionaries". (Henderson, 2015a: 948; emphasis added)

Here we have the views of two completely different participants in the criminal justice system—the first is the mother of a three-year-old whose child was one of four children allegedly abused by a childcare centre owner. The second is that of a researcher and practising barrister. The parent views the criminal justice system as an outsider who has the best interests of her child at heart. The second views the criminal justice system as an insider who praises the insularity of lawyers.

For example, many of the reforms discussed in Chapter 10 were, in previous times, the type of reforms that would have resulted in reformers being told to 'piss off', such as remote rooms, the use of CCTV and pre-recorded evidence. Now they are more or less entrenched within the criminal justice systems in E&W and Australia. Thus, fairness is a mutable concept that changes over time and with greater social awareness of the insularity and rigidity of those systems.

While lawyers are the guardians of a fair trial, they are also practitioners in the art of trauma since to many lawyers, the sacrifice of a child witness's well-being is worth the preservation of 'fairness', a concept that is usually not defined, although it is difficult to see how traumatising a child or vulnerable adult helps preserve the presumption of innocence, the right to silence and the prosecution's burden of proof. Indeed, as discussed in Chapter 8, the concept of fairness is broader than preservation of the rights of defendants and has never included a right to traumatise witnesses.

For example, CDE was a six-year-old who told his mother that he had been sexually abused by a respite carer in the family home. The carer was charged with indecent assault but acquitted at trial. The Director of Public Prosecutions for the ACT noted that during the cross-examination of CDE, the defence used the common practice 'of repeating a series of propositions until the witness accedes to the proposition. He said this style of cross-examination can "work" with children, as they tire, lose energy and effectively start agreeing with the propositions put to them' (Royal Commission, 2017a: 9). This is particularly the case with children and those who have cognitive disabilities.

Nonetheless, fairness is to be measured more widely than merely the interests of the accused. The rights of an accused under the fair trial principle are not absolute and the concept of fairness has been recognised by several courts as taking into account the interests of complainants and the community generally, including the need to minimise the re-traumatisation of sexual assault complainants. It can and should be applied in a way that encourages victims to report sexual offences to the police.

The discussion below, therefore, considers the legal ramifications of the use of rape myths by defence counsel and jurors, as well as the impact of cross-examination on producing inaccurate evidence.

2 Equal Treatment: Reconceptualising the Concept of Fairness

In E&W, the *Equal Treatment Bench Book* (Judicial College, 2013–2019) has a chapter on children and vulnerable adults which contains a number of processes and procedures that are designed to accommodate a vulnerable person's needs as required by:

> case law, the Equality Act 2010, the European Convention on Human Rights, the UN Convention on the Rights of the Child, the UN Convention on the Rights of Persons with Disabilities and the European Directive establishing minimum standards on the rights, support and protection of victims of crime. (Judicial College, 2013–2019: 5-1)

The *Equal Treatment Bench Book* is premised on equality principles, rather than trauma-informed principles, which means that the 'safeguarding responsibilities' of courts for children and vulnerable adults (Judicial College, 2013–2019: 5-1) do not explicitly recognise that the standard of 'equality' embodied within legislation and case law is not consonant with a trauma-informed model.

While 'the exercise of judicial discretion often has a safeguarding dimension' (Judicial College, 2013–2019: 5-1), the criminal justice system is not designed to deal with children's emotional, mental and communication development, nor with the effects of trauma on adults, making it difficult for these vulnerable witnesses to meet the high expectations of consistent and reliable evidence in criminal trials. Without judges who are trained in trauma-informed care, judicial discretion is an inadequate method for overcoming the barriers faced by vulnerable witnesses.

Because vulnerable witnesses 'continue to be adversely affected by an absence of real focus on their needs … the [criminal justice] system itself appears to be unable to maintain a consistent and acceptable level of care as cases pass through it' (HM CPS Inspectorate and HM Inspectorate of Constabulary, 2012). The *Equal Treatment Bench Book* recommends 'that a named individual has responsibility for the vulnerable person's welfare at the hearing, with a line of communication to alert [the judge] to difficulties' and warns that '[s]afeguarding is most at risk when responsibilities are unclear and there is a breakdown of communication' (Judicial College, 2013–2019: 5-5).

The measures discussed in the *Equal Treatment Bench Book* are explicitly designed to enable vulnerable witnesses to give their best evidence on the grounds that:

> Just because a change does not coincide with the way we have always done things does not mean that it should be rejected … . Do proposed changes cause unfair prejudice to the defendant? If so, of course, they cannot happen. If however they make it more likely to enable the truth to emerge, whether favourable or unfavourable to the defendant, then

> let it be done. The truth is the objective. (Judicial College, 2013–2019: 2–12; citing the Lord Chief Justice)[1]

Some examples of the 'flexible approach' instituted under the concept of equal treatment (Judicial College, 2013–2019: 5-2–5-4) include:

- The use of intermediaries, who are trained communication specialists, during the examination and cross-examination of child witnesses;
- Allowing witnesses to write and draw to clarify answers;
- 'Permitting witnesses unable to give evidence (e.g. because of distress ...) to come back the next day ... rather than dismissing the case immediately';
- 'allowing children to briefly pause cross-examination to relieve their stress, without leaving the live link room, by going under a table, behind a curtain or under a blanket, and ... being permitted to leave the room without prior permission to use the toilet';
- 'allowing a fearful eight-year-old to calm herself quickly by taking herself out of sight of the main live link camera (but still visible to the judge on the overview camera). The child and intermediary practised these "in room" breaks beforehand, using a large 30-second egg timer. The judge requested everyone to wait, rather than adjourning the court';
- 'scheduling children with learning disabilities to give evidence for short periods, with breaks, in the morning over several days';
- 'allocating a female judge and counsel to a trial with a[n adult] witness who refused to speak to a man about the alleged offence';
- 'allowing a Registered Intermediary to relay the answers of a witness with autism spectrum disorder and behavioural problems who gave evidence with her back to the live link camera';
- Allowing a registered intermediary to 'relay the replies of witnesses who would only whisper their answers'; and
- 'letting a man with autism spectrum disorder give evidence wearing a lion's tail, his "comfort object" in daily life'.

[1]The Lord Chief Justice 2013, Toulmin Lecture, Half a Century of Change: The Evidence of Child Victims, King's College London; cited in Judicial College (2013–2019: 2).

A perusal of these flexible approaches shows that they are adaptations to the hostile and traumatising environment of the adversarial trial and do not directly address the triggers that may require a witness to 'come back the next day' because of distress, or those that cause a witness to go under a table, behind a curtain or under a blanket to relieve their stress.

The Judicial Commission of NSW (2006–2017: 6103–6108) publishes the *Equality before the Law Bench Book* for judges in NSW which contains a section on the difficulties that children have in giving evidence, although it is not explicitly trauma-informed. Suggestions for overcoming these difficulties in the Bench Book are not all mandated in legislation so that judges are free to ignore the barriers to children giving their best evidence, such as age-inappropriate language and communication by lawyers, children's lack of understanding of court processes and procedures, the cross-examination effect and the use of improper questions (Judicial Commission of NSW, 2006–2017: 6309–6316).

By contrast, if a child is a *defendant* in criminal proceedings, 'several pieces of legislation specifically require [a judge] to explain court proceedings and processes to ensure that the child understands the proceedings' (Judicial Commission of NSW, 2006–2017: 6310). For example, s 12(1) of the *Children (Criminal Proceedings) Act 1987* (NSW), states:

> If criminal proceedings are brought against a child, the court that hears those proceedings must take such measures as are reasonably practicable to ensure that the child understands the proceedings.[2]

However, no such provision exists in relation to children (or vulnerable adults) giving evidence in sexual assault trials in NSW.

3 Where to from Here?

In a sexual assault trial, the complainant is, for all practical purposes, at the centre of the trial, yet her interests or rights, in a legal sense, are no

[2]See also *Children and Young Persons (Care and Protection) Act 1998*, s 95.

greater than those of any other witness. What the complainant said or did not say, did or did not do *before* the alleged assault, at the time of the alleged assault and *after* the alleged assault are matters that are central to both the prosecution's case and the accused's defence.

Most reforms of the sexual assault trial have focused on procedural and evidentiary reforms, such as the enactment of rape shield laws and removal of the requirement for mandatory warnings to be given in relation to the uncorroborated evidence of children and sexual assault complainants. However, it appears that evidentiary and procedural reforms have had little or no impact on reports to police, prosecution and conviction rates (Cossins, 2010a; Daly & Bouhours, 2010; see also Brown, 2011; Cook, 2011; Jordan 2011) and it can take some decades for the implementation of such reforms in day-to-day practice (Connolly, Coburn, & Chong, 2017).

With no evidence that these reforms have improved the conditions under which complainants give evidence in sexual assault trials nor had any discernible effect on wrongful acquittals (see Chapter 1), there have been many suggestions for further reform of the sexual assault trial:

- Specialist sex offences courts (Cossins, 2006, 2010a; Ministry of Justice, 2014; NSW Criminal Justice and Sexual Offences Taskforce, 2005; NSW Joint Select Committee on Sentencing of Child Sexual Assault Offenders, 2014; NSW Standing Committee on Law and Justice, 2002);
- Specialist judges (Cossins, 2010a)[3];
- Restorative justice (Daly, 2008, 2011; Kasparian, 2014; Wager, 2013);
- Abolition of juries (Temkin & Krahé, 2008; Willmott, Boduszek, & Booth, 2017);
- Legal representation for complainants (Chalmers, 2014; Cossins, 2004; Raitt, 2010; Wilson, 2005);

[3]Representations by the author to the NSW Government in 2015 saw the appointment of two specialist judges to the NSW District Court to sit on CSA trials; https://www.justice.nsw.gov.au/Pages/media-news/media-releases/2015/New-specialist-judges-support-victims-child-sexual-assault.aspx, accessed 7 March 2019.

- Expert evidence to educate jurors about the responses of children and adults to sexual assault (Cossins, 2008, 2013; Ellison & Munro, 2009).

However, the focus of this chapter is on reforms that would enact fundamental cultural change—from a system with a narrow view of fairness so that protecting the rights of defendants requires the re-traumatisation of complainants, to a system that is able to counteract the cultural significance of rape myths and is designed to:

- do no harm;
- protect the psychological needs of complainants;
- counteract the cross-examination effect; and
- achieve best evidence.

To that end, this chapter will focus on reforms that are aimed at wholesale reform of the criminal justice system for the prosecution of sex offences: specialist courts based on trauma-informed principles (with or without the use of restorative justice as a post-trial sentencing option).

As discussed in previous chapters, rape myths and misconceptions about children's responses to sexual abuse not only create the cultural context in which a complainant's evidence is interpreted but they can also nullify 'conventional strategies of reform aimed at offence definition', as well as reforms to rules of evidence and procedure (Pether, 2009: 242). This means that solutions are needed to challenge the dominance of those cultural narratives:

> formal attempts to alter statutes and policies must be supplemented by analysis of the social and cultural patterns that shape the implementation, interpretation, and effect of the law. (Frohmann & Mertz, 1995: 835; cited in Pether, 2009: 242)

This chapter is written with this idea in mind although I do not have blind faith in the ability of the criminal justice system to deliver justice—just a strong belief that a *fair* system (from the point of view of victims) of redress, recognition and punishment is required to deal with the entrenched nature of sexual assault in Western societies. For example, Robinson (2015: 169) contends that 'it is vital' for children to testify in criminal trials:

> not only for the administration of justice, but because it has the potential to right some of the wrongs done to their development. … [C]hildren should be encouraged to testify if they are able, as it affords them the opportunity to regain control, offers a sense of empowerment, and provides a feeling of retribution against the abuser.

This observation also applies to adult survivors of CSA and those who are sexually assaulted in adulthood. An accessible system of justice—where the complainant is not 'on trial', where the 'theatre of the trial' which pits the complainant against the defendant is dismantled, where a culture of adversarialism that depends on the complainant's emotional toughness to withstand all that the defendant can throw at her is replaced by a trauma-informed system—may go some way towards healing, and reducing the use of drugs, alcohol and, sometimes, suicide to cope with the trauma of being sexually assaulted.

Reform recommendations are based on a recognition that the legitimate expectations of an accused under the fair trial principle must be balanced against the needs of complainants and the expectations of the community at large. This means that the right to cross-examine prosecution witnesses should not be absolute and ought to be subject to controls where necessary in the public interest as is the case already in some courts in E&W. At present, there is an ad hoc, rather than a formal, approach to reducing re-traumatisation in trials in E&W and NSW through the use of intermediaries, pre-recording of evidence and other special measures although neither jurisdiction has formally confronted the impact of the cross-examination effect. Below I discuss:

- rape myth busting;
- opening and closing addresses;
- mandatory training;

- child- and complainant-friendly environments;
- pre-recording of evidence;
- time-limited cross-examination and vetting of questions;
- changing the cross-examination process: the use of a specialist examiner who is trained in the principles of trauma-informed systems; and
- restorative justice.

But, first, what would a trauma-informed sexual assault trial involve?

4 Trauma-Informed Sexual Assault Trials: A Best Practice Model

As discussed below, because of the triggers that presently exist within the sexual assault trial, and the possible effect this will have on a complainant's ability to give their best evidence, various reforms would be necessary to move to a trauma-informed criminal justice system, in order to equalise the relations between witness and examiner, nullify the cross-examination effect and achieve best evidence.

These reforms, which are based on the 10 principles of trauma-informed care in Table 3, Chapter 11, include:

- Training of all court personnel in trauma-informed principles and practices;
- Reconfiguration of courtroom facilities to diffuse the power imbalance between judge, examiner and complainant so that each is seated on the same level within normal speaking distance (see further Cossins & Rowden, 2020);
- Special interview room for the giving of evidence (known as remote rooms in NSW, for example) where evidence can be pre-recorded or transmitted via CCTV but with additional support in the form of trained personnel to deal with re-traumatisation;

- Employment of specialist examiners to assess a complainant's language and developmental abilities and needs because of age, disability and/or trauma;
- Reconfiguration of the cross-examination process so that defence counsel submit their questions at a pre-trial hearing where questions are vetted by a specialist examiner (i) to determine the age-appropriateness of proposed defence questions; and (ii) to ensure questions are in keeping with trauma-informed principles relevant to the legal system so that all defence questions are not only age-appropriate but they:

  - *Recognise the long-term impact of violence and victimization on development and coping strategies*: complainants may have difficulty regulating their emotions and relating to authority figures so that their participation in the legal process may be impaired, such as coping with intense, humiliating and lengthy courtroom questioning.
  - *Employ an empowerment model*: questions and questioning needs to build on a complainant's existing strengths to participate in the legal process, in light of any pre-existing trauma symptoms, in particular the ability to comprehend questions and communicate an appropriate answer in an alien environment. Thus, examination of the complainant would take place in light of their specific age, disability and psychological needs.
  - *Create interactions that are collaborative, empowering and safe*: best evidence is more likely to be achieved where there is a non-shaming, non-blaming and non-authoritarian relationship between complainant and examiner which will depend on the tone, content and form of questions asked.
  - *Create an environment that provides safety, respect and acceptance*: safe, non-hierarchical relationships require appropriate trauma-informed interactions by all personnel (including through the questioning process) which is particularly pertinent to the criminal trial context in order to promote best evidence.
  - *Minimise re-traumatization*: the minimisation of re-traumatisation is essential to trauma-informed systems including a criminal trial. This would require prohibition of questions that are based on rape

myths and stereotypes to ensure that no further harm is done to the complainant and that she will be able to give her best evidence.
  - *Are culturally competent*: a complainant's capacity to participate in the legal process needs to be understood with respect to her cultural background. This awareness allows legal personnel to understand a complainant's reactions to the court environment.

- In a case with multiple defendants and multiple counsel, one set of questions to be submitted for vetting;
- Employment of a specialist examiner to examine, cross-examine and re-examine the complainant;
- Transformation of cross-examination into a *time-limited* second examination using vetted defence questions;
- Reforms to prohibit questions based on rape myths (see below);
- Appointment of a court-based professional who is responsible for the trauma-informed care of a complainant from pre-trial through to the trial in order to provide psychological support where necessary and to inform the court of threats to the complainant's psychological welfare;
- Pre-recording of a complainant's examination-in-chief and cross-examination—this reform means that both adult and complainants can give pre-recorded evidence as close to the time of their report as possible, rather than having to wait months or years to give evidence during the actual trial;
- Judicial directions to the jury about the (i) the impact of trauma on a complainant's evidence; and (ii) about the fact that inconsistencies in evidence and gaps in memory are not necessarily indicative of veracity but may be a symptom of trauma or the cross-examination effect.

Without a package of reforms that are trauma-informed, re-traumatisation is the likely outcome for any complainant in a sexual assault trial, whether or not there is a conviction. Thus, the utility of a trial process that impedes a complainant from giving their best evidence, and the jury from hearing the best evidence of the prosecution's chief witness, must be questioned, the more so if a non-trauma-informed

trial process results in jury decisions that amount to wrongful acquittals. Neither complainants or the community at large benefits from a non-trauma informed system of justice.
These reforms and others that are compatible with trauma-informed care are discussed in detail in the next sections.

4.1 Rape Myth Busting and Judicial Warnings

Chapters 4 and 5 discussed the extent to which rape myths are used by defence counsel during the cross-examination of rape complainants and the extent to which jurors and mock jurors filter the evidence of complainants through the lens of rape myths. The task for this chapter is to consider how to eliminate or minimise the effects of rape myths on jury and judicial decision-making. The likelihood of success of these methods could be tested in pilot studies, and/or through the commission of mock jury studies.

One of the key findings from the studies discussed previously was the fact that those with higher levels of RMA are more likely to blame a victim, and less likely to perceive a victim as credible and the defendant as culpable (see, e.g. Stewart & Jacquin, 2010). In other words, there is a positive correlation between relatively high levels of RMA and a tendency to acquit in sexual assault trials (Dinos, Burrowes, Hammond, & Cunliffe, 2015).

While expert evidence and/or judicial directions have been recommended by a number of researchers, including myself, as the obvious way to counteract the effect of rape myths and other misconceptions about complainants and sexual assault (Cossins, 2013a; Cossins, Goodman-Delahunty, & O'Brien, 2009; Ellison, & Munro, 2009; Goodman-Delahunty, Cossins, & O'Brien, 2010, 2011; Henderson & Duncanson, 2016), there is some evidence to show that experts are not always available, and expert evidence may not always have the expected impact on counteracting rape myths and misconceptions (Goodman-Delahunty, Cossins, & Martschuk, 2014). Similarly, the efficacy of judicial directions appears to depend on timing (Goodman-Delahunty, Cossins, & O'Brien, 2011; Henderson & Duncanson, 2016; Steblay,

Hosch, Culhane, & McWethy, 2006). In relation to juror comprehension of judicial directions, there are several studies to show that judicial directions are not necessarily effective (Goodman-Delahunty, Cossins, & Martschuk, 2016; Simon, 2012; Trimboli, 2008) or well understood by jurors (Goodman-Delahunty et al., 2016; Law Commission, New Zealand, 1999; Queensland Law Reform Commission, 2009; Thomas, 2010) even if jurors believe they understand them.

As I stated in Chapter 6, jurors do not merely interpret trial testimony and other evidence based on the directions given to them by the trial judge, they actively process that information to 'fit' with their own experiences of, and beliefs about, human behaviour, with pre-decisional distortion a realistic phenomenon that is unlikely to be corrected by judicial warnings.

In fact, Fig. 3 from Chapter 6 (repeated below) shows the limited influence of judicial directions/warnings on jury decision-making.

Most of the research on judicial warnings has 'almost unanimously concluded that a jury's ability to comprehend [directions] is poor and that there is room for considerable improvement' (Comiskey, 2010: 629). For example, Thomas (2010: vi) found that:

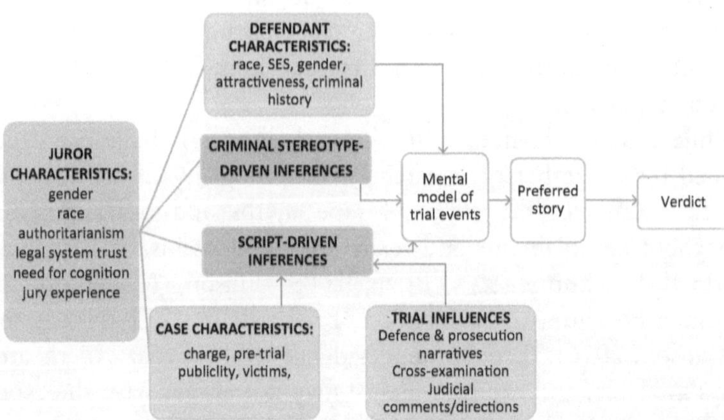

Fig. 1 'Director's cut' model linking juror and defendant characteristics to juror decisions (Adapted from Devine & Caughlin, 2014: 112; with additions by author)

> While over half of the jurors perceived the judge's directions as easy to understand, only a minority (31%) actually understood the directions fully in the legal terms used by the judge … [while] comprehension of directions on the law declin[ed] as the age of the juror increased.

In addition, juries can receive a range of complex directions in a sexual assault trial, such that the desired effects of educative directions may well be counteracted by other directions that are mandatory or requested by the defence (Flynn & Henry, 2012). The NSW Law Reform Commission (2012: 27; citing Devine, 2012; Devine, Clayton, Dunford, Seying, & Pryce, 2001) reported that 'directions that require jurors to ignore information that appears relevant to them, in determining what happened, tend to be less effective than other types of directions'.

Are there more effective options than judicial directions which jurors may or may not understand or ignore? While there have been suggestions to issue jurors in sexual assault trials with 'myth busting packs', these are unlikely to be universally efficacious or endorsed due to concerns about possible prejudice to the accused (Gibb, 2007).

Realistic alternatives would focus on introducing reforms that would *prevent* the use of rape myths within the trial. Perhaps it is time to challenge the entrenched protection of the jury from scrutiny in Australia and E&W with respect to the myths they bring to the jury room. For example, in E&W:

> Around 30,000 cases progress to full trial each year, resulting in approximately 400,000 jurors being summoned … [U]nlike in other countries where those selected are questioned extensively before the trial begins, within England the law prevents jurors from being asked almost anything related to the case. The reasoning for this being that the random selection of jurors, without the need for qualifying features (except for age, sound mental health, and a lack of criminal convictions), is … considered to be fundamental to the fairness of verdicts … [H]uge value (and trust) is placed in the random composition of 12 people … each of whom bring alternative views and opinions … Yet with such a wide spectrum of people … comes a whole host of associated biases. Biases which bring the assumption of juror impartiality, into question. (Willmott et al., 2017: 13)

This quote highlights the assumption that an unscrutinised jury is one that is likely to produce the fairest verdict. Yet in sexual assault trials, the unscrutinised jury, relying on their own myths and misconceptions, is likely to produce an unfair verdict. As research discussed previously shows, various juror characteristics, such as gender, RMA levels and pro-defence biases, influence the verdicts of jurors in sexual assault trials.

One possible solution is the use of compulsory online surveys to measure levels of RMA of all jurors called up for jury duty to prevent those with high levels of endorsement of rape myths from sitting on sexual assault trials. An online survey would be relatively easy to administer prior to jurors' attendance at court by asking them to log into a particular website at the time of notification of jury duty. The availability of software programmes for coding surveys would produce the individual RMA levels of jurors without too much cost.

Jurors with high levels of RMA could then be excluded from being assigned to juries in sexual assault trials, since what is the point of running trials where the evidence is filtered through inaccurate and discriminatory beliefs about women and children who are sexually assaulted?

We also know from a considerable amount of research (see Chapters 5 and 6) that female jurors are more likely to convict in a sexual assault trial, compared to male jurors who are more likely to acquit. This data suggests that a balance of male and female jurors should be empanelled in sexual assault trials to ensure a balance of opinions and scrutiny of the evidence.

While particular reforms to cross-examination are discussed later in relation to vetting of questions, reforms are required to prevent topics that endorse rape myths from being the subject of cross-examination. Below I have drafted a provision to prevent the use of rape myths during cross-examination, with particular reference to the symptoms of sexual victimisation listed in Table 1, Chapter 2. I have decided not to follow the format of s 41 of the NSW *Evidence Act 1995* which refers to improper questions and requires the court to determine if a particular question is improper before prohibiting it, since as discussed in Chapter 8, s 41 has been underutilised by judges in NSW.

Prohibited questions

(1) This section applies to prescribed sexual offence proceedings.
(2) The following topics are prohibited as the subject of questions during the cross-examination of a complainant in a sexual assault trial where they are to be used to challenge the credibility of the complainant or the reliability of her or his evidence:

(i) the sexual history of the complainant with the accused or any other person prior to, or after the alleged sexual activity that is the subject of the charges;
(ii) the sexual reputation of the complainant;
(iii) the state of intoxication (by drugs and/or alcohol) of the complainant before, during or after the events that are the subject of the charges, unless that state of intoxication is to be used by the prosecution to argue absence of consent;
(iv) the style of dress of the complainant before, during or after the events that are the subject of the charges;
(v) the failure of the complainant to physically resist the accused;
(vi) the failure of the complainant to verbally resist the accused;
(vii) the presence or absence of a recent complaint by the complainant;
(viii) the presence or absence of a delayed complaint;
(ix) any psychological or psychiatric treatment, therapy or counselling that the complainant has received, or is receiving[4];
(x) the mental health history of the complainant including but not limited to anxiety disorders, depression, eating disorders, post-traumatic stress disorder, sleeping disorders, self-mutilation, drug overdoses and suicide attempts, unless that mental health history is to be used by the prosecution to argue absence of consent;
(xi) the medical history of the complainant including any pregnancies or abortions, unless that medical history is to be used by the prosecution to argue absence of consent;
(xii) any criminal history of the complainant;
(xiii) any allegations of sexual assault made by the complainant against a person other than the accused.

(3) In consultation with the trial judge and counsel, the specialist examiner appointed by the court must vett all cross-examination questions to ensure that they comply with the prohibitions set out in subsection (2).

In the above list, I have included topics that pertain to the sexual history and reputation of a complainant. While some jurisdictions have relatively strong rape shield provisions, such as s 293 of the *Criminal Procedure Act 1986* (NSW), this is not universally the case. For example, McGlynn (2017: 367) has observed that in E&W, 'despite the clear legislative intent to curtail the use of sexual history evidence in rape trials [under the YJCE Act], it continues to be admitted in a considerable number of trials'. Even the restrictive NSW provision does not impose a blanket ban on sexual experience evidence. Yet the absence of a blanket ban contradicts the model of communicative consent, that is, that a woman's previous sexual experience with the accused (or another person) can never amount to implied consent to future sexual activities with the accused.

Because complainants who become intoxicated by drugs and/or alcohol voluntarily are 'are simply not perceived as credible – not only by juries, but by police and prosecutors as well' (Carlson, 2014: 307), it is necessary to restrict the admissibility of evidence regarding a complainant's voluntary intoxication to the situation where intoxication is only argued by the prosecution as a factor vitiating or negating consent (see Chapter 7). Thus, evidence about a complainant's voluntary intoxication should be inadmissible where the defence seeks to adduce it as being relevant to the facts in issue and/or the complainant's credibility, the risk being that jurors will use such evidence to blame the complainant for the defendant's sexual behaviour (as discussed previously). In other words, it is necessary to eliminate the *cultural* meanings that are associated with women's voluntary intoxication in a sexual assault trial (that they are sexually available, or irresponsible, or 'asking for it') to ensure that jurors focus on the biological significance of intoxication (voluntary or otherwise); that is, the impaired ability to consent due to the effects of intoxication (see Chapter 7 and the *Lazarus* case).

Making such evidence inadmissible, except for the purposes of proving lack of consent by the prosecution, would prevent the defence from adducing prejudicial evidence of the voluntary nature of a complainant's intoxication, such as the amount of alcohol she had

[4] Using the wording of s 278.2(4) of the Criminal Code of Canada.

purchased and drunk, or photographs/videos of the complainant's intoxicated behaviour, all of which has cultural overtones associated with irresponsibility and sexually promiscuous behaviour. Such a prohibition might also encourage prosecutors to rely on medical evidence of blood-alcohol levels and their effect, as discussed in Chapter 7, in order to focus the jurors' minds on a complainant's *capacity* to freely and voluntarily consent.

Arguably, it would be insufficient, as recommended by Carlson (2014: 308), to allow the admissibility of such evidence to be governed by a judicial discretion to exclude on the grounds that the 'probative value of evidence demonstrating the voluntary nature of the victim's intoxication is substantially outweighed by its prejudicial effect'. As discussed in Chapter 7, judges are not necessarily aware of the psychological studies that reveal the prejudicial effect of voluntary intoxication on jurors' decision-making, nor are they necessarily aware of the degree of intoxication that gives rise to an inability to freely and voluntarily consent.

4.2 Opening and Closing Addresses

In order to continue with the theme of preventing the use of rape myths in sexual assault trials, reforms are necessary to the opening and closing addresses of counsel, particularly the defence. Chapter 6 discussed the problems with opening and closing addresses, including the use of these addresses by the defence to encourage jurors to feel empathy towards the defendant, and the misuse by jurors of such addresses as 'evidence' in the trial.

A study on inducing empathy (via defence attorney opening and closing addresses) in a mock murder trial to determine whether or not jurors' empathy for a defendant made them more likely to 'hold the defendant less responsible for his or her actions' (Haegerich & Bottoms, 2000: 423) found that:

> jurors' case-related judgments are affected when an attorney asks them to identify affectively and cognitively with a defendant. … [C]ompared

> to … the control condition, jurors in the empathy condition had more empathy for the defendant, were more lenient in their guilt judgments, [and] considered the defendant to be less responsible for the killing. (Haegerich and Bottoms, 2000: 437)

The degree of empathy inducement in the jurors also meant that some jurors ignored legal instructions regarding their verdict:

> Thirty percent of the jurors in the empathy condition who found the defendant not guilty because of self-defense indicated that they chose that verdict because of the defendant's past history of abuse and the father's alcoholism. For example, a juror … wrote, 'I believe [the defendant] probably wasn't in "immediate danger", but the acts his father had committed in the past justify a not guilty verdict.' Thus, such jurors may have doubted the defendant's claim of being in imminent danger at the moment of the shooting, but believed that the past abuse was a sufficient excuse for killing the father, nullifying the law instructing them to acquit only if the defendant felt … in imminent danger. (Haegerich & Bottoms, 2000: 438)

As discussed previously, 'jurors' biases—either preexisting biases or those induced by trial circumstances—may overshadow … hard evidence … and threaten the integrity of the judicial system by hindering fair, impartial trials for defendants and victims' (Haegerich & Bottoms, 2000: 442). Thus, Haegerich, Salerno, & Bottoms (2013: 90) recommend that judges could:

> inform jurors about the potential bias that attorneys' statements may have on their decision making, even without their awareness, and that they can attempt to resist such biases by being more cognitively aware, critically evaluating the evidence and the conclusions that the attorneys assert about what happened.

However, such instructions are no guarantee against empathy-inducing statements in opening/closing addresses so the better approach would be to devise ways in which these biases are not fostered during a trial.

A later study by Haegerich et al. (2013), discussed in Chapter 6, showed that 'the manner in which case material is presented' in a trial can influence verdicts, 'putting the fairness of the legal system in jeopardy' (Haegerich et al., 2013: 89). Thus, controlling the content of counsels' 'biasing statements about the defendant during opening and closing arguments might be more important in decreasing juror bias' (Haegerich et al., 2013: 90) than other strategies.

How could this be done? Arguably, it would be necessary to restrict the content of opening addresses of both counsel to information that will be supported by admissible evidence and the content of closing addresses to information that has been supported by the evidence adduced in the trial, not merely counsel speculation or commentary.

For opening addresses in a sexual assault trial, a simpler approach would be to limit the prosecutor's opening address to a summary of the elements of the charge(s) against the defendant, followed by a defence opening address which is limited to a denial of the defendant's guilt with respect to the charge(s).

Legislation would be required to prohibit the use of certain information in opening and closing statements in order to prevent the use of supposition, gossip, speculation and rape myths, such as commentary about the complainant, including:

- the complainant's style of dress;
- the complainant's 'flirtatious' behaviour;
- the complainant's voluntary consumption of alcohol and/or drugs;
- the complainant's desire for victims' compensation;
- the complainant's delayed complaint;
- revenge on the part of the complainant;
- a desire by the complainant to protect her reputation; and
- the passivity of the defendant versus the 'titillating' behaviour of the complainant.

4.3 Mandatory Training

As discussed in Chapter 11, mandatory training about the effects of trauma and trauma-informed systems and principles, as well as the triggers within an adversarial trial that could re-traumatise complainants is also required, not only of lawyers (solicitors, prosecutors and defence lawyers) who appear in sexual assault cases, but also all court staff within a court complex—from the security guards at court entrances, to judges, judges' associates and tipstaffs, sheriffs, courts reporters and so on. In addition, all judges and lawyers involved in sexual assault cases should be required to undergo training about child development and language development, as well as the cognitive and language capacities of differently aged complainants who may be suffering from the effects of trauma or living with particular disabilities.

4.4 Child- and Complainant-Friendly Environments

As part of a trauma-informed system, a child- and complainant-friendly environment needs to be created through relaxation of the formality of the court environment, including the removal of gowns and wigs by judges and counsel, an option available in E&W but only upon application by the prosecutor.[5] One of the long-term innovations of some Australian jurisdictions, such as NSW, has been the use of remote rooms (away from the court precinct) from which sexual assault complainants give evidence via CCTV which is likely to remove the possibility of re-traumatisation associated with seeing the defendant and his supporters within the courtroom and its waiting areas. It also means that complainants will not be retriggered by the imposing nature of court architecture and the alien environment of a courtroom filled with strangers. By comparison, remote rooms are secure areas to which the defendant has no access and which include comfortable and spacious waiting areas, with children's toys and refreshments for complainants and supporters (see, further, Cossins & Rowden, 2020).

---

[5]See YJCE Act, s 26.

Future innovations could include a court-appointed psychologist who is able to assist a complainant—adult or child—in coping with trauma symptoms during the giving of evidence in a remote room.

4.5 Pre-recording of Evidence

Pre-recorded cross-examination in a pre-trial hearing represents the best time for exerting control over the type and style of cross-examination questions, in order to prevent the contamination of a complainant's evidence by the defence and to achieve best evidence.

When I was first involved with government to introduce special measures for vulnerable witnesses in the early 2000s, the idea of pre-recording of evidence was radical (see, for example, Spencer & Lamb, 2012). Now is it a relatively unremarkable measure to assist vulnerable witnesses, particularly children, to give their best evidence. With schemes available in both E&W and NSW for the pre-recording of children's evidence, the Royal Commission (2017a: 88) observed that:

> We are satisfied that prerecording the entirety of a witness's evidence is likely to have clear benefits for both the witness and the parties in a prosecution. Where the witness is a child complainant of child sexual abuse, the benefits are even greater in minimising the trauma associated with participating in the criminal justice process.

In fact, one Director of Public Prosecutions in Australia noted that 'using recorded interviews as evidence in chief has contributed to an increase in guilty pleas prior to trial' (Royal Commission, 2017a: 89). It is also likely that the pre-recording of cross-examination would have a similar effect since defendants will not be able to take advantage of any delays resulting in the attrition of their case (such as complainant withdrawal) while the child's performance under cross-examination and re-examination will be known before trial. Thus, pre-recording allows both parties to gauge the strength of the prosecution's case well before trial which assists the prosecution in deciding whether or not to proceed to trial and the defence in deciding whether or not to mount a defence or to plead guilty.

In a review of pre-trial procedures in sexual assault trials, the Australian Law Reform Commission (ALRC) (2010a: 800–801) identified the benefits of pre-recording a child's evidence as follows, although they did not do so within a framework of trauma-informed care:

- improvements in the quality and reliability of evidence;
- facilitating pre-trial decisions by the prosecution and the defence;
- helping with the scheduling and conduct of the trial; and
- minimising systemic abuse of child witnesses.

As a result of the ALRC's review of pre-recording procedures in Australia, it recommended that both child and adult complainants of sexual assault should be able to give the whole of their evidence by way of a pre-recording (ALRC, 2010b: 1233). At the same time, defence counsel objected to this particular reform on the grounds that it is unfair for them to cross-examine the prosecution's chief witness before the trial has begun (ALRC, 2010b: 800) and that further issues for cross-examination are likely to come up during the trial.

In fact, most jurisdictions have provided for this possibility. For example, under s 376(1) of the Victorian *Criminal Procedure Act 2009*, a child complainant (whose cross-examination has already been pre-recorded) may be subject to further cross-examination at trial if the court gives leave. There is a presumption against further cross-examination unless the court is satisfied one of the following matters exist:

(i) the accused is seeking leave because of becoming aware of a matter of which the accused could not reasonably have been aware at the time of the recording; or
(ii) if the complainant were giving direct testimony in the proceeding, the complainant could be recalled, in the interests of justice, to give further evidence; or
(iii) it is otherwise in the interests of justice to permit the complainant to be cross-examined or re-examined.

Overall, the benefits of pre-recording close to the time of report to the police are fivefold:

(i) it increases the reliability of the witness's evidence, and allows the jury to view the witness at the age of report to police, a particular advantage when the witness is a child, which may increase the child's credibility in the jury's eyes;
(ii) allows the witness to get on with their lives, since by reducing anxiety about a trial in the (sometimes distant) future, they are able to seek counselling, return to school/work and other important activities in their lives;
(iii) increases the likelihood of a guilty plea;
(iv) pre-recorded evidence can be used in a re-trial if the first trial is aborted or there is a hung jury or if there is a successful appeal by the defendant[6]; and
(v) allows editing of the pre-recording in relation to any inadmissible evidence and/or irrelevant or improper questions by counsel.

In order to reduce any re-traumatisation associated with delays before trial, it would be necessary to allow for the pre-recording of all sexual assault complainants' evidence as close as possible to the time of the first report to authorities. There is a good case to be made for pre-recording to be available to adult complainants, in addition to children, on the grounds that sexual assault is one of the main traumas leading to PTSD, so that pre-trial anxiety is minimised and best evidence is given.

In E&W, a pilot scheme for the pre-recording of the cross-examination of adult and child complainants under s 28 of the YJCE Act was conducted from 30 December 2013 to 31 October 2014 in Leeds, Liverpool and Kingston upon Thames Crown Courts for children under the age of 16 years and other vulnerable witnesses (HM Government, 2018: 35; see also Spencer & Lamb, 2012).

After a positive evaluation, it was announced that the scheme would be rolled out across the country in September 2017 (Ministry of Justice, 2017). One of the key findings of the evaluation was that, although the process of being cross-examined was still stressful for vulnerable witnesses:

[6]See, e.g., *Criminal Procedure Act 1986* (NSW), ss 306B; 306I.

> Most of the practitioners who attended s.28 cross-examinations … were of the opinion that … [pre-recording] was reducing the level of distress/trauma suffered by witnesses. … [T]he witness experience was improved by the questioning styles adopted, length of cross-examinations and the way [pre-recordings] were listed. The majority of practitioners … agreed that the questions posed to witnesses … were more focused and relevant than at [live] cross-examinations. They thought this was due to the increased scrutiny of Ground Rules Hearings. (Baverstock, 2016: 7)

The evaluation also found that vulnerable witnesses during pre-recording were cross-examined for shorter periods of time, that is, between 20 and 45 minutes, compared to complainants who gave live cross-examination (between 45 minutes and three hours) (ibid.).

In Australia, the idea of pre-recording was first introduced in Western Australia in 1992 for children under the age of 12 years (Jackson, 2012; Standing Committee on Uniform Legislation and Intergovernmental Agreements, 1996: 18) and was one of the recommendations of the National Child Sexual Assault Reform Committee in 2010 (Cossins, 2010a).

Pre-recording of a child's evidence was the subject of a recent pilot scheme in NSW and is now available in two court registries. The biggest problem with the pre-recording of evidence is resources, including the quality of technology used, and the ability of courts to schedule a pre-trial hearing in which the pre-recording of evidence takes place:

> The pre-recorded evidence hearing requires both defence and prosecution to be prepared for trial much quicker than usual, and for continuity of counsel, wherever possible, between the prerecording and … the trial. This has resource implications for both parties: time to prepare for the pre-recording, and then to prepare for … the trial months later. (Cashmore, Taylor, & Parkinson, 2017: 8)

Other procedural problems identified by Baverstock's (2016: 5–8) evaluation of pre-recording in E&W found:

- 'some eligible witnesses were not being identified by the police and CPS at a sufficiently early stage' for pre-recording;

- there were still many months of delay between a witness's ABE interview and pre-recording;
- increases in workload on all practitioners involved because of the expedited framework for pre-recorded cases;
- delays to pre-recorded cross-examinations due to defendants' availability; and
- inadequate technology.

Other drawbacks that have been identified in the Australian context include the quality of the pre-recording which may make it hard to hear and see the child. However, in most modern courtrooms, state-of-the-art technology using large screens and good quality audio facilities have overcome this problem.

While a video-recording of a child's evidence is said to lack 'the immediacy and persuasiveness' of a child's live testimony (ALRC, 2010b: 801), empirical evidence shows that jurors are not adversely affected by this form of evidence, as discussed previously. In fact, although such reforms were designed to address the vulnerability of child witnesses and to remove the traditional barriers that had been thought to prevent the successful prosecution of child sex offences, such reforms do not appear to have any effect on the likelihood of conviction.[7]

[7]In 2004 a comprehensive British study found there was no evidence that conviction rates were affected by the availability of special measures for vulnerable witnesses (Hamlyn et al., 2004). Two Australian studies confirmed these findings. Taylor and Joudo (2005) found that the mode of presentation of evidence had no impact on mock jurors' perceptions of the defendant, the complainant or the defendant's guilt. Similar findings were reported by Cashmore and Trimboli (2006) who found that a majority of actual jurors from 22 child sexual assault trials did not have a negative reaction to viewing a child's pre-recorded interview (as evidence-in-chief), or to a child giving evidence via CCTV. Out of 241 jurors, 84% stated that 'the pre-recorded tape of the child's evidence-in-chief helped either "a lot" … or "quite a bit" … in understanding the child's evidence' (ibid., 5). With regard to the police interview being used as evidence-in-chief, jurors appreciated seeing the child give a first-hand account in their own words close to the time when the report was first made. In addition, 90.3% of 277 jurors in 25 trials considered the use of CCTV as 'quite fair' or 'very fair' to the complainant, while 88% held the same views in relation to the defendant (ibid., 6). There was also a high level of understanding by jurors about the reasons for using CCTV such as the need to reduce the stress on the child, provide a safe environment for the child, the child's age, the nature of the alleged offence or the relationship between defendant and complainant. While this study did not examine the use of pre-recorded cross-examination, there is no reason to expect jurors would react differently to that aspect of a child's evidence. See also Ellison and Munro (2014).

Seven jurisdictions in Australia now permit the pre-recording of the whole of a child complainant's evidence, that is, NSW, Victoria, Queensland, South Australia, the ACT and the NT, in addition to WA.[8] However, most jurisdictions do not permit pre-recording of the evidence of an adult complainant unless they come within the definition of 'vulnerable' or 'special' witness. For example, in WA, pre-recording is usually only available in relation to children under the age of 13 years, with expert evidence required to request pre-recording for older children. If an adult is a special witness (that is, suffers from a physical or mental disability) or is 'likely to suffer severe emotional trauma' pre-recording will be made available to them (Royal Commission, 2017: 54). These restrictions in the legislation highlight the lack of trauma-informed awareness in relation to the conduct of sexual assault trials and the impact of the cross-examination effect.

In CSA trials, NSW only permits the pre-recording of a child's evidence-in-chief at a pre-trial hearing in the two court registries (Downing Centre, Sydney and Newcastle) that were involved in a pilot intermediary scheme. At the time of writing, the child must be available for cross-examination at trial in all other courts.[9]

In Victoria, pre-recording (known as the video or audio taping of evidence (VATE) process) takes place during a pre-trial hearing where, in the absence of a jury, the child is examined in chief in the presence of a judge and the accused's defence counsel. The child's cross-examination is then pre-recorded along with any re-examination. The accused is not permitted to be in the courtroom while the child's evidence is pre-recorded but may observe the child using CCTV facilities and must at all times be able to communicate with his defence counsel. The VATE pre-recording is then admissible as evidence in a subsequent trial as if the recording was the live testimony of the child. It may also be used in any subsequent retrial.

In some jurisdictions, the pre-recording procedure has been extended to cognitively impaired complainants in sexual assault trials. The

[8] *Criminal Procedure Act 2009* (Vic), ss 369–370; *Evidence Act 1977* (Qld), s 21AK; *Evidence Act 1906* (WA), s 106I; *Evidence Act 1929* (SA), s 13; *Evidence (Miscellaneous Provisions) Act 1991* (ACT), s 40S; *Evidence Act 1939* (NT), ss 21A–21B.

[9] *Criminal Procedure Act 1986* (NSW), s 306U.

Queensland legislation, for example, covers 'special witnesses' who are defined as those suffering from a mental, intellectual or physical impairment who would be disadvantaged as a witness, those suffering severe emotional trauma and those who would be so intimidated as to be disadvantaged as witnesses.[10] The South Australian legislation goes even further by allowing the evidence of a vulnerable witness to be pre-recorded if she has been subject to threats of violence or retribution or has reasonable grounds to fear violence or retribution in connection with the proceedings.[11]

For a jury, there is very little difference between a complainant giving evidence from a remote room via CCTV compared to the jury viewing a complainant's pre-recorded evidence but a great deal of difference for a child or vulnerable adult. The pre-recording of evidence, including cross-examination, provides a key opportunity for introducing processes and procedures that are compatible with a trauma-informed system to ensure that a complainant's *best* evidence is given.

Pre-recording should be in the form of a mandatory requirement, rather than leaving prosecutors and judges to decide, since neither are trained in being able to assess the cognitive development or language comprehension of any particular child, or the psychological well-being of a vulnerable adult.

To achieve the benefits of pre-recording, it should occur as soon as practicable after the defendant has been committed to stand trial in consultation with defence counsel to enable her or him to prepare since the fairness of the trial for the accused is likely to be affected if defence counsel has insufficient preparation time for the special hearing where pre-recording will occur. Such preparation time should also include the ability to apply for orders to edit the pre-recorded evidence. It would be appropriate to include a specific timeframe within legislation, rather than leaving the timeframe to judges and the parties, although a legislative timeframe will not be met in practice unless there are personnel, processes, and procedures to facilitate the achievement of the timeframe. The introduction of special hearings for the pre-recording of

[10] *Evidence Act 1977* (Qld), s 21A(1).

[11] *Evidence Act 1929* (SA), s 4.

complainants' evidence is likely to place an extra burden on judges, court staff and resources.

4.6 Time-Limited Cross-Examination and Vetting of Questions

Trial judges ought to be required to ensure that the conditions under which a child is cross-examined are reliable by ensuring that age-inappropriate questions, such as suggestive statements and questions, are not used to elicit a child's agreement. As discussed in Chapter 8, a wide range of studies reveal that cross-examination techniques produce unreliable answers, particularly for vulnerable witnesses.

Anecdotally, cross-examination can take hours or even days, particularly in trials with multiple defendants who each have their own defence counsel. As the *Ward* case demonstrated in Chapter 8, the longer the cross-examination, the more likely it is for a child complainant to become confused, stressed, tired and retraumatised, increasing the likelihood of incomprehension of, and agreement with, defence questions and the production of inaccurate evidence.

In line with the approach of the EWCA in *R v Jonas* [2015] EWCA Crim 562, which rejected the practice of multiple defence counsel each carrying out independent cross-examination of a child of any length, cross-examination needs to be time-limited and limited to questions that have not already been put to the witness. In *Jonas* the Court said:

> [o]ver-rigorous or repetitive cross-examination of a child or a vulnerable witness must be stopped [so that] … the witness is treated fairly overall, and not asked questions on the same topics, to the same end, by each and every advocate. Advocates must accept that the courts will no longer allow them the freedom to conduct their own cross-examination where it involves simply repeating what others have asked before, or exploring precisely the same territory. … [D]efence advocates will now be treated as a group and, if necessary, issues divided amongst them, provided, of course, there is no unfairness in so doing. ([2015] EWCA Crim 562, [31])

For example, if 'a total of two hours' is the norm 'and half a court day at the outside' (Judicial College, 2013–2019: 2–30) then a mandated limit of 2 hours could be set, with an application from defence counsel for an extension of time if sufficient reasons are given for an extension. Given the documented effects of leading questions on vulnerable witnesses, prohibitions on leading questions are essential in order to prevent the defence's manipulation of a witness, the aim of which is to persuade, cajole or force their agreement to defence statements in order to advance the defence case. Thus, questions likely to produce unreliable answers should be prohibited such that greater control over cross-examination should be given to the court. As Caruso (2012: 224; emphasis in original) acknowledges, '[e]very leading question is a non-leading question in a different form. Counsel do not *need* leading questions in order to put the case fairly on behalf of the client'.

In order to increase the fairness of the trial for the vulnerable and traumatised witness, there is also a need to vet the cross-examination questions drafted by the defence. The need for vetting of all cross-examination questions was discussed in Chapter 8. This could be done at a pre-trial or ground rules hearing with questions vetted by a specialist examiner and the trial judge. The aim of the vetting process would be to eliminate complex leading questions and maximise the use of open-ended questions where possible. This would be necessary because:

> in practice, many advocates find it more difficult to adapt key questions than they anticipate. It can also be difficult to keep in mind all aspects of questioning that may be problematic for the individual witness. (Victims Services NSW, 2016: 16)

Vetting of cross-examination questions at a ground rules hearing has been encouraged by the EWCA: 'to avoid any unfortunate misunderstanding at trial, it would be an entirely reasonable step for a judge at the ground rules hearing to invite defence advocates to reduce their questions to writing in advance' (*R v Lubemba* [2014] EWCA Crim 2064, [43]; see also *R v Boxer* [2015] EWCA Crim 1684; *Re FA* [2015] EWCA Crim 209), although the practice is not mandatory in E&W.

A possible draft provision for vetting questions and time-limited cross-examination of complainants in sexual assault trials is set out below. Briefly, this provision allows for a list of permissible questions to be drawn up by the presiding judge and specialist examiner at a pre-trial hearing after defence cross-examination questions are vetted.

Time-limited cross-examination and vetting of cross-examination questions

(1) This section applies to prescribed sexual offence proceedings.
(2) For the purposes of subsection (1), all such proceedings must be preceded by a pre-trial hearing.
(3) All questions to be asked of the complainant in a prescribed sexual offence proceeding must be submitted in writing at the pre-trial hearing.
(4) For the purposes of subsection (3), all such questions are to be reviewed by the presiding judge and a specialist examiner who has been appointed to assist the court to determine if the questions:

  (i) are age-appropriate;
  (ii) able to be understood by the complainant in question; and/or
  (iii) are likely to trigger a trauma reaction in the complainant.

(5) A list of permissible questions for the purposes of cross-examination will then be drawn up by the presiding judge and the specialist examiner at the pre-trial hearing.
(6) For the purposes of subsection (5), permissible questions are limited to those that have been drafted with regard to trauma-informed principles, are age-appropriate and capable of being understood by the complainant with regard to any physical or intellectual disabilities, their age, sex and racial and cultural background.
(7) For the purposes of subsection (5), all questions that are deemed to be age-inappropriate, or unable understood by the complainant and/or are likely to trigger a trauma reaction in the complainant are to be removed from the list of permissible questions to be asked of the complainant, including:

  (i) questions that directly suggest that the complainant is a liar, or is lying, or has lied, such as 'You're lying, aren't you?'; You're a liar, aren't you?'; 'It's all lies'; 'What you've said is a pack of lies';
  (ii) questions that are repetitive in that the content of the question is largely the same as that of a previous question asked of the same complainant; and

(iii) questions about a prior inconsistent statement made by the complainant, unless the court is satisfied that the prior statement:
(a) is in fact inconsistent to the complainant's evidence given in court;
(b) is a prior statement about a matter relevant to a fact in issue in the trial; and
(c) does not relate solely to a trivial or irrelevant matter.

(8) During the cross-examination of a complainant, cross-examination is to be limited to no more than two hours, with breaks as required.
(9) Application for an extension of time can be made to the trial judge.
(10) For the purposes of subsection (9), an extension of time cannot exceed 30 minutes.
(11) For the purposes of subsection (9), the trial judge must consider the following matters before ordering an extension of time:
(i) the likely impact on the complainant of further cross-examination, including:
(a) emotional distress;
(b) confusion;
(c) comprehension of further questions; and
(d) overall ability to give their best evidence;
(ii) any objections by the prosecution; and
(iii) the interests of justice, which include the interests of the defendant, the prosecution and the complainant.
(12) In proceedings where there are multiple defendants with multiple defence counsel, one list of questions only must be submitted at the pre-trial hearing.
(13) One specialist examiner only will be permitted to put to the complainant the questions from the list of permissible questions.

The above recommendation also places restrictions on the use of prior inconsistent statements during cross-examination. This would mean that before any questions about a prior inconsistent statement can be asked, the judge must be satisfied that the statement is a prior statement about a matter relevant to the facts in issue, that it is inconsistent with evidence given in court, and does not relate solely to a trivial or irrelevant matter. This would prevent a complainant from being cross-examined on a prior inconsistent statement which is only relevant to her credibility, on the grounds that there is no evidence that inconsistencies in evidence are the result of lying. For children, they are more likely to be the result of cognitive development (Dent, 1992; Geddie, Fradin, & Beer 2000; Ghetti, Goodman, Eisen, Qin, & Davis, 2002) or the use of leading and suggestive questions. This recommendation is also likely to reduce the length of cross-examination by restricting the number of questions put to the complainant about inconsistencies in their evidence.

Even if cross-examination is time-limited and questions are vetted, what type of second examination would be the most effective in achieving best evidence for those who are vulnerable to the impact of trauma? Zajac and O'Neill (2013: 29–30) observe that:

> [t]o stop children from changing correct responses under cross examination, we know that we should ask open-ended questions … and avoid suggestion … and possibly even yes/no questions … [T]he ideal cross-examination protocol would maximize favourable changes (i.e., changes directed towards the truth) while minimizing unfavourable changes (i.e., changes directed away from the truth). At present, no such interview protocol exists.

While 'the questions that are problematic for children to answer correctly are the same questions that are most likely to effectively challenge credibility' (Zajac & O'Neill, 2013: 30), those questions only challenge credibility *because* they are designed to encourage confusion, engender lack of comprehension and inconsistencies, and, as a result, are likely to produce answers that are directed away from the truth.

It makes no sense to, instead, consider 'training interventions that teach children how to identify and respond to incomprehensible questions … or … provide children with the opportunity to practice difficult questions and gain feedback about their responses' (Zajac & O'Neill, 2013: 30), when such training involves preparing them for a hostile and traumatising court environment. How would this further the trauma-informed principle of doing no further harm?

The key question is, who ought to conduct the cross-examination of adult and child complainants in order to do no harm and achieve best evidence?

4.7 Changing the Cross-Examination Process: The Use of a Specialist Examiner Trained in the Principles of Trauma-Informed Care

Although 'conventional cross-examination is not conceived of as a forensic examination' for eliciting the truth (Henderson, 2014: 99), recent judgements of the EWCA (see Chapter 8) suggest that cross-examination should not be used as a tool for manufacturing incorrect evidence. Changes to cross-examination that have been endorsed by the EWCA mean that 'it is no longer enough that an advocate managed to induce an eight-year-old to retract her allegations. The conditions under which the retraction was obtained must contain a sufficient guarantee of its reliability' (Henderson, 2014: 99). Thus, '[e]ven relevant issues should not be examined unless it can be done in a way likely to produce reliable answers' (ibid., 101).

Throughout E&W, there is now:

> widespread recognition that the questioning of children and other vulnerable persons is a specialist skill … [and that cross-examination] does not achieve best evidence from a vulnerable witness. It is unfit for the task of enabling a jury to assess the credibility and accuracy of the witness's evidence. (Rook, Rafferty, & Ward, 2016: 1553)

While some advocates in E&W have 'acquired the necessary specialist skill' for questioning vulnerable witnesses, concern remains that 'advocacy has not evolved to ensure best practice is universally adopted':

> Questioning which ignores the principles designed to obtain accurate information from a witness and exploits his or her developmental limitations is not only wholly inconsistent with a fair trial but also contravenes the advocate's Code of Conduct. (Rook et al., 2016: 1554)

However, Rook et al. (2016: 1554) consider that it is only 'a matter of time before every criminal and family law advocate will have to be a specialist at handling the vulnerable as part of their basic training'. To that end, the Inns of Court College of Advocacy has designed a specialist training course for criminal lawyers when they question vulnerable witnesses. Called the Advocacy and the Vulnerable Training Programme, it 'has been designed to ensure that all advocates, when dealing with vulnerable witnesses, understand the key principles behind the approach to and questioning of vulnerable people in the justice system'.[12] The ICCA website also notes that '[i]n due course, the training will become mandatory for any advocate wishing to undertake publicly funded work for serious sexual offence cases involving vulnerable witnesses'.[13] A collection of ten toolkits for advocates is available on the Advocate's Gateway for dealing with ground rules hearings and the best practice questioning of vulnerable witnesses.

The above developments in E&W raise the question, how do we ensure that the conditions under which a complainant is cross-examined guarantee the reliability of her answers so that these answers reflect her best evidence, rather than confused responses? Is it sufficient to leave the questioning of children and other vulnerable witnesses in the hands of defence counsel, even if they are trained, as discussed above? Henderson (2014: 108) has observed that:

> In truth, there is very little about conventional cross-examination technique which the average expert in forensic interviewing would consider reliable. The courts and advocates need further help from linguists and experts in forensic interviewing to identify an alternative methodology and a body of appropriate questions and strategies with which to test children's evidence.

Because the intermediary scheme in E&W and NSW does not involve direct communication between the complainant and intermediary, is the advice from a registered intermediary about the acceptability of defence questions sufficient to guarantee conditions of reliability? One intermediary highlighted the passivity of intermediaries in E&W:

> My role is passive in the sense that I'm not there as a second interviewer. I'm there to listen and to monitor the questions put to the child … to

[12] https://www.icca.ac.uk/advocacy-the-vulnerable, accessed 30 March 2019.

[13] https://www.icca.ac.uk/advocacy-the-vulnerable, accessed 30 March 2019.

> ensure that they are appropriate for that person's communication needs. … I alert the judge to the terribly worded question … and then I explain what the problem is with the question … It's then up to the judge to decide what to do with the question … My assistance with rephrasing questions is extended only to me giving suggestions to the judge and then counsel taking them upon him or herself … but at no point do I actually communicate the question to the witness myself. (Royal Commission into Institutional Responses to Child Sexual Abuse, 2017a: 46–47; citing Dr. Mattison)

The passivity of this role is clear in that, without judicial cooperation, the intermediary's intervention would fail.

The use of an specialist examiner is the only way to ensure the necessary conditions of reliability when a vulnerable witness is being cross-examined on their evidence. The efficiency of a specialist examiner would also ensure that cross-examination is conducted within the necessary time limits discussed above, given the tendency of defence counsel towards repetitive questions and those that require clarification or rephrasing.

Where the vulnerable witness has been assessed as requiring emotional support while giving evidence, perhaps because of an existing disability or mental health issue, a trauma-informed court would need to ensure the availability of professional support, in order to manage the witness's emotional state.

In 2010, the National Child Sexual Assault Reform Committee (Cossins, 2010a) recommended the enactment of a provision for an intermediary examiner (Recommendation 6.2) which I have adapted below.

Cross-examination by a specialist examiner

(1) This section applies to prescribed sexual offences proceedings.
(2) Where a child or adult complainant, or other vulnerable witness, is to give evidence in prescribed sexual offences proceedings, the court must appoint a specialist examiner to conduct the cross-examination of that complainant or witness.

(3) The function of the specialist examiner is to:

(a) put to the witness, the list of permissible questions prepared in a pre-trial hearing; and
(b) if necessary, communicate to the court, the answers given by the witness.

(4) For the purposes of subsection (3), the list of permissible questions for the purposes of cross-examination is the list that has been drawn up by the presiding judge and the specialist examiner at a pre-trial hearing.
(5) Any cross-examination of the witness must take place in the presence of such persons as the rules of the court or a direction by the trial judge may provide, but in circumstances in which—

(a) the judge, the prosecutor and legal representatives acting in the proceedings are able to see and hear the cross-examination of the witness and to communicate with the specialist examiner; and
(b) (except in the case of a pre-recorded cross-examination) the jury are able to see and hear the cross-examination of the witness.

(6) The specialist examiner appointed under this provision is to take an oath or make a declaration, in such form as the court thinks fit, that he or she will faithfully perform his or her function under subsection (3).
(7) The specialist examiner appointed under this provision who, while performing or purportedly performing his or her function under subsection (3), wilfully makes any false or misleading statement to the child or to the court commits a crime and is liable on conviction to [insert penalty as appropriate].

Some will argue that the above reform will impede the rights of an accused to a fair trial. Yet, what is the nature of those rights? While there is a fundamental right to cross-examine witnesses, Chapter 8 discussed how this right is not absolute. Nor is there any case law that states that the right to cross-examine extends to attempts to produce or manufacture inaccurate evidence. If cross-examination is considered the best method for testing the accuracy of a witness's evidence, then the present methods used in sexual assault trials is clearly not appropriate to that task since a fair trial necessarily involves *preventing* processes that contaminate a complainant's evidence.

Given that judges play a legitimate role in 'protecting complainants from unnecessary, inappropriate and irrelevant questioning' (*R v TA*

(2003) 57 NSWLR 444 at 446, per Spigelman CJ), these reforms, informed as they are by the research literature, merely restrict the right to cross-examine in ways that will limit the manufacture of inaccurate evidence and will improve the quality of the evidence given by complainants in sexual assault trials.

In conclusion, this discussion has documented the evidence that justifies the need for the reforms set out above. For the transformation of a sexual assault trial into a trauma-informed system, more than training of all court personnel is required. Methods to prevent re-traumatisation and the cross-examination effect and achieve best evidence are required. Arguably, utilisation of a specialist examiner is the best way to achieve these goals.

Some will question why restorative justice (RJ), discussed below, could not achieve the same goals. Since RJ, generally, is a justice option that is dependent on a guilty plea by the defendant, it is an option more focused on the sentencing process, rather than the trial process. For complainants who might be involved in RJ, however, the best interests of the complainant ought to be assessed before RJ is considered. Ideally, this would involve an assessment by trained personnel (such as a social worker, or psychologist) about the complainant's emotional and psychological ability to participate, face-to-face, with their abuser and the risks of re-traumatisation. See, for example, the documented mental health effects on children of seeing the defendant in court or the court precinct (Table 1, Chapter 11). Trauma-informed principles ought to inform the RJ process, as discussed below. In fact, it may be that with a trauma-informed courtroom, child and adult complainants will not need the option of RJ, since their needs will be a priority and their vulnerability will be addressed.

Figure 2 describes what a trauma-informed, specialist court would look like:

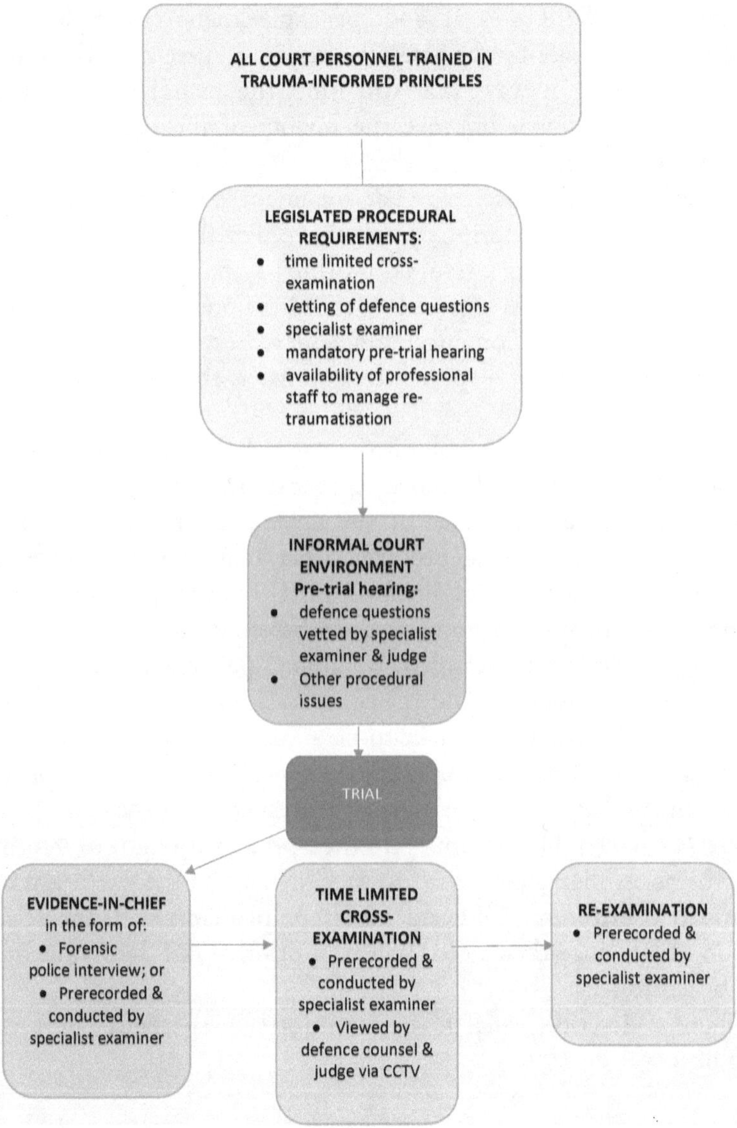

Fig. 2 Trauma-informed, specialist court

5 Where Does Restorative Justice Fit in?

Many articles and books have been written about restorative justice (RJ) and this book does not intend to cover the breadth of the literature on the topic which is covered extensively elsewhere (see, for example, Larsen, 2014; O'Mahony and Doak, 2017; Strang & Braithwaite, 2017; Van Ness & Strong, 2015).

The aim of this section, however, is to consider the compatibility of RJ processes with a trauma-informed sexual assault trial.

Aside from diversionary forms of RJ, where offenders are diverted from the criminal justice system into a RJ conference (see, e.g. Daly, Curtis-Fawley, & Bouhours, 2003), most RJ processes apply at the time of sentencing after a guilty verdict in a criminal trial. RJ may also be used during or after an offender's term of imprisonment if both the victim and offender agree to participate.

RJ conferencing exists in many jurisdictions including Australia,[14] New Zealand and E&W (see Australian Law Reform Commission, 2010a; House of Commons Justice Committee, 2016; O'Mahony & Doak, 2017). RJ, or conferencing as it also known, was first introduced to deal with juvenile offenders who had made an admission or pleaded guilty to an offence, with New Zealand the first country to formalise a conferencing model under the *Children, Young Persons and their Families Act 1989* (NZ) (McElrea, 1998).

RJ and youth conferencing have now become mainstream practices (Larsen, 2014; Strang, Sherman, Mayo-Wilson, Woods, & Ariel, 2013) which are available in various sites in E&W, as well as in all Australian jurisdictions for juveniles (and sometimes adults) usually in relation to less serious, non-violent offences. In Australia, Restorative Justice National Guidelines were adopted in 2013 to ensure consistency in relation to the use of RJ in Australia's six states and two territories (Standing Council on Law and Justice, 2013).

---

[14] *Young Offenders Act 1997* (NSW); *Youth Justice Act* 2018 (NT); *Dispute Resolution Centre Act 1990* (Qld); *Young Offenders Act 1993* (SA); *Youth Justice Act 1997* (Tas); *Children, Youth and Families Act 2005 (Vic); Young Offenders Act 1994* (WA).

It is generally agreed that the term, 'restorative justice', is used to describe a disparate number of practices, such as New Zealand's family group conferences, Australia's diversionary conferences, which divert juveniles (and sometimes adults) out of the criminal justice system, post-sentencing victim-offender mediation, transformative justice, which is used 'to deal with conflict in employment and educational settings' and circle sentencing in Canada and two states in Australia (Strang et al., 2013: 8). Many other practices also exist under the umbrella of 'restorative justice'.

For example, in Australia, youth conferencing exists in all states and territories, adult conferencing is available in NSW and South Australia, victim-offender mediation is available in all jurisdictions except Victoria and the ACT, while circle sentencing is available in NSW and Western Australia (Larsen, 2014: 6). In relation to sex offences, South Australia is the only Australian jurisdiction to offer RJ conferencing as a diversionary scheme from the courts to juvenile sex offenders (Daly, 2006; Daly & Curtis-Fawley, 2006), although sex offences will also be dealt with in the ACT along with other serious offences in phase two of its RJ scheme which works in conjunction with the courts (Larsen, 2014; *Crimes (Restorative Justice) Act 2004* [ACT]).

A RJ conference is 'a planned and scheduled face-to-face conference in which a trained facilitator "brings together offenders, their victims, and their respective kin and communities, in order to decide what the offender should do to repair the harm that a crime has caused"' (Strang et al., 2013: 8; citing Sherman and Strang, 2012: 216). Generally, the endpoint of the conference is 'the formulation of an agreement … which will usually involve some measure of reparation to the victim as well as measures to reintegrate the offender back into the community' (O'Mahony & Doak, 2017: 2).

Typically, both the victim and offender must agree to participate in a conference which will be organised and conducted by a professional facilitator and may be attended by community members, sometimes a police officer along with support people for the victim and the offender. The aim of RJ is to provide a forum in which there may be competing aims: the reintegration of the offender, as well as providing the victim with a space in which s/he can communicate the financial, physical and/or emotional impact of the offence.

Generally, RJ programmes 'define justice as an attempt to repair the harm a crime has caused rather than inflicting harm on an offender' (Strang et al., 2013: 7). Another way of conceiving RJ is as 'a process of justice which maximises opportunities for exchange of information, participation, dialogue and mutual consent between the victim and offender' (Zehr & Mika, 1998: 2). However, with a focus on process and resolution, definitions are light on the type of (ideal) outcomes (Dignan, 2005), other than pointing to vague notions of repair and healing (O'Mahony & Doak, 2017). They also infrequently engage with the possibility of re-victimisation of the victim by the offender and the possible triggers for re-traumatisation. Generally, definitions of RJ do not recognise that RJ programs:

- do not necessarily offer the same forms of resolution to both victims and offenders;
- are not necessarily all underpinned by the same principles;
- are not all grounded in evidence-based research; and
- are not necessarily subject to evaluation or produce knowable results, such as a reduction in recidivism, victim satisfaction and the prevention of re-traumatisation.

Indeed, there are mixed results in relation to the ability of RJ to prevent reoffending (Jones, 2009; KPMG, 2010; Poynton, 2013; Rossner, Bruce, & Meher, 2013). However, in a review of the effectiveness of RJ conferences in ten studies on three continents (involving 1879 offenders and 734 interviewed victims), Strang et al. (2013: 4–5) concluded:

> The evidence of a relationship between conferencing and subsequent convictions or arrests over two years post-random assignment is clear and compelling … The impact of RJCs on 2-year convictions was reported to be cost-effective in the 7 UK experiments, with up to 14 times as much benefit in costs of the crimes prevented (in London), and 8 times overall, as the cost of delivering RJCs. The effect of conferencing on victims' satisfaction with the handling of their cases is uniformly positive.

However, none of the above studies involved sex offences.

By contrast, when Smith and Weatherburn (2012) reviewed various studies on the impact of youth conferencing on reoffending compared to appearances in a children's court, they concluded that there was 'little basis for the confidence that conferencing reduces reoffending at all' (Smith & Weatherburn, 2012: 6). While many studies report favourably on victim satisfaction after RJ conferencing (Larsen, 2014; see, e.g. Koss, 2014), satisfaction may be short-lived if the offender does meet his/her obligations under the RJ agreement.

There are 'different understandings of the concept of restorative justice, with some arguing that it necessarily involves restoration, presumably to some pre-existing emotional/psychological state' (Cossins, 2008: 360). From a practical point of view, however, RJ may amount to no more than engaging in a process that is merely called restorative, since the ability to restore depends on the nature of the relationship between victim/offender and the willingness of the parties to cooperate in the process—that is, to forgive (for the victim) and to be accountable and undergo behaviour change (for the offender). Indeed:

> restoration implies that there was a prior state of freedom that existed for the victim and a prior state of integration into the community for the offender ... In fact, restoration of 'damaged human relationships' (Braithwaite, 2002: 569) may be more theoretical than real where the relationship only exists because the victim was targeted by the offender. (Cossins, 2008: 360)

Strang et al. (2013: 7) observe that '[t]he diverse nature of [RJ] practices makes it difficult to answer the question of whether "restorative justice" defined so broadly works better than conventional justice'. Even with the spread of RJ within Western democracies, such as Australia and E&W, there is still 'considerable divergence and disagreement [about the values and principles of RJ] and it is not at all clear what actually constitutes restorative justice' (O'Mahony & Doak, 2017: 29).

This may be because 'the underlying theory of restorative justice has not kept pace with the divergent range of practice developments ... [leading] to a lack of clarity in the underlying purpose and function of restorative justice' (O'Mahony & Doak, 2017: 1). Larsen (2014: viii) also notes that 'it is difficult to assess whether restorativeness has translated into programs the way it was intended', because of the many variations that are considered to be 'restorative' which is 'complicated by the fact that theory in this space has, and continues to, develop alongside practice'. Daly (2017: 129) considers that 'we need to move away from seeing restorative justice as a "type of justice" and instead see it as one of several mechanisms under a broader innovative justice umbrella' (see also Daly, 2016).

There is also disagreement regarding the way forward for RJ. On the one hand, Strang et al. (2013: 7) believe that the 'primary challenge … is empirical rather than conceptual … [since] [m]ost of the practices described as restorative justice have never been subjected to controlled field tests'. On the other hand, O'Mahony and Doak (2017: 1) consider that because of the lack of clarity regarding the principles underpinning RJ programs, it is necessary to develop 'a new theoretical lens through which the role of restorative justice … can be reimagined'. Larsen (2014: vii–viii), however, is more process-focused and identifies three key future challenges for RJ:

(i) 'whether it is appropriate to extend restorative justice to older offenders';
(ii) whether or not RJ should be extended to serious offences, such as murder, sexual assault and family violence; and
(iii) to determine 'whether "restorativeness" is achieved is highly dependent on the willingness of victims and offenders to engage in restorative justice processes'.

For example, the use of RJ for offences involving violence against women and children, such as sexual assault, CSA and family/domestic violence, continues to be controversial (Anderson, 2016; Cossins, 2008; Daly, 2008, 2011, 2017; Godden-Rasul, 2017; Joyce-Wojtas, & Keenan, 2016; Kasparian, 2014; Keenan & Zinsstag, 2014; Marsh & Wager, 2015; McGlynn, Westmarland, & Godden, 2012; Miller & Iovanni, 2013; Naylor, 2010; Proietti-Scifoni & Daly, 2011; Zinsstag & Keenan,

2017). In a study of the views of survivors and non-survivors of sexual assault, Marsh and Wager (2015) reported that 70% of survivors who had participated in the formal criminal justice system did not support the use of RJ as an alternative to court processes, compared to 45% of survivors who had not reported the offences to authorities.

In fact, many jurisdictions (NSW,[15] the NT,[16] Victoria,[17] WA,[18] ACT[19] and some police areas, known as PCCs, in E&W) exclude sexual offences from RJ conferencing (see Home Office Justice Committee, 2016; Victims' Commissioner, 2016). South Australia is the only Australian jurisdiction that allows RJ to be used for young offenders who have committed a sex offence.

In response to criticisms that RJ was inappropriate for victims of sexual assault and that offenders would be treated too leniently, Daly, Curtis-Fawley, and Bouhours (2003) undertook an analysis of the outcomes in sexual assault cases in South Australia to find out whether these concerns had any basis (reported in Daly, 2006).

By looking closely at the Sexual Assault Archival Study (SAAS) conferencing model (Daly et al., 2003), a RJ process introduced into South Australia for juvenile sex offenders, I demonstrated (Cossins, 2008) that the ideal of empowering victims and prioritiing victims' needs was not necessarily achieved, since:

---

[15] *Young Offenders Act 1997* (NSW), ss 8 and 35. This Act established a youth conferencing scheme. Section 8(2)(d) and (e) excludes the following sex offences 'under section 61E, 61L, 61M, 61N, 61O (1), (1A) or (2), 66C, 66D, 80, 81A or 81B of the *Crimes Act 1900*' and 'an offence under the *Crimes (Domestic and Personal Violence) Act 2007*'.

[16] *Youth Justice Act 2018 (NT)*, s 39(3) excludes, serious offences as prescribed by the regulations, such as murder, attempted murder, manslaughter, terrorism offences, other violent offences and sexual offences.

[17] In Victoria, no offences are specifically excluded under the *Children, Youth and Families Act 2005*, although in practice serious offences, such as murder, manslaughter, serious violent crimes and sex offences are excluded from conferencing. The Victorian Law Reform Commission (2016) made a recommendation to enact a statutory scheme for restorative justice conferencing for indictable offences where a decision is made to discontinue a prosecution or after a guilty plea and before sentencing. However, it was recommended that the scheme should only be extended to sexual violence and family violence offences at a later stage (Recommendations 32, 33 and 34).

[18] *Young Offenders Act 1994* (WA), s 25.

[19] *Crimes (Restorative Justice) Act 2004* (ACT), ss 14(3) and 16.

- victims had no say about whether a case proceeded to conferencing and, therefore, no choice about how they wanted the offender to be punished;
- the model appeared to be designed for first time offenders to divert them from court and to ensure that no conviction was recorded, so that victims' needs were secondary;
- victims may have no say in the terms of the undertaking agreed to by the defendant;
- even when defendants refused to admit to the offence, conferences still proceeded;
- there was no evidence that conferencing encouraged admissions rather than denial—the vast majority of finalised court cases were proved by way of guilty pleas, while defendants who made no admissions tended to have different backgrounds compared with those who admitted (Cossins, 2008: 372–373).
- two conferencing case studies illustrated the ad hoc nature and content of agreements, as well as the emotional consequences when the victim is unwilling to participate or is intimidated, when intra-familial and/or ongoing abuse is involved, when family members are in conflict and when the offender represents a real danger to the victim.

I was later criticised by Daly (2008) for failing 'to mention that 100 court cases were dismissed or withdrawn. What about the victims in these cases?' Given that Daly (2006) reported that it was the police (*not* the victims or the offenders) who had the discretion to decide whether a case went to conferencing in her SAAS study, the fact that 100 cases were not selected for conferencing by the police (the gate-keepers), *despite the existence of that option,* indicates that RJ will not be the solution for every case.

For example, the Arizona-based RESTORE programme for sex offenders over the age of 18 years was not available to repeat sex offenders, those with a history of domestic violence and those who had been arrested for criminal offences involving physical assault (Koss, 2014).

Police and prosecutors will continue to make decisions about proceeding with or withdrawing cases (sometimes because a victim does not want to proceed). So how do we increase the number of cases that are proceeded with? One way, as discussed above, would be the introduction of specialist, trauma-informed sex offences courts to *increase* the number of cases going to trial, thereby *decreasing* the number of cases withdrawn or dismissed and hopefully increasing the guilty plea rate, with trauma-informed processes at the policing and prosecution stages as well. That surely is a more desirable option than cases not being selected for RJ and not proceeding to court.

The primary aim of the SASS conferencing model appears to be to divert offenders from the courts. This aim, together with the risk of re-victimisation and the leniency of agreements, could affect victims', offenders' and the public's perception of the seriousness of child sex offences compared with the efforts of the last three decades, which have improved social and legal awareness of the prevalence and effects of CSA, in particular. The replacement of court proceedings with RJ could also hide from public scrutiny the agreements entered into by offenders, follow-up procedures and the extent of offender compliance. The leniency of agreements is likely to be a consideration that sex offenders would take into account in relation to future offending. When the costs of being caught do not outweigh the rewards of the behaviour, then recidivism is a possible outcome.

Although 'formal justice processes alone cannot effectively handle the complexity and range of sexual violence cases' (Daly, 2017: 108), it is doubtful that RJ will be capable of addressing the key problems associated with the prosecution of sex offences against both children and adults:

- high attrition rates after first report;
- relatively low conviction rates at trial compared with other offences; and
- high rate of cases withdrawn at trial.

Arguably, RJ will have no impact on these issues unless it is assumed that offering a diversion from court encourages more admissions. The SAAS study did not show that RJ had this effect. The main benefit of RJ evident from Daly's (2006) study was associated with the recidivism rate post-conferencing. However, did the reduction in recidivism result from the RJ process itself, or the effectiveness of the treatment programme that the offender agreed to participate in as part of his conferencing agreement? Using Daly's (2006) data, I showed that the same number of defendants pleaded guilty (and went to court) as those who made admissions (and went to conferencing), suggesting that there was no intrinsic benefit *for victims* from diversion to conferencing. But Daly (2006) also reported that recidivism rates were lower for all juvenile sex offenders who had undertaken a treatment programme, irrespective of whether they arrived via court or conferencing. Reoffending rates were high for offenders who had *not* undertaken treatment both post-court and post-conferencing. This suggests that the main issue concerning sex offenders is the need to mandate treatment rather than the process by which the offender arrives in a treatment programme.

The fact that Daly's study showed that an admission to a sex offence was less likely if the offence was serious, the offender was a repeat offender and the relationship between victim/offender was extrafamilial indicates that, in practice, conferencing may only have a small part to play as an alternative if conferencing is mainly used for first-time offenders and less serious offences. In other cases, conferencing and the courts would need to work side by side:

> responses to a single case of sexual violence may have a mix of conventional and innovative justice mechanisms (e.g. criminal prosecution and civil litigation, with a conference post-sentence or settlement). We need to understand how each is perceived and relates to the other, from a victim's perspective. Conventional justice mechanisms should not be disparaged or erroneously termed 'retributive' or 'punitive' justice ... Instead, the task should be to determine the degree to which conventional and innovative justice mechanisms can address one or more victims' justice interests in the aftermath of crime. (Daly, 2017: 129)

The key problem with the adversarial system is that it is best suited for dealing with sexual assault committed by strangers, yet the most common perpetrators of sexual assault are family members or people known to their victims. On the other hand, the adversarial trial process can never realistically be displaced by RJ because CSA, in particular, is typically not a one-off, discrete event; it is usually committed repeatedly and escalates in seriousness over months or years.

Because of their seriousness, the prosecution of sex offences should not become a private conference process, with varying outcomes and no follow-up in relation to offender compliance. Arguably, such prosecutions should continue to be a public process with assured and measureable outcomes.

Daly (2008) criticised my approach by saying that, '[t]hose who are sceptical of restorative justice for sexual violence have not produced evidence to show that established court processes are better for victims'. However, evidence is cited in Cossins (2008: 375) about the benefits and effectiveness of legal reform in the form of specialist courts for prosecuting sex offences which have had a dramatic effect on the number of cases going to trial and conviction rates in countries such as Canada and South Africa (see, further, Cossins, 2010a).

In addition, Hamlyn, Phelps, Turtle, and Sattar (2004) carried out an in-depth empirical study of the benefits of vulnerable witness protections in the UK and reported substantial benefits for vulnerable witnesses (including sexual assault complainants) such as an increase in satisfaction levels with the criminal justice system. They also reported that the protections had probably resulted in cases proceeding to court that might not otherwise have done so because of the greater willingness of witnesses to give evidence. Similarly, the introduction of intermediaries in E&W has provided further protections for vulnerable witnesses and further evidence of cases proceeding to court. (Plotnikoff & Woolfson, 2015).

Nonetheless, I agree with Daly (2008, 2017) that there is a need for significant change to the way cases of sexual assault are dealt with, as discussed throughout this book. Thus:

> [w]e need to see the value of different justice mechanisms and not be tied to just one … [and] to be able to move flexibly across the knowledge gained from research on sexual victimisation and justice in different contexts of victimisation; and … to glimpse the potential for new and emergent justice forms. (Daly, 2017: 130)

The trauma-informed approach discussed in this chapter is one new, emerging form of justice for sexual assault cases. Despite Daly's (2008) call for more radical change, the move to specialisation for sex offences would constitute a fundamental shift in focus to the adversarial system. An even more fundamental shift would be a move to a trauma-informed sexual assault trial, as discussed above.

Ultimately, RJ is unlikely to entirely replace the adversarial trial process. At the same time, there is an ongoing need to critique the trial process as an appropriate forum for dealing with sex offences. As there will always be a need for a fact-finding process (due to the lack of admissions or guilty pleas by defendants) a variety of ways must be considered to deal with the barriers represented by the adversarial system for sexual assault complainants, as discussed in this book.

5.1 RJ for Sex Offenders as a Pre- or Post-sentencing Option

In 2008, Daly (2008: 2) said I had failed 'to mention how court victims felt when cases are dropped by the police or dismissed or acquitted in court'. While we know that victims can be very dissatisfied if their court cases are dropped or dismissed (Lievore, 2005a; see Chapter 1), secondary victimisation as a result of the court process is not an issue for that particular group of victims. However, when it comes to the satisfaction levels of victims after participating in RJ as reported in various studies, little work has been done on the risk of *secondary victimization as a result of participation in RJ* and the fact that some victims might be vulnerable to re-victimisation after RJ.

Because Daly's SAAS study showed that the number of offenders who pleaded guilty and the number who made admissions were equal, most court cases in her study did not have to deal with the 'high evidentiary standards for convictions, that makes proving sex offences difficult' (Daly, 2008: 3). This means that RJ remains, at best, a post-trial, sentencing option for the majority of offenders who plead not guilty but who must be prosecuted in an (adversarial) criminal trial. As well, victims must be informed that RJ, generally, does not impose custodial sentences, which means that the offender remains in the community leaving the victim (and others) vulnerable to re-victimisation, particularly if the victim and offender are in a familial or domestic relationship.

So what could go wrong in a RJ conference with a vulnerable victim? Daly (2008) asserted that I had misrepresented her by 'overlooking the contingent nature of "the power" of the conference process' in relation to offender admissions. I had directly challenged the so-called power of the conference to censure an offender who retracted his admission of guilt and highlighted what could go wrong (Cossins, 2008: 371):

> reliance on conference participants as a way of correcting offender denial is fraught with potential problems, especially in word-against-word cases, since the offender's support people may place responsibility for the crime on the victim.

I then discussed the potential for re-victimisation and the power imbalances that may arise in conferencing and how these issues are dependent on participants' perceptions of justice. Indeed, 'an admission and apology do not necessarily mean that an offender's behaviour will change' (Cossins, 2008: 367), while sincere apologies are difficult to achieve (Daly, 2017: 124).

Recently, Daly (2017: 110–111; references omitted) has written:

> The need to identify a way to assess and compare different justice mechanisms became clear to me when I reflected on Annie Cossins' critique of my research, which compared the court and conference handling of youth sex offences … She said that I did not have sufficient evidence to show that conferences were better than court, from a victim's perspective … In turn, I said that she did not have sufficient evidence that court was better than conferences, from a victim's perspective … We were talking past one another. Would it be possible, I wondered, to establish a set of criteria that could adjudicate research findings and debate on the efficacy of different justice responses to sexual violence? I reasoned that what was required was a systematic way to assess the efficacy of any one justice mechanism and to compare the efficacy of two or more justice mechanisms.

Daly (2017: 111) goes on to say that 'researchers have placed too much emphasis on achieving therapeutic outcomes for victims, as the sole or primary aim of a justice activity', rather than 'the prior moral and political matters of what victims as citizens … should expect in seeking justice'. This is something I agree with, in that neither the adversarial trial nor a RJ conference is an appropriate mechanism for dealing with sex offences (the majority of which are committed by people known to the victim), and neither have the capacity to heal the trauma symptoms of complainants.

The aim of my reform proposals has been to do no further harm, to achieve best evidence *and* to eliminate the moral judgements of complainants so as to convert their status from worthy/unworthy victim to a person with certain rights and expectations, which equate with Daly's (2017: 111) 'victim's justice interests'. These interests include not only interests 'for themselves, but [also] for offenders and the wider society' (Daly, 2017: 115; citing Holder, 2013). Daly (2017: 115–116) also uses 'the term "interests" to signal a political relationship that victims, as citizens, have in pursuing justice in the aftermath of crime'. Arguably, these political interests extend to the ongoing battle that women and girls, in particular, confront when they are cast as dichotomous, moral bodies within the sexual assault trial, a battle that puts their dignity and humanity on the line.

Daly (2017: 114–115) 'identified a parsimonious set of victims' interests: participation, voice, validation, vindication, and offender accountability-taking responsibility' which Daly (2017: 117–124) defines as follows:

- **participation**: access to information and justice options, address offending and ask questions of the offender;
- **voice**: is related to participation—the opportunity to relay their experience as a victim and its impact on them, with 'public recognition and acknowledgement';
- **validation**: the victim's story is believed and their harm acknowledged, with no victim blaming;

- **vindication**: affirmation that the criminal act against the victim 'was wrong, morally and legally', through condemnation and censure of the offence, and various forms of reparation, not just an apology;
- **offender accountability-taking responsibility**: accountability is about calling and holding an offender to account. While an offender's acts of reparation are undertaken 'to vindicate a victim and the polity', responsibility is an active process 'by, for example, sincere apologies or expressions of remorse and completing prescribed justice requirements'.

These interests are possible to satisfy or uphold in a RJ conference because the offender *has pleaded guilty or admitted the offence* so that there is no question about whether the sexual assault occurred and about the harm that was done to the victim.

In a trial, the question of guilt is not determined until the trier-of-fact has reached a verdict so that some of the above justice interests are not compatible with a trial context. Nonetheless, aspects of these justice interests may be possible to achieve within a trauma-informed specialist court if the moral worth of the complainant is no longer on trial, interests such as:

- participation (access to information and psychological support throughout the trial);
- protecting voice (the removal of cross-examination as a tool for introducing rape myths and humiliating the complainant); and
- validation (the removal of victim blaming through the elimination of rape myths and aggressive and humiliating forms of cross-examination).

Vindication is only possible if a criminal trial results in a guilty verdict while offender accountability-responsibility may be obtainable through sex offender treatment programmes and/or RJ as part of a sentencing regime, since punishment, a form of vindication, is not necessarily 'a component of accountability' (Daly, 2017: 125).

My concerns with RJ as a *diversionary* option for sex offenders remain the same (Cossins, 2008), if not heightened because the goals of offender accountability by making amends (such as an apology) and repairing the harm are simplistic in relation to victims of sexual assault who experience a range of mental health issues (see Chapter 11), including PTSD, the symptoms of which may remain with a victim/survivor for life even after intensive counselling. While RJ may have beneficial, therapeutic effects for a victim, it is not a form of therapy (Woessner, 2017). As well, how efficacious is RJ in relation to one or two charged incidents of sexual assault when there may be a long history of sexual assault between the victim and offender? As O'Mahony and Doak (2017: 14) observe, compensation might make amends for stolen goods but:

> it is considerably more difficult to outline how a process can make amends for a sexual offence, or indeed any offence that carries significant and lasting emotional harm or trauma for the victim.

If RJ aims to go beyond the retributive and punishment model represented by the adversarial trial in order to repair the harm, restore relationships and, ultimately, strengthen 'those social bonds that make a society strong' (Larsen, 2014: viii), is it appropriate to conceive of the victim-sex offender dyad as a relationship to be restored and is it appropriate to risk the mental well-being of a sexual assault victim in order to reintegrate an offender?

Other goals of RJ, such as behaviour change, are also naïve since sex offenders require specially designed treatment programmes in order to prevent recidivism while the Royal Commission into Institutional Responses to Child Sexual Abuse (2017a) showed that reconciliation with offenders is not a desirable goal in relation to serial institutional offenders, since many adult survivors wanted denunciation and punishment for the offender, not reconciliation.

When it comes to serial and repeat offenders, reconciliation could also pose a danger for the most vulnerable victims—children. As for reintegration, the Royal Commission (2017a) revealed what happens when sex offender priests are kept within their religious communities and moved from one parish to another—denial, shaming of victims and recidivism. Many parents, for example, might well be aghast at the idea of 'reintegration' of a sex offender into a church or school community.

Nonetheless, Larsen (2014) identifies that one of the future challenges for RJ is whether or not to extend conferencing to serious offences, such as sexual assault. Because there is evidence to suggest that RJ is more effective post- rather than pre-sentence (Larsen, 2014: vii), it is appropriate to consider the use of RJ in relation to sex offences as a post-sentencing option. If victims of sexual assault are seeking justice when they participate in the criminal justice system in the form of an acknowledgement of their traumatic experiences, and public condemnation and punishment of the offender (Daly, 2017; Herman, 2005; Lievore, 2005), their participation in the adversarial trial process is not likely to provide those outcomes without further shaming and humiliation, particularly during defence cross-examination.

Thus, it is useful to compare the principles of RJ with those of trauma-informed care to determine how RJ for sex offenders and their victims could become a safe, empowering and non-traumatising option pre- or post-sentencing.

5.2 The Compatibility of Restorative Justice Theory and Trauma-Informed Care

O'Mahony and Doak (2017) recently proposed 'a new theoretical lens' for RJ and it is worthwhile comparing and contrasting their approach with the principles and practices of trauma-informed care because of the concerns with extending RJ to sex offences. Because of a significant gap 'in our understanding as to how and why restorative justice works as a theory', O'Mahony and Doak (2017: 59) propose:

> a fresh framework to better understand both how restorative justice operates within the context of criminal justice, as well as the normative values which it ought to encapsulate in order to realise its full potential.

Using empowerment theory, a theory that is consistent with a trauma-informed approach, O'Mahony and Doak (2017: 65, 66) have 'mapp[ed] restorative justice values against the broad concepts of "empowering values", "empowering processes", and "empowering outcomes"'. In doing so, they documented the overlap between 'many of the guiding values and principles underpinning both empowerment theory and restorative justice', summarised in Table 1 for ease of reading.

Through this comparison, O'Mahony & Doak (2017: 67) argue that RJ and empowerment theory share the same values and principles, such as reconciliation, reintegration, responsibility, reparation, encounter, empathy, forgiveness and apology/remorse, as well as sharing the same best practices, such as fairness, consent/non-coercion, inclusive participation, listening, respect, non-domination, non-judgement, non-punitiveness and safety.

By way of summary, O'Mahony and Doak (2017: 68) nominate the four common goals of RJ as:

- encounter and participation (process factors), and
- reparation and reintegration (outcome factors).

Based on empowerment theory, they call these goals as either restorative agency or restorative accountability, which together amounts to

Table 1 The principles of restorative justice versus empowerment theory

Restorative justice	Empowerment theory
• to provide victims/offenders the opportunity 'to tell their story and be heard' (agency)	• enables individuals to 'gain control over their lives'
• 'to be recognised as stakeholders' (not just witnesses/defendants[a])	• 'achieve democratic participation within their "community"'
• To ask questions and receive answers	• 'participate in decisions that impact them'
• 'to be able to reconnect with their community'	• Involves 'mutual respect, critical reflection and group participation'
• 'to have meaningful interactions, on their own terms'	
• 'to transform negative impacts of crime ... into community support, shared healing, interaction, reengagement and empowerment'	

Taken from O'Mahony & Doak (2017: 60, 66–67)
[a]The defendant in a criminal trial is a major stakeholder already and has significant power within the trial through the fair trial principle and the rights conferred on him/her under that principle: presumption of innocence, right to silence, right to legal representation, right to defend

the 'agency-accountability framework' (O'Mahony & Doak, 2017: 69). Agency is understood as giving individuals 'the power to make their own decisions and the capacity to make their own choices amongst available alternatives' (O'Mahony & Doak, 2017: 71) which means empowering them to have a voice within the RJ setting.

Accountability within RJ, compared to within the trial process, means 'creat[ing] a space where individuals render *themselves* accountable' (O'Mahony & Doak, 2017: 71; emphasis in original), that is, taking responsibility through admissions, apologies, remorse, appropriate reparation and rehabilitation and even reconciliation. Nonetheless, it does not appear that there is space for a consideration of the risk of reoffending based on past behaviour (including prior convictions) which is problematic for power-based offences, such as sex offences.

In conclusion, the 'empowering concepts of agency and accountability differentiate restorative justice from conventional criminal justice and provide clearer goals and expectations for its delivery within the criminal process' (O'Mahony & Doak, 2017: 73). But does the agency-accountability framework work in practice, by empowering a vulnerable victim who is suffering from the effects of trauma? Agency and accountability are relative concepts that are very much dependent on context, cooperation of the parties and the ability of a victim to manage the often overwhelming physiological effects of trauma on the brain.

As well, reconciliation, encounter, reparation and forgiveness are not values or principles of either trauma-specific services or trauma-informed services (as defined above), since trauma-informed care is focused on the effects of trauma on a client and the *avoidance* of triggers that will result in re-traumatisation.

In order to create a trauma-informed RJ process, it would be necessary to introduce procedures to prevent unavoidable triggers and re-traumatisation of the complainant. Specifically, it is necessary to consider the relevance and applicability of trauma-informed principles (listed in Table 1, Chapter 11) to RJ for sexual offences in order to reduce victim disempowerment, enhance emotional safety and achieve 'agency'.

At the outset, training about the long-term impact of trauma for all those who interact with conferencing victims would be needed, including the facilitator of the RJ conference, any other professional staff and support persons. A review of the policies and procedures of RJ would identify practices that 'replicate trauma dynamics', in particular 'dynamics that characterize abusive relationships', such as boundary violations, practices that deny or invalidate a victim's experiences, or practices that reconstruct reality in a way that 'represent[s] the values and beliefs of the abuser' (Harris & Fallot, 2001: 9).

What then are the common themes between trauma-informed care and RJ which both embrace an empowerment model, as described in Table 1, above?

As discussed in Chapter 11, a trauma-informed process must, first, recognise the long-term impact of violence and victimisation on a victim's development and coping strategies. However, there is no recognition in the model proposed by O'Mahony and Doak (2017) of this long-term impact and the inbuilt triggers (such as being face-to-face with the offender and his supporters) that might re-traumatise a victim and, in turn, impede a victim's 'agency' to participate in RJ. Even speaking about the harm suffered may result in a sexual assault victim re-experiencing the original traumatic emotions. Thus, a process would be required to assess a victim's ability to cope with RJ and being in the presence of the offender.

For example, the Arizona-based RESTORE programme for sex offenders (Koss, 2014) carried out pre- and post-conference testing for post-traumatic stress symptoms on victims who participated in the conferencing programme. A Post-Traumatic Symptoms Scale revealed a decrease in post-traumatic stress symptoms—at the time of referral, 82% of victims satisfied the diagnostic criteria for post-traumatic stress compared to 66% of victims after conferencing. Despite this decrease, two-thirds of victims still exhibited post-traumatic stress at the end of the process, thus placing into question the ability of conferencing to reduce the triggers for victims and to do no further harm.

In other words, while the adversarial trial, generally, denies victims the agency to speak about the impact of sexual assault on them (see e.g. Daly & Wade, 2017), a RJ setting that is not trauma-informed will not necessarily promote agency, nor empower a victim to fully participate in the RJ process.

While the vague term, 'healing', is one of the core values of RJ, clearly, the second principle of trauma-informed care, making recovery from trauma the primary goal, is not a realistic goal of RJ since much of the focus of RJ is on concepts such as reconciliation and reintegration and the offender's offending behaviour, while recovery from trauma is a long-term process.

Indeed, it is not inevitable that employment of an empowerment model (the third principle of trauma-informed care and one of the goals of RJ) will facilitate a person's ability to make conscious choices if there are triggers present which mean the victim is overwhelmed by fear and helplessness, the legacy of victimisation.

As with the trial process, a sexual assault victim may have difficulty regulating her emotions within a RJ setting where her survival/coping strategies were developed as adaptations to traumatic events. Thus, in order to reflect the fourth principle of trauma-informed care, that is, maximisation of a victim's choices and control over her recovery (which could include participation in RJ), the RJ setting would need to be primarily focused on the needs of the victim, rather than trying to promote forgiveness by the victim and reintegration of the offender at any cost. Thus, the relationship established between the facilitator and the victim would need to be one that is collaborative, empowering and safe with a flattened hierarchy (to reflect the fifth principle of trauma-informed care).

One of the ironies of utilising RJ for sex offences is the fact that throughout Australia and E&W, steps have been taken to either remove the complainant from the courtroom so as to avoid the re-traumatising effects of seeing the defendant (using CCTV for live evidence or pre-recording evidence before trial), or placing screens in the courtroom between the complainant and defendant. Thus, in a face-to-face meeting in a RJ conference, there is a risk of creating an unsafe environment for the victim. Steps would need to be taken to equalise the relations between victim and offender within an RJ conference with mechanisms for safely removing the victim or offender if required.

Because the original trauma occurred in an unsafe environment and in order to create an environment that provides safety, respect and acceptance (the sixth principle of trauma-informed care), the physical RJ setting must be a welcoming and safe space for victims in order to remove possible obstacles to participation (agency) such as avoidance or hostility. It is possible that for violent, interpersonal offences, such as sexual assault, the emotional safety of the victim will be compromised when she is in the presence of the offender, who might still exercise some degree of power and control over her (for example, within an employee/employer relationship, a student/teacher or a parent/child relationship or a sexual/other family relationship) so that the victim may be at risk of future violence. For example:

> the child/offender relationship, based as it is on power, control and manipulation, is likely to be re-created in conferencing where an offender denies responsibility or transfers responsibility to the child or where an offender makes apologies and promises in order to re-engage in grooming of the victim. Interestingly, survivors of historical sexual abuse interviewed by Jülich (2006) also expressed similar concerns about restorative justice, particularly their fears that the power relationship would reassert itself during conferencing. (Cossins, 2008: 372)

Since the 'safety of all parties is a prerequisite to providing a secure setting in which agency and accountability can be exercised … in cases where this cannot be achieved restorative disposals will not be appropriate' (O'Mahony & Doak, 2017: 90).

Emphasis of a person's strengths (the seventh principle of trauma-informed care) recognises that rather than something being wrong with them, 'something wrong was done to that person' (Elliott et al., 2005) and that their symptoms constitute adaptations to the original traumatic events. This, coupled with the eighth principle of trauma-informed care, the minimisation of re-traumatisation, are essential features of both trauma-specific services and trauma-informed systems. Since sexual assault involves an abuse of power, the power differential between the victim and the RJ professional staff, as well as between the victim and the offender, may retrigger traumatic experiences. Thus, re-traumatisation prevention processes are needed to manage the trauma symptoms of hyperarousal or avoidance.

Finally, both trauma-informed services and systems should seek to be culturally competent (the ninth principle), where a victim's harm is understood with respect to her cultural background. This is a particular concern since RJ may not have the capacity, as presently structured, to recognise issues of 'structural disadvantage' including the racial, class and gendered backgrounds of victims of power-based crimes (Stubbs, 2007: 171), such as sexual assault.

Overall, it can be concluded that RJ should be considered as a post-trial (that is, a sentencing option) or post-release option for the participation of victims of sexual assault (see, e.g. Jülich & Landon, 2017; Miller & Iovanni, 2013), with recent literature reviews identifying the success of using RJ post-sentencing (Bolitho & Freeman, 2016). Arguably, RJ for sexual offences involving vulnerable victims, in particular children, needs to be a process that is governed by trauma-informed principles to maintain a victim-focus of doing no further harm.

One of the advantages of the use of RJ after the offender has served a sentence is that the victim has sufficient time to participate in counselling in order to prepare for a face-to-face conference with the offender which could be a healing part of the process of recovery from trauma (Miller & Iovanni, 2013). In fact, Jülich and Bowen (2015) document a five-stage recovery model for victims of sexual assault in order to obtain the correct timing for the use of RJ for sex offences—from Stage One (the initial impact of trauma) when it would be inappropriate for a victim to engage in RJ through to Stage Four (the latter stage of the recovery process where victims have gained sufficient emotional strength to engage with RJ but remain vulnerable to offenders' denial and minimisation), and Stage Five which is the last stage of recovery where there has been integration of the sexual assault into the victim's life with little or no vulnerability to offender perspectives. This is the time when victims have the greatest emotional ability to engage with RJ.

Obviously, Stages Four and Five in the recovery process will not necessarily coincide with the criminal justice process and the pressures on a victim to participate in RJ.

6 Conclusion

In conclusion, I wish to list all the recommendations for reform that have been made in this book in order to transform the adversarial sexual assault trial into a trauma-informed system in order to do no further harm to complainants and to achieve their best evidence. These reforms include:

- A best practice model for a trauma-informed sexual assault trial;
- Reform of opening and closing addresses to control the content of counsels' biasing statements about the defendant and the complainant;
- Mandatory training of all court personnel about trauma-informed principles;
- The creation of child- and complainant-friendly environments in order to relax the formality of the court environment and to eliminate possible triggers for re-traumatisation;
- Pre-recording of all evidence of sexual assault complainants;
- Prohibition of cross-examination questions on topics that endorse rape myths;
- Time-limited cross-examination and vetting of cross-examination questions in order to eliminate the cross-examination effect and achieve best evidence;
- The employment of a specialist examiner to prevent the cross-examination effect, thereby reducing re-traumatisation and achieving best evidence; and
- A trauma-informed restorative justice model for sexual assault complainants as a post-sentencing and/or post-release option.

References

Anderson, P. S. (2016). When justice and forgiveness come apart: A feminist perspective on restorative justice and intimate violence. *Oxford Journal of Law and Religion, 5*, 113–134.

Australian Law Reform Commission. (2010a). *Family violence: A national legal response* (ALRC Report No. 114). Sydney: ALRC.

Australian Law Reform Commission. (2010b). *Family violence: Improving legal frameworks* (Consultation Paper). Sydney: ALRC.

Baverstock, J. (2016). *Process evaluation of pre-recorded cross-examination scheme* (Section 28). London: Ministry of Justice. https://www.gov.uk/government/publications/process-evaluation-of-pre-recorded-cross-examination-pilot-section-28.

Bolitho, J., & Freeman, K. (2016). *The use and effectiveness of restorative justice in criminal justice systems following child sexual abuse or comparable harms.* Sydney: Royal Commission into Institutional Responses to Child Sexual Abuse.

Braithwaite, J. (2002). Setting standards for restorative justice. *British Journal of Criminology, 42,* 563–577.

Brown, J. (2011). We mind and we care but have things changed? Assessment of progress in the reporting, investigating and prosecution of allegations of rape. *Journal of Sexual Aggression, 17,* 263–272.

Carlson, C. (2014). 'This Bitch Got Drunk and Did This to Herself': Proposed evidentiary reforms to limit 'victim blaming' and 'perpetrator pardoning' in rape by intoxication trials in California. *Wisconsin Journal of Law, Gender & Society, 29,* 285–315.

Caruso, D. (2012). Proposed reforms for the cross-examination of child witnesses and the reception and treatment of their evidence. *Journal of Judicial Administration, 21,* 191–236.

Cashmore, J., Taylor, A., & Parkinson, P. (2017). The characteristics of reports to the police of child sexual abuse and the likelihood of cases proceeding to prosecution after delays in reporting. *Child Sexual Abuse & Neglect, 74,* 49–61.

Cashmore, J., & Trimboli, L. (2006). Child sexual assault trials: A survey of juror perceptions. *Crime and Justice Bulletin, 102,* 1–20.

Chalmers, J. (2014). Independent legal representation for complainers in sexual offence cases. In J. Chalmers, F. Leverick, & A. Shaw (Eds.), *Post corroboration safeguards review report of the academic expert group* (pp. 185–189). Edinburgh: The Scottish Government.

Comiskey, M. (2010). Initiating dialogue about jury comprehension of legal concepts: Can the 'stagnant pool' be revitalised? *Queen's Law Journal, 35,* 625–677.

Connolly, D. A., Coburn, P. I., & Chong, K. (2017). Twenty-six years prosecuting historical child sexual abuse cases: Has anything changed? *Psychology, Public Policy, and Law, 23,* 166–177.

Cook, K. (2011). Rape investigation and prosecution: Stuck in the mud? *Journal of Sexual Aggression, 17,* 250–262.

Cossins, A. (2006a). Prosecuting child sexual assault cases: Are vulnerable witness protections enough? *Current Issues in Criminal Justice, 18,* 299–317.

Cossins, A. (2006b). Prosecuting child sexual assault cases: To specialise or not, that is the question. *Current Issues in Criminal Justice, 18,* 318–342.

Cossins, A. (2008). Children, sexual abuse and suggestibility: What laypeople think they know and what the literature tells us. *Psychiatry, Psychology and Law, 15,* 153–170.

Cossins, A. (2010a). *Alternative models for prosecuting child sex offences in Australia.* Sydney: National Child Sexual Assault Reform Committee, UNSW.

Cossins, A. (2013a). Expert witness evidence in sexual assault trials: Questions, answers and law reform in Australia and England. *International Journal of Evidence and Proof, 17,* 74–113.

Cossins, A. (2013b). The legacy of the *Makin* case 120 years on: Legal fictions, circular reasoning and some solutions. *Sydney Law Review, 35,* 731–759.

Cossins, A., Goodman-Delahunty, J., & O'Brien, K. (2009). Uncertainty and misconceptions about child sexual abuse: Implications for the criminal justice system. *Psychiatry, Psychology & Law, 16,* 435–452.

Cossins, A., & Rowden, E. (2020). The child sexual assault trial: Redesigning courtroom spaces according to trauma informed principles. In K. Duncanson & E. Henderson (Eds.), *Courthouse design and social justice.* London: Routledge (in press).

Daly, K. (2006). Restorative justice and sexual assault: An archival study of court and conference cases. *British Journal of Criminology, 46,* 334–356.

Daly, K. (2008). Setting the record straight and a call for radical change: A reply to Annie Cossins on 'Restorative justice and child sex offences'. *British Journal of Criminology, 48,* 557–566.

Daly, K. (2011). *Conventional and innovative justice responses to sexual violence* (Australian Centre for the Study of Sexual Assault, Issue 12). Melbourne: Australian Institute of Family Studies.

Daly, K. (2016). What is restorative justice? Fresh answers to a vexed question. *Victims & Offenders, 11,* 9–29.

Daly, K. (2017). Sexual violence and victims' justice interests. In E. Zinsstag & M. Keenan (Eds.), *Sexual violence and restorative justice: Legal social and therapeutic dimensions* (pp. 108–140). London: Routledge.

Daly, K., & Bouhours, B. (2010). Rape and attrition in the legal process: A comparative analysis of five countries. In M. Tonry (Ed.), *Crime and justice: A review of research*. Chicago: University of Chicago Press.

Daly, K., & Curtis-Fawley, S. (2006). Justice for victims of sexual assault: Court or conference? In K. Heimer & C. Kruttschnitt (Eds.), *Gender and crime: Patterns of victimization and offending* (pp. 230–265). New York: New York University Press.

Daly, K., Curtis-Fawley, S., & Bouhours, B. (2003). *Sexual offence cases finalised in court, by conference, and by formal caution in South Australia for young offenders, 1995–2001: Final report*. Brisbane: School of Criminology and Criminal Justice, Griffith University. https://www.gu.edu.au/school/ccj/kdaly.html.

Daly, K., & Wade, D. (2017). Sibling sexual violence and victims' justice interests: A comparison of youth conferencing and judicial sentencing. In E. Zinsstag & M. Keenan (Eds.), *Restorative responses to sexual violence: Legal social and therapeutic dimensions* (pp. 143–178). New York: Routledge.

Dent, H. (1992). The effects of age and intelligence on eyewitnessing ability. In H. Dent & R. Flin (Eds.), *Children as witnesses* (pp. 1–13). Chichester: Wiley.

Devine, D. J. (2012). *Jury decision making: The state of the science*. New York: New York University Press.

Devine, D. J., & Caughlin, D. E. (2014). Do they matter? A meta-analytic investigation of individual characteristics and guilt judgments. *Psychology, Public Policy, and Law, 20*, 109–134.

Devine, D. J., Clayton, L. D., Dunford, B. D., Seying, R., & Pryce, J. (2001). Jury decision making: 45 years of empirical research on deliberating groups. *Psychology, Public Policy, and Law, 7*, 622–727.

Dignan, J. (2005). *Understanding victims and restorative justice*. Maidenhead: Open University Press.

Dinos, S., Burrowes, N., Hammond, K., & Cunliffe, C. (2015). A systematic review of juries' assessment of rape victims: Do rape myths impact on juror decision-making? *International Journal of Law, Crime and Justice, 43*, 36–49.

Elliott, D. E., Bjelajac, P., Fallot, R. D., Markoff, L. S., & Reed, B. G. (2005). Trauma-informed or trauma-denied: Principles and implementation of trauma-informed services for women. *Journal of Community Psychology, 33*, 461–477.

Ellison, L., & Munro, V. E. (2009). Turning mirrors into windows? Assessing the impact of (mock) juror education in rape trials. *British Journal of Criminology, 49,* 363–383.

Ellison, L., & Munro, V. E. (2014). A 'special' delivery? Exploring the impact of screens, live-links and video-recorded evidence on mock juror deliberation in rape trials. *Social & Legal Studies, 23,* 3–29.

Flynn, A., & Henry, N. (2012). Disputing consent: The role of jury directions in Victoria. *Current Issues in Criminal Justice, 24,* 167–184.

Frohmann, L., & Mertz, E. (1995). Legal reform and social construction: Violence, gender, and the law. *Law and Social Inquiry, 19,* 829–851.

Geddie, L., Fradin, S., & Beer, J. (2000). Child characteristics which impact accuracy of recall and suggestibility in preschoolers: Is age the best predictor? *Child Abuse & Neglect, 24,* 223–235.

Ghetti, S., Goodman, G. S., Eisen, M. L., Qin, J., & Davis, S. L. (2002). Consistency in children's reports of sexual and physical abuse. *Child Abuse and Neglect, 26,* 977–995.

Gibb, F. (2007, November 27). Juries to be warned of rape victim 'myth'. *The Times.* https://www.thetimes.co.uk/article/juries-to-be-warned-of-rape-victim-myth-3wv7k9dlrpc.

Godden-Rasul, N. (2017). Repairing the harms of rape of women through restorative justice. In E. Zinsstag & M. Keenan (Eds.), *Restorative responses to sexual violence: Legal social and therapeutic dimensions* (pp. 15–27). New York: Routledge.

Goodman-Delahunty, J., Cossins, A., & Martschuk, N. (2014). Persistent misconceptions about child sexual assault abuse: The impact of specialized educative information and deliberation on mock-jurors. In K. C. Haung (Ed.), *Proceedings of the third international conference of empirical studies of judicial systems: Citizen participation around the world.* Taipei, Taiwan: Academia Sinica.

Goodman-Delahunty, J., Cossins, A., & Martschuk, N. (2016). *Jury reasoning in joint and separate trials of institutional child sexual abuse: An empirical study.* Sydney: Royal Commission into Institutional Responses to Child Sexual Abuse.

Goodman-Delahunty, J., Cossins, A., & O'Brien, K. (2010). Enhancing the credibility of complainants in child sexual assault trials: The effect of expert evidence and judicial directions. *Behavioral Sciences & the Law, 28,* 769–783.

Goodman-Delahunty, J., Cossins, A., & O'Brien, K. (2011). A comparison of expert evidence and judicial directions to counter misconceptions in child sexual abuse trials. *Australian and New Zealand Journal of Criminology, 44*, 196–217.

Haegerich, T. M., & Bottoms, B. L. (2000). Empathy and jurors' decisions in trials involving child sexual assault allegations. *Law and Human Behavior, 24*, 421–448.

Haegerich, T. M., Salerno, J. M., & Bottoms, B. L. (2013). Are the effects of juvenile offender stereotypes maximized or minimized by jury deliberation? *Psychology, Public Policy & Law, 19*, 81–97.

Hamlyn, B., Phelps, A., Turtle, J., & Sattar, G. (2004). *Are special measures working? Evidence from surveys of vulnerable and intimidated witnesses* (Home Office Research Study 283). London: Home Office.

Harris, M., & Fallot, R. D. (2001). Envisioning a trauma-informed service system: A vital paradigm shift. *New Directions for Mental Health Services, 89*, 3–22.

Henderson, E. (2014). All the proper protections—The Court of Appeal rewrites the rules of the cross-examination of vulnerable witnesses. *Criminal Law Review, 2*, 93–108.

Henderson, E. (2015). Theoretically speaking: English judges and advocates discuss the changing theory of cross-examination. *Criminal Law Review, 12*, 929–948.

Henderson, E., & Duncanson, K. (2016). A little judicial direction: Can the use of jury directions challenge traditional consent narratives in rape trials? *The University of New South Wales Law Journal, 39*, 750–778.

Herman, J. (2005). Justice from the victim's perspective. *Violence Against Women, 11*, 571–602.

HM CPS Inspectorate and HM Inspectorate of Constabulary. (2012). *Joint inspection report on the experience of young victims and witnesses in the CJS*. London: HMIC & HMCPSI.

HM Government. (2018). *Victims strategy*. London: Ministry of Justice.

House of Commons, Justice Committee. (2016). *Restorative justice: Fourth report of session 2016–17*. London: House of Commons.

Jackson, H. (2012). Children's evidence in legal proceedings—The position in Western Australia. In J. R. Spencer & M. E. Lamb (Eds.), *Children and cross-examination: Time to change the rules* (pp. 75–94). Oxford: Hart Publishing.

Jones, C. (2009). *Does Forum Sentencing Reduce Re-Offending? Report No. 129*. Canberra: Australian Institute of Criminology.

Jordan, J. (2011). Here we go round the review-go-round: Rape investigation and prosecution—Are things getting worse not better? *Journal of Sexual Aggression, 17*, 234–249.

Joyce-Wojtas, N., & Keenan, M. (2016). Is restorative justice for sexual crime compatible with various criminal justice systems? *Contemporary Justice Review, 19,* 43–68.

Judicial College. (2013–2019). *Equal treatment bench book.* https://www.judiciary.uk/wp-content/uploads/2018/02/equal-treatment-bench-book-february2018-v5-02mar18.pdf.

Judicial Commission of NSW. (2006–2017). *Equality before the law bench book.* Sydney: Judicial Commission of NSW. https://www.judcom.nsw.gov.au/wp-content/uploads/2016/07/Equality_before_the_Law_Bench_Book.pdf.

Jülich, S. (2006). Views of justice among survivors of historical child sexual abuse. *Theoretical Criminology, 10,* 125–138.

Jülich, S., & Bowen, H. (2015). Restorative justice in Aotearoa, New Zealand: Improving our response to sexual violence. *Revista De Asistenta Sociala, 14,* 93–104.

Jülich, S., & Landon, F. (2017). Achieving justice outcomes: Participants of Project Restore's restorative processes. In E. Zinsstag & M. Keenan (Eds.), *Restorative responses to sexual violence: Legal, social and therapeutic dimensions* (pp. 192–212). New York: Routledge.

Kasparian, A. (2014). Justice beyond bars: Exploring the restorative justice alternative for victims of rape and sexual assault. *Suffolk Transnational Law Review, 37,* 377–410.

Keenan, M., & Zinsstag, E. (2014). Restorative justice and sexual offences: Can 'changing lenses' be appropriate in this case too? *Monatsschrift for Criminology, 97,* 93–106.

Koss, M. P. (2014). The RESTORE program of restorative justice for sex crimes: Vision, process, and outcomes. *Journal of Interpersonal Violence, 29,* 1623–1660.

KPMG. (2010). *Review of the Youth Justice Group Conferencing Program: Final Report.* Melbourne: Department of Human Services.

Larsen, J. (2014). *Restorative justice in the Australian criminal justice system* (Research and Public Policy Series No. 127). Canberra: Australian Institute of Criminology. https://aic.gov.au/publications/rpp/rpp127.

Law Commission, New Zealand. (1999). *Juries in criminal trials part two: A discussion paper, preliminary paper 37—Volume 1.* Law Commission, New Zealand.

Lievore, D. (2005a). *Prosecutorial decisions in adult sexual assault cases* (Trends and Issues in Crime & Criminal Justice, No. 291, pp. 1–6).

Lievore, D. (2005b). *No longer silent: A study of women's help-seeking decisions and service responses to sexual assault*. Canberra, Australian Institute of Criminology.

Marsh, F., & Wager, N. M. (2015). Restorative justice in cases of sexual violence: Exploring the views of the public and survivors. *Probation Journal, 62,* 336–356.

McElrea, F. W. M. (1998). The New Zealand model of family group conferencing. *European Journal on Criminal Policy and Research, 6,* 527–543.

McGlynn, C. (2017). Rape trials and sexual history evidence: Reforming the law on third-party evidence. *The Journal of Criminal Law, 81,* 367–392.

McGlynn, C., Westmarland, N., & Godden, N. (2012). I just wanted him to hear me: Sexual Violence and the possibilities of restorative justice. *Journal of Law and Society, 39,* 213–240.

Miller, S. L., & Iovanni, L. (2013). Using restorative justice for gendered violence: Success with a post-conviction model. *Feminist Criminology, 8,* 247–268.

Ministry of Justice. (2014). *Report on review of ways to reduce distress of victims in trials of sexual violence*. London: Ministry of Justice.

Ministry of Justice. (2017). *Press release: Greater protection for rape victims and children at risk of grooming.* https://www.gov.uk/government/news/greater-protection-for-rape-victims-and-children-at-risk-of-grooming.

Naylor, B. (2010). Effective justice for victims of sexual assault: Taking up the debate on alternative pathways. *University of New South Wales Law Journal, 33,* 662–684.

NSW Criminal Justice and Sexual Offences Taskforce. (2005). *Responding to sexual assault: The way forward*. Sydney: Attorney-General's Department of NSW.

NSW Joint Select Committee on Sentencing of Child Sexual Assault Offenders. (2014). *Every sentence tells a story—Report on sentencing of child sexual assault offenders* (Report No. 1/55). Sydney: Parliament of NSW.

NSW Law Reform Commission. (2012). *Jury Directions (Report No. 136).* Sydney: NSW Law Reform Commission.

NSW Standing Committee on Law and Justice. (2002). *Report on child sexual assault prosecutions* (Parliamentary Paper No. 208; Report No. 22). Sydney: Parliament of NSW.

O'Mahony, D., & Doak, J. (2017). *Reimagining restorative justice: Agency and accountability in the criminal process.* Oxford: Hart Publishing.

Pether, P. (2009). What is due to others: Speaking and signifying subject(s) of rape law. *Griffith Law Review, 18,* 237–258.

Plotnikoff, J., & Woolfson, R. (2015). *Intermediaries in the criminal justice system: Improving communication for vulnerable witnesses and defendants*. Bristol: Policy Press.

Poynton, S. (2013). Rates of recidivism among offenders referred to Forum Sentencing. *Contemporary Issues in Crime and Justice, 172*, 1–14.

Proietti-Scifoni, G., & Daly, K. (2011). Gendered violence and restorative justice: The views of New Zealand Opinion Leaders. *Contemporary Justice Review, 14*, 269–290.

Queensland Law Reform Commission. (2009). *A review of jury directions* (Report No. 66). Brisbane: Queensland Law Reform Commission.

Raitt, F. E. (2010). Independent legal representation for complainants in rape trials. In C. McGlynn & V. E. Munro (Eds.), *Rethinking rape law: International and comparative perspectives*. Abingdon: Routledge.

Robinson, J. (2015). The experience of the child witness: Legal and psychological issue. *International Journal of Law and Psychiatry, 42–43*, 168–176.

Rook, P., Rafferty, A., & Ward, R. (2016) Advocacy and the vulnerable. In P. Rook & R. Ward (Eds.), *Rook & ward on sexual offences: Law & practice* (5th ed., pp. 1553–1568). London: Sweet & Maxwell.

Royal Commission into Institutional Responses to Child Sexual Abuse. (2017a). *Final report: Nature and cause* (Vol. 2). Sydney: Royal Commission into Institutional Responses to Child Sexual Abuse.

Royal Commission into Institutional Responses to Child Sexual Abuse. (2017b). *Criminal justice report* (Executive Summary and Parts I–II). Sydney: Royal Commission into Institutional Responses to Child Sexual Abuse.

Royal Commission into Institutional Responses to Child Sexual Abuse. (2017c). *Criminal justice report* (Parts VII–X and Appendices). Sydney: Royal Commission into Institutional Responses to Child Sexual Abuse.

Rossner, M., Bruce, J., & Meher, M. (2013). *The Process and Dynamics of Restorative Justice: Research on Forum Sentencing: Final Report Prepared for NSW Department of Attorney General's and Justice*. Sydney: University of Western Sydney and University of New South Wales.

Simon, D. (2012). More problems with criminal trials: The limited effectiveness of legal mechanisms. *Law and Contemporary Problems, 75*, 167–209.

Smith, N., & Weatherburn, D. (2012). Youth justice conferences versus Children's Court: A comparison of re-offending. *Contemporary Issues in Crime and Justice, 160*, 1–23.

Spencer, J. R., & Lamb, M. (2012). *Children and cross-examination: Time to change the rules?*. Oxford: Hart Publishing.

Standing Committee on Uniform Legislation and Intergovernmental Agreements. (1996). *Evidence law: Eighteenth report in the thirty-fourth parliament*. Perth: Legislative Assembly of Western Australia.

Standing Council on Law and Justice. (2013). *Guidelines for restorative justice processes in criminal cases*. Sydney: Standing Council on Law and Justice. http://www.sclj.gov.au/agdbasev7wr/sclj/restorative%20justice%20national%20guidelines.pdf.

Steblay, N., Hosch, H. M., Culhane, S. E., & McWethy, A. (2006). The impact on juror verdicts of judicial instruction to disregard inadmissible evidence: A meta-analysis. *Law and Human Behavior, 30*, 469–492.

Stewart, D. N., & Jacquin, K. M. (2010). Juror perceptions in a rape trial: Examining the complainant's ingestion of chemical substances prior to sexual assault. *Journal of Aggression, Maltreatment & Trauma, 19*, 853–874.

Strang, H., Sherman, L. W., Mayo-Wilson, E., Woods, D., & Ariel, B. (2013). *Restorative justice conferencing (RJC) Using face-to-face meetings of offenders and victims: Effects on offender recidivism and victim satisfaction. A systematic review*. Oslo: Campbell Collaboration.

Strang, H., & Braithwaite, J. (2017). *Restorative Justice: Philosophy to Practice*. London: Routledge.

Stubbs, J. (2007). Beyond apology? Domestic violence and critical questions for restorative justice. *Criminology and Criminal Justice, 7*, 169–187.

Taylor, N., & Joudo, J. (2005) *The impact of pre-recorded video and closed circuit television testimony by adult sexual assault complainants on jury decision-making: An experimental study* (Research and Public Policy Series No. 68). Canberra: Australian Institute of Criminology.

Temkin, J., & Krahé, B. (2008). *Sexual assault and the justice gap: A question of attitude*. Oxford: Hart Publishing.

Thomas, C. (2010). *Are juries fair?* (Ministry of Justice Research Series No. 1/10). London: Ministry of Justice. https://www.justice.gov.uk/downloads/publications/research-and-analysis/moj-research/are-juries-fair-research.pdf.

Trimboli, L. (2008). *Juror understanding of judicial instructions in criminal trials* (Crime and Justice Bulletin, No. 119). Sydney: Bureau of Crime Statistics and Research.

Victims Commissioner Office. (2016). *A question of quality: A Review of restorative justice part 1—Service providers*. https://s3-eu-west-2.amazonaws.com/victcomm2-prod-storage-119w3o4kq2z48/uploads/2019/02/VC-Restorative-Justice-Part-1-Service-Providers-Review-2016.pdf.

Victims Services, NSW Department of Justice (2016) *Children's Champion (Witness Intermediary) Procedural Guidance Manual (2016)*, Sydney, NSW

Department of Justice (https://www.victimsservices.justice.nsw.gov.au/Documents/child-champ_manual.pdf).

Victorian Law Reform Commission. (2016). *The role of victims of crime in the criminal trial process* (Report No. 34). Melbourne: Victorian Law Reform Commission.

Van Ness, D. W., & Strong, K. H. (2015). *Restoring Justice: An Introduction to Restorative Justice*. New York: Routledge.

Wager, N. (2013). The experience and insight of survivors who have engaged in a restorative justice meeting with their assailant. *Temida, 16,* 11–32.

Willmott, D., Boduszek, D., & Booth, N. (2017). The English jury on trial. *Custodial Review, 82,* 12–14.

Wilson, L. C. (2005). Independent legal representation for victims of sexual assault: A model for delivery of legal services. *Windsor Year Book Access to Justice, 23,* 249–312.

Woessner, G. (2017). On the relationship between restorative justice and therapy in cases of sexual violence. In E. Zinsstag & M. Keenan (Eds.), *Restorative responses to sexual violence: Legal social and therapeutic dimensions* (pp. 248–265). New York: Routledge.

Zajac, R., & O'Neill, S. (2013). The role of repeated interviewing in children's responses to cross-examination-style questioning. *British Journal of Psychology, 104,* 14–38.

Zehr, H., & Mika, H. (1998). Fundamental concepts of restorative justice. *Contemporary Justice Review, 1,* 47–55.

Zinsstag, E., & Keenan, M. (Eds.). (2017). *Sexual violence and restorative justice: Legal, social and therapeutic dimensions.* London: Routledge.

References

Abbey, A. (2011). Alcohol's role in sexual violence perpetration: Theoretical explanations, existing evidence and future directions. *Drug and Alcohol Review, 30,* 481–489.

Abbey, A., & McAuslan, P. (2004). A longitudinal examination of male college students' perpetration of sexual assault. *Journal of Consulting and Clinical Psychology, 72,* 747–756.

Abbey, A., Ross, L. T., McDuffie, D., & McAuslan, P. (1996). Alcohol and dating risk factors for sexual assault among college women. *Psychology of Women Quarterly, 20,* 147–169.

Abbey, A., Zawacki, T., Buck, P. O., Clinton, A. M., & McAuslan, P. (2004). Sexual assault and alcohol consumption: What do we know about their relationship and what types of research are still needed? *Aggression and Violent Behaviour, 9,* 271–303.

Advocacy Training Council. (2011). *Raising the bar: The handling of vulnerable witnesses, victims and defendants in court*. London: The Advocacy Training Council. https://www.icca.ac.uk/wp-content/uploads/2019/07/Raising-the-Bar.pdf.

Agres, K., & Wiggins, G. A. (2015). Schematic processing as a framework for learning and creativity in CBR and CC. In *Proceedings of the ICCBR 2015 workshops*. Frankfurt, Germany. http://ceur-ws.org/Vol-1520/paper16.pdf.

A. Cossins, *Closing the Justice Gap for Adult and Child Sexual Assault*,
https://doi.org/10.1057/978-1-137-32051-3

Ahern, E., Kowalski, M., & Lamb, M. E. (2018). A case study perspective: The experiences of young persons testifying to child sexual exploitation in British criminal court. *Journal of Child Sexual Abuse, 27,* 321–334.

Alaggia, R. (2004). Many ways of telling: Expanding conceptualizations of child sexual abuse disclosure. *Child Abuse & Neglect, 28,* 1213–1227.

Alderden, M. A., & Ullman, S. E. (2012). Creating a more complete and current picture examining police and prosecutor decision-making when processing sexual assault cases. *Violence Against Women, 18,* 525–551.

Allen, J. A. (1990). *Sex and secrets: Crimes involving Australian women since 1880.* Sydney: Allen & Unwin.

Allen, M., Emmers, T., Gebhardt, L., & Giery, M. A. (1995). Exposure to pornography and acceptance of rape myths. *Journal of Communication, 45,* 5–26.

Allum, J. (2017, April 7). SCEGGS principal speaks out over alleged rape of student and violence against women. *The Wentworth Courier.*

American Bar Association. (2014). *ABA policy on trauma-informed advocacy for children and youth.* www.americanbar.org/content/dam/aba/administrative/child_law/ABAPolicyonTrauma-InformedAdvocacy.authcheckdam.pdf. Accessed 8 February 2018.

American Psychiatric Association. (2013). *Diagnostic and statistical manual of mental disorders (DSM-5)* (5th ed.). Arlington, VA: American Psychiatric Publishing.

Anderson, K., Cooper, H., & Okamura, L. (1997). Individual differences and attitudes toward rape: A meta-analytic review. *Personality and Social Psychology Bulletin, 23,* 295–315.

Anderson, J., Martin, J., Mullen, P., Romans, S., & Herbison, P. (1993). Prevalence of childhood sexual abuse experiences in a community sample of women. *Journal of American Academy of Child and Adolescent Psychiatry, 32,* 911–919.

Anderson, M. (2005). Negotiating sex. *Southern California Law Review, 78,* 101–138.

Anderson, P. S. (2016). When justice and forgiveness come apart: A feminist perspective on restorative justice and intimate violence. *Oxford Journal of Law and Religion, 5,* 113–134.

Andrews, S. J., & Lamb, M. E. (2017). The structural linguistic complexity of lawyers' questions and children's responses in Scottish criminal courts. *Child Abuse & Neglect, 65,* 182–193.

Andrews, S. J., Lamb, M. E., & Lyon, T. D. (2014). Question types, responsiveness and self-contradictions when prosecutors and defense attorneys question alleged victims of child sexual abuse. *Applied Cognitive Psychology, 25*, 253–261.

Angiolini, E. (2015). *Report of the independent review into the investigation and prosecution of rape in London*. London: Crown Prosecution Service.

Arata, C. M. (1998). To tell or not to tell: Current functioning of child sexual abuse survivors who disclosed their victimization. *Child Maltreatment, 3*, 63–71.

Aronowitz, T., Lambert, C. A., & Davidoff, S. (2012). The role of rape myth acceptance in the social norms regarding sexual behaviour among college students. *Journal of Community Health Nursing, 29*, 173–182.

Ask, K., & Granhag, P. A. (2005). Motivational sources of confirmation bias in criminal investigations: The need for cognitive closure. *Journal of Investigative Psychology and Offender Profiling, 2*, 43–63.

Atara, Y. (2015). Trauma from an enactive perspective: The collapse of the *knowing-how* structure. *Adaptive Behavior, 23*, 143–154.

Attorney-General's Department of NSW. (2004). *Pilot specialist child sexual assault jurisdiction*. Unpublished document.

Attorney General's National Task Force on Children Exposed to Violence. (2012). *Defending childhood: Report of the Attorney General's national task force on children exposed to violence*. Washington, DC: US Department of Justice.

Australian Bureau of Statistics (ABS). (1996). *Women's safety Australia*. Canberra: ABS.

Australian Bureau of Statistics (ABS). (2012). *Personal safety survey* (Catalogue No. 4906.0). Canberra: ABS.

Australian Bureau of Statistics (ABS). (2017a). *4906.0—Personal safety, Australia, 2016*. https://www.abs.gov.au/ausstats/abs@.nsf/Lookup/by%20Subject/4906.0~2016~Main%20Features~Experience%20of%20Abuse%20before%20the%20age%20of%2015~27.

Australian Bureau of Statistics (ABS). (2017b, June). *3101.0—Australian demographic statistics*. https://www.abs.gov.au/AUSSTATS/abs@.nsf/Lookup/3101.0Main+Features1Jun%202017.

Australian Bureau of Statistics (ABS). (2018). *4510.0—Recorded crime—Victims, Australia, 2017*. http://www.abs.gov.au/ausstats/abs@.nsf/Lookup/by%20Subject/4510.0~2017~Media%20Release~Recording%20of%20sexual%20assaults%20reaches%20eight-year%20high%20(Media%20Release)~16.

Australian Bureau of Statistics (ABS). (2019a). *4510.0—Recorded crime—Victims, Australia, 2018*. https://www.abs.gov.au/AUSSTATS/abs@.nsf/Lookup/4510.0Main+Features12018?OpenDocument.

Australian Bureau of Statistics (ABS). (2019b). *4513.0—Criminal courts, Australia, 2017–18*. https://www.abs.gov.au/Ausstats/abs@.nsf/0/4BC54F34DFC618ACCA2573DA0016FB63?OpenDocument.

Australian Human Rights Commission. (2017). *Change the course: National report on sexual assault and sexual harassment at Australian Universities*. Sydney: AHRC. https://www.humanrights.gov.au/sites/default/files/document/publication/AHRC_2017_ChangeTheCourse_UniversityReport.pdf.

Australian Human Rights Commission. (2019). *Everyone's business: Survey on sexual harassment of members of the shop, distributive and allied employees' association*. Sydney: AHRC. https://humanrights.gov.au/sites/default/files/document/publication/ahrc_sda_survey_report_2019.pdf.

Australian Institute of Criminology (AIC). (2014). *Australian crime: Facts & figures*. Canberra: AIC.

Australasian Institute of Judicial Administration Committee (AIJA). (2014). *Bench book for children giving evidence in Australian courts*. Melbourne: AIJA.

Australian Law Reform Commission. (2010a). *Family violence: A national legal response* (ALRC Report No. 114). Sydney: ALRC.

Australian Law Reform Commission. (2010b). *Family violence: Improving legal frameworks* (Consultation Paper). Sydney: ALRC.

Australian Law Reform Commission and Human Rights and Equal Opportunity Commission. (1997). *Seen and heard: Priority for children in the legal process* (ALRC Report No. 84). Sydney: ALRC.

Australian Law Reform Commission, NSW Law Reform Commission and Victorian Law Reform Commission. (2005). *Uniform evidence law report* (ALRC Report No. 102; NSWLRC Report No. 112; VLRC Final Report). Sydney: ALRC.

Bagley, C., & Thurston, W. E. (1996). *Understanding and preventing child sexual abuse: Critical summaries of 500 key studies*. Aldershot: Ashgate.

Bailey, C., Powell, M., & Brubacher, S. P. (2017). The attrition of indigenous and non-indigenous child sexual abuse cases in two Australian jurisdictions. *Psychology, Public Policy, and Law, 23*, 178–190.

Baker, A., & Duncan, S. (1985). Child sexual abuse: A study of prevalence in Great Britain. *Child Abuse and Neglect, 9*, 457–467.

Banks, S. (2008). An honest but mistaken belief in London legislation: Consent, controversy and sexual offence reform in New South Wales. *The Law Teacher, 42,* 228–235.

Basow, S. A., & Minieri, A. (2011). 'You owe me': Effects of date cost, who pays, participant gender, and rape myth beliefs on perceptions of rape. *Journal of Interpersonal Violence, 26,* 479–497.

Bath, H. I. (2008). The three pillars of trauma-informed care. *Reclaiming Children and Youth, 17,* 17–21.

Baverstock, J. (2016). *Process evaluation of pre-recorded cross-examination scheme* (Section 28). London: Ministry of Justice. https://www.gov.uk/government/publications/process-evaluation-of-pre-recorded-cross-examination-pilot-section-28.

Bavin, J. (1991). Writing about incest in Victoria 1880–1890. In P. Hetherington (Ed.), *Incest and the community: Australian perspectives* (pp. 49–78). Perth: Centre for Western Australian History, University of Western Australia.

Bavin-Mizzi, J. (1995). Understandings of justice: Australian rape and carnal knowledge cases, 1876–1924. In D. Kirkby (Ed.), *Sex, power and justice: Historical perspectives of law in Australia* (pp. 19–32). Melbourne: Oxford University Press.

Bederian-Gardner, D., & Goldfarb, D. (2014). Expectations of emotions during testimony: The role of communicator and perceiver characteristics. *Behavioral Sciences & the Law, 32,* 829–845.

Bederian-Gardner, D., Goldfarb, D., & Goodman, G. S. (2017). Empathy's relation to appraisal of the emotional child witness. *Applied Cognitive Psychology, 31,* 488–499.

Behzadnia, A., & Mehrani, M. B. (2017). Young children's yes bias in response to tag questions. *Early Child Development and Care, 188,* 1663–1672.

Beichner, D., & Spohn, C. (2005). Prosecutorial charging decisions in sexual assault cases: Examining the impact of a specialized prosecution unit. *Criminal Justice Police Review, 16,* 461–498.

Ben-David, S., & Schneider, O. (2005). Rape perceptions, gender role attitudes, and victim-perpetrator acquaintance. In R. Iconcis (Ed.), *Rape myth acceptance in college students: A literature review* (*Contemporary Issues in Education Research—Second Quarter, 1,* 47–52).

Bendixen, M., Hendriksen, M., & Nøstdahl, R. K. A. (2014). Toward rape and attribution of responsibility to rape victims in a Norwegian community sample. *Nordic Psychology, 66,* 168–186.

Benedet, J. (2014). Sexual assault cases at the Alberta Court of Appeal: The roots of *Ewanchuk* and the unfinished revolution. *Alberta Law Review, 52,* 127–144.

Benton, T. R., Ross, D. F., Bradshaw, E., Thomas, W. N., & Bradshaw, G. S. (2006). Eyewitness memory is still not common sense: Comparing jurors, judges and law enforcement to eyewitness experts. *Applied Cognitive Psychology, 20,* 115–129.

Berliner, L., & Conte, J. R. (1995). The effects of disclosure and intervention on sexually abused children. *Child Abuse & Neglect, 19*(3), 371–384.

Bettenay, C., Ridley, A. M., Henry, L. A., & Crane, L. (2014). Cross-examination: The testimony of children with and without intellectual disabilities. *Applied Cognitive Psychology, 28,* 204–214.

Bieneck, S., & Krahé, B. (2011). Blaming the victim and exonerating the perpetrator in cases of rape and robbery: Is there a double standard? *Journal of Interpersonal Violence, 26,* 1785–1797.

Blackstone, W. (1765–1769). *Commentaries on the laws of England* (Book 4, Chapter 15 of Offenses Against the Persons of Individuals). Oxford: The Clarendon Press.

Blackwell, S. (2008, November). *Child sexual abuse on trial in New Zealand.* Paper presented at the Criminal Law Symposium, Auckland, New Zealand.

Blackwell, S., & Seymour, F. (2014). Prediction of jury verdicts in child sexual assault trials. *Psychiatry, Psychology & Law, 21,* 567–576.

Bleecker, E. T., & Murnen, S. K. (2005). Fraternity membership, the display of degrading sexual images of women, and rape myth acceptance. *Sex Roles, 53,* 487–493.

Bloom, B., Owen, B., & Covington, S. (2003). *Gender-responsive strategies: Research, practice, and guiding principles for women offenders.* Washington, DC: National Institute of Corrections.

Blume, J. H., Johnson, S. L., & Paavola, E. C. (2007). Every juror wants a story: Narrative relevance, third party guilt and the right to present a defense. *American Criminal Law Review, 44,* 1069–1113.

Bolitho, J., & Freeman, K. (2016). *The use and effectiveness of restorative justice in criminal justice systems following child sexual abuse or comparable harms.* Sydney: Royal Commission into Institutional Responses to Child Sexual Abuse.

Bollingmo, G. C., Wessel, E. M., Eilertsen, D. E., & Magnussen, S. (2008). Credibility of the emotional witness: A study of ratings by police investigators. *Psychology, Crime & Law, 14,* 29–40.

Bollingmo, G. C., Wessel, E. M., Sandhold, Y., Eilertsen, D. E., & Magnussen, S. (2009). The effect of biased and non-biased information on judgments of witness credibility. *Psychology, Crime & Law, 15,* 61–71.

Bongiorno, R., McKimmie, B. M., & Masser, B. M. (2016). The selective use of rape-victim stereotypes to protect culturally similar perpetrators. *Psychology of Women Quarterly, 40,* 398–413.

Boniface, D. J. (1994). Ruining a good boy for the sake of a bad girl: False accusation theory in sexual offences, and New South Wales Limitations Periods—Gone but not forgotten. *Current Issues in Criminal Justice, 6,* 54–75.

Bordini, S., & Sperb, T. M. (2013). Sexual double standard: A review of the literature between 2001 and 2010. *Sexuality & Culture, 17,* 686–704.

Bornstein, B. H., & Greene, E. (2011). Jury decision making: Implications for and from psychology. *Current Directions in Psychological Science, 20,* 63–67.

Bottoms, B. L. (1993). Individual differences in perceptions of child sexual assault victims. In G. S. Goodman & B. L. Bottoms (Eds.), *Child victims, child witnesses: Understanding and improving testimony* (pp. 229–261). New York: Guildford Press.

Bottoms, B. L., Golding, J., Stevenson, M., Wiley, T., & Yozwiak, J. (2007). Summary of factors affecting juror decisions in child sexual assault cases. In M. Toglia, J. Read, D. Ross, & R. Lindsay (Eds.), *Handbook of eyewitness psychology*. London: Lawrence Erlbaum Associates.

Bottoms, B. L., & Goodman, G. S. (1994). Perceptions of children's credibility in sexual assault cases. *Journal of Applied Social Psychology, 24,* 702–732.

Bottoms, B. L., Peter-Hagene, L. C., Stevenson, M. C., Wiley, T. R. A., Schneider-Mitchell, T., & Goodman, G. S. (2014). Explaining gender differences in jurors' reactions to child sexual assault cases. *Behavioral Sciences & the Law, 32,* 789–812.

Bovin, M. J., Jager-Hyman, S., Gold, S. D., Marx, B. P., & Sloan, D. M. (2008). Tonic immobility mediates the influence of peritraumatic fear and perceived inescapability on posttraumatic stress symptom severity among sexual assault survivors. *Journal of Traumatic Stress, 21,* 402–409.

Bowden, P., Henning, T., & Plater, D. (2014). Balancing fairness to victims, society and defendants in the cross-examination of vulnerable witnesses: An impossible triangulation, *Melbourne University Law Review, 37*, 539–584.

Boyd, R., & Hopkins, A. (2010). Cross-examination of child sexual assault complainants: Concerns about the application of s 41 of the Evidence Act. *Criminal Law Journal, 34,* 149–166.

Bracton, H. (1268/1968). *Bracton on the laws and customs of England* (S. Thorne, Trans.). Cambridge, MA: Harvard University Press.

Bradshaw, T. L., & Marks, A. E. (1990). Beyond a reasonable doubt: Factors that influence the legal disposition of child sexual abuse cases. *Crime & Delinquency, 36*, 276–285.

Braithwaite, J. (2002). Setting standards for restorative justice. *British Journal of Criminology, 42*, 563–577.

Braun, K. (2013). Legal representation for sexual assault victims—Possibilities for law reform. *Current Issues Criminal Justice, 25*, 819–837.

Brehmer, B. (1994). The psychology of linear judgment models. *Acta Psychologica, 87*, 137–154.

Brennan, M. (1994). Cross examinations of child witnesses. *International Journal of the Semiotics of Law, VII*, 51–73.

Brennan, M. (1995). The discourse of denial: Cross-examining child victim witnesses. *Journal of Pragmatics, 23*, 71–91.

Brewin, C. R., Rose, S., Andrews, B., Green, J., Tata, P., McEvedy, C., … Foa, E. B. (2002). Brief screening instrument for post-traumatic stress disorder. *British Journal of Psychiatry, 181*, 158–162.

Bricknell, S. (2008). *Trends in violent crime* (Research Paper No. 359). Australian Institute of Criminology.

Bröder, A. (2000). Assessing the empirical validity of the 'take-the-best' heuristic as a model of human probabilistic inference. *Journal of Experimental Psychology: Learning, Memory, and Cognition, 26*, 1332–1346.

Bronitt, S. (1998). The rules of recent complaint: Rape myths and the legal construction of the 'reasonable' rape victim. In P. Easteal (ed), *Balancing The Scales, Rape Law Reform and Australian Culture* (pp. 41–59). Sydney: Federation Press.

Brown, J. (2011). We mind and we care but have things changed? Assessment of progress in the reporting, investigating and prosecution of allegations of rape. *Journal of Sexual Aggression, 17*, 263–272.

Brown, J. D., & L'Engle, K. L. (2009). X-rated: Sexual attitudes and behaviors associated with U.S. early adolescents' exposure to sexually explicit media. *Communication Research, 36*, 129–151.

Browne, A., Miller, B., & Maguin, E. (1999). Prevalence and severity of lifetime physical and sexual victimization among incarcerated women. *International Journal of Law and Psychiatry, 22*, 301–322.

Bryan, A. E. B., Norris, J., Abdallah, D. A., Stappenbeck, C. A., Morrison, D. M., Davis, K. C., … Zawacki, T. (2016). Longitudinal change in women's sexual victimization experiences as a function of alcohol consumption and sexual victimization history: A latent transition analysis. *Psychology of Violence, 6,* 271–279.

Buchwald, E., Fletcher, P., & Roth, M. (1993). Preamble. In E. Buchwald, P. Fletcher, & M. Roth (Eds.), *Transforming a rape culture* (p. vii). Minneapolis: Milkweed Editions.

Buhi, E. R. (2005). Reliability reporting practices in rape myth research. *Journal of School Health, 75,* 63–66.

Bumby, K. M., & Maddox, M. C. (1999). Judges' knowledge about sexual offenders, difficulties presiding over sexual offense cases, and opinions on sentencing, treatment, and legislation. *Sexual Abuse, 11,* 305–315.

Bunting, L. (2008). Sexual offences against children: An exploration of attrition in the Northern Ireland criminal justice system. *Child Abuse & Neglect, 32,* 1109–1118.

Bunting, L. (2014). Exploring the influence of reporting delay on criminal justice outcomes: Comparing child and adult reporters of childhood sexual abuse. *Journal of Child Sexual Abuse, 23,* 577–594.

Burgin, R., & Flynn, A. (2019). Women's behavior as implied consent: Male "reasonableness" in Australian rape law. *Criminology & Criminal Justice,* online. https://doi.org/10.1177/1748895819880953.

Burt, M. R. (1980). Cultural myths and supports for rape. *Journal of Personality & Society, 38,* 217–230.

Burton, M., Evans, R., & Sanders, A. (2007). Vulnerable and intimated witnesses and the adversarial process in England and Wales. *International Journal of Evidence and Proof, 11,* 1–23.

Butler, J. (1990). *Gender trouble: Feminism and the subversion of identity.* London: Routledge.

Butler, J. (1993). *Bodies that matter: On the discursive limits of sex.* London: Routledge.

Butler, L. D., Critelli, F. M., & Rinfrette, E. S. (2011). Trauma-informed care and mental health. *Directions in Psychiatry, 31,* 177–192.

Campbell, R. (2008). The psychological impact of rape victims. *American Psychologist, 63,* 702–717.

Campbell, R., Wasco, S. M., Ahrens, C. E., Self, T., & Barnes, H. E. (2001). Preventing the 'second rape': Rape survivors' experiences with community service provider. *Journal of Interpersonal Violence, 16,* 1239–1259.

Caprioli, S., & Crenshaw, D. A. (2017). The culture of silencing child victims of sexual abuse: Implications for child witnesses in court. *Journal of Humanistic Psychology, 57,* 190–209.

Carlson, C. (2014). 'This Bitch Got Drunk and Did This to Herself': Proposed evidentiary reforms to limit 'victim blaming' and 'perpetrator pardoning' in rape by intoxication trials in California. *Wisconsin Journal of Law, Gender & Society, 29,* 285–315.

Carlson, K. A., & Russo, J. E. (2001). Biased interpretation of evidence by mock jurors. *Journal of Experimental Psychology: Applied, 7,* 91–103.

Caruso, D. (2012). Proposed reforms for the cross-examination of child witnesses and the reception and treatment of their evidence. *Journal of Judicial Administration, 21,* 191–236.

Carroll, M. H., Rosenstein, J. E., Foubert, J. D., Clark, M. D., & Korenman, L. M. (2016). Rape myth acceptance: A comparison of military service academy and civilian fraternity and sorority students. *Military Psychology, 28,* 306–317.

Cashmore, J. (1995). The prosecution of child sexual assault: A survey of NSW DPP solicitors. *The Australian and New Zealand Journal of Criminology, 28,* 32–54.

Cashmore, J. (2002). Innovative procedures for child witnesses. In H. L. Westcott, G. M. Davies, & R. Bull (Eds.), *Children's testimony: A handbook of psychological research and forensic practice.* Chichester: Wiley.

Cashmore, J., & Bussey, K. (1995). *The evidence of children.* Sydney: Judicial Commission of New South Wales.

Cashmore, J., Katz, I., Shackel, R., & Valentine, K. (2017). *Evaluation of the child sexual offence evidence pilot process evaluation report.* Sydney: Social Policy Research Centre.

Cashmore, J., Taylor, A., & Parkinson, P. (2017). The characteristics of reports to the police of child sexual abuse and the likelihood of cases proceeding to prosecution after delays in reporting. *Child Sexual Abuse & Neglect, 74,* 49–61.

Cashmore, J., Taylor, A., Shackel, R., & Parkinson, P. (2016). *The impact of delayed reporting on the prosecution and outcomes of child sexual abuse cases.* Sydney: Royal Commission into Institutional Responses to Child Sexual Abuse.

Cashmore, J., & Trimboli, L. (2005). *An evaluation of the NSW child sexual assault specialist jurisdiction.* Sydney: NSW Bureau of Crime Statistics and Research.

Cashmore, J., & Trimboli, L. (2006). Child sexual assault trials: A survey of juror perceptions. *Crime and Justice Bulletin, 102,* 1–20.

Cecil, C. A. M., Viding, E., Fearon, P., Glaser, D., & McCrory, E. J. (2017). Disentangling the mental health impact of childhood abuse and neglect. *Child Abuse & Neglect, 63,* 106–119.

Chaiken, S. (1980). Heuristic versus systematic information processing and the use of source versus message cues in persuasion. *Journal of Personality & Social Psychology, 39,* 752–766.

Chaiken, S., & Trope, Y. (1990). *Dual-process theories in social psychology*. New York: Guilford Press.

Chaiken, S. & Trope, Y. (Eds.). (1999). *Dual-process theories in social psychology*. New York: Guilford Press.

Chalmers, J. (2014). Independent legal representation for complainers in sexual offence cases. In J. Chalmers, F. Leverick, & A. Shaw (Eds.), *Post corroboration safeguards review report of the academic expert group* (pp. 185–189). Edinburgh: The Scottish Government.

Chapman, L. (2006). *Review of South Australia rape and sexual assault law: Discussion paper*. Adelaide: Government of South Australia.

Charles, C. (2012). *Special measures for vulnerable and intimidated witnesses: Research exploring the decisions and actions taken by prosecutors in a sample of CPS case files*. London: Crown Prosecution Service.

Charman, E. A., Honess, T. M., & Levi, M. (2001). Juror competence and processing style in making sense of complex trial information. In R. Roesch, R. R. Corrado, & R. J. Dempster (Eds.), *Psychology in the courts: International advances in knowledge* (pp. 83–96). London: Routledge.

Chen, L. P., Murad, M. H., Paras, M. L., Colbenson, K. M., Sattler, A. L., Goranson, E. N., … Zirakzadeh, A. (2010). Sexual abuse and lifetime diagnosis of psychiatric disorders: Systematic review and meta-analysis. *Mayo Clinic Proceedings, 85,* 618–629.

Chen, S., & Chaiken, S. (1999). The heuristic-systematic model in its broader context. In S. Chaiken & Y. Trope (Eds.), *Dual-process theories in social psychology* (pp. 73–96). New York: Guilford Press.

Chen, S., Shechter, D., & Chaiken, S. (1996). Getting at the truth or getting along: Accuracy versus impression-motivated heuristic and systematic processing. *Journal of Personality and Social Psychology, 71,* 262–275.

Children's Commissioner. (2015). *Protecting children from harm: A critical assessment of child sexual abuse in the family network*. London: Children's Commissioner. https://www.childrenscommissioner.gov.uk/wp-content/uploads/2017/06/Protecting-children-from-harm-full-report.pdf.

Clark, H. L., & Nightingale, N. N. (1997). When jurors consider recovered memory cases: Effects of victim and juror gender. *Journal of Offender Rehabilitation, 25,* 87–104.

Clemens, F., Granhag, P. A., Strömwall, L. A., Vrij, A., Landström, S., ad Hjelmsäter, E. R., & Hartwig, M. (2010). Skulking around the dinosaur: Eliciting cues to children's deception via strategic disclosure of evidence. *Applied Cognitive Psychology, 24,* 925–940.

Cleveland, K. C., Quas, J. A., & Lyon, T. D. (2016). Valence, implicated actor, and children's acquiescence to false suggestions. *Journal of Applied Development Psychology, 43,* 1–7.

Clifford, B. (2003). Methodology: Law's adopting and adapting to psychology's methods and findings. In D. Carson & R. Bull (Eds.), *Handbook of psychology in legal contexts* (pp. 605–624). Chichester: Wiley.

Cohn, E. S., Dupuis, E. C., & Brown, T. M. (2009). In the eye of the beholder: Do behaviour and character affect victim and perpetrator responsibility for acquaintance rape? *Journal of Applied Social Psychology, 39,* 1513–1535.

Cole, E. (2018, January 8). Can juries deliver justice to sexual assault victims? *The Sydney Morning Herald*. http://www.smh.com.au/comment/can-juries-deliver-justice-to-sexual-assault-victims-20171220-h0870m.html. Accessed 16 January 2018.

Coles, J., Lee, A., Taft, A., Mazza, D., & Loxton, D. (2015). Childhood sexual abuse and its association with adult physical and mental health: Results from a national cohort of young Australian women. *Journal of Interpersonal Violence, 30,* 1929–1944.

Collier, R. (1998). *Masculinities, crime and criminology: Men, heterosexuality and the criminal(ised) other*. London: Sage.

Collins, K., Harker, N., & Antonopoulos, G. A. (2017). The impact of the registered intermediary on adults' perceptions of child witnesses: Evidence from a mock cross-examination. *European Journal of Criminal Policy and Research, 23,* 211–225.

Collin-Vézina, D., Daigneault, I., & Hébert, M. (2013). Lessons learned from child sexual abuse research: Prevalence, outcomes, and preventive strategies. *Child and Adolescent Psychiatry and Mental Health, 7,* 1753–2000.

Colton, M., & Vanstone, M. (1996). *Betrayal of trust: Sexual abuse by men who work with children—In their own words*. London: Free Association Books.

Comiskey, M. (2010). Initiating dialogue about jury comprehension of legal concepts: Can the 'stagnant pool' be revitalised? *Queen's Law Journal, 35,* 625–677.

Connell, M. (2015). Expert testimony in sexual assault cases: Alcohol intoxication and memory. *International Journal of Law and Psychiatry, 42–43,* 98–105.

Connolly, D. A., Chong, K., Coburn, P. I., & Lutgens, D. (2015). Factors associated with delays of days to decades to criminal prosecutions of child sexual abuse. *Behavioral Sciences & the Law, 33,* 546–560.

Connolly, D. A., Coburn, P. I., & Chong, K. (2017). Twenty-six years prosecuting historical child sexual abuse cases: Has anything changed? *Psychology, Public Policy, and Law, 23,* 166–177.

Cook, K. (2011). Rape investigation and prosecution: Stuck in the mud? *Journal of Sexual Aggression, 17,* 250–262.

Cooper, A., Quas, J. A., & Cleveland, K. C. (2014). The emotional child witness: Effects on juror decision-making. *Behavioral Science & the Law, 32,* 813–828.

Cooper, P., & Mattison, M. (2017). Intermediaries, vulnerable people and the quality of evidence: An international comparison of three versions of the English intermediary model. *The International Journal of Evidence & Proof, 21,* 351–370.

Copeland, W., Keeler, G. P., Angold, A., & Costello, E. J. (2007). Traumatic events and posttraumatic stress in childhood. *Archives of General Psychiatry, 64,* 577–584.

Cossins, A. (1999). Defying reality: Child sexual assault and the delay in complaint rule. *Current Issues in Criminal Justice, 11,* 17–34.

Cossins, A. (2000). *Masculinities, sexualities and child sexual abuse*. The Hague: Kluwer Law International.

Cossins, A. (2001). Complaints of child sexual abuse: Too easy to make or too difficult to prove? *Australian and New Zealand Journal of Criminology, 34,* 149–168.

Cossins, A. (2002). The hearsay rule and delayed complaints of child sexual abuse: The law and the evidence. *Psychiatry, Psychology and Law, 9,* 163–176.

Cossins, A. (2003). Saints, sluts and sexual assault: Rethinking the relationship between sex, race and gender. *Social and Legal Studies, 12,* 77–103.

Cossins, A. (2004). Is there a case for the legal representation of children in sexual assault trials? *Current Issues in Criminal Justice, 16,* 1–23.

Cossins, A. (2006a). Prosecuting child sexual assault cases: Are vulnerable witness protections enough? *Current Issues in Criminal Justice, 18,* 299–317.

Cossins, A. (2006b). Prosecuting child sexual assault cases: To specialise or not, that is the question. *Current Issues in Criminal Justice, 18,* 318–342.

Cossins, A. (2008). Children, sexual abuse and suggestibility: What laypeople think they know and what the literature tells us. *Psychiatry, Psychology and Law, 15*, 153–170.

Cossins, A. (2009). Cross-examination in child sexual assault trials: Evidentiary safeguard or an opportunity to confuse? *Melbourne University Law Review, 33*, 68–104.

Cossins, A. (2010a). *Alternative models for prosecuting child sex offences in Australia*. Sydney: National Child Sexual Assault Reform Committee, UNSW.

Cossins, A. (2010b). Time out for *Longman*: Myths, science and the common law. *Melbourne University Law Review, 34*, 69–105.

Cossins, A. (2011a). Similar facts and consent in sexual assault cases: Filling in the gap left by the high court in *Phillips*. *Monash University Law Review, 37*, 47–88.

Cossins, A. (2011b). The behaviour of persistent sex offenders: Implications for the prosecution of child sex offences in joint trials. *Melbourne University Law Review, 35*, 821–864.

Cossins, A. (2013a). Expert witness evidence in sexual assault trials: Questions, answers and law reform in Australia and England. *International Journal of Evidence and Proof, 17*, 74–113.

Cossins, A. (2013b). The legacy of the *Makin* case 120 years on: Legal fictions, circular reasoning and some solutions. *Sydney Law Review, 35*, 731–759.

Cossins, A. (2015). *Female criminality: Infanticide, moral panics and the female body*. Basingstoke, UK: Palgrave Macmillan.

Cossins, A., & Plummer, M. (2016). Masculinity and sexual abuse: Explaining the transition from victim to offender. *Men and Masculinities, 21*, 163–188.

Cossins, A. (2019). Why her behaviour is still on trial: The absence of context in the modernisation of the substantive law on consent. *The University of New South Wales Law Journal, 42*, 462–499.

Cossins, A. (2020). Feminist criminology in a time of 'digital feminism': Can the #MeToo Movement create fundamental cultural change? In S. Walklate, K. Fitz-gibbon, J. M. Maher & J. McCulloch (Eds.), *Emerald handbook in criminology, feminism and social change* (pp. 69–94). Bingley, UK: Emerald Publishing.

Cossins, A., & Goodman-Delahunty, J. (2013). Misconceptions or expert evidence in child sexual assault trials: Enhancing justice and jurors' 'common sense'. *Journal of Judicial Administration, 22*, 171–190.

Cossins, A., Goodman-Delahunty, J., & O'Brien, K. (2009). Uncertainty and misconceptions about child sexual abuse: Implications for the criminal justice system. *Psychiatry, Psychology & Law, 16,* 435–452.

Cossins, A., Jayakody, A., Norrie, C., & Parkinson, P. (2016). The Role of photographic and video documentation in the investigation and prosecution of child sexual assault. *Journal of Law and Medicine, 23,* 925–937.

Cossins, A., & Rowden, E. (2020). The child sexual assault trial: Redesigning courtroom spaces according to trauma informed principles. In K. Duncanson & E. Henderson (Eds.), *Courthouse design and social justice.* London: Routledge (in press).

Courthouse Dogs Foundation. (2015). *Facility dogs at Children's Advocacy Centers and in legal proceedings: Best practice.* Courthouse Dogs Foundation, Western Legal Advocacy Center and Office of Juvenile Justice and Delinquency Prevention.

Cowan, G., & Quinton, W. (1997). Cognitive style and attitudinal correlates of the perceived causes of rape scale. *Pyschology of Women Quarterly, 21,* 227–245.

Cowan, S. (2007a). Freedom and capacity to make a choice: A feminist analysis of consent in the criminal law of rape. In V. Munro & C. Stychin (Eds.), *Sexuality and the law: Feminist engagements* (pp. 51–71). London: Routledge.

Cowan, S. (2007b). Choosing freely: Theoretically reframing the concept of consent. In R. Hunter & S. Cowan (Eds.), *Choice and consent: Feminist engagements with choice and subjectivity* (pp. 91–105). Abingdon: Routledge-Cavendish.

Cowart, M. (2004). Consent, speech act theory, and legal disputes. *Law and Philosophy, 23,* 495–525.

Coyle, I. R., Field, D., Wilson, P., Cuthbert, C., & Miller, G. (2009). Out of the mouths of babes: The case for an increased use of expert evidence in rebuttal of sexual abuse allegations by child witnesses. *Criminal Law Journal, 33,* 139–164.

Cox, P. (2016). *Violence against women: Additional analysis of the Australian Bureau Of Statistics' Personal Safety Survey, 2012: Key findings and future directions.* Sydney: Australian National Research Organisation for Women's Safety.

Crenshaw, D. A., Stella, L., O'Neill-Stephens, E., & Walsen, C. (2016). Developmentally and trauma-sensitive courtrooms. *Journal of Humanistic Psychology,* online, 1–7. https://doi.org/10.1177/0022167816641854.

Crime and Misconduct Commission Queensland. (2003). *An inquiry into the handling of sexual offences by the criminal justice system.* Brisbane: Crime and Misconduct Commission.

Criminal Justice and Sexual Offences Taskforce. (2006). *Responding to sexual assault: The way forward*. Sydney: Attorney-General's Department.

Cromer, L. D., & Freyd, J. J. (2007). What influences believing child abuse disclosures? The roles of depicted memory persistence, participant gender, trauma history and sexism. *Psychology of Women Quarterly, 2,* 227–245.

Cross, T. P., Whitcomb, D., & De Vos, E. (1994). Criminal justice outcomes of prosecution of child sexual abuse: A case flow analysis. *Child Abuse and Neglect, 19,* 1431–1442.

Crowe, J., & Sveinsson, L. (2017). Intimidation, consent and the role of holistic judgments in Australian rape law. *University of Western Australia Law Review, 42,* 136–154.

Crowley, M. J., O'Callaghan, M. G., & Ball, P. J. (1994). The juridical impact of psychological expert testimony in a simulated child sexual abuse trial. *Law and Human Behavior, 18,* 89–105.

Crown Prosecution Service. (2018a). *Rape and serious sexual offence prosecutions: Assessment of disclosure of unused material ahead of trial*. https://www.cps.gov.uk/sites/default/files/documents/publications/RASSO-prosecutions-Assessment-disclosure-unused-material-ahead-trial_0.pdf. Accessed 2 October 2019.

Crown Prosecution Service. (2018b). *The code for crown prosecutors.* https://www.cps.gov.uk/sites/default/files/documents/publications/Code-for-Crown-Prosecutors-October-2018.pdf.

Dahl, L. C., Brimacombe, C. A. E., & Lindsay, D. S. (2009). Investigating investigators: How presentation order influences participant–investigators' interpretations of eyewitness identification and alibi evidence. *Law and Human Behavior, 33,* 368–380.

Danielson, C. K., Macdonald, A., Amstadter, A. B., Hanson, R., de Arellano, M. A., Saunders, B. E., & Kilpatrick, D. G. (2010). Risky behaviors and depression in conjunction with—or in the absence of—lifetime history of PTSD among sexually abused adolescents. *Child Maltreatment, 15*(1), 101–107.

Daly, K. (1997). Different ways of conceptualizing sex/gender in feminist theory and their implications for criminology. *Theoretical Criminology, 1,* 25–51.

Daly, K. (2002). Restorative justice: The real story. *Punishment and Society, 4,* 55–79.

Daly, K. (2006). Restorative justice and sexual assault: An archival study of court and conference cases. *British Journal of Criminology, 46,* 334–356.

Daly, K. (2008). Setting the record straight and a call for radical change: A reply to Annie Cossins on 'Restorative justice and child sex offences'. *British Journal of Criminology, 48,* 557–566.

Daly, K. (2011). *Conventional and innovative justice responses to sexual violence* (Australian Centre for the Study of Sexual Assault, Issue 12). Melbourne: Australian Institute of Family Studies.

Daly, K. (2016). What is restorative justice? Fresh answers to a vexed question. *Victims & Offenders, 11,* 9–29.

Daly, K. (2017). Sexual violence and victims' justice interests. In E. Zinsstag & M. Keenan (Eds.), *Sexual violence and restorative justice: Legal social and therapeutic dimensions* (pp. 108–140). London: Routledge.

Daly, K., & Bouhours, B. (2010). Rape and attrition in the legal process: A comparative analysis of five countries. In M. Tonry (Ed.), *Crime and justice: A review of research.* Chicago: University of Chicago Press.

Daly, K., & Curtis-Fawley, S. (2006). Justice for victims of sexual assault: Court or conference? In K. Heimer & C. Kruttschnitt (Eds.), *Gender and crime: Patterns of victimization and offending* (pp. 230–265). New York: New York University Press.

Daly, K., Curtis-Fawley, S., & Bouhours, B. (2003). *Sexual offence cases finalised in court, by conference, and by formal caution in South Australia for young offenders, 1995–2001: Final report.* Brisbane: School of Criminology and Criminal Justice, Griffith University. https://www.gu.edu.au/school/ccj/kdaly.html.

Daly, K., & Wade, D. (2017). Sibling sexual violence and victims' justice interests: A comparison of youth conferencing and judicial sentencing. In E. Zinsstag & M. Keenan (Eds.), *Restorative responses to sexual violence: Legal social and therapeutic dimensions* (pp. 143–178). New York: Routledge.

Darby, A. (2004, July 1). Deal struck on paedophile database. *The Sydney Morning Herald*, p. 2.

Davies, E., Henderson, E., & Hanna, K. (2010). Facilitating children to give best evidence: Are there better ways to challenge children's testimony? *Criminal Law Journal, 34,* 347–362.

Davies, E., Henderson, E., & Seymour, F. W. (1997). In the interests of justice? The cross-examination of child complainants of sexual abuse in criminal proceedings. *Psychiatry, Psychology and Law, 4,* 217–229.

Davies, E., & Seymour, F. W. (1998). Questioning child complainants of sexual abuse: Analysis of criminal court transcripts in New Zealand. *Psychiatry, Psychology and Law, 5*, 47–61.

Davies, M. (1997). Taking the inside out: Sex and gender in the legal subject. In N. Naffine & R. J. Owens (Eds.), *Sexing the subject of law* (pp. 25–46). London: Sweet and Maxwell.

Davies, M., Austen, K., & Rogers, P. (2011). Sexual preference, gender, and blame attributions in adolescent sexual assault. *The Journal of Social Psychology, 151*, 592–607.

Davies, M., & Hudson, J. (2011). Judgments towards male and transgendered victims in a depicted stranger rape. *Journal of Homosexuality, 58*, 237–247.

Davies, M., Rogers, P., & Whitelegg, L. (2009). Effects of victim gender, victim sexual orientation, victim response and respondent gender on judgements of blame in a hypothetical adolescent rape. *Legal and Criminological Psychology, 14*, 331–338.

Davis, J. H. (1980). Group decision and procedural justice. In M. L. Fishbein (Ed.), *Progress in social psychology* (pp. 157–229). Hillsdale, NJ: Erlbaum.

Davis, K. C., George, W. H., & Norris, J. (2004). Women's responses to unwanted sexual advances: The role of alcohol and inhibition. *Psychology of Women Quarterly, 28*, 333–343.

Davis, K. C., Stoner, S. A., Norris, J., George, W. H., & Masters, N. T. (2009). Women's awareness of and discomfort with sexual assault cues: Effects of alcohol consumption and relationship type. *Violence Against Women, 15*, 1106–1125.

Dein, J. (2015, September). *Crown Court trial in 2015: A practical update*. https://www.25bedfordrow.com/cms/document/Madrid__edited_pdf.

De Jong, A. R., & Rose, M. (1991). Legal proof of child sexual abuse in the absence of physical evidence. *Pediatrics, 88*, 506–511.

DeKay, M. L. (2015). Predecisional information distortion and the self-fulfilling prophecy of early preferences in choice. *Current Directions in Psychological Science, 24*, 405–411.

Denham, S. A. (1998). *The Guilford series on special and emotional development: Emotional development in young children*. New York: Guilford Press.

Dent, H. (1992). The effects of age and intelligence on eyewitnessing ability. In H. Dent & R. Flin (Eds.), *Children as witnesses* (pp. 1–13). Chichester: Wiley.

Department for Women. (1996). *Heroines of fortitude: The experiences of women in court as victims of sexual assault*. Sydney: Department for Women.

Department of Justice. (2015). *Northern Ireland registered intermediaries schemes pilot project: Post project review*. https://www.justice-ni.gov.uk/sites/default/files/publications/doj/ri-post-project-reviewfeb15.pdf.

DePaulo, B. M., Lindsay, J. L., Malone, B. E., Muhlenbruck, L., Charlton, K., & Cooper, H. (2003). Cues to deception. *Psychological Bulletin, 129,* 74–118.

Devine, D. J. (2012). *Jury decision making: The state of the science*. New York: New York University Press.

Devine, D. J., Buddenbaum, J., Houp, S., Stolle, D. P., & Studebaker, N. (2007). Deliberation quality: A preliminary examination in criminal juries. *Journal of Empirical Legal Studies, 4,* 273–303.

Devine, D. J., Buddenbaum, J., Houp, S., Studebaker, N., & Stolle, D. P. (2009). Strength of evidence, extra evidentiary influence, and the liberation hypothesis: Data from the field. *Law and Human Behavior, 33,* 136–148.

Devine, D. J., & Caughlin, D. E. (2014). Do they matter? A meta-analytic investigation of individual characteristics and guilt judgments. *Psychology, Public Policy, and Law, 20,* 109–134.

Devine, D. J., Clayton, L. D., Dunford, B. D., Seying, R., & Pryce, J. (2001). Jury decision making: 45 years of empirical research on deliberating groups. *Psychology, Public Policy, and Law, 7,* 622–727.

Devine, D. J., Olafson, K. M., Jarvis, L. L., Bott, J. P., Clayton, L. D., & Wolfe, J. M. T. (2004). Explaining jury verdicts: Is leniency bias for real? *Journal of Applied Social Psychology, 34,* 2069–2098.

Dhami, M. K. (2003). Psychological models of professional decision making. *Psychological Science, 14,* 175–180.

Dhami, M. K., & Ayton, P. (2001). Bailing and jailing the fast and frugal way. *Journal of Behavioral Decision Making, 14,* 141–168.

DiBennardo, R. A. (2018). Ideal victims and monstrous offenders: How the news media represent sexual predators. *Socius: Sociological Research for a Dynamic World*. Open Epub. https://doi.org/10.1177/2378023118802512.

Dignan, J. (2005). *Understanding victims and restorative justice*. Maidenhead: Open University Press.

Dinos, S., Burrowes, N., Hammond, K., & Cunliffe, C. (2015). A systematic review of juries' assessment of rape victims: Do rape myths impact on juror decision-making? *International Journal of Law, Crime and Justice, 43,* 36–49.

Dioso-Villa, R. (2015). Is there evidence of a 'CSI-effect'? In K. J. Strom & M. J. Hickman (Eds.), *Forensic science and the administration of justice: Critical issues and directions*. Thousand Oaks, CA: Sage.

Dobinson, I., & Townsley, L. (2008). Sexual assault law reform in NSW: Issues of consent and objective fault. *Criminal Law Journal, 32,* 152–172.

Donnelly, H. (2007). Delay and the credibility of complainants in sexual assault proceedings. *Judicial Officers' Bulletin, 19,* 17–23.

Donnelly, C. L., March, J. S., & Amaya-Jackson, L. (2006). Posttraumatic stress disorder. In M. K. Dulcan & J. M. Wiener (Eds.), *Essentials of child and adolescent psychiatry* (pp. 479–504). Arlington, VA: American Psychiatric Publishing.

Dowler, K. (2006). Sex, lies, and videotape: The presentation of sex crime in local television news. *Journal of Criminal Justice, 34,* 383–392.

Drabble, L. A., Jones, S., & Brown, V. (2013). Advancing trauma-informed systems change in a family drug treatment court context. *Journal of Social Work Practice in the Addictions, 13,* 91–113.

Driesmans, K., Vandenbosch, L., & Eggermont, S. (2015). Playing a videogame with a sexualized female character increases adolescents' rape myth acceptance and tolerance toward sexual harassment. *Games for Health Journal, 4,* 91–94.

Dubowski, K. M. (1977). *Manual for analysis of ethanol in biological liquids: Final report.* Washington, DC: Department of Transportation, National Highway Traffic Safety Administration.

Dulcan, M. K., & Wiener, J. M. (2006). *Essentials of child and adolescent psychiatry*. Arlington, VA: American Psychiatric Publishing.

Du Mont, J., & White, D. (2007). *The uses and impacts of medico-legal evidence in sexual assault cases: A global review.* Geneva: World Health Organization. http://www.svri.org/sites/default/files/attachments/2016-01-19/medico.pdf.

Du Mont, J., & White, D. (2013). Barriers to the effective use of medico-legal findings in sexual assault cases worldwide. *Qualitative Health Research, 23,* 1228–1239.

Du Toit, L. (2007). The conditions of consent. In R. Hunter & S. Cowan (Eds.), *Choice and consent: Feminist engagements with choice and subjectivity* (pp. 58–73). Abingdon: Routledge-Cavendish.

Dwyer, T., Easteal, P., & Hopkins, A. (2012). Law and the media in New South Wales. *Alternative Law Journal, 37,* 249–253.

Eagly, A. H., & Chaiken, S. (1993). Process theories of attitude formation and change: The elaboration likelihood and heuristic-systematic models. In A. H. Eagly & S. Chaiken (Eds.), *The psychology of attitudes* (pp. 303–350). Fort Worth, TX: Harcourt, Brace, & Janovich.

Easteal, P. (2011). Sexual assault law in Australia: Contextual challenges and changes. In N. Westmarland & G. Gangoli (Eds.), *International approaches to rape* (pp. 13–34). Bristol: The Policy Press.

Eastwood, C., & Patton, W. (2002). *The experiences of child complainants of sexual abuse in the criminal justice system*. Brisbane: Queensland University of Technology. http://www.criminologyresearchcouncil.gov.au/reports/eastwood.pdf.

Eastwood, C., Kift, S., & Grace, R. (2006). Attrition in child sexual assault cases: Why Lord Chief Justice Hale got it wrong. *Journal of Judicial Administration, 16,* 81–91.

Edwards, K. M., Turchik, J. A., Dardis, C. M., Reynolds, N., & Gidycz, C. A. (2011). Rape myths: History, individual and institutional-level presence, and implications for change. *Sex Roles, 65,* 761–773.

Edwards, S. R., Bradshaw, K. A., & Hinsz, V. B. (2014). Denying rape but endorsing forceful intercourse: Exploring differences among responders. *Violence and Gender, 1,* 188–193.

Ehlers, A., & Clark, D. M. (2000). A cognitive model of posttraumatic stress disorder. *Behaviour Research and Therapy, 38,* 319–345.

Ehlers, A., Clark, D. M., Hackmann, A., McManus, F., & Fennell, M. (2005). Cognitive therapy for PTSD: Development and evaluation. *Behaviour Research and Therapy, 43,* 413–431.

Ehring, T., & Quack, D. (2010). Emotion regulation difficulties in trauma survivors: The role of trauma type and PTSD symptom severity. *Behavior Therapy, 41,* 587–598.

Eisenberg, T., Hannaford-Agor, P. L., Hans, V. P., Waters, N. L., Munsterman, G. T., Schwab, S. J., & Wells, M. T. (2005). Judge-jury agreement in criminal cases: A partial replication of Kalven and Zeisel's *The American Jury*. *Journal of Empirical Studies, 2,* 171–206.

Ekman, P., O'Sullivan, M., & Frank, M. G. (1999). A few can catch a liar. *Psychological Science, 10,* 263–266.

Elliott, D. E. (2003). *Difficult conversations: A training curriculum on becoming trauma-informed*. Holyoke, MA: Franklin County Women's Research Project.

Elliott, D. E., Bjelajac, P., Fallot, R. D., Markoff, L. S., & Reed, B. G. (2005). Trauma-informed or trauma-denied: Principles and implementation of trauma-informed services for women. *Journal of Community Psychology, 33,* 461–477.

Elliott, S. (2015). The new regime for vulnerable witnesses. *The Criminal Appeals Bulletin*, Issue 3. http://doughty-street-chambers.newsweaver.com/Appeals/5z2g7ifzdun?a=2&p=698889&t=174048.

Ellison, L. (1999). The protection of vulnerable witnesses in court: An Anglo-Dutch comparison. *International Journal of Evidence and Proof, 3,* 29–43.

Ellison, L., & Munro, V. E. (2009a). Of 'normal sex' and 'real rape': Exploring the use of socio-sexual scripts in (mock) jury deliberation. *Social and Legal Studies, 18,* 291–312.

Ellison, L., & Munro, V. E. (2009b). Reacting to rape: Exploring mock jurors' assessments of complainant credibility. *British Journal of Criminology, 49,* 202–219.

Ellison, L., & Munro, V. E. (2009c). Turning mirrors into windows? Assessing the impact of (mock) juror education in rape trials. *British Journal of Criminology, 49,* 363–383.

Ellison, L., & Munro, V. E. (2010). Getting to (not) guilty: Examining jurors' deliberative processes in, and beyond, the context of a mock rape trial. *Social and Legal Studies, 30,* 74–97.

Ellison, L., & Munro, V. E. (2013). Better the devil you know? 'Real Rape' stereotypes and the relevance of a previous relationship in (Mock) juror deliberations. *The International Journal of Evidence & Proof, 17*, 299–322.

Ellison, L., & Munro, V. E. (2014). A 'special' delivery? Exploring the impact of screens, live-links and video-recorded evidence on mock juror deliberation in rape trials. *Social & Legal Studies, 23,* 3–29.

Ellsworth, P. C. (1989). Are twelve heads better than one? *Law and Contemporary Problems, 52,* 205–224.

Elmi, M. H., Daignault, I. V., & Hébert, M. (2018). Child sexual abuse victims as witnesses: The influence of testifying on their recovery. *Child Abuse & Neglect, 86,* 22–32.

End Violence Against Women Coalition. (2018). *Attitudes to sexual consent research.* https://www.endviolenceagainstwomen.org.uk/wp-content/uploads/1-Attitudes-to-sexual-consent-Research-findings-FINAL.pdf.

Epstein, S. (2003). Cognitive-experiential self-theory of personality. In T. Milton & M. J. Lerner (Eds.), *Comprehensive handbook of psychology, personality and social psychology—Vol. 5* (pp. 159–184). Hoboken, NJ: Wiley.

Erez, E., Kilching, M., & Wemmers, J.-A. (2011). *Therapeutic jurisprudence and victim participation in justice: International perspectives.* Durham: Carolina Academic Press.

Evans, A. D., Stolzenberg, S. N., Lee, K., & Lyon, T. D. (2014). Children's difficulty with indirect speech acts: Implications for questioning child witnesses. *Behavioral Sciences & the Law, 32,* 775–788.

Eyssel, F., & Bohner, G. (2011). Schema effects of rape myth acceptance on judgments of guilt and blame in rape cases: The role of perceived entitlement to judge. *Journal of Interpersonal Violence, 26,* 1579–1605.

Fallot, R. D., & Harris, M. (2008). Trauma-informed approaches to systems to care. *Trauma Psychology Newsletter, 3,* 6–7.

Feinstein, J. S., Adolphs, R., Damasio, A., & Tranel, D. (2011). The human amygdala and the induction and experience of fear. *Current Biology, 21,* 34–38.

Feild, H. S. (1979). Rape trials and jurors' decisions: A psycholegal analysis of effects of victim, defendant, and case characteristics. *Law and Human Behavior, 3,* 261–284.

Feldman-Summers, S., & Lindner, K. (1976). Perceptions of victims and defendants in criminal assault cases. *Correctional Psychologist, 3,* 135–150.

Fergusson, D. M., Boden, J. M., & Horwood, L. J. (2008). Exposure to childhood sexual and physical abuse and adjustment in early adulthood. *Child Abuse & Neglect, 32,* 607–619.

Fergusson, D. M., McLeod, G. F. H., & Horwood, L. J. (2013). Childhood sexual abuse and adult developmental outcomes: Findings from a 30-year longitudinal study in New Zealand. *Child Abuse & Neglect, 37,* 664–674.

Ferris, A. L., Smith, S. W., Greenberg, B. S., & Smith, S. L. (2007). The content of reality dating shows and viewer perceptions of dating. *Journal of Communications, 57,* 490–510.

Finch, E., & Munro, V. E. (2004, October). The Sexual Offences Act 2003: Intoxicated consent and drug-assisted rape revisited. *Criminal Law Review,* 789–802.

Finkel, N. J., Burke, J. E., & Chavez, L. J. (2000). Commonsense judgments of infanticide: Murder, manslaughter, madness, or miscellaneous? *Psychology, Public Policy, and Law, 6,* 1113–1137.

Finkelhor, D., Hotaling, G., Lewis, I. A., & Smith, C. (1990). Sexual abuse in a national survey of adult men and women: Prevalence, characteristics, and risk factors. *Child Abuse and Neglect, 14,* 19–28.

Firth, G. (2011). Not an invitation to rape: The Sexual Offences Act 2003, consent and the case of the 'drunken' victim. *Northern Ireland Legal Quarterly, 62,* 99–118.

Fischer, D. G., & McDonald, W. L. (1998). Characteristics of intrafamilial and extrafamilial child sexual abuse. *Child Abuse & Neglect, 22,* 915–929.

Fisher, R. P., Vrij, A., & Leins, D. A. (2013). Does testimonial inconsistency indicate memory inaccuracy and deception? Beliefs, empirical research, and theory. In B. S. Cooper, D. Griesel, & M. Ternes (Eds.), *Applied issues in investigative interviewing, eyewitness memory, and credibility assessment* (pp. 173–189). New York: Springer.

Fitzgerald, J. (2006). *The attrition of sexual offences from the New South Wales criminal justice system* (Crime and Justice Bulletin, No. 92). Sydney: NSW Bureau of Crime Statistics and Research.

Fleming, J. M. (1997). Prevalence of childhood sexual abuse in a community sample of Australian women. *Medical Journal of Australia, 166,* 65–68.

Flynn, A., & Henry, N. (2012). Disputing consent: The role of jury directions in Victoria. *Current Issues in Criminal Justice, 24,* 167–184.

Fogliati, R., & Bussey, K. (2014). The effects of cross-examination on children's reports of neutral and transgressive events. *Legal & Criminological Psychology, 19,* 296–315.

Fogliati, R., & Bussey, K. (2015). The effects of cross-examination on children's coached reports. *Psychology, Public Policy, and Law, 21,* 10–23.

Forbes, G. B., Adams-Curtis, L. E., & White, K. B. (2004). First and second-generation of measures of sexism, rape myths and related beliefs, and hostility towards women: Their inter-relationships and association with college students' experiences with dating aggression and sexual coercion. *Violence Against Women, 10,* 236–261.

Forbes, G. B., Adams-Curtis, L. E., Pakalka, A. H., & White, K. B. (2006). Dating aggression, sexual coercion, and aggression-supporting attitudes among college men as a function of participation in aggressive high school sports. *Violence Against Women, 12,* 441–455.

Ford, J. D., & Blaustein, M. E. (2013). Systemic self-regulation: A framework for trauma-informed services in residential juvenile justice programs. *Journal of Family Violence, 28,* 665–677.

Forster, C. (2009). Sexual offences law reform in Pacific island countries: Replacing colonial norms with international good practices standards. *Melbourne University Law Review, 33,* 833–864.

Foubert, J. D., Brosi, M. W., & Bannon, R. S. (2011). Pornography viewing among fraternity men: Effects on bystander intervention, rape myth acceptance and behavioral intent to commit sexual assault. *Sexual Addiction and Compulsivity, 18,* 212–231.

Franuik, R., Seefelt, J. L., & Vandello, J. A. (2008). Prevalence of rape myths in headlines and their effects on attitudes towards rape. *Sex Roles, 58,* 790–801.

Frohmann, L. (1991). Discrediting victims' allegations of sexual assault: prosecutorial accounts of case rejections. *Social Problems, 38,* 213–226.

Frohmann, L., & Mertz, E. (1995). Legal reform and social construction: Violence, gender, and the law. *Law and Social Inquiry, 19,* 829–851.

Fusé, T., Forsyth, J. P., Marx, B., Gallup, G. G., & Weaver, S. (2007). Factor structure of the Tonic Immobility Scale in female sexual assault survivors: An exploratory and confirmatory factor analysis. *Journal of Anxiety Disorders, 21,* 265–283.

Gabbay, V., Oatis, M. D., Silva, R. R., & Hirsch, G. (2004). Epidemiological aspects of PTSD in children and adolescents. In R. R. Silva (Ed.), *Posttraumatic stress disorder in children and adolescents: Handbook* (pp. 1–17). New York: W. W. Norton.

Gabora, N. J., Spanos, N. P., & Joab, A. (1993). The effects of complainant age and expert psychological testimony in a simulated child sexual abuse trial. *Law and Human Behavior, 17,* 103–119.

Galliano, G., Noble, L. M., Travis, L. A., & Puechl, C. (1993). Victim reactions during rape/sexual assault: A preliminary study of the immobility response and its correlates. *Journal of Interpersonal Violence, 8,* 109–114.

Galvin, H. (1986). Shielding rape victims in the State and Federal Courts: A proposal for the second decade. *Minnesota Law Review, 70,* 763–916.

Gawronski, B., & Bodenhausen, G. V. (2014). Implicit and explicit evaluation: A brief review of the associative-propositional evaluation model. *Social and Personality Psychology Compass, 8,* 448–462.

Geddie, L., Fradin, S., & Beer, J. (2000). Child characteristics which impact accuracy of recall and suggestibility in preschoolers: Is age the best predictor? *Child Abuse & Neglect, 24,* 223–235.

George, W. H., Gournic, S. J., & McAfee, M. P. (1988). Perceptions of post-drinking female sexuality: Effects of gender, beverage choice, and drink payment. *Journal of Applied Social Psychology, 18,* 1295–1317.

Gerger, H., Kley, H., Bohner, G., & Siebler, F. (2007). The acceptance of modern myths about sexual aggression (AMMSA) scale: Development and validation in German and English. *Aggressive Behavior, 33,* 422–440.

Gerkey, L. (2016). Legal beagles, a silent minority: Therapeutic effects of facility dogs in the courtroom. *International Journal of Therapeutic Jurisprudence, 1,* 405–431.

Ghetti, S., Goodman, G. S., Eisen, M. L., Qin, J., & Davis, S. L. (2002). Consistency in children's reports of sexual and physical abuse. *Child Abuse and Neglect, 26,* 977–995.

Gibb, F. (2007, November 27). Juries to be warned of rape victim 'myth'. *The Times*. https://www.thetimes.co.uk/article/juries-to-be-warned-of-rape-victim-myth-3wv7k9dlrpc.

Gigerenzer, G., & Gaissmaier, W. (2011). Heuristic decision making. *Annual Review of Psychology, 62*, 451–482.

Gigerenzer, G., Todd, P. M., & The ABC Research Group (Eds.). (1999). *Simple heuristics that make us smart*. New York: Oxford University Press.

Girard, A. L., & Senn, C. Y. (2008). The role of the new 'date rape drugs' in attributions about date rape. *Journal of Interpersonal Violence, 23*, 3–20.

Glanvil, W. (1170/1965). *The treatise on the laws and customs of the realm of England* (G. Hall & G. Derek, Eds.). London: Nelson.

Godden-Rasul, N. (2017). Repairing the harms of rape of women through restorative justice. In E. Zinsstag & M. Keenan (Eds.), *Restorative responses to sexual violence: Legal social and therapeutic dimensions* (pp. 15–27). New York: Routledge.

Golding, J. M., Fryman, H. M., Marsil, D. F., & Yozwiak, J. A. (2003). Big girls don't cry: the effect of child witness demeanor on juror decisions in a child sexual abuse trial. *Child Abuse & Neglect, 27*, 1311–1321.

Golding, J. M., Bradshaw, G. G., Dunlap, E. E., & Hodell, E. C. (2007). The impact of mock jury gender composition on deliberations and conviction rates in a child sexual assault trial. *Child Maltreatment, 12*, 182–190.

Gobbo, J. A. (1970). *Cross on Evidence*. Sydney: Butterworths.

Goodman, G. S., & Melinder, A. (2007). Child witness research and forensic interviews of young children: A review. *Legal and Criminological Psychology, 12*, 1–19.

Goodman-Delahunty, J. (2014). *Profiling parental child sex abuse* (Trends and Issues in Crime and Criminal Justice, No. 465, pp. 1–8). Canberra: Australian Institute of Criminology.

Goodman-Delahunty, J., Cossins, A., & Martschuk, N. (2014). Persistent misconceptions about child sexual assault abuse: The impact of specialized educative information and deliberation on mock-jurors. In K. C. Haung (Ed.), *Proceedings of the third international conference of empirical studies of judicial systems: Citizen participation around the world*. Taipei, Taiwan: Academia Sinica.

Goodman-Delahunty, J., Cossins, A., & Martschuk, N. (2016). *Jury reasoning in joint and separate trials of institutional child sexual abuse: An empirical study*. Sydney: Royal Commission into Institutional Responses to Child Sexual Abuse.

Goodman-Delahunty, J., Cossins, A., & O'Brien, K. (2010). Enhancing the credibility of complainants in child sexual assault trials: The effect of expert evidence and judicial directions. *Behavioral Sciences & the Law, 28*, 769–783.

Goodman-Delahunty, J., Cossins, A., & O'Brien, K. (2011). A comparison of expert evidence and judicial directions to counter misconceptions in child sexual abuse trials. *Australian and New Zealand Journal of Criminology, 44*, 196–217.

Goodman-Delahunty, J., Martschuk, N., & Cossins, A. (2017a). What Australian jurors know and do not know about evidence of child sexual abuse. *Criminal Law Journal, 41*, 86–103.

Goodman-Delahunty, J., Martschuk, N., & Cossins, A. (2017b). Validation of the child sexual abuse knowledge questionnaire. *Psychology, Crime & Law, 23*, 391–412.

Goodman-Brown, T. B., Edelstein, R. S., Goodman, G. S., Jones, D. P. H., & Gordon, D. S. (2003). Why children tell: A model of children's disclosure of sexual abuse. *Child Abuse & Neglect, 27*, 525–540.

Goodman, G. S., Taub, E. P., Jones, D. P. H., England, P., Port, L. K., Rudy, L., Prado, L., Myers, J. E. B., & Melton, G. B. (1992). Testifying in criminal court: Emotional effects on child sexual assault victims. *Monographs of the Society for Research in Child Development, 57*, 1–159.

Gordon, S. G. (2015). *All together now: Using principles of group dynamics to train better jurors* (Scholarly Works, Paper 896, pp. 1–46). http://scholars.law.unlv.edu/facpub/896.

Grace, S., Lloyd, C., & Smith, L. (1992). *Rape: From recording to conviction.* London: Home Office Research Unit.

Gray, J. M. (2006). Rape myth beliefs and prejudiced instructions: Effects on decisions of guilt in a case of date rape. *Legal and Criminological Psychology, 75*, 75–80.

Gray-Eurom, K., Seaberg, D. C., & Wears, R. L. (2002). The prosecution of sexual assault cases: Correlation with forensic evidence. *Annals of Emergency Medicine, 39*, 39–46.

Granhag, P. A., & Strömwall, L. A. (2000). Effects of preconceptions on deception detection and new answers to why lie-catchers often fail. *Psychology, Crime, & Law, 6*, 197–218.

Granhag, P. A., Strömwall, L. A., & Hartwig, M. (2005). Eyewitness testimony: Tracing the beliefs of Swedish legal professionals. *Behavioral Sciences & the Law, 23*, 709–727.

Gregory, S., & Lees, S. (1996). Attrition in rape and sexual assault cases. *British Journal of Criminology, 36*, 1–17.

Grogan, S., & Murphy, K. P. (2011). Anticipatory Stress Response in PTSD: Extreme stress in children. *Journal of Child & Adolescent Psychiatric Nursing, 24,* 58–71.

Grubb, A., & Harrower, J. (2009). Understanding attribution of blame in cases of rape: An analysis of participant gender, type of rape and perceived similarity to the victim. *Journal of Sexual Aggression, 15,* 63–81.

Grubb, A., & Turner, E. (2012). Rape myth acceptance, gender role conformity and substance use on victim blaming. *Aggression and Violent Behavior, 17,* 443–452.

Gunnell, J. J., & Ceci, S. J. (2010). When emotionality trumps reason: A study of individual processing style and juror bias. *Behavioral Sciences & the Law, 28,* 850–877.

Haegerich, T. M., & Bottoms, B. L. (2000). Empathy and jurors' decisions in trials involving child sexual assault allegations. *Law and Human Behavior, 24,* 421–448.

Haegerich, T. M., Salerno, J. M., & Bottoms, B. L. (2013). Are the effects of juvenile offender stereotypes maximized or minimized by jury deliberation? *Psychology, Public Policy & Law, 19,* 81–97.

Haferkamp, L., Bebermeier, A., Möllering, A., & Neuner, F. (2015). Dissociation is associated with emotional maltreatment in a sample of traumatized women with a history of child abuse. *Journal of Trauma & Dissociation, 16,* 86–99.

Hagemann, C., Stene, L., Myhre, A., Ormstad, K., & Schei, B. (2011). Impact of medico-legal findings on charge filing in cases of rape in adult women. *Acta Obstetrics & Gynecology Scandanavia, 90,* 1218–1224.

Hale, M. (1736/1971). *Historia Placitorum Coronae* (P. R. Glazebrook, Ed., Vol. 1). London: Professional Books.

Hamlyn, B., Phelps, A., Turtle, J., & Sattar, G. (2004). *Are special measures working? Evidence from surveys of vulnerable and intimidated witnesses* (Home Office Research Study 283). London: Home Office.

Hammond, E. M., Berry, M. A., & Rodriguez, D. N. (2011). The influence of rape myth acceptance, sexual attitudes, and belief in a just world on attributions of responsibility in a date rape scenario. *Legal and Criminological Psychology, 16,* 242–252.

Hanna, K., Davies, E., Crothers, C., & Henderson, E. (2012). Questioning child witnesses in New Zealand's criminal justice system: Is cross-examination fair? *Psychiatry, Psychology and Law, 19,* 530–546.

Hanna, K., Davies, E., Henderson, E., Crothers, C., & Rotherham, C. (2010). *Child witnesses in the New Zealand criminal courts: A review of practice and implications for policy*. Auckland: AUT University, Institute of Public Policy.

Hanna, K., Davies, E., Henderson, E., & Hand, L. (2013). Questioning child witnesses: Exploring the benefits and risks of intermediary models in New Zealand. *Psychiatry, Psychology and Law, 20,* 527–542.

Hannaford-Agor, P. L., & Hans, V. P. (2003). Nullification at work? A glimpse from the National Center for State Courts study of hung juries. *Chicago-Kent Law Review, 78,* 1249–1277.

Hannaford-Agor, P., Hans, V. P., Mott, N. L., & Munsterman, G. T. (2002). *Are hung juries a problem?* Williamsburg, VA: National Center for State Courts. http://www.ncsconline.org/WC/Publications/Res_Juries_HungJuriesProblemPub.pdf.

Hansen, L., Mikkelsen, S., Sabroe, S., & Charles, A. (2010). Medical findings and legal outcomes in sexually abused children. *Journal of Forensic Sciences, 55,* 104–109.

Harris, J., & Grace, S. (1999). *A question of evidence? Investigating and prosecuting rape in the 1990s* (Home Office Research Study 196). London: Home Office.

Harris, M., & Fallot, R. D. (2001). Envisioning a trauma-informed service system: A vital paradigm shift. *New Directions for Mental Health Services, 89,* 3–22.

Haslam, N. (2006). Dehumanization: An integrative review. *Personality and Social Psychology Review, 10,* 252–264.

Hastie, R., Penrod, S., & Pennington, N. (1983). *Inside the jury*. Cambridge, MA: Harvard University Press.

Hatzistergos, The Hon. John, Attorney-General, Second Reading Speech. (2007, November 7). *Crimes Amendment (Consent—Sexual Assault Offences) Bill 2007*, *Parliamentary Debates* (NSW Legislative Council, 3584).

Hayes, R. M., Abbott, R. L., & Cook, S. (2016). It's her fault: Student acceptance of rape myths on two college campuses. *Violence Against Women, 22,* 1540–1555.

Hayes, D., & Bunting, L. (2013). 'Just be Brave'—The experiences of young witnesses in criminal proceedings in Northern Ireland. *Child Abuse Review, 22,* 419–431.

Hazlitt, G., Poletti, P., & Donelly, H. (2004). *Sentencing offenders convicted of child sexual assault*. Sydney: Judicial Commission of NSW.

Hebert, M., Tourigny, M., Cyr, M., McDuff, P., & Joly, J. (2009). Prevalence of childhood sexual abuse and timing of disclosure in a representative sample of adults from Quebec. *The Canadian Journal of Psychiatry, 54,* 631–636.

Heger, A., Ticson, L., Velasquez, O., & Bernier, R. (2002). Children referred for possible sexual abuse: Medical findings in 2384 children. *Child Abuse and Neglect, 26,* 645–659.

Heidi, J. M., Marx, B. P., & Forsyth, J. P. (2005). Tonic immobility and childhood sexual abuse: A preliminary report evaluating the sequela of rape-induced paralysis. *Behavior Research and Therapy, 43,* 1157–1171.

Held, M., & McLaughlin, J. (2013). Rape and sexual assault. *Georgetown Journal of Gender & Law, 15,* 155–194.

Henderson, E. (2002). Persuading and controlling: The theory of cross-examination in relation to children. In H. Westcott, G. Davies, & R. Bull (Eds.), *Children's testimony: A handbook of psychological research and forensic practice* (pp. 279–293). Chicester: Wiley.

Henderson, E. (2014). All the proper protections—The Court of Appeal rewrites the rules of the cross-examination of vulnerable witnesses. *Criminal Law Review, 2,* 93–108.

Henderson, E. (2015a). Taking control of cross-examination: Judges, advocates and intermediaries discuss judicial management of the cross-examination of vulnerable people. *Criminal Law Review, 3,* 181–205.

Henderson, E. (2015b). Theoretically speaking: English judges and advocates discuss the changing theory of cross-examination. *Criminal Law Review, 12,* 929–948.

Henderson, E. (2015c). 'Communicative competence? Judges, advocates and intermediaries discuss communication issues in the cross-examination of vulnerable witnesses. *Criminal Law Review, 9,* 659–678.

Henderson, E. (2015d). 'A very valuable tool': Judges, advocates and intermediaries discuss the intermediary system in E&W. *International Journal of Evidence and Proof, 19,* 154–171.

Henderson, E., & Duncanson, K. (2016). A little judicial direction: Can the use of jury directions challenge traditional consent narratives in rape trials? *The University of New South Wales Law Journal, 39,* 750–778.

Henning, T. (2006). Control of cross-examination—A snowflake's chance in hell? *Criminal Law Journal, 30,* 133–137.

Henry, J. (1997). System intervention trauma to child sexual abuse victims following disclosure. *Journal of Interpersonal Violence, 12,* 499–512.

Henry, L., Crane, L., Nash, G., Hobson, Z., Kirke-Smith, M., & Wilcock, R. (2017). Verbal, visual, and intermediary support for child witnesses with autism during investigative interviews. *Journal of Autism and Developmental Disorders, 47,* 2348–2362.

Hergovich, A., Schott, R., & Burger, C. (2010). Biased evaluation of abstracts depending on topic and conclusion: Further evidence of a confirmation bias within scientific psychology. *Current Psychology, 29,* 188–209.

Herman, J. (2005). Justice from the victim's perspective. *Violence Against Women, 11,* 571–602.

Hershkowitz, I., Horowitz, D., & Lamb, M. E. (2005). Trends in children's disclosure of abuse in Israel: A national study. *Child Abuse & Neglect, 29,* 1203–1214.

Hershkowitz, I., Lamb, M. E., & Horowitz, D. (2007). Victimisation of children with disabilities. *American Journal of Orthopsychiatry, 77,* 629–635.

Hester, M. (2015). Reflections on criminal (in)justice in cases of rape. *Papers from the British Criminology Conference, 15,* 26–42.

Hester, M., & Lilley, S.-J. (2017). Rape investigation and attrition in acquaintance, domestic violence and historical rape cases. *Journal of Investigative Psychology and Offender Profiling, 14,* 175–188.

Heyes, C. J. (2016). Dead to the world: Rape, unconsciousness, and social media. *Signs: Journal of Women in Culture and Society, 41*(2), 361–383.

Higgins, P. L., Heath, W. P., & Grannemann, B. D. (2007). How type of excuse defense, mock juror age, and defendant age affect mock jurors' decisions. *Journal of Social Psychology, 147,* 371–392.

Hildebrand, M. M., & Nadjowski, C. J. (2014). The potential impact of rape culture on juror decision making: Implications for wrongful acquittals in sexual assault trials. *Albany Law Review, 78,* 1059–1086.

Hill, M., & Winkler, D. (2000). Juries: How do they work? Do we want them? *Criminal Law Forum, 11,* 397–443.

Hillberg, T., Hamilton-Giachritsis, C., & Dixon, L. (2011). Review of meta-analyses on the association between child sexual abuse and adult mental health difficulties: A systematic approach. *Trauma, Violence & Abuse, 12,* 38–49.

Hopkins, A., & Boyd, R. (2010). Cross-examination of child sexual assault complainants: Concerns about the application of s 41 of the Evidence Act. *Criminal Law Journal, 34*, 149–166.

HM CPS Inspectorate and HM Inspectorate of Constabulary. (2012). *Joint inspection report on the experience of young victims and witnesses in the CJS.* London: HMIC & HMCPSI.

HM Government. (2013). *Working together to safeguard children: A guide to inter-agency working to safeguard and promote the welfare of children.* http://media.education.gov.uk/assets/files/pdf/w/working%20together.pdf.

HM Government. (2018). *Victims strategy*. London: Ministry of Justice.

HM Inspectorate for Constabulary & HM Crown Prosecution Service Inspectorate. (2002). *Report on the joint inspection into the investigation and prosecution of rape offences in England and Wales.* London: HMIC & HMCPSI.

HM Inspectorate for the Constabulary & HM Crown Prosecution Service Inspectorate. (2007). *Without consent: A report on the joint review of the investigation and prosecution of rape offences.* London: HMCPSI and HMIC.

Hobbs, S., Goodman, G. S., Block, S. D., Oran, D., Quas, J. A., Park, A., … Baumrind, N. (2014). Child maltreatment victims' attitudes about appearing in dependency and criminal courts. *Children and Youth Services Review, 44,* 407–416.

Hockett, J. M., Saucier, D. A., Hoffman, B. H., & Craig, A. W. (2009). Oppression through acceptance? Predicting rape myth acceptance and attitudes toward rape victims. *Violence Against Women, 15,* 877–897.

Hodgdon, H., Kinniburgh, K., Gabowitz, D., Blaustein, M. E., & Spinazzola, J. (2013). Development and implementation of trauma-informed programming in youth residential treatment centers using the ARC framework. *Journal of Family Violence, 28,* 679–692.

Hohl, K., & Conway, M. A. (2017). Memory as evidence: How normal features of victim memory lead to the attrition of rape complaints. *Criminology & Criminal Justice, 17,* 248–265.

Hohl, K., & Stanko, E. A. (2015). Complaints of rape and the criminal justice system: Fresh evidence on the attrition problem in England and Wales. *European Journal of Criminology, 12,* 324–341.

Holder, R. (2013). *Just interests: Victims, citizens and the potential for justice* (Unpublished PhD thesis). Australian National University, Canberra, ACT.

Holmes, K., & Sher, L. (2013). Dating violence and suicidal behavior in adolescents. *International Journal of Adolescent Medicine and Health, 25,* 257–261.

Holmgren, J. A., & Fordham, J. (2011). The CSI effect and the Canadian and the Australian jury. *Journal of Forensic Sciences, 56,* S63–S71.

Home Office. (1989). *Report of the interdepartmental working group on the treatment of vulnerable or intimidated witnesses in the criminal justice system.* London: Home Office.

Home Office. (1998). *Speaking up for justice: Report of the interdepartmental working group on the treatment of vulnerable or intimidated witnesses in the criminal justice system*. London: Home Office.

Home Office. (2000). *Setting the boundaries: Reforming the law on sexual offences*. London: Home Office.

Home Office. (2002). *Protecting the public: strengthening protections against sex offenders and reforming the law on sexual offences*. London: Home Office.

Home Office. (2010). *The stern review: A report by Baroness Vivian Stern CBE of an independent review into how rape complaints are handled by public authorities in England and Wales*. London: Home Office.

Home Office. (2011). *Achieving best evidence: Guidance on interviewing victims and witnesses*. London: Home Office.

Honess, M., & Charman, E. A. (2002). Members of the jury—Guilty of incompetence? *The Psychologist, 15*, 72–75.

Hood, R., Shute, S., Feilzer, M., & Wilcox, A. (2002). Sex offenders emerging from long-term imprisonment. *British Journal of Criminology, 42*, 371–394.

Horvath, M., & Brown, J. (2010). Between a rock and a hard place. *The Psychologist, 23*, 556–559.

Hosch, H. M., Culhane, S. E., Tubb, V. A., & Granillo, E. A. (2011). Town vs. gown: A direct comparison of community residents and student mock jurors. *Behavioral Sciences & the Law, 29*, 452–466.

House of Commons, Home Affairs Select Committee. (2013). *Child exploitation and the response to localised grooming: Second report of session 2013–14*. London: The Stationery Office Ltd.

House of Commons, Committee of Public Accounts. (2016). *Efficiency in the criminal justice system: First report of session 2016–17*. London: House of Commons.

House of Commons, Justice Committee. (2016). *Restorative justice: Fourth report of session 2016–17*. London: House of Commons.

Houston, K. A., Hope, L., Memon, A., & Read, J. D. (2013). Expert testimony on eyewitness evidence: In search of common sense. *Behavioral Sciences & the Law, 31*, 637–651.

Howe, M. L. (2013). Memory development: Implications for adults recalling childhood experiences in the courtroom. *Nature Reviews Neuroscience, 14*, 869–876.

Hoyano, L. (2014). What is balanced on the scales of justice? In search of the essence of the right to a fair trial. *Criminal Law Review, 1*, 4–29.

Hoyano, L. (2015). Reforming the adversarial trial for vulnerable witnesses. *Criminal Law Review, 2*, 107–129.

Hoyano, L., & Keenan, (2010). *Child abuse: Law and policy across boundaries.* Oxford: Oxford University Press.

Huang, K.-C., & Lin, C.-C. (2014). Mock jury trials in Taiwan: Paving the ground for introducing lay participation. *Law and Human Behavior, 38,* 367–377.

Hunter, J. (2004). *Battling a good story—The failure of evidence law.* Paper presented at the International Evidence Colloquium, University of Nottingham.

Huntley, J. E., & Costanzo, M. (2003). Sexual harassment stories: Testing a story-mediated model of juror decision-making in civil litigation. *Law and Human Behavior, 27,* 29–51.

Jack, F., & Zajac, R. (2014). The effect of age and reminders on witnesses' responses to cross-examination-style questioning. *Journal of Applied Research in Memory and Cognition, 3,* 1–6.

Jackson, H. (2012). Children's evidence in legal proceedings—The position in Western Australia. In J. R. Spencer & M. E. Lamb (Eds.), *Children and cross-examination: Time to change the rules* (pp. 75–94). Oxford: Hart Publishing.

Jay, A. (2014). *Independent inquiry into child sexual exploitation in Rotherham (1997–2013).* https://www.rotherham.gov.uk/downloads/file/1407/independent_inquiry_cse_in_rotherham.

Jewkes, R., Christofides, N., Vetten, L., Jina, R., Sigsworth, R., & Lotts, L. (2009). Medico-legal findings, legal case progression, and outcomes in South African rape cases: Retrospective review. *PLoS Medicine, 6,* 1–9.

Jewkes, Y. (2004). *Media and crime.* London: Sage.

Jimenez, J. A., & Abreu, J. M. (2003). Race and sex effects on attitudinal perceptions of acquaintance rape. *Journal of Counseling Psychology, 50,* 252–256.

Jina, R., Jewkes, R., Vetten, L., Christofides, N., Sigsworth, R., & Loots, L. (2015). Genito-anal injury patterns and associated factors in rape survivors in an urban province of South Africa: A cross-sectional study. *BMC Women's Health, 15,* 1–14.

Johnson, C. F. (2004). Child sexual abuse. *The Lancet, 364,* 462–470.

Johnson, D., Peterson, J., Sommers, I., & Baskin, D. (2012). Use of forensic science in investigating crimes of sexual violence: Contrasting its theoretical potential with empirical realities. *Violence Against Women, 18,* 193–222.

Johnson, H. (2017). Why doesn't she just report it? Apprehensions and contradictions for women who report sexual violence to the police. *Canadian Journal of Women and the Law, 29,* 36–59.

Johnson, T. J., Wendel, J., & Hamilton, S. (1998). Social anxiety, alcohol expectancies and drinking-game participation. *Addictive Behaviors, 23,* 65–79.

Joint Select Committee, Parliament of NSW. (2014). *Joint select committee on sentencing of child sexual assault offencers* (Report No. 1/55). Sydney: Parliament of NSW.

Jones, C. (2009). *Does Forum Sentencing Reduce Re-Offending?, Report No 129,* Canberra: Australian Institute of Criminology.

Jonas, E., Schulz-Hardt, S., Frey, D., & Thelen, N. (2001). Confirmation bias in sequential information search after preliminary decisions: An expansion of dissonance theoretical research on selective exposure to information. *Journal of Personality and Social Psychology, 80,* 557–571.

Jonas, S., Bebbington, P., McManus, S., & Meltzer, H. (2011). Sexual abuse and psychiatric disorder in England: Results from the 2007 Adult Psychiatric Morbidity Survey. *Psychological Medicine, 41,* 709–719.

Jones, L., Bellis, M. A., Wood, S., Hughes, K., McCoy, E., Eckley, L., … Officer, A. (2012). Prevalence and risk of violence against children with disabilities: A systematic review and meta-analysis of observational studies. *The Lancet, 380,* 899–907.

Jones, M., & Sugden, R. (2001). Positive confirmation bias in the acquisition of information. *Theory and Decision, 50,* 59–99.

Jordan, J. (2011). Here we go round the review-go-round: Rape investigation and prosecution—Are things getting worse not better? *Journal of Sexual Aggression, 17,* 234–249.

Joyce-Wojtas, N., & Keenan, M. (2016). Is restorative justice for sexual crime compatible with various criminal justice systems? *Contemporary Justice Review, 19,* 43–68.

Judicial College. (2013–2019). *Equal treatment bench book.* https://www.judiciary.uk/wp-content/uploads/2018/02/equal-treatment-bench-book-february2018-v5-02mar18.pdf.

Judicial College. (2017). *The Crown Court Compendium: Part 1: Jury and trial management and summing up.* www.judiciary.gov.uk/wp-content/uploads/2016/06/crown-court-compendium-pt1-jury-and-trial-management-and-summing-up-feb2017.pdf. Accessed 24 May 2017.

Judicial College. (2019). *The Crown Court Compendium: Part 1: Jury and trial management and summing up.* https://www.judiciary.uk/wp-content/uploads/2016/06/Crown-Court-Compendium-Part-I-December-2019-amended-19.02.20.pdf.

Judicial Commission of NSW. (2006–2017). *Equality before the law bench book.* Sydney: Judicial Commission of NSW. https://www.judcom.nsw.gov.au/wp-content/uploads/2016/07/Equality_before_the_Law_Bench_Book.pdf.

Judicial Commission of NSW. (2017, Update). *Criminal trial courts bench-book.* https://www.judcom.nsw.gov.au/publications/benchbks/criminal/index.html.

Judicial Studies Board. (2010). *Crown court bench book: Directing the jury.* https://issuu.com/forensicmed/docs/crown_court_benchbook_-_judicial_studies_board/276.

Jülich, S. (2006). Views of justice among survivors of historical child sexual abuse. *Theoretical Criminology, 10,* 125–138.

Jülich, S., & Bowen, H. (2015). Restorative justice in Aotearoa, New Zealand: Improving our response to sexual violence. *Revista De Asistenta Sociala, 14,* 93–104.

Jülich, S., & Landon, F. (2017). Achieving justice outcomes: Participants of Project Restore's restorative processes. In E. Zinsstag & M. Keenan (Eds.), *Restorative responses to sexual violence: Legal, social and therapeutic dimensions* (pp. 192–212). New York: Routledge.

Kahan, D. M. (2015). Laws of cognition and the cognition of law. *Cognition, 135,* 56–60.

Kahlor, L., & Eastin, M. S. (2011). Television's role in the culture of violence toward women: A study of television viewing and the cultivation of rape myth acceptance in the United States. *Journal of Broadcasting & Electronic Media, 55,* 215–231.

Kalven, H., & Zeisel, H. (1966). *The American jury.* Chicago: University of Chicago Press.

Kanin, E. J. (1985). Date rapists: Differential sexual socialization and relative deprivation. *Archives of Sexual Behavior, 14,* 219–231.

Kasparian, A. (2014). Justice beyond bars: Exploring the restorative justice alternative for victims of rape and sexual assault. *Suffolk Transnational Law Review, 37,* 377–410.

Kassin, S. M., Dror, I. E., & Kukucka, J. (2013). The forensic confirmation bias: Problems, perspectives, and proposed solutions. *Journal of Applied Research in Memory and Cognition, 2,* 42–52.

Kassin, S. M., Meissner, C. A., & Norwick, R. J. (2005). 'I'd know a false confession if I saw one': A comparative study of college students and police investigators. *Law and Human Behavior, 29,* 211–227.

Kaufman, G., Drevland, G. C. B., Wessel, E., Overskeidand, G., & Magnussen, S. (2003). The importance of being earnest: Displayed emotions and witness credibility. *Applied Cognitive Psychology, 17,* 21–34.

Kebbell, M. R., Deprez, S., & Wagstaff, G. F. (2003). The direct and cross-examination of complainants and defendants in rape trials: A quantitative analysis of question type. *Psychology, Crime & Law, 9,* 49–59.

Kelly, L. (2002). *Routes to (in)justice: A research review on the reporting, investigation and prosecution of rape cases.* London: Her Majesty's Crown Prosecution Service Inspectorate.

Kelly, L. (2010). The (in)credible words of women: False allegations in European rape research. *Violence Against Women, 16,* 1345–1355.

Kelly, L., & Karsna, K. (2017). *Measuring the scale and changing nature of child sexual abuse and child sexual exploitation.* London: London Metropolitan University. https://cwasu.org/wp-content/uploads/2017/07/18871_CSA_Scoping_paper_web_FA.pdf.

Kelly, L., Lovett, J., & Regan, L. (2005). *A gap or a chasm? Attrition in reported rape cases* (Home Office Research Study No. 293). London: Home Office. https://webarchive.nationalarchives.gov.uk/20110218141141/http://rds.homeoffice.gov.uk/rds/pdfs05/hors293.pdf.

Keenan, M., & Zinsstag, E. (2014). Restorative justice and sexual offences: Can 'changing lenses' be appropriate in this case too? *Monatsschrift for Criminology, 97,* 93–106.

Kerr, N. L., & MacCoun, R. J. (2012). Is the leniency asymmetry really dead? Misinterpreting asymmetry effects in criminal jury deliberation. *Group Processes and Intergroup Relations, 15,* 585–602.

Kerr, N. L., MacCoun, R. J., & Kramer, G. P. (1996). Bias in judgment: Comparing individuals and groups. *Psychological Review, 103,* 687–719.

Kilpatrick, D. G., Acierno, R., Resnick, H. S., Saunders, B. E., & Best, C. L. (1997). A 2-year longitudinal analysis of the relationships between violent assault and substance use in women. *Journal of Consulting and Clinical Psychology, 65,* 834–847.

Kilpatrick, D. G., Resnick, H. S., Ruggiero, K. J., Conoscenti, L. M., & McCauley, J. (2007). *Drug-facilitated, incapacitated, and forcible rape: A national study.* Charleston, SC: National Crime Victims Research & Treatment Center.

King, M., Freiberg, A., Batagol, B., & Hyams, R. (2014). *Non-Adversarial Justice.* Sydney: Federation Press.

Kirchengast, T. (2013). Victim lawyers, victim advocates, and the adversarial criminal trial. *New Criminal Law Review: An International and Interdisciplinary Journal, 16,* 568–594.

Klayman, J. (1995). Varieties of confirmation bias. *Journal of Learning and Motivation, 32,* 385–418.

Klein, R. (2015). An analysis of thirty-five years of rape reform: A frustrating search for fundamental fairness. *Akron Law Review, 41,* 981–1057.

Klemfuss, J. Z., Quas, J. A., & Lyon, T. D. (2014). Attorneys' questions and children's productivity in child sexual abuse criminal trials. *Applied Cognitive Psychology, 28,* 780–788.

Klettke, B., Hallford, D., & Mellor, D. (2016). Perceptions of credibility of sexual abuse victims across generations. *International Journal of Law and Psychiatry, 44,* 91–97.

Klippenstine, M. A., & Schuller, R. A. (2012). Perceptions of sexual assault: Expectancies regarding the emotional response of a rape victim over time. *Psychology, Crime & Law, 18,* 79–94.

Klippenstine, M. A., Schuller, R. A., & Wall, A.-M. (2007). Perceptions of sexual assault: The expression of gender differences and the impact of target alcohol consumption. *Journal of Applied Social Psychology, 37,* 2620–2641.

Kochanska, G. (2003). Emotional development in children with different attachment histories: The first three years. *Child Development, 72,* 474–490.

Kogan, S. M. (2004). Disclosing unwanted sexual experiences: Results from a national sample of adolescent women. *Child Abuse & Neglect, 28,* 147–165.

Kolko, D. J., Hurlburt, M. S., Zhang, J., Barth, R. P., Leslie, L. K., & Burns, B. J. (2010). Posttraumatic stress symptoms in children and adolescents referred for child welfare investigation: A national sample of in-home and out-of-home care. *Child Maltreatment, 15,* 48–63.

Kopper, B. (1996). Gender, gender identity, rape myth acceptance, and time of initial resistance on the perception of acquaintance rape blame and avoidability. *Sex Roles, 34,* 81–93.

Korkman, J., Svanbäck, J., Finnilä, K., & Santt, P. (2014). Judges' views of child sexual abuse: Evaluating beliefs against research findings in a Finnish sample. *Scandanavian Journal of Psychology, 55,* 497–504.

Koski, D. D. (2002). Jury decisionmaking in rape trials: A review and empirical assessment. *Criminal Law Bulletin, 38,* 85–159.

Koss, M. P. (2006). Restoring rape survivors: Justice, advocacy, and a call to action. *Annals of the New York Academy of Sciences, 1087,* 206–234.

Koss, M. P. (2014). The RESTORE program of restorative justice for sex crimes: Vision, process, and outcomes. *Journal of Interpersonal Violence, 29,* 1623–1660.

Kovera, M. B., & Borgida, E. (1997). Expert testimony in child sexual abuse trials: The admissibility of psychological science. *Applied Cognitive Psychology, 11,* 105–129.

KPMG. (2010). *Review of the Youth Justice Group Conferencing Program: Final Report.* Melbourne: Department of Human Services.

Krahé, B., Temkin, J., Bieneck, S., & Berger, A. (2008). Prospective lawyers' rape stereotypes and schematic decision making about rape cases. *Psychology, Crime & Law, 14,* 461–479.

Krahé, B., Tomaszewska, P., Kuyper, L., & Vanwesenbeeck, I. (2014). Prevalence of sexual aggression among young people in Europe: A review of the evidence from 27 EU countries. *Aggression and Violent Behavior, 19,* 545–558.

Kuehnle, K., & Connell, M. (2009). *The evaluation of child sexual abuse allegations: A comprehensive guide to assessment and testimony.* Hoboken, NJ: Wiley.

LaFree, G. D. (1980). Variables affecting guilty pleas and convictions in rape cases: Toward a social theory of rape processing. *Social Forces, 58,* 833–850.

LaFree, G. D., Reskin, B. F., & Visher, C. A. (1985). Jurors' responses to victims' behaviour and legal issues in sexual assault trials. *Social Problems, 32,* 389–407.

Lagnado, D. A., & Harvey, N. (2008). The impact of discredited evidence. *Psychonomic Bulletin and Review, 15,* 1166–1173.

Lalor, K., & McElvaney, R. (2010). Child sexual abuse, links to later sexual exploitation/high-risk sexual behavior, and prevention/treatment programs. *Trauma, Violence, & Abuse, 11,* 159–177.

Lamb, M. E., & Fauchier, A. (2001). The effects of question type on self-contradictions by children in the course of forensic interviews. *Applied Cognitive Psychology, 15,* 483–491.

Lamb, M. E., Hershkowitz, I., Orbach, Y., & Esplin, P. W. (2008). *Tell me what happened: Structured investigative interviews of child victims and witnesses.* Hoboken, NJ: Wiley-Blackwell.

Lamb, M. E., La Rooy, D. J., Malloy, L. C., & Katz, C. (2011). *Children's testimony: A handbook of psychological research and forensic practice.* Oxford: Wiley-Blackwell.

Landström, S., & Granhag, P. A. (2010). In-court versus out-of-court testimonies: Children's experiences and adults' assessments. *Applied Cognitive Psychology, 24,* 941–955.

Langbein, J. H. (2003). *The origin of adversary criminal trial.* Oxford: Oxford University Press.

Langer, E., & Abelson, R. (1974). A patient by any other name: Clinician group difference in labelling bias. *Journal of Consulting and Clinical Psychology, 42,* 4–9.

Larcombe, W. (2011). Falling rape conviction rates: (Some) feminist aims and measures for rape law. *Feminist Legal Studies, 19,* 27–45.

Larcombe, W., Fileborn, B., Powell, A., Hanley, N., & Henry, N. (2016). 'I think it's rape and I think he would be found not guilty': Focus group perceptions of (un)reasonable belief in consent in rape law. *Social & Legal Studies, 25,* 611–629.

Larsen, J. (2014). *Restorative justice in the Australian criminal justice system* (Research and Public Policy Series No. 127). Canberra: Australian Institute of Criminology. https://aic.gov.au/publications/rpp/rpp127.

Law Commission. (2000). *Consent in sexual offences.* London: Law Commission.

Law Commission, New Zealand. (1999). *Juries in criminal trials part two: A discussion paper, preliminary paper 37—Volume 1.* Law Commission, New Zealand.

Law Reform Commission of Western Australia. (2008). *Court intervention programs: Consultation* (Project No. 96). Perth: Law Reform Commission of Western Australia.

Leahy, S. (2014a). Reform of Irish rape law: The need for a legislative definition of consent. *Common Law World Review, 43,* 231–263.

Leahy, S. (2014b). The corroboration warning in sexual offence trials: Final vestige of the historic suspicion of sexual offence complainants or a necessary protection for defendants? *The International Journal of Evidence & Proof, 18,* 41–64.

Lecci, L. B., & Myers, B. (2009). Predicting guilt judgments and verdict change using a measure of pretrial bias in a videotaped mock trial with deliberating jurors. *Psychology, Crime & Law, 15,* 619–634.

LeMaire, K. L., Oswald, D. L., & Russell, B. L. (2016). Labeling sexual victimization experiences: The role of sexism, rape myth acceptance, and tolerance for sexual harassment. *Violence and Victims, 31,* 332–346.

Lens, K. M. E., Doorn, J., Pemberton, A., & Bogaerts, S. (2014). You shouldn't feel that way! Extending the emotional victim effect through the mediating role of expectancy violation. *Psychology, Crime, & Law, 20,* 326–338.

Levett, L., Danielsen, E., Kovera, M., & Cutler, B. L. (2005). The psychology of jury and juror decision making. In N. Brewer & K. D. Williams (Eds.), *Psychology and law: An empirical perspective* (pp. 365–406). New York: Guildford Press.

Levitt, A., & Crown Prosecution Service Equality and Diversity Unit. (2013). *Charging perverting the course of justice and wasting police time in cases involving allegedly false rape and domestic violence allegations: Joint report to the Director of Public Prosecutions.* London: CPS.

Lev-Wiesel, R., & First, M. (2018). Willingness to disclose child maltreatment: CSA vs other forms of child abuse in relation to gender. *Child Abuse & Neglect, 79,* 183–191.

Lewis, T. T., Klettke, B., & Day, A. (2014). The influence of medical and behavioral evidence on conviction rates in cases of child sexual abuse. *Journal of Child Sexual Abuse, 23,* 431–441.

Leyens, J. P., Rodriguez, A. P., Rodriguez, R. T., Gaunt, R., Paladino, M. P., Vaes, J., & Demoulin, S. (2001). Psychological essentialism and the differential attribution of uniquely human emotions to ingroups and outgroups. *European Journal of Social Psychology, 31,* 395–411.

L'Heureux-Dubé, C. (2012). Foreword: Still punished for being female. In E. A. Sheehy (Ed.), *Sexual assault in Canada: Law, legal practice and women's activism* (pp. 1–5). Ottawa: University of Ottawa Press.

Lieberman, J., & Krauss, D. (2009). *Jury psychology: Social aspects of the trial process.* Burlington, VT: Ashgate.

Lievore, D. (2003). *Non-reporting and hidden recording of sexual assault: An international review.* Canberra: Commonwealth Office of the Status of Women.

Lievore, D. (2005a). *Prosecutorial decisions in adult sexual assault cases* (Trends and Issues in Crime & Criminal Justice, No. 291, pp. 1–6).

Lievore, D. (2005b). *No longer silent: A study of women's help-seeking decisions and service responses to sexual assault.* Canberra: Australian Institute of Criminology.

Lima, A. A., Fiszman, A., Marques-Portella, C., Mendlowicz, M., Coutinho, E. S. F., Maia, D. C. B., … Figueira, I. (2010). The impact of tonic immobility reaction on the prognosis of posttraumatic stress disorder. *Journal of Psychiatric Research, 44,* 224–228.

Linz, D. G., Donnerstein, E., & Penrod, S. (1988). Effects of long-term exposure to violent and sexually degrading depictions of women. *Journal of Personality and Social Psychology, 55*(5), 758–768.

Lisak, D., & Miller, P. M. (2002). Repeat rape and multiple offending among undetected rapists. *Violence and Victims, 17,* 73–84.

Lisak, D., Gardinier, L., Nicksa, S. C., & Cote, A. M. (2010). False allegations of sexual assault: An analysis of ten years of reported cases. *Violence Against Women, 16,* 1318–1334.

Littleton, H., Grills-Taquechel, A., & Axsom, D. (2009). Impaired and incapacitated rape victims: Assault characteristics and post-assault experiences. *Violence and Victims, 24,* 439–457.

London, K., Bruck, M., Ceci, S. J., & Shuman, D. W. (2005). Disclosure of child sexual abuse: What does the research tell us about the ways that children tell? *Psychology, Public Policy and Law, 11,* 194–226.

Lonsway, K. A., & Archambault, J. (2012). The 'justice gap' for sexual assault cases: Future directions for research and reform. *Violence Against Women, 18,* 145–168.

Lonsway, K. A., & Fitzgerald, L. F. (1994). Rape myths: In review. *Psychology of Women Quarterly, 68,* 133–164.

Lonsway, K. A., & Fitzgerald, L. F. (1995). Attitudinal antecedents of rape myth acceptance: A theoretical and empirical examination. *Journal of Personality and Social Psychology, 68,* 704–711.

Loughnan, S., Haslam, N., Murnane, T., Vaes, J., Reynolds, C., & Suitne, C. (2010). Objectification leads to depersonalization: The denial of mind and moral concern to objectified others. *European Journal of Social Pyschology, 40,* 709–717.

Lutz-Zois, C. J., Moler, K. A., & Brown, M. J. (2015). Mechanisms for the relationship between traditional masculine ideologies and rape myth acceptance among college men. *Journal of Aggression, Maltreatment and Trauma, 24,* 84–101.

Lynch, K. R., Wasarhaley, N. E., Golding, J. M., & Simcic, T. (2013). Who bought the drinks? Juror perceptions of intoxication in a rape trial. *Journal of Interpersonal Violence, 28,* 3205–3222.

MacCoun, R. J. (1984). Modeling the impact of extralegal bias and defined standards of proof on the decisions of mock jurors and juries. *Dissertation Abstracts International, 46,* 700B.

MacCoun, R. J., & Kerr, N. L. (1988). Asymmetric influence in mock jury deliberation: Jurors' bias for leniency. *Journal of Personality and Social Psychology, 54,* 21–33.

Mackinnon, C. (1989). *Toward a feminist theory of the state*. Harvard, MA: Harvard University Press.

Maheswaran, D., & Chaiken, S. (1991). Promoting systematic processing in low motivation settings: Effect of incongruent information on processing and judgment. *Journal of Personality and Social Psychology, 61*, 13–25.

Malamuth, N. M., Addison, T., & Koss, M. (2000). Pornography and sexual aggression: Are there reliable effects and can we understand them? *Annual Review of Sex Research, 11*, 26–91.

Malloy, L. C., & Lamb, M. E. (2010). Biases in judging victims and suspects whose statements are inconsistent. *Law and Human Behavior, 34*, 46–48.

Mancini, D. E. (2013). The 'CSI effect' in an actual juror sample: Why crime show genre may matter. *North American Journal of Psychology, 15*, 543–564.

Maniglio, R. (2009). The impact of child sexual abuse on health: A systematic review of reviews. *Clinical Psychology Review, 29*, 647–657.

Maniglio, R. (2013). Child sexual abuse in the etiology of anxiety disorders: A systematic review of reviews. *Trauma, Violence, & Abuse, 14*, 96–112.

Mann, S., Vrij, A., & Bull, R. (2004). Detecting true lies: Police officers' ability to detect suspects' lies. *Journal of Applied Psychology, 89*, 137–149.

Marchant, R. (2016). 'Age is not determinative': The evidence of very young children in the English justice system. *Criminal Law and Justice Weekly, 180*, 12–13.

Marks, M. J., & Fraley, R. C. (2006). Confirmation bias and the sexual double standard. *Sex Roles, 54*, 19–26.

Marsh, F., & Wager, N. M. (2015). Restorative justice in cases of sexual violence: Exploring the views of the public and survivors. *Probation Journal, 62*, 336–356.

Marx, B. P., Forsyth, J. P., Gallup, G. G., Fusé, T., & Lexington, J. M. (2008). Tonic immobility as an evolved predator defense: Implications for sexual assault survivors. *Clinical Psychology Science and Practice, 15*, 74–90.

Masser, B. M., Lee, K., & McKimmie, B. M. (2010). Bad woman, bad victim? Disentangling the effects of victim stereotypicality, gender stereotypicality and benevolent sexism on acquaintance rape victim blame. *Sex Roles, 62*, 494–504.

Mathews, B., Bromfield, L., Walsh, K. M., Cheng, Q., & Norman, R. E. (2017). Reports of child sexual abuse of boys and girls: Longitudinal trends over a 20-year period in Victoria, Australia. *Child Abuse & Neglect, 66*, 9–22.

Mathews, B., Walsh, K., Dunne, M., Katz, I., Arney, F., Higgins, D., … Bates, S. (2016). *Scoping study for research into prevalence of child sexual abuse in*

Australia. Sydney: Royal Commission into Institutional Responses to Child Sexual Abuse.

Matthias, C. R., & Zaal, F. N. (2011). Intermediaries for child witnesses: Old problems, new solutions and judicial differences in South Africa. *International Journal of Children's Rights, 19,* 251–269.

McCauley, M. R., & Parker, J. F. (2001). When will a child be believed? The impact of the victim's age and juror's gender on children's credibility and verdict in a sexual-abuse case. *Child Abuse & Neglect, 25,* 523–539.

McCauliff, B. D., & Kovera, M. B. (2012a). When will a child be believed? The impact of the victim's age and juror's gender on children's credibility and verdict in sexual-abuse cases. *Child Abuse & Neglect, 25,* 523–539.

McCauliff, B. D., & Kovera, M. B. (2012b). Do jurors get what they expect? Traditional versus alternative forms of children's testimony. *Psychology, Crime & Law, 18,* 27–47.

McCoy, M. L., & Gray, J. M. (2007). The impact of defendant gender and relationship to victim on juror decisions in a child sexual abuse case. *Journal of Applied Social Psychology, 37,* 1578–1593.

McDonald, E., & Tinsley, Y. (2011). *From "real rape" to real justice: Prosecuting rape in New Zealand*. Wellington: Victoria University Press.

McElrea, F. W. M. (1998). The New Zealand model of family group conferencing. *European Journal on Criminal Policy and Research, 6,* 527–543.

McGlynn, C. (2017). Rape trials and sexual history evidence: Reforming the law on third-party evidence. *The Journal of Criminal Law, 81,* 367–392.

McGlynn, C., & Munro, V. E. (2010). *Rethinking rape law: International and comparative perspectives*. Abingdon: Routledge.

McGlynn, C., Westmarland, N., & Godden, N. (2012). I just wanted him to hear me: Sexual Violence and the possibilities of restorative justice. *Journal of Law and Society, 39,* 213–240.

McGregor, M., Du Mont, J., & Myhr, T. (2002). Sexual assault forensic medical examination: Is evidence related to successful prosecution? *Annals in Emergency Medicine, 39,* 639–647.

McKee, J., Widder, S. L., Paton-Gay, J. D., Kirkpatrick, A. W., & Engels, P. (2016). Ten year review of alcohol use and major trauma in a Canadian province: Still a major problem. *Journal of Trauma Management & Outcomes, 10,* 1–9.

McKimmie, B. M., Masser, B. M., & Bongiorno, R. (2014). What counts as rape? The effect of offense prototypes, victim stereotypes, and participant gender on how the complainant and defendant are perceived. *Journal of Interpersonal Violence, 29,* 2273–2303.

McMillan, L. (2018). Police officers' perceptions of false allegations of rape. *Journal of Gender Studies, 27,* 9–21.

Milburn, M. A., Mather, R., & Conrad, S. D. (2000). The effects of viewing r-rated movie scenes that objectify women on perceptions of date rape. *Sex Roles, 43,* 645–664.

Miller, N. A., & Najavits, L. M. (2012). Creating trauma-informed correctional care: A balance of goals and environment. *European Journal of Psychotraumatology, 3,* 17246/1–8.

Miller, S. L., & Iovanni, L. (2013). Using restorative justice for gendered violence: Success with a post-conviction model. *Feminist Criminology, 8,* 247–268.

Ministry of Justice. (2008). *Ministry of justice report: Judicial and court statistics 2007*. London: Ministry of Justice.

Ministry of Justice. (2011). *Achieving best evidence in criminal proceedings: Guidance on interviewing victims and witnesses, and guidance on using special measures*. London: Ministry of Justice.

Ministry of Justice. (2012). *Swift and sure justice: The government's plans for reform of the criminal justice system.* London: Ministry of Justice.

Ministry of Justice. (2013). *Transforming the criminal justice system (CJS): A strategy & action plan to reform the criminal justice system.* London: Ministry of Justice. https://www.gov.uk/government/publications/transforming-the-criminal-justice-system.

Ministry of Justice. (2014a). *Report on review of ways to reduce distress of victims in trials of sexual violence*. London: Ministry of Justice.

Ministry of Justice. (2014b). *Transforming the criminal justice system strategy and action plan—Implementation update*. London: Ministry of Justice.

Ministry of Justice. (2015a). *Registered intermediary procedural guidance manual*. London: Ministry of Justice. https://www.zakon.co.uk/admin/resources/downloads/registered-intermediary-procedural-guidance-manual-2015.pdf.

Ministry of Justice. (2015b). *Code of practice for victims of crime presented to Parliament pursuant to section 33 of the Domestic Violence, Crime and Victims Act 2004*. London: Ministry of Justice.

Ministry of Justice. (2015c). *Code of practice for victims of crime*. London: Ministry of Justice.

Ministry of Justice. (2017). *Press release: Greater protection for rape victims and children at risk of grooming.* https://www.gov.uk/government/news/greater-protection-for-rape-victims-and-children-at-risk-of-grooming.

Ministry of Justice. (2018). *Limiting the use of complainants' sexual history in sex cases Section 41 of the Youth Justice and Criminal Evidence Act 1999: The law on the admissibility of sexual history evidence in practice*. London: Ministry of Justice.

Ministry of Justice. (2019, March). *Criminal justice system statistics quarterly.* https://www.gov.uk/government/statistics/criminal-justice-system-statistics-quarterly-march-2019.

Ministry of Justice, Home Office & Office for National Statistics. (2013). *An overview of sexual offending in England and Wales. Statistical Bulletin.* London: Ministry of Justice, Home Office and Office for National Statistics.

Miragoli, S., Camisasca, E., & Di Blasio, P. (2017). The narrative fragmentation in child sexual abuse: The role of age and posttraumatic stress disorder. *Child Abuse Neglect, 73C,* 106–114.

Miragoli, S., Camisasca, E., & Di Blasio, P. (2019). Investigating linguistic coherence relations in child sexual abuse: A comparison of PTSD and non-PTSD children. *Heliyon, 5,* e01163.

Miragoli, S., Procaccia, R., & Di Blasio, P. (2014). Language use and PTSD symptoms: Content analyses of allegations of child sexual abuse. *Journal of Forensic Psychology Practice, 14,* 355–382.

Molinaro, P. F., & Malloy, L. C. (2016). Statements from youth in legal contexts: Effects of consistency, legal role, and age. *Behavioral Sciences & the Law, 34,* 139–159.

Monaghan, J., & Mason, G. (2016). Reasonable reform: Understanding the knowledge of consent provision in section 61HA(3)(c) of the Crimes Act 1900 (NSW). *Criminal Law Journal, 40,* 246–261.

Moore, S. E. H. (2014). *Crime and the media.* Basingstoke: Palgrave Macmillan.

Morison, S., & Greene, E. (1992). Juror and expert knowledge of child sexual abuse. *Child Abuse & Neglect, 16,* 595–613.

Mugno, A. P., Klemfuss, J. Z., & Lyon, T. D. (2016). Attorney questions predict jury-eligible adult assessments of attorneys, child witnesses, and defendant guilt. *Behavioral Sciences & the Law, 34,* 178–199.

Muller, R. T., Caldwell, R. A., & Hunter, J. E. (1994). Factors predicting the blaming of victims of physical child abuse or rape. *Canadian Journal of Behavioural Science, 26,* 259–279.

Munro, V. E. (2008). Constructing consent: Legislating freedom and legitimating constraint in the expression of sexual autonomy. *Akron Law Review, 41,* 923–956.

Munro, V. E. (2017). Shifting sands? Consent, context and vulnerability in contemporary sexual offences policy in England and Wales. *Social & Legal Studies, 26*, 417–440.

Murnen, S. K., & Kohlman, M. H. (2007). Athletic participation, fraternity membership, and sexual aggression among college men: A meta-analytic review. *Sex Roles, 57*, 145–157.

Myers, J. E. B., Redlich, A. D., Goodman, G. S., Prizmich, L. P., & Imwinkelried, E. (1999). Jurors' perceptions of hearsay in child sexual abuse cases. *Psychology, Public Policy, and Law, 5*, 388–419.

Myklebust, T. (2012). The position in Norway. In J. R. Spencer & M. E. Lamb (Eds.), *Children and cross-examination: Time to change the rules?* (pp. 147–170). Oxford: Hart Publishing.

Najavits, L. M., Weiss, R. D., & Shaw, S. R. (1997). The link between substance abuse and posttraumatic stress disorder in women. *The American Journal on Addictions, 6*, 273–283.

National Child Traumatic Stress Network. (2009). *Helping traumatized children: Tips for judges*. https://www.nctsn.org/sites/default/files/assets/pdfs/JudgesFactSheet.pdf.

National Child Traumatic Stress Network. (2017). *Trauma: What child welfare attorneys should know*. https://www.nctsn.org/sites/default/files/assets/pdfs/attorneyresourceguide.pdf.

National Union of Students. (2011). *Hidden marks: A study of women students' experiences of harassment, stalking, violence and sexual assault*. https://www.nus.org.uk/Global/NUS_hidden_marks_report_2nd_edition_web.pdf.

Naylor, B. (2010). Effective justice for victims of sexual assault: Taking up the debate on alternative pathways. *University of New South Wales Law Journal, 33*, 662–684.

Nemeth, C. (1977). Interactions between jurors as a function of majority vs. unanimity decision rules. *Journal of Applied Social Psychology, 7*, 38–56.

Newcombe, P. A., van den Eynde, J., Hafner, D., & Jolly, L. (2008). Attributions of responsibility for rape: Differences across familiarity of situation, gender, and acceptance of rape myths. *Journal of Applied Social Psychology, 38*, 1736–1754.

Newell, B. R., Weston, N. J., & Shanks, D. R. (2003). Empirical tests of a fast-and-frugal heuristic: Not everyone 'takes-the-best'. *Organizational Behavior & Human Decision Processes, 91*, 82–96.

Nightingale, N. N. (1993). Juror reactions to child victim witnesses: Factors affecting trial outcome. *Law and Human Behavior, 17*, 679–694.

Northern Territory Law Reform Commission. (1999). *Final report on the laws relating to the investigation and prosecution of sexual assault in the North Territory*. Darwin: North Territory Law Reform Commission.

NSPCC. (2018). *How safe are our children? The most comprehensive overview of child protection in the UK*. NSPCC. https://learning.nspcc.org.uk/media/1067/how-safe-are-our-children-2018.pdf.

NSW Criminal Justice and Sexual Offences Taskforce. (2005). *Responding to sexual assault: The way forward*. Sydney: Attorney-General's Department of NSW.

NSW Department for Women. (1996). *Heroines of fortitude: The experiences of women in court as victims of sexual assault*. Sydney: New South Wales Government.

NSW Department of Attorney-General and Justice. (2013). *Review of the consent provision for sexual assault offences in the crimes act 1900*. Sydney: Department of Attorney-General and Justice.

NSW Department of Justice. (2015). *Children's champions & pre-recording of evidence*. Sydney: Department of Justice.

NSW Joint Select Committee on Sentencing of Child Sexual Assault Offenders. (2014). *Every sentence tells a story—Report on sentencing of child sexual assault offenders* (Report No. 1/55). Sydney: Parliament of NSW.

NSW Law Reform Commission. (2003). *Questioning of complainants by unrepresented accused in sexual offence trials* (Report No. 101). Sydney: NSW Law Reform Commission.

NSW Law Reform Commission. (2008). *Consultation paper 4: Jury directions*. Sydney: NSW Law Reform Commission.

NSW Law Reform Commission. (2012). *Jury Directions (Report No. 136)*. Sydney: NSW Law Reform Commission.

NSW Law Reform Commission. (2019). *Consent in relation to sexual offences: Draft proposals*. Sydney: NSW Law Reform Commission.

NSW Office of the Director of Public Prosecutions. (2018). *ODPP Prosecution guidelines*. https://www.odpp.nsw.gov.au/prosecution-guidelines-0.

NSW Standing Committee on Law and Justice. (2002). *Report on child sexual assault prosecutions* (Parliamentary Paper No. 208; Report No. 22). Sydney: Parliament of NSW.

Nurius, P. S., Norris, J., Macy, R. J., & Huang, B. (2004). Women's situational coping with acquaintance sexual assault. *Violence Against Women, 10*, 450–478.

NUS Women's Department. (2015). *Talk about it: NUS women's department 2015 survey*. National Union of Students. https://d3n8a8pro7vhmx.cloudf

ront.net/nus/pages/144/attachments/original/1454369041/Talk_about_it_Survey_Report.pdf?1454369041.

Oates, R. K., & Tong, L. (1987). Sexual abuse of children: An area with room for professional reforms. *Medical Journal of Australia, 147,* 544–548.

O'Brien, B. (2009). Prime suspect: An examination of factors that aggravate and counteract confirmation bias in criminal investigations. *Psychology, Public Policy, and Law, 15,* 315–334.

O'Brien, K., Jones, C., & Korabelnikoff, V. (2008). *What caused the decrease in sexual assault clear-up rates?* (Crime and Justice Bulletin, No. 125). Sydney: NSW Bureau of Crime Statistics and Research.

Odgers, S. (2008, August 29). *Witness questioning: The role of the judge and the role of the barrister* (lecture delivered at the student forum). Sydney: University of New South Wales Law School.

Office for National Statistics. (2018). *Sexual offending: Victimisation and the path through the criminal justice system: An overview of sexual offending in England and Wales, using a range of national statistics and official statistics from across the crime and criminal justice system.* https://www.ons.gov.uk/peoplepopulationandcommunity/crimeandjustice/articles/sexualoffendingvictimisationandthepaththroughthecriminaljusticesystem/2018-12-13.

Ogden, P., & Minton, K. (2000). Sensorimotor psychotherapy: One method for processing traumatic memory. *Traumatology, 6,* 149–173.

O'Hare, T., Shen, C., & Sherrer, M. (2010). High-risk behaviors and drinking-to-cope as mediators of lifetime abuse and PTSD symptoms in clients with severe mental illness. *Journal of Traumatic Stress, 23,* 255–263.

O'Leary, P., Koh, E., & Dare, A. (2017). *Grooming and child sexual abuse in institutional contexts.* Sydney: Royal Commission into Institutional Responses to Child Sexual Abuse.

Oliver, K. (2015). *Rape as spectator sport and* creepshot *entertainment: Social media and the valorization of lack of consent* (ASJ Occasional Papers, OP 10). http://op.asjournal.org/rape-as-spectator-sport-and-creepshot-entertainment/.

Oliver, K. (2016). *Hunting girls: Sexual violence from the hunger games to campus rape.* New York: Columbia University Press.

O'Mahony, D., & Doak, J. (2017). *Reimagining restorative justice: Agency and accountability in the criminal process.* Oxford: Hart Publishing.

O'Neal, E. N., Tellis, K., & Spohn, C. (2015). Prosecuting intimate partner sexual assault: Legal and extra-legal factors that influence charging decisions. *Violence Against Women, 21,* 1237–1258.

O'Neill, S., & Zajac, R. (2013a). Preparing children for cross-examination: How does intervention timing influence efficacy? *Pyschology, Public Policy, and Law, 19,* 307–320.

O'Neill, S., & Zajac, R. (2013b). The role of repeated interviewing in children's responses to cross-examination-style questioning. *British Journal of Psychology, 104,* 14–38.

Orcutt, H. K., Goodman, G. S., Tobey, A. E., Batterman-Faunce, J. M., & Thomas, S. (2001). Detecting deception in children's testimony: Factfinders' abilities to reach the truth in open court and closed-circuit trials. *Law and Human Behavior, 25,* 339–372.

Ouimette, P., & Brown, P. J. (Eds.). (2003). *Trauma and substance abuse: Causes, Consequences, and treatment of comorbid disorders.* Washington, DC: American Psychological Association.

Pagura, I. (2012). Law report: Protecting massage therapists against sexual assault claims. *Journal of the Australian Traditional-Medicine Society, 18,* 165–166.

Paladino, M. P., Leyens, J. P., Rodriguez, R. T., Rodriguez, A. P., Gaunt, R., & Demoulin, S. (2002). Differential associations of uniquely and non-uniquely human emotions to the ingroup and the outgroups. *Group Processes and Intergroup Relations, 5,* 105–117.

Palusci, V., Cox, E., Cyrus, T., Heartwell, S., Vandervort, F., & Pott, E. (1999). Medical assessment and legal outcome in child sexual abuse. *Archives of Pediatric and Adolescent Medicine, 153,* 388–392.

Park, K., Kim, S., Lee, E., & Seo, H. (2005). Social conformity and cognitive conversation during jury deliberation: A content analysis of deliberation arguments in the first officially simulated jury trial in Korea. *The Korean Journal of Social and Personality Psychology, 19,* 1–21.

Parliament of Victoria, Crime Prevention Committee. (1995). *Combating child sexual assault: An integrated model* (First Report Upon the Inquiry into Sexual Offences Against Children and Adults). Melbourne: Government Printer.

Payne, D. L., Lonsway, K. A., & Fitzgerald, L. F. (1999). Rape myth acceptance: Exploration of its structure and its measurement using the *Illinois Rape Myth Acceptance Scale. Journal of Research in Personality, 33,* 27–68.

Payne, S. (2009). *Rape: The victim experience review.* London: Home Office.

Pennington, N., & Hastie, R. (1986). Evidence evaluation in complex decisions-making. *Journal of Personality and Social Psychology, 51,* 242–258.

Pennington, N., & Hastie, R. (1988). Explanation-based decision making: Effects of memory structure on judgment. *Journal of Experimental Psychology: Learning Memory and Cognition, 14,* 521–533.

Pennington, N., & Hastie, R. (1992). Explaining the evidence: Tests of the story model for juror decision making. *Journal of Personality and Social Psychology, 62,* 189–206.

Pereda, N., Guilera, G., Forns, M., & Gomez-Benito, J. (2009a). The international epidemiology of child sexual abuse: A continuation of Finkelhor (1994). *Child Abuse & Neglect, 33,* 331–342.

Pereda, N., Guilera, G., Forns, M., & Gómez-Benito, J. (2009b). The prevalence of child sexual abuse in community and student samples: A meta-analysis. *Clinical Psychology Review, 29,* 328–338.

Perry, B. D. (2009). Examining child maltreatment through a neurodevelopmental lens: Clinical applications of the neurosequential model of therapeutics. *Journal of Loss and Trauma, 14,* 240–255.

Peter, J., & Valkenburg, P. M. (2009). Adolescents' exposure to sexually explicit internet material and notions of women as sex objects: Assessing causality and underlying processes. *Journal of Communication, 59,* 407–433.

Pether, P. (2009). What is due to others: Speaking and signifying subject(s) of rape law. *Griffith Law Review, 18,* 237–258.

Phelan, P. (1995). Incest and its meaning: The perspectives of fathers and daughters. *Child Abuse and Neglect, 19,* 7–24.

Piaget, J., Cook, M., & Norton, W. (1952). *The origins of intelligence in children* (Vol. 8). New York: International Universities Press.

Pichler, A. S., Sharman, S. J., Powell, M., Westera, N., & Goodman-Delahunty, J. (2019). Association between interview quality and child sexual abuse trial outcome. *Journal of Family Violence*, online, 1–9. https://link.springer.com/article/10.1007/s10896-019-00051-5.

Pickel, K. L., & Gentry, R. H. (2017). Mock jurors' expectations regarding the psychological harm experienced by rape victims as a function of rape prototypicality. *Psychology, Crime & Law, 23,* 254–273.

Pilnik, L., & Kendall, J. R. (2012). *Identifying polyvictimization and trauma among court-involved children and youth: A checklist and resource guide for attorneys and other court-appointed advocates 2.* Safe Start Center, Office Juvenile Justice and Delinquency Prevention, U.S. Department of Justice.

Pineau, L. (1989). Date rape: A feminist analysis. *Law and Philosophy, 8,* 217–243.

Plotnikoff, J., & Woolfson, R. (2007). *Evaluation of young witness support: Examining the impact on witnesses and the criminal justice system.* London:

Ministry of Justice. https://www.lexiconlimited.co.uk/PDF%20files/Young_Witness_Study_Report.pdf.

Plotnikoff, J., & Woolfson, R. (2009). *Measuring up? Evaluating implementation of government commitments to young witnesses in criminal proceedings*. London: NPSCC & Nuffield Foundation.

Plotnikoff, J., & Woolfson, R. (2012). 'Kicking and screaming': The slow road to best evidence. In J. R. Spencer & M. E. Lamb (Eds.), *Children and cross-examination: Time to change the rules* (pp. 21–41). Oxford: Hart Publishing.

Plotnikoff, J., & Woolfson, R. (2015). *Intermediaries in the criminal justice system: Improving communication for vulnerable witnesses and defendants*. Bristol: Policy Press.

Polusny, M., & Follette, V. (1995). Long-term correlates of child sexual abuse: Theory and review of the empirical literature. *Applied and Preventative Psychology, 4*, 143–166.

Porges, S. W. (2011). *The polyvagal theory: Neurophysiological foundations of emotions, attachment, communication, self-regulation*. New York: W. W. Norton.

Porter, S., Woodworth, M., & Birt, A. R. (2000). Truth, lies, and videotape: An investigation of the ability of federal parole officers to detect deception. *Law and Human Behavior, 24*, 643–658.

Powell, M. B. (2013). An overview of current initiatives to improve child witness interviews about sexual abuse. *Current Issues in Criminal Justice, 25*, 711–720.

Powell, M. B., Bowden, P., & Mattison, M. (2014). Stakeholders' perceptions of the benefit of introducing an Australian intermediary system for vulnerable witnesses. *Australian & New Zealand Journal of Criminology, 48*, 498–512.

Powell, M. B., Roberts, K., & Guadagno, B. (2007). Particularisation of child abuse offences: Common problems when questioning child witnesses. *Current Issues in Criminal Justice, 19*, 64–74.

Powell, M. B., Westera, N. J., Goodman-Delahunty, J., & Pichler, A. S. (2016). *An evaluation of how evidence is elicited from complainants of child sexual abuse*. Sydney: Royal Commission into Institutional Responses to Child Sexual Abuse.

Poynton, S. (2013). Rates of recidivism among offenders referred to Forum Sentencing. *Contemporary Issues in Crime and Justice, 172*, 1–14.

Prentky, R. A., Lee, A. F. S., Knight, R. A., & Cerce, D. (1997). Recidivism rates among child molesters and rapists: A methodological analysis. *Law and Human Behavior, 21*, 635–659.

Priebe, G., & Svedin, C. G. (2008). Child sexual abuse is largely hidden from the adult society: An epidemiological study of adolescents' disclosures. *Child Abuse & Neglect, 32*, 1095–1108.

Proietti-Scifoni, G., & Daly, K. (2011). Gendered violence and restorative justice: The views of New Zealand Opinion Leaders. *Contemporary Justice Review, 14*, 269–290.

Quadara, A., Fileborn, B., & Parkinson, D. (2013). *The role of forensic medical evidence in the prosecution of adult sexual assault*. Canberra: Australian Institute of Family Studies.

Quas, J. A., Bottoms, B. L., Haegerich, T. M., & Nysse-Carris, K. L. (2002). Effects of victim, defendant, and juror gender decisions in child sexual assault cases. *Journal of Applied Social Psychology, 32*, 1993–2021.

Quas, J. A., & Goodman, G. S. (2012). Consequences of criminal court involvement for child victims. *Psychology, Public Policy, and Law, 18*, 392–414.

Quas, J. A., Goodman, G. S., Ghetti, S., Alexander, K. W., Edelstein, R., Redlich, A. D., & Jones, D. P. H. (2005). Childhood sexual assault victims: Long-term outcomes after testifying in criminal court. *Monographs of the Society for Research in Child Development, 70*, Serial No. 280.

Quas, J. A., Thompson, W. C., & Clarke-Stewart, K. A. (2005). Do jurors 'know' what isn't so about child witnesses? *Law and Human Behavior, 29*, 425–456.

Queensland Crime and Misconduct Commission. (2003). *Seeking justice: An inquiry into the handling of sexual offences by the criminal justice system*. Brisbane: Crime and Misconduct Commission.

Queensland Crime Commission and Queensland Police Service. (2000). *Project axis-child sexual abuse in Queensland: Responses to the problem*. Brisbane: Queensland Crime Commission.

Queensland Law Reform Commission. (2000). *The receipt of evidence by Queensland courts: The evidence of children* (Report No. 55; Part 2). Brisbane: Queensland Law Reform Commission.

Queensland Law Reform Commission. (2009). *A review of jury directions* (Report No. 66). Brisbane: Queensland Law Reform Commission.

Quilter, J. (2011). Re-framing the rape trial: Insights from critical theory about the limitations of legislative reform. *Australian Feminist Law Journal, 35*, 23–56.

Quilter, J. (2015). From raptus to rape: A history of the requirements of resistance and injury. *Law & History, 2*, 89–113.

Raitt, F. E. (2010). Independent legal representation for complainants in rape trials. In C. McGlynn & V. E. Munro (Eds.), *Rethinking rape law: International and comparative perspectives*. Abingdon: Routledge.

Randall, M. (2010). Sexual assault law, credibility, and 'ideal victims': Consent, resistance, and victim blaming. *Canadian Journal of Women and the Law, 22,* 397–435.

Redlich, A. D., Ghetti, S., & Quas, J. A. (2008). Perceptions of children during a police interview: A comparison of alleged victims and suspects. *Journal of Applied Social Psychology, 38,* 705–735.

Regan, P. C., & Baker, S. J. (1998). The impact of child witness demeanor on perceived credibility and trial outcome in sexual abuse cases. *Journal of Family Violence, 13,* 187–195.

Reitman, K. A. (2011). *Attorneys for children guide to interviewing clients: Integrating trauma informed care and solution focused strategies*. http://www.nycourts.gov/ip/cwcip/Publications/attorneyGuide.pdf.

Reskin, B. F., & Visher, C. A. (1986). The impacts of evidence and extralegal factors in jurors' decisions. *Law & Society Review, 20,* 423–438.

Ridley, A. M., van Rheede, V., & Wilcock, R. (2015). Interviews, intermediaries and witnesses interview. *Investigative Interviewing: Research and Practice, 7,* 21–315.

Rieskamp, J., & Hoffrage, U. (2008). Inferences under time pressure: How opportunity costs affect strategy selection. *Acta Psychologica, 127,* 258–276.

Rieskamp, J., & Otto, P. E. (2006). SSL: A theory of how people learn to select strategies. *Journal of Experimental Psychology: General, 135,* 207–236.

Righarts, S., Jack, F., Zajac, R., & Hayne, H. (2014). Young children's responses to cross-examination style questioning: The effects of delay and subsequent questioning. *Psychology, Crime & Law, 21,* 274–296.

Righarts, S., O'Neill, S., & Zajac, R. (2013). Addressing the negative effect of cross-examination questioning on children's accuracy: Can we intervene? *Law and Human Behavior, 37,* 354–365.

Robinson, J. (2015). The experience of the child witness: Legal and psychological issue. *International Journal of Law and Psychiatry, 42–43,* 168–176.

Rodger, R. (2003, May 1–2). *New specialist child sexual assault jurisdiction for New South Wales*. Paper presented at the Child Sexual Abuse: Justice Response or Alternative Resolution Conference, Australian Institute of Criminology, Adelaide.

Roesler, T. A., & Wind, T. W. (1994). Telling the secret: Adult women describe their disclosures of incest. *Journal of Interpersonal Violence, 9,* 327–338.

Rook, P., & Ward, R. (Eds.). (2016). *Rook & Ward on sexual offences: Law & practice* (5th ed.). London: Sweet & Maxwell.

Rook, P., Rafferty, A., & Ward, R. (2016) Advocacy and the vulnerable. In P. Rook & R. Ward (Eds.), *Rook & ward on sexual offences: Law & practice* (5th ed., pp. 1553–1568). London: Sweet & Maxwell.

Rossner, M., Bruce, J., & Meher, M. (2013). *The Process and Dynamics of Restorative Justice: Research on Forum Sentencing: Final Report prepared for NSW Department of Attorney General's and Justice*. Sydney: University of Western Sydney and University of New South Wales.

Royal Commission into Institutional Responses to Child Sexual Abuse. (2017a). *Final report: Nature and cause* (Vol. 2). Sydney: Royal Commission into Institutional Responses to Child Sexual Abuse.

Royal Commission into Institutional Responses to Child Sexual Abuse. (2017b). *Criminal justice report* (Executive Summary and Parts I–II). Sydney: Royal Commission into Institutional Responses to Child Sexual Abuse.

Royal Commission into Institutional Responses to Child Sexual Abuse. (2017c). *Criminal justice report* (Parts VII–X and Appendices). Sydney: Royal Commission into Institutional Responses to Child Sexual Abuse.

Royal Commission into the New South Wales Police Service. (1997). *The paedophile inquiry* (Vol. 5, Final Report). Sydney: The Government of the State of New South Wales.

Rumney, P. N. (2001). The review of sexual offences and rape: Another false dawn. *Modern Law Review, 64*, 890–910.

Rumney, P. N. (2006). False allegations of rape. *The Cambridge Law Journal, 65*, 128–158.

Rumney, P. N., & Fenton, R. A. (2008). Intoxicated consent in rape: *Bree* and juror decision-making. *Modern Law Review, 71*, 279–290.

Rumney, P. N., & Fenton, R. A. (2011). Judicial training and rape. *Journal of Criminal Law, 75*, 473–481.

Russell, D. E. (1983). The incidence and prevalence of intrafamilial and extrafamilial sexual abuse of female children. *Child Abuse & Neglect, 7*, 133–146.

Saint-Martin, P., Bouyssy, M., & O'Byrne, P. (2007). Analysis of 756 cases of sexual assault in Tours (France): Medico-legal findings and judicial outcomes. *Medicine, Science and the Law, 47*, 315–324.

Saks, M. J. (1997). What do jury experiments tell us about how juries (should) make decisions? *Southern California Interdisciplinary Law Journal, 6*, 1–53.

Salerno, J. M., & Diamond, S. S. (2010). The promise of a cognitive perspective on jury deliberation. *Psychonomic Bulletin & Review, 17,* 174–179.

Salhany, R. E. (2006). *Cross-examination: The art of the advocate.* Sydney: LexisNexis.

Salter, A. C. (1995). *Transforming trauma: A guide to understanding and treating adult survivors of child sexual abuse.* Thousand Oaks, CA: Sage.

Sandys, J., & Dillehay, R. C. (1995). First-ballot votes, predeliberation dispositions, and final verdicts in jury trials. *Law and Human Behavior, 19,* 175–195.

Sas, L. (2002). *The interaction between children's developmental capabilities and the courtroom environment: The impact on testimonial competency.* Ottawa, ON: Department of Justice.

Sas, L. D., Hatch, A., Malla, S., Dick, T., & Hurley, P. (1993). *Three Years After the Verdict: A Longitudinal Study of the Social and Psychological Adjustment of Child Witnesses Referred to the Child Witness Project.* London, Ontario: National Criminal Justice Reference Service.

Saunders, C. (2012). The trust, the half-truth, and nothing like the truth: Reconceptualising false allegations of rape. *British Journal of Criminology, 52,* 1152–1171.

Sauzier, M. (1989). Disclosure of child sexual abuse: For better or for worse. *Psychiatric Clinics of North America, 12,* 455–469.

Sayfan, L., Mitchell, E. B., Goodman, G. S., Eisen, M. L., & Qin, J. (2008). Children's expressed emotions when disclosing maltreatment. *Child Abuse & Neglect, 32,* 1026–1036.

Saywitz, K. J. (1995). Improving children's testimony: The question, the answer and the environment. In M. Zaragoza, J. R. Graham, G. C. N. Hall, R. Hirschman, & Y. S. Ben-Porat (Eds.), *Memory and testimony in the child witness* (pp. 113–140). Thousand Oaks: Sage.

Saywitz, K., Comparo, L. B., & Romanoff, A. (2010). Interviewing children in custody cases: Implications of research and policy for practice. *Behavioral Sciences & the Law, 24,* 542–562.

Schore, A. N. (2003). *Affect regulation and repair of the self.* New York: W. W. Norton.

Schore, A. N. (2016). *Affect regulation and the origin of the self: The neurobiology of emotional development.* New York: Routledge.

Schuller, R. A., & Hastings, P. A. (2002). Complainant sexual history evidence: Its impact on mock jurors' decisions. *Psychology of Women Quarterly, 26,* 252–261.

Schuller, R. A., McKimmie, B. M., Masser, B. M., & Klippenstine, M. A. (2010). Judgments of sexual assault: The impact of complainant emotional demeanor, gender and victim stereotypes. *New Criminal Law Review, 13,* 759–780.

Schuller, R. A., & Wall, A.-M. (1998). The effects of defendant and complainant intoxication on mock jurors' judgments of sexual assault. *Pyschology of Women Quarterly, 22,* 555–573.

Schutte, J. W., & Hosch, H. M. (1997). Gender differences in sexual assault verdicts: A meta-analysis. *Journal of Social Behavior & Personality, 12,* 759–772.

Schweitzer, N. J., & Saks, M. J. (2007). The CSI effect: Popular fiction about forensic science affects the public's expectations about real forensic science. *Jurimetrics, 47,* 357–364.

Scott-Ham, M., & Burton, F. (2005). A study of blood and urine alcohol concentrations in cases of alleged drug-facilitated sexual assault in the UK over a 3-year period. *Journal of Clinical Forensic Medicine, 13,* 107–111.

Scottish Executive Central Research Unit. (2002). *Vulnerable and intimidated witnesses: Review of provisions in other jurisdictions.* Edinburgh: Scottish Executive.

Scottish Law Commission. (2007). *Report on rape and other sexual offences.* Edinburgh: Scottish Law Commission.

Seymour, F., Blackwell, S., Calvert, S., & McLean, B. (2014). Counterintuitive expert psychological evidence in child sexual abuse trials in New Zealand. *Psychiatry, Psychology and Law, 21,* 511–522.

Shapland, J., & Hall, M. (2011). Victims at court: Necessary accessories or principal players at centre state? In A. Bottoms & J. Roberts (Eds.), *Hearing the victim: Adversarial justice, crime victims and the state.* London: Willan Publishing, Routledge.

Sharman, S. J., & Powell, M. B. (2012). A comparison of adult witnesses' suggestibility across various types of leading questions. *Applied Cognitive Psychology, 26,* 48–53.

Sheehan, P. (2006). *Girls like you: Four young girls, six brothers and a cultural timebomb.* Sydney: Pan Macmillan Australia.

Sheehy, E. A. (2012). *Introduction, sexual assault in Canada: Law, legal practice and women's activism* (pp. 7–21). Ottawa: University of Ottawa Press.

Shelton, D. E. (2008). The 'CSI effect': Does it really exist? *National Institute of Justice Journal, 259,* 1–7.

Shin, L. M., Rauch, S. L., & Pitman, R. K. (2006). Amygdala, medial prefrontal cortex, and hippocampal function in PTSD. *Annals of the New York Academy of Science, 1071*, 67–79.

Siegmund, A., & Wotjak, C. T. (2007). A mouse model of posttraumatic stress disorder that distinguishes between conditioned and sensitised fear. *Journal of Psychiatric Research, 41*, 848–860.

Simms, A., & Nichols, T. (2014). Social loafing: A review of the literature. *Journal of Management Policy and Practice, 15*, 58–67.

Simms, C. M., Noel, N. E., & Maisto, S. A. (2007). Rape blame as a function of alcohol presence and resistant type. *Addictive Behaviors, 32*, 2766–2776.

Simon, D. (2004). A third view of the black box: Cognitive coherence in legal decision-making. *University of Chicago Law Review, 71*, 511–586.

Simon, D. (2012). More problems with criminal trials: The limited effectiveness of legal mechanisms. *Law and Contemporary Problems, 75*, 167–209.

Sleath, E., & Bull, R. (2012). Comparing rape victim and perpetrator blaming in a police officer sample. *Criminal Justice and Behaviour, 39*, 646–665.

Sleight, K. (2007, June 27–July 1). *Commentary on the video 'A Case for Balance': The issue of judicial control of cross-examination.* Paper presented at the Biennial District and County Court Judges' Conference, Fremantle, Western Australia.

Smart, C. (1989). *Feminism and the power of the law.* London: Routledge.

Smart, C. (1990). Law's truth/women's experiences. In R. Graycar (Ed.), *Dissenting opinions: Feminist explorations in law and society* (pp. 1–20). Sydney: Allen & Unwin.

Smith, D., Letourneau, E. J., Saunders, B. E., Kilpatrick, D. G., Resnick, H. S., & Best, C. L. (2000). Delay in disclosure of childhood rape: Results from a national survey. *Child Abuse & Neglect, 24*, 273–287.

Smith, N., & Weatherburn, D. (2012). Youth justice conferences versus Children's Court: A comparison of re-offending. *Contemporary Issues in Crime and Justice, 160*, 1–23.

Smith, O. (2017). The practicalities of English and Welsh rape trials: Observations and avenues for improvement. *Criminology & Criminal Justice, 18*, 332–348.

Smith, O., & Skinner, T. (2017). How rape myths are used and challenged in rape and sexual assault trials. *Social & Legal Studies, 26*, 441–466.

Snow, P. C., & Powell, M. B. (2007). *Getting the story in forensic interviews with child witnesses: Applying a story grammar framework* (Report to the Criminology Research Council Grant: CRC 04/04-05). https://www.criminologyresearchcouncil.gov.au/reports/200405-04.pdf.

Spears, J. W., & Spohn, C. C. (2006). The effect of evidence factors and victim characteristics on prosecutors' charging decisions in sexual assault cases. *Justice Quarterly, 14,* 501–524.

Spencer, J. R. (2008). *Hearsay evidence in criminal proceedings*. Oxford: Hart Publishing.

Spencer, J. R. (2009). *Evidence of bad character*. Oxford: Hart Publishing.

Spencer, J. R. (2011). The victim and the prosecutor. In A. Bottoms & J. V. Roberts (Eds.), *Hearing the victim: Adversarial justice, crime victims and the state* (pp. 141–162). Abingdon: Routledge.

Spencer, J. R. (2012). Conclusions. In J. R. Spencer & M. Lamb (Eds.), *Children and cross-examination: Time to change the rules?* (pp. 171–202). Oxford: Hart Publishing.

Spencer, J. R., & Flin, R. (1993). *The evidence of children: The law and the psychology* (pp. 289–291). London: Blackstone Press.

Spencer, J. R., & Lamb, M. (2012). *Children and cross-examination: Time to change the rules?*. Oxford: Hart Publishing.

Sperry, K., & Siegel, J. T. (2013). Victim responsibility, credibility, and verdict in a simulated rape case: Application of Weiner's attribution model. *Legal and Criminological Psychology, 18,* 16–29.

Spertus, I. L., Yehuda, R., Wong, C. M., Halligan, S., & Seremitis, S. V. (2003). Childhood emotional abuse and neglect as predictors of psychological and physical symptoms in women presenting to a primary care practice. *Child Abuse & Neglect, 27,* 1247–1258.

Spohn, C., Beichner, D., & Davis-Frenzel, E. (2002). Prosecutorial justifications for sexual assault case rejection: Guarding the 'gateway to justice'. *Social Problems, 48,* 206–235.

Spohn, C., & Holleran, D. (2001). Prosecuting sexual assault: A comparison of charging decisions in sexual assault cases involving strangers, acquaintances, and intimate partners. *Justice Quarterly, 18,* 651–688.

Standing Committee on Uniform Legislation and Intergovernmental Agreements. (1996). *Evidence law: Eighteenth report in the thirty-fourth parliament*. Perth: Legislative Assembly of Western Australia.

Standing Council on Law and Justice. (2013). *Guidelines for restorative justice processes in criminal cases.* Sydney: Standing Council on Law and Justice. http://www.sclj.gov.au/agdbasev7wr/sclj/restorative%20justice%20national%20guidelines.pdf.

Stankiewicz, J. M., & Rosselli, F. (2008). Women as sex objects and victims in print advertisements. *Sex Roles, 58,* 579–589.

Stanko, E., & Williams, E. (2009). Reviewing rape and rape allegations in London: What are the vulnerabilities of the victims who report to the police? In M. Horvath & J. Brown (Eds.), *Rape: Challenging contemporary thinking* (pp. 207–228). Collumpton, UK: Willan Publishing.

Steblay, N., Hosch, H. M., Culhane, S. E., & McWethy, A. (2006). The impact on juror verdicts of judicial instruction to disregard inadmissible evidence: A meta-analysis. *Law and Human Behavior, 30,* 469–492.

Steel, J., & Herlitz, C. (2005). The association between childhood and adolescent sexual abuse and proxies for sexual risk behavior: A random sample of the general population of Sweden. *Child Abuse & Neglect, 29,* 1141–1153.

Steil, R., Dyer, A., Priebe, K., Kleindienst, N., & Bohus, M. (2011). Dialectical behavior therapy for posttraumatic stress disorder related to childhood sexual abuse: A pilot study of an intensive residential treatment program. *Journal of Traumatic Stress, 24,* 102–106.

Stewart, D. N., & Jacquin, K. M. (2010). Juror perceptions in a rape trial: Examining the complainant's ingestion of chemical substances prior to sexual assault. *Journal of Aggression, Maltreatment & Trauma, 19,* 853–874.

Stoltenborgh, M., van Ijzendoorn, M., Euser, E., & Bakermans-Kranenburg, M. (2011). A global perspective on child sexual abuse: Meta-analysis of prevalence around the world. *Child Maltreatment, 16,* 79–101.

Stolzenberg, S. N., & Lyon, T. D. (2014). How attorneys question children about the dynamics of sexual abuse and disclosure in criminal trials. *Psychology, Public Policy and Law, 20,* 19–30.

Strang, H., & Braithwaite, J. (2017). *Restorative Justice: Philosophy to Practice.* London: Routledge.

Strang, H., Sherman, L. W., Mayo-Wilson, E., Woods, D., & Ariel, B. (2013). *Restorative justice conferencing (RJC) Using face-to-face meetings of offenders and victims: Effects on offender recidivism and victim satisfaction. A systematic review.* Oslo: Campbell Collaboration.

Straus, S. G., Parker, A. M., & Bruce, J. B. (2011). The group matters: A review of processes and outcomes in intelligence analysis. *Group Dynamics: Theory, Research & Practice, 15,* 128–146.

Strömwall, L. A., & Granhag, P. A. (2003). How to detect deception? Arresting the beliefs of police officers, prosecutors and judges. *Psychology, Crime & Law, 9,* 19–36.

Strömwall, L. A., Granhag, P. A., & Landström, S. (2007). Children's prepared and unprepared lies: Can adults see through their strategies? *Applied Cognitive Psychology, 21,* 457–471.

Stuart, S. M., McKimmie, B. M., & Masser, B. M. (2016). Rape perpetrators on trial: The effect of sexual assault–related schemas on attributions of blame. *Journal of Interpersonal Violence, 34,* 310–336.

Stubbs, J. (2007). Beyond apology? Domestic violence and critical questions for restorative justice. *Criminology and Criminal Justice, 7,* 169–187.

Suarez, E., & Gadalla, T. M. (2010). Stop blaming the victim: A meta-analysis on rape myths. *Journal of Interpersonal Violence, 25,* 2010–2035.

Substance Abuse and Mental Health Services Administration. (2013a). *Essential components of trauma-informed judicial practice* (pp. 1–12). https://www.nasmhpd.org/sites/default/files/JudgesEssential_5%201%202013finaldraft.pdf.

Substance Abuse and Mental Health Services Administration. (2013b). *Creating a place of healing and forgiveness: The trauma-informed care initiative at the women's community correctional center of Hawaii* (pp. 1–9). https://www.nasmhpd.org/sites/default/files/7014_hawaiian_trauma_brief_2013(1).pdf.

Süssenbach, P. (2016). Rape myth acceptance and judgments in rape cases: An overview with meta-analysis. *Recht & Psychiatrie, 34,* 35–42.

Süssenbach, P., Albrecht, S., & Bohner, G. (2017). Implicit judgments of rape cases: An experiment on the determinants and consequences of implicit evaluations in a rape case. *Psychology Crime and Law, 23,* 291–304.

Süssenbach, P., Eyssel, F., Rees, J., & Bohner, G. (2017). Looking for blame: Rape myth acceptance and attention to victim and perpetrator. *Journal of Interpersonal Violence, 32,* 2323–2344.

Swim, J. K., Hyers, L. L., Cohen, L. L., & Ferguson, M. J. (2001). Everyday sexism: Evidence for its incidence, nature, and psychological impact from three daily diary studies. *Journal of Social Issues, 57,* 31–53.

Tabak, S. J., & Klettke, B. (2014). Mock jury attitudes towards credibility, age, and guilt in a fictional child sexual assault scenario. *Australian Journal of Psychology, 66,* 47–55.

Tanford, S., & Penrod, S. (1986). Jury deliberations: Discussion content and influence processes in jury decision making. *Journal of Applied Social Psychology, 16,* 322–347.

Tasmania Law Reform Institute. (2018). *Facilitating equal access to justice: An intermediary/communication assistance scheme for Tasmania?* (Final Report No. 23). http://www.utas.edu.au/__data/assets/pdf_file/0011/1061858/Intermediaries-Final-Report.pdf.

Taylor, N. (2007). *Juror attitudes and biases in sexual assault cases* (Trends and Issues in Crime and Criminal Justice, No. 344). Canberra: Australian Institute of Criminology.

Taylor, N., & Joudo, J. (2005) *The impact of pre-recorded video and closed circuit television testimony by adult sexual assault complainants on jury decision-making: An experimental study* (Research and Public Policy Series No. 68). Canberra: Australian Institute of Criminology.

Taylor, N., & Mouzos, J. (2006). *Community attitudes to violence against women survey 2006: A full technical report* (Violence Against Women Community Attitudes Project No. 1). Canberra: Australian Institute of Criminology.

Taylor, R., & Hill-Davies, C. (2004). Parents' and non-parents' beliefs about the cues to deception in children. *Psychology, Crime, & Law, 10*, 455–464.

Temkin, J. (2002). *Rape and the legal process*. Oxford: Oxford University Press.

Temkin, J., & Ashworth, A. (2004). The Sexual Offences Act 2003: (1) Rape, sexual assaults and the problems of consent. *Criminal Law Review*, 328–346.

Temkin, J., & Krahé, B. (2008). *Sexual assault and the justice gap: A question of attitude*. Oxford: Hart Publishing.

Testa, M., & Parks, K. A. (1996). The role of women's alcohol consumption in sexual victimization. *Aggression and Violent Behavior, 1*, 217–234.

Testa, M., Van Zile-Tamsen, C., & Livingston, J. A. (2007). Prospective prediction of women's sexual victimization by intimate and nonintimate male perpetrators. *Journal of Consulting and Clinical Psychology, 75*, 52–60.

The British Psychological Society Research Board. (2010). *Guidelines from memory and the law: Recommendations from the scientific study of human memory*. Leicester: British Psychological Society.

Thomas, C. (2010). *Are juries fair?* (Ministry of Justice Research Series No. 1/10). London: Ministry of Justice. https://www.justice.gov.uk/downloads/publications/research-and-analysis/moj-research/are-juries-fair-research.pdf.

Tolmie, J. (2012). New Zealand's Jane Doe. In E. A. Sheehy (Ed.), *Sexual assault in Canada: Law, legal practice and women's activism* (pp. 53–71). Ottawa: University of Ottawa Press.

Topping, A., & Barr, C. (2018, September 24). Revealed: Less than a third of young men prosecuted for rape are convicted. *The Guardian*. https://www.theguardian.com/society/2018/sep/23/revealed-less-than-a-third-of-young-men-prosecuted-for-are-convicted.

Trickett, P. K., Noll, J. G., & Putnam, F. W. (2011). The impact of sexual abuse on female development: Lessons from a multigenerational, longitudinal research study. *Development and Psychopathology, 23*, 453–476.

Trimboli, L. (2008). *Juror understanding of judicial instructions in criminal trials* (Crime and Justice Bulletin, No. 119). Sydney: Bureau of Crime Statistics and Research.

Ullman, S. E., & Filipas, H. H. (2005). Gender differences in social reactions to abuse disclosures, post-abuse coping, and ptsd of child sexual abuse survivors. *Child Abuse & Neglect, 29,* 767–782.

Ullman, S. E., Karabatsos, G., & Koss, M. P. (1999). Alcohol and sexual assault in a national sample of college women. *Journal of Interpersonal Violence, 14,* 603–625.

Underwood, J. H., Boudreaux, D. O., & Rao, S. (2009). Demographics in civil trials: Biases and implications. *Journal of Business & Economics Research, 7,* 33–42.

United Nations Department of Economic and Social Affairs, Division for the Advancement of Women. (2010). *Handbook for legislation on violence against women* (UN Doc ST/ESA/329).

United Nations Statistics Division. (2015). *The world's women 2015: Trends and statistics.* United Nations. https://unstats.un.org/unsd/gender/aboutWW2015.html.

Vaes, J., Paladino, P., & Puvia, E. (2011). Are sexualized women complete human beings? Why men and women dehumanize sexually objectified women. *European Journal of Social Psychology, 41,* 774–785.

Valentine, T., & Maras, K. (2011). The effect of cross-examination on the accuracy of adult eyewitness testimony. *Applied Cognitive Psychology, 25,* 554–561.

van der Bruggen, M., & Grubb, A. (2014). A review of the literature relating to rape victim blaming: An analysis of the impact of observer and victim characteristics on attribution of blame in rape cases. *Aggression and Violent Behavior, 19,* 523–531.

van der Kolk, B. A. (2005). Developmental trauma disorder: Towards a rational diagnosis for children with complex trauma histories. *Psychiatric Annals, 33,* 401–408.

van der Kolk, B. A. (2006). Clinical implications of neuroscience research in PTSD. *Annals of New York Academy of Sciences, 1071,* 277–293.

van der Kolk, B. A. (2015). *The body keeps the score: Brain, mind, and body in the healing of trauma.* New York: Viking Press.

Vandiver, D. M., & Dupalo, J. R. (2012). Factors that affect college students' perceptions of rape: What is the role of gender and other situational factors? *International Journal of Offender Therapy and Comparative Criminology, 57,* 592–612.

Van Dorn, R. A., Mustillo, S., Elbogen, E. B., Dorsey, S., Swanson, J. W., & Swartz, M. S. (2005). The effects of early sexual abuse on adult risky sexual behaviors among persons with severe mental illness. *Child Abuse and Neglect, 29,* 1265–1279.

Van Ness, D. W., & Strong, K. H. (2015). *Restoring Justice: An Introduction to Restorative Justice*. New York: Routledge.

Ventus, D., Antfolk, J., & Salo, B. (2017). The associations between abuse characteristics in child sexual abuse: A meta-analysis. *Journal Of Sexual Aggression, 23,* 167–180.

VicHealth. (2014). *Australians' attitudes to violence against women: Findings from the 2013 National Community Attitudes towards Violence Against Women Survey (NCAS)*. Melbourne: Australia Victorian Health Promotion Foundation.

Victims Commissioner Office. (2016). *A question of quality: A Review of restorative justice part 1—Service providers*. https://s3-eu-west-2.amazonaws.com/victcomm2-prod-storage-119w3o4kq2z48/uploads/2019/02/VC-Restorative-Justice-Part-1-Service-Providers-Review-2016.pdf.

Victims' Commissioner Office. (2017a). *Victims code is not delivering entitlements to victims*. http://victimscommissioner.org.uk/victims-code-is-not-delivering-entitlements-for-victims/.

Victims' Commissioner Office. (2017b). *Are we getting it right for young victims of crime? A review of children's entitlement in the victims' code*. https://s3-eu-west-2.amazonaws.com/victcomm2-prod-storage-119w3o4kq2z48/uploads/2019/02/VC-Young-victims-of-crime-Review-2017.pdf.

Victims Services, NSW Department of Justice. (2016). *Children's champion (witness intermediary) procedural guidance manual (2016)*. Sydney: NSW Department of Justice. https://www.victimsservices.justice.nsw.gov.au/Documents/child-champ_manual.pdf.

Victorian Law Reform Commission. (2004). *Sexual offences* (Final Report). Melbourne: Victorian Law Reform Commission.

Victorian Law Reform Commission. (2009). *Jury directions* (Final Report No. 17). Melbourne: Victorian Law Reform Commission.

Victorian Law Reform Commission. (2016). *The role of victims of crime in the criminal trial process* (Report No. 34). Melbourne: Victorian Law Reform Commission.

Visher, C. A. (1987). Juror decision making: The importance of evidence. *Law and Human Behavior, 11,* 1–17.

Volchan, E., Souza, G. G., Franklin, C. M., Norte, C. E., Rocha-Rego, V., Oliveira, J. M., … Freire Coutinho, E. S. (2011). Is there tonic immobility in humans? Biological evidence from victims of traumatic stress. *Biological Psychology, 88,* 13–19.

von Helversen, B., & Rieskamp, J. (2009). Predicting sentencing for low level crimes: Comparing models of human judgment. *Journal of Experimental Psychology: Applied, 15,* 375–395.

Vrij, A., & Fischer, A. (1997). The role of displays of emotions and ethnicity in judgments of rape victims. *International Review of Victimology, 4,* 255–265.

Vrij, A., Granhag, P., & Porter, S. (2010). Pitfalls and opportunities in nonverbal and verbal lie detection. *Psychological Science in the Public Interest, 11,* 89–121.

Wager, N. (2013). The experience and insight of survivors who have engaged in a restorative justice meeting with their assailant. *Temida, 16,* 11–32.

Wall, A., & Schuller, R. (2000). Sexual assault and defendant/victim intoxication: Jurors' perceptions of guilt. *Journal of Applied Social Psychology, 30,* 253–274.

Walsh, K., Danielson, C. K., McCauley, J. L., Saunders, B. E., Kilpatrick, D. G., & Resnick, H. S. (2012). National prevalence of posttraumatic stress disorder among sexually revictimized adolescent, college, and adult household-residing women. *Archives of General Psychiatry, 69,* 935–942.

Walsh, K., Resnick, H. S., Danielson, C. K., McCauley, J. L., Saunders, B. E., & Kilpatrick, D. G. (2014). Patterns of drug and alcohol use associated with lifetime sexual revictimization and current posttraumatic stress disorder among three national samples of adolescent, college, and household-residing women. *Addictive Behaviors, 39,* 684–689.

Ward, L. M., Merriwether, A., & Caruthers, A. (2006). Breasts are for men: Media, masculinity ideologies, and men's beliefs about women's bodies. *Sex Roles, 55,* 703–714.

Watts, A. (2014). *To investigate models of Intermediaries for child victim and witnesses in the criminal justice system in England, Ireland, Austria and Norway.* Sydney: The Winston Churchill Memorial Trust of Australia. https://www.churchilltrust.com.au/media/fellows/Watts._Amy_2013.pdf.

Weiner, B. (1980). A cognitive (attribution)-emotion-action model of motivated behavior: An analysis of judgments of help-giving. *Journal of Personality and Social Psychology, 39,* 186–200.

Weiner, B. (1985). An attributional theory of achievement motivation and emotion. *Psychological Review, 92,* 548–573.

Weinstock, M. P., & Flaton, R. A. (2004). Evidence coverage and argument skills: Cognitive factors in a juror's verdict choice. *Journal of Behavioral Decision Making, 17,* 191–212.

Wenger, A. A., & Bornstein, B. H. (2006). The effects of victim's substance use and relationship closeness on mock jurors' judgments in an acquaintance rape case. *Sex Roles, 54,* 547–555.

Wessel, E., Magnussen, S., & Melinder, A. M. D. (2013). Expressed emotions and perceived credibility of child mock victims disclosing physical abuse. *Applied Cognitive Psychology, 27,* 611–616.

Wessel, E. M., Drevland, G. C. B., Eilertsenand, D. E., & Magnussen, S. (2006). Credibility of the emotional witness: A study by court judges. *Law & Human Behavior, 30,* 221–230.

Westcott, H. L., & Page, M. (2002). Cross-examination, sexual abuse and child witness identity. *Child Abuse Review, 11,* 137–152.

Westera, N., Darwinkel, E., & Powell, M. (2016). *A systematic review of the efficacy of specialist police investigative units in responding to child sexual abuse.* Sydney: Royal Commission into Institutional Responses to Child Sexual Abuse.

Westera, N., Zydervelt, S., Kaladelfos, A., & Zajac, R. (2017). Sexual assault complainants on the stand: A historical comparison of courtroom questioning. *Psychology, Crime & Law, 23,* 15–31.

Whatley, M. A. (1996). Victim characteristics influencing attributions of responsibility to rape victims: A meta-analysis. *Aggression and Violent Behavior, 1,* 81–95.

Whelan, P. (2000). Hansard, Legislative Assembly, Second Reading Speech, Child Protection (Offenders Registration) Bill, pp. 6914–6915.

Whitcomb, D., Runyan, D. K., De Vos, E., Hunter, W. M., Cross, T. P., Everson, … Cropper, C. (1991). *Child victim as witness project: Final report.* Washington, DC: Office of Juvenile Justice and Delinquency Prevention (U.S. Department of Justice), U.S. Government Printing Office. https://www.ncjrs.gov/pdffiles1/Digitization/149172NCJRS.pdf.

Wigmore, J. H. (1974). *Evidence in Trials at Common Law (Volume 5).* Boston: Little Brown.

Williams, L. M., Kemp, A. H., Felmingham, K., Barton, M., Olivieri, G., Peduto, A., … Bryant, R. A. (2006). Trauma modulates amygdala and medial prefrontal responses to consciously attended fear. *Neuroimage, 29,* 347–357.

Williams, R. (2007). The psychosocial consequences for children of mass violence, terrorism and disasters. *International Review of Psychiatry, 19,* 263–277.

Williams, Z. (2013, October 19). Keir Starmer: 'The potential for change in our criminal justice system is huge'. *The Guardian.* https://www.the

guardian.com/theguardian/2013/oct/18/keir-starmer-potential-change-criminal-justice.

Williams, Z. (2017, April 10). From Elle to Game of Thrones, why is culture obsessed with rape? *The Guardian*. https://www.theguardian.com/tv-and-radio/2017/apr/10/rape-culture-elle-game-thrones-zoe-williams.

Willmott, D., Boduszek, D., & Booth, N. (2017). The English jury on trial. *Custodial Review, 82,* 12–14.

Willmott, D., Boduszek, D., Debowska, A., & Woodfield, R. (2018). Introduction and validation of the juror decision scale (JDS): An empirical investigation of the story model. *Journal of Criminal Justice, 57,* 26–34.

Wilson, D. R. (2010). Health consequences of childhood sexual abuse. *Perspectives in Psychiatric Care, 46,* 56–64.

Wilson, L. C. (2005). Independent legal representation for victims of sexual assault: A model for delivery of legal services. *Windsor Year Book Access to Justice, 23,* 249–312.

Wilson, W. H. (1891) Criminal Law Amendment Bill, Second Reading, Hansard, Queensland Parliament, pp. 16–17.

Winter, R. J., & Greene, E. (2007). Juror decision-making. In F. Durso, R. S. Nickerson, S. T. Dumais, S. Lewandowsky, & T. J. Perfect (Eds.), *Handbook of applied cognition* (pp. 739–761). Chichester: Wiley.

Wissink, I. B., van Vugt, E., Moonen, X., Stams, G.-J., & Hendriks, J. (2015). Sexual abuse involving children with an intellectual disability (ID): A narrative review. *Research in Developmental Disabilities, 36,* 20–35.

Woessner, G. (2017). On the relationship between restorative justice and therapy in cases of sexual violence. In E. Zinsstag & M. Keenan (Eds.), *Restorative responses to sexual violence: Legal social and therapeutic dimensions* (pp. 248–265). New York: Routledge.

Wood, B., Orsak, C., Murphy, M., & Cross, H. J. (1996). Semistructured child sexual abuse interviews: Interview and child characteristics related to credibility of disclosure. *Child Abuse & Neglect, 20,* 81–92.

Wood, J. (2003, February 12). *Sexual assault and the admission of evidence.* Paper presented at Practice and Prevention: Contemporary Issues in Adult Sexual Assault in New South Wales Conference, University of Technology, Sydney.

World Health Organization. (2014). *Global status report on violence prevention 2014*. Luxemborg: WHO.

Wright, P. J., Tokunaga, R. S., & Kraus, A. (2015). A meta-analysis of pornography consumption and actual acts of sexual aggression in general population studies. *Journal of Communication, 66,* 183–205.

Wundersitz, J. (2003). *Child Sexual assault: Tracking from police incident report to finalisation in court*. Adelaide: Office of Crime Statistics and Research.

Wurtzel, D., & Marchant, R. (2017). Intermediaries. In P. Cooper & H. Norton (Eds.), *Vulnerable people and the criminal justice system: A guide to law and practice*. Oxford: Oxford University Press.

Zajac, R., & Cannan, P. (2009). Cross-examination of sexual assault complainants: A developmental comparison. *Psychiatry, Psychology and Law, 16,* S36–S54.

Zajac, R., Gross, J., & Hayne, H. (2003). Asked and Answered: Questioning children in the courtroom. *Psychiatry, Psychology and Law, 10,* 199–209.

Zajac, R., & Hayne, H. (2003). I Don't Think That's What Really Happened: The effect of cross-examination on the accuracy of children's reports. *Journal of Experimental Psychology, 9,* 187–195.

Zajac, R., & Hayne, H. (2006). The negative effect of cross-examination style questioning on children's accuracy: Older children not immune. *Applied Cognitive Psychology, 20,* 3–16.

Zajac, R., Irvine, B., Ingram, J. M., & Jack, F. (2016). The diagnostic value of children's responses to cross-examination questions. *Behavioral Sciences & the Law, 34,* 160–177.

Zajac, R., Jury, E., & O'Neill, S. (2009). The role of psychosocial factors in young children's responses to cross-examination style questioning. *Applied Cognitive Psychology, 23,* 918–935.

Zajac, R., & O'Neill, S. (2013). The role of repeated interviewing in children's responses to cross-examination-style questioning. *British Journal of Psychology, 104,* 14–38.

Zajac, R., O'Neill, S., & Hayne, H. (2012). Disorder in the courtroom? Child witnesses under cross-examination. *Developmental Review, 32,* 181–204.

Zehr, H., & Mika, H. (1998). Fundamental concepts of restorative justice. *Contemporary Justice Review, 1,* 47–55.

Zeisel, H., & Diamond, S. S. (1978). The effect of peremptory challenges on jury and verdict: An experiment in a Federal District Court. *Stanford Law Review, 30,* 491–531.

Zillmann, D., & Bryant, J. (1982). Pornography, sexual callousness, and the trivialization of rape. *Journal of Communication, 32,* 10–21.

Zinsstag, E., & Keenan, M. (Eds.). (2017). *Sexual violence and restorative justice: Legal, social and therapeutic dimensions*. London: Routledge.

Zurbriggen, E. L. (2010). Rape, war, and the socialization of masculinity: Why our refusal to give up war ensures that rape cannot be eradicated. *Psychology of Women Quarterly, 34,* 538–549.

Zydervelt, S., Zajac, R., Kaladelfos, A., & Westera, N. (2017). Lawyers' strategies for cross-examining rape complainants: Have we moved beyond the 1950s. *British Journal of Criminology, 57*, 551–569.

www.ingramcontent.com/pod-product-compliance
Lightning Source LLC
LaVergne TN
LVHW090253210926
848480LV00001B/7
9781137320506